FEMINIST INTERPRETATIONS OF LUDWIG WITTGENSTEIN

RE-READING THE CANON

NANCY TUANA, GENERAL EDITOR

This series consists of edited collections of essays, some original and some previously published, offering feminist reinterpretations of the writings of major figures in the Western philosophical tradition. Devoted to the work of a single philosopher, each volume contains essays covering the full range of the philosopher's thought and representing the diversity of approaches now being used by feminist critics.

Already published:

Nancy Tuana, ed., *Feminist Interpretations of Plato* (1994)

Margaret Simons, ed., *Feminist Interpretations of Simone de Beauvoir* (1995)

Bonnie Honig, ed., *Feminist Interpretations of Hannah Arendt* (1995)

Patricia Jagentowicz Mills, ed., *Feminist Interpretations of G. W. F. Hegel* (1996)

Maria J. Falco, ed., *Feminist Interpretations of Mary Wollstonecraft* (1996)

Susan J. Hekman, ed., *Feminist Interpretations of Michel Foucault* (1996)

Nancy J. Holland, ed., *Feminist Interpretations of Jacques Derrida* (1997)

Robin May Schott, ed., *Feminist Interpretations of Immanuel Kant* (1997)

Celeine Leon and Sylvia Walsh, eds., *Feminist Interpretations of Søren Kierkegaard* (1997)

Cynthia Freeland, ed., *Feminist Interpretations of Aristotle* (1998)

Kelly Oliver and Marilyn Pearsall, eds., *Feminist Interpretations of Friedrich Nietzsche* (1998)

Mimi Reisel Gladstein and Chris Matthew Sciabarra, eds., *Feminist Interpretations of Ayn Rand* (1999)

Susan Bordo, ed., *Feminist Interpretations of René Descartes* (1999)

Julien S. Murphy, ed., *Feminist Interpretations of Jean-Paul Sartre* (1999)

Anne Jaap Jacobson, ed., *Feminist Interpretations of David Hume* (2000)

Sarah Lucia Hoagland and Marilyn Frye, eds., *Feminist Interpretations of Mary Daly* (2000)

Tina Chanter, ed., *Feminist Interpretations of Emmanuel Levinas* (2001)

Nancy J. Holland and Patricia Huntington, eds., *Feminist Interpretations of Martin Heidegger* (2001)

Charlene Haddock Seigfried, ed., *Feminist Interpretations of John Dewey* (2001)

Naomi Scheman and Peg O'Connor, eds., *Feminist Interpretations of Ludwig Wittgenstein* (2002)

FEMINIST INTERPRETATIONS OF LUDWIG WITTGENSTEIN

EDITED BY
NAOMI SCHEMAN
AND
PEG O'CONNOR

THE PENNSYLVANIA STATE UNIVERSITY PRESS
UNIVERSITY PARK, PENNSYLVANIA

Library of Congress Cataloguing-in-Publication Data

Feminist interpretations of Ludwig Wittgenstein / edited by Naomi Scheman
    and Peg O'Connor.
      p.   cm. — (Re-reading the canon)
    Includes bibliographical references and index.
    ISBN 0-271-02197-7 (cloth : alk. paper)
    ISBN 0-271-02198-5 (pbk. : alk. paper)
    1. Wittgenstein, Ludwig, 1889–1951. 2. Feminist theory.
    I. Scheman, Naomi. II. O'Connor, Peg, 1965– . III. Series.
B3376.W564 F45   2002
192—dc21   2002005455

It is the policy of The Pennsylvania State University Press to use acid-free paper for the
first printing of all clothbound books. Publications on uncoated stock satisfy the
minimum requirements of American National Standard for Information
Sciences—Permanence of Paper for Printed Library Materials, ANSI Z39.48–1992.

Contents

Acknowledgments   ix

Preface   xi
Nancy Tuana

List of Abbreviations   xv

Introduction   1
Naomi Scheman

Section I: The Subject of Philosophy and the Philosophical Subject

1   Philosophy, Language, and Wizardry   25
     Phyllis Rooney

2   Wittgenstein, Feminism, and the Exclusions of Philosophy   48
     Nancy E. Baker

3   Speaking Philosophy in the Voice of Another:
     Wittgenstein, Irigaray, and the Inheritance of Mimesis   65
     Tim Craker

Section II: Wittgensteinian Feminist Philosophy: Contrasting Visions

4   What Do Feminists Want in an Epistemology?   97
     Alice Crary

5   Making Mistakes, Rendering Nonsense, and Moving Toward
    Uncertainty   119
    Sarah Lucia Hoagland

6   *Tractatio Logico-Philosophica:* Engendering Wittgenstein's
    Tractatus   138
    Daniel Cohen

7   The Moral Language Game   159
    Susan Hekman

8   The Short Life of Meaning: Feminism and Nonliteralism   176
    Jane Braaten

Section III: Drawing Boundaries: Categories and Kinds

9   "Back to the Rough Ground!": Wittgenstein, Essentialism,
    and Feminist Methods   195
    Cressida J. Heyes

10 Wittgenstein Meets 'Woman' in the Language-Game of
    Theorizing Feminism   213
    Hilde Lindemann Nelson

11 Using Wittgensteinian Methodology to Elucidate the
    Meaning of "Equality"   235
    Christine M. Koggel

12 Eleanor Rosch and the Development of Successive
    Wittgensteinian Paradigms for Cognitive Science   259
    Nalini Bhushan

Section IV: Being Human: Agents and Subjects

13 Words and Worlds: Some Thoughts on the Significance of
    Wittgenstein for Moral and Political Philosophy   287
    Judith Bradford

14 Big Dogs, Little Dogs, Universal Dogs: Ludwig Wittgenstein
    and Patricia Williams Talk About the Logic of Conceptual
    Rearing   305
    Sandra W. Churchill

15 Developing Wittgenstein's Picture of the Soul: Toward a
    Feminist Spiritual Erotics   322
    Deborah Orr

16 "No Master, Outside or In": Wittgenstein's Critique of the
    Proprietary Subject   344
    Janet Farrell Smith

Section V: Feminism's Allies: New Players, New Games

17 Wittgensteinian Vision(s) and "Passionate Detachments":
    A Queer Context for a Situated Episteme   367
    Wendy Lynne Lee

18 Wittgenstein's *Remarks on Colour* as Remarks on Racism   389
    Bruce Krajewski

19 Culture, Nature, Ecosystem (or Why Nature Can't Be
    Naturalized)   408
    Rupert Read

20 Moving to New Boroughs: Transforming the World by
    Inventing Language Games   432
    Peg O'Connor

    Bibliography   451

    Index   455

    Contributors   469

Acknowledgments

The call for papers for this volume went out in 1995, and the process of editing the volume has been maddeningly drawn out, something for which I take full responsibility. Its finally coming to a successful end, however, is something for which the responsibility goes primarily to my co-editor, Peg O'Connor, whose philosophical acumen is happily combined with organizational efficiency. Nancy Tuana, the series editor, and Sandy Thatcher, the editor at Penn State Press, have been extremely helpful and heroically patient, as have the contributors, despite their understandable frustration at not having their work see the light of day. I am sure they all share my gratitude to Peg. The Introduction remains mine, since, unlike Peg, I do not have an essay in the volume; and I owe her a philosophical, as well as a practical, debt: as her teacher, then dissertation supervisor, and then philosophical colleague, I have learned a great deal from her about the actual social and political processes by which language games can, slowly but significantly, change.

One of the consequences of the volume's delay is that the project of thinking Wittgenstein and feminism in the same breath has proceeded in ways that the volume was meant to prompt. This development is, of course, a welcome one; and while it may make the present collection less groundbreaking, it does not make it less relevant, nor do the particular essays in it have less to contribute to ongoing discussions. There is just more out there now for readers who want to follow up on the possibilities this volume raises and explores. The bibliography is as up-to-date as we were able to make it: thanks to Susan Parry, Linda Wayne, and Tanya Rodrigues for their work on compiling it. In particular, one of the contributors, Cressida Heyes, has published a book that expands on the themes of her essay here; Peg O'Connor similarly has a book due to be published at the same time as this volume, *Oppression and Responsibility:*

A Wittgensteinian Approach to Social Practices and Moral Theory, also with
Penn State Press; and Alice Crary and Rupert Read have edited a volume,
The New Wittgenstein, which, although not explicitly feminist, bears
reading in relation to the present volume.

I would like to also acknowledge the women's studies department at
the University of Gothenburg for providing support, collegiality, and
ideal working conditions during 1997–98, and Douglas Lewis for assuming my duties as director of Graduate Studies in Philosophy for the summer of 2000 to allow me to work on this volume. Neither, needless to say,
bears any responsibility for their generosity's not having done the trick.
My primary gratitude, however, goes to the contributors to the volume,
for the effort they have put into writing and (repeatedly) rewriting their
essays, and, first and foremost, for the quality of those essays and for the
contribution they have already begun—as circulating manuscripts—to
make to conversations drawing together, and thereby enriching, Wittgenstein scholarship, philosophy more generally, and feminist theory. I
am not alone in having "forthcoming" essays from this volume cited in
my notes, and I look forward to seeing many more, less promissory, references in the future.

Finally, this is an awkwardly appropriate place in which to acknowledge my debt to the many feminist philosophers and theorists who over
the years have solicited and published my essays. Since literally everything I have published falls in this category, I owe my entire career to
(mostly) women who have edited anthologies and special issues of journals. It was to (partially) repay that debt that I agreed to edit this volume.
However far short of repayment I remain, the writing and reading public
will be relieved to know that I have no intention of trying again.

Naomi Scheman

I have been fortunate to work with Naomi Scheman for the last eleven
years as her student, advisee, colleague, and friend. Her influence on me
is significant, and her fingerprints can be seen on my thinking. Working
with her on this project provided intellectual stimulation combined with
a good amount of humor.

I owe thanks to Ambryn Melius and Jenny Schiebe, two students at
Gustavus who helped immensely in the final preparation of the manu-
script.

Peg O'Connor

Preface

Nancy Tuana

Take into your hands any history of philosophy text. You will find compiled therein the "classics" of modern philosophy. Since these texts are often designed for use in undergraduate classes, the editor is likely to offer an introduction in which the reader is informed that these selections represent the perennial questions of philosophy. The student is to assume that she or he is about to explore the timeless wisdom of the greatest minds of Western philosophy. No one calls attention to the fact that the philosophers are all men.

Although women are omitted from the canons of philosophy, these texts inscribe the nature of woman. Sometimes the philosopher speaks directly about woman, delineating her proper role, her abilities and inabilities, her desires. Other times the message is indirect—a passing remark hinting at women's emotionality, irrationality, unreliability.

This process of definition occurs in far more subtle ways when the central concepts of philosophy—reason and justice, those characteristics that are taken to define us as human—are associated with traits historically identified with masculinity. If the "man" of reason must learn to control or overcome traits identified as feminine—the body, the emotions, the passions—then the realm of rationality will be one reserved primarily for men,[1] with grudging entrance to those few women who are capable of transcending their femininity.

Feminist philosophers have begun to look critically at the canonized texts of philosophy and have concluded that the discourses of philosophy are not gender-neutral. Philosophical narratives do not offer a university perspective, but rather privilege some experiences and beliefs over others. These experiences and beliefs permeate all philosophical theories whether they be aesthetic or epistemological, moral or metaphysical. Yet this fact has often been neglected by those studying the traditions of philosophy. Given the history of canon formation in Western philosophy, the perspective most likely to be privileged is that of upper-class white males. Thus, to be fully aware of the impact of gender biases, it is imperative that we re-read the canon with attention to the ways in which philosophers' assumptions concerning gender are embedded within their theories.

This new series, *Re-Reading the Canon,* is designed to foster this process of reevaluation. Each volume will offer feminist analyses of the theories of a selected philosopher. Since feminist philosophy is not monolithic in method or content, the essays are also selected to illustrate the variety of perspectives within feminist criticism and highlight some of the controversies within feminist scholarship.

In this series, feminist lenses will be focused on the canonical texts of Western philosophy, both those authors who have been part of the traditional canon, as well as those philosophers whose writings have more recently gained attention within the philosophical community. A glance at the list of volumes in the series will reveal an immediate gender bias of the canon: Arendt, Aristotle, de Beauvoir, Derrida, Descartes, Foucault, Hegel, Hume, Kant, Locke, Marx, Mill, Nietzsche, Plato, Rousseau, Wittgenstein, Wollstonecraft. There are all too few women included, and those few who do appear have been added only recently. In creating this series, it is not my intention to rectify the current canon of philosophical thought. What is and is not included within the canon during a particular historical period is a result of many factors. Although no canonization of texts will include all philosophers, no canonization of texts that excludes all but a few women can offer an accurate representation of the history of the discipline, as women have been philosophers since the ancient period.[2]

I share with many feminist philosophers and other philosophers writing from the margins of philosophy the concern that the current canonization of philosophy be transformed. Although I do not accept the position that the current canon has been formed exclusively by power relations, I do believe that this canon represents only a selective history of the tradition. I share the view of Michael Bérubé that "canons are at once the location, the index, and the record of the struggle for cultural representation; like any other hegemonic formation, they must be continually reproduced anew and are continually contested."[3]

The process of canon transformation will require the recovery of "lost" texts and a careful examination of the reasons such voices have been silenced. Along with the process of uncovering women's philosophical history, we must also begin to analyze the impact of gender ideologies upon the process of canonization. This process of recovery and examination must occur in conjunction with careful attention to the concept of a canon of authorized texts. Are we to dispense with the notion of a tradition of excellence embodied in a canon of authorized texts? Or, rather than abandon the whole idea of a canon, do we instead encourage a reconstruction of a canon of those texts that inform a common culture?

This series is designed to contribute to this process of canon transformation by offering a re-reading of the current philosophical canon. Such a re-reading shifts our attention to the ways in which woman and the role of the feminine is constructed within the texts of philosophy. A question we must keep in front of us during this process of re-reading is whether a philosopher's socially inherited prejudices concerning woman's nature and role are independent of her or his larger philosophical framework. In asking this question, attention must be paid to the ways in which the definitions of central philosophical concepts implicitly include or exclude gendered traits.

This type of reading strategy is not limited to the canon, but can be applied to all texts. It is my desire that this series reveal the importance of this type of critical reading. Paying attention to the workings of gender within the texts of philosophy will make visible the complexities of the inscription of gender ideologies.

Notes

1. More properly, it is a realm reserved for a group of privileged males, since the texts also inscribe race and class biases that thereby omit certain males from participation.

2. Mary Ellen Waithe's multivolume series, *A History of Women Philosophers* (Boston: M. Nijoff, 1987), attests to this presence of women.

3. Michael Bérubé, *Marginal Forces/Cultural Centers: Tolson, Pynchon, and the Politics of the Canon* (Ithaca: Cornell University Press, 1992), 4–5.

List of Abbreviations

BB   *The Blue and Brown Books*
CV   *Culture and Value*
OC   *On Certainty*
PG   *Philosophical Grammar*
PI   *Philosophical Investigations*
RFM   *Remarks on the Foundations of Mathematics*
RC   *Remarks on Colour*
RPP   *Remarks on the Philosophy of Psychology*
TLP   *Tractatus Logico-Philosophicus*
Z   *Zettel*

Introduction

Naomi Scheman

One might say: the axis of our examination must be rotated,
but about the fixed point of our real need.

—Ludwig Wittgenstein, *Philosophical Investigations*

This volume is shaped by the conviction of its contributors that Wittgenstein and feminist theorists have mutually illuminating and substantively constructive things to say to each other—a conviction that is not
(yet) widely shared by others and that frequently seems, equally to feminists and to Wittgensteinians, baffling, if not perverse. Most obviously,
Wittgenstein is widely known as someone who did not much like women
(apparent exceptions to this dislike, notably Elizabeth Anscombe, were,
so the stories go, precisely exceptions that proved the rule). What is more
important, it seems at least odd to make an alliance between someone
who urges us to bring our words back home to their ordinary uses, leaving
everything as it is, recognizing that it is our agreements in judgments and
forms of life that ground intelligibility, and those whose theoretical task

it is to articulate a radical (down to the root) critique of what *we* say, of the commonplaces of everyday life, to problematize and disturb precisely those taken-for-granted agreements in judgments and forms of life. How could there be common ground between a philosopher who would dissolve philosophical problems by drawing our attention to the facts of our natural history and those who want to expose the category of the "natural" as an ideological fiction?

The contributors to this volume have diverse aims and perspectives, diverse readings both of Wittgenstein and of feminist theory, but they are united in rejecting that way of understanding the relationship between them and in believing that through understanding the relationship differently, we will be differently understanding each of the relata. Taken as a whole, these essays give us ways of understanding both Wittgenstein and feminist theory that make better sense of and help move us toward the explicit aims of each: of Wittgenstein to comprehend and come to terms with the wellsprings of philosophical problems in order to put them to rest, and of feminist theory to articulate the constructions of gender subordination in order to change them. Most schematically, what Wittgenstein and feminist theorists have in common is the suspicion that there is something fundamentally wrong with the ways in which what are taken to be "serious" questions are posed and answered, something that gives the game away before it has started to be played (what Wittgenstein calls "the decisive move in the conjuring trick").[1] They share, on these grounds, a suspicion of expertise, especially scientific expertise, as staking a claim to seriousness while obfuscating the social and intellectual grounds of its authority: why *these* questions, *these* methods? For different reasons, Wittgenstein and feminist theorists find themselves—for better *and* worse—radically "unparented," unwilling or unable to make sense in the terms of the traditions from which they come, needing to rely on a variety of other means, including telling stories about everyday life, to make a different kind of sense, to change our ideas of what sense is and of what it is to make it. For both, appeal to grounding—to whatever bedrock might have been, or been thought to be—is problematic, but the groundedness of particular judgments remains a frequent (and not infrequently realized) aspiration, and as such it is in need of understanding.

For feminist theorists, Wittgenstein suggests responses to the often immobilizing tugs between modern, Enlightenment modes of theorizing and postmodern challenges to them, challenges that can seem equally liberating and incapacitating. For Wittgenstein, feminist theory suggests responses to those who would turn him into what he dreaded becoming—a "normal" philosopher, with normal problems and solutions to them. The dis-ease with disciplined philosophy that feminist philosophers have may not be identical with his (there is not, of course, even one form of that dis-ease shared by all feminist philosophers), but the attention to philosophical practice, the refusal to take the terms of its problems and methods for granted, the serious superficiality of feminist critique ("look at *this*, what we're doing *here*, the language that we're using and the ways that we're acting, not just at the arguments and the deep structures presumed to lie beneath the surface of the texts and our discussions") can help to set Wittgenstein in a relation to current philosophy that is neither so marginal as to be irrelevant nor so central as to be unrecognizable.

The felt need for justificatory bedrock, along with other still-vital legacies of early modernity, rests on a picture of the knowing subject as ideally outside of, hence noncomplicit in the construction of, the known world. As the anthropologist Barbara Meyerhoff wrote about ritual, the power of realist discourse requires that we not catch ourselves making it up.[2] Her point, of course, is that ritual *is* powerful, even though we *have* made it up; but it is risky: every time we engage in it, even as in so doing we reinforce its power, we expose it and ourselves to the "scandal" of our own agency. Wittgenstein's exhortation that we attend to what we *do* in using language is similarly risky, as is the frequently reiterated feminist exhortation that we "denaturalize" the ways in which we think sex, gender, and sexuality, in order to reveal in order to challenge, the ways in which those categories work. A point of contact between Wittgenstein and some strains of feminist thinking is shared resistance to the inference from "this is something we *do*, not something we simply discover," to "this is arbitrary; we could just as well do it differently; there are no standards by which we might judge that we are doing it well or badly." These feminist theorists (some of them, such as those in this volume, explicitly indebted to Wittgenstein for the framing of these issues) share with Wittgenstein a respect for the power and seriousness of human practice and human history, and a radical suspicion of what is taken as the implicit contrast when their role in accounting for the shape of a category or the force of an imperative is preceded by "merely," as in "merely conventional." Such respect does not, of course, entail acquiescence, as it clearly doesn't either for Wittgenstein or for feminists, but it redirects transgressive attention toward the crafting of a radical critique that doesn't need to claim for itself practice-transcendent ground.

History is also relevant for feminists, as for Wittgensteinians, in querying the nature of philosophy. The recent salutary turn in (analytic) philosophy toward taking history seriously has illuminated the ways in which the apparently timeless and generic problems that have shaped modern philosophy arose out of the historically specific needs of those who would become bourgeois individuals; and the task of feminist theorists—along with all those, such as postcolonial, queer, and critical race theorists, who theorize from the diverse perspectives of modernity's Others—is to "rotate the axis of our examination" around whatever "real need(s)" might emerge through these struggles. To the extent that those liberatory movements mark a break with, rather than a continuation of, the emancipatory projects and promises of modernity, this historical moment is one that unsettles philosophy's conceptions of what its problems are and might be. While Wittgenstein surely did not share the politics of such liberatory movements, he did share a deep alienation from, in particular, the Europe of his day, an alienation that makes it odd to ascribe to him an attitude of acceptance of "what we do"; and he surely means to unsettle our sense that the problems of philosophy present themselves to us independently of how we live our lives. Wittgenstein and feminist theorists may not fit together comfortably, but they share a respect for discomfort—both attending to it and producing it; and we can learn a great deal both from the discomfort each causes the other and from the discomfort they together can cause both to philosophy and to political theory and practice.

The essays in this collection are all new, and many are by philosophers at the early stages of their careers. There is some previous work, listed in the bibliography at the end of the volume, that explicitly joins Wittgenstein and feminist theory, as there is a somewhat more extensive literature joining Wittgenstein and Marxist theory.[3] There are also discernibly Wittgensteinian influences in the work of feminist philosophers who do not much cite him, notably Marilyn Frye and Sara Ruddick; as well as feminist implications to not explicitly feminist discussions of Wittgenstein, notably Cora Diamond's *The Realistic Spirit: Wittgenstein, Philosophy, and the Mind*, much of the writing of Stanley Cavell, and, especially, Sabina Lovibond's *Realism and Imagination in Ethics*. But it is significant that a large number of the submissions that I received in response to the call for papers for this volume came with a cover letter expressing the author's delighted amazement that others had seen ways of connecting feminism to philosophically serious and attentive readings of Wittgenstein. Such readings show Wittgenstein to be both difficult and simple: simple in ways professional philosophy rarely is, and most difficult for those who professionally philosophize: in his words, "Philosophy unties knots in our thinking; hence its result must be simple, but philosophizing has to be as complicated as the knots it unties" (Z, 452).

Section I: The Subject of Philosophy and the Philosophical Subject

> The real discovery is the one that makes me capable of stopping
> doing philosophy when I want to.—The one that gives
> philosophy peace, so that it is no longer tormented by questions
> which bring *itself* in question.
> —Ludwig Wittgenstein, *Philosophical Investigations*

That much of the time Wittgenstein is philosophizing about philosophy is obvious. Rather less obvious is what to make of that fact: What is it about philosophy that calls for such investigation, and what might the results of that investigation be? What are the relationships between the investigation itself and the objects of investigation—both, after all, in some sense philosophy? If what we are to do with the language the philosopher would sublime—words such as 'meaning' and 'truth', 'knowledge' and 'certainty'—is to bring them back to their uses in our ordinary practices, what are we to make of the practices of philosophers, of what it is that many of *us* "do"? And if philosophy is an illness requiring therapy, is it an illness only philosophers contract? Are others healthy in a way philosophers have to struggle to be—a view of philosophy that makes it of little interest to others—something, in fact, to be avoided. (To adapt the cowboy song: "Mamas, don't let your babies grow up to be philosophers.") Or is it, rather, that the dis-ease of philosophy, the inability to feel at home in one's language and practices, is one we all carry, though only philosophers actually fall ill from it, so that the cure requires a change in the way we (all of us) live, a change that the therapy of philosophy, involving only those who suffer the symptoms, may clear the ground for but cannot effect?

The authors of the essays in Section I explore the ways in which the philosophical self is constituted and contested in order better to understand Wittgenstein's willed critical distance from the characteristic problems and demands that self makes—and the hold those problems and demands can have even on those of us who are only marginally or problematically included within the supposedly universal *we*. Phyllis Rooney and Nancy Baker point to the ways in which the philosophical subject is constituted precisely by the exclusionary forms of disciplining that give rise to its characteristic problems. Rooney examines the feminist characterization of philosophy as masculine through querying specifically the textual constitution of the philosophical subject in explicit and metaphoric contrast to modes of thinking and being that are coded as feminine. She draws our attention to the role of metaphor in structuring a field of inquiry, in this case philosophy. Bringing a feminist eye to reading philosophy (including Wittgenstein) reveals particularly gendered aspects of the metaphors that help to constitute arguments. In Rooney's analysis, gender emerges not as a subject of philosophy, but as deeply implicated in the construction of philosophy as a (disciplined) subject— hence as relevant to Wittgenstein's attention to what is going on when specifically philosophical attention (problematically, he suggests) is brought to bear.

Baker, drawing, as Rooney does, on the work of the feminist philosopher Michèle Le Doeuff, addresses the theme of exclusion—as it plays out both in constituting the philosophical voice and within philosophical discussions—by contrasting it with Wittgenstein's admonitions that we "just *look*," that we attend to differences and particularities and not insist on sharp boundaries and clear distinctions, as we will always be tempted to do in the articulation of a politically usable *we*.[4] Following Le Doeuff, Baker argues that the problem with the "disciplining" of philosophy, with its requirements of defining and boundary-marking, is not a matter of the exclusion of an already-existing something (for example, women), but rather of something's being created *by* the exclusion, as a scapegoat that, by its exclusion, gives definition to what it is excluded from. At the end of her essay Baker speculates about the unendingness of the project of unmasking such moves, given the role they play, and arguably will continue to play, in politically efficacious theorizing. What happens when we recognize the tug between political effectiveness (which seems to call for the wholehearted embrace of the categories that inform political action) and explicit acknowledgment of the provisional nature of those categories? Can we simultaneously "unsublime" our thought—

acknowledging its contingency and our own agency and, hence, responsibility—and remain wholeheartedly committed to liberatory projects "in the name of" the very groups we watch ourselves provisionally, contingently, think into existence?

Tim Craker's essay returns to the topic of the specifically philosophizing subject, and raises questions about philosophical voice. He turns to another feminist philosopher—Luce Irigaray—to explore, in particular, the relation of mimesis—speaking in the voice of another—to questions of autonomy and originality, questions that Craker argues Wittgenstein confronted in relation to the (deeply problematic) discussions of genius, gender, and Jewishness in Otto Weininger's *Sex and Character*.[5] Craker uses his discussion of mimesis to address the difficult (and for Wittgenstein's would-be heirs, painful) questions of Wittgenstein's acknowledged indebtedness to Weininger, whose writing is, in morbidly fascinating ways, anti-Semitic, homophobic, and misogynist. What does such a debt mean, Craker asks, especially in light of Wittgenstein's searching self-critique and, in particular, his characterization of his own voice as "unoriginal" (in other words, mimetic), his linking of originality to "genius," and his concern with finding a responsible, responsive, ethical voice, in and through language?

Section II: Wittgensteinian Feminist Philosophy: Contrasting Visions

> [T]he term 'language-*game*' is meant to bring into prominence the fact that the *speaking* of language is part of an activity, or of a form of life.
>
> —Ludwig Wittgenstein, *Philosophical Investigations*

Wittgenstein was deeply reflective about, and anguished by, the contemporary culture of Europe. Those reflections and that anguish have little explicit place in the writing he prepared for publication, and their place in the broader corpus of his work is difficult to ascertain, in part because what has become available to us reflects the judgments of his executors, concerning both what should be published at all and how what is published is to be organized and framed, judgments that have, for the most part, helped to shape a view of his work as more philosophically "disciplined," less enmeshed in broader cultural concerns, than might have emerged from alternative presentations. Without attempting to attribute to Wittgenstein systematic views about matters of culture that there is no reason to suppose he held or had an interest in developing, it can be illuminating to read his work against the backdrop of the world that he regarded for the most part with differing degrees of discomfort, alienation, and despair. Facing our own world, the complicated heir to his, we can look at *it* in the light of his disciplining of attention, as contrasted with the discipline of theories: how can he help us make usable sense of that world, in part by helping us query what usable sense—or, for that matter, a world—might be?

It is not, of course, just philosophizing that Wittgenstein urges us to see as something we do, as a form of practice. He suggests we think of words as tools and see their meanings in our uses of them. These urgings are not meant as the cornerstones of a philosophy of language; he is not, as he is often read as doing, formulating a "theory of meaning as use," nor is he saying that words *are* tools. Rather, in the face of our trying to formulate some theory of language (or reference, meaning, sense, truth), he wants to draw our attention to what it is we actually do in, with, and through language, to the place of language in our lives. What we are meant to see is not the stuff of a new, better theory, but rather, the complex diversity of the ways in which language is involved in our lives, and the impossibility of extricating it from those involvements in order to discover its essential nature, one supposedly revealed in abstraction from the contingencies of our uses and misuses. The inextricability goes both ways: it makes no more sense to seek *our* essence, supposedly prior to the particular languages through which we live. The mutual implications of languages and language users may preclude independent theories of either, but they do not preclude—they rather invite—attention to how, in particular locations, we do what we do and say what we say, and how it is that we can be held responsible for what we say and do.

Attention specifically to what we do with the texts we read and write, and the theories we develop and deploy, informs Alice Crary's essay. She argues for a rearticulation, rather than an abandonment, of objectivity in light of the insight gleaned from central feminist practices (she discusses in particular early second-wave consciousness-raising groups and the challenges to white-centered feminist analyses by women of color). The "wider" understanding of objectivity she argues for contrasts with the "narrower," more orthodox conception, in terms of point-of-viewlessness, which is, she argues, rightly rejected by feminist theorists. But Crary urges that we resist the claim that "feminist skeptics" take to follow from this rejection: that insights such as those she discusses can be approached *only* through the lens of the particular experiences that typically give rise to them. This relativist position is, Crary argues, both philosophically problematic and politically impotent. One important feature of her "feminist objectivist" approach is that the justifiability of truth claims is not limited to those who share the experiences on which the claims were originally based.

Sarah Hoagland takes from Wittgenstein a sharply contrasting view about the scope of the address of feminist arguments. She argues, however, not for relativism, but for separatism, that is, for the explicit decision to limit the scope of one's discourse, refusing to engage with a discourse that claims for itself universal scope while representing interests inimical to those of women. She raises questions about who speaks and, importantly, to and with whom, in relation to specifically lesbian separatism, as an epistemological strategy, one that focuses, she argues, not on the drawing of boundaries as marking difference (between lesbians, or women, and others), but on the complex and subtle articulation of differences within a space constructed to allow them. She draws on Wittgenstein's engagements with Moore and the skeptic in *On Certainty* to argue for the usefulness for feminists of the sorts of exclusions in terms of which some remarks are not mistaken but meaningless—not moves at all in the discursive games we're playing. Such exclusions are far from arbitrary: they are always politically significant, and can be politically subversive.

Susan Hekman shares with Hoagland the conviction that attention to who is knowing, from where, and with what stakes, is crucial to, rather than undermining of, a usable conception of knowledge. Her particular concern is with moral knowledge, and she defends an account of it, based on Wittgenstein's understanding of language games, that connects moral voices with personhood in a way that shows them to be importantly—not contingently and arbitrarily—diversely plural; and in contrast to Crary, she argues that morality can be (is) serious in the ways it needs to be for us to talk of moral knowledge and to make sense of our moral lives without the presumption of single answers or transcendent grounding. In contrast to Hoagland, however, on Hekman's account there is an inclusive *we* who share a (meta)moral practice that allows for such a plurality of moral voices.

Daniel Cohen's nonrealist sympathies come from a quite different direction, and from engagement with quite different Wittgensteinian texts.

He engages not, as do the other authors in the collection, with Wittgenstein's later work, but with the *Tractatus*.[6] He finds there a respect for the "nonfactual," for ways of characterizing our lived world that are not properly thought of as true or false, but that are nonetheless of great importance, more important, in many cases, than are the facts in which the world consists—and he suggests that we can see gender in this way, as part of what gives our lives meaning. Gender matters to us because it matters to us, not because it truly describes the facts about us: it is an aspect of how we inhabit the world, not a discovered fact about the world we inhabit.

In approaching the question of the relationship of feminist (or other transgressive discourses) to hegemonic discourse, Jane Braaten takes up Wittgenstein's metaphor of the city (as does Peg O'Connor in Section V), one that allows for the deliberate construction of new ways of talking even as it acknowledges a central core of ancient structures and pathways. Both O'Connor and Braaten suggest, however, that it is not only in the newly constructed outlying boroughs that change can occur; rather, moving around in the inner city in different ways can subtly reshape its face, even as we acknowledge the importance of the ancient and nondeliberate history embedded in the old walls and lanes. In particular, Braaten defends Wittgenstein against Habermas's charges that he sees languages as ahistorical and static, and users of a common language as interchangeable. She argues that Wittgenstein's view of language games is much more flexible and open than Habermas allows and that we can in Wittgensteinian terms make sense of the ways in which differently located users of a common language, or participants in different but contiguous language games, can engage critically and transformatively.

Section III: Drawing Boundaries: Categories and Kinds

> We do not know the boundaries because none have been drawn.
> To repeat, we can draw a boundary—for a special purpose. Does it take that to make the concept usable? Not at all! (Except for that special purpose.)
> —Ludwig Wittgenstein, *Philosophical Investigations*

Central to what we do in making sense of the world is settling on the categories in terms of which it is best described and explained, as well as determining that something does or does not belong to some particular category. Questions about philosophy as a (disciplinary) subject and the philosopher as (disciplined) subject that were taken up in Section I are reexamined in the essays in this section around questions concerning theoretical subjects (in other words, objects of study). Such questions about gender—what it is to be a woman and how it is to be decided if some particular person is or is not one—have played central roles in feminist theory. Feminist philosophers in particular have turned to accounts of the nature of categorizing in order to find approaches that meet the needs for a concept of 'woman' sufficiently stable and well defined to ground a political movement, but sufficiently flexible and capacious not to distort the experiences and perspectives of those in whose name that movement exists. Wittgenstein's notion of a family resemblance concept has struck some theorists as a useful and illuminating way of accommodating these apparently contradictory demands.[7]

Cressida Heyes, in her essay in this section, extends such insights through a Wittgensteinian meditation on "woman," moving from what is referred to in feminist theory as "the problem of difference"—which locates that problem in the abstract theoretical apparatus of classification—to attention to what we do in using, refusing to use, or problematizing the use of the term 'woman'. In particular, she draws our attention to the ways in which the unmasking of contingency and undefinability can be as much an expression of privilege as can the uncritical deployment of overly narrow and deceptively generic terms. The construction of theory, she reminds us, is itself a form of political practice: it is something we do and needs to be judged as such, in context.

Wittgenstein's discussions of family resemblances, as well as the private language argument, enable Hilde Lindemann Nelson to chart a middle path between postmodern theoretical evasions of definitional fixity and pragmatic evasions of theory in the name of political efficacy. She sees both these moves as responses to the failure, or abandonment, of attempts to theorize the essence of gender and the supposed consequence that, lacking anything like an essence, gender is not, really, real. If serious theory tells us that gender is not real, these arguments go, we can either be postmodern and go with the theory, or be pragmatic and either dismiss theory or acknowledge it and self-consciously use gender strategically.[8] Nelson's aim is to undermine this way of conceiving the lessons of anti-essentialism. In a critical engagement with the work of feminist philosopher Judith Butler, she argues for taking seriously the rule-governed nature of the language of gender, even as we acknowledge the ungroundedness of those rules. Postmodern nihilism is, Nelson argues, the flip side of modernist demands for foundational certainty, and equally in thrall to the pictures from which Wittgenstein would free us.

Christine Koggel turns explicit attention to the philosophical question of realism versus nominalism, arguing that, while Wittgenstein is usually read as opposing realism about kinds, he is equally opposed to nominalism (a view that he is frequently, at least implicitly, read as—or accused of—holding). Through a discussion of the concept of equality, Koggel articulates the interaction between description and prescription, drawing on Ian Hacking's "dynamic nominalism" to move away from the idea that either we discover kinds in the nature of the world, or they are "just" a matter of how we speak about the world. Rather, she argues, categorizing is a crucial aspect of our engaging in and with the world, engagements that help to shape the world as we inhabit it.

Questions about the status of the distinctions that we draw and the categories that we use receive a strikingly different, though not necessarily incompatible, treatment in the essay by Nalini Bhushan, drawing on different strains in Wittgenstein's discussions. Bhushan is struck by Wittgenstein's appeal to natural history, to the importance of what we actually do, the distinctions we actually draw, the ways we find it natural to divide the world. She connects his way of thinking about categorization without necessary and sufficient conditions to the work of the psychologist Eleanor Rosch: for Rosch and, Bhushan argues, for Wittgenstein, that this is just what we do—not what, because of the nature of reality, we *must* do—is not trivial, nor does it imply that we might, really might, do something different. She argues further that Wittgenstein's appeal to "natural history" intentionally blurs the distinction between nature and culture (a theme picked up on in Rupert Read's essay in Section V). The point is that things' having been this way (that we say and do what we do, that in general the facts of our lives are as they are) *matters*, though nothing dictates what this mattering should come to, and certainly nothing says that things have to continue in the same ways. Her discussion of Rosch also allows her to mark as a misdiagnosis the charge of essentialism as made against, in particular, white feminist theorists who overgeneralized about women based on their own experiences. Essences yield necessary and sufficient conditions for class membership and, as such, are equally applicable to all members of the class. In contrast, Rosch's discussion of class formation as governed not by essences but by the "prototype effect" accurately captures the logic of various forms of "centrism": the dominant group takes its own experiences as prototypical, and those of others as included only insofar as they sufficiently resemble the prototype, and then marked as variously marginal.

In various ways, the authors of the essays in this section insist on the *deep* importance of the apparently superficial, namely "what we do" in our practices and uses of words. The nature of that attention ranges from the political—urging us to take responsibility for our language, rather than fobbing that responsibility off onto Reality, via claims to ultimate referential transparency—to the ontological—urging us to resist the deflationary *merely* that too easily attach to the recognition of our own classificatory agency. But all the authors urge, with Wittgenstein, that we *both* recognize our own historically contingent contribution to how we categorize the world *and* break free of a picture that insists that the price of this recognition is the loss of sustainable claims to reference and truth.

Section IV: Being Human: Agents and Subjects

> How could human behaviour be described? Surely only by
> sketching the actions of a variety of humans, as they are all mixed
> up together. What determines our judgment, our concepts and
> reactions, is not what *one* man is doing *now*, an individual action,
> but the whole hurly-burly of human actions, the background
> against which we see any action.
>
> —Ludwig Wittgenstein, *Zettel*

The mutual implications of languages and persons is connected for Wittgenstein with the social nature of both. The private language argument implicates (at least the possibility of) others in our apparently simplest uses of words, and when it comes to more complex matters of the self— our beliefs, attitudes, desires, intentions, emotions—the complexities of others' lives are inextricably interwoven with our own. The texture and terrain of our lives are meaningfully patterned, intelligible, in light of the stories we tell: the complexities are complexities of significance, not of causal connection; we are who and how we are through our enmeshment with one another and through the patterns of salience that reflect that enmeshment. Feminists have stressed the social nature of the self, even as they have grappled with the difficulties such a conception poses for those who would contest the ways in which people are "made up."[9] Who, what, and how are the selves that stage such contestations? What is it to take responsibility for how we make one another up, or to imagine doing it differently?

Wittgenstein's emphasis on the shared and the social has frequently led to his being misread as a behaviorist, as denying the reality or relevance of our inner lives—a denial he repeatedly returns to, one that needs repeated disavowal. What he wants to block is the philosophical use of the inner, the demand that there be a particular sort of something "in there" that, for example, fixes meaning or reference, something that stands in need of, and admits of, no interpretation, that bears its meaning on its face. There is, he wants us to grasp, nothing that can play that role, because the role is unplayable, nor is it one that needs to be played for us to take ourselves and our inner lives seriously.

Part of such seriousness involves attention to the ways in which what it is like to be the sorts of creatures we are (what one might call human nature) both shape and are shaped by the practices in which we engage. For the authors in Section IV, the relevance of Wittgenstein for moral and political discourse in particular lies in the ways he can help us to understand those discourses and our participation in them, as subjects of experience and as actors: What is it to be a political or moral agent? What is it for moral or political judgments to have claims on us? How can we best think about the nature of subjectivity, and what view of the subject makes sense of and helps us articulate our lives as political actors?

Judith Bradford goes back to Hannah Pitkin's early attempt to draw implications for political theory from Wittgenstein, by stressing the ways in which moral and political discourse call on agents to position themselves, to embrace or repudiate judgments and practices, including, in the case of the political, those that constitute the public *we*. Bradford extends Pitkin's insights in the light of more recent work that problematizes the demarcations between the political and the personal, the public and the private. She argues for a "discursive politics" that opens the possibility for—even as it shows the extraordinary difficulty of—exploring, by moving among, different and differently powerful and privileged ways of constructing selves and *we*'s. As do a number of others in this collection, Bradford draws on the work of María Lugones, a philosopher who has examined questions of subjectivity and agency as these reveal themselves especially from the perspectives of those who move between "worlds" and whose identities are complex or even, in normative terms, impossible.

Deborah Orr finds in Wittgenstein's discussions of our natural history and of the continuing prelinguistic practices that underlie language the resources for a positive alternative characterization of human nature, one that supports feminist ethics and politics by emphasizing the social nature of the self, the continuity of humans with nonhuman nature, and the inseparability of mind and body. Drawing together Diotima of Mantinea and the African American feminist poet and theorist Audre Lorde, Orr sketches what she calls a "feminist spiritual erotics" that moves beyond the political impasses produced variously by views of human nature as either essentially fixed or as wholly socially constructed. Her suggestion that Nagarjuna's Indo-Tibetan Mahayana Buddhism offers an additional resource for liberatory conceptions of personhood intriguingly echoes Nalini Bhushan's discussion of Nagarjuna in connection with Eleanor Rosch's Wittgensteinian cognitive science in her essay in Section III.

Following Wittgenstein's suggestions that we think about how initiations into language are accomplished, Sandra Churchill discusses what she calls "conceptual rearing." She draws on a story told by the critical race theorist Patricia Williams to explore the ways in which the usually implicit teaching of concepts and distinctions serves to discipline attention, specifically around a "logic of sameness," according to which categories are internally homogeneous and differences are boundary marking. Churchill's point is not that concepts do not function like this, but rather, that using them in this way is something that we, many of us, much of the time, *do*, but that we needn't. We ought, therefore, to attend to the consequences of our doing so, to the ways in which, for example, the exclusions of racism and sexism are perpetuated by such a logic.

Starting with Wittgenstein's critique of the picture of the proprietary subject, the owner of experience, Janet Farrell Smith spins out the implications of the conception of property inherent in this picture. She extends Wittgenstein's critique into the political arena, asking how we can best understand political agency and subjectivity. Her critical discussion of the ideal of the "mastery" of the self draws on Patricia Williams's reflections on property and ownership from the complex perspective of a professor of property law descended from both a jurist and a slave: Williams's great-great-grandfather was a lawyer who purchased her great-great-grandmother.

That Churchill and Smith both turn to Patricia Williams is no coincidence. As a leading critical race theorist, Williams is concerned to bring to legal theory the insights of particular socially located narratives; and this project—of showing how a formal system of rules needs always to be interpreted through the lens of particular practices and against the background of particular interests and concerns—is very much of a piece with Wittgenstein's attempts, especially in the philosophy of mathematics, to get us to see that apparently forced moves depend for their force on our understanding them from inside a particular practice. We go on like *this* (as in his example of reciting the series "plus two") because that's what the rule tells us to do; but abstracted from our practice, the rule doesn't specify what counts as doing what it tells us to. Only because we go on as we do is it specifically *that* that the rule dictates.[10] Williams departs from Wittgenstein in explicitly drawing our attention to questions about just who *we* are, and to how practices, and hence the understanding of rules, are shaped by shifts in whose experiences and perspectives inform that *we*.

Section V: Feminism's Allies: New Players, New Games

> The sickness of a time is cured by an alteration in the mode of
> life of human beings, and it was possible for the sickness of
> philosophical problems to get cured only through a changed mode
> of thought and of life, not through a medicine invented by an
> individual.
>
> Think of the use of the motor-car producing or encouraging
> certain sicknesses, and mankind being plagued by such sickness
> until, from some cause or other, as a result of some development
> or other, it abandons the habit of driving.
>
> —Ludwig Wittgenstein, *Remarks on
> the Foundations of Mathematics*

One reason often given for finding Wittgenstein an unlikely ally for feminists is the conservatism that is supposed to follow from his grounding justification in what we do and his oft-cited injunction that philosophy "leaves everything as it is."[11] But the problems that come from the rejection of foundationalist pictures of justification and of accounts of objectivity that abstract from the specificities of social location are ones common to feminist theorizing, quite independently of any explicit connection to Wittgenstein. Analyses of those pictures and accounts as problematically masculinist have featured centrally in feminist epistemology, as have discussions of how, having rejected them, to make sense of and to argue for feminist claims. The need for an alternative to the apparently forced choice between "look, Ma, no hands (or hearts)" objectivism and politically irresponsible playful pluralism has shaped feminist theorizing, and the clear "real need" to find such an alternative, as well as the concreteness with which the problems get posed, makes these discussions useful places to look for readings of Wittgenstein that do not portray him as complacently accepting of a world he so clearly found deeply troubling. Such readings are, in turn, useful in the ongoing attempts to articulate such a middle path, especially once one acknowledges the impossibility of a quick theory-fix: It is not *just* a philosophical mistake to think that without practice-transcendent ground we are deprived of meaningful uses of concepts such as 'truth' or 'reality', and it will take more than a better theory to keep us from veering between demanding such ground or rejecting the concepts.

Wittgenstein's question in the *Investigations:* "What gives the impression that we want to deny something?" has particular resonance here.[12] Many of the critics of objectivist epistemologies and realist metaphysics *are* meaning to deny something—the meaningfulness of talk of truth or of a real world—and it is with good reason that many feminists, along with others who have only recently and still tenuously won the right to be among those who might possess the truth about the real world, should be suspicious of claims that such talk is meaningless or, worse, theoretically naive. Perhaps Wittgenstein's most important contribution to these disputes is to show such claims to be still in thrall to the pictures they take themselves to be denying, still captured by the thought that only something that transcended our practices could make notions such as truth and reality genuinely, fully, robustly meaningful. To truly break the hold of those pictures would be to give up both the demand and the nihilistic response to the demand's not being met.

Think of the cartoon characters who run over the edge of cliffs and fall only when they notice that there is no longer any ground underneath their feet. Outside cartoons we fall whether we notice or not, so it surely behooves us to pay attention to where we stand and not to take as foundation what will not bear the weight we would place on it. But how to take this lesson is not always clear: one might be tempted to derive the impossibility of boats from one's inability to walk on water. An alternative story is this: when I was learning to walk, I needed to be holding onto something—the edge of a couch or an adult's hand or, after a while, just a stick. Empty-handed, I fell down. If an adult had pointed out to me that what I clutched was, in fact, unconnected to any plausible source of support, I might have fallen—but I might instead have realized that I was, actually, walking, without the support I had demanded as a necessary condition. What I was doing is what walking unaided *is*, talismanic stick or no.

The authors in Section V take on the question of how to understand such notions as truth, justification, and objectivity in ways that reject the demand that they be understood—if they are to be meaningful at all—in practice-transcendent ways. They do so by examining specific sites of political dispute and activism, holding theory responsible to real needs: What sorts of claims need to be made and defended, and what resources are available for doing so? Thinking about the issues that arise among feminists especially around issues of sexuality, including bisexuality, Wendy Lynne Lee takes as her starting point the insight from Donna Haraway that it is precisely partial, situated voices, not those that aim to be speaking from nowhere-in-particular, that can contribute to objective knowledge of the world. Lee finds in Wittgenstein's *Remarks on Colour* suggestive resources for fleshing out Haraway's conception of partial perspectives and of the subjects that embody them, emphasizing, through examples drawn from the work of María Lugones and Elizabeth Daumer, the roles of acknowledgement of and responsibility for the positions from which we view the world.

Bruce Krajewski reads the *Remarks on Colour* by situating the text in a world—Wittgenstein's and, somewhat differently, ours—in which color is not simply a feature we find in the world, but a complexly value-laden system in terms of which we see the world, in particular, as it shapes our conceptions and perceptions of race. Like most of the other authors in this volume, Krajewski is "reading into" Wittgenstein's texts: he almost certainly was not thinking about race in the *Remarks on Colour*. But it is not just that, turning to his texts in the light of these concerns, we can find useful tools for thinking about race (or gender). Rather, we equally find illuminating takes on the texts themselves when we think of them (and of philosophical texts generally) not as stable and fixed, but as themselves part of our world, to be used and understood through use, their meaning not a matter of what they are, but of what they do, or rather, of what we (can) do with them.

Rupert Read examines the language of nature and culture as it is deployed by many environmental activists, arguing that responsible politics is better served by evading the debate between nature and culture, dissolving the intelligibility of the distinction. That is, a distinction between nature and culture is something we *make*, and we might learn not to make it: his proposal is that we speak and think instead in terms of ecosystems, and judge them as preferable or nonpreferable, judgments that are contested sociopolitically by sociopolitically constituted and contested *we*'s. Read finds in Wittgenstein not only attention to language as something we do, but also, more specifically, the resources for thinking of humans as always already in an environment that is inextricably cultural and natural. Wittgenstein, Read argues, is, like John Dewey, a "cultural naturalist."

Peg O'Connor is concerned, similarly to Sarah Hoagland in her essay in Section II, with the ways in which the creation of new practices creates new meanings. Both can be seen as addressing Alice Crary's arguments, also in Section II, that some feminists' claims about the inexpressibility of women's experience in male-centered language run afoul of Wittgenstein's arguments against analogous attempts on the part of the skeptic to insist on the truth of something that cannot quite be said. For O'Connor, as for Hoagland, it is not that there are, as Crary shows to be incoherent, truths that preexist the possibilities of their articulation, but there are ways in which participants in language games can be sufficiently ill at ease in those games as to have good reason to make the attempt to create new ones, attempts that as and insofar as they succeed, will be the ground for the emergence of new meanings, new modes of articulation. Such attempts involve learning new competencies and, crucially, unlearning old ones, becoming less than fluent in the language games of racism and homophobia, for example.

As in the case of the philosophical demands for the unambiguous inner "something," Wittgenstein deflects the demands for the unassailable guarantors of truth, deflecting as well the skepticism that would follow from those demands' being unmet. From the perspectives of those whose efforts at accurate description of the world are of practical, political importance (as they are in the essays in this section), the lesson of Wittgenstein's therapy is a crucial one: taking some task (for example, accurately describing the world) to be in theory impossible is a good way of evading recognition of, and responsibility for, how extraordinarily *difficult* it is. Paying close, careful attention to what we do in giving accounts of the world—including to who the *we* are that do this, and to how such accounts shift when that *we* changes—reveals both that justification does, sometimes, come to an end, and properly so, *and* that we may mistakenly think that we have reached such an end when we have yet to engage seriously with a particular critical response that we could not have imagined or that we cannot figure out how to understand. Justification is not less so for being fallible: it is, in fact, demonstrated openness to demonstrable fallibility that marks true justification. The demand for something that would put an end to the process, some bedrock that would ground it, is a demand for the dismantling of what actually makes justification work. Arguing that the demand is for the impossible, while conceding that without it justification is ungrounded, lets one off the hook when it comes to being responsible for what makes justification come to an end (or seem to) when it does, and for creating the conditions under which it could come to a better one.

The cumulative weight of the essays in this section—in fact, of this volume as a whole—despite the differences in opinion and emphasis among the authors, points to the conclusion that Wittgenstein's truest philosophical heirs and most faithful interpreters might well be found among people he would never have acknowledged as allies. His avoidance of explicit political engagement has enabled most of his philosophical heirs to absorb him within the philosophical tradition from which he aimed to free himself and us. But Wittgensteinians ought not to find this fact surprising: philosophy alone, even Wittgenstein's philosophy, cannot liberate us from itself, and he would have been the last to claim that it could. The "real needs" around which our investigations are to turn—to which those investigations are to be accountable—must be just that: *real.* And that means they are to be found where people struggle—concretely, politically—against the very forms of life in which they are enmeshed and that give meaning even to their most radical protests and visions. If we know where, and how, to *just look,* we can answer the theorist's insistence that such a thing can't happen with the observation that it does; and, having liberated practice from the grip of theory, we can in turn liberate theorizing from the grip of its own demands.

Notes

1. Ludwig Wittgenstein, *Philosophical Investigations*, trans. G. E. M. Anscombe (New York: Macmillan, 1958), §308.

2. Barbara G. Meyerhoff, "We Don't Wrap Herring in a Printed Page: Fusion, Fictions, and

Continuity in Secular Ritual," in *Secular Ritual*, ed. Sally Falk Moore and Barbara G. Meyerhoff (Amsterdam: Van Gorcum, Assen, 1977), 200.

3. See Gavin Kitching and Nigel Pleasants, *Wittgenstein and Marxism: Language, Science, and Morality*, forthcoming from Routledge Research. The volume is a collection of papers from an international symposium held in Cambridge in June 1999.

4. There is an extensive feminist literature about this temptation and about related issues concerning the problematic role of identity/ies in political theory and practice. For engagements with these issues and references to this literature, see, in this volume, the essays by Nancy Baker, Cressida Heyes, Hilde Lindemann Nelson, and Sandra Churchill. Heyes explores the issues further in her *Line Drawings: Defining Women Through Feminist Practice* (Ithaca: Cornell University Press, 2000).

5. On Wittgenstein's fascination with Weininger, see Ray Monk, *Ludwig Wittgenstein: The Duty of Genius* (London: Vintage, 1990).

6. For another discussion of the *Tractatus* in relation to feminist concerns, in this case, the nature of the self and of responsibility, see Wendy Lee-Lampshire, "The Moral 'I': The Feminist Subject and the Grammar of Self-Reference," *Hypatia* 7, no. 1 (1992): 34–51.

7. See Judith Mary Green and Blanche Radford Curry, "Recognizing Each Other Amidst Diversity: Beyond Essentialism in Collaborative Multi-Cultural Feminist Theory," *Sage* 8, no. 1 (1991): 39–49.

8. For the move of "strategic essentialism," see Gayatri Chakravorty Spivak, "Criticism, Feminism, and the Institution," in *The Post-Colonial Critic: Interviews, Strategies, Dialogues*, ed. Sarah Harasym (New York: Routledge, 1990).

9. For an early statement of these difficulties, see Marilyn Friedman, "The Social Self and the Partiality Debates," in *Feminist Ethics*, ed. Claudia Card (Lawrence: University Press of Kansas, 1991). For a subtle treatment of the roles we play in the expression—and, hence, the nature—of one another's feelings, see Sue Campbell, *Interpreting the Personal: Expression and the Formation of Feelings* (Ithaca: Cornell University Press, 1997).

10. *PI*, 185–242.

11. *PI*, 124.

12. *PI*, 305. (The Anscombe translation has "anything" in place of "something." I changed it to conform to the original German and, more important, to make it clear that the question is not a rhetorical one: Wittgenstein cares—as, I argue, do his feminist interpreters—about what it is that gives us this impression.)

Section I

The Subject of Philosophy and the Philosophical Subject

1

Philosophy, Language, and Wizardry

Phyllis Rooney

I

The development of, and reaction to, feminist philosophy at this end of the twentieth century bears especially interesting comparison with the development of Wittgenstein's philosophy in the earlier part of the century. On the surface they seem to have little in common. Wittgenstein was not known for political involvement or political insight, a significant marker of feminist thought. His remarks about women, as we glean from biographical accounts especially, leave much to be desired from a feminist perspective.

In his philosophical work, however, Wittgenstein placed himself in an uneasy critical relationship with the tradition of philosophy, a position many feminist philosophers also find themselves in, whether they choose it or not. The claim, for instance, by some philosophers that feminist philosophy is not "real philosophy" has renewed interest in questions about traditional definitions of *philosophy*. It is here that feminists will surely find common cause with Wittgenstein, who, though motivated by quite different concerns, continually focused critical attention on the constitution of philosophy and philosophical questions—this is one of the most distinguishing characteristics of his philosophy, both early and late. My main goal in this essay is to advance this common cause and, specifically, to take it in the direction of a particular focus on language as the working medium of philosophy.

Critical rethinking of traditional views of women and gender relations continues to be central to many feminist projects in moral, social and political philosophy. Over the past two decades there has also been a growing awareness that the theoretical momentum engendered by feminist reassessments cannot be confined to these particular areas of philosophy, or separated off into "applied" philosophy, as some not especially sympathetic to feminist philosophy continue to seek to do. Feminist work has begun to challenge some long-held assumptions about the ways in which many core concepts in these and other areas of philosophy are delineated and theorized, including such central concepts as human nature, rationality, moral goodness, objective knowledge, and political order. In the wake of such scrutiny come concerns about the definition and role of Western philosophy itself, which, as a discipline with a specific history and culture, also lends itself to feminist critique.

It does not take a student of that tradition long to note that in it women were persistently excluded and disparaged, and that many of the ideals of thought and action that philosophers theorized as constitutive of human excellence were regularly denied to women.[1] Philosophy has thereby identified itself as "masculine," in a sense of that term that is something more than the historical fact that it was almost exclusively men who got to do philosophy, to have it published and recognized. The many implications of this and other senses of the "masculinity" or "masculinism" of philosophy have only begun to be fully explored. I propose to develop what I think is one particularly fruitful avenue of such exploration in this essay, one that attends to the linguistic and symbolic aspects of philosophical texts. By drawing on specific Wittgensteinian insights into the relationship between philosophy and language (particularly when philosophy is itself construed as a special kind of working in or with language), I will show how we can secure new feminist insights into some gender dimensions of philosophy, insights that even Wittgenstein couldn't quite entertain. In addition, as we will see, such insights provoke new considerations of Wittgenstein's own reflections on language and philosophy.

Suggestions about exploring the "masculinity" of philosophy, or of concepts and areas in philosophy, meet strong resistance in a discipline that has been significantly invested in its goal of acquiring understandings of truth, goodness, and beauty that are in some sense universal and abstract, that, in effect, transcend the particularities of specific cultures and histories, including particularities of gender. However, feminist re-readings of the canon are continuing to show that gender norms, symbols, and ideals have mattered at various points: in the delineation of philosophical problems, in the directions that solutions to those problems take, and as mentioned, in the conceptualizations of theoretical concepts that would seem, initially, to have nothing to do with gender.[2] And so a puzzling discrepancy emerges, between what philosophers have regularly claimed they were doing (or were attempting to do) and what feminist reconsiderations of philosophical texts have begun to reveal.

One important clue to understanding this discrepancy starts to surface when we examine the ways in which the professed neutrality and universality of philosophy and philosophical concepts have been articulated and theorized. Gender symbolism emerges as a significant element here. When we explore philosophical texts, not simply with a view to what is written there about actual women, but also with a keen eye for the discursive role of the symbolic "woman" and "the feminine," a significant pattern emerges. There is now a substantial body of work that draws attention to *woman* as a deeply embedded cultural, symbolic, and linguistic category that has functioned within philosophy as the foil, "the other" upon which (or whom) is projected disparaged modes of embodiment, locatedness, disunity, disorder, subjectivity, and irrationality.[3] It is important to note that this projection *thereby also inscribes* the ideal philosophical place of reason, order, unity, objectivity, clarity, and control as other than the other, that is, as "masculine." (Here, as elsewhere, *feminine* and *masculine* are fundamentally complementary relational terms, that is, they have sense only in relation to each other in the context of particular understandings of gender.) The problem is not simply that various concepts and locations are marked as masculine or feminine, but that gender terms carry with them a host of cultural associations, assumptions, and divisions that are carried over into the structures of "abstract" philosoph-ical theorizing. Among other things, this results in gender metaphors and symbols doing conceptual work that would not get done without them—as we will see later with specific examples.

But first, I switch attention to Wittgenstein's reflections on the role of language in demarcating philosophy and philosophical problems. The critical reflexive scrutiny that Wittgenstein brings to the philosopher's relationship to language provides an especially interesting framework within which to examine the role of gender imagery in philosophy—to examine the ways in which this and other images and metaphors are often implicated in keeping philosophers "in the grip of a picture," as Wittgenstein might put it. This, in turn (as I will argue in the final sec-tion), helps to expand our understanding of some of the contours of Witt-genstein's own thought—in particular, it helps to shed light on some recurring tensions that arise in his attempts to determine to his satisfac-tion the nature and role of philosophy.

Philosophers have traditionally seen themselves as engaging in system-atic reflections on the nature of things such as reason, knowledge, human nature, goodness, beauty, and social and political order. What they often haven't seen, and what Wittgenstein saw perhaps more clearly than any previous philosopher, is the importance of language in not simply provid-ing a medium for philosophizing, but in significantly framing the en-deavor itself. Language came to the fore for Wittgenstein, no longer as a transparent medium passively recording the mind's descriptions of, and reflections on, the world, but as having an indispensable role in the way the world is pictured in mind and thought (in his early work), and as an active participant in the constitution of both mind and world (in his later work). In addition, both early and late, Wittgenstein argued that philosophical problems regularly have their source in linguistic entangle-ments created by philosophers no less than by nonphilosophers. Because of this, their solution often involves something like a dissolution brought about by a more perspicuous use of language.

It is important to distinguish here between two philosophical projects with language, even though Wittgenstein was involved with both. In *philosophy of language* (as a specific subject area *in* philosophy), we reflect on how language works, what propositions are, how words signify mean-ings, and so on. A second project with language, the one that is a large part of my focus in this essay, is the *metaphilosophical* project of mapping out the nature and role of philosophy itself vis-à-vis language. Here questions such as the following are foregrounded (questions that are as much about philosophy as they are about language): What specific kinds of attention to language are required when one does philosophy? Does philosophy have, or ought it to have, its own special language in the way mathematics and psychology have their discipline-specific languages? Or is philosophy's primary role with language that of bringing order and clarity to language, to "ordinary" language and to discipline-specific languages, and, if so, what constitutes that philosophical order and clarity? While a philosopher can work in philosophy of language without developing any systematic metaphilosophical claims about the nature of philosophy out of that pursuit, this is hardly the case with Wittgenstein. For him the two projects are fundamentally connected. The shift in his views on the nature of philosophy from his early to his later work reflects the shift in his views of language over that time. What remains relatively constant for him, however, is the importance of the philosopher's engagement with language, and especially as that demarcates the enterprise of philosophy itself.

Wittgenstein devotes a significant part of the *Tractatus* to the definition and logical analysis of propositions with sense—for him, propositions that describe possible states of affairs in the world. The attempt by philosophers to make certain kinds of ethical and metaphysical statements is seriously misguided, he thinks, since it involves an attempt to say in language what cannot be said. He sums up his position on "the correct method in philosophy" in one of his concluding paragraphs: "The correct method in philosophy would really be the following: to say nothing except what can be said, i.e., propositions of natural science—i.e., something that has nothing to do with philosophy—and then, whenever someone else wanted to say something metaphysical, to demonstrate to him that he had failed to give a meaning to certain signs in his propositions" (*Tractatus*, §6.53).[4]

Wittgenstein's later reflections on language and philosophy, however, include disabusing himself of the "picture that held [him] captive" in the *Tractatus*, at the core of which is the notion that language and propositions have an "essence" as "something that lies *beneath* the surface . . . [that] *is hidden from us* . . . which an analysis digs out" (*PI*, §115, §92).[5] But what he later sees as this problem of seeking *hidden* essences also has its main source in language. The forms of language that we use in philosophy to express ourselves often stand in our way: for instance, questions such as, What is language? What is a proposition? are framed and presented in a way that makes us seek hidden essences; philosophical discourse makes us invest such concepts as "experience," "language," and "world" with peculiarity and profundity (*PI*, §93, §92, §97). Instead of seeking hidden meanings, structures, and referents, Wittgenstein now continually urges us to shift our attention to *language use* as that is "open to view," and especially to the way words are used in their ordinary or natural settings, "in the language-game which is [their] original home." Thus, a significant marker of his approach to all sorts of philosophical topics such as mind, language, understanding, the self, rule-following and mathematics, involves continually seeking "to bring words back from their metaphysical to their everyday use" (§116). And so, here again, he is also fundamentally concerned with something like a "correct method in philosophy" (his earlier phrase): though the method has changed, it is still primarily bound up with particular kinds of attention to language, and, again, with the ways in which it can lead philosophers astray. It is in such contexts that he asserts what is one of his most prominent (later) claims about the nature and role of philosophy: "Philosophy is a battle against the bewitchment of our intelligence by means of language" (§109).

There has been much debate about more precise understandings of this assertion (as well as its variants in other contexts) and about its relationship to Wittgenstein's other (later) remarks about language and philosophy. Few interpreters claim that these remarks weave together to give an overall clear consistent picture of Wittgenstein's later thought, and I don't intend to claim so either. But I would like to expand the context of interpretation somewhat, and in a way that I think sheds new light on some tensions that directly connect to his "bewitchment" remarks. To do that, I would like to place this discussion about the philosopher's place in or with language in a somewhat broader historical context, one that invites special feminist reflection. Although Wittgenstein advanced this critical focus on language and philosophy in significant new ways, he was also drawing on some recurring themes in the Western philosophical tradition, themes that emerge anew with feminist re-readings.

II

In her book examining woman's relationship to the history of philosophy Nancy Tuana invites us to re-read our traditional texts *as women*, a reading strategy that, she says, is open to both women and men.[6] Reading with special attention to the ways in which women and gender relations are constructed in these texts, she argues, helps us to better understand the basis of women's alienation from philosophy and the ways in which traditional gender biases have informed central categories and philosophical systems. However, this reading that Tuana encourages involves resisting the reading and hearing space we have typically been encouraged to adopt, which, among other things, is the reading space of the "neutral" philosopher subject who knows no gender. Yet, as noted above, a keen awareness of the persistent displacement of woman as "other" in philosophical texts begins to disrupt this putative neutrality.

This reading also includes resisting common assumptions about the peripheral nature of disparaging comments about women. Many still claim that such comments can be set aside as historical curiosities of more sexist times, as extraneous to the real stuff of philosophy. But this suggestion also raises concerns in feminist hearing spaces about who or what is still projected as the authorizing subject of philosophy, that is, who decides what philosophy is, what demarcates the "proper" subject matter of philosophy, including what can and cannot be overlooked in canonical texts. Michèle Le Doeuff articulates this unease well: "If we do not feel authorized to use the usual [critical] method to examine observations in a philosophical text in which 'women' are discussed, this comes down to saying that the problem is unimportant. Or that a thinker may say whatever he likes about 'women' (but not about physics). Or that we do not think we have the right to look critically at what is said about 'women'. Or all three things."[7]

The study of the textual placement of women draws attention to the use of "woman" and gender terms in their metaphorical and symbolic senses no less than in their more literal senses. But then, concerns about a second displacement (or erasure) appear. Taking images and metaphors in philosophical texts seriously also involves resisting common readings of these texts, which treat metaphors as stylistic embellishment not essential to the core content and argument. In another work, *The Philosophical Imaginary*, Le Doeuff addresses this dilemma of the common philosophical use of imagery coupled with the normal viewing of such images "as extrinsic to the theoretical work." She attributes this dismissal to the fact that "[p]hilosophical discourse is inscribed and declares its status as philosophy through a break with myth, fable, the poetic, the domain of the image . . . [i]t is, indeed, a very old commonplace to associate philosophy with a certain *logos* thought of as defining itself through opposition to other types of discourse."[8] At one point, in her discussion of the imaginary portrait of woman in philosophy texts ("a power of disorder, a twilight beauty, a dark continent, a sphinx of dissolution") Le Doeuff notes that the logos/mythos couple is one form of an opposition between definite and indefinite that the man/woman difference is used to signify (113–15).

I want to examine in more detail some important implications of these gender images and associations that are too often drawn in broad strokes. I begin by noting a connection between the two displacements, that is, the displacement of woman as other than the ideal or "normed" philosopher subject, and the displacement of image and metaphor as other than the proper language and discourse of philosophy. This connection involves noting when metaphor is cast as the "feminine" decoration or embellishment of language.

John Locke provides what surely must be one of the most eloquent articulations of this connection. In a chapter titled "Of the Abuse of Words," he claims that "figurative speeches and allusion in language" can scarcely be considered faults in discourses where we seek "pleasure and delight," but where we seek "information and improvement" it is quite another matter:

> [I]f we would speak of things as they are, we must allow that all the art of rhetoric, besides order and clearness, all the artificial and figurative application of words eloquence hath invented, are for nothing else but to insinuate wrong ideas, move the passions, and thereby mislead the judgment . . . where truth and knowledge are concerned [these artificial and figurative application of words] cannot but be thought a great fault, either of the language or person that makes use of them.

Yet he notes how much men are tempted by such entertainments and deceptions of language, and he then ends this paragraph two sentences later with the following statement: "Eloquence, like the fair sex, has too prevailing beauties in it to suffer itself ever to be spoken against; and it is vain to find fault with those arts of deceiving, wherein men find pleasure to be deceived."[9] We are, of course, drawn to Locke's "eloquent" use of a gender metaphor to further persuade us of the entertaining yet deceiving ploys of figurative speech! Furthermore, we note that this metaphor marks the proper place in language (for the philosopher at least) as "masculine."

Since he uses this image in *the same passage* in which he is warning us philosophers—purveyors of truth and knowledge—about the use of figurative speech, we begin to wonder whether this metaphor is visible as such to Locke, whether it even counts. Perhaps, we conjecture, this is some kind of ground metaphor in philosophy, part of some unacknowledged foundation for philosophy, a metaphor that "goes without saying," as Wittgenstein might put it.

It is especially interesting to note a particular edition of Locke's work where the editor, J. A. St. John, adds an editorial comment at the end of this passage. He remarks that the notions that Locke puts forward here on "ornate and figurative style" are "as inconsistent with his own practice as they are with true philosophy." He notes that Locke makes use of a profusion of tropes and figures throughout his works, and St. John continues:

> [N]or, as will be evident to the reader, is his meaning thereby at all darkened, but placed in a broader, clearer, and more perfect light. It is, in fact, nearly impossible to convey truth from one mind to another without the abundant employment of metaphors; and the art of rhetoric, though it may sometimes be used to adorn and recommend falsehood, is no more to be rejected by truth on that account, than dress is to be laid aside by modest women because it is also worn by courtezans.[10]

St. John essentially modifies Locke's distinction between literal-philosophical and metaphorical-rhetorical uses of language to a distinction between good philosophical uses of metaphor (that "consistent with . . . true philosophy") and bad philosophical uses of metaphor (that which "recommends falsehood"). Yet what is additionally noteworthy is that he does this by also using a gender-inflected metaphor that can be read as a modification of Locke's metaphor: the metaphor in St. John's case draws upon a supposed clear distinction between two kinds of women. Now we ask: Does St. John's metaphor automatically count as a "good" philosophical use of metaphor, for St. John at least? This is not only left unsaid, but it is not even clear that, as with Locke, St. John's own metaphor is visible as such to him. Furthermore, it is not at all evident from this note that St. John is even aware of Locke's "fair sex" image as a metaphor: to illustrate his point about Locke's own practice of using metaphors he directs the reader to "§5 of the next chapter, where [Locke] speaks of 'language being the great *conduit* whereby men convey their discoveries" (113). I will return shortly to a further examination of the cognitive work these metaphors do.

It is no longer accurate to say that metaphor is regularly treated as "mere" stylistic embellishment by all (or perhaps even most) philosophers, or treated as "seducing the Reason," a figure Eva Feder Kittay notes that Bachelard used, seductively, to damn it.[11] More recently, as Kittay documents, metaphor has been experiencing renewed attention in some areas of philosophy, in philosophy of language and philosophy of science especially. Some still grant a relatively minimal cognitive role to metaphor: those who subscribe to some version of the *substitution view*, for example, argue that a metaphorical expression is simply a substitution for a typically more long-winded literal expression. Max Black's work on metaphor made an important contribution to this renewed philosophical interest in more robust semantic and cognitive accounts of metaphor. His *interaction view* of metaphor has been quite influential, though with predictable modifications and refinements. Metaphors, he argues, involve an interaction between the secondary domain (the domain or subject area from which the metaphor is drawn) and the primary domain (the "literal" subject area under discussion), which alters, however subtly, our understanding of both domains. In particular, he argues that when a metaphor "works," a system of assumptions and implications is carried over from the secondary domain to help structure meanings and understandings of concepts in the primary domain. In the case of the metaphors under discussion here, this suggests that associations and assumptions linked to gender help to structure "our" understanding of language, particularly as it demarcates the realm of clear philosophical thought and expression.[12]

With the exception of the examination of specific models in science (where models are understood as extended metaphors), many philosophical theories of metaphor have tended to focus on metaphor in a very general way as it is used in everyday speech. Among philosophers who ponder general theories of metaphor, there is also something of a lack of reflexivity in the relatively minimal attention they give to the cognitive role of metaphors and metaphorical themes in philosophical texts, yet many of their arguments apply no less to such metaphors. This is, in part, what makes Le Doeuff's work significant.[13] In addition, more-general accounts or theories of metaphor often proceed with little examination of the cultural and social location of specific metaphors and metaphorical themes. This, as we will see, can be especially illuminating when applied to the kinds of gender metaphors under examination in this essay.

Le Doeuff's remarks on the use and displacement of philosophical imagery are ones that can be quite aptly addressed to these examples from Locke and St. John (and others later):

> it is no longer feasible to go on ignoring the importance of imagery in philosophy. . . . The perspective I am adopting . . . involves reflecting on strands of the imaginary operating in places where, in principle, they are supposed not to belong and yet where, without them, nothing would have been accomplished. . . . Images are the means by which every philosophy can engage in straightforward dogmatization, and decree a 'that's the way it is' without fear of counter-argument, since it is understood that a good reader will by-pass such 'illustrations'—a convention which enables the image to do its work all the more effectively. (*The Philosophical Imaginary*, 2, 12)

What is the cognitive work that Locke's and St. John's examples effectively achieve? I contend that the "straightforward dogmatization" secured by their images involves, at least, injecting unargued claims that seem to remain invisible as such. Locke relies on assumptions about gender difference and gender dimorphism to help deflect attention from the need for arguments for the following claims: there is a clear distinction between literal and metaphorical uses of language; these two aspects of language belong to and help demarcate two quite distinct disciplines, philosophy and rhetoric; philosophy ought to maintain this distanced and disparaging attitude toward rhetoric—this is a significant element in the demarcation of philosophy. St. John's image, on the other hand, replaces an argument for the assertion that there is a clear distinction between good and bad philosophical uses of metaphor. These "effective" metaphors, in effect, carry arguments that do not get carried without them.

Before I return to reflect on the broader social and cultural placement of these metaphors, I want to add another example, from the work of American pragmatist C. S. Peirce. This, like Locke's example, is particularly significant because it occurs in a context where Peirce is stressing the philosophical importance of clear and distinct ideas, precise definitions, and "higher perspicuity of thought." Not unlike Wittgenstein (in the *Tractatus*), who was quite influenced by recent developments in symbolic logic, Peirce was inspired by logic's renewed promise to instill new levels of analysis and precision in language, thought, and philosophy. In the opening section of an essay that is often touted as the "seminal work" in the pragmatist tradition, Peirce again emphasizes the philosophical importance of precise definitions and uses of terms. Lest we are not fully convinced of the urgency of this renewed call to clarity and precision, Peirce ends this opening section with an image of what "a single unclear idea, a single formula without meaning, lurking in a young man's head" will do:

> Many a man has cherished for years as his hobby some vague shadow of an idea, too meaningless to be positively false; he has, nevertheless, passionately loved it, has made it his companion by day and by night, and has given to it his strength and his life, leaving all other occupations for its sake, and in short has lived with it and for it, until it has become, as it were, flesh of his flesh and bone of his bone; and then he has waked up some bright morning to find it gone, clean vanished away like the beautiful Melusina of the fable, and the essence of his life gone with it.[14]

(One can barely begin to imagine what would happen to a young man with three or five unclear ideas!) Again, in a way that resembles Locke's example, we note that recurring symbolic association of woman with the tempting and attractive, yet—for the philosopher bent on clarity and truth—ultimately dangerous and deceptive, aspects of language and thought. And again, we have the sense of an argument being clinched here that perhaps even Peirce suspects might not otherwise be clinched. Wouldn't "we" be less convinced of the dire urgency of ridding ourselves of unclear ideas without this image of the young man's association with and abandonment by the beautiful Melusina?

This leads us to the question, Who are the "we" here? In these contexts it is of particular interest to consider Black's remarks about the cultural placement and efficacy of metaphors. He notes that a metaphor "works" if, among other things, it draws upon a "system of associated commonplaces" shared by the writer and intended readers. He adds: "[T]he important thing for the metaphor's effectiveness is not that the commonplaces shall be true, but that they should be readily and freely evoked. (Because this is so, a metaphor that works in one society may seem preposterous in another.)"[15] The social and cultural settings that locate these and many similar gender metaphors in philosophy are worth amplifying. For a start, what these images project as the immediate setting for these passages is a conversation among men whose identity as such, that is, as other-than-woman, is not incidental to that conversation. It is difficult to see how the systems of "associated commonplaces" evoked by these images could be so readily summoned and deployed among women, which is not to say that women in these cultural settings don't get these metaphors. Many gender metaphors can also be given a more specific historical setting. With St. John's image, for example, it is important to note that the distinction between "modest women" and "courtesans" is less about women than about men in a specific social and class setting who establish and maintain their status among themselves by demarcating their circumscribed relationships to women: they might, for instance, associate in publicly sanctioned marriages with modest women, and their association with courtesans may be condoned if it is kept appropriately discrete. The clarity of the distinction this metaphor deploys (which insinuates a supposedly clear distinction between good and bad philosophical uses of metaphor), thus depends on particular gender-related social norms and institutions in specific historical settings.

On a somewhat broader cultural level, what underlies these and many similar gender metaphors is that familiar male conundrum in the Western philosophical imaginary: what to do about women? In a cultural tradition that is significantly misogynistic, there is that persistent concern with women's proper placement and relationship to men. In particular, we get those recurring agonized images of male heterosexuality as involving attraction and desire yet also elements of revulsion, and possibilities of pleasant seduction that are simultaneously possibilities of destruction—or at least disarray and confusion. The shared background of these images is a cultural imaginary drawn in part from mythological associations carried by the Furies and Sirens in classical times, and by Witches in more modern times—a mythological heritage making its appearance in a discourse which, as Le Doeuff notes, declares its status as *philosophy* through a break with myth and fable.

Wittgenstein's "bewitchment" image (as noted in *PI*, §109: "Philosophy is a battle against the bewitchment of our intelligence by means of language") also draws on this cultural imaginary. (The German word Wittgenstein uses here, *Verhexung*, is appropriately translated as "bewitchment." It is not a very common word in German—compared with

Verzauberung [enchantment], for example. Also, the gender association is marked by the root word *Hexe*, meaning "witch"—in a way that is not the case with *Zaube* [magic].) In addition to recurring patterns in the gender imagery, there are other comparisons with the previous examples that are worth noting. As is the case with Locke's, St. John's, and Peirce's examples, Wittgenstein's metaphor (in §109) appears in a part of the text where he is specifically concerned with language and the misunderstandings it can bring: for each of them, the avoidance of these misunderstandings helps to demarcate the discipline of philosophy itself. Like Locke and Peirce, Wittgenstein *ends* his paragraph with his claim/image, and, again, we get the sense of an argument being clinched or settled in a way that might not happen without it. Rather than treating these images as afterthoughts to the main argument, we might think of them as something like a coda at the end of a literary or musical work which, though often seen as technically separate from the main structure, functions to round out and cast a unifying interpretation back to the main work. With all this in mind, it is now time to turn to a fuller textual examination of Wittgenstein's metaphor, and to see how that image might (as St. John said of Locke's tropes and figures) place his meaning in a broader, clearer, and more perfect light.

III

Wittgenstein, unlike Locke, doesn't directly disparage the philosophical use of metaphor, though, as we will see, some of his remarks about the deceptions of language might be extended to cover specific effects of metaphor use. Like Locke, Wittgenstein himself partakes of a profusion of images and tropes: his eloquent and creative use of metaphor may well be unmatched in philosophy—except perhaps by Plato or Nietzsche.[16] He often uses metaphors (like the *fly in the fly bottle*) to illuminate and name the pictures that he thinks have captivated philosophers. Wittgenstein's (later) battle against the bewitchment of language cannot simply mean, then, a battle to avoid metaphors. While Wittgenstein's thought, overall, presents a more complex picture of the philosopher's dealings with language than Locke (or even Peirce) anticipated, it is instructive to trace the effect of his use of similar metaphorical themes in arguing for his version of a *specifically philosophical* wariness about language.

The *Tractatus* view of language, as noted earlier, can be viewed as an extension of that recurring search for a philosophical-logical place of cognitive clarity and precision in language. It was not the rhetorical figurative embellishment of language that was Wittgenstein's main worry there: rather, he was significantly concerned with the way in which the surface grammar of ordinary language can be misleading. Recent developments in symbolic logic (by Frege and Russell, in particular) could enable more fine-tuned representations of truth-functional relationships among propositions than previous logical systems could sustain. Drawing on such developments, Wittgenstein noted ways in which the regular grammatical structure of sentences can conceal the logical structure of the propositions and thoughts these sentences express: the copula, for example, might variously signify the "is" of identity, of predication, or of existence—each of these has a different logical function, which the logical analysis (and symbolic representation) of propositions could reveal. Wittgenstein captured this concern about language in a metaphor that interestingly resonates with St. John's clothing metaphor: "Language disguises thought. So much so, that from the outward form of the clothing it is impossible to infer the form of the thought beneath it, because the outward form of the clothing is not designed to reveal the form of the body, but for entirely different purposes" (*Tractatus* §4.002). The "correct method in philosophy" at that point thus involved "the logical clarification of thoughts" expressed in propositions with sense.

Wittgenstein later describes his *Tractatus* self (seeking essences and hidden structures) as being held captive by a misleading picture, but he adds that it is a picture that "[lies] in our language and language [seems] to repeat it to us inexorably" (§§114–116). As noted earlier, we are captivated by, among other things, supposedly meaningful philosophical questions such as, What is language? What is a proposition? More specifically, he now rejects the earlier view that there is "something like a final analysis of our forms of language . . . as if there were something hidden in them that had to be brought to light . . . [which] finds expression in [philosophical] questions as to the *essence* of language, of propositions, of thought" (§91, 92). Philosophical misunderstandings concerning the use of words are, he remarks, "caused, among other things, by certain analogies between the forms of expression in different regions of language" (§90). For example, Wittgenstein thinks that we encounter such a misunderstanding when we seek to develop a uniform analysis of substantives (which function analogously as nouns in sentences), when, in particular, we require that they all have or ought to have referents that can be established by ostensive definitions. "The names I give to bodies, shapes, colors, lengths have different grammars in each case. The meaning of a name is not the thing we point to when we give an ostensive definition of the name" (*PG*, 9).[17] As this passage suggests, his later view incorporates a sense of "grammar" that points to the normal *use* of words and expressions, the ways words are used "in the language-game which is [their] original home" (*PI*, §116). He attributes his earlier "false and idealized picture of the use of language" in part to a misleading comparison with scientific analysis revealing "hidden" elements and processes: "My notion in the *Tractatus* . . . was wrong: . . . because I too thought that logical analysis had to bring to light what was hidden (as chemical and physical analysis does)" (*PG*, 210).

The notion that language has a uniform hidden structure that logical analysis will reveal is now replaced by the idea of a multiplicity of language-games. Language is no longer viewed primarily as a means of representing the world, but as a means of communication embodied in a variety of linguistic practices (which may include practices of representing) embedded in social and cultural contexts. Different language-games may share common elements that need not be shared by all of them—like family resemblances (*PI*, §23, §§65–67). This shift in Wittgenstein's view of language is accompanied by something like a shift in vision metaphors. Earlier we had the image of peering into language, looking behind the surface, with logical analysis helping to reveal the hidden workings. Now we have the image of moving away from or above language to get a clearer view of the way words and forms of expression are used in linguistic practices that are inextricably linked to all sorts of communicative activities in specific cultural contexts. Wittgenstein's uses the term *übersicht* to capture this view: it has a topographical sense of "overview," and it is figuratively linked with his new picture of language as an ancient city with different suburbs, older and newer sections, and so on (*PI*, §122, §18).

The earlier need to determine something that all of these language activities have in common, the need, for example, to arrive at some common "essence" of language, is something that Wittgenstein now sees as a specific requirement of a mistaken philosophical picture of language, something that, he claims, is *postulated* by philosophy and the language of philosophy rather than something that is arrived at as a result of investigation (§107). The philosopher's task now shifts to one that involves giving accurate descriptions of "the workings of language" despite the philosophical temptation to misunderstand them. It is in this context that Wittgenstein warns about the bewitchment of language. *Bewitchment* in this and similar contexts, is directed primarily not to the ordinary use of language, but to the philosophical temptation to "explain" language by "freezing" it, setting it "on idle," seeking to analyze and explain words and expressions by removing them from their dynamic roles in human practices which give them their meaning. The remedy in many cases involves "bring[ing] words back from their metaphysical to their everyday use," back to "the language-game which is [their] original home" (§116).

It is useful to examine (as we did with the earlier examples) what Wittgenstein's "bewitchment" image does that wouldn't get done without it—something that, however, conflicts with some of his other (later) remarks about philosophy and language. Like the earlier gender metaphors that suggest a clear division, *bewitchment* also implies a clear demarcation: it has an all-or-nothing sense to it—one is or one is not cast under the spell. It suggests that there is such a thing as a state of non-bewitchment-by-language that is the philosopher's goal. This metaphor also resonates in such phrases as "in despite of an urge to misunderstand [the workings of language]" (§109). Again, this suggests that there is such a thing as a state of nonmisunderstanding (the workings of language)— for him, a state in which the philosopher can give an accurate description of language, that is free of any elements of explanation or foundation seeking (§109, §124). When he talks about philosophers' being "tempted" to misunderstand language, he is suggesting that there is a place of purity or clarity where philosophers can resist or at least battle such temptation, or, if they have succumbed, can seek to purify themselves of the illness or sin. Wittgenstein's images of illness, therapy, and renunciation fill out the imaginary background here. Philosophy is frequently depicted as a form of therapy, as a corrective to the just-about-inevitable misconceptions brought about by language: "The philosopher's treatment of a question is like the treatment of an illness" (§255). Religious images are also sometimes suggested. Anthony Kenny notes that the comparison between philosophy and conversion, between philosophy and renunciation of the world, is quite explicit in Wittgenstein's *Big Typescript*. Kenny's association with the doctrine of original sin is also noteworthy, given Eve's symbolic role in the Fall:

> Wittgenstein's account of why we have to philosophize, or why it
> is worthwhile to philosophize even though philosophy is only use-

ful against philosophical problems, is rather like the Christian doctrine of original sin. According to the Christian doctrine we are all born in a state of sin; according to Wittgenstein we are not born in a state of philosophical sin, but we take it in along with language . . . along with all the benefits which language brings . . . we take in whether we want to or not, certain temptations; we must resist these if we are not to be misled. There are several passages where Wittgenstein speaks of the temptation or bewitchment of language.[18]

It would be a mistake to claim that the view that these images and words suggest represents anything like Wittgenstein's final position on the philosopher's relationship to language. Indeed, they are somewhat at odds with some of his remarks and practice in other places. Elsewhere, he resists the notion that there is some kind of "final" philosophical place of clarity in or with language (and, indeed, such a picture would be too reminiscent of the *Tractatus* view). Since linguistic misunderstandings are "caused, among other things, by certain analogies between the forms of expression in different regions of language" (*PI*, §90), it is instructive to see what Wittgenstein does with one such example. In a passage in *The Blue Book*, Wittgenstein argues that a particular philosophical puzzlement about the measurement of time (Saint Augustine's, in particular) is due to a confusion brought about by treating the grammar of the "measure" of time as analogous to the grammar of the "measure" of length—as in the length of a rod. Again, the philosophical problem here is discussed in terms of "the fascination which the analogy between two similar structures in our language can exert on us" (*BB*, 26). Yet some paragraphs later he notes: "When we say that by our method we try to counteract the misleading effect of certain analogies, it is important that you should understand that the idea of an analogy being misleading is nothing sharply defined. . . . It is, in most cases, impossible to show an exact point where an analogy begins to mislead us."[19]

In a similar vein, some paragraphs after *PI*, §109 Wittgenstein remarks, "We want to establish an order in our knowledge of the use of language: an order with a particular end in view; one out of many possible orders; not *the* order" (§132). He is suggesting that when we seek a clearer understanding of the use of our words, of the grammar of our expressions, we do so in a way that is related to the question at hand, to the specific linguistic misconceptions animating the philosophical problem at hand.

"The work of the philosopher consists in assembling reminders for a particular purpose" (§127). The goal is not some universal reform of language (ordinary language, for him, is in order as it is), and it is not the creation of some ideal philosophical-logical language; instead, the language "reform" is a piecemeal one directed to specific philosophical confusions and the misleading expressions that are implicated: "There is not *a* philosophical method, though there are indeed methods, like different therapies" (§133).

Given that these views are in conflict with the clear delineation and purity implied by his metaphors of bewitchment and temptation, one is invited to apply something of Wittgenstein's own therapy to *his* recurring *philosophical problem* of trying to demarcate philosophy. This is in large part what I have been doing—uncovering some captivating pictures that lie in his language, in specific metaphorical expressions. Some might argue, however, that when Wittgenstein talks about misunderstandings caused by "analogies between the forms of expression in different regions of language" he was not referring specifically to metaphors, but to grammatical similarities in the "kind of statement" we use to talk about different phenomena (*PI*, §90). In response, it is important to note that Wittgenstein at one point remarks: "Doesn't the form of our expression mislead us here? For isn't it a misleading metaphor to say: 'My eyes give me the information that there is a chair over there'?" (*PI*, §356). In addition, metaphors regularly carry aspects of grammatical form with them. For example, when we say that we *see* her meaning or we *grasp* the concept being explained, we are portraying meanings and concepts as substantives that pick out distinct mental entities or processes. This, according to Wittgenstein, is misleading when we overlook the fact that, in normal use overall, the grammars of words such as *meaning* and *concept* are different from the grammar of physical objects or processes that we *literally see* or *grasp*. The point with such examples is not to suggest that we shouldn't use metaphors or other "ordinary" linguistic tropes, but that we need to be more aware of what we are doing when we use them.

Wittgenstein's main aim in these contexts is to direct our attention to linguistic misunderstandings animating specific *philosophical* problems about propositions, names, understanding, rule-following, pains, and so on, that is, concepts and topics *in* philosophy, not philosophy itself. Yet his remarks apply no less at the metaphilosophical level, with philosophers' attempts to delimit the nature and role of philosophy itself—when this too is treated as a *philosophical problem*. As some of the recurring

metaphors I have been examining illustrate, the "problem" here is regularly bound up with a *need* to mark out a distinct place or ground for
philosophy, separate from what is simply posited (or postulated) as the
problematic "feminine" space of confusion and deception. For whom,
exactly, is this a need and a problem? And why? These same metaphors
also point the way toward dissolving the "problem": they help to illuminate specifics of the cultural and historical development of this particular
overarching need or fixation that may still be captivating some philosophers. Feminist therapy surely helps here.[20]

Many feminists and others concerned with social and political change
question what they see as the conservatism in Wittgenstein's foundational endorsement of cultural practices, traditions, and forms of life, as
these are, among other things, embedded in language use. In addition,
when he talks about describing the workings of *our* language, he doesn't
dwell on the fact that in a given cultural context there may be quite
different relationships to various linguistic practices—some may find particular practices problematic, and others not. (For example, one might
contrast the relationships of racists and antiracists to racist linguistic and
other practices.) Some read his claims that it is not the philosopher's task
to reform language, to create a new ideal language, that "ordinary language is all right," that "every sentence in our language 'is in order as it
is'" (*BB*, 28; *PI*, §98) in this conservative vein. But one can also read
such claims as simply pointing out that language is in proper order in
that, when it is described in terms of the historical and current (and
varied) practices of communication that give it meaning, it accurately
reflects or mirrors those practices and the social and cultural contexts
that they inhabit. It thus gives us a hold on those practices, and gives us
more insight into what keeps some of them in place so tenaciously. If it
is the case that, as Wittgenstein states, "in our language there is an entire
mythology embedded" (where *mythology* here is taken to mean "world-
picture" or inherited background), then we are pointed in another direction where we might effectively examine, expose, and seek to change that
background.[21] Wittgenstein nowhere says that forms of life and practices–
including linguistic practices—can never change.

My argument has involved naming and examining one particular form
of the "maleness" of traditional Western philosophy, and showing that it
is not an inconsequential form. As I have emphasized, what is at issue
here from a feminist perspective is not simply the use of gender and gender-related metaphors. It is the specific ways in which such metaphors
draw upon and reinforce a misogyny-inflected cultural imaginary that is

the main concern. But also of concern is the way in which they have at critical points essentially achieved a "straightforward dogmatization" (Le Doeuff's term) of the view that there is a distinct thing called "philosophy," and that its identity, status, and value lie in its distance from less worthy, seductive, and confusing enterprises that those same metaphors simply postulate it excludes. Although not addressed to this precise situation, Wittgenstein's comment nevertheless seems quite appropriate: "One thinks that one is tracing the outline of the thing's nature over and over again, and one is merely tracing round the frame through which we look at it" (PI, §114).

Philosophy, of course, still exists as an ongoing tradition, as a set of practices, and as a set of texts that continue to be read and read anew. Whether we agree or not with many of his individual claims and arguments, Wittgenstein still impresses on us the importance of continually asking what it is that marks a particular question or problem as philosophical, even while we are attempting to answer or solve that question or problem. And the same applies to the question of the nature and role of philosophy itself, even while we continue to engage its practices, reread its texts, and create new ones. Feminist reflections fit especially well into this critical space. Some of the mythologies of philosophy require feminist readings for their recognition and visibility, that is, readings that go against the grain of a tradition that, among other things, displaced both woman and metaphor, and indeed, against the grain of a cultural imaginary that still too readily accommodates sexism and misogyny. Wittgenstein's reflections on the relationship between philosophy and language may well have provided us with some of the best methods and arguments with which to advance feminist re-readings of "our" canon, a canon that, of course, now includes Wittgenstein himself. Le Doeuff remarks: "Far from giving way to disgust, women should know that the sexism of philosophical discourse offers them a hold on that discourse and that they can re-examine it in a way which has never been done before" (Hipparchia's Choice, 14). And, we can now add, that includes holds on that discourse that even Wittgenstein couldn't quite envision.

Notes

1. For helpful collections of philosophers' views of women, see Linda Bell, ed., *Visions of Women* (Clifton, N.J.: Humana Press, 1983); and Mary Briody Mahowald, ed., *Philosophy of Woman*, 3d ed. (Indianapolis: Hackett, 1994).

2. The series that includes this volume, that is, the Re-Reading the Canon series published by Penn State Press, under the general editorship of Nancy Tuana, is one example of the—by now—quite extensive literature on feminist reflections in philosophy.

3. One cannot overlook the significance of Simone de Beauvoir's *The Second Sex*, trans. H. M. Parshley (New York: Knopf, 1952) for an understanding of the philosophical role of woman as "Other." Also see Susan Bordo, *The Flight to Objectivity: Essays on Cartesianism and Culture* (Albany: State University of New York Press, 1987); Rosi Braidotti, *Patterns of Dissonance* (New York: Routledge, 1991); Elizabeth Grosz, "Bodies and Knowledges: Feminism and the Crisis of Reason," in *Feminist Epistemologies*, ed. Linda Alcoff and Elizabeth Potter (New York: Routledge, 1993); Luce Irigaray, *Speculum of the Other Woman*, trans. Gillian Gill (Ithaca: Cornell University Press, 1985); Eva Feder Kittay, "Woman as Metaphor," *Hypatia*, 3, no. 2 (1988): 63–86; Michèle Le Doeuff, *Hipparchia's Choice: An Essay Concerning Women, Philosophy, Etc.* (Oxford: Blackwell, 1991); Genevieve Lloyd, "Maleness, Metaphor, and the 'Crisis' of Reason," in *A Mind of One's Own: Feminist Essays on Reason and Objectivity*, ed. Louise Antony and Charlotte Witt (Boulder, Colo.: Westview Press, 1993); Phyllis Rooney, "Gendered Reason: Sex Metaphor and Conceptions of Reason," *Hypatia* 6, no. 2 (1991): 77–103; and Naomi Scheman, *Engenderings: Constructions of Knowledge, Authority, and Privilege* (New York: Routledge, 1993).

4. Ludwig Wittgenstein, *Tractatus Logico-Philosophicus*, trans. D. F. Pears and B. F. McGuinness (New York: Routledge and Kegan Paul, 1961). This work is cited in the text as *Tractatus*.

5. Ludwig Wittgenstein, *Philosophical Investigations*, trans. G. E. M. Anscombe (New York: Macmillan, 1953). Hereafter this work is cited as *PI*.

6. Nancy Tuana, *Woman and the History of Philosophy* (New York: Paragon House, 1992), 5.

7. Le Doeuff, *Hipparchia's Choice*, 70.

8. Michèle Le Doeuff, *The Philosophical Imaginary*, trans. Colin Gordon (Stanford University Press, 1989), 1.

9. John Locke, *An Essay Concerning Human Understanding*, bk. 3, chap. 10, par. 34. The particular edition I note here is from *The Philosophical Works of John Locke*, ed. and with essay and notes by J. A. St. John, vol. 2 (London: George Bell and Sons, 1894). See 112–13.

10. Ibid., 113. It is not beside the point here to note that "J. A." stands for "James Augustus."

11. Eva Feder Kittay, *Metaphor: Its Cognitive Force and Linguistic Structure* (Oxford: Clarendon Press, 1987), 1.

12. Ibid. See especially her introduction, 1–11. For helpful accounts of the development of this debate about the cognitive role of metaphor, see Max Black, *Models and Metaphors* (Ithaca: Cornell University Press, 1962); and especially Andrew Ortony, ed., *Metaphor and Thought*, 2d ed. (Cambridge University Press, 1993). In many of these theoretical contexts, the term *metaphor* is taken to cover a range of figures of speech, including images, similes, allegories, and models.

13. Le Doeuff, *The Philosophical Imaginary*. This statement is especially true of work located more in the "analytic" tradition, though it is still somewhat the case in the "continental" tradition. Some of Jacques Derrida's works belong among the exceptions here: for example, he develops a substantial examination of the metaphorical feminine in Nietzsche in Derrida, *Spurs: Nietzsche's Styles*, trans. Barbara Harlow (University of Chicago Press, 1979). There have been other studies of the metaphors used by particular philosophers (Plato and Nietzsche, for instance), but very little on a more comprehensive study of recurring metaphorical themes and on their substantive role in framing philosophical topics and questions. This is, of course, not surprising, if, like Locke, many philosophers treated metaphor as largely extraneous to the main content of philosophy. With specific studies of the role of gender metaphors and themes in philosophy, feminist work on metaphor is clearly making a difference here: see, for e.g., Irigaray, *Speculum*; Kittay, "Woman as Metaphor"; Rooney, "Gendered Reason"; and Lloyd "Maleness, Metaphor."

14. C. S. Peirce, "How to Make Our Ideas Clear," in *Pragmatism: The Classic Writings*, ed. H. S. Thayer (Indianapolis: Hackett, 1982), 82–83.

15. Black, *Models and Metaphors*, 40.

16. See Jerry H. Gill, *Wittgenstein and Metaphor* (Atlantic Highlands, N.J.: Humanities Press, 1996) for an extended study of what Gill calls Wittgenstein's "addiction" to metaphor.

17. Ludwig Wittgenstein, *Philosophical Grammar*, ed. Rush Rhees, trans. Anthony Kenny (Berkeley and Los Angeles: University of California Press, 1974). Hereafter this work is cited as *PG*.

18. Anthony Kenny, *The Legacy of Wittgenstein* (Oxford: Basil Blackwell, 1984), 50.

19. Ludwig Wittgenstein, *The Blue and Brown Books* (New York: Harper and Row, 1958), 28. Hereafter this work is cited as *BB*.

20. This is not to suggest that we cannot have legitimate needs for clarity in specific situations, for particular purposes or practices of communication, representation, and expression. The "problem" that is being addressed here is the "problem" of the need for some overarching space of clarity, metatheoretically postulated as the "proper" place of philosophy.

21. Quote from Anthony Kenny, ed., *The Wittgenstein Reader* (Oxford: Basil Blackwell, 1994), 278.

2

Wittgenstein, Feminism, and the Exclusions of Philosophy

Nancy E. Baker

The theme of exclusion runs through all levels of feminist theory and practice. In the case of philosophy, the exclusion of women from its institutions as well as its subject matter has been obvious. At a less obvious level the exclusion of much that is associated with the word *feminine* may actually determine the nature of philosophy itself. This is the view put forth in "Woman and Philosophy" by the French feminist philosopher Michèle Le Doeuff. I would like to show that exclusion is a theme to be found in the later work of Wittgenstein as well. It is not so explicit in his case, but has everything to do with how he saw philosophy and how he practiced it. The included and excluded are, of course, not connected with gender by Wittgenstein, but Le Doeuff would say that gender is often used as a way of symbolizing something else. By drawing attention

to the similarities between Le Doeuff and Wittgenstein, I hope to show
how a particular feminist view of philosophy not only is shared by Wittgenstein but also deepens our understanding of what he was doing.

I

If philosophy is *intrinsically* patriarchal, as some feminists tell us it is, then
we cannot succeed in correcting its patriarchal bias without reconceiving
the nature of philosophy itself. Moreover, if, in order to define itself,
philosophy requires the exclusion of anything, then—like gender and the
self—it is not as autonomous as it takes itself to be. According to Le
Doeuff, philosophy defines itself in opposition to what it excludes, and
fails to see that what it excludes is really a projection onto other discourses and forms of knowledge of its own repressions. In other words,
philosophy authorizes its own autonomy by concealing from itself its de-
pendency on what it excludes. As an example, in "The Shameful Face of
Philosophy," Le Doeuff writes that, in spite of philosophy's dissociating
itself from myth, fable, the poetic and the domain of the image, it is, in
fact, filled with images, myths and ordinary things: "We shall . . . find
statues that breathe the scent of roses, comedies, tragedies, architects,
foundations, dwellings, doors and windows, sand, navigators, various musical instruments, islands, clocks, horses, donkeys and even a lion, representatives of every craft and trade, scenes of sea and storm, forests and
trees: in short, a whole pictorial world sufficient to decorate even the
dryest 'History of Philosophy'."[1] If acknowledged at all, the images appearing in philosophical works are usually thought of as inessential to
that work. Le Doeuff, however, argues that they are necessary for the
proper working of the system which disavows them and that "[v]arious
strategies have been pursued to exorcize this inner scandal. One of them
consists of projecting the shameful side of philosophy on to an other.
This denegration (in which the writing subject disavows what he himself
writes) is simple in its mechanism and variable in its forms."[2] In "Women
and Philosophy," the form considered is the disavowal of women and the
feminine, as opposed to imagery, but the mechanism is the same. In other
words, the feminine is not simply excluded from philosophy but is somehow already in it, repressed and disavowed through projection outward.

What is the "feminine" that philosophy consciously excludes? In its history, Le Doeuff reminds us, women have typically been associated with the practical, the particular, observation, emotion, infinity, multiplicity, and chaos; while men—and philosophy itself—have been associated with the abstract, the universal, principles, reason, limit, and unity. According to Rousseau, "all that tends to wide generalization is beyond the grasp of women."[3] Hegel, however, tells us that "[w]omen may have ideas, taste, and elegance, but they do not have the ideal" (189). Because Le Doeuff can find nothing historical or political to explain what is so threatening about women being capable of philosophy, she concludes that the exclusion of 'woman' must somehow be intrinsic to the nature of philosophy itself. It can be seen as "an attempt to mask the nature of the philosophical, or as effort to reassure its always problematic positivity. 'Woman' was to be invoked here in a strictly fantasy-oriented sense, as a purely negative otherness, as an atrophy which, by contrast, guarantees a philosophical completeness . . . women pay the cost of a defense, as, elsewhere, do children, the people, the common man, or the 'primitive'" (192–93). In other words, in order to deny the lack of genuine autonomy and completeness, a purely negative otherness, an atrophy, is needed as a contrast to give, at least, the illusion of autonomy and completeness. Women and others may pay the cost of defense, but the defense is really against the condition "of never being able to produce any knowledge equal to one's standard of validation. . . . The reference to women (or to any other subject deemed 'unfit' for philosophy) allows this powerlessness to be overlooked" (193).

If philosophy continues to need reassurance through this distribution of roles, then admission of women who can "think like a man" to its institutions is for nothing. It is also for nothing if the dichotomous imagery associated with gender remains in place. As for the origins of this imagery, Le Doeuff does not believe that it can be explained in terms of "an unconscious constituted *prior* to metaphysics. This would mean treating metaphysics as the innocent party, something which seems hardly possible" (194). Rather, the gender dichotomies we are concerned with here are created by philosophy and used for a specifically philosophical exclusion. It is, in particular, a "femininity of chaos" against which philosophy defends itself. It does this by making itself a "discipline":

> [T]he discourse we call 'philosophical' produces itself through the fact that it represses, excludes and dissolves, or claims to dissolve, another discourse, other forms of knowledge, even though this

other discourse or forms of knowledge may not have existed as such prior to this operation. For philosophical discourse is a discipline, that is to say a discourse obeying (or claiming to obey) a finite number of rules, procedures or operations, and as such it represents a closure, a delimitation which denies the (actually or potentially) indefinite character of modes of thought (even if this character is only potential); it is a barrage restraining the number of possible (acceptable) statements. The simple fact that philosophical discourse is a discipline is sufficient to show that something is repressed within it. (195)

What the feminine really stands for, what philosophy tries so hard to "keep at bay" cannot be defined, because it is the indefinite, the indefinable. Because of this we need to resort to metaphor: "[T]he man/woman difference is invoked or conscripted to signify the general opposition between definite and indefinite, that is to say validated/excluded, an opposition of which the logos/mythos couple represents one form. . . . [T]he feminine, as support and signifier of something that, having been engendered by philosophy whilst being rejected by it, operates within it as an indispensable deadweight which cannot be dialectically absorbed" (196).

In spite of this situation, Le Doeuff thinks there are other philosophical possibilities. For example, to be rational does not have to mean to be logocentric. Whatever change along these lines occurs in philosophy "is likely to alter the interlocking of the 'philosophical' and the 'feminine', for it is now possible to cease wishing to mask the incomplete nature of all theorization. That knowledge is always defective, but nevertheless still a necessity . . . enables us to dispense with the logocentric-phallocratic phantasmagoria" (198). As for the future of a philosophy that is no longer antifeminist, it is being performed somewhere in the region of Brechtian drama, which . . . produces unfinished plays which always have a missing act and are consequently left wide open to history (199).

When the unreachable "standard of validation" or the "requirement" (to use Wittgenstein's word) that philosophy be complete is dropped, when philosophy can "abandon its wish to be a speculation that leaves no room for lack of knowledge" (206), then the creation of the dichotomy between "woman," on the one hand, and "philosophy as logocentric-phallocratic phantasmagoria," on the other, can be dropped as well. There is then no need for "dialectical absorption." It isn't that woman or the feminine can finally be included, but rather, the whole framework of dichotomized included and excluded can be dropped. What we can then have is "an unfinished philosophical discourse, never closed, and never concluded, and hence the abandonment of any totalizing aim" (207).

In spite of its religious concepts, Le Doeuff finds herself more at home in Pascal's *Pensées* than in any of the other classical texts: "It is because the religious perspective hints at this penumbra of unknowledge (a penumbra which has nothing to do with the limits of reason), which metaphysics has denied. Here is a form of writing which does not claim to reconstruct and explain everything, which slides along the verge of the unthought" (207–8). Le Doeuff also suggests that those who engage in the practice of philosophizing can be reconceived as members of a collective: "In this kind of practice, at every moment I encounter the fact that the other's discourse being the origin of mine, as well as an unforseeable future, gives it a continuing sense of its own limits. Here, one has the impression of experiencing a new rationality, in which a relationship to the unknown and to the unthought is at every moment reintroduced" (208–9).

II

In considering Wittgenstein's later work in light of what Le Doeuff thinks philosophy could be, the first thing to notice is his style of writing. In place of generalizations or abstractions, we find great attention to detail including many examples of specific words and phrases used in everyday life. We also find an unusual sort of dialogue between the author and himself. There is nothing adversarial or even linear here. Nor is there anything that could be called systematic. The same problems are approached from many different directions. Over and over again, the author seems to start a train of thought, stop, and start again, engaging us in process, as opposed to presenting us with product. The sense of incompleteness one gets from all this is like that of Brechtian plays as described by Le Doeuff, which are, with their missing acts, "left wide open to history," only here what is written is left wide open to context. Everything remains unfinished, not because the author fails to follow through, but because the context-dependent work he is doing is by nature never ending.

We also find in Wittgenstein's later work what Le Doeuff calls "the religious perspective," which points, as she puts it, to a "penumbra of unknowing (a penumbra which has nothing to do with the limits of reason)." In spite of self-confessed vanity about his work, what comes across to the reader is humility, self-deprecation, unusual intellectual honesty, and a great willingness to tolerate "unknowing." Wittgenstein said of himself, "My talent consists in being capable of being puzzled when the puzzlement has glided off your mind. I am able to hold the puzzlement when it has slipped through your hands (and you therefore think you are clear). The art of the philosopher is not to be cheated of his puzzlement before it is really cleared up."⁴ He also said, "I am not a religious man but I cannot help seeing every problem from a religious point of view."⁵ Among other things, this meant for him that, like religious belief, philosophy was worth nothing if it didn't change a person's life. Hence the high moral tone and the demand for authenticity. This is a deeply personal, almost confessional, work. And yet in spite of the utter seriousness of its author, *Philosophical Investigations* is full of whimsy. It is also quite deliberately full of what Le Doeuff would call "images," for example, slabs, blocks, beams, pots, brooms, boilers, brakes, coffee, cheese, flies, a lion, a cow, a beetle, dogs, dolls, a duck-rabbit, and chess pieces, among others. It is also full of so-called nonphilosophical topics having to do with bodies and emotions, for example, pains, shudders, tickles, happiness, sadness, grief, fear, faces, toothaches, and hands.

Although he puts it in very different terms, Wittgenstein also shares with Le Doeuff an understanding of the nature of philosophy as it has been. In fact, one might say that the purpose of using what he called his "method" was to dismantle the philosophical structures that produce exclusion. Also, though not put in exactly these terms, philosophy for Wittgenstein has concerned itself with the universal, reason, limit, unity, Rousseau's "wide generalization," and Hegel's "ideal," what Le Doeuff reminds us have been associated with the masculine. This, of course, has involved excluding the practical, the particular, observation, emotion, infinity, multiplicity, and chaos. As if directly addressing Le Doeuff's description of philosophy in terms of repression and projection, Wittgenstein tells us that philosophy is like an illness (*PI*, §255, §593) and that what is needed is something more like therapy than theory (*PI*, §109, §133).⁶ What is needed for philosophical problems is a cure not an answer,⁷ which means that they are not solved so much as dissolved.⁸ For Wittgenstein, this dissolution comes about by paying attention to how language is actually used as opposed to how we, when philosophizing, are "tempted" (*PI*, §254, cf. §299) to use it. Above all, it means giving up the pictures that "hold us captive," pictures of how things *should* be (*PI*, §115).

A student and friend reports a conversation in which Wittgenstein said: "No, I don't think I would get on with Hegel. Hegel seems to me to be always wanting to say that things which look different are really the same. Whereas my interest is in shewing that things which look the same are really different."[9] The "illness" of the philosopher is, above all else, a "craving for generality."[10] To generalize is to "assimilate" cases that are unalike, as in "assimilating two *games*. (Football has *goals*. Tennis not.)" (*PI*, p. 231). Not only does this prevent us from seeing things as they actually are in all their particularity and multiplicity, but also the kind of generalizing Wittgenstein has in mind leads to essentialism, and thus exclusion: "The tendency to generalize the case seems to have a strict justification in logic: here one seems *completely* justified in inferring: 'If *one* proposition is a picture, then any proposition must be a picture, for they must all be of the same nature.' For we are under the illusion that what is sublime, what is essential, about our investigation consists in its grasping *one* comprehensive essence."[11] This desire for 'unity' is a distortion of our concepts, even the ones philosophy has considered so important: "When philosophers use a word—'knowledge', 'being', 'object', 'I', 'proposition', 'name'—and try to grasp the *essence* of the thing, one must always ask oneself: is the word ever actually used in this way in the language-game which is its original home?" (*PI*, §116).

One purpose of Wittgenstein's notion of a "language-game" is to counteract our tendency to essentialize language itself. Earlier in the text his interlocutor accuses him of taking "the easy way out" because he nowhere says what the essence of a language-game, and hence of language, is. In other words, he never says what is common to all these activities that we call "language." Wittgenstein replies that linguistic phenomena don't necessarily have one thing in common that makes us use the same word for all, but rather they are related to one another in many different ways. He continues with the following:

> Consider for example the proceedings that we call "games." I mean board-games, card-games, ball-games, Olympic games and so on. What is common to them all?—Don't say: "There *must* be something common, or they would not be called 'games' "—But *look and see* whether there is anything common to all.—For if you

look at them you will not see something that is common to *all*, but similarities, relationships, and a whole series of them at that. To repeat: don't think, but look! (*PI*, §66)

These similarities he characterizes with the notion of a "family resemblance" and adds that "we extend our concept[s] . . . as in spinning a thread we twist fibre on fibre. And the strength of the thread does not reside in the fact that some one fibre runs through its whole length, but in the overlapping of many fibres" (*PI*, §67). To look for "a *single* completely resolved form of every expression" (*PI*, §91), not to mention to insist on the "must" mentioned above, is to engage in a form of validation and exclusion, to use Le Doeuff's language. It is an example of what she means by saying that philosophical discourse is a "discipline," that is, a discourse that obeys a finite number of rules or procedures "and as such . . . represents a closure, a delimitation which denies the (actually or potentially) infinite character of modes of thought." We can recognize the origins of this in Socrates' attempt to come up with *definitions*. For Wittgenstein, however, this tendency to think that in order to get clear about the meaning of a word one has to find what is common to all its applications has "shackled" philosophical investigations, "for it has not only led to no result, but has made the philosopher dismiss as irrelevant the concrete cases, which alone could have helped him understand the usage of the general term. When Socrates asks 'What is knowledge?' he does not even regard it as a *preliminary* answer to enumerate cases of knowledge."[12] To "dismiss as irrelevant" is to exclude. Interestingly, individual cases fall outside the boundaries of the 'definite'—they are too particular, too multiple, even chaotic from the point of view of the essentializing philosopher. In order to 'include' them, what is required is noticing them to begin with. One might say that what is required is "observation," another excluded element of our philosophical thinking associated with the feminine, as Le Doeuff reminds us. Or, as it is put over and over in the *Investigations*, "Don't think—look!"

At the same time, Wittgenstein is careful not to exclude legitimate exclusion. For example, the mathematician may in certain circumstances give the concept number rigid limits and exclude much that we might call "number" in other circumstances, but this is done consciously for a particular purpose. The generalizing, namely, the essentializing, philosopher, however, does not recognize that he might be excluding something in one case that he needs in another. One reason this happens is that he has a "preconceived idea" (*PI*, §108) of what is needed in all cases—again, this is what Le Doeuff means by "a discipline." Wittgenstein's interlocutor, for example, wonders how a concept "*not* closed by a frontier," that is, one that is without "rigid limits," one that is "unregulated," "uncircumscribed," "blurred," "indistinct," and "inexact," can be a concept at all (cf. *PI*, §§68–88). Moreover, without an essence, the interlocutor wonders, how should we be able to explain to someone else what a game is? Wittgenstein responds by saying that we give examples of different games and sometimes add "This *and similar things* are called 'games.'" He points out that we ourselves don't have any more of an exact definition than what we are able to give to others. He then adds the following:

> "Inexact" is really a reproach, and "exact" praise. And that is to say that what is inexact attains its goal less perfectly than what is more exact. Thus the point here is what we call "the goal." Am I inexact when I do not give our distance from the sun to the nearest foot, or tell a joiner the width of a table to the nearest thousandth of an inch?
>
> No *single* idea of exactness has been laid down; we do not know what we should be supposed to imagine under this head—unless you yourself lay down what is to be so called. But you will find it difficult to hit upon such a convention; at least any that satisfies you. (*PI*, §88)

The "goal" in cases of measuring is a practical one, not an ideal one. Since what counts as exact will vary depending on the circumstances, we can't generalize and be satisfied as we move from one case to the next.

Another example of the excluded being reproachable is found at the end of *Philosophical Investigations*:

> The concept of 'seeing' makes a tangled impression. Well, it is tangled.—I look at the landscape, my gaze ranges over it, I see all sorts of distinct and indistinct movement; *this* impresses itself sharply on me, *that* is quite hazy. After all, how completely ragged what we see can appear! And now look at all that can be meant by "description of what is seen."—But this is just what is called description of what is seen. There is not *one genuine* proper case of such description—the rest being just vague, something which

awaits clarification, or which must just be swept aside as rubbish. (*PI*, p. 200)

In one of the manuscripts containing remarks on philosophy, Wittgenstein says that "what calms us is that we see a system which (systematically) excludes those structures that have always made us uneasy."[13]

In all these examples our inclination to generalize from one case to all cases or to find what is common, the essence, seems motivated by a desire for the distinct, the regulated, the rigid, the circumscribed, the restricted. To say that something is exact is "praise," whereas inexactness is a "reproach." Other reproaches are "indistinct," "unregulated," "complicated" (*PI*, §182), "more involved" (*PI*, §182), "vague," "ragged," "tangled" (*PI*, p. 200). These are "the rest" awaiting clarification or just "swept aside as rubbish"—in other words, the excluded.

Our need for exactness is a symptom of our striving after a philosophical "ideal." What we require of the ideal is that it be "*utterly simple*": "[N]o empirical cloudiness or uncertainty can be allowed to affect it.—It must rather be of the purest crystal. But this crystal does not appear as an abstraction; but as something concrete, indeed, as the most concrete, as it were the *hardest* thing there is" (*PI*, §97). Again, what is validated has "order," and is "pure," "crystalline," "definite," "clear-cut," "hard," "strict," "perfect"; and what is excluded is "vague," "cloudy," "impure," "indefinite," "uncertain" (*PI*, §§97, 101, 102, 105). "We are dazzled by the ideal" (*PI*, §100), which is contrasted with "our actual language" (*PI*, §§105, 107), "ordinary life" (*PI*, §108), "every-day thinking" (*PI*, §106), "the language of everyday," which we take to be "somehow too coarse and material" (*PI*, §120). This is Le Doeuff's "purely negative otherness . . . an atrophy which, by contrast, guarantees a philosophical completeness." For her "women pay the cost of defense, as, elsewhere, do children, the people, the common man, or the 'primitive.'" For Wittgenstein it is the ordinary, the everyday, our actual language.

In *Culture and Value*, we are given another example of the ideal of 'purity' with which we are familiar from the history of philosophy, the following Platonic one: "The greater 'purity' of objects which don't affect the senses, numbers for instance."[14] In "Remarks on Frazer's *Golden Bough*," Wittgenstein comments on the need to give the soul a purity and simplicity in contrast to the body's "multiplicity," another common idealization and exclusion to be found in the history of philosophy.[15]

Another example of an authorization or validation that leads to exclusion is the idealizing of reason:

> Reason—I feel like saying—presents itself to us as the gauge *par excellence* against which everything that we do, all our language games, measure and judge themselves.—We may say: we are so exclusively preoccupied by contemplating a yardstick that we can't allow our gaze to *rest* on certain phenomena or patterns. We are used, as it were, to 'dismissing' these as irrational, as corresponding to a low state of intelligence, etc. The yardstick rivets our attention and keeps distracting us from these phenomena, as it were making us look beyond.[16]

To return to the *Investigations:* Believing that the only sense a sentence or a word can have is a "definite" one, we look for that definiteness in our actual language as if it were hidden below the surface. We begin to exclude the surface: "When we believe that we must find that order, must find the ideal, in our actual language, we become dissatisfied with what are ordinarily called 'propositions', 'words', 'signs'" (*PI*, §105). But looking for the ideal in our actual language doesn't get us anywhere:

> The more narrowly we examine actual language, the sharper becomes the conflict between it and our requirement. (For the crystalline purity of logic was, of course, not a *result of investigation*; it was a requirement.) The conflict becomes intolerable; the requirement is now in danger of becoming empty.—We have got on to slippery ice where there is no friction and so in a certain sense the conditions are ideal, but also, just because of that, we are unable to walk. We want to walk: so we need *friction*. Back to the rough ground! (*PI*, §107)

Idealizing "turns out to be worthless."[17] Its cure is a return to the rough ground of the ordinary, the everyday—the excluded, the dismissed, the demoted, the unauthorized. This must be done even in the case of the most exalted philosophical concepts: "if the words 'language', 'experience', 'world', have a use, it must be as humble a one as that of the words 'table', 'lamp', 'door'" (*PI*, §97).

The ground is "rough" because our concepts don't have the definiteness nor does language as a whole have the uniformity and coherence that the philosopher insists on. Moreover, actual language is *alive* and changing in a way that its ideal form never could be. Language is *used* by *persons*—whether they be speaking, listening, reading, writing, or understanding: "If I had to say what is the main mistake made by philosophers of the present generation . . . I would say that it is that when language is looked at, what is looked at is the form of words and not the use made of a form of words."[18] Speaking a language is an activity. Moreover, it has many nonverbal components: Language-games consist of "language and the actions into which it is woven" (*PI*, §7). Language-games are practices: "The term 'language-*game*' is meant to bring into prominence the fact that the *speaking* of language is part of an activity, or of a form of life" (*PI*, §23). This is followed by a list of language-games: asking, thanking, cursing, greeting, praying, forming and testing a hypothesis, giving orders, and so forth. At the beginning of the paragraph, Wittgenstein asks how many kinds of sentence there are. His answer is "*countless* kinds." Multiplicity is yet another impurity, another indefiniteness. He ends the paragraph with the following remark: "It is interesting to compare the multiplicity of the tools in language and of the ways they are used, the multiplicity of kinds of word and sentence, with what logicians have said about the structure of language. (Including the author of the *Tractatus Logico-Philosophicus*)" (*PI*, §23).

In addition to the countless language-games we play, we use and understand language in countless kinds of context. For example, the words just spoken, place, time, occasion, practical consequences, and the behavior of the participants all contribute to our words' meaning one thing and not another. Moreover, those who engage in language-games are flesh-and-blood human beings whose gestures, facial expressions, bodily posture, and tone of voice all play a role in determining what is meant and understood: "Our talk gets its meaning from the rest of our proceedings."[19] *Countless* in this context does not mean infinite, but rather indefinite. New combinations of use and context can always arise; they are open-ended, as our concepts are open-ended.

Although Wittgenstein does not use the language of "repression" and "projection," Le Doeuff's claim that the excluded has been there all along and is, moreover, necessary can be found in his work as well. For example, in wanting to exclude the ordinary, the philosopher forgets that it is ordinary language he must use to carry out his exclusion. We can see an example of this in the following remark: "When I talk about language (words, sentences, etc.) I must speak the language of every day. Is this language somehow too coarse and material for what we want to say? . . . your very questions were framed in this language; they had to be expressed in this language, if there was anything to ask!" (*PI*, §120; cf. §108).

Another example of this can be found in the Cartesian dualism that Wittgenstein undermines so thoroughly. The mentalist purports to exclude the body, and hence behavior, from our mental concepts, not seeing that this exclusion is an illusion, for our mental concepts depend on the body for their meaning. This means that the mentalist—and this includes the British Empiricist—in his search for the completely mental referent of, say, "understanding" or "pain" or "anger," has already assumed the inclusion of the body and behavior in meaningfully raising his questions (cf. *PI*, §281, §284).

Wittgenstein's treatment of the notion of a private language is yet another example of this. In demonstrating the incoherence of the idea of a private language, he shows us that any attempt to come up with examples of the so-called private already contains the public (cf. *PI*, §261, §304). In *On Certainty*, Wittgenstein points out that the skeptic denies or "represses" the fact that, in order to be consistent, his skepticism ought to apply to the words with which he expresses his skepticism.[20] In other words, the skeptic needs—and needs to repress—certainty in order to exclude certainty in the expression of his skepticism.

One possible misunderstanding of Wittgenstein is that he is introducing or reintroducing the vague and indefinite into our language, either displacing the definite or at least adding to it. The vague and whatever idea is used to combat it, however, are both ends of the same pole. It is the pole he rejects—a pole that represents a certain misunderstanding about meaning. The same is true of mind and body. It isn't that Wittgenstein includes the body in the sense of adding it to the mentalist view, but rather that he shows how our mental concepts already involve the body and that it could not be otherwise. The early misinterpretations of Wittgenstein as a behaviorist were due to the failure to understand that it was a polar opposition he was rejecting and not one end of a pole in favor of the other (cf. *PI*, §304).

Another point of Le Doeuff's to consider in this regard is that philosophy *creates* its 'other'. When I am attached to the ideal of exactness, the inexactness I exclude is a distortion, created to give exactness its meaning and value. The apparent vagueness of our language is a creation. It has its origins in our attachment to another creation, namely, the ideal. To be sure, language is sometimes vague—sometimes its uses are even deliberately vague—but not always, and certainly not necessarily. Once we see meaning differently, namely, as a function of extremely complex connections to occasion, to other words, and to behavior, we see that language as it is could not be more precise. The problem was not language but our framework: "(One might say: the axis of reference of our examination must be rotated, but about the fixed point of our real need)" (*PI*, §108).

III

Although one might argue that everything Wittgenstein describes as being excluded by the philosopher could be associated with the metaphor "feminine" and even that the alternative kind of philosophizing he offers might be said to have something "feminine" about it, this misses the point of what really brings these two philosophers together. As mentioned earlier, Le Doeuff does not believe that some kind of unconsciously formed gender imagery is at the root of philosophy's polarizations. It is rather in the nature of philosophy itself to invoke "a purely negative otherness, as an atrophy which, by contrast, guarantees a philosophical completeness." Whether the cost of defense is paid by women, "children, the people, the common man, or the 'primitive,'" the "mechanism" remains the same. Wittgenstein would agree, although his awareness of exclusion and projection can be seen in contexts other than the strictly philosophical. In one of his manuscripts, he mentions the scapegoat, "on which one lays one's sins, and who runs away into the desert with them—a false picture, similar to those that cause errors in philosophy."[21] In *Culture and Value*, he draws a parallel between an individual psychological version of this pattern in the case of our own bodies and a national, that is, group anti-Semitism:

> "Look at this tumour as a perfectly normal part of your body!"
> Can one do that, to order? Do I have the power to decide at will
> to have, or not to have, an ideal conception of my body?
>   Within the history of the peoples of Europe the history of the
> Jews is not treated as circumstantially as their intervention in
> European affairs would actually merit, because within this history
> they are experienced as a sort of disease, and anomaly, [and no

one wants to speak of a disease as if it had the same rights as healthy bodily processes (even painful ones)].

We may say: people can only regard this tumour as a natural part of the body if their whole feeling for the body changes (if the whole national feeling for the body changes). Otherwise the best they can do is *put up with* it.

You can expect an individual man to display this sort of tolerance, or else to disregard such things; but you cannot expect this of a nation, because it is precisely not disregarding such things that makes it a nation. I.e., there is a contradiction in expecting someone *both* to retain his former aesthetic feeling for the body and *also* to make the tumour welcome.[22]

In a discussion of Wittgenstein's attitude towards Jewishness, his own and others', Ray Monk treats "the adoption of the illness metaphor" as an example of "anti-Semitic paranoia" and says the following about this passage: "It goes without saying that this metaphor makes no sense without a racial notion of Jewishness. The Jew, however 'assimilated,' will never be a German or an Austrian, because he is not of the same 'body': he is experienced by that body as a growth, a disease."[23] Whatever can be said about Wittgenstein's ambivalence towards his Jewishness, it is worth noting that this paragraph also contains an important understanding of "assimilation" in keeping with what both Le Doueff and Wittgenstein have to say about exclusion. In the case of a tumor, there is a conflict between it and our requirement, namely, between it and my "ideal conception of my body." If I "disregard" the tumor—or any other rejected aspect of my body—I exclude, deny, repress and perhaps project it outward in some way, for example, at certain physical characteristics of others I find imperfect. If I "tolerate" it, I recognize it as mine and "put up with it"—just as philosophy can "put up with" women and the feminine. But that still leaves a conflict—the tumour cannot be "dialectically absorbed," to use Le Doeuff's language. The only way to resolve this is to recognize my requirement as a distortion not only of my body, but also of the polar opposite, the tumor. Giving up the distortion is not easy, since it involves giving up my "ideal conception of my body," otherwise described as my "whole national feeling for the body." A nation is by definition exclusionary, all the more so if it defines its members racially. A nation is like a Socratic definition. When the tumor is acknowledged but remains repugnant, it is a projection of unacknowledged and repugnant parts of my own body, namely, those that don't fit my ideal image. But there are other occasions or contexts in which we reject the entire body in the name of the mind or soul. The whole body—like the feminine and our actual language—is then seen as too "coarse," too "multiple," without the singleness and purity demanded of soul or mind. It takes on the qualities of the rejected tumor. When, however, we reject the tumor in the name of the body, the body then takes on the qualities of the idealized mind. "Dialectical absorption" is impossible in the case of these oppositions. As for "assimilation," it can only be "tolerance," a "putting up with," or "inclusion" through generalization by the authorized. It is only by giving up all requirement that something be a certain way that we can be free of the authorization/exclusion patterns that necessarily result. This cannot be done "to order." As Wittgenstein says elsewhere of our philosophical illnesses, "To convince someone of what is true, it is not enough to state it; we must find the *road* from error to truth."[24] This is why "*slow* cure is all important."[25]

As we can see from the preceding comments, it is not only the philosopher in the narrow metaphysical sense who succumbs to the thought patterns of generalization and exclusion for Wittgenstein: "Philosophy is a tool which is useful only against philosophers *and* against *the philosopher in us*" (italics mine).[26] Because we all are subject to the temptations of "the philosopher in us," namely, the tendency to generalize, project, and exclude, Wittgenstein says that (his) philosophy "is really more a working on oneself."[27] To be free of the temptation to exclude is to be willing to live and philosophize in a world of multiplicity, difference, the ordinary, incompleteness, and not knowing, a world without dichotomies. Moreover, as Wittgenstein reminds us, the job of dealing with this temptation is never done: "Problems are solved (difficulties eliminated), not a *single* problem. . . . 'But then we will never come to the end of our job!' Of course not, because it has no end."[28]

Notes

1. Michèle Le Doeuff, "The Shameful Face of Philosophy," in *The Philosophical Imaginary* (Stanford: Stanford University Press, 1989), 1.

2. Le Doeuff, "Shameful Face of Philosophy," 6.

3. Michèle Le Doeuff, "Women and Philosophy," in *French Feminist Thought*, ed. Toril Moi (Oxford: Basil Blackwell, 1987), 189.

4. Gordon P. Baker and Peter M. S. Hacker, *Wittgenstein: Understanding and Meaning* (Chicago: University of Chicago Press, 1980), 541.

5. M. O'C. Drury, "Some Notes on Conversations with Wittgenstein," in *Ludwig Wittgenstein: Personal Recollections*, ed. Rush Rhees (Totowa, N.J.: Rowman and Littlefield, 1981), 94.

6. All references indicated by *PI*, § and a paragraph number or *PI*, p. and a page number are to Ludwig Wittgenstein, *Philosophical Investigations*, ed. G. E. M. Anscombe and R. Rhees, trans. G. E. M. Anscombe, 3d ed. (New York: Macmillan, 1958).

7. Baker and Hacker, *Wittgenstein*, 486.

8. Ludwig Wittgenstein, *Philosophical Occasions: 1912–1951*, ed. James Klagge and Alfred Nordmann (Indianapolis: Hackett, 1993), 183.

9. Drury, "Some Notes," 171.

10. Ludwig Wittgenstein, *The Blue and Brown Books* (Oxford: Basil Blackwell, 1958), 17.

11. Ludwig Wittgenstein, *Zettel*, ed. and trans. G. E. M. Anscombe (Berkeley and Los Angeles: University of California Press, 1967), §444.

12. Wittgenstein, *Blue and Brown Books*, 19–20.

13. Wittgenstein, *Philosophical Occasions*, 174–75.

14. Ludwig Wittgenstein, *Culture and Value*, ed. G. H. Von Wright, trans. Peter Winch (Chicago: University of Chicago Press, 1980), 26.

15. Wittgenstein, *Philosophical Occasions*, 141.

16. Wittgenstein, *Philosophical Occasions*, 389.

17. Ludwig Wittgenstein, *Last Writings on the Philosophy of Psychology*, vol. 1, ed. G. H. Von Wright and Heikki Nyman, trans. C. G. Luckhardt and Maxmillian A. E. Aue (Chicago: University of Chicago Press), §830.

18. Ludwig Wittgenstein, *Lectures and Conversations on Aesthetics and Religious Beliefs*, ed. Cyril Barret (Berkeley and Los Angeles: University of California Press, 1967), 2.

19. Ludwig Wittgenstein, *On Certainty*, ed. G. E. M. Anscombe and G. H. Von Wright, trans. Dennis Paul and G. E. M. Anscombe (New York: Harper and Row, 1972), §229.

20. Wittgenstein, *On Certainty*, see §456.

21. Wittgenstein, *Philosophical Occasions*, 197.

22. Wittgenstein, *Culture and Value*, 20.

23. Ray Monk, *Ludwig Wittgenstein: The Duty of Genius* (New York: Free Press, 1990), 314–15.

24. Ludwig Wittgenstein, *Remarks on Frazer's "Golden Bough"* (Atlantic Highlands, N.J.: Humanities Press), 1.

25. Wittgenstein, *Zettel*, §382.

26. Anthony Kenny, *The Legacy of Wittgenstein* (Oxford: Basil Blackwell, 1984), 48.

27. Wittgenstein, *Culture and Value*, 16.

28. Wittgenstein, *Philosophical Occasions*, 195.

3

Speaking Philosophy in the Voice of Another

Wittgenstein, Irigaray, and the Inheritance of Mimesis

Tim Craker

There is no inheritance without a call to responsibility. An inheritance is always the reaffirmation of a debt, but a critical, selective, and filtering reaffirmation.

—Jacques Derrida, *Spectres of Marx*

Anecdote: Wittgenstein, during yet another of various attempts to assemble his philosophical remarks into a coherent whole, casts about for a title. A student, M. O'C. Drury, suggests *Philosophy* as a fitting title for Wittgenstein's work. Wittgenstein will not hear of this. To suggest that his work is philosophy itself, rather than simply *one* of the heirs of philosophy, would be saying too much.[1] Given the degree to which Wittgenstein rejects the philosophical tradition, it may seem surprising to hear that he considered himself an heir at all, but Wittgenstein's relation to inheritance is complex, and it affirms Derrida's suggestion that there is no inheritance without a call to responsibility. For example, even though Wittgenstein rejected much of his inheritance (both literal and figural) from his father, he still felt himself an heir with an obligation to discharge the wealth he inherited in a way that would do the least harm. In any case, whether because he rejects the philosophical tradition or because he is only one heir among others, *Philosophy* is a title his work is not entitled to bear.

Question: For those of us who are, in some sense, "heirs" of Wittgenstein, to what work, to what titles, are we entitled? What possibilities, what *futures*, are bequeathed to those of us writing *after* Wittgenstein? What remains to be thought in Wittgenstein's thought?

Scenario 1: Wittgenstein, one heir (among others) of a German (which is also to say, Greek) literary and philosophical heritage, tends to understand the possibilities that lie before him in writing philosophy in terms of that heritage. His various remarks on writers and artists constitute an investigation—though not a sustained one—into at least some of the modes of discourse available to an heir, however marginal, of philosophy. Wittgenstein's chief preoccupation seems to be with a distinction between a masculine, ethical, productive discourse and a feminine, amoral, receptive discourse. Whether Wittgenstein is contrasting Genius and Jews, Genius and Taste, or Milton's and Beethoven's genius with Shakespeare's, at stake is whether the position one takes in writing is that of an autonomous individual, or whether one's position in writing is imitative, heteronomous, perhaps even without "character" at all.

Hypothesis: "Wittgenstein" writes out of the conjunction/disjunction of these two strands (roughly: masculine/feminine) in his philosophical remarks, and what remains to be thought in Wittgenstein's thought is a constellation of issues surrounding the question of "who" speaks in Wittgenstein's work.

Scenario 2: Luce Irigaray, one heir (among others) of a Western philosophical tradition that, since Plato, distinguishes—or seeks to distinguish—between speaking in one's own voice *(diegêsis)* and speaking in the voice of another *(mimêsis)*. This identificatory aspect of mimesis is considered dangerous, formless, malleable—and feminine. Irigaray, like Wittgenstein, sees this typology of discourse as what she inherits. Unlike Wittgenstein, Irigaray seems to have little doubt about what "position" she would write from:

> There is, in an initial phase, perhaps only one "path," the one historically assigned to the feminine: that of *mimicry*. One must assume the feminine role deliberately. Which means already to convert a form of subordination into an affirmation, and thus to

begin to thwart it. Whereas a direct feminine challenge to this
condition means demanding to speak as a (masculine) "subject,"
that is, it means to postulate a relation to the intelligible that
would maintain sexual indifference.

To play with mimesis is thus, for a woman, to try to recover the
place of her exploitation by discourse, without allowing herself to
be simply reduced to it.[2]

Question: For those of us who are, in some sense, "heirs" to investigations into the role(s) of gender in writing, what possibilities, what *futures*
are engendered by such investigations? What remains to be thought in
taking up the possibilities of "feminine" writing?

Hypothesis: To affirm "mimesis" (understood as speaking in the voice
of another rather than in one's own voice) in the way Irigaray does is to
reintroduce into ethical and political thought the very mimesis that was
banished in Plato's *Republic*. The upshot of this would be, finally, to recast
thought about ethics and politics in terms of mimesis and the heteronomous relation to others it inscribes rather than in terms of autonomy.
What perhaps remains to be thought is how to distinguish the affirmation
of alterity in Irigaray's parody of the feminine from subordination to
others.

Approach: What I propose to do here is no more than to *begin* an
investigation of a certain juncture between Wittgenstein and feminism,
a juncture I would call an ethical querying of modes of discourse. I am
not seeking to claim that Wittgenstein and Irigaray are doing the same
thing in their philosophies, but that each responds (albeit in different
ways and with different purposes) to the inheritance of a distinction between "original" and "imitative" modes of writing and thinking. Such an
approach will count as a "feminist" reading of Wittgenstein only if one
accepts Irigaray's claim that this traditional distinction is, as we say, "gendered." In what follows, I will rely on Irigaray's argument that "imitative"
discourses are associated with the feminine as a way of unpacking what is
at stake in Wittgenstein's various attempts to characterize different
modes of discourse. But if feminism brings to Wittgenstein a heightened
awareness of the significance of gender in writing philosophy, Wittgenstein may bring to feminism a heightened awareness of the need to
sharpen questions about how to distinguish between modes of imitation.

This occurs in two ways. First, there is Wittgenstein's general interest
in establishing criteria for language-games. As we shall see, Witt-

genstein's remarks on different modes of discourse may be taken as initial attempts at describing differing practices of "authorship." Where and how do we find criteria to distinguish what is subversive or transformative in discourses produced via imitation from what is not? Wittgenstein does not treat this question with the thoroughness with which he treats other philosophical questions, but his suggestive remarks point to the necessity of asking such a question. And, in addition, Wittgenstein is instructive because we see in his work just how intractable the question of how to distinguish subversive instances of mimesis from reassimilation may be. In the end, I will suggest that Judith Butler's project brings together Irigaray's "quasi-transcendental" argument concerning mimesis with a Wittgensteinian emphasis on criteria that is found in our everyday practices, and I will seek to show the relevance of this to contemporary feminism through a discussion of Butler's and Seyla Benhabib's differing responses to the difficulty of knowing where and how to find criteria to mark different modes of mimesis.

I will not be able to "discharge" either my inheritance or my responsibility to my varied inheritances (including feminism) here. What remains to be thought in Wittgenstein, in Irigaray, and in the philosophical tradition's treatment of mimesis will necessarily remain on the horizon, but perhaps we will see better that implicit in the gendered subjectivities produced in and by various modes of discourse are relations of self and other (other people, other practices, other ways of speaking), which bear continued examination. Perhaps, as Drucilla Cornell argues, this ethical impetus in feminist critiques of representation is what is most important—and needs most clarifying—in feminist thought today. I would suggest that the same holds true for Wittgenstein's thought; for Wittgenstein, at least implicitly, also asks about the ethical implications of the subject-positions marked in different modes of discourse. So, while this essay may not be a "feminist" reading of Wittgenstein in the sense of articulating a political position, it may be feminist insofar as it seeks to develop a certain kind of ethical question, informed by critiques of gender differences, about our modes of reading and writing.

But first, in order to uncover the implications of Wittgenstein's modes of discourse for ethics and for an understanding of the role(s) of gender in philosophy, let us pursue the relations of self and other inscribed in Wittgenstein's thought by asking, In what voice, or with what voices, does Wittgenstein engage in philosophy?

Who Speaks?

One way to begin to address this question is to examine the nascent typology of discourses in those remarks collected by G. H. Von Wright under the title *Culture and Value*. This typology follows closely the eighteenth- and nineteenth-century German philosophical and literary preoccupation with genius. Wittgenstein characteristically understands genius in contrast to something else—whether something opposed to genius or else another type of genius. In the early 1930s Wittgenstein follows Otto Weininger's characterology, which "scientifically" confirms the misgivings of Kant, Schopenhauer, and others about the capacity of women to be autonomous beings capable of putting the stamp of genius on their work and lives. Weininger adds to this the specter of men who are also (like women, and unlike genius) without character. Chief among these "feminine" versions of masculinity is the type "Jew," and Wittgenstein, for a time, uses the term *Jewish* in this sense. It is true, as Ray Monk points out, that Wittgenstein drops this term, but the general opposition (which is found throughout philosophical discussions of genius, though more crudely and insistently in Weininger) between masculine, ethical, productive, autonomous genius and feminine, amoral, receptive/reproductive taste remains.[3]

Wittgenstein's own writing seems to be precariously situated in the interstices of these two strands. As we shall see, sometimes Wittgenstein writes of his own work as if the potent force of a genius's character might be seen there. At other times, Wittgenstein writes as if what one finds in his work is a barren receptivity that, without deep passion, intellectually clarifies and tastefully rearranges the work of others. In short, the question before us (including Wittgenstein), is how far Wittgenstein's mode of writing may fairly be characterized as autonomous, and how far the position he takes when writing might be heteronomous—and how is one to evaluate these positions anyway? Clearly, the heteronomous and "feminine" character of both the type "Jew" and "taste" has traditionally been seen as secondary to its privileged contrast of masculine genius. But, in order to call this hierarchy into question without simply reversing it, one needs to understand more fully the ways in which these modes of discourse are implicated in one another in Wittgenstein's thought.

So: for Wittgenstein, there are three types, or modes, of production of a work. A work may be characterized as having been produced by the masculine type "genius," by the more feminine type "Jew," or by a type, "Shakespeare," which seems to confound this opposition. With the first two cases, Wittgenstein is drawing on the typology of Otto Weininger's infamous *Sex and Character*.[4] In the case of Shakespeare, Wittgenstein is employing Schiller's typology of poetry, for Shakespeare is treated as a "naive" poet.

Setting aside the case of Shakespeare for now, but still addressing the question of who speaks in Wittgenstein's work, let me draw out the types of subjectivity involved in Weininger's and Wittgenstein's typology. The type "Jew" is characterized by a capacity to adopt the thought of others as one's own and to adapt to one's surroundings. Indeed, Wittgenstein's often disconcerting remarks about "Jewishness" seem to subscribe to the stereotype of the formlessness, malleability, and purely intellectual character of "Jews."

> Amongst Jews "genius" is found only in the holy man. Even the greatest of Jewish thinkers is no more than talented. (Myself for instance.)
>
> I think there is some truth in my idea that I really only think reproductively. I don't believe I have ever *invented* a line of thinking, I have always taken one over from someone else. I have simply straightaway seized on it with enthusiasm for my work of clarification. That is how Boltzmann, Hertz, Schopenhauer, Frege, Russell, Kraus, Loos, Weininger, Spengler, Sraffa have influenced me. Can one take the case of Breuer and Freud as an example of Jewish reproductiveness?—What I invent are new *similes*.[5]

> It might be said (rightly or wrongly) that the Jewish mind does not have the power to produce even the tiniest flower or blade of grass; its way is rather to make a drawing of the flower or blade of grass that has grown in the soil of another's mind and to put it into a comprehensive picture. (CV, 19e)

> You get tragedy where the tree, instead of bending, breaks. Tragedy is something un-Jewish. Mendelssohn is, I suppose, the most untragic of composers. (CV, 1e)

> Mendelssohn is like a man who is only jolly when the people he is with are all jolly anyway, or like one who is only good when he

is surrounded by good men; he does not have the integrity of a tree which stands firmly in its place whatever may be going on around it. I too am like that and am attracted to being so. (CV, 2e)

At the risk of taking Wittgenstein's remarks on "Jewishness" and, as he might put it, "straightaway" seizing on them with "enthusiasm" for my own "work of clarification"—a work that cannot properly be said to be one's own—I wish to underscore in the preceding remarks Wittgenstein's affirmation of Weininger's claims that the "Jewish" type (like the type "Woman," for Weininger) lacks the strength of character to be a genius and that, *"because they are nothing in themselves, they can become everything"* (emphasis added).[6]

In contrast to this type of subjectivity (or antitype, since one is at the same time no one and everyone), is the "masculine" genius who stands in relation to the world as a whole and, free and alone, affirms his autonomy. Weininger writes:

The secret of the critique of practical reason is that man is alone in the world, in tremendous eternal isolation.

He has no object outside himself; lives for nothing else; he is far removed from being the slave of his wishes, of his abilities, of his necessities; he stands far above social ethics; he is alone.

Thus he becomes one and all; he has the law in him, and so he himself is the law, and no mere changing caprice. The desire is in him to be only the law, to be the law that is himself, without afterthought or forethought. This is the awful conclusion, he has no longer the sense that there can be duty for him. Nothing is superior to him, to the isolated absolute unity. But there are no alternatives for him; he must respond to his own categorical imperatives, absolutely, impartially. "Freedom," he cries (for instance, Wagner, or Schopenhauer), "rest, peace from the enemy; peace, not this endless striving"; and he is terrified. Even in this wish for freedom there is cowardice; in the ignominious lament there is desertion as if he were too small for the fight. What is the use of it all, he cries to the universe; and is at once ashamed, for he is demanding happiness, and that his own burden should rest on other shoulders. . . . To acquiesce in his loneliness is the splendid supremacy of the Kantian.[7]

In sum, Weininger's genius is a man of character. "He" (genius for Weininger is always masculine, never feminine) is both deeply logical and ethical, and has the courage to stand alone while unifying and putting his own stamp on a swirling, inchoate world. (This contrasts with the way in which, because of an indeterminate identity, logic and ethics are not deep, abiding concerns for either the type "Woman" or the type "Jew").

This "heroic" characterization of genius is echoed by Wittgenstein when he writes, "Genius is *talent exercised with courage*" and, "*Courage* is always original" (CV, 38e, 36e). In addition, Wittgenstein held that the moral character of a "man" marks the difference between the aphorisms of Lichtenberg and those of Kraus. Kraus shows exceptional talent and "flashes" of genius, while Lichtenberg is "no mere intellectual skeleton" but a "complete human being." Thus, "the greatness of what a man writes depends on everything else he writes and does" (CV, 65). Character evinces itself not only in the way a writer stands in relation to everything in his life when he writes, but also in a steadfastness against the influence of others. Weininger writes: "The statement that a great man is most moral towards himself stands on sure ground; he will not allow alien views to be imposed on him, so obscuring the judgment of his own ego; he will not passively accept the interpretation of another, of an alien ego, quite different from his own, and if ever he has allowed himself to be influenced, the thought will always be painful to him."[8] And when Wittgenstein suggests that the antithesis of Mendelssohn is a man who has "the integrity of a tree which stands firmly in its place whatever may be going on around it," he underscores the tragic character of genius, "where the tree, instead of bending, *breaks*" (CV, 1).

How the types "genius" and "Jew" relate to one another, and how they function in Wittgenstein's discourse, is still a matter for debate, despite the efforts of Janik, Monk, and Lurie.[9] For one thing, more attention needs to be given to the way in which autonomous genius is characterized as masculine; and heteronomous, imitative malleability is characterized as feminine. What is more, the introduction of Wittgenstein's use of Schiller's type of the natural or naive poet to this scenario complicates matters further. Like the type "Jew," the naive poet is someone who is himself no one. Schiller and Wittgenstein both remark that in reading Shakespeare (or, for Schiller, Homer), one has the experience of being unable to find the poet in the work. Rather, nature "herself"—or, for Wittgenstein, Shakespeare *as* a natural phenomenon—speaks through the rude genius of the poet. Yet if the naive poet is like the type "Jew," in being without character, he is also like the type genius insofar as there is something originary about Shakespeare's language.

What is the significance of the analysis of these three types in Wittgenstein's remarks?

First, these remarks demonstrate that Wittgenstein was interested in the different modes of existence of a work in culture. One cannot, and Wittgenstein in his probing and *critical* way certainly did not, make any easy assumptions about the relation of an author to his work. Moreover, it is difficult to tell what Wittgenstein's assessment of his "own" mode of production is. At times, as we have seen, he clearly sees his work as "Jewish" in character. At other times he touches on the possibility of his work being that of a genius in a Romantic, even Weiningerian, sense.[10] Even in his critique of Shakespeare, one may find (though Wittgenstein would probably disagree) certain similarities between Wittgenstein's rude genius and that of a naive poet. Thus, there remains a question about the mode of existence of Wittgenstein's work.

This question *remains*, and is what we inherit from Wittgenstein, as he inherited it from the German Romantic tradition. What is our responsibility to this inheritance? No doubt there is much that is problematic in this typology of discourse, but it is nevertheless useful in that it marks differences—differences that remain to be acknowledged. For instance, Wittgenstein writes of Shakespeare: "I am *deeply* suspicious of most of Shakespeare's admirers. The misfortune is, I believe, that he stands by himself, at least in the culture of the west, so that one can only place him by placing him wrongly" (CV, 84e). Given Wittgenstein's trepidations about the relation of his discourse to what he calls "the vast stream of European and American civilization in which all of us stand,"[11] and given his sensitivity to the way this stream (mis)appropriated Shakespeare, what is our responsibility to the differences marked in Wittgenstein's (and it is not just Wittgenstein's) typology? At the least, we ought to avoid an uncritical, unreflective use of this typology. Much of the work on Wittgenstein accords to him the role of "genius," and his much vaunted philosophical integrity, passion for truth, high moral character, and originality—all markers of Weininger's "genius"—serve as hermeneutic devices for interpreting his work. From this perspective, readings that suggest that some mode other than that of "genius" is at work seem to devalue Wittgenstein's work. Yet it should be clear that more is at stake here than Wittgenstein's place in the philosophical canon. The position of the subject in each of these types of discourse has much to tell us about the formation of identity in European culture, along with the moral, cultural, and political repercussions of such formations. In short, more is at stake in questioning the mode of subjectivity at work in "Wittgenstein" ("genius," "Jew," or "Shakespeare") than the philosophical status of the work. Also at stake are the *means* by which one may judge the philosophical (as well as the moral, cultural, and political) import of Wittgenstein's remarks. There are many questions to take up at this point, but I will restrict myself to addressing the one we have been discussing all along: Who speaks?[12]

Mimesis

One way to set the context for a discussion of who speaks in Wittgenstein and Irigaray is by a return to Plato, where the mode of one's discourse—and the position of the speaker to it—*matters*, politically and ethically. Although the modern conception of the subject is foreign to Plato, the question, Who speaks? is nevertheless vital to the infamous act of banishing poets from Plato's republic. Poets are a threat to the republic, not only because of what they say, but also because the way in which they say it exposes the instability of their identities. As Gerard Genette reminds us, while Plato generally divides poetry into three kinds (dramatic, lyric, and epic), these three genres are based on two modes of discourse: diegesis (speaking in one's own voice) and mimesis (speaking in the voice of another). Lyric poetry is the "best example" of speaking in one's own voice, and dramatic poetry (tragedy and comedy) is recognized as employing only mimesis. Epic poetry is a mixture of the two. Plato, in an irony difficult to fathom, banishes all forms of mimetic poetry—while speaking in the voice of another. Mimesis is banished (and lyric poets are allowed to remain) because a form that involves speaking in the voice of another is a threat to the principle of identity (one man/one role) that underlies the republic. Young guardians, for example (but this is more than an example), cannot be allowed, while reading poetry in their education, to play the parts of women, because—as Socrates points out—they are men.[13] Not only are poems dangerous insofar as they provoke a confusion of identities, but also poets themselves are dangerous, and for the same reason. "So if we are visited in our state by someone who has the skill to transform himself into all sorts of characters and represent all sorts of things, and he wants to show off himself and his poems to us, we shall treat him with all the reverence due to a priest and giver of rare pleasure, but shall tell him that he and his kind have no place in our city, being forbidden by our code, and send him elsewhere, after anointing him with myrrh and crowning him."[14] The mimetic poet exemplifies someone who could become anyone at all (and so could do anything). As such, the mimetic poet embodies the threat of mimesis and the loss of identity, and—in a logic made clear by René Girard—is expelled or sacrificed as a way of attempting to reestablish differences. Once mimesis is banished, it would again be possible to distinguish between the good and the bad man. As soon as Socrates escorts the mimetic poet across the borders of the polis, he establishes a difference between what the polis is and what it is not.

This "mimetology," as Philippe Lacoue-Labarthe calls it, rests on taking as fundamental, or as natural, the distinction between speaking in one's own voice and speaking in the voice of another.[15] What is at stake in holding onto this distinction as natural or fundamental? The risks of mimesis that this mimetology seeks to control—as Lacoue-Labarthe, following Irigaray closely here, points out—are "feminization and madness."[16] As Socrates discusses what the guardians should not risk imitating, he gives an hysterical picture of the dangers of general instability and hysteria implicit in mimesis.

> We will not then allow our charges, whom we expect to prove good men, being men, to play the parts of women and imitate a woman young or old wrangling with her husband, defying heaven, loudly boasting, fortunate in her own conceit, or involved in misfortune and possessed by grief and lamentation—still less a woman that is sick, in love, or in labor. . . . "And I take it they must not form the habit of likening themselves to madmen either in words nor yet in deeds. For while knowledge they must have both of mad and bad men and women, they must do and imitate nothing of this kind."[17]

It is this "hystericized" and "feminized" mimesis, the possibility that one will "in the presence of many . . . imitate all things," that Irigaray (among others) has taken up in her ethical and political querying of the modes of discourse that seek to regulate the unsettling dimension of the plasticity marked in and by mimesis. We have seen that Irigaray finds that deliberately imitating a feminine, imitative mode of discourse may transform mimicry from a form of submission to an affirmation of *écriture feminine*. Insofar as mimesis is understood as feminine, and speaking as an autonomous subject is understood as masculine, a "direct feminine challenge to this condition" would involve taking up a masculine mode of discourse, one predicated on autonomy. So, if one writes as a woman, Irigaray says, "one must assume the role assigned to the feminine deliberately." Since the role assigned to the feminine is here understood as mimesis, this amounts to saying that one must mime mimesis. This would recuperate the value of mimesis, changing its value from subordination to another to an affirmation of alterity. That is to say, the act of miming mimesis, the imitation of mimesis as a mode of discourse, highlights the difficulty of setting a boundary to mimesis. After all, if one can not only imitate others, but also imitate imitation "itself," then the traditional hierarchical distinction between the object (or subject) of imitation and the imitation becomes blurred, thereby marking mimesis as potentially originary and radically improper (in the sense of exceeding its "proper" bounds). Thus, miming mimesis would not produce "subordination," but would instead produce an "affirmation" of the feminine that is, finally, an affirmation of the alterity and radical impropriety within mimesis.

But we should remember Judith Butler's cautionary note that parodic or deliberately assumed repetitions are not in themselves revolutionary. As she says: "Parody by itself is not subversive, and there must be a way to understand what makes certain kinds of parodic repetitions effectively disruptive, truly troubling, and which repetitions become domesticated and recirculated as instruments of cultural hegemony. A typology of actions would clearly not suffice, for parodic displacement, indeed, parodic laughter, depends on a context and reception in which subversive confusions can be fostered."[18] If mimesis, identification, imitation, and so on are crucial for rethinking politics and ethics, it nevertheless remains to us to come to grips with the difficulties one has in establishing criteria for the uses of these terms and modes of discourse. One place, perhaps, to begin is with Wittgenstein's typologies, and with the "subversive confusions" that may or may not be found there. Here we may see how Wittgenstein sharpens our questions about how to distinguish between modes of discourse and imitation.

"Jewishness" and "Genius"

Let us look further, then, at this remarkable and little-understood aspect of Wittgenstein. "It is typical for a Jewish mind to understand someone else's work better than he understands it *himself*" (CV, 19). Much work needs to be done to understand the place of remarks such as this one, made in 1931, in considering Wittgenstein's work. Wittgenstein's sub-scription to such a cultural stereotype is largely ignored, but insofar as Wittgenstein's own work is informed by Weininger's characterology or typology, it calls for critical attention. I can here only begin this enormously complex task by noting one direction such an investigation might take. Lacoue-Labarthe, citing Alfred Rosenberg's anti-Semitic work *The Myth of the Twentieth Century*, underscores the way in which the myth that Jews have no proper being leads to the conclusion that Jews threaten the very possibility of society:

> Maurice Blanchot is right when he says "the Jews embody . . . the rejection of myths, the eschewing of idols, the recognition of an ethical order which manifests itself in respect for the law. What Hitler is attempting to annihilate in annihilating the Jew, and the 'myth of the Jew,' is precisely man liberated from myths." This "rejection of myths" is precisely what explains why the Jews do not constitute a type: they have, says Rosenberg, no *Seelengestalt*—and therefore no *Rassengestalt*. They are a formless, unaesthetic 'people', which by definition cannot enter into the process of self-fictioning and cannot constitute a subject, or, in other words, a being-proper (*être-propre*). It is this unassignable (and formidable) improperness of the Jews which makes them, says Rosenberg once again, not the direct opposite (a counter-type) of the Teuton, but his contradiction—the very absence of type. Hence their power—they who are neither *Kulturbegründer* nor *Kulturschöpfer*, but mere *Kulturträger*, bearers of civilization—to insert themselves into every culture and State and then to live a life that is parasitic upon these, constantly threatening them with bastardization. All in all, the Jews are infinitely mimetic beings, or, in other words, the site of an *endless mimesis*, which is both interminable and inorganic, producing no art and achieving no appropriation. They are destabilization itself.[19]

Wittgenstein, following Weininger, is not innocent of what Lacoue-Labarthe calls the Nazi ontotypology, which is a form of the Platonic mimetology that bans from the republic all those who speak in the voice of another. And yet, as we shall see, Wittgenstein is also not unaware of the "positive" character of mimesis. That is to say, not only will Wittgenstein sometimes privilege this normally subjugated term (which reverses the ontotypology but keeps its structure intact), but more significant, Wittgenstein also begins to reinscribe mimesis with the figure of Shakespeare by according to mimesis (paradoxically) an originary status.

How does this work itself out? Most of Wittgenstein's typological remarks bear upon the question of the position of the subject in the work. But Wittgenstein's characterization of the "Jewish" type, following Weininger, is not that of a subject as such, but rather of what is already not a subject insofar as what is "characteristic" of the "Jew" is precisely a lack of character, a capacity to identify with others and become like them. This impropriety, which Wittgenstein at least at one point acknowledges and affirms—"I too am like that, and am attracted to being so" (CV, 2)—is what Plato, under the sign of the poets, seeks to banish from the republic. Insofar as Wittgenstein affirms this lack of being-proper, he is reversing the "Platonic" mimetology while essentially keeping it intact. Moreover, Wittgenstein's fascination with the concept of genius as articulated by Weininger—in which there is no lack of being-proper and in which speaking in one's own voice is a mark of genius—suggests that this reversal is none too sure, and that the impropriety of Wittgenstein's "Jewishness" is not simply attractive, but is also deeply troubling to him. What does it mean for Wittgenstein's work to say that it is produced via mimesis—that is to say, through an identificatory process which is not anchored in any identity? One kind of response to this question may be found in Wittgenstein's suggestion, cited earlier, that his work is never productive, only reproductive ("I think there is some truth in my idea that I really only think reproductively"). This repetition of production both clarifies the "original" and is itself devoid of character. Freud, Wittgenstein suggests in this context, owes whatever greatness lies in his work to Breuer's influence (CV, 36e).

But what if Wittgenstein seeks to reproduce, not only the thought of "Boltzmann, Hertz, Schopenhauer, Frege, Russell, Kraus, Loos, Weininger, Spengler, Sraffa," but also language? Nowhere does Wittgenstein suggest that his "Jewishness" lends itself to the nature of his philosophical project, but it would not be too much to say that Wittgenstein's capacity for the "clarification" and "reproduction" of language-games is, according to the logic of the terms he has set up, a consequence of his "Jewishness"—that is to say, of his status as a *mime*. Wittgenstein mimics language ("The aspect presents a physiognomy which then passes away. It is almost as if there were a face there which at first I *imitate*, and then accept without imitating it").[20] Viewed in this way, one might say of Wittgenstein's work that it is in and by the shifting polylogue of voices, imitated by "Wittgenstein," that one may hear the anonymous murmur of language.

This possibility of interpreting Wittgenstein's text as a defacement of the author before language cannot be entertained so long as one supposes—as many have—that Wittgenstein's work is produced by "genius." Wittgenstein's characterization of genius emphasizes integrity, originality and a quasi-Kantian moral subject. Not surprisingly, many descriptions of "Wittgenstein the man" emphasize just those features. If Wittgenstein's work is that of a genius, then (according to Weininger and Wittgenstein's articulation of the concept "genius") it is a product of his relation to the world as a whole, is only a part of his "true" work, the work on his self. And Wittgenstein indicates that this might be the case when he writes: "Working in philosophy—like work in architecture in many respects—is really more a working on oneself" (CV, 16).

So, is Wittgenstein a genius? Again, at stake in this question is not just the status of Wittgenstein's work, but also the mode of its presentation. Wittgenstein, at one point, describes his talent as one involving "taste" and "sensitivity, which are "purely receptive" and unable to give birth to something new (CV, 59–60). It is true that Wittgenstein suggests that there is a kind of originality and courage in his honest acceptance of the limitations imposed on him by his lack of character, but it is not at all clear that in this case courage constitutes genius.

What happens when Wittgenstein suggests that his "originality" and "courage" might lie in his "honest" acceptance of the limitations imposed on him by his "pure receptivity" and "reproductive" talent? It is impossible to tell, on the basis of Wittgenstein's remarks alone, whether Wittgenstein is seeking to salvage the possibility of a moral life, or whether he is in fact reinscribing the conception of "genius" so that "originality" and "courage" may be found in affirming imitation. In either case, though perhaps more profoundly in the latter case, Wittgenstein weaves together both speaking in one's own voice ("genius") and speaking in the voice of another ("Jewishness"). In the possible case of reinscribing courage as an affirmation of imitation, such an interweaving of the proper and improper would be possible only if there were also a reinscription of the improper mimicry, marking mimesis as neither proper nor improper. This occurs in Wittgenstein's thought of Shakespeare.

Everything and Nothing

There is yet another "type" to be found in Wittgenstein's journals, although it may have only one example: Shakespeare. Unlike those of the other two "types," Wittgenstein's characterizations of Shakespeare do not seem to owe anything to Weininger, but rather are a rendition of Schiller's conception of the naive poet.[21] After declaring that a poet will either *be* nature or will *seek* lost nature, Schiller gives this description of learning to recognize Shakespeare as part of nature:

> When, at a very early age I first made the acquaintance of [Shakespeare], I was incensed by his coldness, the insensitivity which permitted him to jest in the midst of the highest pathos, to interrupt the heartrending scenes in *Hamlet*, in *King Lear*, in *Macbeth*, etc., with a Fool; restraining himself now where my sympathies rushed on, then coldbloodedly tearing himself away where my heart would have gladly lingered. Misled by acquaintance with more recent poets into looking first for the poet in his work, to find *his* heart, to reflect in unison with *him* on his subject matter, in short, to observe the object in the subject, it was intolerable to me that here there was no way to lay hold of the poet, and nowhere to confront him. . . . I was not yet prepared to understand nature at first hand.[22]

For Schiller, the "intolerable" situation of a poet without heart or identity is eased by the discovery that in the case of naive poets nature herself is the subject, and that "[s]o long as man is pure—not, of course crude—nature, he functions as an undivided sensuous unity and as a unifying whole."[23]

Like Schiller, Wittgenstein finds it difficult to read poetry in which one could not "reflect in unison with *him* on his subject matter."

It may be that the essential thing with Shakespeare is his ease and authority and that you just have to accept him as he is if you are going to be able to admire him properly, in the way you accept nature, a piece of scenery for example, just as it is.

If I am right about this, that would mean that the style of his whole work, I mean of all his works taken together, is the essential thing and what provides his justification.

My *failure* to understand him could then be explained by my inability to read him *easily*. That is, as one views a splendid piece of scenery. (CV, 49e)

People stare at him in wonderment, almost as at a spectacular natural phenomenon. They do not have the feeling that this brings them into contact with a great *human being*. Rather with a phenomenon. (CV, 85e)

Wittgenstein's experience in reading Shakespeare's poetry seems to be one of astonishment. Without a sense of "contact" with a "human being," without the ability to see the poetry as the result of the poet's reflection, his experience of Shakespeare's language is like an aesthetic experience of a natural phenomenon. But perhaps it would be still clearer to say that his experience is an experience of astonishment that there is language: "He is *not* true to nature [*naturwahr*]. But he has such a supple hand and such a singular *stroke* [*einen so eigenartigen* Strich], that each one of his characters looks *significant*" (CV, 84–84e; translation modified). Unlike Schiller, Wittgenstein does not seek to shore up the absence of a subject in Shakespeare's work by positing nature as a subject. If Wittgenstein supposes that Shakespeare is like nature, he does so not in order to mystify the subject "Shakespeare," but in order to show that Shakespeare's *language* seems significant, or impressive, in much the same way a natural phenomenon would. Another example of this is Wittgenstein's comparison of Shakespeare's work with dreams. The language of dreams is impressive and significant in a way that differs from reflective language, and yet it is "quite right according to a law of its own" (CV, 83e). Thus, given the absence of identity of character in Shakespeare, one could not "speak of Shakespeare's great heart" as one would speak of "Beethoven's great heart." Rather, "'[t]he supple hand that created new natural linguistic forms' would seem . . . nearer the mark" (CV, 84e). Rather than a poet (*Dichter*), Shakespeare would be a creator of language (*ein Sprach-*

schöpfer). And this is a crucial distinction, for anyone who admires Shakespeare as a *Dichter* in the mold of Milton or Beethoven would be misapprehending the force of Shakespeare's language as a phenomenon. "His pieces give me an impression as of enormous *sketches* rather than of paintings; as though they had been *dashed off* by someone who can permit himself *anything*. . . .—So if someone stands in front of these pieces speechless, I can understand him; but anyone who admires them as one admires, say, Beethoven, seems to me to misunderstand Shakespeare" (CV, 86e). What is impressive in Shakespeare is the singular stroke of his sketches, which is singular insofar as it is "*dashed off* by someone who can permit himself *anything*." As we have seen, according to a certain logic of the term mimesis, only someone who has no character, who is himself or herself "nothing," is capable of becoming anyone or doing anything. Thus, there is in Wittgenstein's "Shakespeare" a resemblance to Weininger's "Jew," who "can become everything" and is himself "nothing." But, like the "Shakespeare" in Jorge Luis Borges's parable "Everything and Nothing," Wittgenstein's "Shakespeare" is not passive, but is the site of the creation of language. In this respect "Shakespeare" differs from the "Jew," who cannot create, but can only improve on the work of others (and so remains subject to others).

In short, in Wittgenstein's hands the naive poet Shakespeare marks a different mode of discourse than we have seen so far. "Shakespeare" signifies neither a proper subject, nor the simple lack of a proper subject, but the emergence of language. That is to say, the corpus embodies neither a work of reflective genius, nor a work of imitation and clarification, but an *event*: "A poet cannot really say of himself 'I sing as the birds sing'—but perhaps Shakespeare could have said this of himself" (CV, 84e).

Many readers have been, no doubt, able only to stare in wonder at Wittgenstein, as at a natural phenomenon, unable to "do" anything with him, as Wittgenstein claims about his relation to Shakespeare: "I could only stare in wonder at Shakespeare; never do anything with him" (CV, 84e). But those who emphasize his rude genius, his lack of philosophical sophistication (in terms of knowledge of the history of philosophy), and his eccentricities seek to make of Wittgenstein a figure of nature or, if you will, a naive poet, without taking into account the transformations Wittgenstein makes of Schiller's typology. This is a mistake, for saying that Wittgenstein (or Shakespeare) *is* a figure of nature rather than identifying Wittgenstein (or Shakespeare) *as* a figure of nature covers over the possibility of mimesis at work in Wittgenstein's work. It would also be a mistake to treat Wittgenstein's remarks on Shakespeare as ironic descriptions of features of his "own" work (as if to foreground the "literariness" of Wittgenstein) without also raising the question of mimesis, for otherwise "literariness" tends to be conceived in terms of a "style" of a subject.[24] At stake here is not only the possibility of finding at work in Wittgenstein's work a "subject" (if one may still speak of a subject here) which is "itself" nothing and capable of becoming anyone, but also the possibility of a critique of an unacknowledged mimetology in interpretations of Wittgenstein that frame his work in terms of an opposition of genius and characterlessness. Shakespeare's "genius" (and, perhaps, Wittgenstein's) confounds this opposition. That is to say, Shakespeare's lack of being-proper, his mimetic (or characterless) "character," is conceived in such a way that it is nevertheless also creative, thereby deconstructing a Platonic mimetology.

Who speaks? Is "Wittgenstein" a "Jew," a "genius," or a "Shakespeare"? Enough, more than enough, has been written about Wittgenstein as a heroic genius. Perhaps it is time to consider the possibility that there is no proper subject "behind" the numerous "voices" in the *Philosophical Investigations*, not even a "communal" subject formed in the "shared" activities and tacit judgments of a form of life—unless that "community" were understood not only as a locus of identity but also as a locus of imitations (and so as a confusion of identities). What if, following the indications of Wittgenstein's typology, one were to suppose that "Wittgenstein" is not himself, but is already other, and that this alterity (whether "Jewishness" or "Shakespeare," but perhaps more profoundly in the latter case) exposes language-games, practices, and discursive modes *as events*? One then might learn to hear in a new way the claim, found in *Philosophical Grammar*, that "[l]anguage must speak for itself."[25] Generally, this is heard as the epistemological claim that attempts to ground language in something outside of language are unintelligible. But there is a tendency to forget that the upshot of this for Wittgenstein would be that language-games, and *not* the players of language-games, are the *primary phenomenon* (*Urphänomene*).[26] Through his partial examination of the grammar of the term *author* as found in our practices of interpreting culture, Wittgenstein points to ways of considering the author as an imitator of language.

Implicit in this is a recognition of "our" heteronomous relation to language-games, and it runs counter to the relation of language-games and players of the games described in the famous "toolbox" analogy, wherein language is seen as a toolbox full of very different kinds of tools. But if language not only is a tool to be wielded by the players of language-games, but is also (at least sometimes) something that might be imitated, Wittgenstein marks this latter possibility almost in spite of himself. I say in spite of himself because, in spite of his affinity with the mimicry of a Mendelssohn ("I too am like that, and am attracted to being so" [CV, 2e]), and in spite of his fascination with Shakespeare, Wittgenstein seems generally to privilege the autonomy and moral character of "genius." In contrast, Irigaray seeks rather to recast ethical thought in terms of mimesis. Rather than subscribe to a masculine ethic of independence, Irigaray might ask why one has to decide between autonomy and heteronomy. By miming mimesis Irigaray privileges a "feminine" heteronomy, but by miming mimesis she reinscribes mimesis as active, as an originary repetition, so that it can no longer be understood as simply the reverse of masculine autonomy. But if one cannot simply decide between autonomy and heteronomy, there nevertheless seem to remain distinctions to make. As we have seen, the figure "Shakespeare" that Wittgenstein describes confounds the distinction between autonomy and heteronomy in much the way Irigaray describes feminine writing doing. But the figure of the "Jew" is passive and is, insofar as he models himself on others or seeks to reproduce the thought of others, informed by the idea of mimesis as adequation or homoiosis. Hence, he remains subject to others. "Shakespeare," on the other hand, is active and (insofar as he is a Sprachschöpfer) somehow a figure of "originary" mimesis. But is it possible to maintain this distinction between a mode of mimesis wherein one remains subject to others and one wherein one does not? Would not the very "lack" of character involved in mimesis make such a "characterization" of a distinction between an active and a passive mimesis problematic? If so, Irigaray's certitude about deliberately occupying the position of a mimic in "her" discourse is remarkable.

At stake here is a question about what to do with the inheritance of mimesis. What would happen if one were to recast philosophy in terms of mimesis (a possibility Wittgenstein entertains, with his discussions of the modes of discourse belonging to "Jews," "taste," and "Shakespeare")? After recognizing that we ought not simply dismiss this possibility (as happens from The Republic onward) as nonphilosophical, what is "our" responsibility here? And this means: in what mode of discourse should a response be made? what would count as a responsible acknowledgment of mimesis?[27] and what would responsible mean if the difference between a mimesis in which one is subject to others and one in which one affirms otherness in one's (repeated, imitated) self cannot be marked?

On the Inheritance of Mimesis

> The relations between these concepts form a landscape which language presents us with in countless fragments; piecing them together is *too hard* for me. I can make only a very imperfect job of it.
>
> —Ludwig Wittgenstein, *Culture and Value*

Where does this leave us? Both Wittgenstein and Irigaray prompt us to take up the question of the mode of one's discourse as an ethical question. Moreover, each—in responding to traditional distinctions between speaking in one's own voice and speaking in the voice of another—calls into question the traditional position that speaking in one's own voice is necessary to "ethical" reflection. This is not to say that Wittgenstein and Irigaray are engaged in the same project, for the ways in which they approach their "inheritances" are very different. I have suggested that it is easier to see what Wittgenstein is up to in his cryptic and problematic remarks on genius, Jewishness, and Shakespeare if one approaches those remarks with an awareness of Irigaray's work on gender differences in discourse. I have also suggested that the upshot of Wittgenstein's remarks is that we do not yet know our way about certain paths opened up by focusing on speaking in the voice of another as a kind of language-game. Is there more than one way of engaging in this practice? What are our criteria for distinguishing such different modes, and what are the ethical implications of such distinctions? These are the kinds of questions Wittgenstein might pose to Irigaray, but his sporadic treatment of these issues stops short of helping us to find our way about. Since such a conclusion is not satisfying, let me go one small step further, and try to show how Judith Butler's and Seyla Benhabib's differing responses to the difficulty of knowing where and how to find criteria to mark mimesis show why Wittgenstein's attempts to find ways of distinguishing modes of discourse are relevant to contemporary feminism.

Drucilla Cornell highlights the importance of mimesis in Irigaray's thought in the following passage: "*Mimesis*, as Irigaray uses the word—as an ethical relation to otherness—is very close to Adorno's usage. *Mimesis*, understood as a non-violent ethical relation to what is Other, and not as a mode of artistic representation that supposedly mimics, or more precisely mirrors, the real in art, is an expression of Adornian non-identity in which the subject does not seek to identify or categorize the object, but rather to let the object be in its difference."[28] This letting the object be in its difference, Cornell goes on to say, involves an identification with what is other, and so "demands the reception of the Other as other. The housewarming that Adorno's ethical understanding of *mimesis* implies is not a reaching out that seeks to appropriate so that the subject is still in control of what it seeks to touch. The Other is embraced, but not absorbed."[29]

One can hear in this lengthy citation the effort required to recuperate or rehabilitate this conception of mimesis. Rather than imitation being a threat to identity and the very possibility of responsibility, the identification with others that may occur in imitation becomes something like a condition of possibility for relations with others that would not be completely circumscribed by a master-slave dialectic.

Seyla Benhabib, in addressing Adorno's conception of mimesis, asks how one can distinguish an identification *with* something (such as is described by Cornell in the quote we just read) from narcissism. Here Benhabib sees in mimesis the opposite of the threat Plato finds (or pretends to find) in mimesis. If, for Plato, mimesis poses the threat of losing one's self, Benhabib suspects that mimesis is indistinguishable from an illusion of oceanic oneness with the world.

> The "non-sacrificial non-identity of the subject," which Adorno describes as "utopia," is identified with giving oneself over to the other via an act of contemplation. Yet what distinguishes this act of giving oneself to the other from an act of narcissism? How can we ever establish that this act of contemplative giving into the other is not merely a *projection* on the part of the self onto the other attributes that the self would gladly acknowledge to be its own? Why cannot the art work become a narcissistic mirror of self-contemplation? Are there immanent constraints in the work of art itself that would bring the self back from its boundless self-adoration to the acknowledgment of the other? Why isn't mimesis a form of narcissism?[30]

Neither Plato nor Benhabib, then, finds in mimesis a condition of possibility for responsibility. Whether *mimesis* designates instability (as in

Plato) or narcissism (as in Benhabib), it would seem that recasting ethical and political thought in terms of mimesis would be irresponsible. Thus, one who inherits the project of reinscribing mimesis also inherits a demand to *respond* to the charge of irresponsibility.

To whom would one respond, however? Well, in this case, it would seem to be Seyla Benhabib. Or would it be the thought and tradition that Benhabib speaks for? For "Benhabib," the answer would seem to be: it depends. We are, she says, responsible both to concrete others and to generalized others. "The standpoint of the generalized other" she says, "requires us to view each and every individual as a rational being entitled to the same rights and duties we would want to ascribe to ourselves."[31] She adds: "In assuming this standpoint, we abstract from the individuality and concrete identity of the other. We assume that the other, like ourselves, is a being who has concrete needs, desires and affects, but that what constitutes his or her moral dignity is not what differentiates us from each other, but rather what we, as speaking and acting rational agents, have in common."[32] However, she suggests, viewing the other concretely "requires us to view each and every rational being as an individual with a concrete history, identity and affective-emotional constitution. In assuming this standpoint, we abstract from what constitutes our commonality, and focus on individuality."[33] For Benhabib, then, the key question is when are we responsible to what we have in common and when to what makes us distinct? When there is conflict between these two responsibilities, she suggests, our responsibility to be impartial in recognizing a generalized other's rights *trumps* our responsibility to care for a concrete other's needs.[34] Yet the question of responsibility may be more complicated than just determining when one is responsible for what we have in common and when for what makes us distinct (as if that weren't already complicated enough). As Judith Butler shows, identification *with* another may be understood, as in her discussion of Freud's conception of mourning, with an emphasis placed on the exposure of the self to something other than it through an experience of loss. As she puts it, for Freud, "identifications are always made in response to loss of some kind, and . . . they involve a certain *mimetic practice* that seeks to incorporate the lost love within the very 'identity' of the one who remains."[35]

A full treatment of this difference between Benhabib and Butler on the character of identification would involve an account of the role of narcissism in relation to an ego already constituted, in part, by its melancholic incorporations of others.[36] Let me, instead, underscore the different conceptions of identification and try to draw some of the consequences of this difference. For Benhabib, without criteria to distin-guish identification with another as an exposure to otherness from an identification with another as an act of narcissism, one loses the possibil-ity of—and responsibility to engage in—critique. Hence Benhabib's sus-picion of Butler's affirmation of drag à la Irigaray; on Benhabib's view, one could not account for the "reinscription" of a term, an act, or prac-tice Butler says may occur through imitation of it, so long as there are no criteria for distinguishing mimesis from narcissism. One might wonder, however, whether Benhabib's demand doesn't presuppose the separate categories of self and other. After all, what would count as a criterion of the difference between mimesis and narcissism but something that en-ables us to decide on the relation of already separated entities, the self and other? For Benhabib, the limit of narcissism would appear when, as she says, "the object of identification is itself capable of acting in such a way as to differentiate between identity and difference, between self and other."[37] On Butler's view, however, the "cission" or cut is not so much between self and other as it is within both self and other: "[T]he self only becomes a self on the condition that it has suffered a separation . . . , a loss which is suspended and provisionally resolved through a melancholic incorporation of some 'Other.' That 'Other' installed in the self thus establishes the permanent incapacity of that 'self' to achieve self-identity; it is as it were always already disrupted by that Other; the disruption of the Other at the heart of the self is the very condition of that self's possibility."[38] (By the way, this may also mean that Cornell's formulation of mimesis as "non-violent" is too quick, too easily understood in terms of a narcissistic "oceanic oneness" with things.)

This formulation of Butler's suggests that "we" are different from our-selves. Stated that baldly and plainly, the "result" of a deconstruction of identity sounds either silly or obvious, but it is no more silly or obvious than the unstated assumption behind Benhabib's version of communica-tive ethics, which is that, whether as a generalized or a concrete other, we are self-identical. When we are responsible to a generalized other, we assume that we are all basically the same. And when we are responsible to a concrete other, we assume that the other is concretely different from me, but not different from him/herself. But what if one may also be obliged to respond to mimesis (or alterity) "itself," both within "others" and one's "own" self?

It is strange to say that one must respond to, be responsible to, mimesis understood as an exposure to alterity, but this may be no more strange than saying that one must recognize the freedom and autonomy in the generalized other. Each idea (freedom and autonomy on the one hand, and mimesis and heteronomy on the other) functions in a transcendental way to mark the conditions of possibility of a self and of ethics, and it is this abstraction from concrete individuals that makes a discussion of responsibility seem strange. But there is an important sense in which the alterity found, each time, in others and in oneself, through the practice of imitation, is not necessarily the same, not quite, because with each imitation a difference may be introduced. If such differences are to be meaningful, we must have criteria for marking them in our practices, and here Butler's attempts to find criteria for what counts as a resignification of a practice from *within* that practice would show how Wittgenstein and Irigaray might be brought together in a thick description of how modes of discourse can be subversive in some ways and nonsubversive in others. (At any rate, I read her work after *Gender Trouble* as an attempt to engage in close readings of our practices and their reinscriptions in a way that is true to Wittgenstein's sense that "[w]hen you can't unravel a tangle, the most sensible thing is for you to recognize this" [CV, 74e].) More important, however, the ways in which imitations of a practice may change a practice in specific ways that are marked in that practice makes the "transcendental" character of the alterity and heteronomy of mimesis somewhat different from that of the transcendental ideas of freedom and autonomy. And this caveat is important, because it is this that—to return to Cornell's claim that mimesis is ethical—would account for the possibility of an attunement to concrete others. One could do worse here than to look to Walt Whitman, who says, after an extraordinary list of people of all kinds,

> And these tend inward toward me, and I tend outward toward them,
> And such as it is to be of these more or less I am,
> And of these one and all I weave the song of myself.[39]

The traces of me in others and of others in me may be woven together in different and unending ways; this "weave" constitutes a self which is always already exposed to others in such a way as to be called upon to respond anew to changes in those traces which occur through repetition and exposure to still other traces. Thus, "The Song of Myself," far from being an exercise in narcissistic romanticism, is profoundly social and interested in what makes us able to respond to others. Whitman both responds to everything and everyone that calls to him *and* calls to us to respond to this changing, contradictory, multitudinous "self" constituted via mimesis:

> You will hardly know who I am or what I mean,
> But I shall be good health to you nevertheless,
> And filter and fibre your blood.

> Failing to fetch me at first keep encouraged,
> Missing me one place search another,
> I stop somewhere waiting for you.[40]

Notes

1. M. O'C. Drury, "A Symposium: Assessments of the Man and the Philosopher," in *Ludwig Wittgenstein: The Man and his Philosophy*, ed. K. T. Fann (New York: Dell, 1967), 68.

2. Luce Irigaray, *This Sex Which Is Not One*, trans. Catherine Porter with Carolyn Burke (Ithaca: Cornell University Press, 1985), 78.

3. Here I am restating in cultural (rather than metaphysical) terms the point made by Yuval Lurie in "Jews as a Metaphysical Species," *Philosophy* 64 (1989): 323–47: "[A]lthough he abandoned the use of the concept of the Jew, Wittgenstein kept returning to the metaphysical idea he was trying to express by it: the idea that a distinction needs to be made between two different forces discernible in men of culture." As Jacques Le Rider comments in his postscript to his "Wittgenstein and Weininger" in *Tradition et rupture: Wittgenstein et la critique du monde moderne* (Brussels: La Lettre Volée, 1990): "Ici, Lurie évoque les remarques de Wittgenstein sur son manque d'originalité, ou sur Mendelssohn." But if the "different forces discernible in men of culture" are to be understood as cultural rather than metaphysical differences, it nevertheless remains to understand the philosophical implications of a culture that engenders such (gendered) differences.

4. Although I am convinced that Weininger plays a crucial role here, I would also see Schopenhauer's remarks on genius and taste (see David Abraham Wiener, *Genius and Talent: Schopenhauer's Influence on Wittgenstein's Early Philosophy* (Rutherford: Fairleigh Dickinson Press, 1992) as formative for Wittgenstein's typology.

5. Ludwig Wittgenstein, *Culture and Value*, ed. G. H. von Wright and Heikki Nyman, trans. Peter Winch (Chicago: University of Chicago Press, 1980), 18e–19e. All subsequent references to this work will be cited as *CV* and are to this edition; citations will hereafter be given in the text.

6. Otto Weininger, *Sex and Character* (New York: G. P. Putnam's Sons, 1907), 174.

7. Weininger, *Sex and Character*, 162.

8. Weininger, *Sex and Character*, 174.

9. Allan Janik, *Essays on Wittgenstein and Weininger* (Amsterdam: Rodpoi, 1985); Yuval Lurie, "Jew as a Metaphysical Species" *Philosophy* 64 (1989): 323–47; Ray Monk, *Ludwig Wittgenstein: The Duty of Genius* (New York: Free Press, 1989).

It is difficult to know how to treat Wittgenstein's serious consideration of Weininger's typology (as found in *Sex and Character*) without seeming to lend philosophical credibility to the sexist and racist stereotypes portrayed there. This may be, in part, why the importance of Weininger's work to Wittgenstein's thought is largely ignored. It is also the case, however, that one cannot without difficulty ignore Weininger's work in interpreting Wittgenstein's. This is true not only for the scholastic reasons Janik gives (that Wittgenstein's understanding of Kant is shaped by Weininger; that there are astonishing similarities in Wittgenstein's and Weininger's philosophical ideas, including the idea that logic and ethics are the same; and that Weininger's thought is important for understanding not only Wittgenstein, but also the "times"); nor only for the biographical reasons Monk gives (that Weininger's conception of the "type" genius was formative for both Wittgenstein's character and his work); but also because it is largely in Weininger's terms (with one important exception, as we shall see) that Wittgenstein addresses the question of the position of the subject in the work.

The largely scholastic orientation of Janik's work on Wittgenstein and Weininger comes close to giving Weininger's racism a veneer of sophistication and respectability, in spite of Janik's careful and astute observations. Monk, however, seeks to separate out what is interesting and compelling in Weininger's thought (namely, the conception of genius) from what is clearly spurious. This has the virtue of enabling Monk to distance his own narrative from any suggestion of racism, but it ignores that Weininger's thought of the type "genius" and his thought of the type "Jew" are of a piece. One cannot understand one without the other. And the consequences of this for Wittgensteinian criticism, which relentlessly portrays Wittgenstein's work as the work of genius, are enormous. As troubling as it is to risk lending philosophical credibility to racism, it is just as troubling for an unacknowledged endorsement of a typological project that is in complicity with racism to pass uncritically in the literature on Wittgenstein through an emphasis on Wittgenstein's work as that of a genius. At the same time, if one seeks to understand Wittgenstein (and the "literary" figure of Wittgenstein), one cannot dismiss Wittgenstein's temptations to wax typological in thinking about Wittgenstein and his work. It is my hope that the following analysis not only demonstrates that what is at stake in Wittgenstein's Weiningerian typology is the question of the mode of production of the work, but also remains critical of this typology. The structural opposition between speaking in one's own voice (*diegêsis*) and speaking in the voice of another (*mimêsis*) that underlies Weininger's opposition of the type "genius" to the types "Jew" and "Woman" is to be supplanted by a reinscription of the mimetic pole of Wittgenstein's typology (the "Jew") in the figure of Shakespeare. Whether it is permissible to focus on these, frankly, philosophical consequences of Wittgenstein's typology without also doing the hard work of linking these matters with more overtly political and historical concerns is another question—one that I doubt could be answered affirmatively, but that I am nevertheless not prepared to address. Still, it seems to me that it is not only necessary but also possible to take up Wittgenstein's typological concerns in a way that underscores their significance while yet remaining critical of philosophical typologies. At the very least, the possibility that Wittgenstein wrote as what he called the type "Jew," or else as a kind of "Shakespeare," prevents one from relying on an *unacknowledged* typology in treating Wittgenstein as a genius, and requires that one take seriously the question of the mode of production of "Wittgenstein's" work.

It also, and this is no small matter, raises the possibility of a nonanthropocentric conception of language at work in "Wittgenstein's" work.

10. "It's a good thing I don't allow myself to be influenced!" (CV, 1). "Working in philosophy—like work in architecture in many respects—is really more a working on oneself" (CV 16).

11. Ludwig Wittgenstein, foreword to *Philosophical Remarks*, trans. Raymond Hargreaves and Roger White (Chicago: University of Chicago Press, 1975), 8.

12. Foucault sketches out a *historical* line of inquiry when he writes that we should ask: "How, under what conditions, and in what forms can something like a subject appear in the order of discourse? What place can it occupy in each type of discourse, what functions can it assume, and by obeying what rules?" (Michel Foucault, "What Is an Author?" in *The Foucault Reader*, ed. Paul Rabinow [New York: Pantheon Books, 1984], 118). In what follows I will focus primarily on the

question of the position of the subject in Wittgenstein's discourse. This leaves aside questions about the emergence of a typological discourse (where it come from, how it is circulated, who controls it) that would need to be fleshed out in order to come to grips with the problem of racism in Wittgenstein's thought.

13. Plato, *The Republic*, in *The Collected Dialogues of Plato*, ed. Edith Hamilton and Huntington Cairns (Princeton: Princeton University Press, 1980), 395d.

14. Plato, *The Republic*, 398.

15. Note, too, that even if mimesis is privileged over diegesis, the same "mimetological" structure is at work. A critique of Plato's conception of mimesis requires more than recuperating the value of mimesis. It also involves disorganizing the binary structure the concept inhabits. One would need, for example, to ask why Plato has recourse to mimesis at the moment it is banished.

16. Phillipe Lacoue-Labarthe, "Typography," in *Typography: Mimesis, Philosophy, Politics*, ed. Christopher Fynsk (Cambridge: Harvard University Press, 1989), n.128.

17. Plato, *The Republic*, 395d.

18. Judith Butler, *Gender Trouble* (New York: Routledge, 1990), 139.

19. Phillipe Lacoue-Labarthe, "The Fiction of the Political," in *Heidegger, Art, and Politics: The Fiction of the Political*, trans. Chris Turner (Oxford: Basil Blackwell, 1990), 96.

20. Ludwig Wittgenstein, *Philosophical Investigations*, 3d ed. (New York: Macmillan, 1958), part II, 210.

21. To the best of my knowledge, no one has yet acknowledged the importance of Schiller for Wittgenstein's remarks on Shakespeare. Besides the congruences cited in the text, one can see parallels in their characterizations of one's response to a naive poet (Schiller adds Homer to this company), as well as in their suspicions of the responses of literary critics to a naive poet. (Schiller is critical of critics' inability to address nature as such, while Wittgenstein—who dislikes Shakespeare—is critical of valorizations of Shakespeare that ignore or forget the difference of Shakespeare from other "great" art.)

Schiller:
From society itself they can never arise; but from outside it they still sometimes appear, but rather as strangers at whom one stares, and as uncouth sons of nature by whom one is irritated. (Friedrich Schiller, *Naive and Sentimental Poetry/On the Sublime*, trans. Julius A. Elias [New York: Frederick Ungar, 1966], 109–10)

Wittgenstein:
I could only stare in wonder at Shakespeare; never do anything with him. (CV, 84e)

Schiller:
By the critics, the true gamekeepers of taste, [the naive poets] are detested as trespassers whom one would prefer to suppress; for even Homer owes it only to the power of more than a thousand years of testimony that those who sit in judgment on taste permit him to stand; and it is unpleasant enough for them to maintain their rules against his example and his reputation against their rules. (110)

Wittgenstein:
It is remarkable how hard we find it to believe something that we do not see the truth of for ourselves. When, for instance, I hear the expression of admiration for Shakespeare by distinguished men in the course of several centuries, I can never rid myself of the suspicion that praising him has been the conventional thing to do; though I have to tell myself that this is not how it is. It takes the authority of a *Milton* really to convince me. I take it for granted that he was incorruptible.—But I don't of course mean by this that I don't believe

an enormous amount of praise to have been, and still to be, lavished on Shakespeare without understanding and for the wrong reasons by a thousand professors of literature. (CV, 48e)

I am *deeply* suspicious of most of Shakespeare's admirers. The misfortune is, I believe, that he stands by himself, at least in the culture of the west, so that one can only place him by placing him wrongly. (CV, 84e)

—So if someone stands in front of these pieces speechless, I can understand him; but anyone who admires them as one admires, say, Beethoven, seems to me to misunderstand Shakespeare. (CV, 86e)

More important, perhaps, than these parallels is the difference between Schiller and Wittgenstein in their conceptions of nature. Although Wittgenstein, like Schiller, seeks to understand Shakespeare in terms of nature, he does not as thoroughly identify Shakespeare with nature as does Schiller. A suspicion about the possibility of nature speaking in human beings can be seen in Wittgenstein's remark on a letter Schiller wrote to Goethe (another important influence on Wittgenstein's conception of nature): "In a letter (to Goethe I think) Schiller writes of a 'poetic mood.' I think I know what he means, I believe I am familiar with it myself. It is a mood of receptivity to nature in which one's thoughts seem as vivid as nature itself. But it is strange that Schiller did not produce anything better (or so it seems to me) and so I am not entirely convinced that what I produce in such a mood is really worth anything" (65e–66e).

22. Friedrich Schiller, *Naive and Sentimental Poetry and On the Sublime*, trans. Julias Elias (New York: Frederick Ungar, 1966), 106–7.

23. Schiller, *Naive and Sentimental Poetry*, 111.

24. One may see this subjugation of "literariness" to a philosophical conception of a subject in Cyril Barrett, "Wittgenstein, Leavis, and Literature"; and in Peter Hughes, "Painting the Ghost: Wittgenstein, Shakespeare, and Textual Representation," both in *New Literary History* 19, no. 2 (1988): 585–401 (Barrett); 371–84 (Hughes).

25. Ludwig Wittgenstein, *Philosophical Grammar*, trans. Anthony Kenny (Berkeley and Los Angeles: University of California Press, 1974), 40.

26. Wittgenstein, *Philosophical Investigations*, 654–66.

27. For example, how does one deal with the dangers of stereotyping found in Wittgenstein's thought of the type "Jew" and in Irigaray's more supple and diverse thought of "the feminine"?

28. Drucilla Cornell, *Beyond Accomodation: Ethical Feminism, Deconstruction, and the Law* (New York: Routledge, 1991), 148.

29. Cornell, *Beyond Accomodation*, 148.

30. Seyla Benhabib, *Critique, Norm, and Utopia: A Study of the Foundations of Critical Theory* (New York: Columbia University Press, 1986), 220–21.

31. Seyla Benhabib, *Situating the Self: Gender, Community, and Postmodernism in Contemporary Ethics* (New York: Routledge, 1992), 158.

32. Benhabib, *Situating the Self*, 158–59.

33. Benhabib, *Situating the Self*, 159.

34. Benhabib, *Situating the Self*, 187–90.

35. Judith Butler, "On Imitation and Gender Insubordination," in *Inside/Out: Lesbian Theories, Gay Theories*, ed. Diana Fuss (New York: Routledge, 1991), 26.

36. One might want to ask what it means to understand mimetic practice in terms of a loss. As Butler notes, Mikkel Borch-Jacobsen (following the work of Girard) and others suggest that "[m]imetism is not motivated by a drama of loss and wishful recovery [as Butler would have it], but appears to precede and constitute desire (and motivation) itself; in this sense, mimetism would be prior to the possibility of loss and the disappointments of love" (Butler, "On Imitation and Gender Insubordination," 26). Both theories take up rather than deny or seek to control imitation, and Butler goes

on to draw the conclusion that "[w]hether loss or mimetism is primary (perhaps an undecidable problem), the psychic subject is nevertheless constituted internally by differentially gendered Others and is, therefore, never, as a gender, self-identical" (27). But while in each case one broaches a thought of alterity, we need to draw out the consequences of each mode of assuming this inheritance of mimesis. One difference that may be worth exploring is a difference in tone between the two. On the one hand, understanding mimesis in terms of an originary loss tends to give weight, seriousness, to the motif of mimesis as a kind of performance or as a kind of "drag" that would be a possible subversive repetition of an identity. On the other hand, beginning with the themes of melancholy and loss, even if that loss is later "reinscribed"—as it is in Elizabeth Bishop's poem "The Art of Losing"—seems to mute more or less comic tonalities in a way that what Butler calls "primary mimetism" does not. If this supposition is right, if there is a difference in tone here, there remains the task of understanding the different ways those tones resound while we respond to our various inheritances of mimesis.

37. Benhabib, *Critique, Norm, Utopia*, 221.

38. Butler, "On Imitation and Gender Insubordination," 27.

39. Walt Whitman, "Song of Myself," in *The American Tradition in Literature*, vol. 2, ed. George Perkins and Barbara Perkins (New York: McGraw-Hill, 1994), lines 327–29.

40. Whitman, "Song of Myself," lines 1341–46.

Section II

Wittgensteinian Feminist Philosophy: Contrasting Visions

4

What Do Feminists Want in an Epistemology?

Alice Crary

Introduction: Mapping Feminist Epistemologies

Feminist theory's preoccupation with epistemological questions is a natural extension of its distinctive aims. Feminist theory is devoted to making the lives of women intelligible, and it begins with the recognition that doing so requires shedding light on forces that contribute to the social

My thanks are due to Nancy Bauer and Jay Bernstein for encouragement and helpful suggestions throughout the writing of this essay, and to Nathaniel Hupert and Elijah Millgram for helpful comments on a previous draft. I presented a version of the essay at a session, devoted to the present volume, at the 2001 American Philosophical Association Pacific Division meeting. I am grateful to Peg O'Connor and Hilde Nelson for their constructive input on that occasion. I am likewise grateful to participants in February 2002 meetings of Women in Philosophy at the New York School, and the Workshop on Gender and Philosophy at MIT.

subjection of women. Some of its most significant contributions to our understanding of women's lives take the form of descriptions of how established bodies and practices of knowledge harm women. Many of these descriptions are specifically concerned with ways in which women have been excluded from knowledge. Feminist theorists have, for instance, underlined ways in which women are excluded as *objects* of knowledge. Classic economic analyses of the relation between labor and capital neglect unpaid work that women do in the home;[1] standard historical narratives routinely ignore women's roles in social and political life;[2] biomedical research often fails to take women as subjects even for studies whose results are alleged to bear on the health of all people;[3] and so on. Feminist theorists have also underlined ways in which women are excluded as *subjects* of knowledge. Women have been deprived of education even concerning the conditions of their own lives;[4] women's perspectives and experiences have been ignored even when they are directly pertinent to the species of knowledge in question;[5] women have been described as irrational and hence as unfit to be knowers[6] and have had their claim to epistemic authority, their credibility, undermined even in cases in which they possess knowledge;[7] and so on.

Over the past decades, a central project of feminist theory has been to give a specifically philosophical inflection to our concern with the ways in which women are excluded from knowledge. Feminist theorists have attempted to deepen our understanding of these matters by arguing that there is an important sense in which received renderings of our most basic logical ideals—or perhaps even these ideals themselves—reinforce sexist (and also classist, racist, and heterosexist) biases. They have focused a great deal of attention, in particular, on questions about how to understand the notion of *objectivity* that is partly constitutive of our image of knowledge.[8] The target of a significant number of these feminist discussions is a prevalent philosophical conception of objectivity that is often glossed in terms of the idea of a 'point of view from nowhere'. Many feminist theorists have argued that the assumption that glimpsing objective reality requires adopting a maximally detached (dispassionate and dehumanized) vantage point is both philosophically and politically defective. Indeed, it is now difficult to find even one feminist theorist who wants wholeheartedly to defend this assumption.[9]

There has been a conspicuous shift in the kinds of claims feminist theorists are prepared to make about how a traditional philosophical conception of objectivity excludes women's voices. Twenty years ago, it was not uncommon for feminist theorists to argue that 'objectivity', conceived as demanding a detached stance, is a logical ideal that governs 'male ways of thinking' and, further, that theoretical discourses that appeal to it therefore *essentially* exclude women's voices.[10] Somewhat more recently, however, many feminist theorists have claimed that these sorts of essentialist arguments (which typically insist on the need for new logical ideals to govern 'female ways of thinking') threaten to deprive us of conceptual resources requisite for treating discoveries of masculine bias as grounds for *criticism* of established bodies of knowledge, and hence that, however laudable their original political motives, such arguments are ultimately both philosophically and politically problematic. Most feminist theorists who propose to defend the claim that a familiar conception of objectivity excludes women's voices now present themselves as doing so on nonessentialist grounds. Feminist theorists tend to agree in holding that the familiar conception describes an epistemic ideal that is illegitimate for *all* modes of thought (not merely for those we might once have thought of as 'female'), and that it contributes to the silencing of women's voices—not by means of any simple 'essential' exclusion, but rather—by obstructing efforts to reveal various forms of sexist bias in received discourses. They tend to agree, further, in wanting to support this view by arguing that, in contrast to what the conception implies, some features of the world (and, in particular, some with profound consequences for women's lives) are only available from perspectives afforded by social positions that women of different backgrounds have historically been made to occupy.

This agreement forms the backdrop for recent feminist conversations about objectivity. The central, ongoing feminist debate about this issue takes place between, on the one hand, theorists who criticize the familiar—'detached'—conception of objectivity as problematic and propose to revise it and, on the other, theorists who maintain that the very notion of objectivity (understood in terms of the detached conception) is hopelessly tainted and that we must therefore reject it wholesale.

The conception of objectivity that is in question, in somewhat different ways, on both sides of this debate is characterized by the *epistemological* assumption that we approach a view of objective reality by abstracting from any local or subjective perspectives, and also by the closely connected *ontological* assumption that 'what there really is' is independent of human subjectivity. Feminist theorists on both sides of the debate believe that we need to reject this pair of epistemological and ontological assumptions. But they differ over whether rejecting it undermines our very ability to offer an authoritative ontology or epistemology, or whether it instead suggests the need to broaden our ontology to include features of the world partly constituted by their relation to subjectivity, while at the same time broadening our epistemology to include perspectival judgments capable of revealing such features. Theorists on one side take the pair of assumptions to be essential to the notion of objectivity. They take it for granted that, if we reject it, we turn our backs on the very notion of objectivity and, by the same token, abandon the enterprises of ontology and epistemology as they are traditionally conceived. Theorists on the other side, in contrast, hold that the pair fails to capture what objectivity is like. They maintain that, if we reject it, we find ourselves called on, not to acknowledge the loss of the notion of objectivity, but rather to refashion it in terms of broader, or more permissive, ontological and epistemological assumptions.

The alternative conception of objectivity that members of this latter group of theorists champion might be described as, in virtue of its more permissive ontology and epistemology, 'wider' than the philosophically more traditional—or 'narrower'—conception that is under attack. Using this terminology, we could say that the ongoing feminist debate about objectivity turns on the question of whether a consistent gesture of rejection of the narrower conception commits us to a form of skepticism about objectivity, or whether it instead commits us to making room for a wider conception of what objectivity is like. The project of this essay is to intervene in this debate on the side of those theorists who appeal to the wider conception—specifically, by attacking the assumption, distinctive of theorists on the other side, that our right to objectivity stands or falls with the narrower conception. In a later section of the essay ("Wittgenstein as Arbitrator"), I approach this project by developing a strand of argument from Wittgenstein's philosophy and in effect allowing Wittgenstein to serve as an arbitrator. But I need to start with an overview of feminist epistemologies that are elaborated in widely objective terms, and of criticisms to which they are subjected.

The Argument Between Feminist Objectivists and Feminist Skeptics

The most well-known feminist epistemologies that aim to incorporate the wider conception of objectivity are presented as *feminist standpoint theories*. The label derives from a line of thought in Marx's critique of capitalism, one commonly associated with Lukács's commentary on Marx, that represents the "standpoint" of the proletariat as conferring an epistemic privilege.[11] The relevant Marxian line of thought starts with an account of consciousness as mediated by the material conditions in which we interact with others. Since material conditions thus structure consciousness in addition to behavior, it follows that, under capitalism, a vision of social relations that is biased in favor of capitalists will appear to be authoritative. For it will tend to capture the conduct of members of both (capitalist and proletarian) social classes, and it will also tend to be reflected in their judgment. However, although members of the proletariat (like members of the dominant class) will generally endorse the received social vision and will in this way be complicit in their own oppression, their lives nevertheless furnish a standpoint from which class relations under capitalism can be recognized as offensive to our natures. Investigations of proletarian lives reveal forms of unease or suffering that the received social vision cannot incorporate, and efforts to accommodate such anomalies move us toward an objectively more accurate account of society. *This* is the conclusion of the relevant Marxian line of thought (namely, that if we actively develop the "proletarian standpoint," we improve our understanding of objective reality). And it depends for its cogency on the wider conception of objectivity.

Feminist standpoint theories extract a basic epistemological insight from this Marxian line of thought and apply it to the case of the social subordination of women. The basic strategy is clearly worked out in the writings of Nancy Hartsock, the first defender of feminist standpoint theory.[12] Hartsock combines the Marxian view that "[m]aterial life not only structures but sets limits on the understanding of social relations" with the feminist observation that, in all actual and historical societies, material life varies in systematic ways with gender. She claims that "[t]he vision of the ruling . . . gender . . . structures the material relations in which all parties are forced to participate."[13] Her goal is to establish that, despite the fact that women are thus made complicit in their own oppression, "women's lives make available a particular and privileged vantage point."[14] Although women (like men) tend to endorse received, sexist accounts of society and their own lives, they at the same time have feelings of unease that don't fit within these accounts. We approach a more just and accurate understanding of social relations by trying to occupy the vantage point of such feelings. This vantage point, Hartsock writes, "exposes the real relations among human beings as inhuman, points beyond the present, and carries a historically liberatory role."[15]

The reception of feminist standpoint theories is marked by a wide-spread impression of *essentialism*. The theories are for the most part understood as resting on the assumption that it is possible to identify a perspective, transcending all cultural differences, as distinctively or essentially that of women.[16] The most familiar criticisms stem from this understanding. Feminist standpoint theories are often taken to be implying that women's subjectivity is untainted by oppressive social systems, or, as one critic puts it, that women "are not in fundamental ways damaged by their social experience."[17] In addition, the theories are often taken to be encouraging us to artificially force all women into one restrictive model and to overlook politically decisive differences in the lives of individual women and groups of women.[18]

A number of feminist standpoint theorists have tried to put these familiar criticisms to rest by arguing that—setting aside any questions we might have about the strengths or weaknesses of particular elaborations of the theories—the theories' fundamental epistemological tenets in any case lack essentialist implications. The most influential theorist to do so is Sandra Harding.[19] Harding starts from the view, characteristic of feminist standpoint theories, that the familiar 'narrower' idea that objectivity "requires 'point-of-viewlessness'" is philosophically and politically bankrupt and that as feminists we need to equip ourselves with a wider—or, in her terms, "stronger"—construal of objectivity that allows certain points of view to count as cognitively authoritative.[20] She presents herself as taking an interest, not in perspectives that are supposedly 'essentially those of women', but rather in the diverse "actual perspectives" that "actual women" occupy at different historical periods and in different social contexts.[21] She claims that women's (and men's) experience is "shaped by social relations" and hence tends to bear the imprint of the various sexist (and also classist, racist, heterosexist, etc.) social forces feminists want to resist. She then argues that, although it follows that treating women's self-understanding as by itself "provid[ing] reliable grounds for knowledge claims about the nature of social relations"[22] would threaten to reaffirm oppressive social forms, it is nevertheless also the case that a successful, objectively valid criticism of these forms needs to include reflections that start from perspectives afforded by women's experience as well as by that of other oppressed peoples. This nonessentialist form of criticism is what Harding has in mind when she declares that perspectives furnished by women's lives provide objective 'standpoints'.[23]

Whatever the merits of the efforts of Harding and others to cast feminist standpoint theory in a nonessentialist light, most feminist theorists continue to associate it with a philosophically and politically troubling essentialism. This includes, significantly, many feminist theorists who themselves hope to defend widely objective, nonessentialist forms of feminist criticism.[24] There is thus a residual problem with the proposal to use "feminist standpoint theory" as a label for theories that describe such forms of criticism[25]—a problem I will sidestep by referring to members of this class of theories as *feminist objectivisms*.[26]

It is no secret that feminist objectivisms come under attack *within* feminist theory. Their critics typically sympathize with the call for rejecting the narrower conception of objectivity, but think that to reject it just is to relinquish the notion of objectivity. The most prominent current of feminist thought characterized by this inference is concerned primarily with its bearing on identity categories such as 'woman'. A recent, widely influential strain of feminist thought proceeds *from* the claim that there are no transcendent truths determining the correctness of applications of identity categories (such as 'woman') in a way that satisfies the narrower ideal of objectivity *to* the conclusion that these categories, far from admitting of the sorts of objective applications that feminist objectivists invite us to envision, are fundamentally unstable.[27]

This criticism of feminist objectivism is often placed under the heading 'feminist postmodernism'.[28] But this way of talking, though widespread, is misleading. It is not unusual to speak of the 'modern' in reference to the cultural and intellectual tradition to which the narrower conception of objectivity belongs and to speak of the 'postmodern' in reference to cultural and intellectual movements that aspire to free themselves from this tradition. Indeed, some feminist objectivists, adopting this terminology, present themselves as 'postmodernists'.[29] Given the terminology, our willingness to understand 'feminist postmodernism' in terms of the form of skepticism about objectivity described in the preceding paragraph will seem to imply sympathy for the view that our claim to objectivity stands or falls with the narrower conception. And it will thus seem to commit us to prejudging the very issue that separates feminist objectivists from their critics. Moreover, even if, while adopting this way of talking about feminist postmodernism, we explicitly leave room for the possibility of a wider conception of objectivity, we run the risk of obscuring the fact, just noted, that some self-avowed feminist postmodernists likewise insist on this possibility.[30] In order to avoid these risks, I will refer to the relevant set of critics of feminist objectivisms (that is, those who assume that in relinquishing the narrower conception we lose our very entitlement to objectivity) simply as 'feminist skeptics'.[31]

A feminist skeptic might express her worries about feminist objectivisms in the following terms:

> What is troubling about feminist objectivisms is simply their attachment to the notion of objectivity. Advocates of these theories are plainly right to point out that the narrowly objective ideal of 'point-of-viewlessness' functions, illegitimately and in a manner harmful to women, to make it seem as though there is nothing to be learned from investigating perspectives afforded by women's lives. They are also right to insist that any politically viable feminist theory must rely on perspectival modes of thought. The problem is that these theorists try to combine these insights with an aspiration to objectivity with which the insights are deeply in tension. Admittedly, they don't aim to put themselves in this conflicted position. They assume that there are modes of thought tied to particular perspectives that are capable of revealing how things objectively are. But this assumption is simply false. In their concern with objective reality, feminist objectivists undermine their own, politically decisive efforts to legitimize the perspectival. The upshot is that if we want a theoretical or epistemological outlook that truly serves feminist political purposes, we need to describe one that, unlike feminist objectivisms, is free from any lingering attachment to the notion of objectivity.

Notice that the feminist skeptic who presents this criticism need not have any interest in attacking the *political* motives of feminist theorists who take objectivity to be worth preserving. Feminist skeptics often acknowledge that the prospect of having "no objective basis for distinguishing between true and false beliefs," and of being in a position in which "power alone will determine the outcome of competing truth claims" is a genuinely frightening one, especially for those who "are oppressed by the power of others."[32] Their main goal is simply to discredit the presupposition, distinctive of feminist objectivism, that it is possible to consistently combine an attachment to objectivity (however well motivated) with a commitment to including perspectival modes of thought.[33]

The philosophical debate central to recent feminist discussions of epistemology takes place, as I can now put it, between feminist objectivists, on the one hand, and feminist skeptics, on the other. My larger aim here is to adduce considerations that weigh in favor of feminist objectivists. But I want to preface my discussion of these matters by noting that any balanced account of the criticisms to which these theorists' work is submitted needs to reach beyond this debate.

Since it is unusual for feminist theorists to defend the narrower conception of objectivity, it is rare for feminist objectivists to be criticized within feminist theory for attacking this conception. But outside feminist theory, this criticism is anything but rare. Indeed, the most frequently recited external criticism of contemporary feminist theory is that it betrays an allegedly thoughtless and irresponsible tendency to depart from our logical ideals, where these ideals are understood in narrower terms.[34] This criticism is sometimes given a specifically feminist twist. The idea is that the 'perspectival' innovations of feminist theorists, including those who defend wider objectivisms, make it impossible for us (feminists) to present ourselves as concerned with purging our discourses of sexist bias and approaching an objectively more accurate account of social reality.[35] This criticism of feminist objectivism is an expression of a 'narrow', philosophically more orthodox objectivism—or, as I will put it, of a *traditional objectivism*.[36]

A traditional objectivist might express her worries about feminist objectivisms as follows:

> What is troubling about feminist objectivisms is that they forfeit their entitlement to the notion of objectivity. This forfeiture is, admittedly, not an aim of the theories' advocates. These theorists assume that there are modes of thought tied to particular subjective standpoints that are capable of revealing how things objectively are. But this assumption is simply false. In relying on perspectival modes of thought, feminist objectivists—in spite of comforting rhetoric about 'wider' (or 'stronger') conceptions of objectivity—effectively give up any claim to be concerned with objective reality. This is worrisome because it places us, as feminists, in a position in which we can no longer represent accounts of the social world that we devise as genuinely, objectively superior to any competing sexist (or classist or racist or heterosexist, etc.) descriptions we hope to discredit. The upshot is that if we want a theoretical or epistemological outlook that truly serves feminist political purposes, we need to describe one that, unlike feminist objectivisms, is free from any reliance on perspectival modes of thought.

Comparison of this criticism of feminist objectivism with the kinds of criticisms leveled by feminist skeptics reveals a striking analogy.

Although the two criticisms disagree about whether an unqualified commitment to the notion of objectivity is something feminist objectivists ought to want, they nevertheless agree that a thinker's willingness to draw on perspectival modes of thought invariably represents a qualification of her commitment to the notion of objectivity. Moreover, this agreement expresses, plainly and directly, the internal logic of the narrower conception of objectivity. The narrower conception is composed of epistemological and ontological assumptions from which it follows that any perspective afforded by subjectivity has an intrinsic tendency to interfere with access to objective reality. So there is a basic respect in which feminist skeptics and traditional objectivists agree in holding that this conception accurately captures all that objectivity amounts to.

This observation makes it possible to offer a more precise description of the main philosophical difference between feminist objectivists and feminist skeptics. Where the former differ from the latter is in maintaining that the narrower conception misrepresents what objectivity is like. Notice, moreover, that if feminist objectivists could be shown to have the advantage in this disagreement with feminist skeptics (who complain that their insistence on objectivity amounts to a betrayal of perspectives afforded by women's experience) it would mean that they also have a decisive rejoinder to traditional objectivists (who complain that their commitment to perspectival modes of inquiry amounts to a betrayal of objectivity). The kind of wider conception of objectivity at play in the writings of feminist objectivists represents a strategy for simultaneously answering both groups of critics.

Wittgenstein as Arbitrator

It may seem counterintuitive to appeal to Wittgenstein in this connection. On some of the most influential interpretations of his later writings, Wittgenstein is taken to be moving—in a manner that resonates with the work of feminist skeptics—from a doubt about the applicability of the narrower conception of objectivity to our linguistic practices, toward a conclusion about how our practices are therefore less than fully objective. Indeed, for this reason many feminist skeptics take themselves, even in the absence of any specific engagement with Wittgenstein's writings, to be entitled to portray themselves as treading in his footsteps.[37] So it may seem anything but helpful for feminist objectivists to sound themes from his philosophy.[38]

Let me begin my discussion of Wittgenstein by mentioning basic features of the interpretations that seem to suggest an alignment between his philosophical concerns and the philosophical concerns of feminist skeptics. The point of departure for these interpretations, which is not contentious in itself, is the recognition that Wittgenstein is hostile to views of meaning that invite us to conceive language as—in the terminology of this paper—narrowly objective. What is in question here is a line of argument in Wittgenstein's thought that starts with a restriction on the kind of thing a bit of language or linguistic expression can be, a restriction which might aptly be described as derived from the narrower conception of objectivity. Insofar as the narrower conception carries a demand for 'point-of-viewlessness,' it seems to imply that no objective property can stand in an internal relation to our attitudes, and it thus seems to force us to restrict objective reality to items that can be adequately conceived in merely causal terms—to items, that is, that are in themselves incapable of imposing normative classifications on the world. Given this restriction, it appears that a linguistic sign cannot be anything but a mere noise or mark which, considered by itself, lacks the ability to sort things into those that do or don't accord with it. (As Wittgenstein at one point puts it: "Every sign *by itself* seems dead" [*Investigations*, §432; Wittgenstein's emphasis].) The restriction may at first seem philosophically innocuous. If signs are items that by themselves cannot classify things into correct and incorrect, then—we might figure—it must be the case that what does the classificatory work is not such an item but rather such an item under some interpretation. But an appeal to interpretation simply repeats, and does not eliminate, the problem. Any interpretation we offer—i.e., any new set of signs—will, considered alone, be normatively inert and will itself seem to call for yet another interpretation to give it normative shape. And so on. Our predicament is that "any interpretation still hangs in the air along with what it interprets and cannot give it any support" (*Investigations*, §198). Our sympathy for views of meaning that ask us to look at language through a narrowly objective lens starts us on a hopeless regress of interpretations.

It seems clear that Wittgenstein's attitude toward such endlessly iterated demands for interpretations or explanations is that we should refuse to meet them directly. It is characteristic of him to rebuff demands of this sort by, first, simply describing how whatever sign is in question is used in some (actual or imagined) linguistic practice and, then, adding that "explanations [or reasons] come to an end" (see, e.g., *Investigations*, §1). This gesture has suggested to many commentators that Wittgenstein takes it to follow from his regress argument that we should abandon more traditional views of meaning on which the correct use of a sign is in some sense a consequence of its meaning and exchange them for views on which the use of a sign—our public techniques with it—somehow constitutes its meaning. This basic interpretative approach underwrites a familiar image of Wittgenstein as championing what gets called a "use-theory of meaning"—i.e., a theory on which the ways in which a linguistic expression is integrated into a shared way of life fixes or determines its meaning.

A significant portion of the philosophical interest surrounding this theory of meaning has to do with the fact that it appears to threaten the possibility of objective scrutiny of our linguistic practices. Many commentators who read Wittgenstein as endorsing the theory point out that, consistently developed, it represents the meanings of even our most basic logical concepts as fixed by linguistic conventions. This presents a problem for what we might think of as "external" forms of criticism—forms of criticism that endeavor to round on our linguistic practices and survey them as a whole. The problem, very roughly, is that these forms of criticism depend for their success on bringing into question the very practices within which whatever critical or normative concepts they employ function and are intelligible. The result is that our inquiry, by dint of its very structure, seems to force us into a certain sort of incoherence. We seem to be running up against a barrier installed by the nature of language—one that we would have to get past if we were somehow to show that our linguistic practices are objectively defensible. The point isn't that this precludes all criticism of language. We can raise questions about, for example, whether a given sign is being used consistently if, in doing so, we take for granted that what counts as consistency is determined by our linguistic practices. Nevertheless, even though such "internal" forms of criticism (as we might think of them) remain within reach, external forms are proscribed. Our linguistic practices themselves are inviolable, or immune to rational criticism.

Interpretations with these basic commitments—hereafter "inviolability interpretations"—are a staple of discussions about the bearing of Wittgenstein's philosophy on ethics and political thought.[39] Such discussions typically assume that Wittgenstein excludes the possibility of an objective defense of, in particular, ethical modes of thought and at the same time asks us to conceive ethics as a less than objective undertaking. Further, they typically represent him as extending this exclusionary gesture both to methods of instruction that originally bring us to moral maturity and, in addition, also to methods suitable for arbitrating differences among adults. What's in question in the latter case is the thought that, given our supposed inability to provide an objective defense of our own ethical practices, we're in no position to demonstrate that our practices are *objectively* superior to those of people who arrive at divergent ethical conclusions. In the final analysis, we are obliged to place our hopes for agreement, not in techniques of reason, but rather in methods that are merely rhetorical or "persuasive."[40]

This allegedly Wittgensteinian position resembles, in its main outlines, the theoretical position of feminist skeptics. Feminist skeptics reject a view of language as narrowly objective, and they take it to follow from this gesture of rejection—in a manner that tacitly presupposes that the narrower conception contains an accurate picture of what objectivity is like—that our modes of thought and speech are therefore, in an unqualified sense, less than objective. Similarly, within inviolability interpretations, Wittgenstein rejects the idea that language respects a narrowly objective restriction, and he takes it to follow from this gesture of rejection—in a manner that likewise presupposes that the narrower conception captures all that objectivity amounts to—that our modes of thought and speech (including those that belong to ethics) are, in an unqualified sense, nonobjective.

There are, however, good grounds for questioning the interpretations that bequeath to us this image of Wittgenstein as a philosophical ancestor of feminist skeptics. This is not to say that it is impossible to put together a suggestive textual case in their favor. In fact, it is not difficult to find in Wittgenstein's opus remarks about the relationship between meaning and use that, considered in relative isolation, might plausibly be interpreted as expressions of a use-theory of meaning. The most famous of these remarks is *Investigations*, §43: "For a *large* class of cases—though not for all—in which we employ the word "meaning" it can be defined thus: the meaning of a word is its use in the language."[41] Nor is it difficult to find remarks that, considered in relative isolation, might plausibly be interpreted as expressions of the view that our linguistic practices are at bottom non-objective. For Wittgenstein often says that linguistic competence is inseparable from forms of instruction that shape our contingent responses—or, in his parlance, that it is inseparable from "persuasive" methods or "drill" or "training."[42] Nevertheless, despite the suggestiveness of the textual support they are thus capable of mustering, inviolability interpretations are confronted with the fact that Wittgenstein simply never makes the more general theoretical claims constitutive of the sort of use-theory of meaning they ascribe to him. Champions of these interpretations often chalk up this putative omission to (what they call) Wittgenstein's "quietism." Roughly, their idea is that we should understand the gap between his actual remarks, on the one hand, and the view of

meaning he is alleged to hold, on the other, as an expression of a reluctance to fully spell out what he wants to communicate, a reluctance that
is somehow both principled and also intellectually unnecessary. The
trouble with this strategy is that at bottom it amounts to little more than
an excuse for disregarding, at least to some degree, the specificity of what
Wittgenstein actually says about meaning.

The mark of inviolability interpretations is the idea of some sort of limit
preventing us from submitting our linguistic practices to objective criticism.
The interpretations imply that the structure of language keeps us from
bringing critical concepts intelligibly to bear on our linguistic practices.
There is supposed to be a clash or incompatibility—one resulting in a species of unintelligibility—between these concepts, on the one hand, and
descriptions of the practices, on the other. What is noteworthy about this
account of the unintelligibility of certain utterances is that it presupposes
that they are unintelligible because of the particular things they fruitlessly
aim to express. It presupposes that, despite being unintelligible in one sense,
they nevertheless remain intelligible in yet a further sense: namely, in that
we can grasp the kind of thing that, in virtue of the logical contributions
made by their constituent expressions, they are trying—unsuccessfully—to
say. Yet Wittgenstein himself repeatedly and emphatically distances himself
from the that idea that when a combination of words is rejected as nonsense, it is because we somehow grasp the 'senseless sense' that it attempts
to impart.[43] This idea is, he suggests, fraught with an internal tension. The
difficulty is that here our rejection of an utterance as *lacking* any sense both
depends for its force on, and at the same time is also vitiated by, our (supposed) identification of the impermissible sense its constituent expressions
endeavor vainly to convey.[44]

Wittgenstein's own view of the limits of sense is characterized by the
repudiation of the idea that we can somehow identify the logical categories of expressions outside contexts of their significant use, contexts in
which they are used to perform complete acts of speech. Wittgenstein
maintains that an inscription, or utterance, is rejected as nonsense—not
when there is something defective about what we might think of as the
sense (or logical organization) it does have, but—when it's not clear what
it's saying at all, what logical character (if any) it possesses. What distinguishes the view of the limits of sense he thus describes is, we might say,
its freedom from any suggestion that we can make sense of what lies on
the far side of such limits, what we are—we imagine—prohibited from
ever saying or thinking.

This view provides the background against which we can first understand Wittgenstein's emphasis on the importance of attending to ways in which we *use* expressions. When, in presenting his view of the limits of sense, Wittgenstein dismisses the idea that we can somehow identify the logical categories of expressions outside contexts of significant use, he is at the same time dismissing the idea that we can somehow determine whether particular utterances or inscriptions make sense without drawing on the contingent responses characteristic of us as participants in particular linguistic practices. It is thus an implication of the view—and this brings us to the feature of Wittgenstein's thought most foreign to analytic philosophy of language—that, in determining what is and isn't intelligible, we invariably rely on our *sense* of what it is for an expression to be consistently projected. There is, for Wittgenstein, no way to bypass our *appreciation* of the significance of the similarities and differences constitutive of our practices with the expressions in question. Moreover, Wittgenstein thinks that, in the midst of philosophizing, we are inclined to betray our own appreciation of such significance and, as a result, to lose track of what we ourselves want to say. When he urges us (philosophers) to direct our attention to ways in which we ordinarily *use* expressions, his larger aim is accordingly to return us to the sort of feeling for language which he takes to be internal to ordinary linguistic competence—and which he thinks we are inclined to disown in philosophy. The upshot is that we entirely miss the point of his willingness to speak of equating the meanings of expressions with our public practices with them if we fail to observe that he thinks the patterns traced out by those practices are only available from the perspective of certain feelings.

Part of the interest of this moment in Wittgenstein's thought has to do with its implications for how we conceive of appropriate philosophical methods. Given both the demand for an appreciation of, or feeling for, the texture of language and, further, also the very natural assumption that it is internal to the idea of a theory that it yields claims about what can and cannot be said in a manner independent of the pertinent form of appreciation—given both of these things, there can be no question of developing a *theory* of meaning. This means that, by Wittgenstein's lights, the philosopher's role is not to issue theory-sanctioned permissions and prohibitions; rather, the role of the philosopher is—we might say—to elicit our *acknowledgment* that a particular form of words we are inclined to come out with in philosophy does (or does not) say something that we ourselves want to say.[45] Consequently, there is no reason to follow fans of inviolability interpretations in regarding the fact that Wittgenstein doesn't give his remarks on the relationship between the meaning and use of expressions the form of a theory as a sign of an intellectually, at least, problematic quietism. It would be more appropriate to say that the style of Wittgenstein's remarks needs to be understood as directly contributing to the expression of his distinctive vision of language.

We might describe the role Wittgenstein fashions for the philosopher, in very general terms, as a *persuasive* one. What he is suggesting is that the role of the philosopher is to *persuade* us to return to, and perhaps deepen, our appreciation of the similarities and differences that make up our everyday practices with particular expressions. Here we come to a decisive point of difference from inviolability interpretations. Although what are at issue are methods that engage and shape responses that might properly be classified as affective, the point is not that Wittgenstein is claiming that our linguistic practices are cut off from full objectivity. His thought is, rather, that forms of instruction that address our sensibility are capable of making an internal contribution to genuine (objective) linguistic competence insofar as they do so.

The suggestion that we need to rely on forms of instruction that shape contingent, affective responses may seem to indicate a departure from objectivity. But the suggestion seems threatening to objectivity only granted the assumption that we can make sense, at least to some degree, of the idea of an independent perspective on language from which any and all such responses could be impugned as intrinsically distorting. And, as we saw, one of the objects of Wittgenstein's discussions of the limits of sense is to demonstrate that this idea is inherently unstable. It is inseparable from an internally inconsistent understanding of some utterances as unintelligible because of the particular kind of thing—they are intelligible at least to the degree that we can make this out—they try but fail to say. To liberate ourselves from the idea is to put ourselves in a position in which we can greet the incursion of our contingent responses into linguistic abilities as philosophically innocuous in the sense of leaving intact our entitlement to epistemic ideals such as objectivity, and as philosophically consequential only in the sense of altering—or, in the terms of this paper, widening—our understanding of what this entitlement amounts to.

This puts me in a position to describe the parallel that interests me between Wittgenstein's philosophical orientation and the philosophical orientation of feminist objectivists. Feminist objectivists insist that, in order to arrive at a more objective understanding of social relations, we need to undertake investigations that start from perspectives afforded by women's experiences (as well as from perspectives afforded by the experiences of members of other marginalized groups). The point of such investigations is not, according to feminist objectivists, simply to catalogue the deliverances of different subjectivities. Such investigations are supposed to be capable of revealing forms of suffering that established linguistic practices neglect and, as a result, to be capable of impressing on us the importance of (politically significant) similarities and differences among aspects of our lives to which received modes of thought and speech are blind. It would be possible to describe the kind of value feminist objectivists attach to such perspectival investigations—drawing on the Wittgensteinian terminology introduced above—by speaking of their *persuasive* force. A central tenet of feminist objectivisms is, as we can now put it, that the persuasive force exerted by perspectival investigations of the relevant sort is capable of directly promoting a more objective understanding of the lives of women and men. It is in this respect that the theoretical position of feminist objectivists depends for its appeal on the same— wider—conception of objectivity that Wittgenstein defends.

Conclusion: A Plea for Feminist Objectivism

Let me touch again briefly on the central philosophical and political issues at stake in the dispute between feminist skeptics and feminist objectivists. Recall its basic structure. On the one hand, both feminist objectivists and feminist skeptics tend to agree in their sense of the importance for feminist politics of a commitment to investigating social relations from perspectives afforded by women's lives and experience; on the other, members of these two groups of feminist theorists tend to disagree about whether this commitment is compatible with a commitment to seeking an objective understanding of our lives. Feminist skeptics claim to detect an incompatibility between these two commitments, and they call on us to eliminate it by surrendering the very notion of objectivity. What I have been arguing here is that this demand for theoretical austerity is philosophically unwarranted. The appearance of incompatibility is no more than a function of an artificially restrictive ('narrower') conception of what objectivity amounts to. There is no obstacle to widening our conception of objectivity so that no such appearance remains. We have good reason to follow feminist objectivists in insisting that we can remain committed to the kinds of perspectival investigations that have historically played an important role in uncovering sexist (and other forms of) bias without losing our politically empowering understanding of ourselves as committed to developing modes of thought and conduct that are truly—objectively—more just and consistent.

Notes

1. Feminist concern about such neglect is, for instance, what drives the "domestic labor dispute" (that is, the dispute about whether Marxian analysis is capable of providing an adequate account of women's domestic labor). For a classic discussion, see Heidi Hartman, "The Unhappy Marriage of Marxism and Feminism," reprinted in *Women and Revolution*, ed. Lydia Sargent (Boston: South End Press, 1981).

2. The resurgence of feminism since the 1960s brought about a striking growth in interest in the historical study of women's lives. Feminist contributions to women's history typically call, not for mere supplements to older, nonfeminist histories, but rather for corrective reworkings. Thus, to mention one representative compilation, Nancy Scott and Elizabeth Pleck open the introduction to their edited volume *A Heritage of Her Own* (New York: Touchstone, 1979) with the declaration that "all readings of the past . . . are fatally defective if lacking women's outlook or failing to treat women's position" and that most written history therefore "compels a thorough re-viewing" (9).

3. Decades of feminist activism led to the creation, in 1991, of the Office of Research on Women's Health at the National Institutes of Health and the inauguration, in 1992, of the Women's Health Initiative, a large-scale clinical intervention and prevention trial that takes women as research subjects. (For helpful discussion, see Bernadine Healy, "Women's Health, Public Welfare," *Journal of the American Medical Association* 264, [1991]: 566–68, and Paul Cotton, "Women's Health Initiative Leads Way as Research Begins to Fill Gender Gaps," *Journal of the American Medical Association* 267, no. 4 [1992]: 469–70.) Feminist publications such as the Boston Women Health Collective's *Our Bodies Ourselves* (New York: Touchstone, 1998) also aim to supply needed health information about women.

4. For a discussion of feminist efforts, during the first wave of the women's movement, to improve women's access to education, see Eleanor Flexner, "Early Steps Towards Equal Education," chap. 2 of *Century of Struggle: The Women's Rights Movement in the United States* (New York, Atheneum, 1971), 23–40.

5. Many feminist memoirs from the 1960s and 1970s emphasize women's sense of a misfit between their own experience and 'official' accounts of what they went through. Thus, for example, Sheila Rowbotham writes that she suffered a "sense of dislocation between [her] sense of self inside and [her] behavior outside" (*Women's Consciousness, Man's World*, London, Penguin, 1973, 20–21), and Adrienne Rich tells us that she felt "[p]aralyzed by the sense that there exists a mesh of relationships . . . which, if [she] could see it, make it valid, would give me back myself, make it possible to function lucidly and passionately" ("When We Dead Awaken: Writing as Re-Vision," in *On Lies, Secrets, and Silence: Selected Prose, 1966–1978* [New York, Norton, 1979], 44). A great deal of feminist theorizing takes women's descriptions of this kind of "discrepancy between . . . 'official' . . . definitions of their identity (who they are supposed to be) and their feelings (or what they are supposed to feel)" as a point of departure. (The inset quote is from Jean Grimshaw, *Philosophy and Feminist Thinking* [Minneapolis: University of Minnesota Press, 1986], 87–88.)

6. A classic feminist account of philosophical representations of reason as 'male' and hence out of women's reach is Genevieve Lloyd, *The Man of Reason: "Male" and "Female" in Western Philosophy*, 2d ed. (Minneapolis: University of Minnesota Press, 1993).

7. For a helpful treatment, see Lorraine Code, "Credibility: A Double Standard," chap. 6 of *What Can She Know? Feminist Theory and the Construction of Knowledge*, New York, Cornell University Press, 1991.

8. Any satisfactory list of the most interesting and influential contributions to the (now vast) body of feminist literature on the nature of objectivity would have to include Code, *What Can She Know?*; Donna Haraway, *Simians, Cyborgs, and Women: The Reinvention of Nature* (New York, Routledge, 1991); Sandra Harding, *The Science Question in Feminism* (Ithaca: Cornell University Press, 1986); Harding, *Whose Science? Whose Knowledge? Thinking from Women's Lives* (Ithaca: Cornell University Press, 1991); Nancy Hartsock, *The Feminist Standpoint Revisited and Other Essays* (Boulder, Colo.: Westview Press, 1998); Sally Haslanger, "On Being Objective and Being Objectified" in *A Mind of One's Own: Feminist Essays on Reason and Objectivity*, ed. Louise Antony and Charlotte Witt (Boulder, Colo.: Westview Press, 1993), 85–126; bell hooks, *From Margin to Center* (Boston: South End Press, 1984); Evelyn Fox Keller, *Reflections on Gender and Science* (New Haven: Yale University Press, 1985); Elisabeth Lloyd, "Objectivity and the Double Standard for Feminist Epistemologies," *Synthese* 104 (1995): 351–81; Helen Longino, *Science as Social Knowledge: Values and Objectivity in Scientific Inquiry* (Princeton, N.J.: Princeton University Press, 1990); Catharine MacKinnon, *Towards a Feminist Theory of the State* (Cambridge: Harvard University Press, 1989); and Naomi Scheman, *Engenderings: Constructions of Knowledge, Authority and Privilege* (New York, Routledge, 1993).

9. The point here is not that every recent feminist treatment of objectivity attacks a 'detached' conception of it, but only that there are next to no treatments that specifically aim to preserve such a conception. Some recent feminist discussions of objectivity are, however, concerned with the harm done to women by norms of objectivity that can be considered independently of the question of whether objectivity is taken to call for detachment. See, e.g., Haslanger's discussion in "On Being Objective."

10. Contributions to feminist epistemology that *explicitly* defend essentialist arguments about objectivity include Susan Bordo, *The Flight From Objectivity: Essays on Cartesianism and Culture* (Albany: State University of New York Press, 1987); Mary Daly, *Gyn/Ecology* (Boston: Beacon Press, 1978); Andrea Nye, *Words of Power* (New York: Routledge, 1990); Sheila Ruth, "Methodocracy, Misogyny, and Bad Faith: The Response of Philosophy," in *Men's Studies Modified: The Impact of Feminism on Academic Disciplines*, ed. Dale Spender (New York, Pergamon Press, 1981); and Liz Stanley and Sue Wise, *Breaking Out: Feminist Consciousness and Feminist Research* (London: Routledge and Kegan Paul, 1983). In addition to these explicitly essentialist arguments, it is also possible to identify a set of feminist arguments about objectivity that are characterized by a tacit, unacknowledged slide into essentialist modes of thought. See, e.g., Lorraine Code's discussion of how some feminist theorizing slides unwittingly into essentialism in "Knowledge and Subjectivity," chap. 2 of *What Can She Know?* I discuss such 'slides' in "A Question of Silence: Feminist Theory and Women's Voices," *Philosophy* 76, no. 96 (2001): 371–95.

11. See especially Georg Lukács, "Reification and the Standpoint of the Proletariat," *History and Class Consciousness* (Cambridge: MIT Press, 1971), 149–222.

12. Hartsock's classic article, "The Feminist Standpoint: Developing the Ground for a Specifically Feminist Historical Materialism," was originally published in Sandra Harding and Merrill Hintikka, eds., *Discovering Reality: Feminist Perspectives on Epistemology, Metaphysics, Methodology, and Philosophy of Science* (Dordrecht, Holland: D. Reidel, 1983), 283–320. It was reprinted in 1998 in Hartsock, *Feminist Standpoint Revisited*, 105–32. All citations here are to the reprinted version.

13. Harding, "The Feminist Standpoint Revisited," 107.

14. Ibid.

15. Ibid., 108.

16. For a catalog of the work of critics who charge feminist standpoint theory with essentialism, see Hartsock, "The Feminist Standpoint Revisited," 230–33. Hartsock here defends her original discussion of feminist standpoint theory against this charge while also allowing that some of her early formulations helped to invite it. I am inclined to think that there is more merit to the charge, directed at Hartsock's original piece, than she admits, but I cannot discuss this matter further here.

17. Jane Flax, "Postmodernism and Gender Relations in Feminist Theory," in *Feminism/Postmod-*

emism, ed. Linda Nicholson (London, Routledge, 1990), 56. Hartsock discusses this criticism in *The Feminist Standpoint Revisited*, 230–31 and 233–34.

18. For a clear statement of this charge, see Lorraine Code's treatment of feminist standpoint theories in *What Can She Know?* Code argues that the idea of a feminist standpoint is "both remote and suspect" in that "it would presuppose an artificial unity in diversity" (317). See also Donna Haraway's presentation of the same criticism in "Situated Knowledges," reprinted in Haraway, *Simians, Cyborgs, and Women*. Hartsock discusses the criticism (but not Code's or Haraway's versions of it) in *The Feminist Standpoint Revisited*, 236–38.

19. Harding's most complete description of the version of a feminist standpoint theory she favors is in Harding, *Whose Science? Whose Knowledge?* For her repudiation of the suggestion of essentialism, see especially 49, 68, 134, and 173ff.

20. Harding, *The Feminist Standpoint Revisited*, 109. For her discussion of a "strong" conception of objectivity, see esp. chap. 6.

21. Ibid., 123.

22. Ibid.

23. Ibid. See also 127ff. and 167.

24. See, e.g., Lorraine Code's discussion of feminist standpoint theory in *What Can She Know?* and in *Rhetorical Spaces: Essays on Gendered Locations* (New York, Routledge, 1995), 180–81. This is perhaps the appropriate place to mention that a number of the most powerful (widely objective) descriptions of how women are made complicit in their own oppression are found *outside* treatments of feminist standpoint theory. A classic case is Marilyn Frye's discussion of "arrogant perceivers" in *The Politics of Reality: Essays in Feminist Theory* (Freedom, Calif., Crossing Press, 1983). Frye writes that the arrogant perceiver "manipulates the environment, perception and judgment of her whom he perceives so that her recognized options are limited, and the course she chooses will be such as coheres with his purposes . . . [his perception] manipulates the other's perception at the root by mislabeling the unwholesome as healthy, and what is wrong as right" (67 and 70). See also Catharine MacKinnon's discussion of how, when the arrangement of social and legal institutions fails to reflect the wrongness of rape and sexual harassment, women who suffer these harms are often deprived of resources for understanding what they have been made to go through (*Feminism Unmodified: Discourses on Life and Law* [Cambridge: Harvard University Press, 1988], esp. 105). Some of the most perceptive feminist commentators on MacKinnon fail to notice that she is concerned with how oppressive social institutions thus shape women's judgment. Sally Haslanger's recent commentary on MacKinnon ("On Being Objective"), although deeply insightful in other respects, fails to acknowledge this dimension of her thought.

25. I am grateful to Nancy Bauer, Hilde Nelson, and Peg O'Connor for helpful discussion about this point.

26. In speaking of 'feminist objectivism' in connection with the wider conception of objectivity, I do not mean to be denying that some intellectuals whose political inclinations are decidedly feminist are committed to defending "narrower" objectivisms. (I discuss the work of such intellectuals later in this section.) I am simply taking advantage, for the purposes of a perspicuous terminology, of the fact that *within feminist theory* almost all defenses of objectivism lay claim to the wider conception.

27. The classic elaboration of this—now familiar—position is Judith Butler, *Gender Trouble: Feminism and the Subversion of Identity* (New York, Routledge, 1990).

28. This terminology is used alike by many feminist defenders of, and many feminist detractors from, the relevant form of skepticism about objectivity. For a representative defender who speaks in these terms, see Jane Flax, *Thinking Fragments: Psychoanalysis, Feminism, and Postmodernism in the Contemporary West* (Berkeley and Los Angeles: University of California Press, 1990). For a representative detractor who does so, see Seyla Benhabib, "Feminism and Postmodernism: An Uneasy Alliance," in Seyla Benhabib et al., *Feminist Contentions: A Philosophical Exchange* (London, Routledge, 1995).

29. Thus, e.g., Sandra Harding describes her own work in these terms (see esp. *Whose Science? Whose Knowledge?* 47ff.). See also Nancy Fraser and Linda Nicholson, "Social Criticism with Philos-

ophy: Feminism and Postmodernism," in Nicholson, *Feminism/Postmodernism*, 19–38, and especially 34–35. This Nicholson anthology, the classic source for discussions of the relation between feminism and postmodernism, contains both essays such as this one of Fraser's and Nicholson's that interpret postmodernism to include the wider conception and also essays that associate postmodernism with skepticism about objectivity (see, e.g., the essay by Jane Flax).

30. This is not an idle worry. Many feminist critiques of 'feminist postmodernism' that understand it in terms of a certain skepticism about objectivity obscure fundamental epistemological differences among thinkers who call themselves feminist postmodernists. For a clear and relatively recent illustration of the problem, see Miranda Fricker, "Feminism in Epistemology: Pluralism Without Postmodernism," in *The Cambridge Companion to Feminism in Philosophy*, ed. Miranda Fricker and Jennifer Hornsby (Cambridge: Cambridge University Press, 2000), 146–65.

31. One further note about terminology is in order. Skeptical critics of feminist objectivisms are sometimes referred to as 'anti-epistemologists' in virtue of their hostility to the very ideal of objectivity that is partly constitutive of the object of epistemological research (as traditionally conceived). But this terminology turns out to be no more helpful here than talk of postmodernism. This is because feminist objectivists are *also* sometimes referred to as 'anti-epistemologists'—now in virtue of their hostility to the idea of a point of view external to responses and reactions we learn in learning language (that is, a 'point of view from nowhere') from which we can make theoretical claims about the structure of knowledge.

32. Jane Flax, "Postmodernism and Gender Relations," 42.

33. The tendency of thought distinctive of feminist skeptics (i.e., the tendency to move from rejecting the narrower conception of objectivity to insisting on some qualification of our entitlement to objectivity) tacitly informs the work of some feminist objectivists. Consider, e.g., the writings of Lorraine Code. Although one of the central claims of Code's work is that feminists should refashion objectivity along wider lines (see, e.g., *What Can She Know?* 4–5), she repeatedly characterizes her attack on the narrower conception as a departure from "a perfect, ideal objectivity" (215). Code differs from feminist skeptics in resisting the conclusion that we should give up the pursuit of objectivity. Indeed, she encourages us to try "to occupy as objective a standpoint as possible" (215). Nonetheless, she maintains that our best efforts in this pursuit won't take us farther than a "mitigated relativism" (251, 264, and 320).

34. The enthusiasm with which this somewhat patronizing criticism of feminist theory is rehearsed reveals what Elizabeth Lloyd ("Objectivity and the Double Standard") correctly describes as a "double standard" for feminist research. Although *nonfeminist* critiques of 'narrower' metaphysics are often discussed within mainstream philosophical circles, they are rarely assessed in the same patronizing terms.

35. In a somewhat discouraging turn, this tired criticism of feminist theory is leveled even by some philosophers who themselves draw on the wider conception of objectivity. See, e.g., Martha Nussbaum, "Feminists and Philosophy," *New York Review of Books*, no. 41 (1994), 59–63. Although Nussbaum herself doesn't believe that perspectival modes of thought as such have a tendency to depart from objectivity (one of her central contributions to Anglo-American ethics is an attack on this belief) she nonetheless wrongly represents the perspectival leanings of all feminist theorists—feminist objectivists as well as feminist skeptics—as an expression of disdain for the very notion of objectivity. And she accordingly takes it upon herself to urge feminist theorists to retain robust renderings of this and other basic logical notions.

36. More familiar names for members of the group of feminist intellectuals who endorse what I am calling traditional objectivisms include 'feminist empiricists' (see, e.g., Harding, *Whose Science? Whose Knowledge?* 111ff.) and "liberal feminists." I prefer to avoid these more familiar names because I am inclined to think that it is possible to be an empiricist or a liberal without insisting on the narrower conception of objectivity. But I cannot discuss these matters here.

37. Thus, to mention but one representative case, Judith Butler occasionally indicates that she regards her work as Wittgensteinian in spirit. Nevertheless, despite the fact that Butler's gesture has

analogies in the writings of a number of other feminist skeptics, I have been unable to find even one who enters into a detailed discussion of Wittgenstein's work.

38. This is not to say that matters have seemed this way to all feminist objectivists. Two works that draw on Wittgenstein's philosophy in defending forms of feminist objectivism deserve mention: Sabina Lovibond's *Realism and Imagination in Ethics* (Minneapolis: University of Minnesota Press, 1983) and Naomi Scheman's *Engenderings*. Although I admire Lovibond's work in many respects, I am not entirely comfortable with her manner of appropriating Wittgenstein. It would, however, take me too far afield to enter into the relevant interpretative issues here. (For a helpful critique of Lovibond's approach to Wittgenstein, see Jim Conant, "On Wittgenstein's Philosophy of Mathematics," *Proceedings of the Aristotelian Society* 97 (1997): 195–222.) I am generally sympathetic to Scheman's approach to Wittgenstein. But it is not clear to me how she would negotiate the specific exegetical questions that concern me here.

39. What makes an interpretation an "inviolability interpretation" in my sense is that—irrespective of whether it is developed by a critic or champion of Wittgenstein's thought—it (a) represents Wittgenstein as advocating some version of a use-theory of meaning and (b) represents him as holding that this theory excludes the possibility of objective criticism of linguistic practices.

40. An enormous secondary literature depicts Wittgenstein as advancing the view that ethical discourse thus falls short of strict objectivity. The class of contributors to this body of commentary—which includes both champions and critics of Wittgenstein's philosophy—splits into (a) those who think it's a consequence of the view that we can't regard our own ethical practices as correct and must therefore embrace some form of ethical relativism (see, e.g., David Bloor, *Wittgenstein: A Social Theory of Knowledge* [New York: Columbia University Press, 1983]; H. O. Mounce and D. Z. Phillips, *Moral Practices* [New York: Schocken Books, 1970]) and (b) those who insist that the view lacks any such relativistic implications (see, e.g., Richard Rorty's more recent writings on Wittgenstein's thought).

41. A significant number of suggestive remarks along similar lines can be found in Wittgenstein's writings in the early 1930s.

42. One of the more famous of these remarks is in *On Certainty*, §612: "At the end of *reasons* comes persuasion" (Wittgenstein's emphasis).

43. See, e.g., *Investigations* §500: "When a sentence is called senseless, it is not as it were its sense that is senseless. But a combination of words is being excluded from the language, withdrawn from circulation."

44. In a set of lectures in 1933–34, Wittgenstein explains his perception of a problem in these terms:

> It is queer that we should say what it is that is impossible, e.g., that the mantle piece cannot be yellow and green at the same time. In speaking of that which is impossible it seems as though we are conceiving the inconceivable, When we say a thing cannot be green and yellow at the same time we are excluding something, but what? Were we to find something which we described as green and yellow we would immediately say this was not an excluded case. We have not excluded any case at all, but rather the use of an expression. And what we exclude has no semblance of sense. (*Wittgenstein's Lectures, Cambridge 1932–35*, 63–64)

45. I am here invoking Stanley Cavell's discussion of what he sees as a moment of "acknowledgment" in Wittgenstein's conception of our judgments about 'what we say when.' Cavell's thought is that, insofar as, for Wittgenstein, no empirical survey of usage can save us from the need to appeal to our *sense* of whether an expression is being projected along a smooth and natural course, we might say that Wittgenstein thinks that we are forced to *acknowledge* that it says something we ourselves want to say (or to refuse to do so). See "Knowing and Acknowledging," *Must We Mean What We Say? A Book of Essays* (Cambridge: Cambridge University Press, 1976), 238–66. See also Cora Diamond's talk of a demand for "recognition" internal to Wittgenstein's vision of our conceptual lives. (See, esp., "Losing Your Concepts," *Ethics* 98 [1988]: 255–77.)

5

Making Mistakes, Rendering Nonsense, and Moving Toward Uncertainty

Sarah Lucia Hoagland

Ludwig Wittgenstein opens *On Certainty* by remarking, "If you do know that *here is one hand*, we'll grant you all the rest," and proceeds to explore the language-game of knowing, including 'proving', 'doubting, 'making a mistake'. The impetus for this work is Moore's "Proof of an External World," and "Defense of Common Sense" (in Moore 1966). In graduate school I loved Moore's common sense, realist reaction; his analyses, such as what counts as an external object, are obvious and brilliant and, as analyses, challenge the skeptic.

By virtue of his opening remark, I would say Wittgenstein was also

My discussion of Moore and Wittgenstein is excerpted from my Ph.D. dissertation (Hoagland 1975). This essay was developed at the NEH Summer on Feminist Epistemologies run by Nancy Tuana, and has benefited from the attentive comments of Naomi Scheman, Wendy Lee-Lampshire, and Nancy drawn to Moore's reaction. What he challenged was Moore's *strategy* of claiming to know the propositions of Common Sense. While Moore's approach was initially satisfying, Wittgenstein's approach helped orient me for my subsequent criticism of the hegemonic language-games of white Western heteropatriarchy, particularly in terms of strategy.

Much of On *Certainty* investigates conditions under which one makes knowledge claims, professes certainty, claims doubt, ascribes mistake. Moore, of course, was trying to argue that the skeptic was wrong, mistaken. Wittgenstein argues that claiming to know "Here is one hand" renders it a particular empirical proposition, capable of being doubted and verified *and ipso facto* incapable of refuting the skeptic.

On a particular occasion a firefighter searching a burned building may question whether something is a hand, trying to determine if there is a body in the debris. But within this context "Here is one hand" is no longer a Proposition of Common Sense; it is an ordinary empirical proposition and as such it may be verified, it may be doubted or believed, it may be investigated and proven false or true.

Moore took the Propositions of Common Sense to be fundamental, grounding: if he doesn't know that "Here is one hand," he doesn't know anything at all. Wittgenstein argues that this is not a normal empirical proposition (e.g., OC, §308), but a foundational one (OC, §401). Transforming the concept of 'foundation', he suggests that foundations are like an axis, held in place by all that surrounds it (e.g., OC, §152)—for instance, doing research with a microscope *while* using one's hands, writing a skeptical treatise . . . *with one's hands*—and as such go unquestioned. In other words, the foundations of our knowledge are not grounds/ building blocks but rather what never gets questioned?[1]

In fact Moore thinks it is *because* we know that here is one hand that we know the things we do in science and our everyday life. Wittgenstein's strategy is to suggest, rather, that it is *because* of our everyday activity and what we do in science that whether what I type with are hands or not never gets questioned. Its solidity is accomplished not because of basic truth or reality but because of our activity. Everything we do confirms it, to misstate the point. If it were in question, we would be unable to carry on as we do.

In effect Moore was claiming that the Propositions of Common Sense

Tuana. As always, Anne Throop Leighton has carefully combed this essay for extraneous rubble and provided immeasurable insight.

are unconditionally true, absolute. Wittgenstein remarks, "Here *once more* is needed a step like the one taken in relativity theory" (OC, §305). That step involves showing that an absolute claim is nonsense, makes no sense, rather than attempting to prove it false. This strategy I want to explore further.

Much of what I understand Wittgenstein to be doing in relation to Moore, and by extension the conceptual traps of the skeptic and the idealist, I found useful as I began to recognize conceptual traps of white Western heteropatriarchy. Feeding my imagination, radical feminists such as Kate Millett and Mary Daly have contributed enormously to an understanding of conceptual reversals (Millett 1969; Daly 1978). They address questions of power, questions Wittgenstein stopped short of, questions perhaps he avoided as he avoided addressing his Jewish and his gay identities (Jarman).

(A Few) Conceptual Traps

When I was in graduate school, men around me claimed that with the exception of a few aberrant suffragists and crazed bra-burning radical feminists, women were content with their lot. I knew this to be false, as Moore knew the skeptic's position to be. But just saying "I know women aren't content" didn't work. I also noticed that these men have means of disseminating their worldview in a way I and other radical feminists do not. Questions of power, of course, never arose for Moore. He enjoyed legitimacy in academic institutions in just the way the skeptic did.

So I asked what would *count* as women's resistance, and realized that the answer was *nothing*.[2] And I began to develop my sabotage thesis, initially in relation to white ideology about black slaves as a result of my earlier immersion in Black Power literature. I considered stereotypes of slaves: docile, childlike, clumsy, lazy. I argued the very behaviors, such as breaking a tool, that support a white supremacist language-game are themselves indications of slave resistance, sabotage. Comparably, I argued the very behaviors that contribute to the feminine stereotype indicate women's discontent and resistance, sabotage—from the "fluffy-headed" housewife who sends raw eggs in her husband's lunch bucket all the way to the wife who burns her husband to death as he sleeps.

Significantly, anger and insanity converge in the concept, 'mad'. And the anger of those oppressed, female slaves who killed their masters, for example, is represented as insanity.

'Femininity' functions to obscure female resistance to male domination. Challenging the solidity of 'femininity' involves challenging our form of life (*PI*, §241) (not merely modifying it, reforming it, fitting in better). Understanding this can help identify certain forms of academentia (Daly), help show the fly the way out of the fly bottle (*PI*, §309).

Women undeniably not feminine; clearly not accepting of men's dominance, are not counterexamples, instead we are discounted as real women. A normal woman is male-identified, she who challenges that identification is stamped abnormal, mad, or stupid. Similarly, slaves not docile were deemed mad, not revolutionary. Resistance rendered invisible . . .

. . . In order that dominance remain invisible. 'Masculinity' and 'femininity' are not empirical concepts. In psychology there are, after all, experimental methods and *conceptual confusions* (*PI*, 232). Men confuse the cause of their passion with the object of it (*PI*, §476, Z, §488, §492), imagining women attract predators. So they depict women as objects of predation (when a woman says, "No," men "know" she means yes) and as objects of protection (by portraying us as helpless, they make us targets). A man can't be a protector unless there is something vulnerable to predation, his masculine identity (as a protector) requires that women be vulnerable to attack. To prove we do not fall into the category of those deserving predation, women must seek male protection and approval. When a woman steps out of the feminine line (for example, says no, won't marry to have children, comes out as a lesbian, works in the trades, reports incest), she is guilty (has sinned) and hence subject to attack: the women men beat are the object of male aggression and so considered its cause.

Thus we have the phrase "battered woman" emerging from linguistic transformations: "John beat Mary," to "Mary was beaten by John," to "Mary was beaten," to "Mary is a battered woman." Something he did to her becomes something that happened to her which becomes part of her character, and John disappears altogether (Penelope 1990). Then studies investigate the peculiar nature of women (feminine creatures) to whom these things happen, suggesting that something about the "feminine character" evokes men's abuse. This is part of the logic of white Western heteropatriarchy.

In the seamless walls of ignorance and resistance men erected in response to Women's Liberation, I realized 'femininity' is part of the foundation (axis) of mainstream U.S. understanding.[3] Consider equal rights: one is supposed to consider "both" sides of the issue—that women should and that women should not be granted equal rights. But this is only one side; the other concerns whether men should be allowed to retain their rights. There's good reason to suggest they should not, but the idea is treated as nonsense. So if I engage in the debate as laid out by men, even if I brilliantly argue that women should be given equal rights, I am at a deeper level agreeing (not disagreeing [PI, §§240–42]) that it is possible that women should not have equal rights, that women's—but not men's—rights are debatable. (Similarly for arguments that Blacks are not genetically inferior, or that there was a Jewish Holocaust.)

Trying to defeat skepticism by claiming to know the Propositions of Common Sense grants the skeptic credibility. I think this is why Wittgenstein focused on Moore's strategy. After all, the skeptic couldn't prove his case, he could only capture imagination by casting doubt. And by trying to prove women deserve equal rights, feminists grant proponents of male domination credibility. But one difference between Moore's dealings with the skeptic and radical feminists' dealings with heteropatriarchs is that while a skeptic couldn't prove his case, he also couldn't *enforce* it. Heteropatriarchs can and do enforce their worldview, their Weltanschauung. And they enforce the norms of 'femininity'. Men who kill their wives/girlfriends are often either not charged or let off lightly. Women who successfully fight back against their abusers are convicted of murder. This is the role of power, and this is not a mistake.

Mistake

At the end of part II in the *Remarks on the Foundations of Mathematics*, Wittgenstein complains that he has not yet made the concept of 'miscalculating', of 'making a mistake', clear (*RFM*, 111). And he wonders about the difference between calculating wrong and not calculating at all (*RFM*, 120). Addressing the "foundations" of empirical knowledge in his later work, *On Certainty*, he returns to the concept of a 'mistake' and argues that not all false beliefs are mistakes.

Moore thought that all false beliefs are adjustments of the mind to some "fact" (Moore 1953, 292). Equating 'mistake' with 'false belief' he argues, if a person falsely believes he is hearing the noise of a brass band, the essence of the mistake consists in a fact, his "being hearing the noise of a brass band," to which his mind has a positive attitude, but which fact is not in the Universe (278 ff.).

Wittgenstein argues: some beliefs are false, but properly called, are not mistaken (OC, §72; note OC, §155). First of all, should it turn out that we are wrong about some things, we would be unable to be sure about anything. This is not just a psychological remark (OC, §494): if we began to feel unsure about certain (basic) things, we would be unable to make judgments about anything at all (OC, §66, §§69–70).

Second, Wittgenstein argues that not all beliefs held by one person are regarded as mistakes by others. If a person sincerely (i.e., is not lying) says he is a given age, from a certain place, and so on, and yet it turn out that this is not true, we would not regard him as mistaken (OC, §67). Here Wittgenstein distinguishes between mistake and "mental illness."

So how can one tell whether a particular false belief is a mistake or not? Wittgenstein suggests that a mistake not only has a cause, it also has a ground, "I.e., roughly: when someone makes a mistake, this can be fitted into what he knows aright" (OC, §74). Basically, a mistake is something that occurs in a frame of reference within which it makes sense as a mistake.

And that is to say, if one regards Moore's claim to know "Here is one hand" as a claim about which he is not mistaken, then one must first have an idea of the possibility Moore is ruling out and how an error might be put aright, or at least how one would know when it is put aright. . . . And the mistaken person needs to judge in conformity with other human beings (OC, §§155–56). One who considers that this might not be a hand—while staring at their own hand—does not so judge.

Relativity

But suppose the question concerned the possibility of error not as it re-lates to a particular instance but as it relates to all our empirical knowl-edge. Wittgenstein notes that not all corrections of our view are on the same level (OC, §300; note also OC, §292): "Here once more, is needed a step like the one taken in relativity theory" (OC, §305). To discover this step, I was sent by Elizabeth Anscombe to Albert Einstein's discussion of relativity in his popularized account.

Einstein considers how to decide the truth of an assertion that two lightning flashes occurred simultaneously at a great distance from each other. To define 'simultaneity' we need an empirical decision-procedure because the concept "does not exist for the physicist until he has the possibility of discovering whether or not it is fulfilled in an actual case." Einstein suggests finding a midpoint, M, on a railway track between two points of great distance, A and B, where an observer would stand with two mirrors, allowing her to observe both A and B. Stipulating that light travels at a constant rate of speed, we now have a definition that can give an exact meaning to as many events as we want, a definition of "time" in physics.

This works relative to a frame of reference. Once a different frame of reference is brought in, say a train traveling along the track, and the same definition of simultaneity is given relative to the train, one might go on to ask whether simultaneous events relative to the embankment are simultaneous relative to the train. The answer is, not for an observer on the train. She is moving toward B and will see the flash from B earlier than the flash from A. By definition, she must conclude the events are not simultaneous. Consequently, "[e]very reference-body (coordinate system) has its own particular time; unless we are told the reference-body to which the statement of time refers, there is no *meaning* in a statement of the time of an event" (Einstein 1907, 21–26, my emphasis).

The step taken in relativity theory concerns what is to be said of the assertion that there is an absolute time at which two events take place. One is tempted to say that absolute theory is wrong and that anyone adhering to it is mistaken.

Moore suggests as much in *The Commonplace Book* when he analyzes the proposition "There was a time at which I was seeing St. Paul's" as "($\exists$x): Px & I was seeing St. Paul's at x." He then says that absolute theory asserts this analysis is correct, the relative denies it; in other words, relativity theory denies there is any *property* such that the proposition can be analyzed in this way (Moore 1962, 91). This suggests that if Moore believed relativity theory to be accurate, he would say of someone who asserted there is such a property, that he was mistaken.

But the step Einstein took was to claim that a statement of absolute time is *meaningless* not *mistaken*. Scientists were not mistaken in their previous assumptions about time. Their assumptions were meaningless.

Insofar as actual scientific investigations did make sense, it was because they were applied within a framework (even if unacknowledged). What did not make sense was the idea that the investigations apply absolutely and independently of any frame of reference. So the step taken in relativity theory that interests Wittgenstein involves noting that something taken out of all context is meaningless, not mistaken.

By claiming to know "Here is one hand," Moore was in effect maintaining that the Propositions of Common Sense are *unconditionally the truth* (OC, §425). Relating this to a claim about mistakes, we might think Moore is addressing himself to the possibility of error not about whether this is a hand, but about whether physical objects exist, whether we might be mistaken about our whole physical object/external world ontology and metaphysics. At which point the claim to know seems superfluous.

However, saying "I am not mistaken" while staring at one's own hand is not superfluous. The meaning is not (yet) determined by the situation (OC, §348). To make sense of a claim concerning a mistake, a frame of reference needs to be determined, and that relates the question of mistake to quite particular circumstances. An absolute claim is meaningless.

Significantly, Einstein introduced a relativity of *location* of the perceiver, not of the perceiver herself. One has not the freshman ploy of "Whatever you perceive is true for you, whatever I perceive is true for me." The concept of 'mistake' still functions within a frame of reference or context. If there were nine people on the railway embankment and eight of them saw the lights flash simultaneously while one saw them flash in sequence, one or the other would be wrong. Similarly for a group traveling on the railroad car. Relativity does not render the concept of 'mistake' meaningless; we have not lost the capacity to judge, to say intelligibly that someone is mistaken. So long as we function within the same frame of reference. So long as we agree on our form of life.

So *within* a language-game or frame of reference, Wittgenstein distinguishes between a mistake and mental illness. With regard to the *whole* frame of reference, Wittgenstein distinguishes between being mistaken and uttering nonsense (or not yet playing the game).

Strategy

Much feminist resistance to the idea of relativity has to do with wanting to prove men are mistaken, as opposed, say, to arguing that men exhibit a peculiar mental illness, perhaps a form of dissociative disease. (Consider women's reactions to men's assessment of Anita Hill: a popular saying was "Men just don't get it." And indeed they didn't, still don't, aren't going to.) I find ways in which hegemonic discourse appropriates, co-opts, or renders feminist discourse nonsense fascinating. And I find the academic feminist effort to get entrenched colleagues to admit they're mistaken itself mistaken.

Wendy Lee-Lampshire comments that while accusing men of conspiracy credits them with too much, consigning them to mental illness credits them with too little. Men in power's backlash to the Women's Movement is itself a product of cognition: they are perfectly aware of their privilege and don't want to lose it. I agree, and that means along with mistake and mental illness comes willful resistance, something Wittgenstein never considered.

Wittgenstein is exposing a disease. What is the difference between miscalculating and not calculating at all? My interest lies in understanding the limits of a language-game as indicated by what gets counted as a mistake and what is discarded as nonsense, what the dominant discourse excludes. For it is not just absolute claims that are rendered nonsense. Claims not fitting the dominant frame of reference are also rendered nonsense, radical lesbian feminist claims, for example.

In fact, using the axis metaphor, by considering what is rendered nonsense we can detect what goes unquestioned and is held in place by what surrounds it—male supremacy, for example. Investigating whether the concept of 'mistake' applies is one way of determining whether what one is questioning is a particular matter within a field of understanding in which we agree, or whether one is questioning the field of agreement, the language-game, itself.

Initially, this wave of Western feminists demanded liberation. But for that to not be an absolute (meaningless because contextless) concept, many feminists played it out in a particular context—capitalist democracy, itself grounded in social contract theory—arguing in effect that men were mistaken to exclude women.

Carole Pateman argues that contract grounds a certain concept of legitimate political right, but this particular political right includes (hetero)patriarchal right or sex-right. The "freedom won is by sons who cast off their natural subjection to their fathers and replace paternal rule by civil government." But the original pact also establishes men's political right over women and establishes orderly access by men to women's bodies

(Pateman 1988, 2). The original theorists incorporated conjugal right into their theories and transformed the law of male sex-right into its modern civil, contractual form, constructing what it is to be men and women. And (are we surprised?) only "masculine beings are endowed with the attributes and capacities necessary to enter into contracts, only men, that is, are individuals" (Pateman 1988, 5–6).

The feminist shift to Equal Rights thus involved entering men's conceptual framework, thereby agreeing that women's political status needs to be justified in a way that men's need not: women must show men how women's liberation fits with how men understand and go about things. Men handily finessed that endeavor.

The next stage in the dialogue, spearheaded by academic feminists, carries on the attempt to show men to be mistaken about women by showing how women fit through efforts to positively value 'femininity' and valorize women's traditional roles—caretaking men and children and old people (who are portrayed as children in the literature). Some men are willing to consider this.

We've moved from *liberation* from male dominance to *equality* with men to *care* for men (and children). And the specter of the Women's Liberation Movement has been rendered nonsense. What's wrong with this picture?

Well, talking feminist talk, while it is an act of resistance to treat men as if they have been mistaken about women, it is also a strategic mistake.

The strategy that I think helps one to keep from falling back into the dominant frame of reference is separatism,[4] conceptual separatism at least,[5] constructing new language-games, lesbian language-games. Participating in a male-identified framework, one with dominant men at the center, retains dominant men at center. And engaging in "debates" within an androcentric, racist, heterosexist, classist, capitalist, abelist, anti-Semitic, ageist, imperialist framework, while resistance, nevertheless nurtures that framework (Hoagland 1978, 1988). We want a shift in our form of life, not a debate/validation of the terms of the existing language-game.

Again, Wittgenstein did not consider the question of power;[6] nor did he consider the question of competing language-games, nor willful resistance. But he did consider questions of sense and nonsense. And his disagreement with Moore concerns the strategy of claiming to know (to not be mistaken about) the Propositions of Common Sense (propositions taken out of all context). Moore grants the skeptic credibility by claiming to know the Propositions of Common Sense, attempting to prove that the skeptic is mistaken and that he, Moore, is not. Similarly, attempting to prove men mistaken, feminists grant the subordination of women credibility.

Skepticism

While claims out of all context are meaningless, still the assertion "I don't know p" is not the same as asserting the negation of p. With "I don't know . . . ," a new element is added to the language-game (OC, §593). Thus Wittgenstein considers the extent to which knowledge is threatened by the fact that humans do have doubts and make mistakes.

He notes that Moore need not show he can do something. In reply to the skeptic, one can simply note that knowledge claims make sense (OC, §390); the language-game works: very often when people claim to know things or assure us they are not mistaken, they are right. That is, doubt is not necessary even where it is possible (OC, §392, §596).

This is connected to the role of contradiction in mathematics (OC, §392). A contradiction is problematic if it can make us lose our way in the game, make the game lose sense (RFM, 103). But if it can be isolated, the rest of the game is not affected. Contradictions such as the Barber Paradox have been isolated as self-referentials and do not cause us to lose our way in logic.

Similarly, the existence of a language-game does not depend on there being no doubt at all. What matters is there be no doubt that makes us lose our way in the rest of the game. The problem is not that we are sometimes not absolutely sure about something, nor is it even a problem if some matter is never resolved. Doubt is only harmful if it blocks all ability to make judgments.

Doubt introduced by radical feminism is harmful to heteropatriarchy: as a result of the creation of feminist contexts, more women are remembering/talking about experiences of incest, daughter rape, cult ritual abuse, child abuse. To doubt the fathers this way yields a contradiction— self-proclaimed protectors are in fact abusers—which makes one lose one's way in a patriarchy. (A contradiction made apparent by Marxists is that profit is theft.)

Wendy Lee-Lampshire suggests that in logic, other contradictions such as Godel's theorems or Russell's paradox don't make us lose our way only because we are willing to ignore their implications. Similarly, the hetero-patriarchal language-game contains strategies built into its institutions for ignoring/isolating oppression and violence at the heart of its "logic." As Nancy Tuana argues, white privileged men isolate the violence by constructing particular groups of men as predators, most notably in the United States, black men. Thus engaging in activity designed to protect (white) women holds white male supremacy in place, like in axis. This is another part of the logic of white heteropatriarchy.

The contradiction that makes us lose our way, so the axis of patriarchy collapses, is that the fathers, particularly ruling fathers—self-designated protectors—are the predators. And to avoid this, they isolate and gaslight survivors first with Freud's "rape fantasy,"[7] more recently with the "false memory syndrome." (Hence the impossibility of getting women's reports of sexual abuse to make sense in law courts.) In the process, the feminist frame of reference in which daughters' reports make sense and hold fathers accountable flows like sand through our fingers. The skepticism of white Western heteropatriarchy has captured social imagination by casting doubt. And it is making women doubt the confidence of our per-ceptions, displacing a feminist foundation of woman-identification. I want a lesbian moral revolution, a change in our form of life.

Moving Toward Uncertainty:
"What Chou Mean, We, White Boy?"[8]

As Wittgenstein argues, Moore's propositions are not presupposed by our language-games. What is presupposed is a *kind* of certainty. This certainty is not an intellection of truth or even of sense. It is a way of acting, a form of life.

My discussion of 'femininity' has focused on conceptual coercion em-bedded in white Western heteropatriarchy. The point of my work has been to emerge from the isolation that such coercion left me in, isolation with regard to other women, isolation that one way or another leaves women male-defined, male-identified. What moves me is my desire to connect with other women/lesbians.

And so I work to extract my thinking from the realms of signification of privileged men. I work with others to make meaningful different everyday practices that hold in place different axes. I want different things treated as meaningless, nonsense (for example sexism, anti-Semitism, racism, currently held in place by the practices of debating women's rights, the Holocaust and black biology, things that animate the practices of rape, pogroms, and lynchings), things many feminists treat as (horrible) mistakes.

I work to wrest the meanings of women from a masculine/ feminine construction. Some theorists have made valiant efforts to revalue the feminine, but I think this a mistake. Ultimately animating the feminine spaces of masculine discourse is neither sufficiently ambitious nor sufficiently imaginative.

Nor is the category 'woman' unproblematic. Chandra Mohanty argues the "assumption of women as an already constituted, coherent group with identical interests and desires, regardless of class, ethnic or racial location, or contradictions, implies a notion of gender or sexual difference or even patriarchy which can be applied universally and cross-culturally" (Mohanty 1991, 55). It assumes that "men and women are already constituted as sexual-political subjects prior to their entry into the arena of social relations," when in fact "women are produced through these very relations as well as being implicated in forming these relations" (Mohanty 1991, 59).

Chandra Mohanty charges that use of an analytic (in effect, absolute, contextless) concept of 'woman' is an act of colonization because Western feminist scholars thereby presuppose Western culture/form of life and "codify others as Other" (Mohanty 1991, 52, 62) such that "Western feminists alone become the true 'subjects' of this counterhistory" (71). Third World women are not mere victims of the production process, but resist, challenge, subvert, re-create. And that resistance and re-creation emerges within particular contexts as does white middle-class U.S. women's resistance and re-creation (Mohanty 1991).

The doubt which Third World women and U.S. women of color engender challenges U.S. white feminists. Rendering colonial discourse nonsense, it exposes U.S. white feminist entrapment therein. And this points to deep problems in Wittgenstein's thinking.

Wittgenstein's capacity to dispense with the skeptic resides in distinguishing between sense and nonsense. Epistemic certainty is agreement in judgments—not as opinion (or, decision) but as activity, something beyond being justified or unjustified, a form of life (*PI*, §241; *OC*, §§358–59): we put pen to paper, we cook cereal. Presumably he thought such activity, this physical-object-aspect of our form of life, generalizable to all humans. Failing to address questions of power, or consider politically competing language-games and willful resistance, he never asks who is this "we" who distinguishes sense and nonsense.

In judging sense and nonsense, this "we" also legislates. To what extent did this legislation affect Wittgenstein's sense of participation and alienation? To what extent did it affect his sense of himself as a Jew? As a homosexual? As a Viennese Jewish homosexual caught up with the language-game of World War II? Located at Cambridge? To what extend did it affect his bouts with depression, perhaps insanity? Wittgenstein challenged Modern notions of epistemic foundationalism. He did not challenge the solidity of his "we" who distinguishes sense and nonsense. Who is this "we"?

Analyzing an essay by Minnie Bruce Pratt, a white, U.S. southern-raised lesbian, Biddie Martin and Chandra Mohanty argue that the apparent solidity of white identity, of a white "we" in the United States, is derived from marginalization of difference (Martin and Mohanty 1986, 193), supported by "exclusion of specific histories of oppression and resistance, the repression of differences even within oneself" (196). They show how home is an illusion of coherence and safety based on suppression of 'others', secured by men's terror (197), and built on women's surrendering responsibility, in particular white women not noticing the Othering of others in the name of our alleged protection (198).

U.S. white feminists have focused on creating safe spaces/homes/community that locates the frame of reference for meaning in our realms of sense. As a result, the choices of many Third World women appear unintelligible to many white feminists; in effect these choices become nonsense. For example, many white women could not make sense of Iranian women who put on the veil in resisting the shah, dismissing this as incomprehensible, which indeed it is in a white Western framework.

Nayereh Tohidi, however, argues that although mistaken, Iranian women's willingness to put on the veil made great deal of sense, was in fact an act of resistance, resisting Western modernization and capitalist development that undermined Iranian women's economic independence as merchants (Tohidi 1991, 73 ff.).

Rey Chow asks how Chinese women would be recognized beyond victim status. And what would a film by Chinese women about American female China scholars be like? (Chow 1991, 93) White Western women's focus on equal rights in a capitalist, imperialist nation posits a counterpoint to dominant masculine Third World traditions, which yields a fissure through which Third World women disappear (Chow 1991, 88). Noting that the space of the Westernized, non-Western subject is multiply organized (95), Rey Chow begins to articulate a space in between for modern Chinese women to come forth on their own terms (97).

My focus on women/lesbians is a choice I make. However, the form of that focus matters. The certainty presupposed in the U.S. imperialist framework engenders disbelief about what is strange, different. It is this certainty I want to question. When U.S. white feminists focus on commonality, equating unity with sameness (Lugones, conversation), we appeal to a category of women arising out of colonial discourse/form of life. The real and productive challenge to the mistakes of white Western feminism and to a category of 'women' has to do with acknowledging the diversity of women by addressing the actual contexts women live in.

Marilyn Frye argues that a category of 'women' can be constructed not by creating a list of common attributes, but by working differences into the structure (Frye 1996, 1001). A (logically) positive category is "a plurality with internal structure whose elements are differentiated and differentiable . . . in a significant variety of relations with each other, and that is, by virtue of this structure, coalesced as a distinguishable 'something.'" (1002) In other words the category is not a tool for but a product of analysis. And she notes this in turn points to a political strategy of "deliberately, creatively, elaborating and articulating the differences among women . . . as a means to constructing . . . a web of meaning of and among women (Frye 1996, 1002). A new form of life.

Significantly, as Biddie Martin and Chandra Mohanty note, the one unifying element for Minnie Bruce Pratt as she crossed borders, gaining perspective on her "we" and her home, was her lesbianism, her love of women (Martin and Mohanty 1986, 202). However, "a careful reading of the narrative demonstrates the complexity of lesbianism, which is constructed as an effect, as well as a source, of her political and familial positions. Its significance, that is, is demonstrated in relation to other experiences rather than assumed as essential determinant. What lesbianism becomes as the narrative unfolds is that which makes 'home' impossible" (202). Consequently, community is the product of work and struggle. It must be constantly reinterpreted and revalued, and it is inherently unstable and contextual (210).

So in my quest to connect with women and lesbians and make meanings, I have found myself moving toward *uncertainty*, a suspension of disbelief necessary for what María Lugones calls playful world travel (Lugones 1987).

By traveling to the world of another who is quite different from me without trying to destroy it or them, I can work to "understand *what it is to be them and what it is to be [me] in their eyes*. Only when we have traveled to each other's 'worlds' are we fully subjects to each other" (Lugones 1987, 17). This "we" can cease to colonize.

World-traveling involves finding oneself to be another person there, finding one's practices holding another axis in place. It involves finding things one thought true no longer true. It involves finding one has something to learn from others that can challenge one's position, one's certainty, one's sense of reality, one's form of life.

By this same token, it is crucial not to world-travel/play with conquerors. By his own admission Western man is an imperialist when he plays, his goal to kill or conquer (Lugones 1987), sometimes through assimilation and appropriation.

For the ability that comes of world-travel is the ability to engage in counterhegemonic struggle, the ability to recognize women's willful resistance and engage in liberatory work. I believe the work of feminist epistemologists is to undermine hegemonic discourses by helping to establish counterdiscourses, to shift the ground of epistemic sense. (Note Hoagland 2001.) That's the point of separatism, to emerge from the mystification of dominant discourse. One may be quite adept at recognizing one's own counterlogic, but if one does not engage in world travel, one will have only the dominant frame of reference/sense with which to understand other counterhegemonic practices (Lugones, forthcoming).

If I understand only my own resistant logic, I read slaves' breaking tools, lesbian alcoholism, teens' pregnancies, gang economies, women's recovered memories, teens' drug use, guide dogs' running their people into poles, old women in nursing homes' being "troublemakers," all through dominant logic that renders them nonsense or meaningless as choices and erases their oppositional (and potentially liberatory) nature. A feminist epistemological project involves finding resistant logics, engaging to transform them to liberatory ends, and in particular resisting the logic/language-games of hegemonic medical, legal, and scientific models. My point in moving toward uncertainty is letting go of the disbelief that keeps me from dis-covering new worlds of sense.

And as we world-travel, we find we all belong to more than one language-game and that many are incommensurate. Still, it is possible to travel to different language-games/worlds just as it is possible to travel to different countries. But to not do so as a tourist/spectator/colonialist, one must learn the practices. And that involves time, engagement, and acknowledging the trickster—being willing to be made a fool of.[9] It involves leaving home, even the concept of home. And as Anne Throop Leighton argues, it involves a willingness to hold a connection with other women and lesbians even though there are gaps, leaps, awkward moments, stumblings, mistakes, and confusion—a willingness, finally, to enter the realm of nonsense.

World travel involves turning our attention from white men in power to women and lesbians in many places within our town and within the world. Such world travel involves flexibility, playfulness, and *epistemic uncertainty*. And that involves a change in our form of life, a moral revolution.

Notes

1. Naomi Scheman points out that Wittgenstein also appeals to a riverbed metaphor (OC, §§96–97). However, this occurs relatively early and is part of his speculations about how to treat Moore's propositions. Subsequently Wittgenstein develops his strategy in answering Moore. For example, "To say of man, in Moore's sense, that he *knows* something; that what he says is therefore unconditionally the truth, seems wrong to me.—It is the truth only inasmuch as it is an unmoving foundation of his language-games." (OC, §403) My interest in the axis metaphor is that the immobility of the axis lies in the movement/activity around it. Our beliefs/practices don't rest on a shifting riverbed; they hold certain things in place, unquestioned.

2. This discussion of conceptual traps is excerpted from chap. 1 of *Lesbian Ethics* (Hoagland 1988) and Hoagland 1977, 1978.

3. Another foundational concept is 'private property'.

4. Black separatism, for example, was not about whites being mistaken, it was/is about undermining the universality of white-centered contextualization, and rendering white supremacy nonsense.

5. What I mean by conceptual separatism is a resistance to engaging in debate within the confines of the dominant logic, resisting being limited by the assumptions framing hegemonic reason.

6. Wendy Lee-Lampshire rightly argues, nevertheless, that there are real issues of power in many of his examples. (See her chapter in this volume.)

7. As Florence Rush reports, in 1896 Freud identified childhood sexual abuse as the trauma that brought on hysteria, failing however to publicly indict the fathers. In private correspondence to W. Fliess, which Freud ordered destroyed, he wrote that almost all his women patients told him they had been molested by their fathers, and named seduction by fathers as the essential point in hysteria. Subsequently he wrote that the number of fathers named by his patients alarmed him and he eventually shifted his theory to the realm of fantasy: the daughter's wish to be seduced (Rush 1980, chap. 8). Florence Rush goes on: "More at ease with the fantasy rather than reality of sexual abuse, Freud was even more comfortable when he could name the mother rather than the father as the seducer"

(Rush 1980, 83) As Nancy Tuana notes, had these women reported that their servants abused them, they would have been believed.

8. Shiftingly adapted from Lorraine Bethel's question "What Chou Mean, We, White Girl?" (Bethel 1979), which invokes the joke of Tonto talking back to the Lone Ranger, saying, "What d'you mean we, white man?"

9. Of course once one becomes adept, one is capable of judging mistakes (and, in turn, being mistaken).

References to Ludwig Wittgenstein's work are as follows:

OC   1969. *On Certainty*. Oxford: Basil Blackwell.
RFM   1967a. *Remarks on the Foundations of Mathematics*. Oxford: Basil Blackwell.
Z   1967b. *Zettle*. Oxford: Basil Blackwell.
PI   1958. *Philosophical Investigations* New York: Macmillan.

Other References

Bethel, Lorraine. 1979. "What Chou Mean, We, White Girl?" *Conditions* 5:86–92.

Bulkin, Elly, Minnie Bruce Pratt, and Barbara Smith. 1984. *Yours in Struggle: Three Feminist Perspectives on Anti-Semitism and Racism*. Ithaca, N.Y.: Firebrand.

Chow, Rey. 1991. "Violence in the Other Country: China as Crisis, Spectacle, and Woman." In *Third World Women and the Politics of Feminism*, ed. Chandra Mohanty et al. Bloomington: Indiana University Press.

Daly, Mary. 1978. *Gyn/Ecology*. Boston: Beacon Press.

de Laurentis, Teresa, ed. 1986. *Feminist Studies/Critical Studies*. Bloomington: Indiana University Press.

Einstein, Albert. 1907. *Relativity: The Special and the General Theory*. London: Methuen.

Frye, Marilyn. 1996. "The Necessity of Differences: Constructing a Positive Category of Women." *Signs* 21 (Summer): 991–1010.

Hoagland, Sarah Lucia. 1975. "The Status of Common Sense: G. E. Moore and L. Wittgenstein, a Comparative Study." Ph.D. diss., University of Cincinnati.

———. 1977. "On the Status of the Concepts of Masculinity and Femininity." *Proceedings of the Nebraska Academy of Sciences* 4 (August): 169–72.

———. 1978. "Coercive Consensus." *Sinister Wisdom* 6 (Summer): 86–92.

———. 1988. *Lesbian Ethics: Toward New Value*. Institute of Lesbian Studies, P.O. Box 25568, Chicago, IL 60625

———. 2001. "Resisting Rationality." In *Engendering Rationalities*, ed. Nancy Tuana and Sandra Morgan. New York: State University of New York Press.

Jarman, Derek, director. 1999. *Wittgenstein*. 75 mins. Kino Video. Videocassette (film).

Lugones, María. 1987. "Playfulness, 'World'-Travelling, and Loving Perception," *Hypatia* 2, no. 2:3–19.

———. 1990a. "Hispaneando y Lesbiando: On Sarah Hoagland's *Lesbian Ethics*." *Hypatia* 5, no. 3:138–46.

———. 1990b. "Structure/Antistructure and Agency Under Oppression. *Journal of Philosophy* 87, no. 10:500–507.

————. Forthcoming. "Boomerang Perception and the Colonizing Gaze."

Martin, Biddy, and Chandra Talpade Mohanty. 1986. "Feminist Politics: What's Home Got to Do with It?" In *Feminist Studies/Critical Studies*, ed. Teresa de Laurentis. Bloomington: Indiana University Press.

Millett, Kate. 1969. *Sexual Politics.* New York: Doubleday.

Mohanty, Chandra. 1991. "Under Western Eyes: Feminist Scholarship and Colonial Discourses." In *Third World Women and the Politics of Feminism*, ed. Chandra Mohanty et al. Bloomington: Indiana University Press.

Mohanty, Chandra, et al., eds. 1991. *Third World Women and the Politics of Feminism.* Bloomington: Indiana University Press.

Moore, G. E. 1953. *Some Main Problems of Philosophy.* New York: Collier.

————. 1962. *The Commonplace Book.* Ed. C. Lewey. New York: Macmillan.

————. 1966. *Philosophical Papers.* New York: Collier.

Pateman, Carole. 1988. *The Sexual Contract.* Stanford: Stanford University Press.

Penelope, Julia. 1990. *Speaking Freely: Unlearning the Lies of the Fathers' Tongues.* New York: Pergamon Press.

Pratt, Minnie Bruce. 1984. "Identity: Skin Blood Heart." In *Yours in Struggle: Three Feminist Perspectives on Anti-Semitism and Racism*, ed. Elly Bulkin, Minnie Bruce Pratt, and Barbara Smith. Ithaca, New York: Firebrand.

Rush, Florence. 1980. *The Best-Kept Secret: Sexual Abuse of Children.* Englewood Cliffs, N.J.: Prentice-Hall.

Tohidi, Nayereh. 1991. "Gender and Islamic Fundamentalism: Feminist Politics in Iran." In *Third World Women and the Politics of Feminism*, ed. Chandra Mohanty et al. Bloomington: Indiana University Press.

6

Tractatio Logico-Philosophica

Engendering Wittgenstein's *Tractatus*

Daniel Cohen

Introduction: Although many points of contact have been noted between contemporary feminist theories and the philosopher Ludwig Wittgenstein, for the most part, these fall into two large clusters. One consists largely of drawing out the connections between his own life and issues of concern for feminisms. And this is indeed a rich source to be mined. The extent of Wittgenstein's own misogyny and any effect it might have had on his work, for example, are worthy subjects for research and debate.[1] Of more broadly philosophical interest are the questions of identity that plagued Wittgenstein throughout his life and with which he wrestled throughout his career. His life is a veritable case study in self-denials: an antipatrician patrician who gave away his inheritance rather than be corrupted by it, an Austrian expatriate who returned to fight for the Fatherland in the Great War but finally renounced his citizenship during World War II, a homosexual struggling with homophobia,[2] an occasional anti-Semite of Jewish descent,[3] and a lifelong potential suicide whose last words were "Tell them [his friends] I've had a wonderful life."[4] And perhaps symbolic of all of these, he was the consummate antiphilosopher among twentieth-century philosophers.

If his self-denials were notorious, the philosophical affirmations that resulted were heroic, particularly the antiessentialism of his *Philosophical Investigations*. It is around this great work that the second cluster of feminist commentaries has formed. The conceptual tools he developed and the uses to which he put them have become part of the intellectual heritage of contemporary Western society, generally, but also of feminisms, especially. For example, the "family-resemblance" approach to concepts and universals, when applied to being-female, has been used to defend the idea of a genuinely radical feminist philosophizing from some French criticisms that the whole enterprise is inherently essentialist and, consequently, both continuous with and tainted by the sins of the past.[5] Similarly, situating and analyzing discourses within society's power structures would have been unthinkable without Wittgenstein's prior notions of "language-games" and "forms of life."

What I would like to explore here are connections between certain feminist lines of thought and Wittgenstein's earlier work, the *Tractatus Logico-Philosophicus*. Even if the agonies of his life and thought are not as patently manifest in the *Tractatus* as they are in the *Investigations*, they are acutely present nonetheless. And it is here that the groundwork for his subsequent contributions is put in place (although it is, I suppose, disingenuous to speak of the groundwork for antifoundationalism!). In the end, most of the philosophy in the *Tractatus* must be rejected, but feminist readings need not become exercises in "hermeneutical ventriloquism" in order to find great value in the text. Its philosophical contribution remains vital, so it need not be subjected to deconstructionist contortions in order to justify a *reductio ad absurdum* reading of everything that it seems to say. This is certainly not to deny that these strategies are fertile critical techniques when used judiciously—especially when applied to a text as oracular and polysemous as the *Tractatus*. Rather, it is to affirm that there are also important insights and deep truths that are positively present here.

Of all the insights in the *Tractatus* none is more philosophically profound than the important truth that truth per se is not all that important.

In many ways this is both a continuation of and a concluding chapter to the Enlightenment project of optimistic rationalism. Science may well tell us all there is to know about the world, but that is not nearly enough for philosophical beings like us. Wittgenstein opened the *Tractatus* by declaring that the facts, and just the facts, determine everything in the world. By the end, however, he has given us reason to invert Hamlet's assessment completely: for human purposes, there must be more things dreamt of in our philosophy than there are in heaven and earth. In what follows, I suggest an interpretive context for reading the *Tractatus*, the most technical of Wittgenstein's works, that identifies the significance of his linguistic philosophy for Wittgenstein personally, as well as for his readers as persons, and not merely as technical academic philosophers. What emerges from this in specific application is a vital and fertile framework for thinking about gender as an important but "nonfactual" conceptual category.

§1. Pre-text. The *Tractatus* is a text that is at once both celebrated and neglected. It is celebrated as the epitome of analytic philosophy. It is where the metaphysics of logical analysis is most clearly distilled and articulated, and where the "linguistic turn" in philosophy is most sharply executed. Outside the discourse circles of metaphysics, logic, and philosophical methodology, however, the *Tractatus* has received more lip service and perfunctory mention than detailed attention. Feminist discourses are no exception, and the reasons for this are not hard to fathom. For starters, the text is so highly abstract and logical as to seem impersonal and irrelevant to the topics of greatest concern for feminists. There is no mention at all of sexuality, gender, society, or class (except for mathematical classes!), to cite just a few examples. Second, the philosophical orientation is problematic: Wittgenstein's assumptions can, with all fairness, be characterized as "essentialist" and his methodology is indeed thoroughly "logocentric," both labels now uncritically used by critical theorists as terms of abuse. Last, he reached the unpalatable conclusions that nothing at all sensible can be said about the soul or about ethics. All attempts at such talk must be nonsensical. The nature of the soul and the subject matter of ethics are, in the final analysis, beyond the limits of what can be sensibly said. All questions of ethics and personal identity, therefore, are not merely to be ignored but should be positively avoided. And, beyond these, didn't Wittgenstein himself finally repudiate the philosophy of the *Tractatus*?

There are, of course, good and sufficient reasons for confronting the text, even should it ultimately be rejected as inexorably androcentric. For good or ill, it is undeniably a "seminal" text for much of this century's philosophizing. It has been a touchstone for philosophers on both sides of the Atlantic and it continues to capture the imaginations of philosophers around the world. Furthermore, a full appreciation of Wittgenstein's *Philosophical Investigations* requires coming to terms with the *Tractatus*, whether as fruitful soil or a failed foil for the later thought.

In the final analysis, however, it is the philosophy itself that is compelling. At its heart there is a curious and profound identification of logic and ethics. Thus, even though the text appears to be primarily about logic, Wittgenstein could still claim that the real point of the *Tractatus* was ethical.[6] A text seemingly concerned solely with logical matters cannot be dismissed as irrelevant to ethics, if logic and ethics are somehow one and the same. Moreover, since important elements of this identification persist into his later philosophy, neither can a patronizing attitude toward the *Tractatus* as being of merely historical significance be defended. (Some care needs to be taken here, because both "saying" and "logic" are technical terms in the context of *Tractatus*. They have, respectively, restricted and extended applications relative to their ordinary language counterparts. Accordingly, the claims that ethics, like logic, is unsayable, and that ethics and logic are in some fundamental sense the same need to be glossed.)

The *Tractatus*, then, is a text deserving attention. It deals with profound issues of human existence that are of great relevance to ethical theory and the metaphysics of identity. And, one way or the other, it has had an immense effect on subsequent philosophy. Some feminist thinkers have come to the conclusion that much of that effect has been negative. The exact charge is that *Tractatus* epitomizes the logocentrism of the analytic tradition, and that this is incompatible with tenets that are common to many of the central strands of feminist thought.[7] Among the questions that need to be addressed, then, are first, whether the text really is logocentric; second, if so, whether the logocentrism of the *Tractatus* does indeed presuppose or entail some form of androcentrism; third, regardless of the answers to the previous questions, whether something valuable of ethical substance, in addition to abstract metaethical theory, can be extracted; and last, what, if anything, feminists can take anything from the *Tractatus*, or from reading the *Tractatus*.

In brief, the answers that I offer to these questions are that the *Tracta-*

tus is indeed logocentric insofar as it treats philosophical debates as fundamentally linguistic phenomena that can be resolved by logico-linguistic analysis. Moreover, there are some objectionably androcentric aspects implicit in Wittgenstein's essentialism. For example, the explicit fact- and object-atomisms are paralleled by an underlying atomism with respect to individual souls that valorizes autonomy and privileges the associated model for human interaction. However, many of the objectionable aspects are not themselves essential to the overall philosophy. Nonetheless, what remains still exhibits all the problems associated with extreme realism. Especially troublesome is the crucial, but dubious, assumption that there is, at least potentially, a privileged scientific vocabulary for truthful description. However, the final assessment must be that the *Tractatus* remains an achievement of the first rank if only because it demonstrates so concisely exactly how irrelevant a value neutral science would be—and, given the necessity and omnipresence of value in the world, how thoroughly misguided a scientific philosophy would be, even were such a philosophy possible.

§2. Context. On the surface, Wittgenstein's denial of the soul and ethics as subjects for sensible discourse looks like a continuation of the positions taken by his mentor, Bertrand Russell, during the first two decades of the century. From the beginning, both were concerned with fact ontologies,[8] and neither includes values among the facts: Russell joined with some positivists in segregating facts and values by entertaining various forms of emotivism,[9] while Wittgenstein seemed to be taking an even more strident positivist approach in rejecting ethical discourse as altogether meaningless.[10] Either way, values do not count as part of the furniture of the world. Accordingly, ethical discourse is excluded from the vocabulary of careful description. Serious, "hard-headed" philosophers ignore or avoid ethics altogether. Russell and Wittgenstein both concede that philosophical progress on ethical questions is not forthcoming.

Compared with the differences, however, these similarities are superficial. Russell's reluctance to broach ethics in his more technical writings on logic, epistemology, and metaphysics has two sources. First, following Hume's classical empiricist lead, Russell accepted a radical distinction in kind between facts and values. At times during his atomist years, his fact ontology seems to have included general facts; he seriously entertained the possibility of negative facts; he clearly rejected molecular facts;[11] but he seems never to have even considered countenancing value-facts. Discussions of value are matters for social psychologists, anthropologists, or culture critics, not philosophers. (At least not for consistent empiricistically minded philosophers. G. E. Moore's ethical intuitionism recognized value-facts, but despite the methodological elegance and sensitivity of his linguistic analyses, Moore's conclusions were manifestly heretical for classical empiricists.) Second, despite the revolutionary aspects of his philosophical methodology, Russell's overall metaphilosophy was very traditional. For the most part, he thought of philosophy as an activity that was continuous with the natural sciences.[12] It seeks descriptions of the world in which we find ourselves, and its theories are measured in terms of truth and falsity. What distinguishes philosophy, and what gives it pride of place among disciplines, is simply its rarefied level of abstraction, which makes it both completely general and absolutely fundamental. Philosophy's failings arise from not being scientific enough. Russell's logical analysis was supposed to provide philosophy with the kind of exact methodology that would, at long last, enable philosophy to make the same kind of progress as the natural sciences.

Wittgenstein's project could not have been in greater contrast. His reasons for excluding ethics have more to do with his respect for the integrity of ethical discourse than deference to scientific and logical methods. Russell and Wittgenstein can both be said to have regarded ethics as unamenable to scientific treatment: if "progress" is measured as it is in the sciences, then ethics is an obstacle to progress in philosophy. But one philosopher's *modus ponens* is another's *modus tollens*, so while Russell largely ignored ethical theory to preserve the possibility of a scientific and progressing philosophy, Wittgenstein drew the contrary conclusion: the quest for philosophical progress and for a "scientific" philosophy will have to be abandoned because ethics will always resist such methods. Wittgenstein, no less than Russell, was aware of the power and promise of the techniques of logical analysis. He was also acutely sensitive to the limits of analysis, so he did not join in Russell's optimism about the future of philosophy. The conclusions he reached are largely negative. What can be "said" in philosophy can be said forthwith and without much ado, but none of that is to the point. Wittgenstein saw the limits to factual, scientific discourse. Ethics is beyond that limit, but that just serves to devalue scientific discourse, not ethics. Science aims at describing the world. Complete success in this endeavor would yield a complete catalog of all the mundane and contingent facts of the world. Philosophy, in contrast, aims at *understanding* the world. For success in this project, the individual facts are not enough. What would have to be cataloged here are the world's transcendental and necessary features—including its essentially value-laden character. These are, of course, just the features that escape a scientific vocabulary and transcend description, according to Wittgenstein.

The reasoning leading to this will be examined in the next section. What is of immediate importance is Wittgenstein's attitudes toward science. Unlike Russell, he did not have complete faith in the universal applicability of scientific method. In drawing the limits to sensible discourse, Wittgenstein was trying to purge philosophy of its pseudoscientific pretensions. Russell, too, was trying to purge philosophy of its unscientific elements, but he was doing so in order to make philosophy more scientific. The Tractarian endeavor was aimed at driving philosophy and science further apart so that they would never be confused again. "Philosophy is not one of the natural sciences" (TLP, 4.111). They are altogether incommensurable activities. And if, as Wittgenstein insisted at 4.11, "The totality of true propositions is the whole of natural science," then philosophy does not traffic in truths.

How is it, then, that the Tractatus has come to be seen as the epitome of scientism—the "physics envy" that has plagued so much twentieth-century analytic philosophy? The early positivist commentaries are partly responsible, but so is Wittgenstein himself. In his conversations with members of the Vienna Circle in the decade after the Tractatus was written, Wittgenstein sometimes tended to read his own text as they did, seeing what they wanted to see in their "adopted father."[13] The boundaries Wittgenstein had seen for science are boundaries for philosophy, too, so there was also a negative conclusion about philosophy to be drawn. Thus, while Wittgenstein maintained that the important part of his work was the part not written, namely, the negative discourse space that was created by the limitations on factual discourse, there were also grounds for a peremptory dismissal of any positive conclusions. As he wrote in the preface: "[I]t shows how little is achieved when [philosophical] problems are solved." What was too often read as the relegation of metaphysics and ethics to the ineffable is, in better faith, read as their *elevation*. Closing the circle on the philosophical system of Tractatus does contain—and even quarantine—truth. But it also creates a space for something else.

One way to understand this positivistic misreading of the Tractatus that inverted the relation between philosophy and science is by comparing it with a relevant precedent. The subsequent history of Wittgenstein's distinction between science and philosophy bears a striking parallel with another revolutionary dichotomy in the history of philosophy: Descartes's dualism of mind and body. Originally, the radical separation of the physical from the mental was intended to protect the emerging modern science from the occult elements of Scholastic philosophy. Physical phenomena were to be provided with wholly physical explanations. The final cause of dualism, so to speak, was the elimination of final-cause explanations from the physical sciences. However, isolating the physical also isolated the mental, thereby licensing the kind of inward, psychologistic philosophizing culminating in Berkeley, Hume, and Kant. The theoretical wall that was built to keep physics pure of metaphysics became, for some, a wall to keep metaphysics safe from the progressive encroachments of physics. Physicalistic positivism is more in line with the original Cartesian motivation than today's dualisms seeking to preserve a space for mind or soul.

The irony of this history is paralleled by the career of the *Tractatus*. The motivation for finding the limits to "what can be said" in Wittgenstein's philosophy was to preserve the autonomy of a *non*scientific discourse, not to establish the hegemony of science. It is better to read the final cause of Tractarian philosophy as trying to keep science out of ethics, metaphysics, and philosophy generally rather than the reverse. However, as with the next generations of Cartesians, things got turned around, and the positivists were more concerned with keeping metaphysics out of physics. If physicalistic positivism is taken as the rightful heir to the original grounds for Cartesian dualism, then perhaps the spirit of the *Tractatus* calls for some sort of Kantian transcendentalism.

Russell's logical atomism was only one of many discernible and significant influences on the development of Tractarian thought. Together with the works of Frege, it is certainly the strongest determinant of the purely logical and linguistic doctrines of the *Tractatus*. However, if Wittgenstein's own assessment of the point of the book as ethical is to be taken seriously, other predecessors should be highlighted. Schopenhauer, Tolstoy, and William James are among the more commonly cited philosophers whose thoughts are supposed to hold the hermeneutical key to reading Wittgenstein, but all manner of idiosyncratic extensions to the list of influential and parallel thinkers have been offered. Among the influences that Wittgenstein himself noted, the most interesting for current purposes is Otto Weininger.[14] Weininger was something of a romantic hero in turn-of-the-century Vienna, but in all too many ways he is a reprehensible figure. He was explicitly and obsessively anti-Semitic, homophobic, and misogynist—despite being Jewish, homosexual, and thus, by his own reckoning, "psychologically female." Perhaps because of this, he gets little or no mention in most books on either Wittgenstein, the person, or his early philosophy. Neither Anscombe, nor Black, nor Finch, nor Findlay, nor Grayling, nor Griffin, nor Hacker, nor Kenny, nor Malcolm, nor Pears (to cite just some of the authors of the more prominent memoirs of early Wittgenstein and commentaries on his early philosophy) so much as gives Weininger an index entry, and yet his impact on Wittgenstein seems to have been profound.[15]

To begin, there are conspicuous parallels between Wittgenstein's life situation and Weininger's. Weininger's "resolution" of his self-hatred was suicide, a dramatic and romanticized course of action that Wittgenstein apparently had to struggle to resist throughout his life.[16] Weininger thought that genius alone could justify and transcend the miseries of life. Otherwise, suicide was the only philosophically honest response. Wittgenstein's response was to try to justify his existence by establishing his genius.[17] Philosophy was to be the medium.

The dichotomy of genius-or-suicide may seem an unnatural one, but it is explicit in Weiningerian thought. It is almost an inevitable consequence to Weininger's broader worldview pitting the "masculine" against the "feminine" in the grand history of humanity and the individual histories of humans. In brief, all individuals were thought to have both masculine and feminine characteristics to some degree. Man and Woman, as Platonic archetypes, embody pure ideals that transcend what any individual man or woman could achieve. Feminine elements were identified with the earthly and the sensual. Masculine elements were held to be the source of civilization and spirituality. Genius, then, is the highest manifestation of Man. An existence as "pure" Woman, devoid of absolutely anything that is higher, would not be a worthy life. The combination of a highly developed aesthetic sensibility—the ability to appreciate the highest cultural achievements—with a consciousness of one's own self as completely Woman would surely be more than any refined sensibility could bear.

The final ingredient in all this is another Weiningerian psychological archetype: "the Jew." The Jew represents a negative possibility for everyone but was thought to be most exemplified among actual Jews, just as Woman was thought to be most often and best exemplified in women.

And like Woman, who is concerned above all else with pairing for reproduction, the Jew is characterized by a greater sense of community than of
self. As a result, Jews do not achieve individual souls and do not develop
a real sense of good and evil. Jews are essentially feminine. In contrast to
Christianity, Judaism was regarded as merely a historical tradition rather
than offering a genuine sense of something higher or being an authentic
expression of religiosity. Thus, Man, Christian, and Genius stand historically and personally opposed to Woman, Jew, and Beast.

In this schema, only by exhibiting genius can one conclusively establish the worthiness to claim a right to life. Genius offers a way out for
someone already plagued with suicidal tendencies or pathological self-
doubts—and Weininger and Wittgenstein both qualified. Such a person
would have to completely purge herself or himself of the characteristics
of the Jew and of Woman. For anyone too imbued with Woman-ness or
Jewish-ness, that could only mean suicide.

There is plenty in Wittgenstein's life and work to suggest that this
framework had an effect on him, both consciously and unconsciously. For
example, even though Wittgenstein as a young boy was baptized into the
Roman Catholic faith, he often thought of his own thought and person
as somehow Jewish—and he felt this was something that he had to overcome.[18] His notebooks indicate that he was troubled by the belief that he
had a "Jewish mind" insofar as he thought his philosophical contributions were really derivative, developing the ideas of others, rather than
being genuinely original; and there are also entries that show he thought
there was something "feminine" about his way of thinking in pictures.[19]
The essentialism that is implicit in this self-analysis is, of course, patently
inconsistent with Wittgenstein's simultaneous critiques of essentialism.
Not even the greatest philosophers can escape all the irrational forces
within their own psyches.

§3. Text. Wittgenstein identifies the "fundamental idea" of the *Tractatus*
as the recognition that the logical constants are not representatives. In
other words, they do not serve to name objects in the world.[20] This immediately leads to the distinction between showing and saying, which he
also identified as the most important contribution. In a letter to Russell
in 1919, from a prisoner of war camp, Wittgenstein wrote: "Now, I'm
afraid that you haven't really got hold of my main contention to which
the whole business of logical propositions is only corollary. The main
point is the theory of what can be expressed (*gesagt*) by propositions, i.e.

by language (and, which comes to the same thing, what can be thought) and what cannot be expressed by propositions, but only shown (*gezeigt*); which I believe is the cardinal problem of philosophy."[21] But *why* are these important? They must be something other than just interesting facts about language, because facts are the contingent and independent configurations of objects that constitute the world, and facts are without higher value.[22] What makes these important is also what makes them meaningful, namely, the ineffable soul, which is not itself part of the world. The will imparts *meaning*, it is the "meaning locus,"[23] but it also is the source of *value*. That is, the will is the source of meaningfulness in two senses—it is the source of the meaning of words as well as the meaning of life. It is precisely their common source in the will that makes both semantics and ethics ineffable. Indeed, it is central to the *Tractatus* that "meaning" is univocal in the two cases.[24]

These conclusions are integral to the entire philosophy of the *Tractatus*. Briefly, the ontology of the *Tractatus* is that the world consists of facts, which are objects in configuration. Wittgenstein's account of language at this stage is that language consists of propositional signs or "pictures" that represent facts (and possible facts or "states-of-affairs"). Insofar as the propositional signs are themselves configurations of objects—for example, ink marks on a page or sound waves in succession or even the spatial arrangements of blocks of wood that are used in courtrooms to represent vehicles in an accident[25]—they are all facts in their own right (which is not to say that what they assert, the represented states-of-affairs, are true). Any fact can be used as a picture of another fact, provided that the picture and the pictured have the same "logical form." However, although any fact *can* be a picture, not every fact *is* a picture. That requires a projective act of the will.

Now, whether or not a fact is a picture is *not* itself a fact about that fact. This is of the utmost importance for understanding the worldview and philosophy of language in the *Tractatus*. There can be no configurations of objects representing semantic relations. In part this is because Wittgenstein denies that the soul, which mediates meaning, is itself an object in the world, but there is a deeper reason concerning the general logic of representation. A complete description of the world would have to identify all the objects and their configurations, but it would not have to include the additional information that some specified configuration *stands for* some other one. That is, semantic claims add nothing to descriptions of the world. The resulting picture of the world would not change with the addition of the semantic information. Meaning, then, must be somehow interpretative, or intuitive, or incommensurable with the vocabulary of scientific description . . . or *ineffable*.

In the picture theory of meaning, propositions are the primary units of meaning. They are understood as pictures of a sort, namely, configurations of ink marks, sounds, or other objects (in other words, facts), that are willed to represent other possible configurations of objects. The theory, then, limits meaningfulness proper to descriptive pictures. It is this insistence that all literally meaningful vocabulary must somehow contribute to "changing the picture" that establishes the limits to discourse. Consider for example, the description of a piece of white paper with the letters *S, N, O,* and *W* written on it in black ink. A fine grid might be superimposed on the page with an indication for each small square whether it was ink-filled or not. The picture that is given could be made as accurate as desired by refining the grid, but it would not include the meaning of the word *snow*. Knowing what the ink marks mean does not change the picture at all. Meaning is not included in a complete description. In one respect, then, meaning is not part of the world.

There is, of course, another respect in which knowing the meaning of the printed word changes everything. A letter-by-letter account of Homer's *Odyssey*, for example, would completely determine the text, even for someone who knows no Greek, but it would hardly tell us everything we want to know. Indeed, in a very real sense it would not tell us *anything* at all about the text, because it would not tell us anything important. Understanding the text requires more than being able to describe it.

The connection between semantics and ethics is now visible: the picture afforded by a complete description of the world is not changed by adding any semantic information. Neither is it changed by adding ethical information, for instance, that it is good. Ethical discourse, like the discourses of semantics and logic, does not contribute to describing the world; it contributes to understanding the world. In a model in which values are supervenient, the notion of two factually identical possible worlds with different valuations is incoherent, but that is not Wittgenstein's model. The ethical is neither part of, nor determined by, the factual. But while the use of ethical predicates might not change anything internal to the picture itself, their use changes everything *about* the picture. "Ethical facts" might not make a difference to any part of a complete picture of the world, in other words, to describing the world, but when it comes to understanding, ethics makes all the difference in the world: "The world of the happy person is a different one from that of the unhappy person."[26]

Within the solipsistic framework of the *Tractatus*, the soul, which is the source of all meaning and value, is a transcendental soul. It cannot be part of the world of factual discourse because, as the necessary "origin" for all coordinate systems for the world, it is both a logical prerequisite for any discourse and an inviolate limit to discourse.[27] Consequently, the "ethical point" of the *Tractatus* is a vanishing point: ethics, too, is ineffable. But, as already noted, removing the ethical from the sayable was not intended to be part of a positivistic depreciation of ethics. Rather, it is an affirmative appreciation of the ethical dimension of life. The driving force behind it all was neither Russell's epistemological agenda nor the positivists' antimetaphysical one; it was Wittgenstein's own profound ethical sensibility.

Implicit in the identification of logic and ethics is a parallel identification of the transcendental or metaphysical soul and what might be called the "ethical soul."[28] In part, this equation is justified on purely logical grounds—the picture theory of meaning, the fact-ontology of objects in configuration, and the need for a meaning-locus that is itself outside the realm of factual discourse. But there is still the lingering question of what makes this transcendental, metaphysical soul at all *ethically* relevant? Insofar as it is transcendent, it is apart from all the contingent facts of the world. Further, it would have to be absolutely simple, because any parts would have to have some configuration, which would make it a contingent matter. The soul could not, therefore, change—or be involved in change—in any way. It could have no effect on the world at all: "The world is independent of my will."[29] Wouldn't the soul, then, as a logically necessary posit for even the possibility of any experience or representation, in other words, as necessary for a world, be altogether irrelevant—as irrelevant as a beetle in a closed box, to appropriate Wittgenstein's own, later analogy?[30]

In order to provide the desired negative answer to this last question, the logical considerations need to be complemented by more recognizably ethical ones. However, since ethical matters are "ineffable," in other words, outside the realm of literal, factual, descriptive, or scientific discourse, Wittgenstein can say very little about ethics in the *Tractatus* itself. What he does say is negative, indicating what ethics is not: ethics is not about consequences, not about reward and punishment.[31] The consequences of action are contingent, empirical matters. A genuine ethics can be neither.

§4. Subtext. What is ethical about the logico-linguistic analysis that leads to the radical "bracketing" of the soul and all ethical discourse? What is ethical about ignoring—and even excluding—all talk of race, class, gender, and the other categories that we use to define ourselves to ourselves? More pointedly, how can someone who sometimes seems to identify logical error with ethical error and nonsense with sin,[32] castigate his own homosexuality as sinful? Is there something confused or confusing about homosexuality—more so than other forms of sexuality?[33] I think these issues were not far from the thoughts of the author of the *Tractatus*. They are problems he wrestled with, and they are questions that can be answered within the framework he provided.

Although it is often risky business to retroject contemporary concerns and concepts into past discussions, I think the risk is worth it here. In particular, I think there is a way to introduce some contemporary notions about gender into the logical framework of the *Tractatus* that increases our understanding of both the concepts involved and Wittgenstein's project.

The positivists read Wittgenstein's *Tractatus* as a continuation and culmination of the Enlightenment project of rationalism (albeit according to their own empiricist agenda). And the text does seem to champion the supremacy of "natural philosophy" insofar as the range of science is the totality of true propositions. If there are truths about the soul, then there will be a science of psychology; if there are truths about society, then there will be a science of sociology; and so on. Truth is a relation between pictures and what they picture, between language and the world, so truth presupposes the accurate applicability of our categories of thought and the predicates of our language.

Accuracy, however, is a by-product of clarity. To that end, Wittgenstein was trying to isolate the logical form of the proposition in order to identify the essential structures of facts. What he found was the logical form of the constituent objects, and their logically proper names, which mark the end to analysis.[34] The ethical soul is not one of these objects. It has neither internal, formal properties nor external, material ones. It is as if Wittgenstein stripped away all the contingent accidents to get to the very core—and found nothing left. The ethical value of the soul, or of anything else, must be inherent in the thing in itself, and not dependent on any contingencies. An ethical subject would have to be subject to universal and categorical imperatives. Any restrictions that would compromise universality would be inconsistent with the unconditional necessity presupposed by genuine ethical discourse.

What this means is that facts about biological sex, economic class, or racial identity (if indeed these are to count as "facts" in the technical sense of the *Tractatus*) must all be ethically neutral. The imperatives of Enlightenment universalizing begin in the abstract but inevitably become impersonal and, finally, irrelevant. Contrapositively, what is relevant is not factual. Therefore, if the Tractarian framework were to be adopted (or the contemporary conceptual vocabulary were to be retrojected), then a category such as gender would be ethically relevant only if, strictly speaking, it were not a matter of fact. Gender could not be important if it were a factual matter, and we know that the question of his own sexuality was important enough to trouble Wittgenstein greatly.

To deny that questions of gender are matters of fact is to say only what they are not, not what they are. The *Tractatus* is silent on this, as it must be, but there are several options available besides reducing the ethical to the sociological, the psychological, or some other species of the factual. The options range from castigating it as nonsense to elevating it as part of *das Mystiche*, making it higher and transcendental. In between, ethical discourse can be read emotivistically, as expressive; or metalinguistically, as imperative; or, as has already been suggested, critically, as interpretive.

In the preface to the *Tractatus*, Russell wrote, "The essential business of language is to assert or deny facts."[35] And the *Tractatus* does indeed posit this as the essence of all language, so Russell, as an exegete, is right on target. If there is any lesson to be learned from Wittgenstein's later *Philosophical Investigations*, however, it is surely that Russell, as a philosopher of language, completely missed his target. Asserting facts is not the essential business of language. Language is better understood as an unimaginably vast collection of tools, or of "language games," for an equally vast array of human purposes: social interaction, describing our world, controlling the world, inventing ourselves, and more. So perhaps we ought not judge Russell and Wittgenstein too harshly for missing the target, because there never was a target to hit in the first place: language does not have an essential business.

However, Russell can be taken to task on another score: his use of the word *essential*. If he meant "important," he has invoked the language of valuations, rather than facts. There could be no grounds for this assertion, even were it to count as a proper assertion. However, if he did mean to be saying something factual, for example, that metaphorical, interrogative, and other forms of discourse are derivative from factual-indicative discourse, or that a logically perfect language would concern itself only with these functions, then not only has he made a much stronger and controversial claim, he has transgressed Tractarian (and his own!) strictures against linguistic self-reference. Essentialism is presupposed, but in both its ethical and logical senses, it is ineffable. There is no room in the extensional language of the essentialist *Tractatus* for essences.

There is reason for harping on this use of this particular word. The implicit identification of what is essential about something and what is important about it has a venerable pedigree in the history of philosophy. Aristotelian essences, for example, were defined in terms of what was important for Aristotle's science; and Descartes's redefined concept of essence, the knowable truth about an object, was what was important about an object for his epistemological agenda. Wittgenstein apparently buys into the identification of the essential and the important. In accordance with his logical turn, he understood essence in terms of logical form. Equating logic and ethics preserves the traditional importance of essence. It is one of the chief virtues of the *Tractatus* that it makes this identification explicit—if only because it makes it easier to reject it![36] There is an inherent tension here, one bordering on contradiction, that needs to be resolved. Perhaps writing the *Tractatus* was Wittgenstein's way of working it out.

The tension is this: Wittgenstein rejects the thesis that ethics is a factual matter. A genuine ethics must be somehow "higher" than the mundane facts of the world. Real value cannot be dependent on contingent configurations of objects. Rather, whatever value there is must precede all facts. In short, facts are ethically neutral and altogether irrelevant for philosophy.[37] However, if genuine values are transcendental, like logic, then they are independent of the world's contingencies. In that case, they would be necessary and immutable, and there would be no sense in worrying about them. This violates Hume's principle "ought implies can," which captures the crucial intuition that an ethical life must be *possible* for moral agents. We cannot be held responsible for that which is beyond our control, and transcendental values would indeed be beyond our control. Ethics becomes otiose. Thus, the framework of the *Tractatus* immediately presents us with a dilemma: ethics is either factual but ultimately irrelevant (because it is not higher); or else it is transcendental and "essential" but immutable, and therefore irrelevant because it is beyond us.

At several points along the way, I have suggested a reading of the *Tractatus* that aligns the distinction between saying and showing with the distinction between scientific truths and both logical form and ethical values. In addition, it is fruitful to think of these in connection with the difference between descriptions and interpretations. This might provide a way to resolve the dilemma. Interpretive categories are transcendent insofar as they are nonfactual. Furthermore, they can be independent of, and even prior to, experience. Nonetheless, they are not altogether immutable. We are not inexorably imprisoned by the conceptual categories we bring to the world. Above all, however, our interpretive categories are important. For example, on this reading of the Wittgensteinian scheme, categorizing oneself as male or female by gender would not be a factual matter, in contrast, perhaps, to biology's sexual categories. No collection of "scientific facts"—definite configurations of objects in the world—could serve to decide the issue of one's gender. But gender identity is exceedingly important. It is a way of being in the world that makes all the difference in the world. It is something that we bring to all our experiences, something that determines our world. That is, the identity of the transcendental soul is given in just this sort of interpretive category. The logic of interpretation that constrains our understanding of the world, no less than the logic of representation that constrains our descriptions of the world, begins in the transcendental soul. And yet, even though an interpretive identity is a prior condition for the experiences we have, it is not beyond our reach. Gender identity is not immutable.[38]

Although Wittgenstein does not mention sex, gender, class, or race in the *Tractatus*, he does use these categories in other writings.[39] They are clearly useful and important categories for thinking about oneself and one's place in the world. Even so, Wittgenstein was in a position to have concluded that there is no legitimate place for these concepts in the linguistic scheme of purely factual discourse. But again, the facts are not important, so if there are important issues at stake, it is to the nonfactual conceptual apparatus that we must turn. Of special importance for Wittgenstein as he wrote the *Tractatus*, and throughout his life, was the issue of his own gender identity. If this can be regarded as a nonfactual matter, then Wittgenstein may have provided himself with a kind of exculpation for his "sins." Homosexual *activity*, to choose the most pertinent example, would be no more ethically relevant than any other contingent fact in the world. What would be relevant is homosexuality as part of one's ethical identity, as a gender, but that would not be part of the world.

Self-loathing, then, is a permanent (and even justified) possibility for anyone who is really intent on it, regardless of all behavior. Conversely, any behavior can be forgiven, or, more precisely, overlooked as insignificant. We can be as hard on ourselves as we want. But if we are easy on ourselves instead, what changes? Nothing. And everything. The exercise of the will does not change any facts in the world but it can change the significance of those facts. Because ethics so thoroughly permeates the world, the world itself changes. Perhaps that is why Wittgenstein could write, "The world of the happy person is a different one from that of the unhappy person."[40] Did recognizing the important truth that truth *per se* is not all that important make Wittgenstein happy in the end? I like to think so.

Notes

1. See, e.g., Monk 1990, 72–73 and 498.

2. Again, Monk's biography is an excellent source for a sensitive reconstruction of Wittgenstein's life. The appendix, "Bartley's Wittgenstein and the Coded Remarks," is particularly relevant.

3. Wittgenstein's attitude toward Judaism and his discomfort with what he perceives to be his own "Jewish" traits are made evident in several passages in his *Culture and Value*. Relevant passages can be found at 18–19, 21–22, and 35–36; The issue of the Wittgenstein family's attitudes is addressed in Janik and Toulmin 1973, 172f.

4. Reported in Malcolm 1984, 81.

5. See, for e.g., Lee-Lampshire 1991, 313–31. A family-resemblance account is also suggested in Winant 1987, 123–48. In the first chapter of *Essentially Speaking: Feminism, Nature, and Difference*, Diana Fuss (1989) provides an overview of the essentialist-constructionist debate as it relates to feminist thought.

6. Wittgenstein claimed this in a letter to the writer and editor Ludwig von Fickel. See Janik and Toulmin 1973, 192.

7. Harriet Baber (1989) in a letter to the *APA Newsletter on Feminism and Philosophy*, suggested that this is a distressingly widespread attitude in the profession; Naomi Scheman's (1992) response, also in the *APA Newsletter on Feminism and Philosophy*, goes a long way to explaining, but ultimately rejecting, that attitude.

8. Bertrand Russell began his lectures on *The Philosophy of Logical Atomism* with "the first truism" that "the world contains facts." These have been reissued as Russell 1985. Wittgenstein opened the *Tractatus Logico-Philosophicus* (hereafter referred to as *TLP*) with the lines "The world is all that is the case. The world is the totality of facts, not of things."

9. See Matson 1979.

10. For example, *TLP*, 6.421: "It is clear that ethics cannot be put into words."

11. Russell addressed the issue of the kinds of facts throughout the lectures on logical atomism cited in note 8. An excellent discussion can be found in Urmson 1967, 60–75.

12. Russell's expressed thoughts during the first decades of the century on the nature of philosophy itself are often at odds with his practice and with one another. E. R. Eames (1969) provides a helpful cataloge of his pronouncements on philosophy (34ff.).

13. This felicitous phrase is from Shields 1993, 8.

14. In *Culture and Value*, Wittgenstein (1980, 19) lists Boltzmann, Hertz, Schopenhauer, Frege, Russell, Kraus, Loos, Weininger, Spengler, and Sraffa.

15. Of the 5,868 entries of secondary sources in Shanker and Shanker 1986, a bibliography of materials on Wittgenstein, the index cites *only one* as including the name "Weininger" in its title (although at least one other was missed by the indexer and Janik 1985 was too late to be included). There has been a marked increase of scholarship on Weininger and his influence on Wittgenstein recently, especially since the publication of Monk 1990, See, e.g., Harrowitz and Hyams 1995 or Klagge 2001.

16. Three of Wittgenstein's brothers committed suicide, and his journal entries often turn to suicidal thoughts.

17. This is the central thesis sustained in Monk's (1990) biography. The subsequent discussion of Weininger's thought is largely based on Monk's biography and Janik and Toulmin's (1973) book. There is an oft-repeated anecdote in which Russell (1985) gives a late-night reassurance to Wittgenstein that he did indeed have significant philosophical talent. Although Russell offers this flippantly, this event assumes greater significance in the overall scheme of Wittgenstein's life.

18. See Janik and Toulmin 1973, 172–73, for a discussion of the family's attitudes toward its Jewish ancestry; see also the reference to *Culture and Value* in footnote 19.

19. Wittgenstein 1980, 18–19e and 31e, respectively. Ironically, some of Wittgenstein's examples of non-Jewish geniuses were in fact Jewish, but aren't the facts always irrelevant to our prejudices?

20. *TLP*, 4.0312. Richard McDonough (1986) provides an excellent development of the logico-linguistic significance of this and its importance for the associated conception of philosophical truth. Questions of ethics are altogether ignored.

21. Quoted in Griffin 1964, 18.

22. *TLP*, 6.4–6.421.

23. McDonough 1986, 162ff.

24. Wittgenstein's (1961) *Notebooks 1914–1916* include the passage "Things acquire 'significance' only through their relation to my will." The univocality thesis is defended in Cohen 1988–90, 126–40.

25. Wittgenstein (1961) offers this sort of example in the 29 September 1914 entry in his *Notebooks*. This may have even been the genesis for the picture theory.

26. *TLP*, 6.43: "Die Welt des Glücklichen ist eine andere als die des Unglücklichen."

27. *TLP*, 5.632.

28. This distinction is based on Appiah's distinction between metaphysical and ethical identities in Appiah 1990, 493–99. He apparently embraces the conclusion that any metaphysical identity reached by a strictly logico-linguistic analysis (specifically, Kripke's account of "rigid designators") would not be ethically relevant.

29. *TLP*, 6.373.

30. Wittgenstein, *Philosophical Investigations*, §293.

31. *TLP*, 6.42–6.423. Consideration of the consequences may be prudent, but not really ethical. It hardly counts as ethical, for example, on the part of a second-grader to turn over lunch money to a fifth-grade bully. Similarly, neither should it count as ethical when someone behaves in accordance with a perceived ethical system in order to reach heaven or avoid hell. A divine bully is still a bully.

32. Shields 1993, 74–75.

33. In his private diaries, Wittgenstein could adopt a very matter-of-fact tone with regard to his sexual activity, but Weininger's attitudes are never very removed. According to Monk (1990), 25, Weininger thought all "sexuality is incompatible with the honesty that genius demands" and that this resonated with Wittgenstein's own attitudes. However, Monk also records (117) that Wittgenstein recognized a positive correlation between his sexual urges and his ability to work on logic. Monk's conclusion (585) is that "Wittgenstein was uneasy, not about homosexuality, but about sexuality itself." The idea of Wittgenstein as a tormented homosexual seems to have a strong hold on the imagination of parts of the philosophical community.

34. *TLP*, 3.25.

35. Preface to *TLP*, x.

36. Appiah (1990) for example, severs the connection between what is "essential" about an object insofar as it is necessary and what is "essential" insofar as it is ethically relevant. If we are to be responsible for our "ethical identities," they must be within our control, to some extent. The identities we make for ourselves, for example, using socially constructed categories such as gender and ethnicity, are therefore more important than any (putatively!) immutable "essences" such as sex and race.

37. See, e.g., *TLP*, 4.1122 and 6.4–6.432.

38. Once gender is dissociated from the biological sexual categories, the assumption that there are only two should lose whatever hold it might have had on our imaginations. A fuller sense of the variety of sexual roles and social roles, more generally, may require a finer conceptual grid than what has traditionally been offered. For example, "lesbian" might well count as a useful gender category, different from both "female" and "male." In other contexts, so might "butch" and "femme." Different categories may be applicable at different stages of a life. But are these *really* genders? If the question is asked, the point has already been missed. There is no *really*—if by that we mean a single privileged description—when it comes to interpretive categories.

39. *Culture and Value*, for example, includes comments on Englishness, Austrian national character, and other similar categories, in addition to its notorious passages on Jewishness and femininity. These comments are dated as early as 1929 and 1930. In contrast, Wittgenstein's *Notebooks 1914–1916* do not contain comparable passages. This is no doubt largely due to the selective editing of the surviving notebooks. Most were destroyed at Wittgenstein's insistence. Monk (1990, 114) cites a passage from Wittgenstein's "secret" war diaries from the same period describing himself as "German through and through" *(ganz und gar deutsch)*. Alternatively, the shift may be due in part to a change in his philosophical focus from abstract logical matters to the more personal ethical questions with which he became increasingly preoccupied, as has been suggested by Marjorie Perloff (1993).

40. *TLP*, 6.43.

References

Anscombe, Gertrude Elizabeth Margaret. 1959. *An Introduction to Wittgenstein's Tractatus*. Philadelphia: University of Pennsylvania Press.

Appiah, Anthony. 1990. "But Would That Still Be Me? Notes on Gender, 'Race,' Ethnicity, as Sources of Identity." *Journal of Philosophy* 87, no. 10:493–99.

Baber, H. Letter to the Editor. 1989. *APA Newsletter on Feminism and Philosophy* 89, no. 1:90–91.

Black, Max. 1964. *A Companion to Wittgenstein's "Tractatus."* Ithaca: Cornell University Press.

Cohen, Daniel. 1988–90. "The Word as Will and Idea: Semantics in Wittgenstein's *Tractatus*." *Philosophical Studies* (Dublin), 32:126–40.

Eames, Elizabeth Ramsden. 1969. *Bertrand Russell's Theory of Knowledge*. New York: George Braziller.

Finch, Henry Le Roy. 1971. *Wittgenstein: The Early Philosophy*. Atlantic Highlands, N.J.: Humanitites Press.

Findlay, John Niemayer. 1984. *Wittgenstein: A Critique*. London: Routledge and Kegan Paul.

Fuss, Diane. 1989. *Essentially Speaking: Feminism, Nature, and Difference*. New York: Routledge.

Grayling, A. C. 1988. *Wittgenstein*. Oxford: Oxford University Press.

Griffin, James Patrick. 1964. *Wittgenstein's Logical Atomism*. Seattle: University of Washington Press.

Hacker, Peter M. S. 1986. *Insight and Illusion*. Oxford: Clarendon Press.

Harrowitz, Nancy A., and Barbara Hyams, eds. 1995. *Jews and Gender: Responses to Otto Weininger*. Philadelphia: Temple University Press.

Janik, Allan, and Stephen Toulmin. 1973. *Wittgenstein's Vienna*. New York: Simon and Schuster.

Kenny, Anthony. 1973. *Wittgenstein*. New York: Penguin Books.

Klagge, James. 2001. *Wittgenstein: Biography and Philosophy*. Cambridge: Cambridge University Press.

Lee-Lampshire, Wendy. 1991. "History as Genealogy: Wittgenstein and the Feminist Deconstruction of Objectivity." *Philosophy and Theology* 5, no. 4:313–31.

Malcolm, Norman. 1984. *Ludwig Wittgenstein: A Memoir*. 2d ed. Oxford: Oxford University Press.

Matson, Wallace I. 1979. "Russell's Ethics." In *Bertrand Russell Memorial Volume*, ed. G. W. Roberts. London: George Allen & Unwin.

McDonough, Richard. 1986. *The Argument of the "Tractatus."* Albany: State University of New York Press.

Monk, Ray. 1990. *Ludwig Wittgenstein: The Duty of Genius*. New York: Free Press.

Perloff, Marjorie. 1996. *Wittgenstein's Ladder*. Chicago: University of Chicago Press.

Pears, David F. 1986. *Ludwig Wittgenstein*. Cambridge: Harvard University Press.

Russell, Bertrand. 1985. *The Philosophy of Logical Atomism*. Ed. D. Pears. La Salle, Ill.: Open Court.

Scheman, Naomi. 1992. Letter to the Editor. *APA Newsletter on Feminism and Philosophy* 91, no. 2:49–51.

Shanker, V. A., and S. G. Shanker. 1986 *Ludwig Wittgenstein: Critical Assessments*. Vol. 5: *A Wittgenstein Bibliography*. London: Croom Helm.

Shields, Philip. R. 1993. *Logic and Sin in the Writings of Ludwig Wittgenstein*. Chicago: University of Chicago Press.

Urmson, James O. 1967. *Philosophical Analysis*. Oxford: Oxford University Press.

Winant, Terry. 1987. "The Feminist Standpoint: A Matter of Language." *Hypatia* 2, no. 1:123–48.

Wittgenstein, Ludwig. 1953. *Philosophical Investigations*. Trans. G. E. M. Anscombe. New York: Macmillan.

———. 1961. *Notebooks, 1914–1916*. Ed. and trans. G. E. M. Anscombe. New York: Harper Torchbooks.

———. 1974. *Tractatus Logico-Philosophicus*. Trans. D. Pears and B. McGuinness. London: Routledge and Kegan Paul.

———. 1980. *Culture and Value*. Ed. G. H. von Wright. Trans. P. Winch. Oxford: Basil Blackwell.

7

The Moral Language Game

Susan Hekman

In the past several decades feminist moral theorists have been engaged in a thorough deconstruction of modernist moral theory. This deconstruction has taken several forms. They have questioned the existence of one, true, universal morality that transcends gender, race, class, and culture. Following the pathbreaking work of Carol Gilligan, they have questioned the hegemony and definition of what Gilligan calls the "justice voice." Arguing that the justice voice is thematically gendered, and that women tend to speak in a "different" moral voice, they have begun to develop the implications of this voice for moral theory. The feminist deconstruction of modernist moral theory has focused on the critique of the disembodied, disinterested, transcendent subject that grounds modernist epistemology. Most feminist moral theorists have argued instead for a relational conception of the subject. They posit moral subjects who are connected and engaged, who define morality in relational terms rather than as a function of abstract, universal principles.

The radical reconceptualization of moral theory entailed by the feminist critiques has stimulated a vast literature.[1] It has profoundly altered the direction of contemporary moral theory. But it has also raised fundamental questions that feminists are only beginning to answer. Two stand out as central. First, feminist moral theorists must address the question of how to conceptualize moral theory in the absence of a moral metanarrative. If, as many feminist moral theorists argue, we must abandon the masculinist moral metanarrative that defines modernist moral theory, does this entail that we must abandon moral theory altogether? Does the absence of a moral metanarrative necessarily condemn us to moral anarchy, to the babble of conflicting moral voices? Second, if, following Gilligan, we conceptualize moral theory in terms of moral voice, then we must develop a new account of the relationship between morality and subjectivity. The relational subject that is at the center of much feminist moral theory calls for a radically different conceptualization of moral theory because it jettisons the grounding concept of modernist moral theory: the disembodied subject. Relational subjects are constituted by discursive, cultural, historical, and societal factors; these subjects develop moral voices that are a product of those factors; abstract universal principles do not figure into the equation at all. Feminist moral theorists must develop an account of this understanding of moral development and its connection to subjectivity itself.[2]

My thesis in this essay is that Wittgenstein's later philosophy provides a way of theorizing about morality and moral subjectivity that addresses these questions raised by feminist moral theory. I argue that Wittgenstein's understanding of language games and his rejection of the possibility of an ideal language provide the outline for a reconstruction of moral theory along feminist lines. My thesis does not rely on Wittgenstein's explicit statements about ethics. These statements are much too sparse to provide the basis for a moral theory; worse, they suggest that he embraces an individualistic, even idiosyncratic approach to ethical issues. My deployment of Wittgenstein's approach relies instead on his conception of the language game. I attempt to develop a theory of an entity that Wittgenstein never discusses: the moral language game. Specifically, I use Wittgenstein's approach to explain how subjects are connected to their moral voices and how moral voices can be diverse and plural without being arbitrary or anarchic. My argument is organized around two theses. The first is that moral voices are central, integral parts of what it means to be a subject; becoming a subject and developing a moral voice are inseparable. We do not recognize someone as a subject unless she/he possesses a moral voice; our social definition of *subject* is connected to our definition of *moral*. Second, moral voices are unique: they are not subject to the vagaries of preferences that characterize other aspects of subjectivity. What makes a moral voice specifically *moral* is its connection to who we are and the certainty that that entails.

The centerpiece of Wittgenstein's later philosophy is the concept of the language game. Language games emphasize that there is no neat division between words and actions, but, rather, that language is something we *do*. For Wittgenstein, language is a form of life, not "mere words" that can be contrasted with "real life." Further, Wittgenstein emphasizes that, like a form of life, the justification for a language game is internal to the practice itself, not an external standard. Fundamental to his argument is the assertion that, at some point, justification must stop and we say, "This is simply what we do."[3]

At the beginning of *Philosophical Investigations* Wittgenstein states his aim in a deceptively simple manner.[4] What we need, he asserts, is "a clear view of the aim and functioning of words" (*PI*, §5). This far from simple statement must be interpreted in light of Wittgenstein's earlier philosophy. "Getting a clear view of the aim and functioning of words," for the later Wittgenstein, no longer means seeking an ideal language that supersedes the inexactness of everyday language. Rather, it involves plunging into the messiness of that everyday language because, as he puts it, "to imagine a language means to imagine a form of life" (*PI*, §19). His definition of *language game* reflects this thesis: "Here the term 'language game' is meant to bring into prominence the fact that the *speaking* of a language is part of an activity, or a form of life" (*PI*, §23).

In *The Blue and Brown Books* Wittgenstein describes what might be called the methodology of language games that he employs in the *Investigations*.[5] "Language games are the forms of language with which a child begins to make use of words. The study of language games is the study of primitive forms of language or primitive languages" (*BB*, 17). In this and other passages Wittgenstein presents language games as a kind of protolanguage: "Children are taught their native language by means of such games" (*BB*, 81) and "When we look at such simple forms of language the mental mist which seems to enshroud our ordinary use of language disappears" (BB, 17). But he also asserts that language games are not incomplete parts of language, but complete systems of human communication (BB, 81).

Wittgenstein acknowledges at the outset that taking "this line of investigation" will be "difficult." What stands in our way, he asserts, is our "craving for generality," the desire to define an "essence" to words, to find clear boundaries between them (BB, 17). This is a not-so-subtle reference to Wittgenstein's own previous effort to do precisely this—to construct an ideal language that avoids the confusions of ordinary language. Wittgenstein is now arguing that we must abandon that goal, that we must embrace the complexities and contradictions of ordinary language, to describe what it is that we actually *do* with words. Our culture's preoccupation with the method of science has caused us to try to reduce everything to a series of laws. One of the results of this is that we have been disdainful of the particular case (BB, 18), subordinating cases to universal laws. Wittgenstein is now claiming that we must take particular cases seriously.

The logical positivists believed that philosophy must mimic the method of science; what this meant is that the task of philosophy was to find the exact definition of words, to uncover what is common to all uses of a word. This goal, Wittgenstein asserts, stems from our tendency to "sublime the logic of our language" (PI, §38). The method that Wittgenstein is now proposing assumes instead that there is no essence to words, but that we use them in different ways. We can, however, define what Wittgenstein calls a "family resemblance" among the different uses of a word. The uses of a word, although they may not share a single common element, are related to one another much as members of a family share a resemblance. It is impossible to precisely define a family resemblance, but it is apparent in, for example, family pictures. To illustrate his concept Wittgenstein refers to the term *game* itself. Although it would be impossible to specify the essence of the concept "game," it is nevertheless the case that games form a family the members of which resemble one another in certain ways (PI, §§64–71).

Wittgenstein's description of language games focuses on grammar. Games have rules and language games have grammar.[6] "Our investigation," Wittgenstein declares, "is therefore a grammatical one" (PI, §90); "Grammar tells us what kind of object anything is" (PI, §373). But the analogy between grammar and the rules of a game goes only so far. Rules of games are, in most instances, precisely stated. Grammar, however, can create confusions; knowing "our way about" can be difficult (*PI*, §664). These and other comments on language games lead to the conclusion that the new method that Wittgenstein is proposing is in sharp contrast to the exact method of the logical positivists. It involves much messing around in what Wittgenstein calls the "toolbox" that constitutes both language games and language itself. The toolbox metaphor is central to Wittgenstein's approach. Knowledge is no longer identified as the product of an idealized logical language. Rather, "[k]nowledge is the hypothesized reservoir out of which the visible water flows. . . . It is as if I get tools in the toolbox of language ready for use."[7] The rules (grammar) by which we decide which tool (word) to use will not be exact, but variable. The reason for this is that, as Wittgenstein puts it, for a large class of cases, although not for all, "the meaning of a word is its use in the language" (*PI*, §43). Which tool we select will depend on the use to which we are to put it.

One of the central elements of Wittgenstein's position is his claim that the ultimate justification for language games is found in our "form of life." This position is particularly relevant to my attempt to theorize about moral language games. Wittgenstein claims that our language is grounded not in the universal metanarrative of logic, but rather, in our activity. The ultimate justification for our claims to knowledge, thus, is not logic but simply "what we do." "It is what human beings *say* that is true and false; they agree in the *language* they use. That is not agreement in opinions but in forms of life" (*PI*, §241). Our concepts rest not on "a kind of seeing on our part; it is our *acting* which lies at the bottom of the language game."[8] Philosophers since Plato have looked for ultimate justifications, for complete explanations. What Wittgenstein is advocating, in contrast, is an end to justifications not in logic, but in human activity itself: "What people accept as a justification is shown by how they think and live" (*PI*, §325); "the chain of reasons has an end" (*PI*, §326). And, finally, "[o]ur mistake is to look for an explanation where we ought to look at what happens as a 'proto-phenomenon.' That is, where we ought to have said: *this language game is played*" (*PI*, §654).

At a crucial point in his argument, Wittgenstein appears to go beyond a description of human activity as the justification for our knowledge and to appeal once again to a universalistic grounding. His discussion of "general facts of nature" and "natural history" seems to suggest that he is not content with the contextual account he has given and is looking for more reliable, universal criteria. But a careful reading of the relevant passages suggests a different conclusion. Our "natural history" for Wittgenstein includes not just our biological or "natural" activities, but our linguistic activities as well: "[c]ommanding, questioning, recounting, chatting, are as much a part of our natural history as walking, eating, drinking, playing" (*PI*, §25). Our language games are as natural to human life as our biological life. Most important, language games literally *give* us a world in which to live; our concepts are part of the fabric of our form of life. Wittgenstein's point in his famous statement "If a lion could talk, we could not understand him" (*PI*, §223) is not that our biology differs from that of lions, but rather that the lion's concepts would create a world that we could not comprehend. Wittgenstein summarizes:

> I am not saying: if such and such facts of nature were different people would have different concepts (in the sense of a hypothesis). But: if anyone believes that certain concepts are absolutely the correct ones, and that having different ones would mean not realizing something that we realize—then let him imagine certain very general facts of nature to be different from what we are used to, and the formation of concepts different from the usual ones will become intelligible to him. (*PI*, p. 230)

Wittgenstein's theory of language games is appropriate to feminist discussions of moral discourse in a number of important respects. He emphasizes the multiplicity and diversity of language games, the internal character of justification, and, most important, the rootedness of language games in forms of life. It is even possible to interpret Wittgenstein's theory as an extension of Carol Gilligan's discussion of the different moral voice of women. Joining the two approaches has interesting results: a theory that identifies the "care voice" as a distinct moral language game rooted in the particular experiences of most women in our culture. The logic and justification of this language game are different from that of the justice voice, but, like the justice voice, the criteria of rightness are internal to the language game. The difference between the two moral language games, furthermore, can be attributed to the fact that the "form of life" that most women experience in our culture is distinct from that of men. Women do most of the nurturing, caring work in our culture. Men, by contrast, are dominant in the public realm in which questions of abstract justice figure prominently.

One conclusion that flows from this interpretation is that, contrary to modernist moral theory, there is more than one moral language game and, thus, more than one standard of moral rightness. Another conclusion is that although there is more than one moral language game, nevertheless there are identifiable similarities among moral language games that set them apart from other language games. In Wittgenstein's terminology, they share a family resemblance.

There is, however, a significant problem with this theory: this appropriation of Wittgenstein's approach is apparently inconsistent with what Wittgenstein has to say about the subject of ethics. Although his references to ethics are infrequent, his position, especially in the *Tractatus*, appears to be completely consistent with the logical positivist relegation of ethics to the realm of the inexpressible.[9] But there are hints even in the *Tractatus* that Wittgenstein holds a very different view. He begins the book with the famous statement that "what can be said at all can be said clearly and what we cannot talk about we must pass over in silence." References to this silence recur throughout the book. In a letter he wrote to Ficker about the *Tractatus*, he states explicitly what is only implicit in the book: "The book's point is an ethical one. . . . My work consists of two parts: the one presented here plus all that I have *not* written. And it is precisely this second part that is the important one. My book draws limits to the sphere of the ethical from the inside as it were, and I am convinced that this is the ONLY *rigorous* way of drawing those limits."[10]

I would like to advance two theses with regard to Wittgenstein's approach to ethics: first, although Wittgenstein retains the logical positivists' definition of ethics as linked to aesthetics, he does not share their repudiation of ethics; and second, although Wittgenstein's attitude toward language in general changes radically from his earlier to his later work, his attitude toward ethics appears to change hardly at all. In his "Lecture on Ethics"[11] which clearly belongs to his later period, Wittgenstein reaffirms the similarity between ethics and aesthetics that he advanced in the *Tractatus*. He also restates the rigid dichotomy between facts and values that characterized his earlier work. In this later lecture, ethics is once more defined as running against the boundaries of language, a realm excluded from the province of science. Wittgenstein also reaffirms the respect for ethics that characterized his earlier work. He defines ethics as documenting "a tendency in the human mind which I personally cannot help respecting deeply and I would not for my life ridicule it."[12] What is peculiar, if not outright contradictory, about this attitude toward ethics in Wittgenstein's work is that although in his later philosophy he advances a rigorously social conception of language, he excludes ethics from this conception. For the later Wittgenstein, language is exclusively a social activity: meanings are defined by use; justification is conventional and relative to language games; private languages are impossible. Ethics, however, does not seem to have any place in this social world. For Wittgenstein ethics remains personal, individual, idiosyncratic. Wittgenstein's position is perhaps most reminiscent of Weber's well-known ethic of responsibility. Like Weber, Wittgenstein seems to be espousing an individualistic existentialism in which endowing the world with meaning is a mystical act.

It is even possible that Wittgenstein shares another famous Weberian belief: that the disenchantment of the modern world is regrettable and that it is this unfortunate state of affairs that is the cause of the modern privatization of ethics. A short passage in *Culture and Value* suggests that Wittgenstein believes that a privatized ethics is not the ideal relationship between individuals and ethical beliefs. "A culture is like a big organization which assigns each of its members a place where he can work in the spirit of the whole. . . . In an age without culture on the other hand forces become fragmented and the power of an individual man is used up in overcoming opposing forces and frictional resistances."[13] These passages suggest a number of theses: our culture *should* supply us with an ethics, an ethical language game that is a central element of our form of life; our culture's failure to do so is a result of the "disenchantment" of the modern world; and finally, it is only in such a disenchanted world that the individual is forced to choose an ethics without social guidance.

This interpretation of Wittgenstein's approach to ethics, however, is highly speculative. The interpretation I would like to advance is a more modest one. Although Wittgenstein's approach to language underwent a sea change from his earlier to his later work, this change did not apply to his view of ethics. Wittgenstein offers no discussion of morality as a language game, even as a unique language game with special qualities. There is evidence that Wittgenstein saw beliefs, even religious beliefs, as constituting a form of life, a perspective on the world that provides a context for knowledge and its justification. On religious belief, he states: "Hence, although it's a *belief*, it's really a way of living, or a way of assessing life. It's passionately seizing hold of *this* interpretation."[14] But for Wittgenstein ethics does not constitute a belief. Thus he does not extend his identification of belief as a form of life to the ethical realm.[15] It is precisely this extension, however, that I want to pursue.

A central aspect of Wittgenstein's concept of the language game is the claim that the justification for knowledge claims is internal to the language game itself, a function of the fact that language games are activities, forms of life. He does not apply his understanding of how knowledge claims are justified to the issues of ethics and morality, but his position is particularly appropriate to some of the questions that have been raised in moral philosophy. Modernist moral philosophers have been obsessed with the question of justification; they have insisted that unless moral claims have unimpeachable foundations, unless they are disembodied and universal, they cannot be counted as moral at all. Wittgenstein's approach to the question of justification offers an effective deconstruction of this position.

Wittgenstein's most extended discussion of the relationship between justifications and language games is found in *On Certainty*. His principal concern in the statements collected in this book is the central role of science and education in our form of life. His thesis is that the concepts fundamental to science and education form the commonsense ground of our form of life. They are not in themselves provable, but rather, provide the basis by which anything is proved and the definition of proof itself.

Wittgenstein never refers to ethics or moral philosophy in these statements. Yet much of what he says here is relevant to the dominant language game of moral philosophy, especially as it has been articulated since Kant. Wittgenstein emphasizes that the absolute certainty that science seeks is an impossible goal. As he puts it, "At the foundation of well-founded belief lies belief that is not founded" (OC, §252). He also asserts that justifications must come to an end because "at the end of reasons comes persuasion" (OC, §612). Most important, the end we reach is not an absolute, unimpeachable reason but, rather, the activity that grounds our language games: "If I have exhausted the justifications I have reached bedrock, and my spade is turned. Then I am inclined to say 'This is simply what I do'" (PI, §217).

Wittgenstein's remarks can quite profitably be used to deconstruct one of the central goals of modernist moral philosophy: grounding moral judgments in absolute certainty. He argues that the goal of absolute certainty is an epistemological impossibility. He asserts that instead of looking for absolute grounds, we should look at what it is that we actually *do*; our certainty comes from our form of life, not epistemology. Wittgenstein's approach here is closely related to what Gilligan is doing in her exploration of moral voices. Gilligan asks us to look at what we *do* morally, to stop seeking in moral matters certainty that is akin to the certainty of science. Wittgenstein claims that philosophers "are like savages, primitive people, who hear the expressions of civilized men, put a false interpretation on them, and then draw the queerest conclusions from it" (*PI*, §194). The philosophers Wittgenstein has in mind here are the logical positivists who abstract from the concreteness of ordinary life and language in order to formulate an ideal language. But it applies just as well to modernist moral philosophers who have attempted, with concepts such as Kant's categorical imperative and Rawls's original position, to abstract from moral practice to the realm of the universal and absolute. Both Wittgenstein and, in a different way, Gilligan encourage us to avoid this error by listening to linguistic practice.

One of the most vivid metaphors that Wittgenstein employs to make his point is that of the riverbed (*OC*, §§96–98). He argues that our language games, our forms of life, are like water flowing through a riverbed. The riverbed shapes the direction of the water that flows through it, just as the fixed beliefs that are central to our form of life shape what we mean by an argument, proof, and evidence. The riverbed can shift over time, propositions that were fluid can harden, others that were hard can become fluid. Despite these changes, however, it is nevertheless the case that at any given time the riverbed provides the ground of our language games, our form of life. When, driven by the philosophical quest for certainty, we search for the indubitable ground of our reasons, the riverbed is the hard rock that we hit, causing our spade to turn; it is the end of reasons. Thus: "[a]ll testing, all confirmation and disconfirmation of a hypothesis takes place already within a system. And this system is not a more or less arbitrary and doubtful point of departure for all our arguments: no, it belongs to the essence of what we call an argument. The system is not so much the point of departure, as the element in which arguments have their life" (*OC*, §105). It follows that "[i]f language is to be a means of communication there must be agreements not only in definitions but also (queer as this may sound) in judgments" (*PI*, §242). The tradition of modernist philosophy since Descartes and Kant has been driven by what Wittgenstein calls the "illusion" that the point of their investigation is to grasp "one comprehensive essence."[16] What Wittgenstein suggests as a counter to this is that we accept what looks like a preliminary solution, our form of life, as *the* solution: "The difficulty here is: to stop."[17]

Wittgenstein's attack on the possibility of absolute certainty is closely related to his attempt to deconstruct the logical positivists' belief that the goal of philosophy is to articulate an ideal, logical language in which statements can be made with absolute clarity and precision. The aim of such a language is to clear up the ambiguities and confusions of ordinary language, make the truth and falsity of statements apparent, and reveal the single comprehensive essence of things. Against this Wittgenstein argues that we should "go back to the rough ground," to return to the messiness of ordinary language. He argues: "We have got on to slippery ice where there is no friction and so in a certain sense the conditions are ideal, but also, just because of that, we are unable to walk. We want to walk: so we need *friction*. Back to the rough ground!" (*PI*, §107). This metaphor goes a long way toward explaining Wittgenstein's later philosophy. The smooth, icy ground of the ideal language is so perfect that it is useless. It has no connection to the concrete roughness and ambiguity of the phenomenon it seeks to explain: human life.

Wittgenstein's attempt to bring philosophy back to the rough ground of ordinary language closely parallels the efforts of many feminist moral theorists to listen to and valorize the moral voice of women. Modernist moral philosophers' attempt to define the one, true morality, the one correct moral discourse, is motivated by the same desire as the logical positivists' attempt to define an ideal language: getting it right once and for all. In contrast, the approach to moral discourse advocated by many feminist moral theorists represents an attempt to get back to the rough ground, to return to the complexities of everyday language. To make this argument I will refer to the well-known and influential work of Gilligan, although other feminist theorists would serve as well. Gilligan explicitly calls for the need to account for the "messiness" of human life. The attempt to define something like Kant's categorical imperative or Kohlberg's Stage 6 as the "essence" of morality closely parallels the logical positivists' attempt to define an ideal language. Gilligan's attempt to listen to moral voices, to see what it is we *do*, parallels Wittgenstein's turn to ordinary language. Wittgenstein attacks philosophers' craving for generality, the desire to reduce everything to abstract principles. Gilligan attacks the same impulse in moral-development theory; her work entails that moral discourse is something about which we cannot fashion a single set of rules. Wittgenstein's work suggests a similar conclusion for all the subjects that philosophers study. One commentator has suggested that Wittgenstein's style, his rejection of the linear, doctrinaire method of philosophy, is a symptom of his rejection of the linear tradition in philosophy itself.[18] Gilligan's reliance on musical metaphors—themes, fugues, counterpoints—also evinces a rejection of the linear.

Wittgenstein argues that language games are inseparable from forms of life; language is an activity, a doing that is part of our natural history. Gilligan's work also parallels this aspect of Wittgenstein's theory. If we assume that moral discourse constitutes a language game (which Wittgenstein does not), then it would seem to follow that different moral discourses constitute different forms of life. And this is, of course, exactly what Gilligan found. She found that the care voice is thematically feminine, that is, that it is not spoken only by women but is associated with culturally defined feminine values. Most significant, it corresponds to women's form of life, the fact that, in our society, women usually fill the role of caregivers. She also found that the justice voice is associated with qualities that our culture defines as masculine and that this voice defines the public realm, the realm that, until quite recently, excluded women. The private realm, in contrast, is the realm of women, the realm of the moral voice of care and connection. In Wittgensteinian language, Gilligan has defined two language games of morality rooted in two different forms of life. One of these language games, however, is hegemonic and has been defined as the only "truly moral" discourse.[19]

The goal of my consideration of Wittgenstein's work is to employ some of his central concepts—language games, certainty, the ideal language—to construct an approach to morality that is appropriate to feminist concerns. The first element of my argument is that moral language games are unique in that they are inseparably tied to subjectivity itself; in other words, we recognize a subject as fully human only if she can participate in moral discourse. Second, I argue that moral language games negotiate the boundary between the conventional and the nonarbitrary in a unique way. It is beyond question that moral language games are cultural products, that they are multiple and varied; Gilligan's research has revealed that they even differ within cultures. I refer to this as the *content* of the moral language game, a content that is always contextual, historical, located. What makes moral language games unique, however, is that in *form* they are neither conventional nor arbitrary. To make a moral argument is not to claim that such and such is right for me or for my culture, but that it is *right*. Moral language games, like all language games, provide internal criteria of justification. What these criteria justify in the case of moral language games, however, is *moral* rightness. Thus within the parameters of a particular moral language game, I can rely on definable standards of moral judgment. In the context of a different language game, for example, that of anthropology or moral philosophy, I may acknowledge that the morality of my culture is a historical product, that other moral language games exist. But when I am actually engaged in moral argument or action or both, the discourse provides standards of right and wrong that are stable and enduring.

The point of departure of my argument is a consideration of subjectivity. Although Wittgenstein never discusses the subject as such, the concept of the subject implicit in his ordinary language philosophy offers a sharp contrast to the subject that grounds modernist philosophy. Wittgenstein's discussion of language games, certain knowledge, and most significant, the status of "private" sensations implies a subject far removed from the transcendental, self-constituting subject of the modernist tradition. His deconstruction of the very foundations of Western/modernist philosophy necessarily entails the deconstruction of the centerpiece of modernism: the Cartesian subject. In a sense Wittgenstein does not need to discuss the subject, because its deconstruction is implicit in his whole philosophical project.[20] The question that I want to address is in what sense this subject can be said to be moral. My argument is that morality is a practice, a habit in Oakeshott's sense, that the members of cultures teach their children.[21] Although habits/practices vary widely among cultures and even within cultures, and the content of the moral practices that are taught varies, the teaching of moral practice appears to be common to all human cultures. Being taught a moral practice is not an optional part of childhood education, but central to the process of becoming a person. Another way of putting this is that in any culture that we have any knowledge of, to become a person is to become a moral person. Furthermore, in any culture, and most particularly in ours, the ability to employ moral arguments, to discriminate between right and wrong, is definitive of mature adulthood. Our legal system provides an excellent example of this point. We exclude juveniles and the mentally ill from the full force of the law precisely because they are unable to tell right from wrong. The ability to make moral distinctions thus constitutes *the* criterion of full legal and political personhood in our society.

The second aspect of my thesis involves the claim that the content of moral language games is culturally relative, while the form of their employment is not. But by *form* I mean something quite different from a standard such as Kant's categorical imperative. Kant argued that there is a universal standard for moral rightness, that the content of this standard is invariable. In contrast, I am arguing that standards for moral rightness are internal to moral discourses and, thus, that their content varies, but that moral discourses are similar in form: they all make the claim to rightness. My thesis can best be illustrated by comparing two language games that exemplify the extremes of my argument. If I were to assert that I like chocolate ice cream, that I prefer it to any other flavor of ice cream, it would be compatible with this assertion that I accept the arbitrariness of this preference. I might admit that it is mere chance that I prefer chocolate ice cream, that I have not always liked it, or even that I may lose my taste for it in the future. The language game of taste preferences can accommodate all of these statements. If I were to assert, however, that I believe in Jesus Christ as my personal savior, it would be compatible with this statement to acknowledge that not everyone has this belief and even that the Christian religion has its roots in a particular culture. But it would not be compatible with this statement that my belief is arbitrary, that I might just as well believe in another god or that if I were born into another culture I would believe in another god. For me, my belief in Christ is absolute and true; he *is* the savior even if that fact is not universally acknowledged. Furthermore, my belief makes me the kind of person I am: a Christian. Being a Christian constitutes a way of life for me. The language game of religious belief, unlike that of taste preferences, does not include vacillation or willy-nilly choice.

The moral language game has more in common with the religious language game than with that of taste preferences. Although moral and religious language games are not identical, they share an important quality: nonarbitrariness. In any culture, growing into personhood means growing into moral personhood. I can acknowledge that other cultures have different moral systems, but it does not follow that my beliefs are arbitrary. My moral beliefs constitute who I am as a person. When I make a moral statement, I am not saying that I believe this is right but I could just as well believe that something else is right. I am asserting that this *is* right; I would be a different kind of person if I believed differently. Wittgenstein's famous lion statement is relevant here. If I had different moral beliefs I would be a different person; I cannot fully understand what my form of life would be with a different set of moral beliefs, because they are so central to who I am.

Making this point in Kuhnian language might help to clarify my argument. I am asserting that moral beliefs are a, if not the, paradigm of mature subjectivity. Our moral beliefs define us as persons, they give us a world to inhabit and endow that world with meaning. Moral beliefs vary both across and within cultures. Although they provide standards for moral judgments, not all cases will be clear and unambiguous; it is the nature of moral judgments that they involve dispute and disagreement. But it does not follow that moral beliefs are fickle. A change in moral beliefs entails a profound change in worldview, a conversion; it entails inhabiting a new world. Very few, if any, other language games are similarly fundamental. Changing my taste in ice cream will have little effect on my perception of myself as a person; changing my moral language game, however, will make me a different person.

The greatest obstacle to the approach to moral theory that I am advocating here is construing the claim to rightness implicit in moral statements.[22] My argument is that this requirement can be met by focusing on the form of moral arguments rather than their content. When I make moral arguments I am making a claim to rightness, I am asserting that my moral statements are not arbitrary. This claim is rooted in the centrality of my moral beliefs to my status as a person: I am the kind of person that I am because I have certain moral beliefs. Neither my subjectivity nor my morality are arbitrary; they are my way of being in the world. But they are not "right" in a universalistic sense, because, quite obviously, other kinds of persons and other kinds of moral beliefs exist in the world. My understanding of my world, however, is substantially constituted by my necessarily moral subjectivity; I cannot fully understand any other kind of world. My "understanding" of other beliefs, other subjectivities, is of a different order: it is an intellectual understanding constituted by the language game of cultural critique.

It is my argument that this conception of the moral subject can provide the basis for a feminist moral theory. It addresses the issues raised by feminist critiques of masculinist moral theory in two central respects. First, it highlights the connection between morality and subjectivity. It emphasizes that to be a subject is to be a moral subject, to have a moral voice. It entails that different kinds of subjects will have different moral voices, that there is not one paradigm for either morality or subjectivity. Second, it focuses on the plurality of moral language games, allowing for the analysis of hegemonic and marginalized moralities. But it can also accommodate the nonarbitrariness of moral language games, the claim to rightness that is implicit in moral judgments, and, hence, the uniqueness of the moral language game.

Many critics of feminist moral theory and, indeed, even many feminist theorists, have been concerned that rejecting the moral metanarrative necessarily entails moral anarchy, a moral Tower of Babel. Consequently, there has been a tendency among some feminist theorists to refashion the masculinist moral metanarrative, to replace it with a feminist metanarrative, or to remove or deny its gendered connotations. I think this is the wrong direction for feminist moral theory. I think we should instead attempt to articulate a new paradigm of morality, a paradigm rooted in a relational, discursive subject and the acknowledgment of multiple paths to moral truth. It has been my argument here that Wittgenstein's later philosophy provides a useful tool for such a feminist articulation of moral theory.

Notes

1. See especially Carol Gilligan, *In a Different Voice* (Cambridge: Harvard University Press, 1982); Eva Kittay and Diana Meyers, eds., *Women and Moral Theory* (Totowa, N.J.: Rowman and Littlefield, 1987); Claudia Card, ed., *Feminist Ethics* (Lawrence: University of Kansas Press, 1991); Virginia Held, *Feminist Morality* (Chicago: University of Chicago Press, 1993); Sarah Ruddick, *Maternal Thinking* (Boston: Beacon Press, 1989); Nel Noddings, *Caring* (Berkeley and Los Angeles: University of California Press, 1984); Sarah Hoagland, *Lesbian Ethics* (Palo Alto: Institute of Lesbian Studies, 1988); and Iris Young, *Justice and the Politics of Difference* (Princeton: Princeton University Press, 1990). See also my *Moral Voices/Moral Selves* (University Park: Penn State Press, 1995). This essay is another version of chap. 4.

2. See my *Moral Voices, Moral Selves*.

3. For my purposes, it is unfortunate that Wittgenstein employs the word *game* in this context, because it connotes the frivolous and arbitrary. My argument about the moral language game is quite the opposite of these connotations.

4. Ludwig Wittgenstein, *Philosophical Investigations* (New York: Macmillan, 1958). Hereafter this work is referred to as *PI*.

5. Ludwig Wittgenstein, *The Blue and Brown Books* (New York: Harper and Row, 1960). Hereafter, this work is referred to as *BB*.

6. *Ludwig Wittgenstein, Philosophical Grammar* (Berkeley and Los Angeles: University of California Press, 1974), 60.

7. *Philosophical Grammar*, 49.

8. Ludwig Wittgenstein, *On Certainty* (New York: Harper and Row, 1969), §204. Hereafter this work is referred to as *OC*.

9. Ludwig Wittgenstein, *Tractatus Logico-Philosophicus* (London: Routledge and Kegan Paul, 1961).

10. Quoted in Paul Engelmann, *Letters from Ludwig Wittgenstein* (New York: Horizon Press, 1968), 143.

11. Ludwig Wittgenstein, "Lecture on Ethics," *Philosophical Review* 74 (1965): 3–12.

12. Ibid., 12.

13. Ludwig Wittgenstein, *Culture and Value* (Chicago: University of Chicago Press, 1980), 6.

14. Ibid., 64.

15. Other commentators on what I have identified as the contradiction in Wittgenstein's thought are Hanna Pitkin, *Wittgenstein and Justice* (Berkeley and Los Angeles: University of California Press, 1972) and Sabina Lovibond, *Realism and Imagination in Ethics* (Minneapolis: University of Minnesota Press, 1983).

16. Ludwig Wittgenstein, *Zettel* (Berkeley and Los Angeles: University of California Press, 1970), §444.

17. Ibid., §314.

18. Stephen Hilmy, *The Later Wittgenstein* (Oxford: Basil Blackwell, 1987).

19. See *In a Different Voice*; Lyn Mikel Brown and Carol Gilligan, *Meeting at the Crossroads* (Cambridge: Harvard University Press, 1992); Gilligan et al., eds. *Mapping the Moral Domain* (Cambridge: Harvard University Press, 1988); and Gilligan, Nona Lyons, and Trudy Hanmer, eds., *Making Connections* (Cambridge: Harvard University Press, 1990).

20. For a discussion of Wittgenstein's attitude toward subjectivity, see Wendy Lee-Lampshire, "Moral 'I': The Feminist Subject and the Grammar of Self-Reference," *Hypatia* 7 (1992): 34–51; Vincent Descombes, "A Propos of the 'Critique of the Subject' and the Critique of This Critique," in *Who Comes After the Subject?* ed. Eduardo Cadava et al. (New York: Routledge, 1991), 120–34; and Iris Murdoch, *Metaphysics as a Guide to Morals* (New York: Penguin, 1992).

21. Michael Oakeshott, *Rationalism in Politics* (New York: Basic Books, 1962).

22. In *Wittgenstein and Moral Philosophy* (New York: Routledge, 1989), Paul Johnson attempts to deal with the claim to correctness implicit in moral discourse by positing a form of moral objectivism. Murdoch (*Metaphysics*) does much the same.

8

The Short Life of Meaning: Feminism and Nonliteralism

Jane Braaten

In this essay, I argue that Ludwig Wittgenstein's theory of linguistic meaning is "nonliteralist," and that as such, it makes sense of radical linguistic critique. A nonliteralist theory of meaning is one that rejects the view that there are literal, or fully determinate, meanings of words and sentences, or to put it a little differently, that rules of linguistic usage are fully determinate. A radical linguistic critique is, at the very least, one that challenges some political presumption of linguistic usage (where the existence of such a presumption must be shown) at the level of the rules of usage themselves. If such challenges are to be successful, then alternative rules of usage must also be available, and so it is necessary to establish the possibility of viable alternatives.

In more ordinary terms, the argument is this: Wittgenstein's likening of communication to an ensemble of games that people play, each with its own set of rules, is one that allows not only for constant flux in the rules, but also for the introduction of new language games, and the disappearance of unused games. The difference between changing the rules of an existing language game and the introduction of a new game is not a sharp one, but my argument does not depend upon a rigorous distinction here. It does depend upon a basic open-mindedness, or freedom of thought and imagination, which is barely tolerated and rarely nurtured in most human societies.

The most important background assumption in my argument, one that I will not put in Wittgenstein's mouth, is that human beings are fundamentally open to communication of any kind. What this premise means in practice is that people are capable of recognizing something that might be communication before they are fully capable of interpreting it. They may find something that appears to be an ordered arrangement of symbols that they never interpret as a message, and come to the conclusion that maybe there is a message that curious people will decipher in the future, or maybe the appearance of meaning is an illusion. If you accept the possibility that people can suspend judgment about whether something is communication or not, then you accept my assumption, as far as is necessary to support the argument in this essay. Since it is a background assumption, I will not make further mention of it here, though it is an interesting claim that is worth thinking about. Of Wittgenstein, I assume only that he would not deny this claim outright.

When I have made the argument for Wittgensteinian nonliteralism, I will picture within its framework a feminist critique of language as a response to gender-specific rules of interpretation and understanding, which mask underlying injustices. The conception of feminist linguistic critique that I frame here is, therefore, more conservative of ordinary language than those that equate "radical" with "incommensurable with the status quo," but there is room for plenty of extreme difference, in my view, within "ordinary" language.

To begin my argument, I will use as a foil a passage from Jürgen Habermas that is, uncharacteristically, mistakenly uncharitable to Wittgenstein. I will use the feminist analysis of the politics of naming as an instance of radical linguistic critique, and defend the claim that such a critique is easily accommodated in a Wittgesteinian theory of linguistic usage.

In a discussion of H. G. Gadamer's theory of hermeneutics, Habermas argues that Wittgenstein's theory of language games in the *Investigations* is, in contrast to Gadamer's "3-dimensional" theory, only "one-dimensional."[1] Although Wittgenstein recognized the plurality of language games (the first dimension), so Habermas argues, he overlooked the "interpretive-dialogical" and historical qualities of linguistic practice (the second and third dimensions). This claim seems to be false, if it is saying that Wittgenstein adhered to a solipsistic model of linguistic understanding, since Wittgenstein's private language argument—widely recognized as an important, if vexing, argument—allegedly shows the necessity of intersubjectivity for the very possibility of linguistic meaning. But if the publicity or intersubjectivity of meaning is so important to Wittgenstein, how could he be charged with having failed to investigate interpretation, dialogue, and the historicity of usage?

The charge is potentially a serious one for my argument, since feminist dialogue has always been conducted in awareness of its dialogic and experimental character; being historically situated, in flux. Presumably, the interest of the *Investigations* to any radical theorist begins with its insight into the dynamically social character of meaning.

For example, feminist theorists have argued that naming is a political act.[2] This line of thought can be summarized in the following way. Naming is essentially a *social* act, one that somehow brings about not a picture of a reality that is specifiable *independently* of human communication, but rather of a reality whose durability is based upon consensual recognition. The names that we give could be said to comprise our social relations: our orientations to ourselves and others, and the orientations of social entities to the world at large. If these relations are oppressive, then the oppressed, at least, would have a stake in changing them. If these relations are embodied in linguistic practice, such change would take the form of linguistic change.

Many feminist theorists emphasize the importance of a critique of language to the feminist goal of transforming culture. Existing linguistic resources have been found to be at least inadequate, if not detrimental, to women's self-expression and communication. By some, the problem has been treated as though it is "skin deep"; a gender-neutral language can be created, through lexical adjustment, without significantly altering the conceptual resources available to us. On this view, a few terms (e.g., "sexual harassment," brought into the language in 1976, largely as a result of the work of Catherine MacKinnon) need to be introduced, a few (e.g., "hysterical") dropped or modified, and pronominal reference to persons should reflect the mixed company.[3] A problem with this approach is that it does not recognize the misogynistic assumptions built into our conceptual resources in less surgically removable ways.

A few feminist theorists, for example, Mary Daly, hold to the arguably extreme view that existing languages are "languages of the father" rather than "mother tongues," allowing expression only of misogynistic perceptions, norms, and theories.[4] A similarly radical view is held by some critics of Lacan's "phallocentric" theory of language. On these views, women's language, and thereby women's subjectivity, would need to be remade from the ground up. A problem that such views face is that the radical doubt they cast upon our existing means of expression is not clearly coherent. Such radical doubt invites the Wittgensteinian response: if the language itself is suspect, how are we to formulate the doubt? "When I talk about language (words, sentences, etc.) I must speak the language of everyday. Is this language somehow too coarse and material [alternatively, too misogynist] for what we want to say? Then how is another one to be constructed?—And how strange that we should be able to do anything at all with the one we have!" (PI, §120).

The problems faced by these two approaches—the first "shallow," the other, dogmatically radical—suggest that if the politics of naming is to be understood on a deeper level than the first, but without the skeptical absolutism of the second, a richer understanding of linguistic change is needed. But if Habermas is right, Wittgenstein's position obviates such change.

Habermas makes four charges against the theory of language that emerges in the Investigations. The first charge is (1) that Wittgenstein's conception of language games is "monadological" or "closed" (OLSS, 147). Three further charges apparently unpack the first: (2) Wittgenstein fails to recognize the "openness" of life forms to interpretation, for instance, by a participant in a differing life form (OLSS, 147–48). This challenge is significant to our inquiry if it entails that interpreting a language is nothing more than understanding that language, and that the real work of interpretation ends when one has learned a language. But this would suggest that there are no deep areas of contestation underlying usage, and that usage is universally consistent and conflict-free within a linguistic community. (3) Wittgenstein's conception of language is ahistorical and thus does not allow for linguistic change (OLSS, 149). This would imply further that language games are opaque to reflection on their roles over time, removing the significance from any critique of language.

(4) Such a rigid and "nonporous" form of linguistic practice would eradi-
cate the differences between persons, bringing about a "mute union" just
as confining as the "mute isolation" of the private language speaker
(*OLSS*, 150). This challenge is more difficult to understand, but I take it
to mean that if there is no interpretive depth or historical conflict in
linguistic practice, then the very idea of a critique of language or the
politics of naming (other than narrowly technical additions to existing
language games) must collapse altogether.

The Politics of Naming: Is It Possible?

In evaluating Habermas's argument, it would be useful to look in greater
depth at what is being said in saying that naming is political. In some
feminist discussions, the view has been expressed that the entire English
language blocks feminist expression. Suppose that the claim that these
critics of language are making is the following:

   (a) Some thoughts (propositions, and so forth) cannot be expressed
       in English.

To make sense of this claim, we would need an account of English (or
any other natural language in question) that would show that some propositions are beyond its limits of expressibility. However, as Donald Davidson has argued, this strategy seems to collapse instantly.[5] If we could show
that such propositions existed, they would already be expressible. First,
one cannot identify a proposition without stating it, and second, one
cannot show that a proposition does have sense without at the same time
providing an interpretation of it in one's own language of reference.

Davidson's argument is compelling, and it bodes ill for the view that
feminist, or any other radical, thought might take the form of a thoroughly incommensurable conceptual scheme. But why can his conclusion
be so dissatisfying to radical philosophers? One possible reason is that
people do in fact experience varying degrees of misunderstanding between one another, and some misunderstandings seem at the same time
extremely important and practically irresolvable. The philosophical conclusion that radical failures of understanding are impossible conflicts with

experience, since radical thinkers have many such experiences in the heat of political debate.

Let us try another claim:

(b) Some language games are not played in English (or any other actual natural language).

This claim, in contrast, can easily be supported by induction. For example, the language game of consciousness-raising has not always been played; the same holds for psychoanalysis, jurisprudence, psychometrics, Episcopalianism, and any other number of language games, including induction itself. As an aside, it is arguable that such novel language games can alter our self-perceptions deeply; the language of demon possession bears consequences both personal and social for its players, which would not emerge in using, say, the language of psychoanalysis. Moreover, cultural and subcultural differences between speakers of the same natural language show that some language games played by some sublinguistic communities are novel to other sublinguistic communities. It is thus reasonable to suppose that there are language games that could be played but aren't, yet, anywhere, and that there are others just now taking shape. If Wittgenstein's concept of a language game allows us to contrast actual usage with as yet unrealized language games, it could be useful in articulating the underlying philosophical commitments of the politics of naming. But we must first address a possible objection, again coming from the Davidsonian corner. Doesn't (b) entail (a), namely, that there are propositions that cannot be expressed in (today's) English?

The apparent paradox is quickly dissolved if we read (a) as being about possible usage, and its in-principle limits (which is Davidson's intention), and (b) as being about actual usage. We note that (b) is a weaker claim than (a). Nonetheless, (b) clearly allows for politically significant linguistic change, as the example of the "game" of consciousness-raising shows. But now we face another question: How does ordinary usage allow for the rise of such a game? Recalling Habermas's challenges, does the Wittgensteinian model of the language game allow for such developments?

Looking to what Wittgenstein wrote reveals there is some immediate evidence that he believed that there are new language games, as well as language games that wither away: "There are *countless* kinds [of language games]: . . . And this multiplicity is not something fixed, given once and for all; but new types of language, new language games, as we may say, come into existence, and others become obsolete and get forgotten" (*PI*, §23).

If so, however, how is such change possible? In the following section, I shall defend a view of linguistic meaning, drawing from Wittgenstein's philosophy of language and in particular his private language argument, which allows for "reformist" (in other words, not skeptical or "revolutionary") challenges to the ideological content of language. Such a view must avoid the assumption that some "standpoint outside the language" or "Archimedean point" is necessary to support the critique. To do so, I shall argue that Wittgenstein believed that some assumptions about "literal meaning" are unsupportable, and that his conception of linguistic meaning has more play in it than Habermas thinks.

Nonliteralism and Language Games

The conclusion of Wittgenstein's private language argument is widely taken to be the following:

(c) There is no fact about a speaker taken in isolation that would determine what she/he means by any sentence p; and

(d) Linguistic meaning must then necessarily be public (see for example *PI*, §202).

Item (c) reiterates the point that there is no thought or intention that is both (1) expressible privately and (2) inexpressible in public language; (d) is taken to imply that there is something essentially shared in the proper usage of an expression. This conclusion raises obvious conundrums in that it would seem there must be *something* about a speaker (for example, a "brain state") that shows she is using those rules correctly. Contemporary philosophical psychology is friendly to this view, though a "committee" view of content, such as Dennett's, or a "neural networks" view, would make what she means more fuzzy. Wittgenstein apparently would have seen this view as chimerical, since it seems to conflate the "correct" brain state for determining correct usage with the brain state that determines whether or not usage is correct, so to speak.[6] Here, however, I shall set this issue aside, and accept Wittgenstein's conclusion as a provisional assumption. I will try to show that Wittgenstein's philosophy of language allows for the kind of refashioning of language that I have alluded to earlier.

Saul Kripke argues that the publicity of language follows in Wittgenstein's argument from the *normativity* of linguistic usage, because a person's actual usage or actual linguistic dispositions alone cannot account for the fact that there is correct and incorrect usage.[7] Paul Boghossian summarizes Kripke's reading of the fulcrum of the private language argument as follows:

> If I mean something by an expression, then the potential affinity of truths that are generated as a result [of this being the case] are *normative* truths: they are truths about how I *ought* to apply the expression, if I am to apply it in accordance with its meaning, not truths about how I *will* apply it. . . . Now, this observation may be converted into a condition of adequacy on theories of meaning; any proposed candidate for being the property in virtue of which an expression has meaning must be such as to ground the normativity of meaning.[8]

If this is a suitable reading of Wittgenstein's argument, and its conclusion is sound, then it is by virtue of belonging to a linguistic community, and of relying upon the normative basis constitutive of that community, that we do know what we mean. We know what we mean precisely to the extent that we can make ourselves understood; precisely to the extent that we can communicate.

What does normativity guarantee that makes communication possible? The normativity governing linguistic usage would have to guarantee, among other things, the following:

(e) The rules of language are uniform across a community of speakers (see *PI*, §242)

(f) The rules of language are temporally stable (see *PI*, §§207–8).

Item (e) would have to obtain because any (recognized) norm must be binding, and a linguistic norm cannot be binding unless it is (more or less) uniform across speakers of the language. Item (f) would have to obtain as a precondition for (e); the rules of a language cannot be uniform across speakers of that language if their binding character is of too short a duration. But must usage be strictly uniform and unchanging across the linguistic community?

Note that *the question of whether or not* (e) and (f) *actually do obtain* is a *sociological or pragmatic matter*, and usage may conform to (e) and (f) only to varying degrees. Uniformity of usage must contain some slack, to allow for the possibility of incorrect usage, adaptation to novel circumstances, and so on. Admittedly, linguistic change in some "regions" of language, such as mathematics, occurs only in agreement with certain fundamental concepts (what counts as a function, or a space), and once the required definitions are in place usage of terms must agree completely (see *PI*, p. 226). But other regions, such as perhaps the language game of "genuine expression of feeling," evolve more chaotically, drawing heavily upon "knowledge of mankind" and "experience" (see *PI*, p. 227). Although it is true that Wittgenstein did not show much interest in such sociological niceties as dialect, linguistic syncretism, and so on, it is not evident that he intended to rule out "narrow streets" and a proliferation of variously disciplined "suburbs" (*PI*, §18). Moreover, the makeup of Wittgenstein's "city" is not only variegated, as Habermas concedes, but also historically layered. This passage implies that it is *never* clear that a language is either complete (a finished product) or incomplete. (Indeed, could the Wittgenstein of the *Investigations* imagine such a thing as a complete language?) Finally, Wittgenstein explicitly acknowledges the possibility that novel language games evolve from current practice.

> New types of language, new language games, as we may say, come into existence and others become obsolete and forgotten. (*PI*, §23)

> We remain unconscious of the prodigious diversity of all the everyday language games because the clothing of our language makes everything alike. Something new (spontaneous, 'specific') is always a language game. (*PI*, p. 224)

The normativity that binds usage is not, in other words, a fixed, well-bounded entity. Actual usage can survive, in Wittgenstein's view, with some play, variety and indefiniteness or awkwardness about the edges. Furthermore, in comparing natural language to the ideal language of logic, Wittgenstein remarks that the rules of application for any language game are only indefinitely bounded. There are "holes" in language games, which leave correct usage in part an open matter and where uniformity fades into spontaneity. "It is only in normal cases that the use of a word is clearly prescribed. . . . The more abnormal the case, the more doubtful it becomes what we are to say" (*PI*, §142).

But if the use of a sentence is partly unregulated, how can it have any meaning at all? Wittgenstein presents this objection to himself in section 99:

> The sense of a sentence—one would like to say—may, of course, leave this or that open, but the sentence must nevertheless have a definite sense. An indefinite sense—that would really not be a sense at *all*.—This is like: An indefinite boundary is not really a boundary at all. Here one thinks perhaps; if I say "I have locked the man up fast in the room—there is only one door left open"— then I simply haven't locked him in at all; his being locked in is a sham. One would be inclined to say here: "You haven't done anything at all." An enclosure with a hole in it is as good as *none*.—But is that true? (*PI*, §99; see also §§68–77)

In response, Wittgenstein challenges the assumption that language must be "crystalline," "pure," "super-ordered" (an ordering of something that is already in order, as it is), its usage closed to change or variation (*PI*, §97). Wittgenstein argues that language games are already in order as they are; to suppose that a language game might itself stand in need of ordering by a further, perfect game is to misunderstand its nature. The ideal of a perfect language is itself a language game, one among many:

> "But still, it isn't a game, if there is some vagueness *in the rules*,"— But *does* this prevent its being a game?—"Perhaps you'll call it a game, but at any rate it certainly isn't a perfect game." This means: it has impurities, and what I am interested in at present is the pure article.—But I want to say: we misunderstand the role of the ideal in our language. That is to say: we too should call it a game, only we are dazzled by the ideal and therefore fail to see the actual use of the word "game" clearly. (*PI*, §100)

Habermas's mistake, I think, lies in his reading Wittgenstein as a "literalist"—as holding the view that terms have one and only one "literal meaning," and that the normativity of language is strictly universal and stable over time. I have tried to show that Wittgenstein held a "nonliteralist" position on meaning. I must be cautious in using this nomenclature, however, since it is clear that Wittgenstein believed in literal meanings to the extent that there are distinctions between correct and incorrect usage. For this reason, I think it's wrong to attribute to Wittgenstein the view that meaning is a chimera, as Boghossian, for example, has found in Kripke's reading of the private language argument.[9] The nonliteralism I have in mind can be expressed as a joint assertion:

(c) There is no fact about a speaker taken in isolation that would determine what she/he means by a sentence p; and
(d) Language must then necessarily be public; and
(g) The uniformity and stability of the rules of language partly fail.

This position neither holds that meaning is uniform and fixed nor that meaning is a complete mystery. As long as it is recognized that it is the (albeit unbounded) normativity of a public language that keeps its meaningfulness in place, rather than prelinguistic intentions or dispositions of speakers, no puzzle presents itself. However, Wittgensteinian nonliteralism does entail that the normative requirements on literal meanings (or ordinary usage)—in other words, that they are uniform and stable—hold only incompletely. If those meanings are not completely determined by states of the isolated speaker, then they are, to the extent that public language leaves them indefinite, unbounded, in flux. It is the partial *failure* of (e) and (f) at any given time in any given natural language that allows for, and indeed motivates, the emergence of new language games and the critique of existing ones.

Before turning to the question of how these developments might find use in feminist linguistic practice, I will quickly address another reading of Wittgenstein's private language argument, which Paul Boghossian has found in Kripke's reading of the private language argument: that Wittgenstein was committed to "semantic irrealism."[10] Semantic (or content) irrealism is the view that there simply is no fact, of any kind, that would determine what I mean, or in other words, that meaning is fundamentally indeterminate, both in private and in public, so to speak. Intension is merely apparent—like the offerings of Descartes's evil demon.

Whether or not this reading of Wittgenstein is correct (it probably isn't), the view that content is radically indeterminate (in other words,

that there is no certainty of any kind about what a person means by [p])
may seem attractive for political reasons, in that it allows us to explain
the experiences of radical misunderstanding alluded to earlier. For example, women have commonly had the experience of being held, sometimes
violently, to interpretations of their words that "are not what they
meant," while finding it difficult to communicate what it is that they did
mean to the person threatening them. This theme emerges frequently in
the work of Luce Irigaray, who apparently responds with the view, I think
disastrously, that women's thought is always elusive. There is at least a
kernel of truth—also elusive—to Irigaray's intuition, however: some of us
find ourselves thinking that we meant something else indeed, but are at
a loss to say much more than, say, "It's not quite what you'd ordinarily
mean by (p)." The relevant worry is that "ordinary" ("androcentric")
psychological and behavioral explanations might, by their very nature,
distort or otherwise fail to allow expression of female experience (for
example, for any sexual act involving a female, she wanted it; if she is
critical of a man, then she hates men). Thus it might be tempting to
suppose that all content- or meaning-ascriptions to women or by women
to themselves in the available language are either false or chimerical.
However, even the political implications of this view of content surely go
too far, since they cut both ways, depriving any speaker of authority over
what she, or he, meant at any point in time. Once again the problem is
unavoidable: if the entire language throws female experience into
shadow, then from what direction is the light to be brought to the caves?

Nonetheless, there is something worth investigating in another, perhaps less problematic, suggestion that might be made here; namely, that
there are gender-specific language games. There is nothing technically
problematic about this suggestion for Wittgenstein, since he recognizes
the existence of indefinitely many "subcultures" of language. I will pursue
this suggestion next.

Feminist Theory and Wittgensteinian Nonliteralism

The feminist practice of naming our own experience might well be regarded as an emergent language game. However, it is one that appears,
on the face of it, to presume the existence of idiosyncratic, prelinguistic,
previously inexpressible content, and thus to rub against the grain of the

private language argument. Naming our experience can be likened to what in philosophical psychology would be called content *self*-ascription—attributing a thought, belief, or desire, among other things, to oneself. But Wittgenstein insists that there is no fact *about the individual alone* regarding what one privately thinks or feels. If by "naming our own experience" we mean that we find words, for the first time, to name previously unspoken experiences—experiences previously not on the consensual psychic map—then surely Wittgenstein's views run afoul of this practice.

But just as surely, Wittgenstein allows that content self-ascription is a language game. Numerous passages in the *Investigations* and other later writings such as the *Remarks on Psychology* refer to the language games of sensation, pain, fear, grief, and joy; and of wishing, willing, thinking, believing, and knowing. These discussions deal in the attribution of such states not only to others but also to ourselves. If, as I argued earlier, the *Investigations* does support linguistic change, and it also supports content self-ascription, it would naturally support *innovative* content self-ascription. If so, then how does critique emerge in a linguistic community in which the language game of content self-ascription includes, for example, the female gender-specific rule "blame yourself for everything that goes wrong?"

It is with respect to the question of political critique that Wittgenstein's relative silence about conflict and misunderstanding looms large. That he is silent on the social dimensions of linguistic experimentation in general is odd, given that consequences in this direction would seem to be the among the most interesting entailments of his approach to language and thought. Unfortunately, Wittgenstein's rare remarks about new language games are spare, and mention of conflict between players of the "same" language games is even rarer. But since Wittgenstein explicitly adheres to the view that linguistic practice is not completely uniform and stable, and this entails that his view is consistent with political linguistic critique as well as other kinds of experimentation, his theory is quite hospitable to the possibility of a female-specific language game such as "naming our own experience."

To a certain extent, Wittgenstein seemed to regard as obvious the possibility that a given language game might only be available to or played by a distinctly qualified subclass of speakers in a linguistic community. He quite clearly allows for the possibility of a proliferation of distinct technical languages spoken only by specialists, for example. In his metaphor of the city, he likens chemistry and calculus to distinct suburbs. Certainly, not everyone plays these games (occupies, or is able to navigate, these suburbs). Furthermore, he doesn't seem to think that speculating about the shape that novel language games might take is conceptually irresponsible or, in principle, off limits. In the section following the city metaphor, he declares the ease of imagining a language "consisting only of questions and expressions for answering yes or no," and lyrically remarks that "to imagine a language means to imagine a form of life" (*PI*, §19; see also §23, cited earlier.) It is important to note, however, that he does not picture such specialized language games as incommensurable with one another, in the sense that a player of one could not possibly play another. It is quite clearly a corollary of the private language argument that any language game is learnable; access to any language game is in principle open to all.

Mathematics, one of Wittgenstein's own favorite linguistic regions, offers at least one interesting case for our consideration of gender-specific language games. To see it properly, we need to historicize mathematics (a move that is, as I have argued, unproblematically Wittgensteinian); that is, to look at it as an evolving language game.

An early nineteenth-century French gentlewoman named Sophie Germain was awarded the *prix extraordinaire* by the Institut de France for her work in mathematics. Among other things, she shared her ideas with Karl Gauss, who is known for his work in developing non-Euclidean geometry. In 1806, Gauss wrote to her:

> [T]he charms of [the mysteries of numbers] in all their beauty reveal themselves *only to those who have the courage to fathom them* [italics mine]. But when a woman, because of her sex, our customs and prejudices, encounters infinitely more obstacles than men in familiarizing herself with their knotty problems, yet overcomes these fetters and penetrates that which is most hidden, she doubtless has the most noble courage, extraordinary talent, and superior genius.[11]

What is interesting about this excerpt is that it illustrates a challenge to one of the most sacred "rules" of the language game of mathematics: that all mathematical geniuses must be male. Indeed, the rules of this game determine that mathematical genius is inherently *masculine*, precisely because, as Gauss observes, its true nature is *courageous*. A woman might aspire to understand the intricacies of these knotty problems, but daring to bend the very axioms to her will, so to speak, would violate some very deep taboos against women's intellectual freedom.

Germain continued to correspond with Gauss, even writing to him for a while after he stopped responding. It cannot but have profoundly affected her, intellectually, that she was so excluded from the exchange of ideas; that no one could talk to her, except as a gentlewoman. Intellectual historians Louis Bucciarelli and Nancy Dworsky remark of her that "[e]very conversation was a formal social event requiring letters of invitation, planning for transportation, requests for permission. Sophie Germain could not stop to chat with friends at meetings of the Institut nor get into serious conversation over cigars and brandy after dinner."[12] The obstacles to thought, and even more so to complete intellectual achievement, posed by social prohibitions against women freethinkers, are still formidable today. By bringing these "rules"—which amount to little more than primitive taboos—to light, however, women are beginning to break their grip on the boundaries of consensual reality.

I have argued that Wittgenstein's theory of language countenances the possibility of gender-specific language games, that such language games do in fact exist, and that insofar as they are obstacles to expression, they are natural targets for revisionist energies. How deeply can revisions be planned? Wittgenstein himself would probably reject this question as unanswerable. His city metaphor appears to suggest that natural languages are "built" around an ancient "center," which, although it is chaotic—a jumble of alleys and squares—remains unchanged, and functions as the point of reference for more peripheral additions. This could be taken as suggesting that there is a "core" of any language in which everyone communicates in the same patterns, regardless of gender, race, or class. Would this entail that the languages of radical theory have to "flee to the suburbs," to recognize some logical or conceptual sine qua non of language? Presumably, the purpose of a radical critique of language is not to construct a "cantonement" at the outer reaches of the metropolis, "for radicals only." Stretching the metaphor, a radical transformation of language might be likened instead to an urban renewal project; the planting of gardens and boulevards, the expansion of public space and public services, and so on. Although the *Rathhaus* and *Stadtsopernhaus* (like the ancient words in the language) remain standing, their uses may be subject to dispute, and their functions and relative importance may shift considerably. One could liken the divide between gender-specific language games to a citywide debate over the uses of and access to urban space; about which neighborhoods (language games) to target for renewal.

Not wanting to rest my case on, or pin Wittgenstein to, the metaphor alone, let us consider the point in terms of language games new and old. The emergence of a new language game may exert varying influences upon other linguistic practices. Possibly, some new language games leave the rest of linguistic practice virtually unchanged (say, developments in nonlinear topology), at least for the while. Others, however, might immediately give rise to disturbances, by generating misunderstanding, say, or upsetting social routines or rituals, or running afoul of someone's heretofore unquestioned assumptions. Conceivably, such disturbances might provide rich grounds for linguistic experimentation and critique.

For example, suppose there were a rule for the content self-ascription of anger, applying only to women, which required that hysteria be self-ascribed anytime anger is self-ascribed. Suppose further the existence of a complementary rule applying only to men, ascribing reasonable grounds along with any self-ascription of anger. As long as these gender-specific rules were consistently applied, they arguably could, conceivably, exist as perfectly good Wittgensteinian language games. Wittgenstein quite explicitly denied the existence of any a priori or rationalist constraints on language games. More important, the apparent irrationality of this pair of rules, taken out of context, fades into normality once we recall the countless other class-specific rules of deference and authority that we call upon every day. In other words, the lack of reasonableness about a language game doesn't preclude its being perfectly normal.

Suppose, finally, that this state of normalcy were to be challenged, and the pair of complementary rules articulated. This could happen in any number of ways, slowly or quickly, as a result of confusion or of concentrated analysis. For a while, interactions would be disturbed in new ways as women questioned whether recognition of anger entailed a confession of madness in the pathological sense, or men were to question whether recognition of anger entailed recognition of violated rights. These disturbances would not merely be a matter of upset routine. Far more interesting, they would locate adjustments occurring in the web of belief concerning the distinction between reason and insanity, and the nature of human rights, respectively. The latter language games, call them the language games of rationality and rights, are certainly near the "core" of the language if any of them are. And yet it is not at all difficult to see how a challenge to an apparently trivial ritual of emotional management ("don't mind my rage, it must be my period, and so forth") might lead to challenges to fundamental assumptions about social status.

I have argued that Wittgenstein's concept of a language game opens up a useful vocabulary for formulating ideas about the nature of feminist linguistic critique, without imposing any obvious barriers to the possibility of such critique. I have done so by way of arguing that Habermas's four challenges to Wittgenstein are off the mark: Wittgenstein's conception of language is neither ahistorical nor closed to change, and thus it does not entail that to share a language is to be conceptually regimented or homogeneous. Instead, I have argued, Wittgenstein rejected one or two rather simple assumptions about public usage, neither of them anywhere near self-evident, which I have called "literalism." However, I think, Habermas is on the right track about the importance to liberation movements of close scrutiny of the unwritten rules of deference and dominance encoded in communicative practice. His own confidence in the vitality and creativity of human communication, and the longing for freedom it expresses, probably exceeds Wittgenstein's, though I won't try to argue this here.

Notes

1. Jürgen Habermas, *On the Logic of the Social Sciences*, trans. Shierry Weber Nicholsen and Jerry Stark (Cambridge: MIT Press, 1988), 146–50. Hereafter this work is referred to as *OLSS*. Unless otherwise specified, all Wittgenstein citations are from Ludwig Wittgenstein, *Philosophical Investigations* (New York: Macmillan, 1958), referred to as *PI* followed by section number.

2. One of the most substantive defenses of the politics of naming, also drawing from Wittgenstein, is Naomi Scheman's "Anger and the Politics of Naming," in her *Engenderings: Constructions of Knowledge, Authority, and Privilege* (New York: Routledge Press, 1993), 22–35.

3. MacKinnon herself endorses a more radical conception of feminist linguistic critique.

4. See, e.g., Mary Daly and Jane Caputi, *Websters' First New Intergalactic Wickedary of the English Language* (Boston: Beacon Press, 1987).

5. See Donald Davidson, "On the Very Idea of a Conceptual Scheme," in *Inquiries into Truth and Interpretation* (Oxford: Oxford University Press, 1984), 184–98.

6. Naomi Scheman has defended this extension of Wittgenstein's position.

7. Saul Kripke, *Wittgenstein on Rules and Private Language* (Cambridge: Harvard University Press, 1982).

8. Paul Boghossian, "Rule-Following Considerations," *Mind* 98, no. 392 (1989): 509.

9. Kripke, *Wittgenstein on Rules*.

10. See Kripke, *Wittgenstein on Rules*; and also Paul Boghossian, "The Status of Content," *Philosophical Review* 99, no. 2 (1990): 168.

11. Louis Bucciarelli and Nancy Dworsky, *Sophie Germain: An Essay on the History of the Theory of Elasticity* (Dordrecht: D. Reidel, 1980), 30. As cited in Margaret Alic, *Hypatia's Heritage* (Boston: Beacon Press, 1986), 149–50.

12. Ibid., 150.

Section III

Drawing Boundaries:
Categories and Kinds

9

"Back to the Rough Ground!": Wittgenstein, Essentialism, and Feminist Methods

Cressida J. Heyes

Philosophical Investigations (In a Feminist Voice)

And we extend our concept of number as in spinning a thread we twist fibre on fibre. And the strength of the thread does not reside in the fact that some one fibre runs through its whole length, but in the overlapping of many fibres.

—Ludwig Wittgenstein, *Philosophical Investigations*

1. Let us consider the construct that we call "women." I don't just mean white, middle-class, heterosexual, able-bodied, young, attractive, western

women, but all women. What is common to them all? Don't say: "There must be something in common or they wouldn't be called 'women.'" Likewise, don't ask: "If women have nothing in common, then how can feminism form a political movement?" Look and see what the construct of women consists of, and what women might have in common. For if you look, you will not see something that is common to all, but similarities, relationships, and a whole series of them at that. Look, for example, at heterosexual women. They are attracted to, and may form sexual relationships with, men. Now pass to bisexual women: some features drop out and others appear! Think now of a woman of color (if you haven't already). How is she like a white woman? And what is the relationship of a Jewish lesbian to a straight Chicana? Does a poor woman in England have anything in common with a wealthy one in South Africa? "And the result of this examination is: we see a complicated network of similarities overlapping and criss-crossing: sometimes overall similarities, sometimes similarities of detail."[1]

2. Furthermore, even when I talk about one woman, it is not correct to find the logical sum of these individual interrelated concepts: if I am white, anglophone, middle class, young . . . , then the concept of "me" is not an additive product of these different parts (*PI*, §68). I cannot abstract from the rest that part of me that is race, that which is sexuality, and so on. (Yet obviously I can still *use* the concept of myself.) Likewise, when I compare myself to a woman of color, whom I resemble in many other respects, I cannot say "add some color, and we are the same."

3. "So how can you talk about 'women' at all?" Well, when I talk about them, I give examples that I intend to be taken in a particular way, so that they may be *used* (in the game of politics perhaps). The danger of this is that we may not recognize that these are just examples and not an ideal, an inexpressible common thing that represents all women. For what does the mental picture of a woman look like when it does not show us any particular image, but what is common to all women? I think that if you see *women* in a certain light you will use the term in a certain way, and because your account does not apply to all women, but only to those you are thinking of, in using an ideal, you will be guilty of a generalization that is quite unjustified. "The idea now absorbs us, that the ideal '*must*' be found in reality. Meanwhile we do not as yet see *how* it occurs

there, nor do we understand the nature of this 'must.' We think it must be in reality; for we think we already see it there" (*PI*, §101).

4. "So what is the purpose of this ideal, if it is not found in reality?" In this case, the ideal comes to serve a political purpose for you, as my examples serve my political purposes. The ideal woman can be held up as a metaphysical necessity that comes to legislate my identity. So when we identify similarities and differences, we must be quite clear that this is a pragmatic exercise: "How should we explain to someone what a game is? I imagine that we should describe *games* to him, and we might add: "This *and similar things* are called 'games'" (*PI*, §69).

5. "But if you are a feminist, then you need to make generalizations about women, for this is the essence of feminist politics!" Exactly. I have never denied that. When I look around a classroom, for example, I see women having common experiences of being excluded and trivialized. But that is not to say that even we are all the same. I can draw a boundary around us, for a special purpose. (Perhaps I want to show you something.)

6. The ideal becomes an empty notion, which muddles me, and prevents me from seeing what I have to do. What feminist action should I take if I am pursuit of a chimera? We have taken out all the substance of *women*, and are left with a vacuous concept: "we have got onto slippery ice where there is no friction and so in a certain sense the conditions are ideal, but also, just because of that, we are unable to walk. We want to walk: so we need *friction*. Back to the rough ground!" (*PI*, §107).

7. Sometimes you draw a boundary around concepts to use them yourself. (This may be called a stereotype.) What matters is that you look and see whether or not you have drawn the boundary self-consciously. Sometimes the boundary is oppressive; sometimes it acts as an object of comparison: "For we can avoid ineptness or emptiness in our assertions only be presenting the model as what it is, as an object of comparison—as, so to speak, a measuring-rod; not as a preconceived idea to which reality *must* correspond. (The dogmatism into which we fall so easily in doing philosophy.)" (*PI*, §131).

8. But now you will say: "This is nonsense. All women do have something in common; namely, their bodies. Do you want to deny that?" All right,

the concept of "women" is bounded for you by the physical reality of sexed existence. It need not be so. You have given the physical character of "women" particular limits, but I can use the term so that its extension is not closed by the same frontier.

9. This much I will allow you: some aspects of male and female bodies are different. But why have we drawn the most important boundaries there? Why do we not draw them around other differences between us? Certainly it matters that some women menstruate, have breasts, vaginas, bear children. But do all women share these features? And how will we describe them? The physical boundaries of gender are elective foundations, supported by the walls of social practice. The discourse we weave around our bodies is what creates what we think of as a reality in correspondence with nature.

10. So now you agree: "bodies don't matter" (on this I am still only partly in agreement) and ask again, "if even bodies aren't simply 'real,' how is the social construct of 'women' bounded?" By a set of rules that regulate it very well, yet that leave some gaps.

11. "*Essence* is expressed by grammar" (*PI*, §371). The category of "women" has been confirmed by language—such as the gendered pronouns some languages use to divide the world in two. This obscures the contingency of that division and leads us to assign it more importance than we otherwise might: "Philosophy is a battle against the bewitchment of our intelligence by means of language" (*PI*, §109).

12. The category of sex is created and defined by a fluid boundary. For what matters about being a woman? Look and see. We can claim things in common, such as perhaps motherhood, or sexuality, or emotional sensibilities, but that is not to say that we will all, always, have these things in common. I use my own experience to find out what the women I know have in common. The construction of gender identity is a complex thing, and it varies among people; that is to say, it is mutable. (We have approached the problem from the other side, and now we know our way about!): "One might say that the concept 'game' is a concept with blurred edges.—'But is a blurred concept a concept at all'—Is an indistinct photograph a picture of a person at all? Is it even always an advantage to replace an indistinct picture by a sharp one? Isn't the indistinct one often

exactly what we need?" (*PI*, §71). So, perhaps we don't need to specify what the concept "women" is at all. In fact, specifying might not be to our advantage. Rather we need to take the longer path toward discovering who we are, and who we are not.

And we extend our concept of women as in spinning a thread we twist fiber on fiber. And the strength of the thread does not reside in the fact that some one fiber runs through its whole length, but in the overlapping of many fibers.

• • •

Wittgenstein, Essentialism, and Feminist Theory

What does the preceding Wittgensteinian conversation tell us about feminist theory? First, it elaborates a familiar stalemate: namely, that any feminist theory that tries to incorporate the multiplicity of differences among women will not be able to make the generalizations required for feminist politics. This leaves feminist theory trapped between an acute gender skepticism and the use of crude and exclusive generalizations. Much of the debate around this dichotomy has focused on "essentialism" as a central term of critical analysis that allegedly defines the latter position. These polar accounts are sometimes presented as the only options for feminists, yet by inquiring both into meaning and into feminist method, a Wittgensteinian feminist critique of essentialism helps us to locate ourselves outside the terms of the dichotomy. In this essay I use my own "Philosophical Investigations" to show how to continue with feminist theory and practice without falling into the methodological traps commonly labeled "essentialism." I argue that by paying close attention to Wittgenstein's remarks in a central section of his *Philosophical Investigations* (roughly §§66–131), we can undermine the theoretical bases of essentialism through his challenge to one traditional philosophical picture that "holds us captive."

I proceed by briefly locating Wittgenstein's critique of essentialism, before showing how it connects to feminist antiessentialism, offering a solution to certain methodological problems within feminist theory. In particular, I present an articulation of the connection between Wittgenstein's notion of family resemblance, on the one hand, and problematic forms of essentialism with regard to the category "women," on the other. I indicate how this relates to Elizabeth Spelman's analysis in *Inessential Woman*, and point out how Wittgenstein's arguments for purposive boundary-drawing and his notion of "objects of comparison" provide insight into contemporary feminist theorizing about sex and gender identities, making the case that conceptual delimiting is a matter of political strategy, not of ontological necessity.[2] Finally, I indicate that Wittgenstein's injunction to "look and see" might constitute more than a mere slogan for feminist social theory, and I outline the contours of a feminist method that offers a way to go on using antiessentialist insights. Wittgenstein's skepticism toward theory moves our attention away from the "problem of difference" as a philosophical trope, toward normative questions about feminist practice. If we accept the Wittgensteinian argument that meaning is constructed through, rather than prior to, our use of language, then an antiessentialist method must look at the deployments of the term *women* and their political implications.

Wittgenstein's conception of essentialism was primarily linguistic, his targets being contemporary philosophy of language, logic, and metaphysics. He viewed essentialism as a linguistic phenomenon entailed by the claim that members of a particular class share a common key property by virtue of their common name. He rejects the notion of a single "essence" to these classes, where *essence* implies a statement of the necessary and sufficient conditions for the application of a particular term. Wittgenstein conceives many of the linguistic "mistakes" associated with essentialism as arising from misguided metaphysical assumptions.[3] He thus seeks to undermine linguistic essentialism by challenging both an account of language whereby terms refer to things existing as "natural kinds" in the world, and the belief, in its various forms, that meaning emerges prior to the use of language. He raises two implicit objections to linguistic essentialism: first, that it relies on *a priorism* at the expense of empirical inquiry, and second, that linguistic essentialism is a theory that does not reflect our actual use of language.

General claims made about women that are based on the experience of only some women often exhibit the same *a priorism* and failure to examine empirical evidence that Wittgenstein criticized. An essentialist ontology that takes the use of the word *women* to represent a collection of people with specified characteristics existing prior to the application of the term erases both the diversity of women and the fact that women's identities as women emerge from their particular social locations. Thus linguistic essentialism encourages us to assume, on the one hand, that all women are women by virtue of fulfilling a finite set of necessary and sufficient conditions, thereby inviting the assumption that the word *woman* describes merely an instance of these general conditions.

It also obscures the varied contexts of the social construction of gender identity, encouraging feminists to posit a general definitional account of *women* that is allegedly specific to no particular woman. Not only is this latter story epistemologically problematic in Wittgensteinian terms, but also it is susceptible to sustained feminist political critique. Numerous feminists have pointed out that many putatively general accounts of women's oppression reflect only the experiences and identities of those women with power over the construction of theory. In the absence of linguistic and methodological essentialisms, there is no reason to suppose that the experiences of some women can represent those of all women, and the picture that has held (some of) us captive is revealed as a political strategy rather than "the truth about women."

Additive Analyses and Family Resemblances

Spelman criticizes essentializing generalizations in feminist theory and in so doing employs an approach that is implicitly Wittgensteinian. An explicit rendering of the connections between *Inessential Woman* and the *Philosophical Investigations* offers a powerful language for navigating our way out of the labyrinths she describes. Wittgenstein articulates an anti-essentialist method more scrupulously than Spelman, gives a more detailed sense of how the philosophical "therapy" works, and demonstrates how to go on, given the recognition of essentialist errors. Most notably, Wittgenstein's concept of family resemblances is an alternative to certain kinds of mistaken additive analyses (the phenomenon Spelman criticizes). Rather than offering an account of the linguistic essence of any particular term, he points to a variety of connected ways the term is used in language, none of which is definitive (*PI*, §§65–67). If we adopt the notion that women bear family resemblances to one another, we can avoid a misleading ontology that sets up mutually exclusive, bounded categories.

Recognizing the limitations of such categories leads to two ontological questions about political identity: first, how, if at all, can (or should) we justify the subsumption of some characteristics under others (for example, by stressing the primacy of gender in explaining oppression)? Second, can (or should) we separate one characteristic from others (for example, by claiming that all women share certain experiences that are "the same" regardless of their race and class)? Spelman develops an analysis of the former question using an analogical argument about proceeding through labeled "doors." For example, if we choose to classify people (by ask-ing—or requiring—them to walk through the doors into separate rooms) as either "women" or "men" and thereafter as "homosexual" or "hetero-sexual" (all problematic categories in any case), then we end up with categories prioritizing gender, and lesbians and gay men appear to have less in common than if we had first ordered people according to sexual identity, and then gender. This illustrates the problems inherent in both the very possibility of subsuming some characteristics under others, and in the decision-making processes that build and order the doors. With regard to the second question, Spelman argues that no individual should be conceptualized merely as the sum of discrete elements of her identity, be these race, gender, class, sexuality, or any of a host of self-defining characteristics that are more or less important to a person's description of herself. Thus, just as the concept of a game is not expressed by some bounded and essentialist definition, but rather is developed through mul-tiple uses of the term, so it is metaphysically misguided (albeit often politically expedient) to treat personal identity as conveniently com-pound. Spelman is concerned primarily with revealing essentialist prac-tices, and pointing out how in fact we are often required to categorize ourselves and others in ways that both establish and reinforce certain similarities and differences.

On this account there need be no definitive set of characteristics that all women share, but rather we can understand ourselves as connected to one another by a network of overlapping similarities, some of which may be biological—such as breasts, a vagina, a uterus, the capacity to conceive and bear a child and XX chromosomes; others of which may be more obviously socially constructed—such as a particular relation to one's mother, ethical attitudes, experiences of subordination, and so on. But no characteristic is necessary to make an individual a woman, and none is sufficient. Thus, on this view, it is perfectly possible to make sense of the fact that two "distantly related" individuals can both be women and share none of the same characteristics except that they are called "women." A male-to-female transsexual woman, for example, might have XY chromosomes, experience of being raised as a boy in a white, urban bourgeois nuclear family, and conventionally feminine self-presentation. A butch woman might have XX chromosomes, experience of being raised "as a girl" by lesbian parents in a small northern community, and conventionally masculine self-presentation. On my Wittgensteinian-feminist view, it is not "wrong" to call them both "women" even though they do not share any common features potentially definitive of womanhood. This is not to suggest that linguistic usage can never be changed (the argument commonly leveled against Wittgenstein's account of meaning as use). In what follows, I develop the feminist possibilities for this view of language in the context of the need both to change conventional sexist meanings and to offer justifications for political decisions about inclusion and exclusion.

Wittgenstein anticipates several objections to these considerations, all of which are helpful for my antiessentialist feminism. First, he argues that all instances of concepts such as "game" (or, we might add, "women") do not have a disjunctive shared property—some characteristic(s) we can identify as being common to all games—but rather the common term gathers together multiple instances that have overlapping similarities. Our attempts to find common properties are examples of our being led astray by the single word that links these family resemblances. Second, a concept is not the logical sum of subconcepts, each of which can be rigidly defined—board games, card games, Olympic games, and so on—since we can, and often do, use it in a way that is not bounded. That is, we invent new games, or make the case that something not previously thought of as a game should be included in that concept. Wittgenstein rejects the idea that a concept without rigid boundaries is useless, and he shows us a variety of ways in which we use concepts despite the openness of their frontiers. Thus explanation of a particular phenomenon by example is not necessarily subsequent to explanations that posit essences, but rather may be a better strategy for articulating the use of a particular term.

This attack on linguistic essentialism has important implications for feminism. It provides an alternative ontology that sidesteps the view that there is an essential womanness, separable from class, race, and other contexts, that all women share. This approach also sidesteps the ontological (if not the political) need to have people pass through classifications of the sort Spelman describes. However, we can still use the term *women*, make generalizations about women, and engage in feminist politics. Wittgenstein's notion of family resemblances offers not only a supplementary ontological critique of essentialist practices, but also a solution—a new way of thinking about the similarities and differences among people. Of course, to describe women as bearing family resemblances to one another only constitutes an ontological therapy, or a way of freeing ourselves from the misleading philosophical picture that holds us captive, not necessarily a riposte to those (myself included) who see political reasons for positing gender commonality. It does, however, reveal these reasons as purposive rather than predetermined, and therefore as carrying a concomitant demand for justification.

The way the stale debate surrounding essentialisms in feminist theory "holds us captive" is similar to the problems that the *Philosophical Investigations* sets out not to solve, but to dispel. Feminists of many kinds seek a way of thinking—a philosophical imagination—that embraces plurality, starting from the realities of women's lives, not from the exigencies of a theory unselfconsciously trapped in essentialism. Wittgenstein's later work is one of the most profound modern sources of skepticism toward "philosophy" for its detachment from the world, offering a critique of theory that resonates with much contemporary feminist writing. A Wittgensteinian feminist view does not preclude, however, a kind of philosophy that attempts a careful picking apart of damaging philosophical pictures, and a better kind of thinking that recognizes its own location. It is impossible to imagine a world without theory, in the broadest sense of the term, where people did not inquire into different conceptualizations and seek to explain a variety of events within a single framework. This process itself is rightly prized, moreover, as one of the attributes of a self-determining individual or community.

The focus on essentialism as a *theoretical* problem is nonetheless an example of the kind of philosophy that Wittgenstein's critique is directed against. To talk about essentialism as a purely ontological or linguistic problem can be a distancing strategy, a way of removing oneself from the particular and focusing on the general. Echoing Wittgenstein's remark, "instead of 'craving for generality' I could also have said 'the contemptuous attitude towards the particular case,'"[4] "theory" undermines specificity, not only by denying difference in language, but in reality. María Lugones pinpoints this sentiment:

> The white woman theorist did not notice us yet, her interpretation of the question placed the emphasis on theorizing itself, and the generalizing and theorizing impulse led the white theorizer to

think of all differences as the same, that is, as underminers of the truth, force, or scope of their theories. Here racism has lost its character and particular importance—a clear sign that we have not been noticed. This trick does not allow the theorizer to see, for example, the need to differentiate among racism, colonialism, and imperialism, three very different interactive phenomena.[5]

The verbal sameness of the term *difference* and the multitude of arguments feminists have advanced under its banner again direct attention to linguistic uniformity rather than to the many political issues surrounding "different differences" that exist in real lives. A philosophy of generality serves to delegitimate the needs of particular women. If we have a simple theory that explains sexism in one tidy slogan, then why look for different realities? The most crucial lesson is that the prerogative to define identity is not equally shared. Decisions about which similarities are to count (and which differences really don't matter) are usually made by those with the most power.

Line Drawings

Apart from looking at diversity within the group usually referred to as "women," we can challenge essentialism by examining some attempts to defy conventional boundaries around the term. In locating feminist theorists between methodological essentialism and principled antiessentialism, a Wittgensteinian approach gives us reason to see the decisions we make about definitions as deeply political. In Wittgenstein's remarks on the possibilities of setting the boundary of a concept in many different places, and further on the need to set a boundary at all, I see radical possibilities for feminism. It might initially seem as if I am ignoring my own advice and using philosophy to obscure biological difference, if the word *women* actually corresponds to the category of women bounded by the physical reality of the female body. Indeed we do need to recognize the reality and significance of biology, not as presocial or extralinguistic "facts" about chromosomes or genitalia, but as lived experience of embodiment with politically significant cultural meaning. Others have argued in more detail that the female body has been erased both from canonical political theory and from certain feminist theories, and that both feminist and nonfeminist discourses make uncritical assumptions about the natural reality and necessity of sexual dimorphism.[6] Simultaneously afraid that our bodies would be erased, or that we would be reduced to our bodies, or that our bodies would overdetermine our selves, we have struggled with how to locate the sexed body in feminist philosophy.

The specific contribution of a Wittgensteinian feminism to these debates lies in the argument that where we draw the boundary around the category "women" constitutes a political act, which should be scrutinized for its particular purpose, no less when biological characteristics feature on one side or the other of the boundary. "To repeat, we can draw a boundary—for a special purpose. Does it take that to make the concept usable? Not at all! (Except for that special purpose.)" (PI, §69). Thus feminists can aim for semantic influence over the category of "women" and redefine its boundaries with the explicit acknowledgment that this is a political activity (not an unproblematically "objective" scientific or medical one) within which power differentials affect the semantic authority of the participants, including different women.

Perhaps we can also take up the Wittgensteinian notion of foundations as axes: "I do not explicitly learn the propositions that stand fast for me. I can discover them subsequently like the axis around which a body rotates. This axis is not fixed in the sense that anything holds it fast, but the movement around it determines its immobility."[7] If we posit "women" as that bounded group of people held in place on its axis by various popular, medical, and scientific discourses, not fixed in the sense that a preexisting reality "holds it fast," we can also see how adding feminist challenges to "the movement around" women might lead to a further displacement of those who are accepted as women, by way of an alteration in the meaning of that term.

Such methodological possibilities for the subversion of sex and gender identities form a key part of undermining simplistic and rigidly imposed binary definitions of women and men—an integral part of the task of any feminist theory. If we agree that gender is a social construct, then there is no reason why it need reflect a binary sex distinction. The notion that male and female bodies create two discrete groups that are "bounded" obscures the fact that we almost never identify an individual's gender by unequivocal reference to primary or even secondary sexual characteristics (except, crucially, at birth, although even then intersexed infants can cause discursive chaos), although these characteristics usually are posited as the "cause" of gender identity.[8] In fact, physical gender cues can be overridden to a remarkable degree by social context.[9]

So in what ways can we challenge gender binaries, and what justifies strategic boundary drawing around particular groups of people? Some of the deepest challenges to the boundary of the term *women* in western societies come from those who change their gender presentation and/or the physical sex of their bodies or both (transgendered and transsexed persons), or those who have sexual characteristics this culture defines as "ambiguous" (intersexuals). While an obsession with "genital status" can serve merely to reinforce the myth that sex and gender are determinately linked, transsexuality and intersexuality remain deeply fascinating from feminist perspectives, especially in the way they have been treated in literature and popular culture. The extreme reactions of confusion and distaste toward those whose bodies do not accommodate gender demonstrate its deeply ingrained nature. Thus it is partly through the historical and contemporary examination of the treatment of sexually ambiguous individuals that we gain a clearer perspective on the contingency of gender identity.[10] In a growing literature in transfeminism, we can see further efforts to highlight the potentially fluid yet socially significant boundaries of gender.[11] And when Jacquelyn Zita, in her widely cited article, "Male Lesbians and the Postmodernist Body," poses the question "Can men be lesbians?" she points not to an affirmative answer, but to the need for justificatory strategies that emphasize the political gains and losses of boundary-drawing in specific contexts.[12] These and other examples act as case studies, which, if explored, would illuminate the politically salient, as well as the variously constructed, qualities of sex and gender boundaries. They highlight the fluidity of the boundary around the concept "women," the possibilities for challenges to our conventional usages.[13]

While our ontological concerns give us some freedom in leaving terms open, however, the strategic imperatives of politics require objects of comparison; they demand that we draw boundaries around terms to use them as "measuring rods." Making a concept comparatively useful might entail that its boundary be firmly, albeit not immutably, fixed. Wittgenstein recognizes the need for some conceptual delimiting; however, he urges us to acknowledge the contingent nature of our terms, and to view them as tools rather than as "a preconceived idea to which reality must correspond" (*PI*, §131).

None of the foregoing implies that all categories are oppressive and that women should therefore cease to lay claim to gender as an explanatory element of social theory. The excessive reluctance to draw boundaries around terms can be just as ontologically misguided and politically unhelpful as essentialism, not least because I sometimes suspect that this kind of theory is written by those who can afford to let their philosophical imaginations run away with them, leaving more prosaic politics behind for the less privileged. Some antiessentialist philosophical strategies give the impression that their exponents toy with, or are titillated by, the kind of examples that make an antiessentialist case, rather than examining how, in the light of antiessentialism, we can move on and construct useful feminist theory. To claim, for example, that "woman can never be defined" may constitute a valuable critical contention within an existing philosophical discourse, yet it does not obviously further feminist projects that must draw on the notion of specific groups of women, united in some identifiable set of experiences or political objectives.[14]

I have come up against a familiar paradox: namely, that at the same time as feminists try to subvert the stereotypical categories established by patriarchy, we may wish to defend the conceptual limits of the categories women create for ourselves. Otherwise everything becomes available for co-optation, and in the process feminist claims lose their political saliency. Overcoming the "bewitchment of our intelligence by means of language" is not simply a matter of opening every conceptual boundary and inviting everybody in. It consists in careful attention to the political and ethical implications of where we draw lines around terms, not on philosophical well-wishing.

Between the poles of radical deconstruction and rigid essentialism lies a large philosophical terrain, and it is here that Wittgenstein sets us down. His choice is plain: we can leave a concept open (using it in the knowledge that its constituents have no common disjunctive property) or we can draw a line around it for a purpose. Here there is a case for taking very seriously the possibly negative political implications of that boundary, yet even a concept with "blurred edges" is identifiable. In some cases refusing to allow any politically motivated limits on meaning might have negative political connotations. Some commentators on categories such as "women" and "lesbians" seem excessively reluctant to draw boundaries and, in leaving terms gaping, risk political vacuity and ineptitude. There are good political reasons for being inexact about what we mean in many cases, yet at other times philosophy must not be allowed to run ahead of the political reality with which it contends, lest it participate in the creation of deconstructive theories that are as far from usage and experience as the metaphysics they seek to undermine.

From "Slippery Ice" to "Rough Ground"

Implicit in my argument so far is the belief that antiessentialism, in all its versions, has become a set of key insights into "difference," exclusion, and feminist theoretical method. These insights, co-opting Judith Butler's words, are "notions which have entered into an historical crisis that no amount of reflection can reverse."[15] Few feminist theorists, however, have taken up the challenge of exploring how antiessentialist philosophy might relate to empirical social research paradigms, or to political practice—that is, what to *do* with antiessentialism. And while feminist political practices have engaged with exclusion, difference, and power in numerous sites, this engagement deserves to be articulated in closer connection with antiessentialist feminist theory. These are strange lacunae in light of the fear of vapid generalization and the desire to contextualize that supposedly characterize all antiessentialist feminisms. We know that "there are no short cuts through women's lives," but where are the better paths?[16]

Any antiessentialist claim is underdetermined by feminist theory. Any account of the similarities and differences among women must be informed by some empirical considerations: Which group of women do we mean? At what time? In what place? And the materiality of sex and gender oppression constrains and directs legitimate generalization. But these questions cannot simply be labeled "empirical" or "material" without further investigation into the social construction of material reality. The Wittgensteinian injunction to "look and see," occasionally invoked by philosophers as the last word, seems to me to be only the beginning of feminist investigation into antiessentialism.

In putting forward "antiessentialist" ways of thinking about feminism, I have interdependent philosophical and political reasons for avoiding the purely critical project of pointing out homogenizing tendencies in political theorists' invocations of social groups. I am concerned that "accusations" of essentialism are not only theoretically confused, but also politically stifling.[17] For example, two well-known feminists who are among those most often labeled "essentialist," both in published critiques and in academic conversation, are Carol Gilligan and Catharine MacKinnon. Antiessentialist challenges to their work have, in some cases, been both theoretically sophisticated and politically compelling, bringing out buried assumptions about gender and hidden exclusions that require correction. I cannot help noticing, however, that both women are feminists deeply concerned with political action: in MacKinnon's case, as a feminist litigator and antipornography activist, and in Gilligan's, as a social psychologist involved in the empowerment of adolescent girls. This very concern with political action leaves them open to charges of essentialism.[18]

Neither the interminable deconstruction nor the uncritical reification of the category "women" is adequate to the demands of feminist practice. Debates about antiessentialism are in fact often making normative claims about *how to do* feminism. That is, arguments that feminist theory should be contextual, or should pay attention to differences between women, or should use generalizing categories only with the explicit recognition that they are contingent constructions, are claims not only about how to construct new and more sophisticated theoretical accounts of women's oppression, but about how more obviously empirical feminist goals should be met. This seems to me a point where the professed interdisciplinarity of women's studies might most fruitfully be developed. For surely questions about the nature and legitimacy of generalizations about women are *empirical*, however we understand this term?

We draw boundaries around "women" in order to use that category for a specific purpose. I take a corollary of this to be an important antiessentialist point, namely, that we deconstruct and reconstruct meaning *through* our use of categories. Such feminist processes, however, also take place in patriarchal contexts where ideas about "women" are constructed through the material conditions of different women's lives. The justification of boundaries around the use of terms will never be a purely abstract linguistic undertaking. The points that anchor these boundaries are themselves defined by the material conditions and lived experiences of women. But these conditions and experiences (including lived experience of the female body) are always already socially constructed. The fragility of resistance can be exacerbated by theoretical and political insistence on the rejection of those categories that enable us to make sense of our opponents.

Thus I want to suggest that feminists move to examine some of the practice-oriented ways in which antiessentialism might be relevant, in direct response to the tail-chasing that dominates the essentialism debates, as well as to a Wittgensteinian skepticism toward theory. Divorcing claims about generalization from concrete political contexts within which those claims are relevant puts us onto "slippery ice." That is, when we talk about the pitfalls of making generalizations, or the need to emphasize difference over sameness, we run the risk of privileging abstract philosophical discussion over the "rough ground" of practice. Again, there is no straightforwardly accessible truth about the right kinds of categories to invoke; we cannot simply point to reality to make objective claims about the similarities and differences that unite and divide women.

• • •

I have sketched the usefulness of Wittgenstein's philosophical method to antiessentialist feminism, showing not only how it offers a critique of certain ways of thinking, but also a way to go on, a philosophical therapy. His notion of family resemblance provides a way of reconceptualizing the similarities and differences among women, and his account of purposive line drawing provides a tool for halting the extreme fragmentation some forms of antiessentialism seem to recommend. Wittgenstein's skepticism toward philosophy and his injunction to "look and see" are part of what motivates the interdisciplinary feminist project I have outlined here. From a vantage point outside the disciplinary boundary of contemporary western philosophy, many of my arguments seem self-evident, and the rough ground appears as familiar terrain. "Of course," many feminists might say, "when have we ever done anything *but* start from women's lives?" But for those who remain "bewitched" by essentialism, whether as reluctant advocates or as stalwart critics, a developed Wittgensteinian feminism could offer a methodological path between two extremes: one extreme affirms the unity of women in ways that are inattentive to difference and that reify artifacts of oppression, while the other toys with the philosophical limits of categories in ways that discredit valuable generalizing analyses of the oppression of women and undermine unifying feminist political goals.

Notes

1. Ludwig Wittgenstein, *Philosophical Investigations*, 2d ed., trans. G. E. M. Anscombe (1953; Oxford: Blackwell, 1997), §66. All further references to this text will be indicated by the abbreviation *PI* followed by section or page numbers.

2. Elizabeth V. Spelman, *Inessential Woman: Problems of Exclusion in Feminist Thought* (Boston: Beacon Press, 1988).

3. For example, the assumption that terms in aesthetics and ethics can be conclusively defined (*PI*, §77), or from the characteristics of logic (*PI*, §§107–8).

4. Ludwig Wittgenstein, *The Blue Book* (Oxford: Blackwell, 1958), 18.

5. María Lugones, "On the Logic of Pluralist Feminism," in *Feminist Ethics*, ed. Claudia Card (Lawrence: University Press of Kansas, 1991), 41.

6. See, e.g., Elizabeth Grosz, *Volatile Bodies: Toward a Corporeal Feminism* (Bloomington: Indiana University Press, 1994); Anne Fausto-Sterling, "The Five Sexes: Why Male and Female Are Not Enough," *Sciences* 33 (1993): 20–24; Suzanne J. Kessler, *Lessons From the Intersexed* (New Brunswick: Rutgers University Press, 1998).

7. Ludwig Wittgenstein, *On Certainty*, ed. G. E. M. Anscombe and G. H. von Wright (New York: Harper Torchbooks, 1969), §152.

8. See Suzanne Kessler, "The Medical Construction of Gender: Case Management of Intersexed Infants," *Signs* 16, no. 1 (1990): 3–26.

9. See the case studies in Holly Devor, *Gender Blending: Confronting the Limits of Duality* (Bloomington: Indiana University Press, 1989); and for a more popular treatment of female masculinities, Del LaGrace Volcano and Judith "Jack" Halberstam, *The Drag King Book* (London: Serpent's Tail, 1999).

10. See Michel Foucault's introduction to Herculine Barbin, *Herculine Barbin: Being the Recently Discovered Memoirs of a Nineteenth-Century French Hermaphrodite* (New York: Pantheon Books, 1980); Alice Domurat Dreger, *Hermaphrodites and the Medical Invention of Sex* (Cambridge: Harvard University Press, 1998); Julia Epstein and Kristina Straub, *Body Guards: The Cultural Politics of Gender Ambiguity* (New York: Routledge, 1991).

11. For example, Kate Bornstein, *Gender Outlaw: On Men, Women, and the Rest of Us* (New York: Vintage Books, 1995); Leslie Feinberg, *Trans Liberation: Beyond Pink and Blue* (Boston: Beacon Press, 1998); Jay Prosser, *Second Skins: The Body Narratives of Transsexuality* (New York: Columbia University Press, 1998).

12. Jacquelyn Zita, "Male Lesbians and the Postmodernist Body," *Hypatia* 7, no. 4 (1992): 106–27.

13. I do explore these case studies in more detail elsewhere; see Cressida J. Heyes, *Line Drawings: Defining Women Through Feminist Practice* (Ithaca: Cornell University Press, 2000), esp. 88–96.

14. Julia Kristeva, "Woman Can Never Be Defined," in *New French Feminisms: An Anthology*, ed. Elaine Marks and Isabelle de Courtivron (Amherst: University of Massachusetts Press, 1980).

15. Judith Butler, "For a Careful Reading," in *Feminist Contentions: A Philosophical Exchange* ed. Seyla Benhabib, Judith Butler, Drucilla Cornell and Nancy Fraser, with introduction by Linda Nicholson (New York: Routledge, 1995), 132.

16. Spelman, *Inessential Woman*, 187.

17. For a related discussion, see Marianne Hirsch and Evelyn Fox-Keller, eds., *Conflicts in Feminism* (New York: Routledge, 1990).

18. For a detailed treatment of the case of Carol Gilligan, see Cressida J. Heyes, "Anti-Essentialism in Practice: Carol Gilligan and Feminist Philosophy," *Hypatia* 12, no. 3 (1997): 142–63.

10

Wittgenstein Meets 'Woman' in the Language-Game of Theorizing Feminism

Hilde Lindemann Nelson

The problem of difference has been plaguing feminist theory for at least a decade, and it does not look like it will disappear in the near future. An early (and classical) discussion of how feminists inadvertently essentialized 'woman' as white, middle class, and academic is María Lugones and Elizabeth V. Spelman's "Have We Got a Theory for You!" which was quickly followed by a spate of other essays and books grappling with this difficulty—including a number of articles published in the spring 1994 issue of *Signs*.[1] Iris Young has formulated the problem thus:

My thanks to Margaret Urban Walker, Judith Bradford, James Lindemann Nelson, and Naomi Scheman for many helpful suggestions and criticisms.

> The search for the common characteristics of women or of women's oppression leads to normalizations and exclusions. [Yet] there are pragmatic political reasons for insisting on the possibility of thinking about women as some kind of group. Clearly, these two positions pose a dilemma for feminist theory. On the one hand, without some sense in which "woman" is the name of a social collective, there is nothing specific to feminist politics. On the other hand, any effort to identify the attributes of that collective appears to undermine feminist politics by leaving out some women whom feminists ought to include.[2]

Feminist theorists have generally employed one of two strategies to solve this dilemma. The first is to dismiss the efforts to define women's nature altogether, on theoretical grounds. The mistake, according to this strategy, has been to suppose that feminism required a subject at all. As Judith Butler argues in *Gender Trouble*, the feminist insistence on a female subject for feminism obscures the necessarily social and discursive means by which identities are produced. Gender, Butler argues, is performative, a production of the fantasy of a binary opposition of masculine and feminine played out on the surface of the body through the denial and exclusion of other, more fluid possibilities. Gender is imposed by an unwritten law, namely, the taboo against incest, which imposes heterosexuality at the same time as it imposes gender. Because the incest taboo institutes the exogamy that allows a culture to reproduce itself, it presupposes a prohibition against homosexuality; gender is thus not only the identification with one sex, but also entails the direction of sexual desire toward the other sex. It can therefore be seen that the "disciplinary production of gender effects a false stabilization of gender in the interests of the heterosexual construction and regulation of sexuality within the reproductive domain. The construction of coherence conceals the gender discontinuities that run rampant within heterosexual, bisexual, and gay and lesbian contexts in which gender does not necessarily follow from sex, and desire, or sexuality generally, does not seem to follow from gender."[3] Resisting this oppressive, mutual reinforcement of gender and an oppositional sexuality requires that these categories be destabilized by recognizing them for the fantasies they are. Feminist discourse, on Butler's view, could then remain fluid, open to the constant shifts in contingent relations among social practices.

The second solution to the dilemma is pragmatic. At the point where theory interferes with the possibility of political action, theory ought to be suspended so that we can get on with feminist political practice. This is the strategy María Lugones employs when she says that in interpreting the "problem of difference" as a problem for feminist theory, white feminist theorizers have made theory, instead of racism, their main concern.[4] Ditto Susan Bordo: "In shifting the focus of crucial feminist concerns about the representation of cultural diversity from practical contexts to questions of adequate theory, [we are] diverted from attending to the professional and institutional mechanisms through which the politics of exclusion operate most powerfully in intellectual communities."[5]

Young thinks there is much to be said for both the postmodernist and the pragmatist critiques, but argues that neither succeeds in solving the dilemma; instead, they swing back and forth between its two poles. Her own solution is to bracket the two problematic strategies and reconceptualize gender as a collective, without identifying common attributes of all women or implying common identities. While I agree with Young that both strategies are problematic (for reasons I will say more about in a moment), I think they are too valuable to bracket, so I will attempt instead to augment them. The project of this essay is to set theoretically defensible limits to postmodern fluidity while at the same time offering the pragmatic position a means of building coalitions that does not require suspending theory. In short, I aim to supplement both strategies so that the dilemma of difference is resolved. To do this, I turn to Wittgenstein's remarks on rule-following in the *Philosophical Investigations*.

'Woman' as Signifying Practice

While Butler has properly—indeed, brilliantly—pointed out that gender is socially constructed and that this construction has well served hegemonic sexism and heterosexism, any claim of a radical discontinuity between signified and sign—between the "I" who am woman and the "woman" I am—requires careful scrutiny. The description of signifying practice, Wittgenstein might have commented, is the first step, "the one that altogether escapes notice. We talk of processes and states and leave their nature undecided. Sometime perhaps we shall know more about them—we think. But that is just what commits us to a particular way of looking at the matter. For we have a definite concept of what it means to learn to know a process better. (The decisive movement in the conjuring trick has been made, and it was the very one that we thought quite innocent.)" (*PI*, 308). Let us look at Butler's decisive moment and see if with Wittgenstein's help we can show that it is not so innocent. She says,

> That the gendered body is performative suggests that it has no ontological status apart from the various acts which constitute its reality. . . . Acts and gestures, articulated and enacted desires create the illusion of an interior and organizing gender core. . . . If gender attributes and acts, the various ways in which a body shows or produces its cultural signification, are performative, then there is no preexisting identity by which an act or attribute might be measured; there would be no true or false, real or distorted acts of gender, and the postulation of a true gender identity would be revealed as a regulatory fiction. (136, 141)

The image of proliferating gender configurations and radical destabilizing of gender identity that Butler offers in place of this fiction edges her argument in the direction of limitless engendering, an infinitely varied performance of gender identities. What Butler gives with one hand, however, she takes back with the other. Her project in *Gender Trouble* has been to deny the existence of a subject for feminism at all, yet in the end she reins in the radically protean plasticity she has claimed for gender identity and acknowledges that the process of signification through which a gendered "I" is asserted occurs within "the structure of signification, the rules that regulate the legitimate and illegitimate invocation of that pronoun, the practices that establish the terms of intelligibility by which that pronoun can circulate" (143). We are then left wondering where these limits on language come from—why signifiers can't be every bit as plastic and protean as the concepts they purport to signify. The conjuring trick was to destabilize a binary sex-gender system by opening up the possibility of continual and multivariant performative engenderings, but then constraining this process by pointing to the public and social nature of signification. But wasn't it just that public and social nature of signification that constrained gender identity in the first place? If the binary constraint is illegitimate and enforced only through unjustifiable exercises of power, why aren't all other constraints on signification equally unjustified?[6]

Pace Bordo, what is required to keep Butler's argument from being a piece of special pleading is more theory, not less. Butler is quite right to criticize the notion of gender as fixed, binary, and biologically given, but when in its place she offers a performative ideal of ceaseless textual play and then reins it in, she owes us an explanation of why the play can't really be ceaseless. If she leaves this question unanswered, we don't know why the "rules that regulate the legitimate and illegitimate invocation" of words have any more authority than the rule (which she dismisses as fantasy) that there are only two, sexually oppositional, genders.

The Private Language Discussion

A serviceable answer is available in Wittgenstein's remarks on private language. He begins these remarks (at *PI*, 243) by asking if we could imagine a language in which a person could express his inner experiences for his private use—not in ordinary language, but in a language whose words refer to what can be known only to the person speaking, so another person cannot understand. This, I suggest, is the Humpty Dumpty theory of language:

> "But 'glory' doesn't mean 'a nice knockdown argument,'" Alice objected.
> "When *I* use a word," Humpty Dumpty said, in rather a scornful tone, "it means just what I choose it to mean—neither more nor less."
> "The question is," said Alice, "whether you *can* make words mean so many different things."
> "The question is," said Humpty Dumpty, "which is to be master—that's all."[7]

Humpty Dumpty, like other postmodern theorists, is tempted to allow the slippage of the signified under the sign to be ceaseless and unbounded. If he were to succeed in this, he would perplex not only Alice, but any other of his auditors as well—he would, in fact, be using a private language. Wittgenstein's observations, of course, are intended to show that he can't succeed—that the notion of private language is incoherent.

He begins by exploring two senses of the term *private* ("only I can know" and "only I can have") and shows how we go wrong when we lift 'knowing' and 'having' out of the ordinary grammatical criteria inhering in the concept of privacy and turn them into mystical, metaphysically authoritative superfacts. Having made this preliminary observation, he scrutinizes the notion of reference that appears to be operating here. It's at this point (*PI*, 258) that feminist theorists might want to start reading closely.

The diarist Wittgenstein posits, who wishes to write down a sign in a calendar for every day he experiences a certain sensation, has to make the sign refer to the sensation somehow, even though he can't formulate a definition of the sign. He baptizes the sensation by concentrating his attention on it as he writes the sign down on his calendar; he is, as it were, pointing to it inwardly. Why does he do this? So that in the future he will be able to make the correct connection between the sign and the sensation. But what can his criterion for correctness be? What standard allows him to judge that he has remembered the name-object correlation accurately? He can only say that whatever seems right to him will be right.

This "standard" of rightness is so bizarre that Wittgenstein says it shows one can't speak of rightness here. In making this judgment about the incorrect application of 'rightness' for what the diarist is doing, Wittgenstein demonstrates that he has what the diarist lacks: a rule-governed, publicly shared linguistic practice whose rules can be followed or broken. The possibility of following the rules or violating them provides Wittgenstein, but not the diarist, with the criteria for judging whether a particular application of a concept is a success or a failure.

Why has the diarist's application of 'right' failed? It's not so much that an outside observer is unable to verify that the diarist has remembered correctly, nor that Wittgenstein is engaging in a *reductio* that here reaches its absurd conclusion.[8] The application fails because the private-language user, unlike the user of the word *right*, only thinks he is following rules. He is actually doing nothing of the kind. "To *think* one is obeying a rule is not to obey a rule. Hence it is not possible to obey a rule 'privately': otherwise thinking one was obeying a rule would be the same thing as obeying it" (*PI*, 202). And again,

> Are the rules of the private language *impressions* of rules?—The balance on which impressions are weighed is not the *impression* of a balance. " 'Well, I *believe* that this is the sensation E again.'—Perhaps you *believe* that you believe it! . . . What reason have we for calling "E" the sign for a *sensation*? For "sensation" is a word of our common language, not of one intelligible to me alone. So

the use of this word stands in need of a justification which everybody understands. (*PI*, 259–61)

The trouble here is not that the diarist may not be correctly remem-
bering the sensation that goes with the sign, but that he can neither
forget nor remember, go wrong nor go right. "Because the private language user has nothing on which to rest distinctions among according
with a rule, seeming to accord with a rule, and failing to accord with a
rule, appeal to memory cannot be made to support the rule-governedness
of linguistic usage."[9]

Another way to put this is that the only standard the diarist has for
applying the rule that would govern his private sign's application to his
private sensation is his own internal self. But this is just the trouble: if he
is the standard, what sense does it make to say he has applied the rule
correctly? The diarist is in something like the position of a person trying
to measure off twelve inches of a piece of paper with a foot-rule that
keeps shrinking and expanding—and is the only footrule in existence.
How would one know when the ruler is exactly twelve inches long? What
could you use to measure it by? "Imagine," Wittgenstein says at *PI*, 279,
"someone saying: 'But I know how tall I am!' and laying his hand on top
of his head to prove it." A measure must be independent of what it
measures, but there is no way to give the private reference any independence from the private self who attempts to refer.[10]

The discussion of private language, then, can be offered as theory in
support of Butler's closing claim that performances of gender are never
fully self-styled (139). A fully self-styled performance is an incoherent
concept. 'Woman' requires a grammar, a certain conventionally determined positioning in the language, a place in our life forms. And it requires criteria for application whose correctness can be determined
independently of the person wielding them. This means that whatever I
think 'woman' means for me can't be the final word on the subject, no
matter how tempting it is to say that I'm to be master.

That there are grammatical limits on 'woman', however, shouldn't be
taken to mean that the concept can't be rescued from certain illicit usages, even ubiquitous ones.[11] The reason is that language, like the forms
of life in which it is embedded, contains within it the possibilities of self-
challenge and change, of insubordination and learned indifference. If a
player of the language-game of theorizing feminism wishes to issue a challenge to the rule whereby 'woman' is constructed in binary opposition to

'man', she has only to look to the liberatory strategies already in place in the feminist theorizing game to find the resources that allow the players to alter their practice. She can find additional possibilities of irony, resistance, and innovation in the other multiple and overlapping language-games that are played as a background to this one—games having to do with queer theory or Foucauldian or Marxist analyses of power or (especially) ordinary language. As Sabina Lovibond explains:

> Wittgenstein envisages a process of change in which the revision of the existing practice is demanded, at first, by 'only a few.' Those few speakers will initially have to engage, without reference to any already constituted authority, in a language-game which they themselves have invented—a game regulated by norms which, as yet, lack the kind of institutional backing enjoyed by the norms that regulate the dominant practice. But if they succeed in drawing in the bulk of the community, the time will eventually come when they will be described—with all the authority of the altered consensus which it is their purpose to create—as the far-sighted pioneers of an altogether superior approach. . . . This is the material possibility in which critical thinking is grounded.[12]

What motivates revision of the existing practice in the first place will be a belief that it is inapt or inaccurate, that it leaves out something important, that it perpetuates other practices the speaker finds morally repugnant, that (with Butler) it fails to fit the speaker's experience. Whether the player will in fact succeed in revising the rule depends on whether she is heard and whether other players find the proposed revision to be a sensible one. Butler has certainly been heard; her modification of the binary-genders rule governing the use of 'woman' is gaining acceptance in several allied language-games.

'Woman' as Politics

If the postmodern response to the problem of difference has been to deny that there is an "existing identity, understood through the category of women, who constitutes the subject" of feminism,[13] the pragmatic response to the problem of difference has been to suggest that at the point where theorizing interferes with feminist practice, one should stop theorizing and get on with it. The claim is that a deep skepticism about using gender as an analytical category at all can be so paralyzing that we lose sight of feminism as critique—as the struggle for a better understanding of the way social life is and ought to be. When, for example, questions about social policy concerning interventions into female bodies arise (think of Norplant as a condition for probation, or court-ordered cesarean sections), feminists not only can but should mount a concerted response without having to get embogged in postmodern debates about multiple embodiment. Bordo puts it this way:

> Most of our institutions have barely begun to absorb the message of modernist social criticism; surely it is too soon to let them off the hook via postmodern heterogeneity and instability. . . . Rather, we need to reserve *practical* spaces both for generalist critique (suitable when gross points need to be made) and for attention to complexity and nuance. We need to be pragmatic, not theoretically pure, if we are to struggle effectively against the inclination of institutions to preserve and defend themselves against deep change.[14]

The pragmatist move is not unlike G. E. Moore's gesture refuting philosophical skepticism. Moore, it will be remembered, held up his hands and so demonstrated that at least two physical objects exist in the external world.[15] But just as any number of philosophers over the years have found Moore's gesture inadequate,[16] so should feminists find the pragmatic equivalent, while intuitively appealing, inadequate unless it is supplemented by theory. For one thing, not all practices that harm or wrong women wear warning labels to that effect. And it's just at the point where it's difficult to discern which of, say, four options for policy better serve the interests of the women involved, that something vital is apt to be overlooked unless good theory helps one to see it.[17] For example, Iris Young's reconceptualizing justice as shared power helps us to see that distributive theories of justice actually perpetuate injustice, because they overlook inequitable differentials of power in the institutions that produce the goods to be distributed.[18] If the four policy options just look to see that women get their fair share, the sexist biases in the structures of production will be left unchallenged.

Besides, if "getting on with it" is left simply as a matter of getting together a coalition for action, then feminist politics would seem to be arbitrary. As Young observes,

> Some women choose to come together in a political movement, to form themselves as a group of mutually identifying agents. But on the basis of what do they come together? What are the social conditions that have motivated the politics? Perhaps even more important, do feminist politics leave out women who do not identify as feminists? These questions all point to the need for some conception of women as a group prior to the formation of self-conscious feminist politics, as designating a certain set of relations or positions that motivate the particular politics of feminism.[19]

Family Resemblance

A strategy for arriving at the needed conception of women as a group is available in Wittgenstein's discussion of family resemblance. At *PI*, 66, Wittgenstein invites the reader to reflect on a word in everyday use—*games*. "I mean board-games, card-games, ball-games, Olympic games, and so on. What is common to them all?—Don't say: 'There *must* be something common, or they would not be called "games"'—but *look and see* whether there is anything common to all.—For if you look at them you will not see something that is common to all, but similarities, relationships, and a whole series of them at that. To repeat: *denk nicht, sondern schau!*" If we canvass enough examples of games and reflect on them imaginatively, we will see a complicated network of similarities—sometimes overall similarities, sometimes similarities of detail. These similarities are called "family resemblances" because they overlap and crisscross in the same way that build, features, color of eyes, gait, temperament, and so on do among family members.

Not all words are characterized by this notion of family resemblance: think of *hiccuping*. However, *woman* clearly qualifies as a family-resemblance term in that there is no one characteristic all women hold in common, even on the crudest physical level, let alone on the basis of shared experience. A woman who has undergone a double mastectomy has no breasts (and anyway, men have breasts). A woman doesn't stop being a woman when she has a hysterectomy, and some women are born without a uterus. Some are born without a vagina, too. Women have estrogen, but so do men, and women, like men, manufacture testosterone. Even chromosomal differences aren't always reliable. Women with Turner's syndrome have only one X, while men with Klinefelter's have XXY. There are XX males who have a piece of the Y chromosome on one of their Xs, and XY females whose Y lost the masculine gene. There are women with XXX chromosomes, and mentally retarded people of both sexes who have four, five, or even six sex chromosomes. And consider the case of a person with gender dysphoria, born with a penis and testicles and XY chromosomes, but strongly aware from early childhood that her body is the wrong shape: she has sex reassignment surgery at the age of twenty and lives as a woman from then on. Why shouldn't she count as a woman?[20]

Because 'woman', like 'game', is a family-resemblance concept, one's knowledge of 'woman' is completely expressed in the explanations that one could give (*PI*, 75). That is, one could describe various women one knows, show how other women could be identified because of their similarity to these, say that one would scarcely include a ten-year-old girl in the concept, and so on. And if someone were to draw a sharp line at the age of sixteen for some purpose (say, to delimit the age for statutory rape) and another person didn't want to draw a line at all because she thinks rape is far more problematic than this line makes it appear, then her concept of 'woman' and that of the first person are not the same but akin to each other: the kinship is just as undeniable as the difference. This leads to a new worry—or, to be more precise, it swings us back into the worry about the postmodern strategy with which this essay began. Namely, if the edges of the concept get too blurry, if we include girl babies and hermaphrodites and female impersonators and woman-identified men, then we might as well say that anything—and nothing—counts as a woman.

At this point, Wittgenstein has a further suggestion. "In such a difficulty always ask yourself: How did we *learn* the meaning of this word? . . . From what sort of examples? in what language-games? Then it will be easier for you to see that the word must have a family of meanings" (*PI*, 77).

We can say more about this if we return to an earlier passage in the *Investigations*. At *PI*, 43, Wittgenstein points out that for a large class of cases—though not for all—the meaning of a word is its use in the language. How do we grasp its use? By understanding how to go on applying it. If we understand how to follow the rule for using the word, knowing in which situations its use is appropriate, we've grasped its meaning. One can answer the question, How am I able to follow the rule for using the term *woman*? in one of two ways. If the question meant, How did I come to know how to apply the term properly? the answer is that I have been trained to react in a particular way, and now I do so react to it. If the question meant, How does it happen that my way of applying the term counts as correct? the answer is that there is a regular use, a customary way of following the rule that constitutes its correctness (*PI*, 198). More-over (to return for a moment to the Humpty Dumpty theory), it is not possible that there should have been only one occasion on which some-one obeyed a rule. "To obey a rule, to make a report, to give an order, to play a game of chess, are *customs* (uses, institutions)" (*PI*, 199). As a point of grammar, rules can be followed only within a community and a historical context where they are customary.

The pragmatist feminist, like her postmodern sister, has the resources for both following and changing the rules governing the use of 'woman' ready to hand within many of the language-games that can be played with the word. These games overlap and reinforce, stand in tension with and resist one another, and in the interplay among them as well as within each there is considerable—but not unbounded—room for movement. The great thing is to be aware that many of the games are played locally and particularly, and we will then have to ask ourselves which women we are talking about. As Spelman points out,

> to refer to the power "all men have over all women" makes it look as if my relationship to the bank vice president I am asking for a loan is just like my relationship to the man who empties my wastebasket at the office each night; similarly it makes it look as if their relationship to me is no different from their relationship to the woman who cleans the halls of the administration building. Whenever we feel tempted to talk about women "as women," we might remember what the poet Gwendolyn Brooks once said in a somewhat different context: "The juice from tomatoes is not called merely *juice*. It is always called TOMATO juice."[21]

The Language-Games of 'Woman'

The Wittgensteinian reflections on rule-following and the language-games in which we learn how to follow the rules, coupled with the corollary concept of family resemblance, offer feminist pragmatists as much corrective to essentialism as they require while at the same time setting philosophically defensible limits on the postmodern fantasy of unbounded slippage of the signified under the sign. Wittgenstein's approach is itself pragmatic, resisting grand totalizing theories in favor of localized descriptions. If I am right about his usefulness to feminism, whether as critique or as theory, as pragmatic or postmodern, the task that remains is to show how this approach works out in practice by examining the way 'woman' is employed in various language-games.

Learning the Games

A logical place to begin this investigation is to look to how we learn the concept. We learn it, of course, within a given linguistic community, somewhere between the ages of one and four, and most of us probably learn it from the older members of our family. What we learn is what a woman is. As Stanley Cavell put it, "In 'learning language' you learn not merely what the names of things are, but what a name is; not merely what the form of expression is for expressing a wish, but what expressing a wish is; not merely what the word for 'father' is, but what a father is; not merely what the word for 'love' is, but what love is."[22]

We also learn who we are in relation to this concept. I was in an airport washroom recently when a woman came in with her three-year-old daughter. "Why are we coming in here?" asked the little girl. "Because this is the ladies' room. This is where we use the toilet." "Then you can come in here because you're a lady, but I can't because I'm not a lady—I'm a baby." "Well, you're a baby lady."

The little girl probably already knew that babies like herself grow up into ladies, but she was learning that the age distinction between ladies and babies isn't always scrupulously maintained. She was also learning how to extend the concept to include other sorts of ladies besides those that are mothers. For her, however, Mother might well be the most important lady there is, and to the extent that this is generalizable it may have a bearing on the degree to which one's personal concept of 'mother' carries over into one's concept of 'woman', particularly given the patriarchal aggregation of 'woman' (but not 'man') with 'procreative capacity' and the aggregation of that aggregate (but not 'man') with 'nurturer'.

We learn more about 'woman' as we see it played out in the persons of our teachers, day-care providers, TV and movie images, advertising fantasies, and the ordinary experiences of living. We are told that girls can't do math or throw a baseball straight. We are aware that where unpaid care is needed in the family—whether for children, ill adults, or a frail elderly family member—women are expected to do it. We learn that witches are women.

Along with these various applications of the concept, however, we also learn strategies for resisting and correcting particular applications. There is, first, the kind of correction that invokes a rule (the mother's correction of the little girl's blunder in supposing you had to be an adult to use the ladies' room); and then there is the kind of correction that revises the rule. We learn, for example, to revise the rule that the indefinite pronoun takes the masculine form, although in a particular context—for example, Aristotelian scholarship—we might follow the rule as a way of underscoring Aristotle's misogyny. This can be done without the safety of an explanatory footnote, perhaps, only against the background of an ordinary-language game in which there is broad agreement not to play by the masculine pronoun rule, so that doing it jars the sensibilities. Where the Aristotelian scholarship takes place against a background that still follows the rule, it will be necessary to draw attention to that fact. We cannot change this rule or any other single-handedly (except in our own idiolects), but because 'woman' is a family-resemblance concept, we can rule out certain uses and modify others without necessarily doing violence to the integrity of the concept.

The Language-Game of 'Woman' as Coalition Builder

The question for practical feminist politics is how to frame the problem that requires political action, how to form groups to take the required action, how to decide what action to take, and then how to act—without, at any of these stages, unjustly excluding or normalizing either the people or the processes. The temptation is to paper over differences so that the group can achieve consensus and get something done. Feminists have taken seriously the need to resist this temptation; however, paying careful attention to able-bodiedness, race, ethnicity, sexual preference, age, class, performative engendering, important personal projects, and "that exasperated 'etc.' that so often occurs at the end of such lines"[23] can be a paralyzing prospect.

Consider the case of a black woman in Detroit, a foster mother to two little boys. One of the boys is healthy, but the other is HIV-positive and has had repeated hospitalizations for opportunistic infections of various kinds. The foster mother has been heavily involved in his care, but under Michigan law she has no standing to make treatment decisions on his behalf. As a ward of the state (in the person of an overextended social worker who is suffering burnout and sees the boys for ten minutes or so every three months), the little boy's care is pretty much what the resident at the hospital says it will be, and the resident's care plan is to treat each new infection vigorously, even though it is clear that the child will soon die. The foster mother objects to the resident's approach, believing he has lost sight of the overall goals of treatment and so is subjecting her son to needless suffering. The child dies, having endured one painful medical procedure after another.

The foster mother is outraged at the impersonal state bureaucracy that failed this child and that does not acknowledge the importance of the fostering relationship. She resolves to spearhead a campaign to get the law changed so that foster parents will have the authority to make treatment decisions for the children in their care.

She was active in the civil rights movement in the 1960s and campaigned hard to pass the Equal Rights Amendment, so she has some experience of grassroots organizing. She begins by asking the hospital for the names of other foster mothers who have cared for children with AIDS. She assumes that these will be black women like herself and she anticipates that their agenda is the same as hers. At the first meeting of this group, she and four of her friends do most of the talking, and one or two other horror stories of overtreatment are told.

Later into the evening, however, it becomes clear that not all the people in the room frame the problem as she does. Some believe that the white establishment has inflicted AIDS on the black community as a form of genocide, and that the best way to look out for the community's interests is to demand everything medicine has to offer. Some of the women think the local ministers should be the visible lobbyists, since they are the leaders of the African American community in Detroit. Two Latina women who are present disagree with this strategy; they deny that they are part of the black community. They and other women think that the foster mothers who do the actual hands-on caring should be the spokespeople. Some want to open the group to foster mothers who have cared for children ill with other diseases besides AIDS; others think the group would then be too large to be effective. Should the group include older women who have fostered, but are no longer looking after, children? Doctors of color who understand the intricacies of treating AIDS? White doctors, but only if they are women? Does being a woman necessarily make you sensitive to the mother-child relationship that's being trampled on here? Isn't this really more—despite the Latina presence—about being African American than about being a woman? Bernice Johnson Reagon offers a word of caution about this last move: "At some point, you cannot be fighting oppression and be oppressed yourself and not feel it. . . . You tried to talk to these movement people about how you felt. And they say, 'Well let's take that up next week. Because the most important thing now is that Black people are being oppressed and we must work with that.' Watch these mono-issue people. They ain't gonna do you no good."[24] Wittgenstein's advice is the same. "A main cause of philosophical disease—a one-sided diet: one nourishes one's thinking with only one kind of example" (*PI*, 593). In nourishing one's thinking with only the example of black oppression, one excludes other ways of framing the problem, which in turn leads to excluding people unjustifiably and arbitrarily ruling out certain courses of action. "We remain unconscious of the prodigious diversity of all the everyday language-games," Wittgenstein observes, "because the clothing of our language makes everything alike" (*PI*, p. 224). If we insist on framing the problem in terms of black oppression only, we may, for example, fail to see that not all black people are oppressed in the same way. Deferring to the leadership of the male clergy may ratify, rather than challenge, the patriarchal expectation that men, but not women, are to speak for the community, while women, but not men, are to look after the children.

In the language-game of coalition building, wielding the criteria for the legitimate inclusion and exclusion of people and procedures requires practice. Correctness in discriminating between differences that are salient and those that are not

> will generally issue from the judgments of those with better knowledge of mankind. Can one learn this knowledge? Yes; some can. Not, however, by taking a course in it, but through 'experience.'—Can someone be another's teacher in this? Certainly. From time to time he gives him the right *tip*.—This is what 'learning' and 'teaching' are like here.—What one acquires here is not a technique; one learns correct judgments. There are also rules,

but they do not form a system, and only experienced people can apply them right. Unlike calculating-rules. What is most difficult here is to put this indefiniteness, correctly and unfalsified, into words. (*PI*, p. 227)

What is Wittgenstein's tip to the coalition builder? Differences among the players can be respected and put to good use by conceptualizing the members of the coalition as having no core defining characteristic, but rather, bearing a family resemblance to one another. By refraining from insisting on a core characteristic, it is possible to open the group so that relevant people needn't be excluded; at the same time, the family-resemblance tip allows one to avoid totalizing falsely.

The Language-Game of the Parodic 'Woman'

If the game of coalition-building serves as an example of Wittgenstein's usefulness to feminist activists, the game of gender parody can do the same for feminist theorists. Butler points to the practices of drag, cross-dressing, and butch/femme stylizing for their ability to parody the notion of a primary or original gender identity. Drag is always parodic, but not all cross-dressing is drag. Transsexuals cross-dress to relieve a felt dissonance between anatomical sex and gender identity, while transvestites often cross-dress because they find it erotically comforting. (Is an anatomically male but woman-identified transsexual cross-dressed when she is in man-tailored pants or when she is in a skirt? Is a woman cross-dressed when she wears a shirt that buttons to the right?)

Just as not all cross-dressing is drag, so not all drag is performed by cross-dressing. "Garbo 'got in drag' whenever she took some heavy glamour part, whenever she melted in or out of a man's arms, whenever she simply let that heavenly-flexed neck . . . bear the weight of her thrown-back head. . . . How resplendent seems the art of acting! It is all *impersonation*, whether the sex underneath is true or not."[25] In this sense, Dolly Parton has performed drag for many years, while the famous cover photo for *Vanity Fair* in which a scantily clad Cindy Crawford gave k. d. lang a shave features everybody in drag, although only Lang is cross-dressed. Context being everything, in drag as elsewhere, I would argue that Lang's drag performance ended when she left the barber chair, even if she kept the same pants and shirt on for the rest of the day.

As Butler points out, drag performance subverts the fiction of a unity of anatomical sex and gender identity. Drag as performed by gay men arguably mocks femininity, butch stereotyping, the social construction of gay behavior as deviant, and the self whose identity is bound up with being gay. When Cher vamps, she is both complicit in and sending up certain culturally entrenched rules for expressing the relationship between heterosexuality and gender identity. And the film *The Adventures of Priscilla, Queen of the Desert* features multiple and complex destabilizations of the coherence between gender and (hetero)sex, as Terence Stamp imposes on his own gender performatives the role of a postsurgical male-to-female transsexual who performs as a gay drag queen and who, not as a gay man but as a woman, takes a male lover: a man playing the role of a woman who used to be a man, playing the role of a man playing a woman—heterosexual here and there, but certainly not everywhere. Butler claims,

> *In imitating gender, drag implicitly reveals the imitative structure of gender itself—as well as its contingency.* . . . The notion of gender parody defended here does not assume that there is an original which such parodic identities imitate. Indeed, the parody is *of* the very notion of an original; just as the psychoanalytic notion of gender identification is constituted by a fantasy of a fantasy, the transfiguration of an Other who is always already a "figure" in that double sense, so gender parody reveals that the original identity after which gender fashions itself is an imitation without an origin.[26]

It is not as clear to me as it is to Butler, however, that drag is a sendup of gendered identity altogether. The insistence on, for example, a radical proliferation of gay identities and the insistence on an essential gay identity would seem to take in each other's washing. Don't both "there *can't* be" and "there *must* be" falsely totalize what it is to be gay? Gay drag is played not only against the background of a rigidly structured, oppositional coupling of sex and gender (a construction Butler rightly uncouples), but also against the background of a gay community that has its own well-developed rules. Against that double backdrop, drag may be doubly subversive, cocking a snook at hegemonic constructions of gender identity that it finds oppressive while at the same time resisting certain rules of the same-sex community in which it is embedded. Parodic gendering does not demonstrate that there is *no* original after which gender fashions itself—on the contrary, there can be no parody without an original. But the original need not and should not be thought of as essential.

The Wittgensteinian tip here is not to confound *breaking* a rule with the *absence* of a rule. It is enough for Butler to show that there needn't be an invariable binary correlation between 'man' or 'woman' and oppositional sex. This rule turns out not to be an essential feature of gender identity. But, Wittgenstein asks, "how can I decide what is an essential, and what an inessential, accidental, feature of the notation? Is there some reality lying behind the notation, which shapes its grammar? Let us think of a similar case in a game: in [checkers] a king is marked by putting one piece on top of another. Now won't one say it is inessential to the game for a king to consist of two pieces?" (*PI*, 562). It is inessential to the game because the "king = two pieces" rule is regulatory but not constitutive of checkers. The rule can be broken without altering the game unrecognizably. A constitutive rule, on the other hand, must be followed if the game is to be played at all. "Let us say that the meaning of a piece is its role in the game.—Now let it be decided by lot which of the players gets white before any game of chess begins. To this end one player holds a king in each closed fist while the other chooses one of the two hands at random. Will it be counted as part of the role of the king in chess that it is used to draw lots in this way?" (*PI*, 563). So too the meaning of 'woman' is its role in the game, its use in the language. The connection with heterosexual intercourse is arguably inessential, merely regulatory.[27] One can, many people think, do without this rule. But to draw the further conclusions that Butler draws—to say that gender parody reveals that there is no gender—is to suppose that one can play without rules of any kind. "So I am inclined to distinguish between the essential and the inessential in a game too. The game, one would like to say, has not only rules but also a *point*" (*PI*, 564). And again, "Orders are sometimes not obeyed. But what would it be like if no orders were *ever* obeyed? The concept 'order' would have lost its purpose" (*PI*, 345). It is impossible to play the language-game of the parodic 'woman' except against the background of the rules for applying the original concept. They are what give the parody its meaning. The parody can break the regulatory rules—a woman performing a man in the barber's chair—but the refusal to see the family resemblance that is constitutive of 'woman' is no longer parody. It is performance without a point.

Where to Get Off

As our look at the language-games of 'woman' reveals, the problem of difference is actually two different problems. For the pragmatist feminist, who does not deny that there is a subject for feminism, the problem is to arrive at the criteria for correctly including certain women and excluding others for a given practical purpose. The difficulty is that one may not play the language-game of theorizing feminism long enough, and so use arbitrary rather than well-chosen criteria for inclusion.

The postmodern feminist has a different problem. She requires a means of keeping all the differences among women and within the individual self—the "precarious, conflicted, and complex" self[28]—from dissolving 'woman' altogether, for if she does not preserve at least a rough integrity to the concept, her feminist theorizing will consist of words that mean anything—and nothing. The attending difficulty, as Wittgenstein put it, "is not that of finding the solution but rather that of recognizing as the solution something that looks as if it were only a preliminary to it. . . . This is connected, I believe, with our wrongly expecting an explanation. Whereas the solution of the difficulty is a description, if we give it the right place in our considerations. If we dwell upon it, and do not try to get beyond it. The difficulty here is: to stop" (Zettel, 314).

The essentialist trap for feminists was always inadvertent. They meant merely to stop marginalizing women who were already too often unseen and unheard. But the responses to this problem swung between "There must be" and "There can't be," between "Let a thousand women bloom" and "There's no such creature." To insist on the overriding importance of categories such as race or ethnicity or to deny ontologic status to anything other than linguistic practice is to turn the concepts 'race', 'ethnicity', and 'language' into superconcepts—to endow them with a metaphysical halo that sets them outside communal practices and their histories and gives them a gratuitous authority. Whereas, of course, if words such as *ethnicity*, *language*, and *gender* have a use, it must be as humble a one as that of the words *table*, *lamp*, and *door* (PI, 97). It's when we come to these concepts in the spirit of description rather than by surrounding them with a halo that we become capable of stopping work on this problem when we want to.

Notes

1. María C. Lugones and Elizabeth V. Spelman, "Have We Got a Theory for You! Feminist Theory, Cultural Imperialism and the Demand for 'The Woman's Voice,'" *Women's Studies International Forum* 6, no. 6 (1983): 573–81; Jean Grimshaw, *Philosophy and Feminist Thinking* (Minneapolis:

University of Minnesota Press, 1986); Elizabeth V. Spelman, *Inessential Woman: Problems of Exclusion in Feminist Thought* (Boston: Beacon Press, 1988); Denise Riley, *"Am I That Name?" Feminism and the Category of "Women" in History* (Minneapolis: University of Minnesota Press, 1988); Linda Alcoff, "Cultural Feminism Versus Post-Structuralism: The Identity Crisis in Feminist Theory," *Signs* 13, no. 3 (1988): 405–36; Diana Fuss, *Essentially Speaking* (New York: Routledge, 1989); Judith Butler, *Gender Trouble: Feminism and the Subversion of Identity* (New York: Routledge, 1990); Linda J. Nicholson, ed., *Feminism/Postmodernism* (New York: Routledge, 1990), especially Nancy Fraser and Linda J. Nicholson, "Social Criticism Without Philosophy: An Encounter Between Feminism and Postmodernism," 19–38; and Donna Haraway, "A Manifesto for Cyborgs: Science, Technology, and Socialist Feminism in the 1980s," 190–233; Angela P. Harris, "Race and Essentialism in Feminist Legal Theory," *Stanford Law Review* 42 (1990): 581–616; Jane Roland Martin, "Methodological Essentialism, False Difference, and Other Dangerous Traps," *Signs* 19, no. 3 (1994): 630–57; and many, many others.

2. Iris Marion Young, "Gender as Seriality: Thinking About Women as a Social Collective," *Signs* 19, no. 3 (1994): 713–38, at 713–14.

3. Butler, *Gender Trouble*, 135–36.

4. María C. Lugones, "On the Logic of Pluralist Feminism, " in *Feminist Ethics*, ed. Claudia Card (Lawrence: University Press of Kansas, 1991), 35–44, at 41.

5. Susan Bordo, "Feminism, Postmodernism, and Gender-Skepticism," in *Unbearable Weight: Feminism, Western Culture, and the Body* (Berkeley and Los Angeles: University of California Press, 1993), 218.

6. In *Bodies That Matter: On the Discursive Limits of "Sex,"* Butler responds to various criticisms of *Gender Trouble*—in particular, that the body's materiality is an argument against its being constructed, and that the idea of gender as a construction forecloses agency, as it denies a subject who performs the activity of construction. The "discursive limits" she discusses, however, are social and political ones, not the linguistic limits I shall theorize here.

7. Lewis Carroll, *Alice's Adventures in Wonderland* and *Through the Looking-Glass* (London: Methuen, 1978), 171.

8. The reasons other philosophers have offered are numerous. Some, like Norman Malcolm and Hector-Neri Castañeda, see the treatment of private language as an argument that takes the form of a *reductio* that here reaches its absurd conclusion: see Norman Malcolm, "Wittgenstein's *Philosophical Investigations*," *Philosophical Review* 63 (1954): 530–59; and Hector-Neri Castañeda, "The Private Language Argument as a *Reductio ad Absurdum*," in *The Private Language Argument*, ed. O. R. Jones (London: Macmillan, 1971). Others, most famously perhaps A. J. Ayer, think the diarist's failure of reference occurs because the recognition of his sensation can't be verified independently; see his "Can There Be a Private Language?" delivered to the Aristotelian Society and reprinted in *Wittgenstein*, ed. George Pitcher (New York: Doubleday, 1966). Both Castañeda and Ayer think the argument is unsuccessful.

9. See James A. (Lindemann) Nelson, "Wittgenstein's Grammatical Turn," in *Wittgenstein, the Vienna Circle, and Critical Rationalism*, ed. H. Berghel et al. (Vienna: Verlag Holder-Pichler-Tempsky, 1979), 113.

10. Anthony Kenny argues in a way that is reminiscent of this, but his argument derives "from the picture theory of the proposition in the 1910s." See his "Verification Principle and the Private Language Argument," in Jones, *The Private Language Argument*.

11. See Sabina Lovibond's discussion of this in *Realism and Imagination in Ethics* (Minneapolis: University of Minnesota Press, 1983), secs. 33, 38.

12. Lovibond, *Realism and Imagination in Ethics*, 164.

13. Butler, *Gender Trouble*, 1.

14. Bordo, "Feminism, Postmodernism, Gender Skepticism," 242–43.

15. G. E. Moore, "A Proof of the External World," in *Proceedings of the British Academy* 25 (1939), reprinted in Moore's *Philosophical Papers* (London: George Allen and Unwin, 1959).

16. "If," Wittgenstein famously retorts in *On Certainty*, "you do know that *here is one hand,* we'll grant you all the rest."

17. For the distinction between *defending* women's interests and *discerning* their interests, see Hilde Lindemann Nelson and James Lindemann Nelson, "Other 'Isms' Aren't Enough: Feminism, Social Policy, and Long-Acting Contraception," in *Coerced Contraception? Moral and Policy Challenges of Long-Acting Birth Control,* ed. Ellen Moskowitz and Bruce Jennings (Washington, D.C.: Georgetown University Press, 1996).

18. Iris Marion Young, *Justice and the Politics of Difference* (Princeton: Princeton University Press, 1990).

19. Young, "Gender as Seriality," 722.

20. For a good account of the physical variations in male and female bodies, see John Money and Anke A. Ehrhardt, *Man and Woman, Boy and Girl: Differentiation and Dimorphism of Gender Identity from Conception to Maturity* (Baltimore: Johns Hopkins University Press, 1973).

21. Spelman, *Inessential Woman,* 186.

22. Stanley Cavell, *The Claim of Reason: Wittgenstein, Skepticism, Morality, and Tragedy* (Oxford: Clarendon, 1979), 177.

23. Butler, *Gender Trouble,* 143.

24. Bernice Johnson Reagon, "Coalition Politics: Turning the Century," in *Home Girls: A Black Feminist Anthology,* ed. Barbara Smith (New York: Kitchen Table/Women of Color Press, 1983), 356–68, at 363.

25. Parker Tyler, "The Garbo Image," quoted in Butler, *Gender Trouble,* 128.

26. Butler, *Gender Trouble,* 137–38.

27. As Monique Wittig and Catherine MacKinnon see it, of course, the "woman = heterosexual fuckee" rule is *not* inessential: individuals such as lesbians or nuns can break the rule but it does define the game. Whether they are right depends on whose game it is, and who gets to decide what rules are constitutive.

28. The phrase is Patricia Elliot's, in *From Mastery to Analysis: Theories of Gender in Psychoanalytic Feminism* (Ithaca: Cornell University Press, 1991), 75.

11

Using Wittgensteinian Methodology to Elucidate "Equality"

Christine M. Koggel

The prescriptive statement "Equality for all people!" seems unambiguous enough. It suggests that inequality still exists for some, and it expounds equality as a worthy goal. Yet, from the time of Aristotle, political theorists have given different accounts of what makes people equal, and they have come up with conflicting and controversial prescriptions for achieving equality. In this essay, I shall use the seemingly simple strategy of examining how the concept "equality" functions in ordinary cases in which we describe things as equal to explore whether this sheds light on more complex cases in which "equality" is used to prescribe treatment. In what is probably the best-known conceptual work on equality, Peter

I am grateful to Christine Overall, Christine Sypnowich, Susan Babbitt, and Andrew Brook, who commented on early drafts of this essay and to Naomi Scheman and the readers of the volume for help in preparing the essay for publication here.

Westen writes that "the advantage of conceptual analysis is that, being grounded in ordinary language, it rests on matters on which each of us is already an authority" (Westen 1990, xix). But he then draws the disappointing conclusion that a conceptual analysis has "nothing to say about what many people above all wish to know—nothing about what equalities actually exist or ought to exist" (xix). While it is true that an examination of the ordinary use of "equality" will not give substantive answers to what sorts of inequalities are unjust or how a state of equality can be obtained, I think it can provide a framework for those answers.

What I do when I examine how *equality* is used is different from what ordinary language philosophers who study our moral concepts do. Rather than engage in the project of determining the necessary and sufficient conditions for applying a term like "equality," I shall argue that we need to think ourselves into the contexts in which determinations of equality are made and speech acts prescribing equality are used. This is precisely the central feature of Wittgenstein's method for explaining meaning as use, imagining simple language games in which people communicate with one another for various purposes. By using Wittgenstein's famous example of the builders and adding increasingly sophisticated kinds of speech acts to their simple language, ones that Wittgenstein did not himself imagine, the complex and taken-for-granted background activities that go into making determinations of equality come into sharp relief. While Wittgenstein focuses on the implications of meaning as use for language, his methodology of describing what people *do* when they learn to communicate and interact with others can be used to examine the relationships formed in and through social practices and affected by the standards and rules of a community. We can learn about the meaning of "equality," its use and function in moral and political contexts, by highlighting the underlying relational features, both of language and of people. I shall then use these relational insights to discuss briefly feminist critiques of essentialist accounts of difference underlying theories of equality.[1] Despite Wittgenstein's own conservatism, his method can be fruitfully employed to highlight the complexity of moral arguments for equality and to reveal particular inequalities not recognized by traditional equality theorists.

The Framework: Wittgenstein's Theory of Meaning

In his later work, Wittgenstein attempted to undermine previous theories of meaning (including his own earlier account) that took words to be just labels for objects—whether those objects were things in the world or ideas in the head.[2] Wittgenstein's method of illuminating what words mean is "to study the phenomena of language in primitive kinds of application in which one can command a clear view of the aim and functioning of the words" (Wittgenstein 1976, §5). He asks us to think of words as having their home in language games, the context of human activity and purpose. He uses the method of describing language games both as a critique of traditional theories of meaning and as a way to develop his own positive account of meaning as use. Words have functions in purposeful activity in the same way that particular objects have functions. "Think of the tools in a tool-box: there is a hammer, pliers, a saw, a screw-driver, a rule, a glue-pot, glue, nails and screws.—The functions of words are as diverse as the functions of these objects. (And in both cases there are similarities.) Of course, what confuses us is the uniform appearance of words when we hear them spoken or meet them in script and print. For their *application* is not presented to us so clearly. Especially when we are doing philosophy!" (Wittgenstein 1976, §11, his emphasis).

By paring down the description of a language to such simple language games as what builders *do* when they identify different kinds of building stones and learn to fetch them when asked, Wittgenstein has us focus on purposive activity as central to an account of the meaning of words. Consider Wittgenstein's example of the simple language of the builders. "The language is meant to serve for communication between a builder A and an assistant B. A is building with building-stones: there are blocks, pillars, slabs and beams. B has to pass the stones, and that in the order in which A needs them. For this purpose they use a language consisting of the words 'block', 'pillar', 'slab', 'beam'. A calls them out;—B brings the stone which he has learnt to bring at such-and-such a call.—Conceive this as a complete primitive language" (Wittgenstein 1976, §2).

The first observation to make about Wittgenstein's description of the language of the builders is that the successful application of such simple concepts as "slab" reveals the importance of the human capacity to recognize relationships of similarity and difference, a capacity that is vital to being able to identify kinds of building blocks correctly.[3] For each order "slab," builder B fetches that stone by identifying the slabs in the pile that she has learned to differentiate from other kinds of stones.[4] But by immediately placing the capacity to identify similarities and differences into the context of the activity of building, Wittgenstein moves us away from the idea that the meaning of a word is given in the connection between word and object to the whole context of activity and purpose in which the word has its use.

Part of learning what a word means is learning to connect word and object, but there is more than one way to do this (think about connecting *gray* with the object slab) and for more than one purpose. The builders build, but we could just as easily imagine a language in which people were taught to perform some religious ritual when presented with the word *slab*. Perhaps in that language, people would be taught to interpret the way the stones are placed as different messages from the gods: when a slab points north, the gods are angry, for example. Here, the word *slab* would refer to the same object, but the placement of the object would be relevant and result in different rules for the use of *slab* and different social practices and interactions. "With different training the same ostensive teaching of these words would have effected a quite different understanding" (Wittgenstein 1976, §6). Words do refer to things in the world and, in this sense, Wittgenstein is a realist. But to know the meaning of words is to be familiar with the standards, rules, and practices of a community of language users. The builders learn their language in the context of responding to the speech acts of others engaged in the activity of building. The rules of the language involving religious rituals represent social practices that result in different sorts of interactions and relationships among the language users than those that we find in the builders' language.

Things in the world are categorized for particular purposes, and people learn what counts as similar and different at the same time as they learn how to interact and communicate with others in purposive activity. They learn the standards and rules for use in a community and behave accordingly. So far in our description of the meaning of concepts such as slab, we are dealing with standards of comparison and rules for use that are stripped down and basic. Yet even in the context of such a simple language, Wittgenstein's account of meaning as use can already handle more complicated kinds of speech acts in which mistakes are made: an appeal to the agreed-upon and established standards and rules for application could be made. A builder who brings a slab when asked to bring a pillar can be shown how slabs differ from pillars. An inability to apply the concepts and follow the rules may be corrected by training the builder to focus on the relevant similarities and differences for purposes of classifying things and by conveying the importance of building to one's inclusion in a community.

Imagining new language games and the various uses and functions that words and speech acts can have not only emphasizes the endless possibility and variety of language games but also demonstrates just how complicated the descriptions of some activities can become.[5] Not only do members assume agreement about how to identify, compare, and judge items, but it is a feature of language that the agreements are integral to their day-to-day engagement with others in purposeful activity. Such interaction also involves disagreements, doubts, and challenges about standards and rules and it is through these kinds of interaction that changes to the meaning of our concepts and speech acts occur.

When we classify things and use them for particular purposes, we can imagine what might happen when cases of disagreement arise concerning the standards and rules. In the simplest version of the language of the builders, we could imagine that a builder engaged in the activity of building suddenly claims that slabs do not function as useful building materials. We can also imagine various resolutions to this kind of disagreement: the builders decide to eliminate slabs as building materials, they decide that slabs can be used for other purposes, they decide that the builder is wrong about slabs and continue to make the same distinctions and follow the same rules, and so on. In the case of the first two sorts of resolutions, perhaps a period of readjustment to new standards or rules and some retraining are needed. When disagreement involves objects in the world, this interaction, cooperation, interpretation, and changing of standards is a reflection of ordinary purposive human activity. However, the last kind of resolution involving a judgment that the builder is wrong begins to highlight the complexity underlying the activity of describing people and establishing rules for social interaction.

In cases of judgments involving people, beliefs about difference can become institutionalized in ways that affect the lives and interactions of members of a moral community. For example, builders who are incapable of following the rules because of some cognitive or physical disability might be excluded from building activities, and rules for their exclusion could be provided. If the incapacity is intermittent (say a builder is debilitated by depression), we could imagine the judgments and the rules for treatment that accompany perceptions of this kind of incapacity. The person, for example, could be judged to be lazy or unwilling to build. People judged to have similar incapacities might all be subjected to the same rules for treatment. These examples reveal part of what happens when people are themselves judged to be different from other people and rules are established for what the difference will mean in that community.

I have concentrated on what Wittgenstein tells us about the use of words in order to highlight elements that are not always clearly in view, ones that form the background conditions for learning a language and being a member of a community.[6] Wittgenstein draws our attention to the mundane things that we fail to notice when we try to say what a word means. We are beings with such basic capacities as noticing similarities and differences and fitting what we perceive when confronted with a new case under concepts that are already established for particular purposes. Judging things as equal is basic to learning a language at all. We also live in social contexts in which those judgments assume background agreements about the rules to follow in order to make what are taken to be *correct* comparisons and judgments. Language grows out of the interactive and purposeful activity of people in relationships in communities.

Wittgenstein uses the idea of a language game, describing the meaning of words as they are used by people in contexts, to highlight the taken-for-granted background of purposeful *activity* that is integral to learning standards and following rules. While his aim is to undermine accounts that take the meaning of words to be mere labels for objects or for ideas, I want to use these descriptions of background activity to highlight certain relationships that are central to an understanding of how moral concepts function: relationships of similarity and difference are shaped in social practices by community members; standards and rules are established in relationships with others and for particular purposes; and learning the standards and following the rules are conditions for being understood by others and accepted in relationships in communities. Aspects of "equality" in its prescriptive sense as an element in how we ought to treat people come into sharper focus when we keep these relational features of language and of people in mind.

Describing Features and Prescribing Treatment

The determinations of equality that are made in the simple language of the builders are fairly easy to describe and understand. They involve becoming familiar with the established standards of comparison and identifying the things that share the same descriptive features. These kinds of determination are generally referred to as statements or judgments of descriptive equality. When the builders note the relevant similarities and differences and classify building blocks accordingly, they determine what things are equal. When they respond to orders at the appropriate time and in the appropriate context, they apply the rules of treatment for similar cases. Notice, however, that unlike describing what "slab" means, in describing what *equality* means, we no longer describe how to use one word, but capture what is involved in using all words. To pin down what equality means in Wittgensteinian terms is to describe the background conditions of being familiar with the standards and applying the rules in various language games. Each meaningful speech act assumes the background activities of subjecting some thing, person, or event to an agreed-upon standard of measurement and then judging the particular case to be the same as or different from the standard. *Equal* is the word used to describe the outcome of determining relationships of similarity.

The statement that opened this chapter, "Equality for all people," is an example of a prescriptive statement of equality in that it prescribes treating all people equally. But notice that this rallying cry implies a number of equality claims: the claim that all people are equal (they all share some relevant descriptive feature[s]), the claim that these equals ought to be treated equally (they ought to have the same treatment because they share those features), and the claim that achieving a state of equality is a morally worthy goal (we ought to provide conditions that remove inequalities for some people). Once we try to imagine applying standards of comparison first for identifying people as descriptively equal and then for prescribing treatment to those descriptive equals, we quickly notice why the kinds of statements that prescribe equality are "more elusive and problematic" (Westen 1990, 10) than statements that describe what things, events, and states of affairs are equal. When we try to say what *equality* means when it is used in the context of moral arguments for achieving equality, it seems as though Wittgenstein is right to say of ethical judgments in general that "[a]nything—and nothing—is right" (Wittgenstein 1976, §77). Yet Wittgenstein's method of describing what people *do* in contexts in which they interact with others not only sheds light on the meaning of *equality* when it is used prescriptively, but it also clarifies Wittgenstein's own notoriously perplexing comments on ethics.

In his rather obscure remarks about morality in the early work of the *Tractatus*, Wittgenstein takes ethics to lie beyond the realm of what can be expressed in language. Some of these remarks suggest that he held a mystical view of ethics as ultimately a personal outlook on the world, one that frames a way of being in the world and about which we ought to remain silent. "We feel that even when *all possible* scientific questions have been answered, the problems of life remain completely untouched. Of course, there are no questions left, and this itself is the answer" (Wittgenstein 1961, 6.52, his emphasis). Wittgenstein then has this to say about ethics and its place in his work in a letter about the *Tractatus*: "[T]he book's point is an ethical one. . . . My work consists of two parts: the one presented here plus all that I have *not* written. And it is precisely the second part that is the important one" (Engelmann 1967, 143).

In *Ludwig Wittgenstein: The Duty of Genius*, Ray Monk succeeds perhaps more than any other Wittgenstein scholar not only in making sense of the relationship between the two parts of the *Tractatus*, but also in showing that in the transition from his early to his later work, Wittgenstein maintained a view of ethics as a kind of outlook, a way of being, that frames one's actions and interactions in the world.[7] I want to defend Monk's interpretation of Wittgenstein's view of ethics as a kind of "outlook" or "framework" and his argument that Wittgenstein held this view throughout his life. Yet many theorists take this view of ethics to be in tension with the later Wittgenstein's account of meaning as use.

Susan Hekman points out that even though Wittgenstein advances a "rigorous social concept of language" in his later work, he excludes ethics from this conception. "For the later Wittgenstein, language is exclusively a social activity: meanings are defined by use; justification is conventional and relative to language games; private languages are impossible. Yet ethics does not seem to have any place in this social world" (Hekman 1995, 120). Hekman finds a place for ethics in Wittgenstein and in the social world he describes by making a case for viewing moral discourse as a language game and by arguing for a multiplicity of language games representing kinds of moral discourses and outlooks. Yet Hekman also wants to argue that moral behavior and beliefs are integral to what it is to be a member of a community: "[M]oral voices are central—even integral— aspects of what it means to be a subject, that becoming a subject and developing a moral voice are inseparable" (113). The latter point seems to speak against treating morality as a kind of language game distinct from other language games. It would seem instead to support the view that morality reflects persons acting and interacting in all language games. As Seyla Benhabib puts it, "The domain of the moral is so deeply enmeshed with those interactions that constitute our lifeworld that to withdraw from moral judgment is tantamount to ceasing to interact, to talk and act in the human community" (Benhabib 1992, 125–26).[8] Such an account of morality as the very framework within which one acts and interacts in a community fits well with the relational features of language and of people that I have been highlighting thus far.

I think a good strategy for discussing morality in the context of Wittgenstein's later work is to heed the advice he gives in one of the few references to moral concepts that he makes in the *Philosophical Investigations* and then to expand on this in a way that Wittgenstein did not (and perhaps would not): "Anything—and nothing—is right.—And this is the position you are in if you look for definitions corresponding to our concepts in aesthetics or ethics. In such a difficulty always ask yourself: How did we *learn* the meaning of this word ('good' for instance)? From what sort of examples? in what language-games?" Then it will be easier for you to see that the word must have a family of meanings" (Wittgenstein 1976, §77, his emphasis). Not only does this advice fit with Wittgenstein's description of the meaning of concepts as intersecting, criss-crossing, and weaving through various language games, it also lends support to the view that ethics is a whole outlook, the participation and interaction of moral agents in a community.

Wittgenstein tells us that in the more complicated case of defining our moral concepts we should still follow the same procedure of examining the contexts in which the concepts and statements are used. His advice can be implemented by revisiting the builders' community and adding the more complex language and activity associated with the making of prescriptive statements of equality to their language. What happens when the builders learn to group people on the basis of descriptive features they are judged to have in common and to follow rules that prescribe treatment for members of those groups highlights the relational features I have identified thus far—only this time, people are themselves subjected to judgments about similarities and differences. Think of the complex of relationships identified earlier, only now in the context of concepts that group people: relationships of similarity and difference are shaped in social practices by community members; standards and rules are established in relationships with others and for particular purposes; and learning the standards and following the rules are conditions for being understood by others and accepted in relationships in communities.

Suppose that when builder B fetches two slabs after builder A gives the order "two slabs," builder A refuses to take them. Builder B shows that she understood the meaning of builder A's order by telling him that she brought two, not three, and slabs, not pillars. He agrees that she understood the meaning of *two slabs*, but explains that the order was intended for builder C, a man, and that he is following the rule "only males give and receive orders to build." We can provide a purely descriptive account of the use and meaning of equality for builder A in his interaction with builder B (who, for now, is more appropriately called aspiring builder B). He learns what *pillar* means by learning to identify the features that differentiate pillars from other building blocks and by understanding the place given to pillars in the activity of building. We can say that he learns what *woman* means by being able to identify the features that differentiate women from men and by understanding their role with respect to building. If the rule is "only males give and receive orders to build," he is not making a mistake in this language when he refuses to interact with aspiring builder B. But notice that he is following a very different sort of rule from the one he follows when he gives the order "two slabs" instead of "three pillars." The rule he follows *in relation* to aspiring builder B is one that takes the information about *who* responds to his orders to be relevant to the activity of building. When a woman responds to his orders, he takes the case to be different from when a man brings the stones. In other words, he operates with the rule that women are not like men and ought to be treated differently.

When we describe the meaning of *equality* in prescriptive statements about equality of the sort exemplified in the builders' new rule, the same features basic to our application of other concepts reappear: the basic background capacities of comparing and judging cases and following the rules of a community of language users in applying the concept to particular cases. Builder A *knows* how he ought to treat aspiring builder B because he exhibits the ability to identify cases that fall under the descriptive class "woman" and to follow the rule that excludes women from building. But describing the activity in the way we have done so far may make it seem as though similarities and differences are merely discovered, classifications capture real and essential features in the world apart from our interpretations, and judgments are neutral reflections about how the world is actually ordered. These are features characteristic of an essentialist view of the world and a realist picture of language. Certainly, builder A's immersion in the practices supporting his perceptions of and interactions with women would have him believe that the world is structured in this way and that *woman* means nonbuilding person.

The realist holds that there are real essences of things that are discoverable and identifiable through investigation of the world. The descriptive features that are constitutive of a given person or thing are taken to determine the universal categories under which particulars fall independently of human interpretation. We will need to question this realist account of categories and descriptions given the emphasis we have placed on purposeful activity in social interaction. A nominalist account of meaning takes the categories that people assign to things that share descriptive features to be purely a matter of convention and convenience. But this does not seem to be an accurate depiction of categories and descriptions either. Identifying difference(s) and prescribing treatment are activities that are entrenched in *real* social practices and in political contexts that have an *actual* impact on people's lives. When the project is precisely to identify inequalities that *ought* to be removed because they are *unjust*, an account of categories and descriptions as arbitrary social conventions hardly seems adequate to the task.

Debates about realism versus nominalism and essentialism versus constructionism are notoriously complex and raise big topics in philosophy of language, metaphysics, and epistemology. Feminists have played a key role in debates about whether judgments of difference(s) are real in the sense that they capture some essential difference or whether they are socially constructed and mere arbitrary conventions. I intend to discuss only some of the issues for the purpose of defending the claim that descriptions are neither real nor nominal *in the senses just outlined*. A relational approach as captured thus far in insights about the relational features of language and of people supports rather than undermines the idea that categories that group objects capture features in and facts about the world, but human interpretation determines what features and facts are attended to and made significant in the structuring of social practices and human relations. Weighing the arguments on each side of realism and nominalism tips the scale on the side of realism, but only when care is taken to clarify what is meant by realism. Perhaps there is no better way to articulate the kind of realism I shall defend than to differentiate it from Aristotle's, or what might be better described as an "Aristotelian," understanding of equality.

Descriptive Similarities: Real or Constructed?

Consider the following comments from Aristotle about equality and justice: "All men think justice to be a sort of equality. . . . [T]hey admit that justice is a thing and has a relation to persons, and that equals ought to have equality" (Aristotle, *Politics*, 1282b18–22). Out of Aristotle's comments about equality *as* justice and justice *as* treating equals equally has emerged the well-established idea that equality as a prescription for how people ought to be treated means that "like cases ought to be treated alike." In remarks from the *Politics* that immediately follow the prescription that equals ought to have equality, Aristotle asks a question of which, in the end, he seems not to realize the full significance: "But there still remains a question: equality or inequality of what? here is a difficulty which calls for political speculation" (Aristotle, *Politics*, 1282b22–24). The question and answer indicate that determinations of equality presuppose comparison to some standard—equal or unequal with respect to some descriptive feature or features. In other words, treating like cases alike requires that judgments about what cases are alike be made according to what are determined to be relevant criteria of likeness or similarity for purposes of treatment. This account may seem to be compatible with the descriptions of the builders' community in which language users construct categories by determining relevant criteria of similarity and do so for particular social purposes. As is well known, however, Aristotle took differences among people to be inherent and natural and not socially determined in this sense.

The standard interpretation of Aristotle is that he based his conception of applying rules for treating like cases alike on the view that real or essential descriptive properties determine the categories under which people could be identified and classified. The Greek conception of essence was of the "whatness" of a thing, its irreducible, unchanging, and sometimes unknowable "form." The idea in this conception is that "there is some one determinate structure to the way things are, *independent of all human interpretation*" (Nussbaum 1995, 68, my emphasis). Martha Nussbaum refers to this kind of essentialism as "metaphysical realism" (67–68), a useful term for clarifying a sense of realism that most realists no longer defend.[9]

In the domain of moral and political arguments for equality, once the metaphysical realist "discovers" the descriptive facts that sort people into categories, there is little room left for prescription except to exhort people to find their "station" in life and perform its "duties."[10] Aristotle established a close connection between descriptions and prescriptions in his "discovery" of particular properties that then served as justifications for circumscribing the activities and roles of all people who shared those properties, justifications that restricted the realm of moral and political agents by denying membership in the political community to women and slaves on the basis of essential differences. The descriptions work to define the categories and then to justify the roles and functions of those who fit the categories.

Feminists have been critical of this sort of essentialism and point to the historical legacy of arguments for the essential nature of women and of other disadvantaged groups: "Essentialist claims about what makes certain groups of people the way they are . . . are the political-philosophical constructs of conservatism. The history of essentialist arguments is one of oppressors telling the oppressed to accept their lot in life because 'that's just the way it is.' Essentialist arguments were used to justify slavery, to resist the Nineteenth Amendment (which gave women the vote), and to sustain colonialism by arguing 'altruistically' that 'the natives are unable to run their own governments'" (Tong 1989, 135). Minow provides an apt description of the effects of an Aristotelian conception of equality when she writes that "society assigns individuals to categories and, on that basis, determines whom to include in and whom to exclude from political, social, and economic activities. Because the activities are designed, in turn, with only the included participants in mind, the excluded seem not to fit because of something in their own nature" (Minow 1990, 21).

I think the first step to understanding what is real and what is constructed is to reject metaphysical realism and thereby undermine the idea that the descriptions are secure and fixed outside of human activity and purpose. In other words, we focus on the *activity* and reject the notion that categories reflect the structure of the world apart from human interpretation. However, an account of human purposes and interpretation does not clinch the case for a thoroughgoing account of social constructionism or of nominal categories either. This then raises the question of whether and what sort of realism is left to defend, a question for which we can begin to find answers by returning to a discussion of Wittgenstein.

In highlighting the background activity involved in identifying difference and determining what the difference will mean, it may *seem* as though Wittgenstein shifts the focus from a realist account of differences as objectively determined and discoverable to a nominalist account of language users classifying things as a matter of "arbitrary definitional conventions. The only thing uniting classes of similar things, according to nominalists, is a name" (Babbitt 1996, 133). Yet Wittgenstein himself distinguishes his account from nominalism. "[I]t may look as if what we were doing were Nominalism. Nominalists make the mistake of interpreting all words as *names*, and so of not really describing their use, but only, so to speak, giving a paper draft on such a description" (Wittgenstein 1976, §383, his emphasis). When we describe the activity of the builders as though we ourselves might be there in those relationships in which the standards and rules are established, we discover that neither a realist emphasis on essential differences nor a nominalist emphasis on arbitrary social constructions captures the builders' background activity of learning to identify relevant similarities and differences in the purposive context of the language games of members of a community. Wittgenstein's account of meaning as use can be understood as a rejection of both nominalism and realism in their strict and stripped-down versions.

Nominalism as traditionally formulated cannot explain why some categories assigned on the basis of arbitrary conventions, as nominalists put it, have universal or widespread connections with social arrangements, for example, a point captured by Jane Flax when she writes that "physically male and female humans resemble each other in many more ways than we differ. Our similarities are even more striking if we compare humans to, say, toads or trees. So why ought the anatomical differences between male and female humans assume such significance in our sense of selves as persons?" (Flax 1990, 51). History shows widespread discrimination on a global scale against people not only on the basis of gender but also on the basis of differences such as race, color, levels of ability, and sexual orientation. A proper account of meaning cannot ignore these facts of the historical significance that particular differences have had and continue to have and of the impact of them on the *actual* lives of community members identified on the basis of difference(s). We can reject metaphysical realism and still retain a version of realism that allows us to state emphatically that particular inequalities exist and ought to be removed. Conceding too much to the side of arbitrary social conventions and nominal categories would appear to undermine this political project so central to feminism, for example.

The Wittgensteinian view of meaning as use need not be a rejection of the realist insistence that there are facts. The realist "finds it amazing that the world could so kindly sort itself into our categories. He protests that there are definite sorts of objects in it . . . which we have painstakingly come to recognize and classify correctly" (Hacking 1986, 227). With respect to the real features of people, the "robust realist does not have to argue very hard that people also come sorted. Some are thick, some thin, some dead, some alive" (227). Yet, a realist account that emphasizes the discovery of facts in a world that comes already sorted does not adequately explain the close connection that obtains between categories and the purposeful functions for which people create and use categories, purposes that lead them to focus on some features and to ignore others. Slabs have real features that we notice and categorize, but what features we decide to focus on are determined by the function that slabs have in our language. As Martha Minow puts it, "Of course, there are 'real' differences in the world. . . . But when we simplify and sort, we focus on some traits rather than others" (Minow 1990, 3). *Slab* can mean "object of religious worship" as well as "object for building" and in the two cases, different features of slabs are noticed and taken as relevant and particular interactions and relationships are thereby created. This may appear to correspond with arbitrary conventions for describing objects in the sense that it is arbitrary whether slabs are objects for building or for religious worship. But human purposes and interpretation are more than arbitrary factors and mere conventions, as is evident in the consequences for women and slaves of Aristotle's inquiry into human essence as the basis for his account of equality and justice.

One of my goals has been to dislodge the discussion of difference from the metaphysical question of real or essential differences to moral and political questions about social practices that identify difference(s) as the basis for describing, defining, and circumscribing people's lives, activities, and relationships. In this way, the inadequacy of both a realist account of independent facts and a nominalist account of arbitrary categories is apparent. When people are identified, compared, and judged on the basis of descriptive differences, these practices have consequences for determining who can engage in what activities and how the activities function in communities. In the case of the builders who exclude women from building, these practices determine the kind of relationships and interactions that can take place between various community members and the meaning given to the very actions and interactions of people in that community.

The categories we use to group people describe features in the world that people have and share, and in this sense our categories are not arbitrary. When we classify people by identifying differences, we structure relationships in a community in ways that affect how people are treated, who they can be, and what they can do. We learn to identify similarities and differences in relationships in which factors such as authority and power play a role in the establishment and maintenance of the standards and rules, factors that are particularly deep running when we identify differences and categorize people accordingly. The builders learn a language by learning what *others* know and by being trained to perform speech acts in the context of purposeful activity. Those others are language users who already know the standards and rules and are in a position to teach those who do not yet know and who need to learn in order to become participating members of communities. Parents teach children, teachers instruct students, employers train employees, politicians convince citizens, and builders teach nonbuilders or at least those who are perceived as potential builders. While relations of power and authority are implicated in the activity of establishing and maintaining standards and rules in general, they are particularly evident when the standards and rules apply to people.

I have been focusing throughout on speech acts as interactive communicative processes in purposive contexts as a way of reflecting on how concepts and categories shape relationships, social practices, and human interaction. I now want to go well beyond Wittgenstein by examining the role of relationships of authority and power to the meaning of categories by highlighting the moral and political implications of describing people. What happens to people assigned to categories of disability, for example, affects in advance how their behavior and speech acts are understood, what relationships they can enter into with other people, and what level of influence they have for changing the meaning of the categories to which they are assigned. We need to keep these relational features in mind and then get inside the language of the builders who perceive women as different in order to understand what happens to relationships when that kind of determination is made.

Moral and Political Implications
of Describing Difference(s)

What is disturbing about the builder who identifies women for the purpose of excluding them from the activity of building is that the category "woman," and the rule "only males give and receive orders to build," determine the meaning of difference in ways that specify and circumscribe activities, roles, and relationships. For example, the sentence "Women can build too" would be a false statement or perhaps be understood as a joke in a social context in which the rules that exclude women are settled and fixed. Women are just not perceived as having building capacities. If we assume the rule to be not only well understood and accepted but backed by relations of power or entrenched in tradition, then two kinds of consequences result for aspiring builder B: she may accept descriptions of what her difference means, not perceive herself as a builder, and never challenge the description of her as a nonbuilder; or she may perceive herself as having the capacity to build and even aspire to be a builder, but have no power to change the meaning of her difference in the context of an established practice that excludes her from building. The agreement about the meaning of her difference in relation to the norm of male builder has consequences that limit the choices she has for interacting, participating, and acting in this social context that excludes descriptions of her as a builder.

Other consequences flowing from describing women as nonbuilders can be imagined. Women are excluded from building altogether and from contexts in which building skills and practices are learned and discussed. We can imagine that *work* is defined as engagement in building activities and that "workers" are builders. In defining some kinds of human activity as "work" and in determining that some kinds of "work" are appropriate for certain people, all sorts of repercussions with respect to circumscribing, evaluating, and valuing human activities emerge. Who takes care of children and those who are unable to build, who gets paid, who makes meals, who runs for office, and the different values given to these activities go along with the identification and labeling of people. Another example illustrates a similar point. If we go back to the example of the builder who is told that he is wrong to consider slabs as useless building materials, we can imagine that a number of judgments about his ideas being "off" would result in his being ostracized or identified as mentally incompetent. Various purposes and social conditions determine the value placed on possessing the right skills and making the correct judgments. All these valuations and judgments happen in the context of social practices in communities. Judgments about the value and worth of various kinds of activity go with the practice of labeling people as different. As Carol Gilligan points out in the context of giving voice to the ethic of care, "It is difficult to say 'different' without saying 'better' or 'worse'" (Gilligan 1982, 14). And as Gilligan has attempted to show, caring for others has been predominantly women's work and judged to be of inferior worth to the "real" work that takes place outside the home.

There are two things I would like to clarify to forestall possible objections, objections that I cannot address fully here. First, I am not suggesting that all inferences from descriptions of difference to prescriptions for treatment are morally reprehensible. An example of describing people that we might not condemn is using builder C's physical weakness and inability to carry slabs as a reason for exempting him from the activity of building. But even in this example, the need for a heightened awareness of and sensitivity to the moral and political implications of constructing a category such as "disability" and establishing rules of treatment for those fitted into the category is apparent when we examine the relationships that are thereby formed. Second, I am not suggesting that only descriptions of *people* lead directly to moral prescriptions. Our treatment of nonhuman animals depends on how we classify and describe them, and these actions have moral implications because they determine our "way of being" in the world in our interactions with nonhumans and the environment. In both cases, the weight needs to rest on an examination of the social context that results in inequalities and injustices rather than on an appeal to facts about descriptive properties of things in the world in abstraction from facts about the social practices and political contexts that give those properties meaning.

Feminists have been critical of traditional approaches to metaphysical questions about the structure of the world and the nature of personhood, to epistemological questions about what we can know and how, and to moral and political questions about the interpersonal relationships and social arrangements that we should strive to achieve. Perhaps the single most important contribution in all these areas has been the insistence that accounts of human interpretation, social practices, and political contexts are crucial for providing adequate answers to these questions. There is no point of view outside human interpretation and practices. I have argued that Wittgenstein's account of meaning as use provides further and, some might say, unsuspected support for feminists in these areas of inquiry; unsuspected because I have departed from Wittgenstein quite radically in connecting speech acts with social practices to argue that equality gets its meaning in social and political contexts where standards that measure inequalities and rules that apply treatment for unequals create injustices that ought to be addressed.

Standards are created and maintained by members who have the power to identify and assign meaning to difference and the authority to apply and maintain the rules for use. Identifying difference(s) assumes a standard of comparison, a norm, from which the difference is identifiable and defined as meaningful. "A reference point for comparison purposes is central to a notion of equality. Equality asks, equal compared with whom?" (Minow 1990, 51). When language learning is successful, norms and purposes become so much a part of the background that they are taken for granted and hidden. When people are classified according to some descriptive feature or features, this has consequences for who can participate in the activities of creating and changing meaning and who can be a contributing member in the purposeful activities of a community. I have argued that these descriptions of the relational features of language and of people neither establish the case for a thoroughgoing account of social constructionism nor call for the outright rejection of essentialism or realism.

Feminists have had good reason to be critical of those accounts of essentialism and realism that result in arguments for the unequal status of women and minorities and in justifications for their unequal treatment. However, the very rejection of these arguments for essential differences relies on the notion of what it means to be a *human being* that the difference(s) of gender or race or level of ability are then taken to be irrelevant to questions about worth and membership in a community. Susan Babbitt defends essentialism along these lines when she claims that "to the extent that political theorists assume they ought to *look* for things like real essences, they end up defining concepts like 'humanity' or 'women' *incorrectly* (Babbitt 1996, 16, my emphasis). She goes on to argue that "a woman is not *different* from men, with respect to being oppressed, unless she can somehow be identified as a person of the same sort—namely, human. But that kind of judgment is only possible in light of at least some kind of more general, unifying vision—one that at least involves some conception of how people *ought* to think of humanity" (33, her emphasis). Furthermore, the analysis of how social practices and political conditions structure relationships and people's lives in ways that are unjust is critical to the project of eliminating inequalities and reconceptualizing difference. It is precisely this project, so central to feminism, that provides a strong argument for retaining an account of realism: "We want to know whether there are *determinate* answers to questions about how *best* to order things and, consequently, of how *best* to proceed—answers, in particular, that are not simply the result of certain discriminatory traditions" (17, my emphasis).

The kind of realism defended in this essay emphasizes the need to evaluate the social practices that give meaning to difference and make it significant to one's life prospects. This emphasis can both explain and help avoid pernicious essentialist tendencies that have come under attack within feminist theory itself. To take but one familiar example, Gilligan has been accused of essentialism in her failure to pay attention to factors of race and class, for example, in describing the ethic of care as a woman's voice. Rather than reject the insights of an ethic of care altogether, however, I think a better strategy is to examine the social practices in particular political contexts that result in the devaluation of care and the significance this has in the lives of those whose identities and roles are associated with caring for others.[11] Gilligan is right to suggest that these roles tend to be relegated to women, but wrong to universalize this to all women. Attention to social practices in particular contexts can explain that the meaning of gender need not be fixed across all cultures. It can also explain that the meaning given to differences such as race, class, levels of ability, and sexual orientation intersect with and depart from gender in ways that call for careful analyses of the social practices and their effects on the lives of those identified on the basis of these and other differences. Such analysis is important to projects of understanding oppression in particular contexts and devising effective strategies for eliminating all sorts of oppressive relations.

Drawing Conclusions and Looking Ahead: Implications for Equality Theory

The account of the builders' language and of the impact of their discourse on others when prescriptive statements of equality are added to their language makes what started as a very simple language much more complicated and complex than Wittgenstein ever imagined. Noticing similarities and differences and judging items to be the same as or different from standards is a logical feature of language. Yet these human capacities of comparing and judging are so inextricably intertwined with the activities of communicating and interacting with others that descriptive accounts of relationships of similarity and difference removed from accounts of people in purposive relationships miss important elements of moral concepts. We can now understand what underlies the kind of account of morality provided by Hekman and Benhabib, namely the embeddedness of moral judgments and behavior in all aspects of a person's life. People are social beings whose actions and interactions take place in, are shaped by, and have meaning in particular social practices and political contexts. People deliberate and make decisions in the context of planning a life in response to and in relationships with members of a community. Thus, moral beliefs, moral judgments, and moral behavior are not incidental aspects of people's lives, but are embedded in being a person in a community. To return to a point made in the context of interpreting Wittgenstein on ethics, morality forms the kind of personal outlook that frames our actions in the world and our interactions with others.

Prescriptive statements of equality need to be understood in the broader context of a variety of many different language games, how these speech acts function in relationships in communities. When we are dealing with people, descriptions of them affect how they can be, to whom they can relate, and what they are understood to contribute or are permitted to communicate. It will be important to an analysis of equality to be aware of relations of power and of who is excluded from participating in particular social and political contexts. The kinds of inequalities that emerge when we look at the actual details of how and why people are identified on the basis of distinctive features, what effect this has on the possibilities for interactive and purposeful activity, and what implications and consequences for identity and self-concepts emerge from the activity of labeling have not been recognized by traditional equality theorists. These inequalities manifest themselves when we focus on the relational features of language and of people.

To be complete, a theory of equality must take on the task of uncovering and evaluating who or what counts as equal, for what purposes, and in what sorts of relationships. Together, in their interconnectedness and inseparability, the relational features of language and of people in communities can contribute to an understanding of the meaning of difference and its relevance to a theory of equality in a way not dealt with by traditional equality theory. When aspiring builder B is subjected to the agreements reached about what her particular features will mean in particular social contexts, this has consequences for how and who she can be. Aspiring builder B is herself the object of the activity of identifying similarities and differences. Perceptions of her and of the roles appropriate for someone like her will affect the range of choices available to her, including opportunities for her to participate in the activity of changing or challenging meaning, for her to enter into and develop particular kinds of relationships, and for her to acquire the kind of confidence and self-respect that allow her to develop her talents and pursue her goals. And how she is perceived and what levels of power she has for changing her circumstances will vary again when factors such as class or race or sexual orientation are given meaning in social practices and made significant to her life.

Notes

1. I provide a more complete treatment of feminist interpretations of and reactions to theories of equality in *Perspectives on Equality: Constructing a Relational Theory* (1998).

2. My discussion of Wittgenstein's theory of meaning will be limited to a bare outline: what is needed to elucidate how a concept like equality is used. I provide a fuller account of his theory in *Paradigms: The Later Wittgenstein's View of Meaning* (Koggel 1981).

3. In explaining how a child learns a language, Quine defends the centrality of the basic human capacity to notice similarities and differences. "If the child is to be amenable to such training, however, what he must have is a prior tendency to weight qualitative differences unequally. He must, so to speak, sense more resemblance between some stimulations than between others" (Quine 1960, 83).

4. The use of *she* in this context is meant to be jarring. Wittgenstein would never have thought of the builders as women, and readers fall into the same assumptions about the builders being men. If the use of *she* surprises, this too should tell us something about language. I put women in this context of the builders' community throughout as a way of startling people out of their expectations and assumptions.

5. The following remark from Wittgenstein shows the complexity of speech acts:

> [W]e do the most various things with our sentences. Think of exclamations alone, with their completely different functions.
> Water! Away! Ow! Help! Fine! No!
> Are you inclined still to call these words "names of objects"? (Wittgenstein 1976, §27)

6. These remarks on background conditions for rule-following are also connected to insights central to Wittgenstein's *On Certainty*. Consider the following set of comments. "The game of doubting itself presupposes certainty" (Wittgenstein 1969, §115). "The child learns to believe a host of things. I.e. it learns to act according to these beliefs. Bit by bit there forms a system of what is believed, and in that system some things stand unshakeably fast and some are more or less liable to shift" (Wittgenstein 1969, §144). "In order to make a mistake, a man must already judge in conformity with mankind" (Wittgenstein 1969, §156). "The child learns by believing the adult. Doubt comes *after* belief" (Wittgenstein 1969, §160, his emphasis).

7. Monk describes the goal of his book as attempting to bridge the gap in Wittgenstein scholar-

ship between "those who study his work in isolation from his life and those who find his life fascinating but his work unintelligible" (Monk 1991, xvii–xviii).

8. Teresa Iglesias makes a similar point about the human subject being essentially a moral subject and argues that the Wittgenstein of the *Tractatus* held this view in his comments about the import of ethics as contained in what could be shown and not said (Iglesias 1988–90, 146–54).

9. Nussbaum goes on to argue, however, that Aristotle was not a metaphysical realist by examining Aristotle's criticisms of Platonism and referring us to her own work in support of this interpretation of Aristotle (Nussbaum 1995, 68).

10. Terminology used by F. H. Bradley in "My Station and Its Duties," a chapter of *Ethical Studies* (Bradley 1927).

11. Joan Tronto's (1993) analysis of caring practices in *Moral Boundaries: A Political Argument for an Ethic of Care* is one example of important work along these lines.

References

Aristotle. 1941. *Politics*. Trans. Benjamin Jowett. In *The Basic Works of Aristotle*. Ed. Richard McKeon. New York: Random House.

Babbitt, Susan. 1995. "Political Philosophy and the Challenge of the Personal: From Narcissism to Radical Critique." *Philosophical Studies* 77:293–318.

———. 1996. *Impossible Dreams: Rationality, Integrity, and Moral Imagination*. Boulder, Colo.: Westview Press.

Benhabib, Seyla. 1992. *Situating the Self: Gender, Community, and Postmodernism in Contemporary Ethics*. New York: Routledge.

Bradley, Francis Herbert. 1927. *Ethical Studies*. Oxford: Clarendon Press.

Engelmann, Paul. 1967. *Letters from Ludwig Wittgenstein with a Memoir*. Oxford: Blackwell.

Flax, Jane. 1990. "Postmodernism and Gender Relations in Feminist Theory." In *Feminism/Postmodernism*, ed. Linda J. Nicholson. New York: Routledge.

Fuss, Diana. 1989. *Essentially Speaking: Feminism, Nature, and Difference*. New York: Routledge.

Gilligan, Carol. 1982. *In a Different Voice: Psychological Theory and Women's Development*. Cambridge: Harvard University Press.

Hacking, Ian. 1986. "Making Up People." In *Reconstructing Individualism: Autonomy, Individuality, and the Self in Western Thought*, ed. Thomas C. Heller, Morton Sosna, and David E. Wellbery. Stanford: Stanford University Press.

Hekman, Susan J. 1995. *Moral Voices, Moral Selves: Carol Gilligan and Feminist Moral Theory*. Cambridge: Polity Press.

Iglesias, Teresa. 1988–90. "Russell and the Ethical Concern of Wittgenstein's *Tractatus*." *Philosophical Studies* 32:141–55.

Koggel, Christine. 1981. "Paradigms: The Later Wittgenstein's View of Meaning." Master's thesis, Carleton University. Ottawa: National Library Microfiche.

———. 1998. *Perspectives on Equality: Constructing a Relational Theory*. Lanham, Md.: Rowman and Littlefield.

Minow, Martha. 1990. *Making All the Difference: Inclusion, Exclusion, and American Law*. Ithaca: Cornell University Press.

Monk, Ray. 1991. *Ludwig Wittgenstein: The Duty of Genius*. London: Vintage.

Nussbaum, Martha. 1995. Introduction to *Women, Culture and Development: A Study of*

Human Capabilities, ed. Martha Nussbaum and Jonathan Glover. Oxford: Clarendon Press.

Quine, Willard V. O. 1960. *Word and Object*. Cambridge: MIT Press.

Tong, Rosemarie. 1989. *Feminist Thought: A Comprehensive Introduction*. Boulder, Colo.: Westview Press.

Tronto, Joan. 1993. *Moral Boundaries: A Political Argument for an Ethic of Care*. New York: Routledge.

Westen, Peter. 1990. *Speaking of Equality: An Analysis of the Rhetorical Force of "Equality" in Moral and Legal Discourse*. Princeton: Princeton University Press.

Wittgenstein, Ludwig. 1976. *Philosophical Investigations*. Trans. G. E. M. Anscombe. Oxford: Basil Blackwell.

———. 1964. *The Blue and Brown Books*. Oxford: Basil Blackwell.

———. 1961. *Tractatus Logico-Philosophicus*. London: Routledge and Kegan Paul.

———. 1969. *On Certainty*. Ed. G. E. M. Anscombe and G. H. von Wright. New York: Harper Torchbooks.

12

Eleanor Rosch and the Development of Successive Wittgensteinian Paradigms for Cognitive Science

Nalini Bhushan

Introduction

The ability to categorize has been taken to lie at the heart of all cognition. In humans, language aids in the task of categorization and is indispensable for the possession of more-abstract concepts. An investigation into the nature and structure of our concepts and categories therefore typically proceeds via an investigation of our language—names, predicates, and other syntactic and semantic tools of categorization. In this essay I focus upon some areas of Wittgenstein's work that bear on

I thank Naomi Scheman for helpful comments on an earlier draft that improved the content and readability of this essay.

(a) the topic of categorization, and (b) the nature of human cognition more generally, with an eye to exploring his influence upon the work of a woman cognitive psychologist at Berkeley, Eleanor Rosch. In the early 1970s Rosch played a central role in the development of a new paradigm for categorization research in psychology and for cognitive science in general. She took Wittgenstein's "family resemblance" approach to assessing category membership, in sharp contrast to the classical criterion given by a set of necessary and sufficient conditions, and used this philosophical insight in a powerful and empirically revolutionary way with her theory of prototypes.[1] In my discussing Rosch's approach to the study of human categorizing abilities, the relevance to more general feminist concerns (such as the centrality of the body, of the method of taking up the other's perspective, of rendering differences visible) is illustrated. I conclude with a few general remarks about the connections between Wittgensteinian and Buddhist views on the nature of cognition, connections that in recent years have led, interestingly enough, to the forging of a quite different paradigm for cognitive science, spearheaded once again by Rosch and her colleagues.[2]

Since the aim in this essay is not so much to document the trajectory of Rosch's writings and all her sources of influence as it is to explore Wittgensteinian themes that arise both directly and indirectly in her earlier and later work, I will restrict my discussion to relevant areas of her research as well as to those sections of Wittgenstein's work that connect in the most interesting ways with that of Rosch. As we will see, the Wittgensteinian insights that she articulates in her earlier work on categorization and the ones that preoccupy her today are in many ways quite different, taken from Mahayana Buddhism as expounded by Nagarjuna. And yet in going this route, in looking to this quite different tradition to flesh out the details of a new paradigm for cognitive science, in a certain sense she comes full circle, back to Wittgenstein. And so I begin with Wittgenstein.

Key Wittgensteinian Insights

Uniform Appearance Masking Functional Diversity

In the opening pages of *Philosophical Investigations* (1953) Wittgenstein demonstrates his interest in *kinds* of things, or categories, in his skepticism about the plausibility of the Augustinian picture of language. On this latter picture, individual words are names for individual things; in using language, one interacts with objects as particular entities. As Wittgenstein points out, here there is no distinction made between kinds, or categories, of words. Words belong to a single category, nouns, and perform a single kind of function. This is an implausible conception of language, as is clear from the variety of examples that Wittgenstein uses to demonstrate in a decisive way that there are many categories of words whose uses are very different, grounded in the functions that they play. The rest of his book can be read as a series of demonstrations that a certain classical picture of language that has its roots in this simple Augustinian conception of the way language classifies our world is fundamentally misguided.

I would like to begin with Wittgenstein's analogy between the parts and functions of language and the repertoire of a toolbox: "Think of the tools in a tool-box: there is a hammer, pliers, a saw, a screw-driver, a rule, a glue-pot, glue, nails and screws. The functions of words are as diverse as the functions of these objects. Of course, what confuses us is the uniform appearance of words when we hear them spoken or meet them in script and print. For their *application* is not presented to us so clearly. Especially when we are doing philosophy!" (1953, pt. I, sec. 11, p. 6).

I extract two insights from the above section that are pertinent to our discussion. First, if we wish to ascertain what words actually do, it is simply bad methodological practice to study them in abstraction from the way in which people in fact use them. The function of words and the fact of *their functional diversity* is made clear in the context of their actual application, as is the case for tools. Wittgenstein's point here about diversity is not, I take it, that hammers, nails, and the like can be arbitrarily used for tasks for which they were not intended (although one could take this view); for certainly there are correct and incorrect procedures that govern their use. It is that one can appreciate the function of those tools by watching carefully and attentively how they are procedurally used in practice. So too with language. In order to figure out what language is, as well as how it operates, one has to figure out how language works in actual practice.

I turn next to his remark about the "uniform appearance" of words, which confuses us about their application. This is a remark whose point is at the outset difficult to decipher. What does Wittgenstein mean by "uniform appearance"? Do words in fact appear uniform to us? Developmentally it is surely the difference in appearance that is salient; the letters look different from one another, being of different shapes and sizes, and we learn that differences in sound and appearance are not correlated with differences in use. Gradually we are taught the differences between parts of speech in a tradition that goes back as far as Aristotle. In addition, we are often made (painfully) aware of differences in the ways the words sound, and in what they mean, as we wield, and are buffeted by, them in the hustle and bustle of daily life. Understood in these ways, Wittgenstein's remark about the uniform appearance of words seems at best counterintuitive. But no, the point here is, I think, a more subtle one: it is that the previously mentioned diversities seem *so natural, and inevitable*, to us, layperson and philosopher alike (although philosophers are the more culpable group), that one can, precisely in seeing transparently how these different parts work, *render invisible* the fact that there might be other kinds of diversity, other kinds of functions, that are not apparent on the surface of the operation of our language.

And as we find throughout his work, the practices that matter aren't just our own; he has in mind linguistic and other cultural practices of communities that are outside the realm of those with which we are familiar. Indeed, many of the diverse 'cultures' that Wittgenstein examines are hypothetical: that of the solitary language-wielder; that of the wielder of a radically different arithmetical rule 'quus', that of the tribe that is entirely color-blind, and so on. Again, the point is not that languages and their rules are arbitrary; it is that languages and rules that govern their functioning are culturally and historically rooted, that one cannot understand their behavior by an examination that ignores the fact of this rootedness.

These insights are relevant to our special concern with categories and the activity of categorization. For as we shall see, the advice we extract from them, to pay close attention to what people actually do in figuring out the functional categories of language, leads us to a view about the notion of a category and what we are doing when we categorize that constitutes a conceptual shift from the approach to categories that was taken as a given before Wittgenstein.[3]

Categories: Open Borders Revealing Family Resemblances

Let us begin with what Lakoff has called the "classical" view of categories and some of its implications. On this view, categories have clearly delineated boundaries and clearly identified members, each of which must satisfy necessary and sufficient conditions for category membership. These conditions constitute what the members have in common, the invisible thread that places them squarely into the same category. Two important implications of this view are the following. (1) Since each member satisfies the conditions as completely as any other (they either satisfy them or they don't), they are "equivalent" in the sense that one member of a category is as solidly a member of that category as any other. The notion that some members are better representatives of that category than others makes no sense. (2) Since the defining properties are to be found inherently in the members of a category, the delineation of categories is independent of details of the cognizers of those categories: whether they are adults or children, men or women, whether they belong to a current or ancient time, their interests and purposes, indeed, even their neurophysiological makeup.

Two connected ideas in particular in Wittgenstein that made possible the conceptual break from this way of thinking about categories were family resemblances and language games (including the idea that language itself is a language game). Language games are played with clusters of items that are *in some sense* similar, as in a family, in contrast to the eternal games that are played with items having essential properties in common. "I can think of no better expression to characterize these similarities than 'family resemblances'; for the various resemblances between the members of a family: build, features, color of eyes, gait, temperament, etc. etc. overlap and criss-cross in the same way.—And I shall say: 'games' form a family" (1953, pt. I, sec. 67).

Wittgenstein's criticisms on several quite specific topics such as what constitutes following a rule, how one grasps the concept of a game, the nature of mental acts, and so on may be seen as stemming from a deeper and more general worry about whether there is one clear sense that can be attached to the conception of "having attributes in common." If there is none, then this has consequences for all concepts that assume some fundamental notion of what makes for commonality of items. Thus Wittgenstein raises doubts about the very conception of a category as a container of items that all have some specific characteristics in common. Also, rule-following, which involves a commitment to going on in the same way, is in trouble, as is the notion of understanding a game on the basis of attributes that are common to all games, and that of mental acts as being directed in a predictable (namely, law-governed) way onto specific objects.

He also raises doubts about the boundaries and contents of quite specific categories that are under the purview of scientists and philosophers of cognition: of mind and of language, as containers of similar mental and linguistic items respectively. Of the category of language, he says: "Instead of producing something common to all that we call language, I am saying that these phenomena have no one thing in common which makes us use the same word for all,—but that they are *related* to one another in many different ways. And it is because of this relationship, or these relationships, that we call them all 'language'" (1953, pt. I, sec. 65, p. 31). What follows is his famous passage with the illustration of the category "game," where Wittgenstein demonstrates (1) that the category 'game' lacks necessary and sufficient conditions, in other words, does not possess a set of attributes common to all games; and (2) yet we have no difficulty judging that something is a game. He concludes that the category of games is an identifiable category even though it lacks a clear boundary demarcation in terms of necessary and sufficient conditions.

The key Wittgensteinian insight for our purposes here is that one can intelligently talk about categories even after one has given up the assumption that any such talk presupposes the concept of "properties held in common." This was primarily a philosophical breakthrough in conceiving of category and category membership, but it was Rosch who in her work on categorization converted it into a breakthrough with empirical bite.

The Wittgenstein-Rosch Connection I

Functional Diversity, Uniform Appearances, Category Boundaries, Family Resemblances

The Wittgensteinian challenge to the classical view was made concrete and empirically vivid by a psychologist Eleanor Rosch and her colleagues in the early 1970s at Berkeley. Given Wittgenstein's antipathy to theory, a natural question to raise is whether and to what extent he would have endorsed the kind of shift in thinking about categories suggested by Rosch's work.[4] It seems pretty clear that her approach has as key elements a genuine[5] turning away from necessary and sufficient conditions, a recognition of the importance of theory construction in concrete situations, and a refusal to interpret her own "theory of prototypes" as a theory of some entity, a 'prototype', with its own set of essential properties.[6] In effect, Rosch showed that one could "theorize" about categories without having to resort to a reification of either the prototype or its properties. For these reasons I think that Wittgenstein would have found Rosch's approach to theory quite congenial to his way of thinking.[7]

The bulk of Rosch's experiments are designed to uncover what the functions of particular words are for people, by seeing how they categorize common everyday objects.[8] In fact, it is fair to say that Rosch revolutionized the traditional thinking about categorization by making two crucial points in a series of experiments involving physical objects found in the actual world.[9] The first is that the categories that are "basic" or fundamental from the point of view of the cognizer-in-the-world are not the "pure" primitives such as lines and colors and shapes, nor even the more inclusive higher-level categories pertinent to objects-in-general such as 'furniture,' 'cutlery', or 'vehicle'. Instead, objects were cognitively processed at a midlevel of resolution: namely, the level at which the subjects actually interact with objects (functional salience), the highest level at which the object could be concretely imaged (imagistic salience), the level at which most number of members were proffered (frequency salience), and so on. Thus the categories that were of significance for subjects were 'chair' rather than 'wicker chair' or 'furniture'; 'knife' rather than 'penknife' or 'cutlery'; 'car' rather than 'Porsche' or 'vehicle'. Rosch chose to apply the term *basic* to this midlevel of categorical resolution, sandwiched between the subordinate and superordinate levels.

Second, she found that with respect to the contents of categories, certain members were regarded as more representative of a category than others. For instance, in the category of 'vegetable', peas were regarded as the most representative, followed closely by carrots, with green beans, asparagus, corn, and celery being less representative and garlic being among the least representative, being the lowest-rated and least-mentioned member of the category.[10] Rosch used the technical term *prototype* to refer to the most representative members of a category. She concluded that (*a*) the boundaries of a category were not determinate, since some members were at times included or not included in a category; and (*b*) within a category, members varied in degree of prototypicality.

Further, by correlating a subject's rating of a category member with the number of attributes it shared with other members, she found that members that have the most attributes in common with other members of a category are the ones that subjects judged as most prototypical. But there are no attributes that are common throughout the members of the category. The criterion for membership in a category thus seemed to be not a rule specifying necessary and sufficient conditions for admission, but rather resemblance by a kind of rough-and-ready statistical comparison to the appropriate prototypes. In Rosch we come to have a statistically grounded equivalent of Wittgenstein's more metaphorical notion of family resemblance.

In connecting the experimental results to Wittgenstein's insights about category boundaries, Rosch takes the Wittgensteinian point here to be that one does not need to care about boundaries in order to ascertain the nature of a category, which can be assessed by looking to "clear cases" (1978, 36). The moral is to concentrate on the center rather than on the periphery of a category in making category judgments. It is, however, crucial to recognize that for Rosch, a prototype, conceived of as the statistical center of a category, is not a covert substitute for the traditional necessary and sufficient conditions criterion, only now made flesh. Her theory of prototypes stands as a genuine alternative to the classical theory of categories. I will return to a more careful exploration of Rosch's notion of a prototype later on.

Wittgenstein's general philosophical point about uniform appearance masking functional diversity is made particularly vivid in Rosch's early experiments with children's categorizations.[11] Earlier experimenters had found that given items like the ones we encountered in Wittgenstein's toolbox, such as screws, nails, glue, and so forth, three-year-old children did nothing systematic with them, in contrast to adults, who fairly straightforwardly put them into a category such as "things you find in a toolbox." The conclusion drawn was that three-year-olds had not yet developed the ability to categorize.

What Rosch and her colleagues found instead was that the results had to do with the kind of sorting task that the children were given. Instead of the typical sorting task that was pitched at the super ordinate level for adults, they designed an "odd item out" task that was pitched at the basic level. That is, they gave children different instances of the same thing along with one different instance: for instance, three different sizes and colors of screwdrivers and a hammer. They found that the children now performed the categorization task successfully, by putting the screwdrivers together (just as adults would, given the same task). This success prompted Rosch to make the astute observation that since adults in ordinary circumstances do not find that there is a problem that requires categorization unless it is called for at the superordinate level, researchers up to that point had not considered the possibility that a basic-level task like the 'odd item out' task just described would be a legitimate method of testing for a child's *categorizing* ability. At the level of the adult categorizer, a group of objects that consisted of five differently colored screwdrivers and one hammer would not be one that required a significant categorizing ability, since all it meant was putting instances of screwdrivers into the category 'screwdriver'. Since adults tend to see instances of a kind of thing as a single thing, this would not be a task worth proposing. What Rosch and her colleagues found, however, was that *for children* the ability to categorize successfully at the basic level did provide evidence of significant categorizing ability. Now although it is true that Wittgenstein in this particular context was not making a specific point about differences between adults' and children's perceptions of words and their functions, here we have a concrete illustration of Wittgenstein's claim that what is perceived to be uniform (or equivalent) may not be. Certainly, what was perceived to be "uniform" by adults—screws, hammers, and screwdrivers (under the unifying description "things that belong in a toolbox")—is not so perceived by children. But when the task was altered in design to an odd-item-out task, then both adults and children categorized the objects in the same way.

What is interesting about the change in the design of the experiment in running them on three-year-olds is that it required a conceptual shift in what constitutes a categorization task. Remaining within the realm of adults, the behavior of the children on the task could only be interpreted as "incomplete mastery of categorization." Putting themselves in the others' shoes, being able to ask, How do they see these objects? while proposing that perhaps their method was not *deficient* but *different*, was a big breakthrough in experimental thinking about categorization. It is crucial to understanding this point that it is not taken to be equivalent to the following position: "as enlightened individuals, let us no longer call certain cognitive deficits 'defiencies': instead, let us call them 'differently cognized.'" This position may have its own merits and may well have powerful arguments in its favor; but it is not the point that Rosch makes here. Rosch's conceptual breakthrough with these experiments lay in the realization that it was the *design* of the earlier categorization tasks, rather than the children's *performance* on these tasks, that was flawed. The criterion for their being flawed was that they failed to reveal real and indisputable categorizing capabilities possessed by children. Rosch was able to demonstrate this empirically, by redesigning the task in a way that revealed that children do categorize objects successfully, *and according to the same kinds of principles* that adults use in performing categorization tasks. Thus Rosch's point should not be taken to be that interpreted a certain way, children's performances can be judged to be different rather than deficient. What she showed was that although the level at which categorization became a "task" for children was one at which from the point of view of adults there was no task on the table at all, and thus that what constitutes a "categorization task" in the first place depends upon the individuals performing the task, still the basic principles involved in carrying them out were the same across age groups.

I will return to this view about the existence of universal, species-specific psychological principles of categorization later on in the essay, as I discuss points of departure between Rosch and Wittgenstein.

In order to see the way in which she rendered concrete Wittgenstein's notion of family resemblance, we need to take a look at Rosch's theory of prototypes. I begin the following section with Wittgenstein's skepticism of the notion of a sample, as it helps to show what Rosch is and is not committed to in her use of the notion of a prototype.

Wittgenstein on Samples, Rosch on Prototypes

Wittgenstein worries about using samples as the central idea in constructing a general model of how categorization proceeds in language. Now, there is no question that samples are useful in conveying essential information about specific objects in certain restricted domains. Color is a good example. "When someone defines the names of colors for me by pointing to samples and saying 'This color is blue,' this case can be compared in many respects with putting a table in my hands, with the words written under the color-samples" (1953, pt. I, sec. 73). However, one quickly moves to inappropriately extend the notion of a definition-by-sample thus: "to have understood the definition means to have in one's mind an idea of the thing defined, and that is a sample or picture. So if I am shown various different leaves and told, 'This is called a leaf,' I get an idea of the shape of a leaf, a picture of it in my mind. But [responds Wittgenstein] what does the picture of a leaf look like when it does not show us any particular shape, but what is common to all shapes of leaf? Which shade is the 'sample in my mind' of the color green—the sample of what is common to all shades of green?" (ibid.).

Wittgenstein's point is that this approach to thinking about concepts and the way in which they delineate and categorize objects—the model of samples against which individual items are to be assessed—is intuitively appealing at first glance only. The problem with this categorize-by-sample approach is that (1) it works best for those objects or properties that can be demonstrated;[12] but, more seriously, as Wittgenstein points out, (2) one is tempted to overextend its use to the domain of more general concepts. Since there are no demonstrable instances of general samples, this extension results in the construction of "patches in the head" that are to stand for samples of general concepts. With this invention is the analytically connected invention of that which is to be the content of the sample, "that which is common" to all the particular instances of that general concept. Wittgenstein's point is that talk of samples, particularly samples of general concepts, presupposes the feasibility of talk about what is common to all instances that are categorized by the concept. But this is deeply problematic. It is useful to keep in mind Wittgenstein's skepticism about the explanatory value of the notion of a sample as "embodied rule" or master as we move to a discussion of Rosch's use of 'prototypes'.

In an influential article, Rosch (1978) proposes two psychological principles of categorization as universal across the human species: the principle of cognitive economy, and the principle of structure in the perceived world. The first principle determines the levels in a categorical hierarchy, while the second determines the structure within a particular category. Rosch refers to these as the vertical and horizontal dimensions of categories, respectively.[13] It is in explicating the horizontal dimension of categories that the notion of a prototype assumes primary importance.

I will begin by describing the way in which Rosch uses the notion of a prototype and suggest how a connection may be made between Wittgenstein's insight about family resemblances and this more theoretical notion of a prototype. Rosch's notion of a prototype is operationally defined by agents' actual judgments about the goodness of examples for membership in a category. It is therefore distinct, on the one hand, from the notion of an actual, external object that is to serve as the prototype of a category and provide the basis of the activity of agents' comparing objects (matched against that prototype) in making category judgments; and, on the other hand, from the notion of a prototype as something internal to the agent, in virtue of which she processes information that leads to the formation of her category judgments. Rosch stresses that "there is little evidence" (1978, 28) for the hypothesis that internal prototypes are actually used by agents in learning or in the representation of objects or states of affairs. She underscores this point later when she says: "To speak of *a prototype* at all is simply a convenient grammatical fiction; what is really referred to are judgments of degree of typicality" (40).

This point is crucial to understanding her position and yet it is precisely on this point that her notion of prototype has been misunderstood. This is because it is tempting to conceive of a prototype as a 'sample'. Once you give up on being able to specify a set of logically necessary and sufficient conditions for category membership, perhaps the conception of a sample against which all potential members of a category are to be judged provides a more viable alternative. And once one conceives of the possibility of samples, one has external as well as internal candidates for the position: thus, one might think of an actual vegetable, say a carrot, against which all vegetables are to be assessed; alternatively, one can think of an image, an internal sample, that is to be the basis of comparison. Thought of in this way, a sample is akin to a set of necessary and sufficient conditions, now "embodied" in the sample. But this is precisely the problem with the notion of a sample: it is no advance over necessary and sufficient conditions because (*a*) if it is to be a substantive criterion, the attributes of the sample must be seen as critical to categorical membership; but then it collapses into a set of necessary and sufficient conditions and is susceptible to the problem of counterexamples; (*b*) on the other hand, if it is to be understood more loosely, as a way of describing what goes on when we categorize, then it does not do any useful work in explaining categorization.

In a sense, it is better to talk of the phenomenon of prototypically than of prototypes. In a series of experiments, Rosch and her colleagues (Rosch and Mervis 1975; Rosch et al. 1976) tested the proposal that items that are 'prototypical' have most attributes in common with other members within the category and the least attributes in common with members of another category. Interpreting prototypicality, and typicality effects in general, as equivalent to Wittgenstein's idea that members within a category "resemble" one another, analogous to the way that members of a family resemble one another, they concluded that the relation of family resemblance was a viable alternative to the classical requisites for category membership in terms of specifiable features.

There remains a significant difference between their positions. For although Rosch's prototype does not suffer from the problems Wittgenstein worried about with samples, she does take prototypes to be statistically real phenomena, capturing the central tendency of the category of which they are prototypes. Prototypes are thus empirically determined structural facts about categories. They are therefore not subject to historical or cultural whimsy, although one would expect them to vary somewhat historically and culturally. Her position is nicely captured by her response to the following delightful taxonomy of animals from a fictional Chinese encyclopedia titled *Celestial Emporium of Benevolent Knowledge,* which Rosch herself quotes at the beginning of her essay (1978): "On those remote pages it is written that animals are divided into a) those that belong to the Emperor, b) embalmed ones, c) those that are trained, d) suckling pigs, e) mermaids, f) fabulous ones, g) stray dogs, h) those that are included in this classification, i) those that tremble as if they were mad, j) innumerable ones, k) those drawn with a very fine camel's hair brush, l) others, m) those that have just broken a flower vase, n) those that resemble flies from a distance" (Borges 1966, 108).

Here is Rosch's response: "Conceptually, the most interesting aspect of this classification system is that *it does not exist.* Certain types of categorization may appear in the imagination of poets, but they are *never* found in the practical or linguistic classes of organisms or of man-made objects used by any of the cultures of the world . . . human categorization should not be considered the arbitrary product of historical accident or of whimsy but rather the result of psychological principles of categorization, which are subject to investigation" (1978, 27, emphases mine).

What strikes one as significant about Wittgenstein's position, in marked contrast to that of Rosch, is precisely that he would deny (*a*) the existence of universal psychological principles of categorization; and (*b*) that psychological regularities of any kind could be independent of history and culture to the degree suggested by Rosch. Rosch in her later work substantially modifies this position, in a phase that I describe in the section "The Wittgenstein-Rosch Connection II." But in this earlier phase of her thinking, the contrast with Wittgenstein is evident particularly in her conclusions about color categories and her criticisms of the Whorfian hypothesis of linguistic relativity. And so we turn to the case of color.

Color Categories: Universal or Culture-Specific?

Of the properties that we perceive in the world of physical objects, it is color that intrudes the most directly and dramatically upon our sensibilities. For this reason philosophers and psychologists have historically made color the focus of their analyses in their study of human perception. This focus continues today in newer fields such as artificial intelligence, especially computer vision. Wittgenstein (1950, 1953) was interested in the logic and psychology of color concepts and their relationship to other visual properties of objects, such as shape. Rosch did early work on color and was clearly influenced by the research of Berlin and Kay (1969), researchers at Berkeley in the 1960s, especially by their view that there exist "basic" color categories that are universal for the human species. In her most recently co-authored book (Varela, Thompson, and Rosch 1991, 157–71) she takes up color again "as a study case," in which she gives up on her earlier commitment to color as a perceived structure in the physical world and embraces the view that "color categories are experiential . . . [and yet] "belong to our shared biological and cultural world" (172). In this section I will explore Wittgenstein's and Rosch's conceptions of color as a category.

Wittgenstein in several of his writings invites us to consider the language-game of color, the practice of which requires the tools of ostension (direct experience: "that's the color I was thinking of!"), samples, color names, and color categories. In his *Remarks on Colour* (1950), he raises the question of the objectivity and universality of people's judgments of color by asking us to consider the possibility that there could exist a cultural practice of naming and discriminating between colors and shades of color that are very different from our own. "What is there in favor of saying that green is a primary color, not a blend of blue and yellow? Would it be right to say; 'You can only know it directly by looking at the colors'? But how do I know that I mean the same by the words 'primary colours' as some other person who is also inclined to call green a primary color? No,—here language-games decide" (1950, I:6). Here we find the thought that colors aren't part of the fabric of the objective world transparently available to all human beings.[14] Colors are identifiable by what we are inclined to say about them, and this can vary to a great degree depending upon the color vocabulary possessed by the group in question. The assessment of the "primariness" of a color does not depend simply upon the color itself as it exists and appears to us from "out there," but on the degree of fine- or coarse-grainedness of the agent's vocabulary.

And again: "Even if green is not an intermediary color between yellow and blue, couldn't there be people for whom there is bluish-yellow, reddish-green? I.e. people whose color concepts deviate from ours—because, after all, the color concepts of color-blind people too deviate from those of normal people, and not every deviation from the norm must be a blindness, a defect" (1950, I:8). Here he seems to be imagining the possibility that color concepts (apart from language) could be radically different between cultures. That is, where we would pick green as the category between yellow and blue, perhaps another might draw the categorical line in a different place, picking out bluish yellow or reddish green as the next category. "Can't we imagine certain people having a different geometry of color than we do?" (1950, I:66). Here the interlocutor is posing the possibility that the difference could be due to a different physiological hardware and therefore that the differences can be attributed to difference in physiology[15] rather than linguistic or cultural practice. Wittgenstein counters by saying that what is really meant here is that we are imagining people whose color concepts are sufficiently related to ours in such a way that we would also call them "color concepts." Again, the point is that "different geometries of color concepts" can mean no more than "concepts sufficiently similar to ours that we recognize them as *color* concepts, but find being categorized by others very differently." His rejection is of the objective constraint on color concept formation rather than of the possibility of the existence of radically different schemes of categorization.

Wittgenstein concludes, "[L]ooking [at colors in nature] does not teach us anything about the concepts of colors" (1950, I:73). His conclusions about color were thus the result not of experimental observation, but of raising philosophical questions about what it *means* to see the same color and how we can tell whether this is so. For Rosch the answer must lie in looking not at colors in nature either, but at people's *judgments* of color. In having this as her focus, she was in the spirit of Wittgenstein's insistence that in learning more about language games one should look at what people do.

Since Rosch's early thinking on color was influenced more directly by the work of anthropologists Berlin and Kay than by Wittgenstein, she conceived of color as a "natural" category. She found compelling the view that certain colors were "basic" for human beings across cultures and historical epochs. Berlin and Kay had undertaken an extensive study of the use of color vocabulary in ninety-eight languages and concluded that although there was considerable variation in the number and kinds of words used to describe colors (some as few as two), the number of basic colors cognized could be reduced to a set of eleven.[16] Rosch's early work (1971) was devoted to establishing experimentally various theses connected with their position. Thus she established, for instance, that it was the case that human beings, in being given a range of hues of a basic color, say red—magenta through bright red through soft red—typically picked the same hue (in this case, bright red) as the best example of that category of color, although they disagreed in their judgments about which examples were on the periphery or even where the boundary of the category should be drawn.

At this stage Rosch's expressed commitment to a view of categorization that is grounded in real psychological facts rather than historical or cultural circumstance and her maintaining of a sharp dichotomy between biology and culture, is attributable to this strand of influence. Thus she disagreed with a version of the Whorfian hypothesis of linguistic relativity by demonstrating in the color case that although some cultures have as few as two color words, their cognitive categories for color, far from being limited to the surface translations of the two words (white and black), in fact cover the color spectrum as we know it.[17] Color cognition outstrips the resources of the language's color vocabulary. In a series of papers, Rosch and her colleagues demonstrated that color cognition was not simply dependent upon color naming, as shown in experiments that demonstrated that even without having a rich vocabulary of names, subjects could recognize color differences (Rosch 1972; Rosch and Olivier 1972; Rosch 1973, 1974). They concluded that color categories could not be an arbitrary result of contingent naming practices across cultures, but appeared to have a deep connection with human physiology. They were universal and species specific, as Berlin and Kay had hypothesized. Since it is tempting to interpret Wittgenstein's position as that of a cultural relativist, even with respect to the domain of color, here is a clear difference in their approaches to color categories.

In more recent work Rosch and her colleagues draw upon the results of more recent work on color vision research to underscore the more complex character of color categories: on the one hand, there are cultural and linguistic factors that influence color categories, so that the earlier notion of there being "basic" color categories across cultures must be given up; on the other, there is a clear biological constraint on our perceptions of color, so that our categories are not totally dependent upon the contingencies of one's cultural and linguistic heritage. However, Rosch is careful to separate herself from "the received view" within the cognitive science community that the history of our interaction with the environment is not arbitrary but is grounded in evolutionary considerations: thus, that the color categories we actually have, for instance, are the ones that have the greatest survival value. Instead, she emphasizes, "our perceived world of color is, rather, a result of one possible and viable phylogenic pathway among many others realized in the evolutionary history of living beings" (Varela, Thompson, and Rosch 1991, 183).

On her modified view, vision is an active cognitive achievement that involves a complex set of cognitive capacities interacting with one another and with the environment of the perceiver. What properties are seen, indeed, the determination of the boundaries of the object of vision, is dependent upon the type of perceiver, her interests, and her cultural and historical embeddedness. Vision does not involve the simple representation of objects that "possess" properties such as color, shape, size and so on. In the case of color vision in particular, since color contrast delineates the object that we see, it is impossible to separate the object sensed from its color. This interdependence of object and sensory properties is grounded in a deeper philosophical position about the interdependence of subject and object in what they term "enactive cognition," which they suggest as a new paradigm for cognitive science. And so it is to this more general position that we now turn.

The Wittgenstein-Rosch Connection II

Against Representation: The Link with Buddhism

The view that we are all held captive by quite specific and equally illegitimate metaphysical and epistemological pictures, of our selves, of the world, and of the nature of the relationship between the two, is one that constitutes an underlying theme in all of Wittgenstein's work. It is also a crucial theme in the Mahayana Buddhist tradition as Nagarjuna expounds upon it. I will concentrate on those features of the pictures that

are critically appraised by both Wittgenstein and Nagarjuna. Eleanor
Rosch and her colleagues make use of the ideas in the Mahayana Buddhist tradition, particularly the Madhyamika, in developing their newest
paradigm for cognitive science, which they term "embodied cognition."
I shall be claiming that these ideas are also there in Wittgenstein, although they are distinct from the ideas that inspired Rosch in the earlier
phase of her career.[18]

Wittgenstein's writings are offered as therapy, as a way of breaking free
of these pictures by confronting them, challenging them, questioning
their assumptions, the preconceived "givens" that are their source.
"What is your aim in philosophy?—To shew the fly the way out of the
fly bottle" (1953, pt. I, sec. 309). In other words, a liberation of the
understanding by practical means. The main culprit here is language itself, the tool with which the structural properties as well as the content
of the pictures are forged. "Philosophy is a battle against the bewitchment of our intelligence by means of language" (1953, pt. I, sec. 109).
One must therefore pay close attention to languages and how we use
them if one is to clear away the metaphysical and epistemological cob-
webs. The Madhyamikas espouse a similar goal: that of liberation
grounded in a recognition that it is language that creates false metaphysical and commonsense pictures. "What human beings perceive as distinct
entities or segments of existence is a result of mental fabrication. These
entities, Nagarjuna claims, do not exist in themselves; they exist because
they are "named"—distinguished from something else" (Streng 1967, 69, emphasis mine).

In their recent work, Rosch and her colleagues too aim to liberate
cognitive science from the stranglehold of the Cartesian dichotomy between inner and outer. They propose an approach that topples the notion
of 'representation' as the key to understanding the nature of cognition.
In this critique they impugn both realism—the view that the cognizer's
task is to "recover," via representations, the externally existent properties
of the world—and idealism—the view that the cognizer's task involves a
"projection," via representations, of her own conceptual apparatus upon
an external world. They express their goal thus: "Our intention is to
bypass entirely this logical geography of inner versus outer by studying
cognition not as recovery or projection but as embodied action" (Varela,
Thompson, and Rosch 1991, 172). This is language and expressed intent
very similar to that of Wittgenstein as well as of the Madhyamikas, although Rosch and her colleagues go further, locating the discussion in a

modern context in their development of the concept of embodied action as central to the concerns of cognitive scientists.

The blueprint for cognition they suggest to such researchers would contain:

1. Experiences of cognizers that are inextricably tied to a body that navigates a world with the help of various sensory and motor capacities;
2. The cultural, historical, psychological and biological contexts in which these cognizers have the kind of experiences cited in (1).

Thus perceiving (and intending in general) and acting are cognitive acts that are inseparable in cognizers. "An intention is embedded in its situation, in human customs and institutions" (Wittgenstein 1953, pt. I, sec. 337). Accordingly, neither the model of "recovery" nor of "projection" makes sense as an account of how cognizers do what they do vis-à-vis the world.

There remains a significant difference between Rosch and Wittgenstein. For Wittgenstein stresses the connection between intending and acting as "internal," in the sense of its being a grammatical or logico-normative connection rather than an "exernal" causal relation. Thus it is part of the language game of intentionality that "mental acts" such as saying, wishing, desiring, perceiving are regarded as what "guide" behavior. This is quite different from taking them to actually do so. "Our mistake is to look for an explanation where we ought to look at what happens as a 'proto-phenomenon'. That is, where we ought to have said: *this language-game is played*" (1953, pt. I, sec. 656). In contrast, for Rosch this inseparability is not merely grammatical, in Wittgentein's sense, although people's linguistic and cultural institutions constitute a part of its source. This inseparability is additionally grounded in evolutionary biological facts about us as embodied experiencers. This may appear as a difference at least in emphasis, with Wittgenstein stressing the historical and cultural, while Rosch, although much more cognizant than in her earlier work of historical, cultural, and generally experiential factors in cognition, seeks to provide an explanation of cognition that is, additionally, firmly rooted in biology. But even this difference begins to fade as one considers the fact that although Wittgenstein often asks us to imagine how things might be radically other than what they are for us (biologically, as well as culturally and historically), he forces our attention on our own natural historical trajectories, which we see are not whimsical in the least, but are, on the contrary, deep and rooted, although not in metaphysical or even biological necessity.

That this difference in emphasis does not signal a deep divide between Wittgenstein and Rosch is further clarified in the *kind* of biological explanation she proposes. On her biological model, "organism and environment are mutually enfolded in multiple ways, and so what constitutes the world of a given organism is enacted by that organism's history of structural coupling. Furthermore, such histories of coupling proceed *not through optimal adaptation but rather through evolution as natural drift*" (Varela, Thompson, and Rosch 1991, 202, emphasis mine). This is no view of biological or evolutionary necessity; it allows for the possibility of different actions, subject only to the constraint of "maintain[ing] the integrity of the system and/or its lineage" (205). This view forces us to see intentionality in a way that is different from the classical picture that Wittgenstein criticized. In their words, "[A] . . . way to express this idea would be to say that cognition as embodied action is always about or directed toward something that is missing: on the one hand, there is always a next step for the *system* in its perceptually guided action; and on the other hand, the actions of the system are always directed toward *situations* that have yet to become actual" (205).

There is much more that one could comment and elaborate on here. The important point is that Rosch and her colleagues are well aware of the different forms in which the old Cartesian dualism of inner and outer could surface, not only in philosophy and cognitive psychology but in biology as well. Suffice it to say that their proposal, which I do not defend but merely mention here, in its attempt to reconceptualize the inner/outer dichotomy, to do away with the commitment to representations, and to build historical and cultural contexts into biological explanations, and particularly in its emphasis on the actual lived experiences of individuals, is deeply Wittgensteinian in spirit.

In order to bring lived experiences of individuals to the fore, Rosch and her colleagues recommend that we reorient ourselves with respect to the "I," taking it as a nonunified *experiential* phenomenon that can be studied using not the standard Western analytic techniques but rather those of the Buddhist tradition of meditative practice.[19] The reason is that they see the West as concerned only with human science, not with human experience. Since the book begins with the conviction that both "the sciences of the mind" as well as "lived" everyday experience must be part of the study of a complete cognitive science, and the West lacks the tools to study experience, we need to unearth those tools from another tradition. "It is our contention that the rediscovery of Asian philosophy, particularly of the Buddhist tradition, is a second renaissance in the cultural history of the West, with the potential to be equally important as the rediscovery of Greek thought in the European renaissance" (22). And although none of this is suggested in the least in Wittgenstein, I speculate that his worry about the deep roots laid down in us by Cartesianism and the inescapable danger of constantly falling back into the old ways of conceptualizing ourselves and our relationship to the world, would have made any concrete alternative approach that highlighted lived human experience seem to Wittgenstein to be an avenue well worth pursuing.

Conclusion

We have come full circle. Although Rosch did groundbreaking work in categorization using Wittgenstein's notion of family resemblances, she nonetheless belonged to the mainstream of cognitive scientists in taking as given the view of cognition embraced by researchers in the field: that human beings are cognizers of a physical world that exists apart from them, that there are structural properties of that world, and that these are recovered by cognizers via internal representations. Thus in her research on categorization, although she challenged (a) the assumption that the categorical judgments of adult cognizers constitute the standard against which the judgments of other cognizers (such as children) are to be evaluated; (b) the traditional conception of a category and the importance of boundaries, and proposed that the categories in fact had a structure reflected in people's graded responses, with internal differences between members belonging to that category, and that boundaries per se did not matter for one could focus on "clear cases" in assessing category membership; and (c) the notion that people in fact 'recovered' the structure of the world by categorizing what they saw at the most fundamental hierarchical level, demonstrating instead that what categories people saw had to do with the level at which they represented these structures in their everyday lives (thus seeing a chair rather than lines and circles enclosing a certain area), at the deepest level Rosch nonetheless adhered to the general classical model of cognition.

In her latest work, of which the collaborative book with Varela and Thompson (Varela, Thompson, and Rosch 1991) is an illustration, Rosch gives up on this picture; in doing so she moves closer to the more fundamental ideas of Wittgenstein. For in the alternative they propose, cognition is not a matter of representing structures that exist in the world independently of the cognizing subject. In place of the picture that constitutes classical cognition for both the realist and idealist: self, world, and inner systems of representation, grounded in a distinction between inner and outer, we are to conceive of cognition as embodied action.[20] The mind as a category that is uniform and with firm boundaries distinct from the body is replaced by one that is embodied, and therefore subject to the vagaries of change that connection with bodies, histories, cultures, and biologies brings.

The view of cognitive scientific activity that they collectively propose is radical: "The inquisitive scientist . . . asks, How can we imagine, embodied in a mechanism, that relation of codependence between mind and world? The mechanism that we have created (the embodied metaphor of groundlessness) is that of enactive cognition, with its image of structural coupling through a history of natural drift" (237–38). Rosch and her colleagues go on to point out that this activity is not possible without compassion; for although 'groundlessness' (sunyata) is understood by the madhyamikas as 'emptiness', it is also understood by them as 'compassion'.[21] Thus Rosch's conception of the reflective cognitive scientist is of one driven, not by the truth but by an "embodied metaphor of groundlessness," an image of being in a world without internal or external foundations, where lived experiences of interaction (enactive cognition) form the subject as well as the means of study. In moving away from a focus upon finding the truth to a focus on "lived experience," in their emphasis on the crucial role of the body in structuring one's experiences, in the method of their theorizing that acknowledges the use of powerful metaphors in theory construction and even in their thinking about the nature of a "mechanism"; and finally in their recognition of the necessity of fusion of the intellect and feeling in order to practice the kind of cognitive science they advocate, they echo many of the insights provided by feminists in other domains.[22] The value of the work of Rosch and her colleagues resides in bringing these insights to bear on the field of cognitive science.

In this essay I have described a certain trajectory in the thinking of the psychologist Eleanor Rosch and her role in the evolution of two quite distinct paradigms in the fledgling interdisciplinary field of cognitive science. I have argued that we have here, in the person of Rosch, a woman scientist, instrumental in the development of both paradigms, using fundamental Wittgensteinian insights in her early work as a starting point for a fresh look at categories, and in her later work, for a more dramatic recasting of the very framework of human cognition itself.

Notes

1. For a nice summary of the work on categorization by Rosch and her colleagues, see Lakoff 1987.

2. In Varela, Thompson, and Rosch 1991.

3. This is not to suggest that the history of categorization research was marked by agreement on the nature of categories or on the research methodology of psychologists. Certainly this was not the case; my point here is that underlying the disputes there were common assumptions about categories. I describe these in the following section.

4. Wittgenstein seems to be more critical of the dichotomy between theory and practice than of the activity of theorizing itself. In contemporary times the difference between being anti-theory and pushing to break down the split between theory and practice surfaces in the debate between theorizing versus using statistics discussed by Andy Clark (1993).

5. I say "genuine" because other researchers who claimed to shift from necessary and sufficient conditions to prototypes often ended up thinking of prototypes as satisfying the necessary and sufficient conditions requirement. So it was not a genuinely alternative approach.

6. I say more about her notion of a prototype later in the essay.

7. In fact, it seems to me that the thinking of the later Rosch, who gives us a sketch of the cognitive scientist as guided quite explicitly by "the embodied metaphor of groundlessness" (also discussed later in the essay), is even more congenial to Wittgenstein's approach to theory and the activity of theorizing.

8. See, e.g., Rosch 1975; Rosch et al. 1976.

9. Rosch conducted her experiments on nine "natural" taxonomies of objects: vegetable, fruit, bird, furniture, vehicle, toy, weapon, sports, and carpenter's tool.

10. Her result was of course relative to the culture in which the children were reared. Other researchers have since conducted similar experiments in other cultures; the conclusion currently endorsed by Rosch and her colleagues is that while some results of categorization research are biology specific, others are culture and language specific. Results in the case of color make this point vivid. (See Varela, Thompson, and Rosch 1991, chap. 8, 157–71, for an excellent and thorough analysis of the various dimensions of color perception.)

11. See, e.g., Rosch and Mervis 1976.

12. Even for things that can be demonstrated, though, the problem arises about which demonstrated leaf or shade of the color green is the appropriate referent of the term. This leaves out of account the more fundamental problem of the act of demonstration itself: how can we be sure that the pointer is in the direction of the extended finger and not intended to be taken the other way?

13. See Lakoff 1987 for a summary of Rosch's influence on different areas of linguistics (markedness, phonology, for instance) where research has demonstrated "prototype effects" (in other words,

asymmetrical relations between category members, with some regarded as better examples than others) of the kind that Rosch documented for the categorization of colors and for physical objects.

14. This is one way of being an objectivist about color.

15. This is another way of being an objectivist about color.

16. According to Berlin and Kay (1969), there are eleven "basic" colors: red, green, blue, yellow, black, white, gray, orange, purple, brown, and pink. This number is currently in dispute.

17. Rosch's work was on Dani, a New Guinean language that had two basic color categories, named *mili* and *mola* (roughly, "dark-cool" and "light-warm"). That they made finer-grained distinctions within the two categories, however, was evidenced by the fact that individuals, when asked to give the best example of a category, differed in their choice of example. For instance, examples offered of the color category "mili" would be green, or blue, or black. Similarly, examples offered of the category "mola" would be yellow, or red, or white. Rosch found, though, that this did not mean that the differences between colors within each of these categories did not matter. For although the experiments based on color *naming* gave this result, the experiments based on color memory for both English and Dani revealed that the color differences of the entire color spectrum were cognitively significant.

18. Interestingly, in this latest work of which Rosch is a co-author (Varela, Thompson, and Rosch 1991) wherein the new paradigm for cognitive science with Buddhist concepts is crafted, the primary Western philosophical connection made is to the work of French philosopher Merleau-Ponty and the phemenological andstructuralist tradition. No mention is made of Wittgenstein.

19. In Varela, Thompson, and Rosch 1991, see esp. sec. V, titled " 'Worlds Without Ground."

20. Varela, Thompson, and Rosch 1991; see esp. chap. 8.

21. "[S]unyata, the loss of a fixed reference point or ground in either self, other, or a relationship between them, is said to be inseparable from compassion like the two sides of a coin or the two wings of a bird" (248).

22. Although the relationship I describe, of these ideas to those found in feminist writings, is not specifically addressed by them in their work.

References

Berlin, Bernard, and Paul Kay. 1969. *Basic Color Terms: Their Universality and Evolution.* Berkeley and Los Angeles: University of California Press.

Borges, Jorge Luis 1966. *Other Inquisitions, 1937–1952.* New York: Washington Square Press.

Clark, Andy. 1993. *Associative Engines.* Cambridge: MIT Press.

Gudmunsen, Chris. 1977. *Wittgenstein and Buddhism.* New York: Macmillan Press.

Hyman, John, ed. 1991. *Investigating Psychology.* New York: Routledge.

Johnson, Paul. 1993. *Wittgenstein: Rethinking the Inner.* New York: Routledge.

Lakoff, George. 1987. *Women, Fire, and Dangerous Things.* Chicago: University of Chicago Press.

Mervis, Carolyn B., Jack Catlin, and Eleanor Rosch. 1976. "Relationships Among Goodness-of-Example, Category Norms, and Word Frequency." *Bulletin of the Psychonomic Society* 7, no. 3:283–84.

Mervis, Carolyn B., and Eleanor Rosch. 1981. "Categorization of Natural Objects." *Annual Review of Psychology* 32:89–115.

Rosch, Eleanor. [Heider]. 1971. "Focal Color Areas and the Development of Color Names." *Developmental Psychology* 4:447–55.

———. 1972. "Universals in Color Naming and Memory." *Journal of Experimental Psychology* 93:10–20.

Rosch, Eleanor [Heider], and D. C. Olivier. 1972. "The Structure of the Color Space in Naming and Memory for Two Languages." *Cognitive Psychology* 3:337–54.

Rosch, Eleanor. 1973. "Natural Categories." *Cognitive Psychology* 4, no. 3:328–50.

———. 1974. "Linguistic Relativity." In *Human Communication: Theoretical Explorations*, ed. A. L. Silverstein. New York: Halsted Press.

———. 1975. "Cognitive Reference Points." *Cognitive Psychology* 7, no. 4:532–47.

———. 1977. "Human Categorization." In *Advances in Cross Cultural Psychology*, ed. N. Warren. Vol. 1. London: Academic Press.

———. 1978. "Principles of Categorization." In *Cognition and Categorization*, ed. E. Rosch and Barbara B. Lloyd. Hillsdale, N.J.: Lawrence Erlbaum Associates.

———. 1988. "Coherences and Categorization: A Historical View." In *The Development of Language and Language Researchers: Essays In Honor of Roger Brown*, ed. Frank S. Kessel Hillsdale, N.J.: Lawrence Erlbaum Associates.

Rosch, Eleanor, and C. B. Mervis. 1975. "Family Resemblances: Studies in the Internal Structure of Categories." *Cognitive Psychology* 7, no. 4:573–605.

Rosch, Eleanor, and C. B. Mervis.1976. "Children's Sorting: A Reinterpretation Based on the Nature of Abstraction in Natural Categories." *Developmental Psychology* 7:211–21.

Rosch, Eleanor, C. B. Mervis, W. Gray, D. Johnson, and P. Boges-Braem. 1976. "Basic Objects in Natural Categories." *Cognitive Psychology* 8, no. 3:382–439.

Rosch, Eleanor, Carol Simpson, and Scott, R. Miller. 1976. "Structural Bases of Typicality Effects." *Journal of Experimental Psychology: Human Perception and Performance* 2, no. 4:491–502.

Stcherbatski, T. 1979. *The Central Conception of Buddhism and the Meaning of the Word "Dharma."* Delhi: Motilal Banarasidas.

Streng, F. J. 1967. *Emptiness: A Study in Religious Meaning*. Nashville: Abingdon Press.

Varela, Francisco J., Evan Thompson, and Eleanor Rosch. 1991. *The Embodied Mind: Cognitive Science and Human Experience*. Cambridge: MIT Press.

Wittgenstein, Ludwig. 1950. *Remarks on Colour*. Ed. G. E. M. Anscombe. Trans. Linda McAlister and Margaret Schattle. Berkeley and Los Angeles: University of California Press.

———. 1953. *Philosophical Investigations*. 3d ed. Trans. G. E. M. Anscombe. New York: Macmillan.

Section IV

Being Human:
Agents and Subjects

13

Words and Worlds

Some Thoughts on the Significance of Wittgenstein for Moral and Political Philosophy

Judith Bradford

Rather than sacrifice the notion of "ignorance," then, I would be more interested in trying, as we are getting used to trying with "knowledge," to pluralize and specify it. That is, I would like to be able to make use in sexual-political thinking of the deconstructive insight that particular insights generate, are lined with, and at the same time are themselves structured by particular opacities. If ignorance is not—and it evidently is not—a single Manichean, aboriginal maw of darkness from which the heroics of human cognition can occasionally wrestle facts, insights, freedom, progress, perhaps there exists instead a plethora of ignorances, and we may begin to ask questions about the labor, erotics, and economics of their human production and distribution. Insofar as ignorance is ignorance of a knowledge—a knowledge that may itself, it goes without saying, be seen as either true or false under some other regime of truth—these ignorances, far from being pieces of the originary dark, are produced by and correspond to particular knowledges and circulate as part of particular regimes of truth. We should not assume that their doubletting with knowledges means, however, that they obey identical laws identically or follow the same circulatory paths at the same pace.

—Eve Sedgwick, *Epistemology of the Closet*

The significance of Wittgenstein's philosophical and grammatical investigations for subsequent moral, political, and epistemological inquiry has been the subject of much debate in post-Wittgensteinian philosophy. Logical positivists, ordinary-language philosophers, and moral contextualists have all used a more or less "Wittgensteinian" set of approaches to think about problems in contemporary *philosophy*. These attempts at application have stressed various strands of Wittgenstein's work as the most important, and followed those strands out in theories and methodologies. I would like to explore some of these, as well as some less often emphasized aspects of Wittgenstein's work, starting with Hanna Pitkin's analyses of moral and political discourse in *Wittgenstein and Justice* and continuing with an alternate reading of the themes of the *Philosophical*

Investigations as relevant to contemporary philosophical thinking—including Foucauldian inquiries into discourse and what Wittgenstein may offer to such political thinking about theory.

As Pitkin discusses in her introduction (Pitkin 1972, x–xiii) there are several problems involved in the idea of "getting Wittgenstein right" as a philosopher or political theorist. The themes and insights of the *Philosophical Investigations* seem immediately to suggest various ways of going about "doing" philosophy, or thinking about political and social theory: using the method of examining the grammar of concepts to clarify or even dissolve traditional conceptual problems, examining the theoretical pictures that inhabit and underlie such theories, and seeking the meaning of our linguistic habits in the use to which our linguistic expressions are put have all suggested rich uses to various readers of Wittgenstein. Yet finding in, or making from, Wittgenstein's work a new methodology or epistemology may already be a fundamental mistaking of his intents and insights—a new embroilment in another set of lifeless problems, creating a new set of pseudo-issues rather than attending to Wittgenstein's often expressed concerns about what I shall call, rather sheepishly in light of the old-fashioned ring of the term, "human flourishing." Like Nietzsche, Wittgenstein was clearly less concerned with philosophy than with life; his pedagogy in the *Investigations* is certainly meant to be more of a therapeutic, illuminative untraining than a didactic training in the use of another philosophical method.[1]

Pitkin couches her acknowledgment of the problem of "getting Wittgenstein right" in terms of Wittgenstein's aphoristic and obscure style and the possible losses of "restating" the themes of the *Investigations* in a form less difficult and more direct: "There is a real danger that, in trying to make his ideas accessible, lucid, and systematic, I may make their real content and significance inaccessible." While acutely aware of the intimate connection of Wittgenstein's "style" to the content of his philosophical intent, and thus the ambiguities involved in translation of his writing to a systematic endeavor, she finds that such a systematic exploration of the "implications of some philosophical themes for our understanding of politics and society." While agreeing with Pitkin that such uses of Wittgenstein in philosophy or political theory "need not be trivialized or trivializing," it may also be possible to examine philosophically the implications of his style for thinking about pedagogy, social and political theory, and political practice (Pitkin 1972, xii). Of course, in saying something about the implications of Wittgenstein's style, in which the reader is allowed—or forced—to find for himself the truths relevant to him, I will not be doing philosophy in Wittgensteinian fashion so much as explicating what that fashion says about human learning and thus about human capacities to learn.

The Concepts of the Moral and the Political

One of the frequently followed "strands" of the academic appropriation of Wittgenstein has been the importance of looking at the place of moral and political discourse in our lives: that is, looking for the meaning of such discourse in what we do with it. Hanna Pitkin's reading, following Cavell, is an examination of these areas of linguistic activity that avoids the excesses of emotivist ethicists such as Ayer by refusing to reduce the content of moral terms to the purpose of individual approval or disapproval of the action under consideration in moral discourse. Moral discourse cannot be reduced to an addition of such prescriptive elements ("value") to statements about the world ("facts") because one of the most important features of moral discourse is that the question of what the action under discussion is, is part of moral discourse. "Moral discourse is normally not legislative but adjudicative; it assesses conduct by fitting it into a traditional systematic vocabulary" (Pitkin 1972, 151).

Moral discourse is personal without being private; it takes place between speakers but in the contexts of their "vocabularies of action and morality," which are "the concepts in terms of which we accuse, excuse, characterize our conduct" (Pitkin 1972, 150). These vocabularies, as she notes, are inherited and relatively fixed; we can apply the terms and concepts of our vocabularies in various but not unlimited ways; not just anything can be an admissible application. Moral discourse shows the "nature" of any act which has "gone wrong" enough to occasion moral discussion to be in a sense interpersonal and contextual; individual agents do not, and cannot, determine alone what the action is or what it means. "That means both that we do not always see the implications of our own position, who we are; and that we do not always see the reality of our own action, what we have done" (Pitkin 1972, 154). Another sense of the personal, but not private, status of moral discourse is that part of the point of moral discourse is the situation of moral speakers with regard to their actions (linguistic or otherwise). In moral discourse the elaboration of our position is as much an elaboration of ourselves. What sorts of people we are are under consideration, along with what positions we are willing to take responsibility for and what others will expect us to acknowledge, do, or say. Pitkin illustrates this element of moral discourse through Arendt's phrase; in moral discussion we disclose and discover "the agent together with the act." Pitkin, perhaps, underplays the triangular relationship that is actually in place in such disclosures between agent, act, and the rules under which agents and acts are understood. It is clear that acts are understood through a set of rules and going moral understandings, but less prominent in Pitkin's discussion is the point that agents too are understood through such rules, and that there can be different rules for different sorts of agents (Walker 1996). One's agency is understood in relation to one's identity, and different social identities encode different evolutions and expectations. Thus, if moral discourse on this reading is about understanding agents and actions, it also inevitably brings in the operation of the rules of social identities and what can morally be expected of whom. Questions of social understandings, then, are not separate from moral discourse. When we reason morally we are already employing rules of social discrimination and categories of persons and responsibilities, rules that make up the contexts in which we are embedded.

The point of moral discourse, on this reading, is the truthful elaboration of the agent in relationship to the act and the truthful understanding of each speaker through his or her position. Such an understanding of the "rationality" of moral discourse, of course, leads to a much different formulation of rationality than the "objective" or "scientific" rationality that aims at producing agreement between competent speakers. "[I]n science, everyone competent knows what constitutes a valid challenge to, or substantiation of, a claim that has been made. In morality, by contrast, one participant may competently and rationally reject the valid, rational position taken by another. What he cannot do . . . is to reject the relevance of the other's concern; and we related this to the requirement that the other be treated as a person, with attention to his cares and commitments" (Pitkin 1972, 207). While the scientific rationality to which Pitkin contrasts moral rationality measures the competence of speakers by their ability to get the "right" scientific answers, moral rationality is not (or should not be) focused on agreement; there can be rational disagreement between competent users of a moral language or vocabulary, and the function of moral discourse is often that of healing or maintaining social relationships; moral competence involves the ability to see and understand the cares, commitments, and positions of another in a way that does not enter into positivistic scientific rationality—a condition possibly related to the relatively narrow field and function of scientific discourse, what it produces and how it goes about producing, compared with the very broad field of human living that is addressed by moral discourse. One interesting facet of this reading of moral discourse is that it does not require convergence on one moral point of view in order to succeed. To reach a consensus on one's relationship with another may, in fact, be to reach a consensus that you and the other should leave each other alone. The repair and maintenance of social understandings leaves open the possibility that one might understand another to be outside the pale of one's moral point of view and that trying to convert or change the other's position may be impossible or unnecessary (Shrage 1994).

In this kind of examination of moral discourse, Pitkin is aware that she, as well as similar readers, like Cavell, are saying things that Wittgenstein himself considered better left out; morality, he thought, was higher than rationality. Yet in sketching out some of the ways moral discourse is used, its internal logics and social function, neither Pitkin nor Cavell wished to imply that morality is only this function of social adjudication; one of the peculiar criteria of intelligibility of moral discourse is an openness to certain kinds of repudiations, repudiations that are intelligible but not fully explainable within the terms of moral discourse. Such repudiations as Kierkegaard's or Nietzsche's question moral discourse, especially its settled and habitual meanings in the resolution of conflicts about behavior, in the name of what is higher.

One of Pitkin's points about morality's openness to repudiation is that "as a realm of discourse it is limited by the traditional concepts men have developed for assessing and accusing and excusing action." Thus its concepts are continually open to revision to fit new and unforeseen applications. The ways in which different persons and their responsibilities are understood may change; actions may come to be understood as falling under a different rule than previously. Another is that morality "must be open to repudiation also in a different sense, one that has to do less with its concepts than with what Waisman would call its "logic"— the kinds of truth, evidence, principles of reasoning, standards of rationality, appropriate to it. These concern not the limitations of morality as a whole, but the limitations—the openness to repudiation—of particular moral claims and positions" (Pitkin 1972, 152). Here I think that Pitkin's analysis might be made more clear by the use of Wittgenstein's formulation of the "criterial relation" in thinking about concepts; it seems that the different kinds of repudiations of morality that "make sense" to moral discourse have to do with questions of either the correct application of a concept or the correctness of the criteria for a concept. To ask whether a particular action "falls within" a concept is not quite the same as posing a challenge to the definition of that concept. Neither sort of questioning is aimed at destroying the concept, and many questions about morality can be seen as doing both at the same time; but to ask whether a particular state of affairs "qualifies" as, say, an example of a moral act may not be the same as asking whether our criteria for seeing something as moral are adequate for our purposes in a given context.[2] The second kind of repudiation brings one moral context and set of understandings to bear not on a single action but on the rules by which persons and actions are understood, challenging not a single judgment but an entire practice of traditional or familiar judgments that make up a cultural moral norm.

In her subsequent examination concerning political discourse, Pitkin asks many of the same sorts of questions about political rationality and political vocabularies. Although there are similarities between political discourse (as she sees it) and moral discourse, there are significant differences as well. Political discourse, like moral discourse, uses vocabularies of human action, agency, and responsibility; these vocabularies of concepts (and their accustomed uses) apply peculiarly to what political speakers take to be human actors, and implicitly define what shall count as human action and accountability. In the use of these terms, political discourse centers upon the question of "what shall we do"; the content of the *what*, as well as the *we*, are part of the debate in political discourse. The assessment of "who we are" in political discourse is a question of the definition of our past and of our projected future, the regulation of which is the point of political discourse. Political rationality, as Pitkin interprets it, depends not on agreement but in the maintenance of equilibrium; political discourse is the linguistic endeavor of a society in "trying to act and remain a community" (Wolin, *Politics and Vision*, 62; quoted in Pitkin 1972, 216). Political discourse presupposes a plurality of interests in the definition of the general interest of a society; the reconciliation between partial perspectives in any politically achieved policy "will always be temporary, partial, and provisional" (Pitkin 1972, 217). Of course, the partiality of political equilibrium can be viewed in several ways. To interpret politics as the maintenance of equilibrium begs the question of what kind of equilibrium exists to be maintained and whether the partiality of political solutions reflects the interests only of the "we" whose understandings are dominant in the social group (Addelson 1995).

In analyzing the use of political discourse, Pitkin discovers that any attempt to articulate a concept of the political seems to presuppose a certain form of political organization. In sketching out various definitions of *the political*, such as Aristotle's and Arendt's, Pitkin attempts to make sense out of the meaning of *the political* as that area of discourse in which participation of citizens is essential and each citizen is free to both govern and be governed by his equals. The concept of "the political," she argues, contains an inherent tension. On the one hand, political discourse functions as the mechanism for continual redefinition and decision among conflicting interests; on the other, political discourse is defined as that area of contention "between equals" where all are free as citizens. The concept of the political captures, for Pitkin, the area of contestable power, negotiation of what is commonly understood in a community to be open to decision rather than determined by necessity. The members of a body politic pursue their political interests in a space marked apart, by those very actors, from the powers and interests of nonpolitical "private" affairs. For Pitkin this tension between private interest and public equality, the dispute about the political, is "central to the nature of the political. For the rival definitions are both very much bound to the grammar of the word, and both illuminate it" (Pitkin 1972, 214). She concludes that

> [p]erhaps what characterizes political life is precisely the problem of continually *creating* unity, a public, in the context of diversity, rival claims, unequal power, and conflicting interests. In the absence of rival claims and conflicting interests, a topic never enters the political realm; no political decision needs to be made. But for the political collectivity, the "we" to act, those conflicting claims and interests must be resolved in such a way as to preserve the collectivity. (Pitkin 1972, 215)

Thus, for Pitkin, the very concept of the political is intimately bound up with the question of the "we"; when we speak politically, it is always of a "we" rather than an "I." Also, political matters are those about which there is a public question—a matter that citizens view as changeable, open to debate, that affects groups of citizens' concerns rather than a single person's concern. "Of course one can have personal conversations about politics, and some personal conversations can have absolutely crucial effects on political events. Just so, as we said, one can also speak publicly about moral issues. But public sermons are not what moral discourse is for, what it is primarily about; and personal relationships are not the point of political discourse. There is no such thing as private politics, intimate politics" (Pitkin 1972, 204).

Contestations of the Political

Pitkin's 1972 analysis of "the political," from the vantage of twenty years later, seems in one sense still quite accurate and in others very dated. The elements of the "grammar" of the concept of the political she focuses on, especially the necessary publicity of political discourse, are now themselves seen as part of the functioning of the concept—its use in dividing the "natural" power of the private sphere from the contestable power of the public. Pitkin's tension between the conflictual and consensual meanings of *the political*, while retained in the actual operation of public political discourse, seems more of an etymological than grammatical point in the much broader conception of the "use" of the term. The ways in which we theorize the concept of the political have indeed undergone a catastrophic, earthquake-like shift; rather than ask what things are "political" in the sense of "property is the subject of communal deliberation and decision making," we now also ask after the specifically political aspects of who gets to make such divisions at all. The marking off of certain domains of concern and the articulations proper to their expression into *the political* is now seen as a political division of contestable versus noncontestable, naturalized social arrangements—a division that has functioned to keep the concerns of most humans off the political agenda. The boundaries of what is considered political are now a hotly debated political question.

The boundaries of the political domain have entered as an important part of the "what" of political discourse, one of the issues that can and must be debated: what is political? The second-wave feminist challenge to the public-private split has politicized many areas of power relations that have for centuries been seen as merely personal. The power relations of slavery and gender subordination that Aristotle contrasted to political relations, the "household" relations that enabled citizens to interact freely, have entered the domain of the political with explosive consequences for our traditional understandings of citizenship, freedom, and publicity. The "we" encoded in our political tradition has come under intense scrutiny, and judged to reflect the interests, viewpoints, and concerns of the most powerful members of a given community. Yet much of Pitkin's analysis of the features of the political remains true for post-second-wave understandings of the political. Many systematic power relations that have been excluded from political consideration have, in Nancy Fraser's phrase, become matters "subject to legitimate state intervention" through becoming "debated across a wide range of discourse publics" (Fraser 1989, 166). Yet the criteria for the entrance of such a matter as a political concern remain close to those examined by Pitkin. A matter can become part of a political discourse if it affects groups of citizens systematically, involves the definition of a political we, and is thus differentiated from merely personal or private matters. What becomes effectively politicized does so by becoming rearticulated in civil discourses rearticulated in ways that fit the criteria for inclusion as not merely able to be contested, but proper to be contested within political institutions and institutionalized political terms. A matter must be rearticulated forcefully enough by politicizing civil discourses to merit its recognition as a public, rather than individual (even if the individuals form a large group) or private, problem (Fraser 1989). In practical politics, the strategy has been one of stretching the concept to include more citizens' concerns than of challenging the formulation of the concept, the way most people think about and use the word *political*. The way the use of the term has been extended has not changed very much its criteria of application; it is still used mainly to describe situations and conditions that the user of the term considers in need of, and amenable to, change.

Indeed, in light of feminist and antiracist challenges to traditional understandings of politics, it seems to have been part of the grammar of the concept of the political that it divide contestable relations among the powerful from the naturalized and oppressive relations of the powerful to those who are their "niaterial conditions." Yet this notion of the grammar of a concept is closer to Foucault's use of *technology* than Wittgenstein's *technique*. Wittgenstein, in finding that the use of language and the "baseline" recognitions common to a way of life presupposed masteries of certain techniques, did not consider these techniques or the trainings involved in mastering them to be a political matter, although pedagogy includes relations of power. It seems part of the grammar, the possible and sensible use, of the concept of the political that it so divide the concerns of a citizenry; this division is not something people "mean" to do in using the concept, yet it is part of the use of the concept as we understand it.

It is a short step (yet a significant, even revolutionary step) from Wittgenstein's remarks about the learned techniques that underlie and make possible our use of concepts and the thought that such techniques, as they enable, also form and limit, our thinking and speaking. Consideration of these formations as political—the trainings and techniques that "we" use in common and that make us who and what we are rather than otherwise—challenge the concept of the political in its criteria rather than its range of applications. It is thus not surprising that the question of the politics of the concept of the political has not entered institutionalized political discourse; there is no place for it to enter, no way for such a challenge to be articulated within the techniques of using that concept. Yet various postmodern and feminist challenges to the concept of the political suggest important consequences for human social organization, knowledge construction, and subject formation. In Wittgensteinian terms, the possibility of a politics of language and concepts that questions the differentiation of the effects of learning techniques along lines of race, ethnicity, gender, class, and sexual orientation implies that politically differentiated groups, even "within" a culture, have different ways of life. Even with a common vocabulary, some of "us" use it differently from how others use it, and are used differently by it. Using the same words, we inhabit different worlds.

The Politics of the Obvious

Following the implications of the postmodern, especially Foucauldian, reformulation of the political—in terms of the specific limiting and enabling characteristics of initiation into ways of life in a politically differentiated linguistic field—has suggested various new emphases in thinking about moral and epistemological problems. In Pitkin's terms, the concepts and rationality of moral and political discourse employ social rules about identities, responsibilities, and envisaged possibilities of change or continuance within a community. The possibility of politically differentiated learnings and positionings by the inherited "common vocabularies" of moral consideration leads to moral consideration of what may be required to reach such understandings. What must already be in place, economically and socially, for our visions of political freedom to be realized? What relations of persons and identities make our moral understandings and communications possible? The very rules by which we identify moral and political problems become seen as moral and political problems, along with the already-in-place rules of delineating actors and persons. If those rules of personhood and agency are formulated by, and in the interests of, the most powerful members of a community, then they may be deeply problematic for rightly understanding the agency of less powerful members; those concepts may have no "entrance" to describe or recognize the agency, point of view, or concerns of many or most persons (Walker 1995).

The ways in which we learn to recognize, and attribute, human agency and accountability become deeply problematic with the recognition of our own formation by those "techniques" and their possible insufficiency or inappropriateness for understanding agency and accountability for those differently positioned by those concepts. Bakhtin's concept of "dialogic heteroglossia" is useful for thinking about the conflicts and intersections between such uses of our inherited vocabularies (which, of course, have been imposed upon many inappropriately by others) yet is not quite sufficient—these patterns of use and subject positionings produce conflicts along lines of what I shall call "discursive capital"—the ability of the common vocabulary of concepts adequately to articulate the concerns of some language users more than others. In addition, the modes of articulation in which we communicate "formally," "properly," "informally," and so forth are differentially valued and stratified in distribution. For moral discourse to occur dialogically between such speakers, we must regard one another as "concrete others" rather than "general others"—as formed in fundamentally different ways rather than somehow deeply "the same,"[3] varying only in our proficiency in a language game rather than marked variant by the language. In moral speech we must learn to understand the doer along with the deed in relation to the available ways to speak about it—both "our" relation to those concepts and their positional relationships to them. "Translation is always interpretative, critical, and partial. Here is a ground for conversation, rationality, and objectivity—which is a power-sensitive, not pluralist, 'conversation'" (Haraway 1991, 195).

The awareness of the discursive politics of human language use and the learned techniques of their mastery that suggests interrogation of the relationship of the "doer and the deed" to moral discourse suggests an analogous political interrogation of the epistemological problem of the knower and the known. Donna Haraway's remarkable work on "situated knowledges" can be seen in this light; her model of epistemological accountability as the acknowledgment and critical examination of our techniques and positionings vis-à-vis our conceptual vocabularies and our proficiencies with them. Our "visual practices," using her metaphor of sight, require a critical practice of recognizing our own "semiotic technologies" of making meanings (Haraway 1991, 187). With such a model of epistemological accountability, "we might become answerable for what we learn how to see" (190). In science as well as morality, Haraway suggests, it is the norms and criteria of how we are able to see that need to be acknowledged as political products.

Such radical transformations of the traditional concepts of moral and epistemological discourse in light of the politicization of subject formation through initiation into ways of life move problems of morality and of knowledge into a register of "translation" between ways of speaking (and thus living) rather than of adjudication between them—or, worse, transcendence of them. Learning to understand others clearly involves a much more fundamental and difficult endeavor than the familiar, but insufficient, technique of subsuming their concerns and ways of seeing under "our" categories. Rather, those who are discursively advantaged in terms of the current systems of valued articulation must be initiated into others' worlds to make their communications meaningful. So to evaluate our own positionings we must become at least conceptually bilingual; the obviousnesses of our ways of life must be constantly interrogated, seen as our particular obviousnesses learned in our situated trainings. For such "partial perspective" to work, in Haraway's terms, we must learn to recognize that every seeing is made possible, made the particular seeing it is, by the mastery of particular practices of cognition and recognition.

Some Pedagogical Consequences

The tracing of some lines of the appropriation of Wittgenstein in academic philosophy and some consequences of the "politicization" of concepts and language leads me back, in circuitous intersection, to the first question of the essay. What can be said about Wittgenstein's "style" and his often-quoted desire to release philosophers from their fly bottles? Despite the tendency of philosophers "after Wittgenstein" to systematize his thought into various theories about moral and political life, Wittgenstein was deeply disturbed by the thought of creating "a new jargon." The *Philosophical Investigations* does not tell us things that we must accept, but shows us things that we may see for ourselves and tries to warn us away from certain deep-rooted tendencies toward attachment to philosophical pictures that make philosophers unable to see in ways other than "with" their pictures. This attachment to particular schemes of understanding— "visual practices?"—seemed to Wittgenstein a kind of disease; the obstinate unwillingness to attend to the disease, even when shown its tenacious operation, seemed to him a kind of sin. The *Investigations*, however, is not a sermon, but a series of therapy sessions aimed at understanding; "in philosophizing we may not terminate a disease of thought. It must run its natural course, and the slow cure is all important" (*Zettel*, §382, quoted in Pitkin 1972, xii). For Wittgenstein the false pictures in which philosophers are trained and their attachment to such pictures led to a kind of interpretive calcification—an inability to see a particular fact as one fact among others, and perhaps the inability to see the irrelevance of that particular fact to any living problems of human existence. This suggests to me why Wittgenstein so abhorred the philosophical problems generated by the reference model of language; its problems were of deep importance only to philosophers, and were the result of an unduly narrow and technical mode of interpretation. Unlearning those habits of thought and learning others was, on his view, the proper "answer" to such questions. A theory could not answer the need for looking at something else in another way; thus the *Investigations* is less a theory than a set of exercises.

The pedagogy of the *Investigations*, its suggestive force and indirection, its wearing-out of traditional questions grown from mistaken pictures, indicates that Wittgenstein was aware of the recalcitrance and tenacity of such pictures and the delicacy involved in showing someone the way out without telling him or her where to go. It suggests that the kind of interpretive flexibility Wittgenstein thought valuable in human life could be taught not by doctrine but by example; techniques of interpretation are "caught on to," not memorized or deduced. Changing the way we look at things is an interactive venture—like therapy, it cannot work on the unwilling, and the same cure will not work on different people. The *Investigations* tried to show its readers something, produce an illumination that will enable us to "move about on our own"—a knowing-how that cannot be "taught" in the sense of mastering a theory, that must be approached through exercises. Only through going through all the steps, being exhausted by them, feeling the bewilderment and eventual point-lessness of clinging to our pictures, can we figure out the trick of letting go. It is altogether unclear, in addition, whether the kind of flexibility Wittgenstein reminds us of is attainable, or even explainable, to someone who does not see the need to break their habits of thought. As in psycho-analysis, the analysand who does not enter willingly into therapy and work together with the analyst will find no cure; such flexibility cannot be done to one, or given to one, but must be worked for.

Although I would like to draw an analogy between "philosophical therapy" and the learning of a conceptual multilingualism (Lugones 1987), I fear that the *Investigations* provides both an attempt to produce such flexible awareness and a warning about its extreme difficulty. Witt-genstein, after all, sought to break our philosophical attachments to the techniques, particular trained ways to interpret according to mistaken pictures. Attachment to those pictures, dependence on their techniques, is something that we learn at a very late stage of "becoming minded." How much more difficult, then, to learn to let go of (or at least see the parochial nature of) the bedrock of "obvious" interpretive practices that forms our baseline organization of reality? Wittgenstein's "seeing the world aright" was a personal accomplishment that led to a "safety" be-yond attachment to the world; he thought that changing the way philoso-phers looked at things would lead to their silence on many matters rather than better philosophy about them. What cautions are there in Witt-genstein's work on "training" and ways of life that warn us about the difficulty of a project such as Haraway's, or the project of becoming bilin-gual in the arts of seeing and reading expressions? Spelman and Lugones (1983) point out that learning how things are seen by a group different from one's own requires that the learner undergo long practice and initia-tion into that group, that the learner "begin again" from the status of a child rather than from the viewpoint of an outside investigator or theore-tician; a theory cannot help one learn how another sees. Wittgenstein was worried about aspect-blindness; how more worried should we be about the project of learning to see aspects according to different living cultures?

Concluding Cautionary Remarks

The further I get with the description of the radical social
constructionist programme and a particular version of
postmodernism, coupled to the acid tools of critical discourse in
the human sciences, the more nervous I get.
—Donna Haraway, *Simians, Cyborgs, and Women*

One of the points of wariness, if not outright discouragement, implied
by the pedagogy of the *Investigations* for the project of deep interpretive
flexibility is in its recognition that someone who does not want to see in
the way the *Investigations* teaches will be unable to do so. To create interpretive flexibility across a wide range of situated discourses and speakers
it would be necessary to create the desire to change the way in which we
hold our discursive frameworks. Such a desire, and such an ability, could
be taught by no didactic program, but would have to be encouraged and
fostered through a wholesale revision of teaching methods. Spelman and
Lugones suggest that someone must want to learn the ways that another
sees in order to be able to do so; friendship or love could be such a motive.
Various feminist standpoint epistemologies have shown that it is indeed
possible (even necessary for some people in a politically differentiated
linguistic culture) to learn conceptual bilingualism. One tenet of standpoint theory is that oppressed persons must learn to see in the ways that
their oppressors see, and frequently go through life using two sets of interpretive criteria: how we see things and how they see things. Yet such
familiarity with both one's "subjugated" worldview and the language of
the hegemonic discourse depends on the necessity of such bilingualism
for survival.

Wittgenstein's comments on the initiation of each learning child into
a world picture with his natural language involves implicit common facts
about our capacities to learn—capacities that are not universally but
"normally and naturally" human. We are taught our obviousnesses, and
need them to function; it may well be the case that we need to have such
obviousnesses "in place" to be able to go on linguistically. We learn and
use ways of seeing in order to get along with the others we need to get
along with; shall it be necessary to impose the exigencies of oppression
on all, in various ways, to produce world-crossing abilities? How can persons who do not need to learn other ways of seeing in order to survive

learn to do so in order for others to survive? Perhaps Haraway's cyborg heteroglossia requires the full recognition of the fragmented and untranslatable character of language regions and language users in such a way as to put all, in learning worlds, in different positions of needing to know and needing to understand. Yet the bilingualism of border-crossers, in the politically stratified terrain of official and unofficial discourse, is painfully acquired, involving not merely a recognition of oneself as a neophyte in another language game but the constant awareness of one's shaming by the dominant discourse, one's exclusion from and denigration by it. What motivations could make us such that we want and need to recognize concrete others as such, and learn their ways? The revolutionary character of the project of training ourselves and our children to world-crossing without shame should serve to remind us that it may not be possible. What would cognition look like with "contingent foundations"—can we learn on a bedrock we no longer see as solid? We do not know what other "forms of life" are possible for human beings.

One more aspect of Wittgenstein's thought remains in thinking about possible revolutions in the way we learn and think about our framework propositions, the obviousnesses without which we have not yet been able to function. Wittgenstein's concern with aspect-seeing and flexibility of interpretation—the skills of expression and of hearing expression rightly—stemmed from his convictions about the place of flourishing tradition in the flourishing of individual existence. Clearly he thought that the "gestalt-blind," those who could not take part in the humor, artistic enjoyment, and common expressions of a culture, were in a deep way lost to the most important and joyous activities and possibilities of the fully human person. Yet the concern for the loss of such traditions and the emphasis on the importance of interpretive flexibility does not lead, in Wittgenstein, to political activism. Common culture and interpretive flexibility are in some ways fostered, not prevented, by systematic domination; indeed, it seems that the flexibility that Wittgenstein thought important is more available to the subjugated of a culture than to those "on top." Stubborn inflexibility seems to be a problem of privileged ignorance, a habit of not needing to change one's mind or see things differently; yet the flourishing of "living tradition" is both encouraged by the exigencies of communal survival and threatened by it. Can we make ourselves need to understand others without the kind of political stratification that produces anguish and shame along with multilingual, supple conceptual abilities? How can we become joyously, rather than painfully, fragmented selves? To find out, we must try in ways that have never been tried. For as Wittgenstein noted, "the sickness of a time" is cured only "by an alteration in the mode of life of human beings," through alternative modes of "thought and life, not through a medicine invented by an individual" (Wittgenstein, *Remarks on the Foundations of Mathematics*, p. 57, quoted in Pitkin 1972, 340). Perhaps we cannot be trained to freedom, or made to practice liberty; we can only be shown the way out of our messes, not told how to live without them.

Notes

1. In distinguishing philosophy from life I use those terms gingerly; clearly Wittgenstein thought that the way people were doing philosophy was far distant from, and possibly detrimental to, thinking about the more important questions and exigencies of human living. The parallel with Nietzsche seems to me very fruitful in that Wittgenstein, like Nietzsche, sought to teach people something with philosophy that would have profound implications for their lives—"philosophizing with a hammer" was meant to wake people up, not put them to sleep; Wittgenstein tried to free us from particular fly bottles, not give us a new and improved fly bottle.

2. Pitkin's discussion of the "uselessness" of the fact-value distinction in ethics would also, I think, be strengthened by more attention to the criterial relation in determining the operations of "what will count" in moral and political discourse.

3. I am of course borrowing terminology, as well as insight, from Seyla Benhabib's critique of Habermas's discourse ethic. Her critique seems to me right on target; I would also like to add the thought that a discourse ethic must include considereration of the politics of who must learn to speak whose language in order for mutual comprehension' to occur. In the formulation of the ideal speech situation, it is worth pointing out that in a great many actual communications between speakers the requirements of "true, "comprehensible in this context," and "sincerely meant" may be in tension, if not outright conflict.

References

Addelson, Kathryn Pyne. 1991. *Impure Thoughts: Essays on Philosophy, Feminism, amd Ethics*. Philadelphia: Temple University Press.

———. 1994. *Moral Passages: Toward a Collectivist Moral Theory*. New York: Routledge.

Alcoff, Linda, and Elizabeth Potter, eds. 1993. *Feminist Epistemologies*. New York: Routledge.

Anzaldúa, Gloria, ed. 1990. *Making Face, Making Soul*. San Franscisco: Aunt Lute Books.

Baier, Annette C. 1995. *Moral Prejudices: Essays on Ethics*. Cambridge: Harvard University Press.

Barrett, Michele. 1991. *The Politics of Truth from Marx to Foucault*. Stanford: Stanford University Press.

Barrett, Cyril, ed. 1967. *Wittgenstein: Lectures and Conversations on Aesthetics, Psychology, and Religious Belief*. Berkeley and Los Angeles: University of California Press.

Benhabib, Seyla. 1992. *Situating the Set*. New York: Routledge.

Bordo, Susan, and Alison Jaggar, eds. 1989. *Gender/Body/Knowledge*. New Brunswick: Rutgers University Press.

Butler, Judith, and Joan W. Scott, eds. 1992. *Feminists Theorize the Political*. New York: Routledge.

Cavell, Stanley. 1969. *Must We Mean What We Say?* New York: Cambridge University Press.

Code, Lorraine. 1991. *What Can She Know? Feminist Theory and the Construction of Knowledge*. Ithaca: Cornell University Press.

Collins, Patricia Hill. 1990. *Black Feminist Thought: Knowledge, Consciousness, and the Politics of Empowerment*. Boston: Unwin Hyman.

Diamond, Irene, and Lee Quinby, eds. 1988. *Feminism and Foucault: Reflections on Resistance*. Boston: Northeastern University Press.

Flax, Jane. 1993. *Disputed Subjects: Essays on Psychoanalysis, Politics, and Philosophy*. New York: Routledge.

Fraser, Nancy. 1989. *Unruly Practices: Power, Discourse, and Gender in Contemporary Social Theory*. Minneapolis: University of Minnesota Press.

Frye, Marilyn. 1983. *The Politics of Reality*. New York: Crossing Press.

Haraway, Donna. 1991. *Simians, Cyborgs, and Women: The Reinvention of Nature*. New York: Routledge.

Hartsock, Nancy. 1983. *Money, Sex, and Power*. New York: Longman.

hooks, bell. 1981. *Ain't I a Woman? Black Women and Feminism*. Boston: South End Press.

————. 1984. *Feminist Theory from Margin to Center*. Boston: South End Press.

Lovibond, Sabina. 1983. *Realism and Imagination in Ethics*. Minneapolis: University of Minnesota Press.

Lugones, María. 1987. "Playfulness, 'World'-Travelling, and Loving Perception," *Hypatia* 2, no. 2 (Summer): 3–19.

Monk, Ray. 1990. *Ludwig Wittgenstein: The Duty of Genius*. New York: Penguin.

Pitkin, Hanna. 1972. *Wittgenstein and Justice*. Berkeley and Los Angeles: University of California Press.

Rabinow, Paul, ed. 1984. *The Foucault Reader*. New York: Pantheon.

Shrage, Laurie. 1994. *Moral Dilemmas of Feminism*. New York: Routledge.

Smiley, Marion. 1992. *Moral Responsibility and the Boundaries of Community: Power and Accountability from a Pragmatic Point of View*. Chicago: University of Chicago Press.

Spelman, Elizabeth V. 1988. *Inessential Woman: Problems of Exclusion in Feminist Thought*. Boston: Beacon Press.

Spelman, Elizabeth V., and Lugones, María. 1983. "Have We Got a Theory for You! Feminist Theory, Cultural Imperialism, and the Demand for 'The Woman's Voice.'" *Women's Studies International Forum* 6, no. 6:573–81.

Walker, Margaret Urban. 1996. "Feminist Skepticism, Authority, and Transparency." In *Moral Knowledge*, ed. Mark Timmons and Walter Sinnott-Armstrong. Oxford: Oxford University Press.

————. 1998. *Moral Understandings*. New York: Routledge.

Wittgenstein, Ludwig. 1965. *The Blue and Brown Books*. New York: Harper and Row.

————. 1968. *Philosophical Investigations*. 3d ed. Trans. G. E. M. Anscombe. New York: Macmillan.

————. 1970. *Zettel*. Ed. G. E. M. Anscombe and G. H. von Wright. Trans. Anscombe. Berkeley and Los Angeles: University of California Press.

14

Big Dogs, Little Dogs, Universal Dogs:

Ludwig Wittgenstein and Patricia Williams Talk About the Logic of Conceptual Rearing

Sandra W. Churchill

A picture held us captive. And we could not get outside it, for it lay in our language and language seemed to repeat it to us inexorably.

—Ludwig Wittgenstein, *Philosophical Investigations*

Introduction

The practices of philosophical reflection that occupy Wittgenstein early in his philosophical career, especially in the *Tractatus Logico-Philosophicus,* are more concerned with logic than with the experience and uses of language. Wittgenstein's early philosophy of language as well as his practices of writing—uses of language and forms of language—are subordinated to a logic in which language and reality are mimetically sealed, yielding a precision that he hoped would permit completely lucid representation. In this early philosophical vision, language-as-used is no more than a mirroring device whose representative capacity is under the guidance of strict logical requirements. Thought is thus contained in language's mimetic function and is precise and lucid when it is more like a photograph than a painting.

The later Wittgenstein struggled to break away from his early views. Especially in *Philosophical Investigations* and in *On Certainty*, logic takes a backseat to language, which increasingly is seen as richly textured, nuanced, and varied—full of twists, turns, and multiple voices that are no longer seen as problems or errors, but as constitutive of what language is. In both style and content, Wittgenstein's later thinking shows a growing preoccupation with what Creel Froman has called "languaged reality" (Froman 1992). The philosophical task emerging from the later Wittgenstein is to escape from the maze of confusions that entrap us when language is misused and misunderstood and thus leads to a reconfiguration of our philosophic convictions.

To engage in such a philosophic task involves learning to *change our minds*—to undo systems of thought and structures of power in which we, ourselves, are both caught and invested. I believe such *undoing*—in its particular reconsiderations as well as in its more transformative revaluations—is what Wittgenstein spends the majority of his life trying to responsibly carry out.[1] This transformative undoing, what I call intellectual activism, is also fundamental to what it means to be a responsible theorist and feminist thinker.[2] It will become clear that change of mind is not simply a cognitive effort. Such change is required for the displacement of any ideological prejudice. It involves undoing the thought, as well as the comfort, embedded in customs and habits of practice. I refer to both the cognitive and the practical elements of this undoing as making changes in *conceptual rearing*.

"Big Dog, Little Dog, Universal Dogs"

Patricia Williams places this vignette, which she calls, "The Brass Ring and the Deep Blue Sea (some parables on learning to think like a lawyer)," in the opening essay of her book *The Alchemy of Race and Rights: The Diary of a Law Professor*.

> Walking down Fifth Avenue in New York not long ago, I came up behind a couple and their young son. The child, about four or five years old, had evidently been complaining about big dogs. The

mother was saying, "But why are you afraid of big dogs?" "Because they're big," he responded with eminent good sense. "But what's the difference between a big dog and a little dog?" the father persisted. "They're *big*," said the child. "But there's really no difference," said the mother, pointing to a large slathering wolfhound with narrow eyes and the calculating amble of a gangster, and then to a beribboned Pekinese the size of a roller skate, who was flouncing along just ahead of us all, in that little fox-trotty step that keep Pekinese from ever being taken seriously. "See?" said the father. "If you look really closely you'll see there's no difference at all. They're all just dogs." (Williams 1991, 12)

There are two places of difference in the story: (1) the differences between big and little dogs (versus "all dogs are the same"), and (2) the differences between the child's and the parents' perceptions. Both reflect instances of conceptual rearing in which thinking stands still—in the sense that it is locked into and insistent upon imposing a transcendental universalist logic premised on and enforcing sameness. There is action here, to be sure; however, it is violative action that stops the players from being able to use their experience as a legitimate ground for thinking about difference. The logic in "Big Dogs, Little Dogs, Universal Dogs"— the method of considering and the norms/warrants for what counts in our understanding of experience—brings thinking to a standstill. It does so by setting the terms for what the experience of difference can mean in the abstract. The problem is not that the parents try to quiet their son's fears of the "big" dog by appealing to some sense that "all dogs are the same." Rather, the problem comes about—for them and for all of us conceptually reared in this manner—in how we *arrive* at that position, in other words, whether experienced differences count as the location for understanding, whose experiences we count, and how flexible and inclusive we can be, given our desire for absolute certainty and assurance from the methods and the logic(s) we employ. Contextualized attention to experience is brought to a stop in this story, while standstill thinking that suppresses experience of difference as well as different experiences upholds an absolutist logic of sameness. This kind of logic is part of the logical problem in racism and sexism.

The logic at work in the "Big Dogs" story is akin to that of Wittgenstein's *Tractatus Logico-Philosophicus*. This logic pictures relations between thought and reality through a static mimetic theory of the meaning of language in which a structured language is used to force thought and reality into formal sameness. This kind of a priori logic, which sets the terms for understanding experience through conceptual definition, means that we are to judge experience by reference to categorical sets that privilege sameness, rather than testing the grounds of sameness against what experience shows us. This makes illegitimate the effort to understand differences arising within experience, even though the categorization of different "kinds" of dogs and "types" of animals is a logic of difference. A logical framework that represses experience, especially experiences of sameness and difference, can ultimately reinforce prejudiced fears. The logic of sameness teaches fundamentally conflicting norms for consideration: it asks that we *look* and then *not* credit or make use of what we see. But the requirement that some differences be ignored cannot, of course, be sustained in real life.

Patricia Williams calls her vignette "a paradigm of thought" that entails, in a vividly condensed fashion, "the rhetoric of power relations." The focus of my analysis is both on the *logic* of language displayed in the story, and on the connections between that logic and universalist thinking. One outcome of this logic and universalist thinking is that differences (plural) in perspectives of the players in the story cannot be taken seriously, cannot be given equal consideration. Those with power—the parents here—enforce their perspective, as the only logical perspective, over and against the child's. This logic is parallel to the dominant understanding of scientific logic. Sandra Harding talks about the monopoly this kind of scientific logic holds as well as the epistemological position embodied in it: "[There is] a conventional Western tendency to start thought from 'the view from nowhere'. . . . This tendency, which might be called transcendental or ahistorical foundationalism, leads to parochialism because it can never recognize the possible *greater* legitimacy of views that claim to be historically situated but contradict the speaker's."[3] In a similar vein, Patricia Williams calls the epistemological position of the parents "high objectivity" and "high Episcopalianism," referring to the epistemic dimensions of the situation that make this position blind to its blinders and more generally connote relative coolness, distance, and class.

Wittgenstein's philosophical work, taken as a whole, represents his own struggles to move from "high objectivity" to "low objectivity." During the last year of his life he wrote, "Am I not getting closer and closer to saying that in the end logic cannot be described? [There is no metalanguage, no transcendental point of view.] You must look at the practice of language, then you will see it" (*On Certainty*, §501, my interjection in brackets). "Low objectivity" moves away from a disembodied point of view to embrace lived, existentially contingent and experientially diverse points of view. "Low objectivity," which situates the logical and epistemic requirements of language and thought within "languaged reality," is actually more true to the practices of science than the transcendental and monistic requirements of "high objectivity."[4]

The parents in the "Big Dogs" story insist that their son look at two very different kinds of dogs, wolfhound and Pekinese, and perceive only one kind. Their insistence functions not only as a proposition about these two particular dogs; it teaches their son to dismiss his experience of the particular differences between these two dogs and believe *only* their proposition about *all* dogs. This insistence is the kind of move Elizabeth Minnich describes as reproducing "hierarchically invidious monism" (Minnich 1990), and it is characteristic of both orthodox science and patriarchy. Particular differences—between dogs and between the parents' and child's diverse points of view—are dominated by one scientifically oriented, proposition about how things are. We must disentangle ourselves from the textbook logic of this representation of dogs so that we might be in a better position to critique the so-called naturalness of its appeal. In this disentangling, Wittgenstein is particularly helpful.

Disentangling Pictures of the Way Words and Things Hook Up

Wittgenstein says, "The general form of propositions is: 'This is how things are' [*Tractatus*, 4.5].—This is the kind of proposition that one repeats to oneself countless times. One thinks one is tracing the outline of the thing's nature over and over again, and one is merely tracing round the frame through which we look at it" (§114, my interjection in brackets). Changing the frame, transforming the very activity of consideration, requires changing logical assumptions. Speaking of his own early philosophy developed in the *Tractatus*, Wittgenstein observes, "A *picture* held us captive. And we could not get outside it, for it lay in our language and language seemed to repeat it to us inexorably" (§115). One reason *pictures* remain so alluring is that they appeal by way of sublimity.

Wittgenstein asks, "In what sense is logic something sublime?" (§89) It is, he answers, in the concept of language as a rigid, precise calculus; the conviction that language has an essence; the belief in atomic names and objects that are isomorphically related such that their relations can be precisely expressed in propositions. None of these elements in logic's "sublimity" results from empirical research; they derive rather from an a priori ideal. This ideal must be exposed for what it is: "a blind demand, not based on facts of observation but contradicting them" (§101, §105, §107). In the *Investigations* §§89–109, Wittgenstein realizes that no half-way measures to fix the syndrome will do: "The *preconceived idea* of crystalline purity can only be removed by turning our whole examination around. . . . For the crystalline purity of logic was, of course, not a *result of investigation:* it was a requirement. . . . Back to rough ground" (§107, §108, §109).

Wittgenstein struggles to displace his own desires for sublime clarity, crystalline purity and certainty—to change the very activity of those considerations. This struggle often takes place in the *Investigations* through a dialogue between his early and later philosophical selves, enacted by a textual interlocutor. This dialogical form, which foregrounds voices and multiple agencies as well as philosophical technique, is part and parcel of the deconstructive activities of reconsidering the philosophical task and is the duty of the philosopher, according to Wittgenstein.[5] To that end, he throws the reader off guard every time she seeks formal systematic clarity in the content. He consistently and systematically deconstructs the usual or obviously available means whereby the reader could systematize her thought or her thought about his thought. An example of this deconstructive turn is in the way he qualifies his own criticism of the logic of the *Tractatus*. In his early work he characterizes the philosophical method as if it were a kind of science, in which we advance a kind of theory. This theorizing often pushed him (as it pushes the parents in our "Big Dogs" story) to generalize what are genuine insights beyond appropriate boundaries so that they become distorting. This urge to push theory was a large part of what Wittgenstein tried to undo in his later philosophy where he teaches how important "limits" and "will" are to the task of doing philosophy honestly, as well as to honest philosophy. He had thought that a proposition was, in effect, a picture. This was a genuine insight that he then mistakenly tried to apply to *all* propositions of any kind, so that all language must be pictures. If propositions did not look like pictures (if experience dictated conclusions contrary to the proposition), then the fault did not lie with the view of logic he was espousing; rather, he thought, this must be because *we* could not see through them. If we could see sufficiently deeply inside, propositions really would be revealed as pictures.

It is important to the breadth and complexity of Wittgenstein's philosophical methods, however, that he did not systematically reject the use of "pictures"; what he rejected was the inclination to reify the picture (just as the parents reify a scientific, categorical picture of "dogs" and force the child's proposition about particular dogs to conform to it). Such a singularizing overextension of the picture seeks to make *all* the different sentences of our multiple and diverse language activities come under *the same* logic.

> I had used a simile (a proposition is a picture), but because of the grammatical illusion that a concept word has a single thing corresponding to it, the common element in all the objects it applies to, the simile did not seem like one. Now we have a *theory* . . . but it does not look like a theory. It is typical of such a theory to look at a particular case which is in clear view and say "*That* shows how matters stand in general: this case is the paradigm of every case." . . . We have reached a form of representation which appears *self-evident* to us. This tendency to generalize the clear case seems to be strictly justified in logic: here we seem to be fully justified in concluding: "If one proposition is a picture, then every proposition must be a picture, because they must all share a common essence." (*Philosophical Investigations* [MS 220, 92] quoted in Kenny 1982, 7–8)

Here Wittgenstein qualifies his rejection of the "picture *theory*" of language. This move allows us to learn from him that changes in philosophical positions do not have to become wholesale refutations; changes do not have to proceed along a dichotomous either/or fault line where *all-or-nothing* thinking controls both what counts as an acceptable argument and what counts as an acceptable conclusion. This opens up our critique of the parents' attachment to their own picture of their son's experience of dogs such that we do not have to require them to drop *their* understanding of experience in order to embrace the differences their son's perspective includes. Indeed, the possibility of recognizing and logically accrediting diverse understandings of sameness and difference is what is most appealing about Wittgenstein's later philosophy, as well as what is deeply compelling about the feminist, antiracist, critical legal theory Patricia Williams deploys.

Pictures of Dogs and Conceptual Rearing

The parental logic painted in Williams's vignette exerts its power from the way in which it brings material-empirical reality under control: big and little dogs are lifted from experience—the child's as well as the parents'—into the land of a priori, universal, and categorical sameness. Yet this is no seamless a priori. Big and little dogs are turned into *a* dog, which then becomes definitive for *all* dogs. The universalist norm operates independently of what we see or think about actual dogs; it establishes a definition of *dogs* and of *experience* such that appeal to the latter to define the former, is incorrect. The parents teach the child *not* to see (even as he is encouraged to look), because experientially divergent seeing threatens the control the parents have acquired by virtue of the logic of sameness, a logic that says that all dogs are *essentially* the same and we must all *experience* them as such.

Ultimately, this is a story about *conceptual rearing*: the parents pass to their son one of Western culture's characterizing philosophical desires, the desire to have logical control of the random differences of experience—different peoples, facts, situations, relations, and thinking. Wittgenstein shows that this desire for logical purity sets up logic as the requirement, rather than the result, of inquiry. When we try to understand this logic's appeal—why we are drawn to a universalist norm that relies on an empirical untruth—we realize that it is the monolithic nature of logic that is, perhaps, more faulty than the desires we bring to it. Experience is denied its play, as when the parents' logic *reduces* experienced differences to *only* one relevant truth. The regulation of experiences of difference becomes powerfully encased in hierarchically invidious monistic reasoning.

It is helpful in understanding this reduction of difference to notice what Wittgenstein says about how propositions behave. He demonstrates that internal, rather than external, relations have been the dominant focus for logic. Logic's appeal to internal relations is the basis through which we take for granted a picture of the connections between language, thought and reality (Wittgenstein 1961, 4.014). Once Wittgenstein had discovered the secret of the proposition, and thereby of language, thought and language appeared to him "as the unique correlate, picture, of the world. These concepts: proposition, language, thought, world stand in the line one behind the other, each equivalent to each" (§96).

The linear and hierarchical logical surveillance is an appeal to essential universal equivalence, what I have been calling a logic of sameness. We do have dog shows with many breeds and individual dogs subsumed by the category "dogs." But in dog shows there are breed standards, not dog standards. The Afghan is not judged with the Pekinese. Every Pekinese is judged by a breed norm, regardless of which particular dog is loved more. Even when differences *are* relevant, as in best of breed, the context, including issues of power, determines *which* differences are, and are not, relevant.

Logic and Power: Controlling Differing Points of View

The logic of the picture painted in our story, the one sustained by the parents' insistence on universal sameness even in the face of their son's cries of experienced differences, does not allow for a *shifting* focus of attention between sameness and differences. The child's pleas spring out of two kinds of differences. First, he is trying to introduce his own point of view, which is different from his parents'. He is suggesting that his experience of dogs is different from theirs and that it has a logic of its own. He interjects his own difference, and with it the dogs', into a logic that controls differing experiences through universal norms that are actually not relevant to the walking-down-the-street situation (if they are relevant elsewhere). Second, he is empirically and epistemologically dependent upon his parents to teach him the meaning of this "language game" about dogs in which they are engaged. This situation bespeaks a lived difference between his power and theirs. He is, after all, a child. The question of his own different social and epistemic point of view logically cannot matter to his parents' kind of transcendental a priori logic. They have chosen this logic to teach him *as if* it were the *only* source of accurate judgments.

In some ways, this is scientific logic gone rampant—a logic that essentializes and thereby reduces particular differences under the norm of general sameness. Transcendental ideals of logic enforce standards of thinking that teach us that we should pull experienced differences into order without attention to point of view. Points (plural) of view are, by definition, epistemically irrelevant. Making point of view (except its own) irrelevant to logic encourages paradigms of thought devoid of lived social and cultural contingency; it also encourages points of view divorced from a bodily situated perspective that, in turn, perpetuates faulty conceptual rearing. The parents' logic reinforces "a static, unyielding, totally uncompromising point of reference . . . (where) people learn so well the idiocies of High Objectivity . . . and (where) they learn to capitulate so uncritically to a norm that refuses to allow for difference" (Williams 1991, 12).

This logic of sameness sustains its sway over our imaginations in part because it fulfills our desire for control, order and certainty, and "[i]t is in language that an expectation and its fulfillment make contact" (§445).

> Language is the bottle, the labyrinth in which we lose our way. Not this or that statement, tucked away in a tome of Hegel, or uttered in a classroom. Nothing that isolated or that infrequent, and therefore nothing that superficial or limited in its effects. No, the source of our difficulties is the whole conceptual system in which we live and move and have our being from the moment we are born; this second nature, this air we breath. The difficulties with which Wittgenstein deals are, correspondingly, widespread, deep-rooted, and tenacious. "They are deep disquietudes; their roots are as deep in us as the forms of our language and their significance is as great as the importance of our language." (§111) (Hallett 1977, 34)

Audre Lorde talks about the "deep disquietudes" hidden in our language as an "energy drain" that constantly keeps us from stopping, looking at differences, and redefining "ourselves and devising realistic scenarios for altering the present and constructing the future" (Lorde 1984, 115). She points out that Western European culture has taught us to respond to human differences "with fear and loathing." Indeed, one of the complicated features of the "Big Dogs" story is that the parents are teaching their child two things, at least, at once. The parents teach the child to distrust the differences between himself (and his perceptions) and his parents (and theirs). They teach him to *copy* their point of view, to bring his point of view to their (same) level. Lorde characterizes this dominant logic as a response that obliterates difference in three ways: "We ignore it, and if that is not possible, copy it if we think it is dominant, or destroy it if we think it is subordinate. But we have no patterns for relating across our human differences as equals" (Lorde 1984, 115). Lorde is not saying that each person sees "the other" in distorted ways, but rather that each person sees difference through the lenses of white supremacy, male dominance, heterosexism, and so forth. We are too often guilty of availing ourselves of the logic of dominance by claiming the superiority and "commonsensical assumptions" of that logic. It is part of the legacy of the later Wittgenstein that he offers us a philosophy of language—a logic—that can help us learn to relate across our human differences as equals.

Logic That Recognizes Cultural Effects

Lorde maintains that "differences [between people] have been misnamed and misused in the service of separation and confusion. Certainly there are very real differences between us of race, age, and sex. But it is not those differences between us that are separating us. It is rather our refusal to recognize those differences, and to examine the distortions which result from our misnaming them and their effects upon human behavior and expectation" (Lorde 1984, 115). Both racist and sexist beliefs partake of a transcendental logic of sameness that is taught in, among other places, routine instances of conceptual rearing such as the one we witness in "Big Dogs." What the parents are teaching their child amounts to a first primer on the mistrust and fear of difference—differences in fact and differences in thought. Their logic enforces control over the fear that differences will erupt and become uncontrollable, and it disables the capacity to "develop tools for using human difference as a springboard for creative change" (Lorde 1984, 13).

Wittgenstein's understanding of this logic helps us better understand these parents. The form of representation—universal dogs—appears "self-evident" to them. This marks the conservative nature of conceptual rearing: The "self-evident" logic seems impenetrable to change because it naturalizes its own norms and trains us to streamline our thinking and generalize incorrectly the real particular differences—between types of dogs in this story, or between types of persons and experiences of sameness and difference in stories of gender and race. Through a kind of vertical epistemological streamlining, actual empirical differences, such as size as well as kind of dog, for instance, "big," "wolfhounds," "little," and "Pekinese," are dismissed as unimportant. One major difference being denied is that between the parents' and the child's size relative to the dogs: the child looks down on the Pekinese and is towered over by the wolfhound. The parents look down on both.

Part of what is going on here is early and thorough training by these lawyer parents in the cultural supremacy of science's "high objectivity"— lessons about a science-worshiping culture. The power of this kind of logic and epistemological perspective within even the most innocent-sounding familial talk about dogs marks the hegemonic nature of this logic, which appears within countless other instances of conceptual learning. Once "*all* dogs are the same" assumes ideological supremacy, its logic of sameness easily justifies and relegitimates the "high objectivity" that was actually already assumed as the only norm for rule-making and experience-testing. Thus, scientific norms become monolithic standards. These standards frequently are used by analogy in different places and for different purposes, including in matters of racism and sexism.

Wittgenstein observes that it is typical of such analogical reasoning to look at *a* particular case (or particulars in a case) that is in (or are) clear view and say, "*that* shows how matters stand in general" (§101). He does not take his concerns about faulty analogical generalizations in the direction Lorde does. He is struggling to unthink the picture of thought and reality obtained from an atemporal crystalline sublimity and thus come to terms with the power and practice of conceptual rearing. He is struggling to do philosophy in the thick of a "radical break with the idea that language always functions in one way" (§304), an idea that "stands in the way of our seeing the use of the word as it is" (§305). On a broader level Wittgenstein is, as Naomi Scheman says, "struggling to shatter the crystal [the crystalline purity of logic], to show it to be a hall of mirrors, in which what we take for metaphysics are the reflections of our own activity, the long accretions of human community and practices, our natural history and forms of life" (Scheman 1993, 57; my interjection in brackets). Scheman asks: "But what are we to do once we have broken free from the grip of a picture that says that this is how things *have* to be, once we see that our practices [those of science and of the parents in this story] constitute the patterns of meaningfulness . . . ? What, especially are we to do if those practices and consequently those patterns are in deep ways abhorrent to us?" (57; my interjection in brackets).

The movement of Wittgenstein's thinking from the secure conceptual certainty and mirrored reality of his early thought to the breakup of that picture in his later thought helps us to understand Audre Lorde's criticisms of institutional and cultural power—a power that reaps its position of authority out of a logic of sameness and plays itself out as "institutional rejection of difference" (Lorde 1984, 115).

Thinking Through Differences: Undoing Conceptual Rearing

If we want to unthink our own dependence on the purity of logical pictures, we must begin a hard task. Lorde calls this "thinking through difference," by which she means dismantling the monolithic logic of sameness that can act out a logic of racist reaction and metaphysical untruths. One manner in which this kind of logic operates in prejudiced reactions is that it tacitly encourages uncritical or thoughtless judgments—thoughtless in two senses. First, we exercise them often through custom; we accept their efficacy as part of our conceptual rearing, without critical reflection on these "blind" assumptions. We do not see the necessity of stepping aside from their cultural dominance. Second, the enactment of these judgments blocks our thinking so that we do not recognize difference as a resource; we *do* recognize difference *from us* as difference, but only in using these monolithic judgments as our standard of reference for difference in general. We are cut off from lived and particular differences. Thus, the very cultural and intellectual resources that we need for changing our minds and practices are the ones we are blind to recognize, even as we reinscribe the cultural norms that keep us trapped. By so doing we isolate and distance ourselves, and those persons and objects of difference we behold, from a different kind of logic—one that might uphold us and help us value change more than sameness. As Lorde points out, "Difference must not be merely tolerated, logically or experientially, but seen as a necessary fund of polarities between which our creativity can spark like a dialectic. Only then does the necessity for interdependence become unthreatening. . . . Within the interdependence of mutual differences lies that security which enables us to descend into the chaos of knowledge and return with true visions of our future" (Lorde 1984, 112).

The logic of sameness prevalent in the "Big Dogs" story, in addition to concealing its more obvious transcendental ordering and control dynamics, also conceals domesticated/colonial imperial tendencies. The child in the story is domesticated much in the same way that an "anthropological other" is domesticated by the logic of opposition operative in the language of "primitive" and "civilized." The parents want the child to be just like them; the child's "primitive" conceptual thinking is the target of the parents' instruction. Ordering him to behave "well" absorbs his personal difference; he is made to look, act, and speak the same as his parents. The child's "primitive" empirical thinking, replete with a rich capacity to notice differences, is made to conform, is brought under control. This is all the more shocking because the scene depicted is *routine*. This is no extreme case of cultural dominance.[6] It shows a set of customary, ordinary, everyday practices used by parents to civilize (educate) their child.

The domestication of thought inherent in the "primitive"/"civilized" opposition, when coupled with the monolithic adherence to "high objectivity," renders unruly differences invisible by reduction or absorption into customary cultural norms. In both cases that which is "different" or "other" is "civilized" by it being made to look conceptually and customarily the same. This brings imperial and colonial hegemony very close to home, indeed. As a parent, I am frightfully familiar with the conservative nature of the domesticating duties of child rearing. How to undo the powerful tendency in Western thought to order, control, and erroneously universalize and generalize is one of the "deep disquietudes" that troubles Wittgenstein, Patricia Williams, and myself.

Conclusion

What Wittgenstein came to understand is that it is very difficult, if not impossible, to entertain a reflexive and critical conceptual attitude when the pictorial relationship between propositions and states of affairs is taken to be a *complete* account of language and understanding. He also recognized that once the certainty of "pure" logic is dismantled, philosophy as a foundational project must also be relinquished. He gave up on "the characteristic of modern scientific thought [which is] to claim universal validity by subsuming the purposes that might lie behind such constructions into the single one of distanced and dominating control, and to render that purpose either invisible or apparently inevitable. The purposefulness of the alternative epistemology which emerges from Wittgenstein's later work is by contrast both manifest and various" (Scheman 1993, 124). My own effort in this essay has been to launch a similar kind of critique of the social and conceptual rearing of one boy by one set of parents in order to point out the need for a philosophical criticism of the epistemology of everyday practices such as parenting. I do not think I would have undertaken this particular kind of critique if I had not also reared children of my own, but as Sara Ruddick says: "Engagement in the practices [of child rearing] gives license to criticism. . . . When mothers (or parents) engage in self-criticism, their judgments presuppose a knowledge of the efforts required to respond to their children's demands that those unpracticed in tending to children do not have" (*Maternal Thinking*, 1989, 26). Scenes such as the one in the "Big Dogs" story illuminate the conceptual practices and problems in rearing the next generation.

We are rearing children-thinkers, socializing them into modes of thought and action. Transforming these modes for the next generation, as in changing any paradigm of thought and the logic that governs it, involves changing our minds about the conceptual and cultural realities we take to be "self-evident"—the ones in which we "naturally" or customarily find ourselves at home. Breaking free of the manifold ways in which a transcendent a priori logic of "high objectivity" privileges a "view from no/every where," and moving toward a situated, experience-based logic of "low objectivity," is one way to describe the contextualizing activities of Wittgenstein's later philosophy. Those activities involve new ways of noticing how differences are linguistically constructed and practiced and how agreement across differences can be reached without following a logic of essential, universalist sameness. They also point the way toward new modes of conceptual rearing.

Notes

1. Annette Baier devoted a chapter to the discussion of change of mind in her book *Postures of the Mind*. She thinks that change of mind, "occurs against a background of procedures and in the calm between revolutionary transvaluations of values." However, she describes "transvaluation of

values" as "a radical shift in the method of considering . . . and, with it, what counts as things to consider" (1985, 60). Wittgenstein can be read for both levels of change. However, in his most radical assaults on fundamental thinking styles it is how he questions "transvaluation of values" that interests me. Parallel to this level of consideration, the transvaluation offered by feminist intellectual activism, an activism determined to transform the very activities of considering has been fundamental to my own work. It has afforded me both personal and conceptual space/positions from which to re-read Wittgenstein's philosophy of language for its "transvaluation of values."

2. I am particularly indebted to the following feminist philosophers: Susan Bordo, Sandra Harding, Audre Lorde, Elizabeth Minnich, Naomi Scheman, Rosemarie Tong, and Patricia Williams. Each of these feminist thinkers stands as critic within her own academic discipline. Each writes in new ways in order to change her own mind about previously held notions of what constitutes philosophic problems. Each sees as fundamental to feminist criticism the transformation of categories in which thinking and speaking are experientially and professionally constructed. All these thinkers could be considered radical, yet conservative, feminist thinkers—probing to the level of "deep disquietudes" in philosophical inquiry. In each case I have learned to take seriously my own philosophical and experiential prejudices as a profoundly important starting place for more systematic critical thinking. I have also learned, in different ways from each one, the importance of personal honesty and depth of inquiry in philosophic reformation. Each of these feminist reformers works diligently to keep her own mind open to change and to enable the very best of the philosophic tradition to cary forward, even if under the influence of profound feminist criticism.

3. Harding goes on to characterize another, opposite, tendency in reaction to historical foundationalism, one that she calls "experiential foundationalism." In this view, "the spontaneous consciousness of individual experience provides a uniquely legitimating criterion for identifying preferable or less false beliefs. This can be thought of as experiential foundationalism—which obviously also tends to parochialism" (Harding 1991, 269).

4. Sandra Harding speaks about the way in which scientific models are inadequate to the tasks of science, especially in "Why 'Physics' is a Bad Model for Physics" (Harding 1991). Her arguments about "strong" versus "weak" objectivity in Whose Science? Whose Knowledge? is also germane to this discussion. The philosopher of science Michael Polanyi spent his entire career showing why "high objectivity" does not make for good science any more than good logic, good language use, or good epistemology, and how, upon a more holistic investigation into the language and practice of science, a different epistemological framework becomes evident. He calls this kind of epistemology "personal knowledge."

5. "We know that Wittgenstein's hostility toward philosophy was a hostility toward its love of generalization and "contempt for the particular case." His own method could be described as a systematic and regulated leakage, or deconstruction, across the boundaries of established categories, a method for allowing what seemed accidental to acquire cognitive centrality—at least momentarily. Deconstruction is not a defense of formlessness, but a regulated overflowing of established boundaries" (Staten 1984, 24).

6. Sara Ruddick worries about similar questions in her book Maternal Thinking: Towards a Politics of Peace. The conservative conceptual ideology reproduced by the nature of thinking required by parenting, even though necessary for enculturation and socialization, is a subtext of this book that has received less attention than I would like.

Acknowledgments

I thank Elizabeth Minnich and Naomi Scheman for their encouragement and careful reading of the initial drafts, and Brenda Denzler for her skillful editing of the final version.

Bibliography

Baier, Annette. 1985. *Postures of the Mind*. Minneapolis: University of Minnesota Press.

Froman, Creel. 1992. *Language and Power*. Books 1 and 2. New York: Humanities Press.

Hallett, Garth. 1977. *A Companion to Wittgenstein's Philosophical Investigations*. Ithaca: Cornell University Press.

Harding, Sandra. 1991. *Whose Science? Whose Knowledge? Thinking from Women's Lives*. Ithaca: Cornell University Press.

Kenny, Anthony. 1982. "Wittgenstein on the Nature of Philosophy." In *Wittgenstein and His Times*, ed. Brian McGuinness. Chicago: University of Chicago Press.

Lorde, Audre. 1984. *Sister Outsider: Essays and Speeches*. Trumansburg, N.Y.: Crossing Press.

Minnich, Elizabeth. 1990. *Transforming Knowledge*. Philadelphia: Temple University Press.

Rhees, Rush, ed. 1984. *Recollections of Wittgenstein*. New York: Routledge and Kegan Paul.

Ruddick, Sara. 1989. *Maternal Thinking: Towards a Politics of Peace*. New York: Ballantine.

Scheman, Naomi. 1993. *Engenderings: Constructions of Knowledge, Authority, and Privilege*. New York: Routledge.

Staten, Harry. 1984. *Wittgenstein and Derrida*. Omaha: University of Nebraska Press.

Williams, Patricia. 1991. *The Alchemy of Race and Rights: The Diary of a Law Professor*. Cambridge: Harvard University Press.

Wittgenstein, Ludwig. 1953. *Philosophical Investigations*. Ed. G. E. M. Anscombe and Rush Rhees. New York: Macmillan.

———. 1961. *Tractatus Logico-Philosophicus*. Trans. D. F. Pears and B. F. McGuinness. Introduction by Bertrand Russell. London: Routledge and Kegan Paul; and New York: Humanities Press.

———. 1969. *On Certainty*. Ed. G. E. M. Anscombe and G. H. von Wright. Trans. Dennis Paul and G. E. M. Anscombe. New York: J. & I. Harper Editions.

15

Developing Wittgenstein's Picture of the Soul:

Toward a Feminist Spiritual Erotics

Deborah Orr

Introduction

The question, What kind of creature am I? has been at the heart of Western philosophy since its recorded beginnings. Since it was first asked, no doubt well before the recorded beginnings of Western philosophy, it has given rise to a host of related questions and issues that continue to exercise philosophers to this day and that are of vital concern to feminist philosophers as well as to individual seekers after self-understanding: What kind of question *is* this? How can we make sense of it? How to answer it? Is its answer to be given by appeal to natural kinds, as essentialism proposes? Or through the examination of language as a humanly constructed artifact, as nominalism and its contemporary variant, constructionism, would do? Will its answer, if it has one, be the same for all women? For women and men alike? Can it overarch race? Class? Sexual orientation?

The concern of feminist philosophers with these and associated questions and issues lies in the import that their answers have not only for virtually all areas of philosophy but also for a wide range of political, social, policy, and ethical issues. While a huge amount of time and thought has been expended on them, there is little consensus in results, and debates continue to energize, and often divide, feminists. In this essay, I will demonstrate that Wittgenstein brings a new, but historically far from original or unprecedented, perspective to this fundamental philosophical question that can, in turn, show philosophers a middle path between the extremes of essentialism and nominalism/constructionism; shed light on the questions and problems that have grown up around the fundamental philosophical question with which I opened; and perhaps also provide some direction for the social, political, and ethical issues that feminist philosophers hinge on it. In what follows, Wittgenstein's picture of the soul will be fleshed out by the work of two important feminist philosophers, Diotima of Mantinea and Audre Lorde, and yogic meditation techiques will be introduced to provide practices that can bring their insights to life.

In following Wittgenstein in his reading of the depth grammar of natural language, we find revealed there a picture of the human that is anchored in the body and in human lived experience which includes both "instinctive" and "prelinguistic" behaviors as well as social practices, habits, and activities. The body and lived experience are, he shows, the weft into which language is woven to create the patterning of our lives. Wittgenstein's work reveals a logically primitive, holistic picture of human being in which mind and body are separated only in logically later and dependent moves, through the imposition of linguistic categories that cannot claim ontic referents. The mind/body bifurcation of patriarchal culture is parasitic on this primitive, holistic picture of the human. In consequence, we can see that much understanding and knowledge production happen not "in the mind," nor even "in the body," but rather "in the person," or better, in Wittgenstein's logically primitive sense of the word, "in the soul." Here we have the key to Wittgenstein's belief that a philosophically clarified understanding might lead to a better way of life; understanding involves the state of the soul and how we live.

At the same time that his philosophical investigations of language return time and again to the embodied and relational self, they leave the person strangely out of focus, underexposed and blurry, so to speak. His work was to provide the therapy that would help us overcome dysfunctions of the understanding, think more clearly, and live better lives; however, the biases of the dominant philosophical paradigm led him to focus sharply, even obsessively, on language and the specific sorts of bewitchments, confusions, and diseases of the understanding that language may lead us into. At the same time that focus led him inexorably back to the living person, and while he did attend to the nature of the person in a way and to a degree unique to the philosophy of his time and place, his work repeatedly shifted back to "words" and the way they work at the expense of an investigation into human lived experience and what he called "human natural history."[1] Developing an understanding of lived experience and "human natural history" is important to logic both in that it is internal to the logic of concepts, and in that it forms part of an individual's and of society's shared "world-picture," including its picture of the human.

With the development of the methodology of his mature period and especially his notion of language-games, Wittgenstein has provided a powerful therapy for the understanding, but as a feminist philosopher I am left with a host of further questions by his work. Among the most pressing are questions around the nature of the relationship between how we think and how we live. While Wittgenstein's picture of the human does not fall into either essentialism or nominalism/constructionism, by and large it fails to represent either historical women's experiences; nor does it explore those aspects of the human that have been culturally designated female and feminine. Fortunately, feminist philosophy, art, and literature is rich in the pictorial detail we need to produce a more fully detailed and accurate study, and so I will supplement the Wittgensteinian depiction developed in this essay with additional detail supplied by two women philosophers who worked at either historical end of the Western patriarchal philosophical tradition, Diotima of Mantinea and Audre Lorde. Together their work provides a sketch of the soul that illuminates distinctly human forms of love and generativity and provides us with a feminist spiritual erotics that is consonant with Wittgensteinian peacefulness while opening the way to practical measures designed to achieve that peacefulness. For those practical measures designed to achieve the existential personal transformation that may issue in broader social, political, and cultural change I end with a brief discussion of meditation.

Pictures, Grammar, and Language-Games

It is in the human social world and out of people's experiences there that language-games are developed and what Wittgenstein called a world-picture is produced.[2] A world picture is a complex and stratified structure rooted at different levels in the experience of the person whose world picture it is as well as in the common culture and history of the community of which she is a part. Its logical function is to provide the matrix of certainty within which language-games and various activities, including decision procedures, function. While not immune to change in some areas, many of the logically most primitive elements of this "scaffolding of our thoughts" (OC, §211) is so rooted in human ways of being in world and so fundamental to thinking and living as to be impervious to change: "[e]very human being has parents" is one example Wittgenstein gives. World-picture certainty may never be articulated; "My life shews that I know or am certain that there is a chair over there, or a door, and so on.—I tell a friend e.g. Take that chair over there," "Shut the door," etc etc" (OC, §7). Nevertheless, it is a part of the human "form of life" (OC, §358), which functions to guide the way one lives. Wittgenstein calls it "something animal" (OC, 359) to bring out both that having a world picture is itself a part of "human natural history," and that one's world picture is an outgrowth of pre- and nonconceptual aspects of human life (Z, 541). This is what gives some aspects of it both such unshakable certainty for the person whose world picture it is, and also such stability over historical time for social groups. Wittgenstein's work on the logic of natural language shows it to be rooted in human lived experience, which is, to a far greater degree than Western philosophy has recognized, pre- and nonlinguistic. I have said that Wittgenstein's philosophy provides us with a "picture" of human being. Let me explain this with some further discussion of what Wittgenstein meant by a picture, how his picture of the human is developed, and why the term *human* rather than *female* or *male being* is used. What follows in this section of the essay will not be news to Wittgenstein scholars with respect to what I have to say about language and his investigations of it; what I wish to achieve here is to shift the philosophical lens to focus more sharply on human lived experience as it relates to linguistic usage and also to the deep mutual implication of epistemology and human ontology that that reveals.

Wittgenstein used the term *picture* in a family of related ways.[3] For my purposes I will focus on two ways that he distinguished in his mature work: pictures generated by the surface grammar of language and pictures generated by depth grammar and embedded in a world picture. Famously, *Philosophical Investigations* opens with the powerful but misleading "picture" of "the essence of human language," found in Augustine's *Confessions*, that words name objects (*PI*, §1). This is a picture of the type projected by the surface grammar (*PI*, §664) of language and in this case its crystallization in words and hasty generalization gives rise to a philosophical "idea," or what we may call a prototheory, more a model for a theory than a full-blown theory.[4] Augustine's model is pervasive in Western philosophy. It underlies referential theories of meaning, essentialism, rationalism, mentalism, theories of human ontology such as mind/body dualism, grand theories such as that of the *Tractatus Logico-Philosophicus*, and much else. It can be described in three theses: "Every word has a meaning. This meaning is correlated with the word. It is the object for which the words stands" (*PI*, §1). Wittgenstein argues that philosophers are misled by the fact of surface grammar, that some nouns function to name objects, to take the mistaken position that *all* words function as names of things, thus generating Augustine's referential model of language and its variants that have dominated so much of philosophical, scientific, and linguistic theory in the modern period.

An example of a powerful picture projected by surface grammar is the dualistic picture of a human being as composed of an outer, public, material body that contains an inner, private, spiritual/cognitive subject. This is the germ from which has grown many of the theories of the human in the modern period. Its most influential theoretical articulation has been Descartes's radical separation of the "thinking substance," (mind/soul) from the "material substance" (body).[5] The major alternative to Cartesian dualism, developed in response to it by Thomas Hobbes, denies the independent existence of the inner dimension and reduces the human to the material, to matter-in-motion.[6] The linguistic theory of choice of this model and its variants is nominalism; language functions not to pick out natural kinds, but creatively to construct and designate groups of things. In the formation of these theories and their variants, the pictures that misled the philosopher into them, their underlying dualistic or monistic models, Wittgenstein argued, are nothing but "full-blown pictorial representation[s] of our grammar. Not facts; but as it were illustrated turns of speech" (*PI*, §295). The effect of this type of picture can be subtle but powerful in that it is "not articulated but . . . guides our thinking."[7] This sort of picture is thus pretheoretical and proto- or prephilosophical[8] and it is pernicious if it is not properly understood as merely the shadow of grammar and so is allowed to develop into theories such as those developed by Descartes or Hobbes or any of the wide range of other linguistic and logical positions that have been developed out of Augustine's picture or language.

Thus Wittgenstein used the notion of surface grammar to refer, roughly, to the domain of textbook grammar, the relationships between words as parts of speech (*PI*, §664), and he showed that this superficial level of grammar is philosophically misleading; it generates "grammatical illusions" (*PI*, §110) that can seduce the philosopher into confusion. For example, by mistaking the proposition "sensations are private," a logical proposition that states a rule of a language-game (*PI*, §248), for a statement of empirical fact one may be inclined to accept the Cartesian picture. One major source of the problem with surface grammar projections is that these pictures can function outside one's awareness and so are hard to detect or combat, but they gain great strength when they play into other inclinations, beliefs, values, and theories which a philosopher holds.

Wittgenstein developed the notion of depth grammar in making his shift from dominant conceptions of logic (including his own earlier views), to an understanding of logic as a family-resemblance concept.[9] The preconceived idea of logic as a structure of crystalline purity lying behind mundane uses of language was itself an illusion generated by surface grammar working together with the "craving for generality" (*BB*, 17) that lies at the heart of science. This view of logic was radically challenged in his later work. In his new view logic remains concerned with rules for use and the limits of sense, but now "the philosophy of logic speaks of sentences and words in exactly the sense in which we speak of them in ordinary life . . . we are talking about the spacial and temporal phenomenon of language, not about some nonspatial, nontemporal phantasm" (*PI*, §108). Depth grammar describes the rules of language use, and the move away from the abstractness of traditional logic enabled Wittgenstein to see that the description of rules of use could only be given by including the "surroundings" (*PI*, §250) in which that use takes place. These surroundings may include a wide variety of things ranging from the "special circumstances" in which the expression "This is here" makes sense (*PI*, §117) to the whole of human "natural history"

(*PI*, §25, §415, 230), and the rich array of practices, customs, and institutions in which language has its life. In his new view the logical relationship between a word and the surround that gives it sense (for example, the experience of a sensation, the particular social circumstances, the expression of feeling by another) is internal, not contingent.[10]

It is from this logical investigation of the surroundings of linguistic usage, its conditions of sense, that the depth grammatical picture of the human begins to emerge. Thus this picture is not generated by the misleading workings of surface grammar; it is embedded at the deepest logical level of the use of natural language and, as part of the logic of that language, requires and can have no justification beyond itself. This is what humans do, these are the language-games they play, Wittgenstein has said repeatedly and in many different ways, and this picture of the human is what we see when we look at the primitive language-games they play. The description of this picture is a part of what Wittgenstein called in *On Certainty* a "world-picture." There he compared world pictures to a sort of mythology, the "inherited background" (*OC*, §95) of thought. Calling it an "inherited background" helps to foreground the historical-cultural dimension of parts of a world picture, however much of it arises out of human natural history and lived experience. "My life" gives up a world picture and provides its certainty, and one by logic can no more doubt it than a cat that this is a mouse, or a squirrel that it must save up nuts (*OC*, §287).

Primitive uses of concepts and features of the world picture they reveal lie sedimented under, and often obscured by, layers of uses built up over the course of human history. In comparing language with a river in *On Certainty*, Wittgenstein noted that empirical propositions—we might add ideological, sexist, racist, and other types of propositions—can harden and themselves function as channels that guide the direction of part of the river (*OC*, §96–99). Concepts and propositions such as those of Augustine, Descartes, and Hobbes can themselves become rules of socially constructed language-games but, like stones in the river, they may eventually be worn down and washed away. The power of the river analogy is that when we study the flow of the river, our attention is inevitably turned to its bed. That bed may contain sediment, but at some level the riverbed merges with the earth itself and so our study of the river must end in describing the natural processes of the earth and linguistically in describing human natural history. At this level, what logic shows "is not an ungrounded presupposition: it is an ungrounded way of acting" (OC, §110) a human way of being in the world. Thus, the study of logic leads us to the study of primitive and prelinguistic, but often obscured, levels of human life.

Wittgenstein's heuristic tactic of asking how a child might learn a particular language-game both reveals logically more primitive uses of words (a child learns these primitive uses of words before she learns scientific theories about them), and focuses attention on the surround of linguistic usage. Attention to this surround revealed that in many respects language acquisition can best be undertood as a training process that depends on "normal learner's reactions" (PI, §143), which act as a part of the "scaffolding" of use. In his extended treatment of rules in *Philosophical Investigation*, Wittgenstein juxtaposed two very different types of language, mathematical concepts and sensation words, to make this point. Human agreement (PI, §241) and agreement in judgments, as well as constancy in the results of measurement (PI, §242), provide the framework in which mathematical language can function. Description of this framework is part of the description of the family of language-games of mathematics. Similarly, learning the language of sensations depends on nonlinguistic regularities of behavior and experience, on "the primitive, the natural, expressions of the sensations" (PI, §244). Wittgenstein argues that we might replace the Augustinian picture in which words name sensations with one in which the language of sensation replaces natural expressions. Here learning language constitutes learning, e.g., "new pain behaviour" (PI, §244). This new behavior may be finely nuanced by culture and can have the effect of suppressing or enhancing aspects or kinds of physical sensation experience. This is also true of the closely related category of emotions. Alison Jaggar has argued that expressions of emotion may be continuous with instinctive responses; however, complex linguistic and other social preconditions are necessary for the experience, that is, for the existence of human emotions. Consequently, the emotions that we feel reflect prevailing forms of social life.[11] This social channeling and molding of subjective experience—not only of physical sensations and emotions, but also of such abstract activities as thinking through math calculations—is deeply implicated in the formation of gendered experience, but this social construction is only possible within the context of regularities of human expression and experience that precede and exceed language. Thus a human soul is shaped by the language-games she

plays—not only the words but also the shaping of her lived experience—
and consequently any genuine change must affect not only her words but
how she lives her life.

I have argued in this section that Wittgenstein's mature philosophy
has uncovered a picture of the human that is embedded in the depth
grammar of natural language. This picture depicts a being with natural,
primitive, prelinguistic, and nonlinguistic ways of behaving in the world
out of which language is developed and then woven into new patterns.
For instance, humans interact with others and react to their expressions
and behaviors, and it is out of this complex of behaviors that interpersonal language-games develop. This fact of depth grammar shows solipsistic and socially atomistic conceptions of the human to be the outgrowth
of a distorted picture. Thus, "My attitude towards him is an attitude
towards a soul. I am not of the *opinion* that he has a soul" (*PI*, 178) is a
logical statement descriptive of an aspect of the world picture that resists
cultural and historical variation. To paraphrase Wittgenstein, "My life
shows she is a soul and not either matter in motion or a material casing
housing a ghostly mind." Neither of these pictures fit. The holistic picture of human being flows from the bedrock of our interpersonal experience and is a core element of the natural language concept of the human.
If someone hurts their hand, Wittgenstein points out, "one does not
comfort the hand, but the sufferer: one looks into his face" (*PI*, §286).
"Pain-behaviour can point to a painful place—but the subject of pain is
the person who gives it expression" (*PI*, §302). Thus Wittgenstein's
primitive picture of the human is holistic in the sense that it shows mind
and body as an integrated whole. "If the picture of thought in the head
can force itself upon us, then why not much more that of thought in the
soul?" he asks. He continues, "The human body is the best picture of
the human soul" (*PI*, 178). This picture undercuts dualistic views of the
Cartesian sort that have been used to such destructive effect in the social
enforcement of gender, race, and other oppressive divisions; it undercuts
materialism, behaviorism, and various forms of material reductionism;
and it undercuts radical constructionism's textual reductionism as well.

Focusing on the "bed-rock" of language helps to uproot the dominant
culture's foundational mind/body dichotomy and reveals a holistic picture of the person. At this deep logical level of human being, body and
soul are a primordial unity; however, this bedrock of human experience
is sedimented under by deep layers of historically developed practices,
customs, and habits that are manifest in locally situated conceptual struc-

tures and which function to structure the subjectivity of living persons. It is out of these culturally imposed formations that the oppositional dualisms of gender, as well as those of race, class, sex, and others, circulate within what Karen Warren has described as a cultural "logic of domination"[12] which structures them as oppositional, mutually exclusive, hierarchical, and oppressive. Thus, this logical investigation reveals that an adequate analysis of the concept "woman" must take account of its family-resemblance character, that is, the multitude of social and cultural uses to which it is put, and in doing so trace out the practices, customs, and habits, as well as "the words themselves," that are the many fibers that make up the thread of language embedded in this one word."[13] At the same time, and of equal importance, it must also include an account of women as human souls.

Toward a Feminist Spiritual Erotics

Wittgenstein used the notion of language-games in a multitude of related ways. Thus he was able to both distinguish and examine very minute segments of language and even to invent games, for instance the famous builders' micro game of *PI*, §2, and also to explore broad macro structures of culture such as science, mathematics, psychology, art, and religion. However, in light of the deep antiessentialism of his work and his repeated demonstrations that humans set conceptual boundaries in accord with their purposes, needs, and projects, a feminist philosopher is as suspicious of dividing up human life into these macro categories as she is of dividing the human soul into a radically distinct mind and body. Why these macro catagories and not others? Do they not, as much as the dichotomies of gender, race, class, and sex, reflect and entrench the interests of patriarchal culture? A feminist reading of the speech of Diotima of Mantinea in Plato's *Symposium* will begin to address this concern by showing one way in which this terrain can be resurveyed in order to reveal a very different geography.

Feminist philosophers have long struggled with the "fact" of women's biological role in human reproduction and the implications of this role for women's lives. In spite of vigorous and often radical efforts to shift the terms of the debate away from masculinist presuppositions and categories, and in spite of the thorough questioning the public/private distinction that it structures has received, the debate has, by and large, bought into and reproduced its founding patriarchal move, to conceptually cordon off biological reproduction from other generative and creative activities.[14] This move was challenged and resisted by the first feminist philosopher in recorded Western history, Diotima of Mantinea, who proposed an alternative model of generativity that begins with physical desire, which may issue in begetting and raising children, but which opens up to include all the forms of creativity that aim to do the work of love, to create the circumstances in which human life can flourish. We might also call Diotima's model of generativity a macro language-game, one that is played out in everyday life and revealed by depth grammar, although its early appropriation and reduction to the categories of patriarchal culture by Platonic philosophy has erased it from most philosophical and theoretical consideration for millennia. I propose that a feminist reading of Diotima of Mantinea reveals in her work a different surveying of the boundaries of human generativity, one that encloses physical desire and biological reproduction (both male and female) in a common conceptual territory with all other forms of creative action aimed at human flourishing: the production of virtue and wisdom, of states and families, of laws, of education, and finally of wisdom itself.[15]

In concert with Wittgensteinian philosophy, Diotima reminds us that "I" does not refer to a self-subsistent entity, but arises out of the matrix of a person's life in relationship with other existing beings. "A man [sic]," she reminds us, is called "the same" throughout his life although every attribute of his body and soul—hair, flesh, bones, and blood, character, habits, opinions, desires, pleasures, pains, and fears—undergoes change, death, and replacement." It is only because we "use the same word" that we give "a spurious appearance of uninterrupted identity to that man."[16] In spite of the blinding power of the Platonic appropriation of Diotima's words, we do not see her affirming an essentialized human ontology here, only the conventional usage of words. At the same time, and contrary to Irigaray,[17] we do not need to "deconstruct" her words; she was not using language in a way necessitating poststructuralist intervention.[18] She was speaking the natural language of daily life,[19] the "illogical" discourse of "mortal opinion" that, philosopher Andrea Nye[20] argues, patriarchal philosophers and logicians from Parmenides onward have sought to supplant.

Parmenides rejected "mortal opinion" as illogical because it did not function on a dualistic logic ruled by the laws of noncontradiction and excluded middle, logical preconditions for the production of the type of "absolute truth" that Wittgenstein argued is illusory. Parmenides' logic is, in fact, precisely the structure of the logic of domination that Warren has identified and that underpins patriarchal oppression. This logic has served as the sine qua non justification of patriarchal power throughout the history of Western culture. A nondichotomous logic that eschews its master laws and does not assume a referential theory of meaning, as clearly Diotima did not in her understanding of identity, presents a powerful challenge to the ontology and epistemology of patriarchy and consequently to the cultural formations that have been founded on them.

As does Wittgenstein, Diotima radically undercuts the distinction between ontology and epistemology; unlike her male counterpart, in doing so she expands the conceptual boundaries of procreation as well. It is the generative force of love, she explains, initially the desire for physical beauty in others, that sparks creative actions. She proceeds to explore a model of generativity that may begin with the procreation of physical children, but broadens out to include all other kinds of creativity. In her discussion, as Andrea Nye points out, she uses the language of procreation throughout, "to bear or bring forth," "to be pregnant" (Nye, "Rethinking Male and Female," 267), for both male and female activity. This use of language is not metaphorical; the family of procreative activities is held together as the many manifestations of a generative force whose "object is to procreate and bring forth in beauty"[21] in all its forms, from children, to acts, to ideas and institutions, to wisdom itself. The generic concept of love, Diotima says, "embraces every desire for good and for happiness"[22] and it expresses itself in many ways.

In her explication of Diotima's philosophy, Andrea Nye notes that "[f]or Diotima, love cannot exist in isolation from the needs and desires of others, or in isolation from the practices and institutions that support relationships. Our proper activity then as lovers is naturally deflected towards the beauty of these more general consideration" ("The Subject of Love," 150). For Diotima, personal identity emerges from the never static relationships between elements of the individual soul (flesh, ideas) as well as among that soul and other souls. Thus we are led to a realization of the interdependence of personal and social good. There is no clear boundary here, as there is no clear boundary between the procreation of children and the creation of the environment necessary to nurture and sustain them. If procreation cannot be isolated as the action of the body, and if thought cannot be confined to the mind, as Wittgenstein has also argued, then Diotimean lovers are, in all they do, in loving conversation productive of all forms of good, both personal and social. For Diotima, "intercourse and not opposition is the model for interaction both within a person and between persons" ("Rethinking Male and Female," 270). The human soul seeks intimacy, community, and generative intercourse with others, which issues in the creative production of all aspects of the human world.

Since Diotima rejects the dualistic logic of mind and body, we cannot divide human creativity up as *either* procreative physical, sexual action that produces children, *or* creative action of the mind that issues in ideas, laws, philosophy, and so forth. However, there is something potentially misleading about saying that for Diotima (or Wittgenstein) it is 'the body that thinks' (Nye, "Rethinking Male and Female," 265). Better, as Wittgenstein has suggested, thought, which we now see as one form of human procreative action, happens in the soul; the whole person is engaged in it. If this is so, if the traditional predicates of mentation—knowledge, belief, understanding, and so forth—involve the actions of a living soul, then living well and having wisdom are deeply, mutually implicated. To know or to understand or to be wise comes out in how a person lives, in what they do, not in the things they have "in their heads."

Rescued from its impression into the service of patriarchy, the few words we have of Diotima's philosophy are a rich resource for feminist philosophy and theory, one that I have barely begun to explore here. I have argued that in radically realigning the conceptual boundaries around procreation, she adds greatly in detail to our picture of a person, and does so in ways that are useful to feminists. Procreation can no longer be confined to women and it can no longer be limited to the bearing and raising of children, nor situated in the domestic sphere. Following the work of Andrea Nye, I have indicated that Diotimean lovers live in loving conversation with each other, the fruits of which include the creation of the social and cultural conditions in which human life can flourish. I have indicated as well that Diotima, in company with Wittgenstein, provides an ontology of the self that is rooted in the lived experience of human persons and that refuses reification. Diotima describes the life of the self as being like a journey that begins with physical desire and love, but that moves through ever more inclusive forms of love toward its *telos*, the vision of "a beauty whose nature is marvelous indeed,"[23] which Andrea Nye calls the " generative principle at the heart of natural existence" ("The Subject of Love," 150). Thus, in her picture of the human soul, Diotima of Mantinea outlines for us a feminist spiritual erotics.

Audre Lorde rearticulated a Diotimean conception of the human form of life in contemporary feminism's most powerful and straightforward statement of a feminist spiritual erotics, her "Uses of the Erotic: The Erotic as Power."[24] Here she reclaims the erotic from its trivialized, dehumanized, and destructive uses in patriarchal pornography which functions through the severing of sensation from feeling, and reconstitutes it as an integration of the spiritual and the physical dimensions of life.[25] Living within the erotic bridges the physical, the emotional, the psychic, and the intellectual and enables generative and joyful work. In a powerful and resonant statement, Audre Lorde has said, "Within the celebration of the erotic in all our endeavors, my work becomes a conscious decision—a longed-for bed which I enter gratefully and from which I rise up empowered" (*Sister Outsider*, 55). The *telos* of this work is, as Diotima also held, to make human life "richer and more possible." Thus the erotic encompasses all of life's activities—dancing, building a bookcase, writing a poem, examining an idea are some of Audre Lorde's examples. To live and act erotically is not simply a matter of what we do, it is also a matter of "how acutely and fully we can feel in the doing" (54); it is experiencing and sharing joy.

Audre Lorde maintains that "recognizing the power of the erotic within our lives can give us the energy to pursue genuine change within our world, rather than merely settling for a shift of characters in the same weary drama" (54). In this she shares with Diotima and Wittgenstein a felt need for a different way of living and the belief that personal change is a necessary component of broader sociopolitical change. We must individually change the games we play. But how is this personal change to be effected? How might we come to "feel the power of the erotic in our lives," to be moved by the generative force at the heart of all things, when our lives are so deeply structured by the categories and practices of patriarchal culture? By itself, philosophical inquiry as practiced within the Western patriarchal tradition seems impotent to effect significant levels of change. Even as powerful and persistent a critic and seeker as Wittgenstein was unable to fully free himself from its categories or use it to find much joy in his own life. Further, in light of the holistic conception of the human uncovered by Wittgenstein, Diotima, and Lorde, it seems unreasonable to seek access to this form of life by solely intellectual means. Where else might we look? What other way might we try?

Can feminist philosophy provide a real alternative? The responses of feminist philosophy, while powerful in their critique, have been limited and unsatisfactory in their ability to move women, or men, toward the experience of Audre Lorde's joyful spiritual eroticism, or Diotima's lov-ing, procreative conversations. Essentializing philosophy is widely recog-nized to be problematic for feminism for a range of reasons, largely summed up by the observation that in its ontological forms it has been used to shore up patriarchy by endowing women with a "nature" deter-mined by the "fact" of their biological reproductive function that places them in the subordinate position (defined by difference and lack) in the patriarchal logic of domination. Feminist appropriations of biological dif-ference that seek to foreground the "superiority" of this difference such as we find in the work of Mary Daly, Adrienne Rich, and others are unsatisfactory in their failure to adequately account for difference amongst women, and in their inevitable reproduction of an unbridgeable divide between men and women.[26]

In response to the perceived problems with essentialist feminisms, postmodernist feminisms have sought, through theorization of the "textu-ality of subjectivity," to both avoid biologism and to provide a means of accounting for the social and political production of difference,[27] but they have done so at the expense of the erasure not only of the subject[28] but also of the body as a site of knowledge production, wisdom, and resis-tance. Arguing from a somewhat different perspective from my own for a theoretical recognition of prediscursive erotic subjectivity, Gad Horowitz has succinctly put his finger on the impasse reached by those who look to constructionist theorizing in the formulation of their liberation proj-ects: "If power and resistance are always everywhere how could we realis-tically hope for any change more radical than the alteration of the balance between them?"[29] If both voice and body are radically con-structed, then from what point do we seek liberation? Who and what do we seek to liberate? And, compounding the problem, as Diana Fuss has argued at length, these theories make their own essentializing moves.[30] Is there no way out of this impasse?

While both of these major feminist camps' responses to patriarchal oppression are less than fully satisfactory for feminists, there is no denying that they have each produced major insights into the nature of that op-pression. However we theoretically account for it, the destructive binaris-tic categories of patriarchy are imposed on the consciousness of women to structure their subjectivity; their bodies are inscribed and rendered docile by the technologies of power; and their lives are constrained by restrictive social practices.[31] Thus feminism now stands in need of a phi-losophy that can both unite the best insights of essentialist and postmodernist responses to patriarchy, and also move us beyond responses to patriarchal oppression which themselves break down along the doing/ knowing divide. We need a response that will build from the picture of the human soul developed out of Wittgenstein's work and reflected in the works of feminists as diverse as Diotima of Mantinea and Audre Lorde; one that can provide not only liberating theory but also liberating spiritual practices, which together might form liberatory praxis.

Anne Klein, arguing from the perspective of Indo-Tibetan Mahayana Buddhism, which claims Nagarjuna as its founder, has shown that this is a spiritual tradition that has much to offer the feminist philosopher and the personal seeker of access to the spiritual erotic. Klein demonstrates that Buddhist philosophy offers an analysis of selfhood that foregrounds existential and relational experience, supplemented by a set of meditative techniques designed to change the emotional and psychological character of the self by contesting misleading and destructive conceptual formations. Buddhism, in company with its mother tradition Hinduism, which also offers complimentary intellectual and physical practices, stresses that change in both these areas must be pursued together to bring about personal and spiritual growth. Buddhism's importance to feminism lies in its rejection of the bifurcation of epistemology and ontology, and within epistemology the severing of experience and knowledge.[32] Thus, Klein points out, while Western philosophy does not specify how questioning the ontology of identity will affect the epistemological state of an individual, and Western psychology fails to recognize the import of its ontological assumptions about the self, Buddhism takes both of these into account theoretically, as well as in yogic and meditative practices designed as a therapy of the self (Klein, "Finding a Self," 194). In this respect, then, Buddhism goes well beyond the simple provision of an alternative epistemology and ontology that can serve as an antidote to patriarchal discourse. It provides a middle path between the warring camps of essentialist and postmodernist feminisms[33] and also provides in yogic meditation practices the tools we need to gain access to the feminist spiritual erotic that is described by Diotima and Audre Lorde and that is implicit in the underdeveloped philosophical picture of human being provided by Wittgenstein.

Philosopher Laura Kaplan grounds her philosophical exploration of the importance of yoga[34] for feminism in her personal practice as a yoga student and teacher. In her comparison of hatha yoga classes with aerobics classes she argues that "hatha yoga emphasizes interiority in resistance to a culture of exteriority."[35] Because not only the *asansas* (postures) themselves but also the environment, the style of teaching, the ethos of yoga, focus the student's attention inward, it is possible to create a site of resistance, a place of personal empowerment from which to counter the Foucauldian regimes of power and domination, such as the aerobics and beauty industries, which permeate contemporary culture and oppress women. Here a Wittgensteinian theoretical paradigm of the self derived from natural language's picture of the human soul can ground Kaplan's argument while she in turn opens up for us the yogic practices that can bring his insights to life. Wittgenstein's concept of language-games show that in learning new physical practices we learn new ways of being. The new ways of being that yogic meditation practices can access are unoccupied sites and so potential platforms from which to mount resistance to oppressive regimes. More important, they provide a way to excavate the sediment of oppressive language-games and recover the eroticized soul.

It is in facilitating this development of the self not structured by an oppressive logic of domination that yoga and meditation might give women access to a site for resistance, for they are, in Kaplan's words, "a set of . . . practices designed to create a person who does not serve the aims of a particular powerful institution" ("Physical Education," 71). Audre Lorde speaks of the erotic as a source of power but one that has been appropriated and turned against women by patriarchy through reduction of it to mere sensation, sexuality cut off from feeling. As Lorde describes it, reclaiming the erotic as an expression of one's whole being gives one the sense of empowerment that Kaplan also describes in her work on yoga and Klein affirms for meditation. It is by this reclamation that the erotic can exist as "the life-force of women" (Lorde, "Uses of the Erotic," 55), the energy by which they are able to create the families, institutions, ideas, and wisdom that, Diotima reminds us, are the works of love.

In Audre Lorde's account the uses of the erotic far exceed the heavy work of direct resistance to patriarchal power; it is also a source of the "self connection" and joy that she experiences in all that she does and which she can share with others. Her descriptions of dancing, loving, and working are of total, energized absorption in what she is doing, and while the joy she experiences clearly has an element of pleasure, it is not simple hedonism; it springs from the total engagement of her being in all that she does, a mode of acting that resonates with Anne Klein's meditative action. Erotic joy is experienced in activities that are not typically considered work, but it may be intimately bound up with struggle and work, and does not preclude these. In this way the erotic can make all of one's activities a form of resistance to oppression.

Conclusion

I have argued in this essay that Wittgenstein's mature philosophy is a valuable resource for feminists in providing some conceptual and logical tools with which to begin to dismantle the master's house and build a new one out of the materials provided by feminist and other antioppressive work. At the same time, he provides a reminder that that house must be built to suit the human soul. He has provided us with a picture of the embodied sexually undifferentiated and holistic human soul that foregrounds its "natural history," as well as its nonlinguistic practices. He has shown that language-games are instrumental in the production of human subjectivity as well as society and its institutions, and that language is as fluid and open to change as the lives in which it is rooted. The logical importance of the picture of the human soul is that it guides not only thinking but also the formation of both individual and sociopolitical life. Since language-games are formed, and malformed, by the deep grammatical pictures we hold, it is crucial to develop this picture as accurately as possible by drawing out fully those aspects of "human natural history" that shape it.

Diotima of Mantinea and Audre Lorde flesh out our picture of the human soul through their understanding of an important aspect of human natural history, spiritual erotics, which shows that the human soul is generative and seeks intimacy and communion with others. The work of the eroticized soul is done with energy and joy and includes the production of all aspects of the human world but, as Diotima also reminds us, it is not only creative and sustaining; it includes death and decay. Thus when it is more fully developed we see that Wittgenstein's picture of the human soul contains not only the light, orderly, and rational; it contains the dark, chaotic, and mysterious as well, and so no particular philosophical understanding and no set of practices in themselves can guarantee the lifting of oppression.[36] Buddhist and Hindu yogic meditational practices have been introduced for two reasons: on a philosophical level Mahayana Buddhism offers a picture of the human soul strikingly similar to Wittgenstein's, especially when that is supplemented by the work of Diotima and Audre Lorde. But what is potentially most useful for feminism is that this picture is complemented by a set of liberatory practices that have been developed to effect release from restrictive conceptual structures, beliefs, and practices. As Diotima has reminded us, we love and call beautiful that which makes us happy, but on the path in search of happiness we are questing pilgrims who are easily led astray. Philosophical clarity in our ideas about ourselves may help us to avoid some wrong turns, but that clarity shows us that we also need spiritual practices that can free us from old, oppressive ideas and ways of living and prepare the ground for new directions of development.

I have used the following abbreviations for Wittgenstein's works:

BB   *The Blue and Brown Books*. Oxford: Basil Blackwell, 1975.
CV   *Culture and Value*. Ed. G. H. von Wright. Trans. Peter Winch. Chicago: University of Chicago Press, 1980.
OC   *On Certainty*. Ed. G. E. M. Anscombe and G. H. von Wright. Trans. Denis Paul and G. E. M. Anscombe. New York: Harper and Row, 1969.
PI   *Philosophical Investigations*. Trans. G. E. M. Anscombe. Oxford: Basil Blackwell, 1968.
Z   *Zettel*. Ed. G. E. M. Anscombe and G. H. von Wright. Berkeley and Los Angeles: University of California Press, 1967.

Notes

1. His use of "human natural history" is discussed at *PI*, §25, §415, and 230. Its role in logic is foregrounded in much of his later work, for instance in the formation of the concepts of mathematics and subjective sensations (*PI*, §240–44), which I discuss below.

2. See *On Certainty*.

3. I do not present what follows as an exhaustive account of the uses Wittgenstein made of *picture* in his work. There are other important uses that I will not touch upon, inter alia, the picture of language he develops in his *Tractatus Logico-Philosophicus*.

4. Merril Ring has carefully delineated the distinction between a picture and an idea in "Baker and Hacker on Section One of the *Philosophical Investigations*," *Philosophical Investigations* 6, no. 4 (1983): 259–75.

5. René Descartes, *On Method and The Meditations*, trans. F. E. Sutcliffe (Great Britain: Penguin Books, 1968), 54.

6. Thomas Hobbes, *Leviathan*, parts 1 and 2 (Indianapolis: Bobbs-Merrill, 1958). In this edition, chap. 46, "Of Darkness from Vain Philosophy and Fabulous Traditions," Hobbes's answer to Descartes and a succinct statement of his own materialism and nominalism, are printed as an introduction.

7. Ring, "Baker and Hacker," 262. This metaphor is developed by Wittgenstein in his riverbed analogy in *On Certainty*. It will be developed more fully in this text. See also my "Did Wittgenstein Have a Theory of Hinge Propositions?" *Philosophical Investigations*, 12, no. 2 (1989): 134–53.

8. Ring, "Baker and Hacker," 262. Ring notes that this position is also found in G. P. Baker and P. M. S. Hacker, *Wittgenstein: Meaning and Understanding* (Oxford: Blackwell, 1980), 61.

9. Some aspects and implications of this new conception of logic have been developed in my "On Logic and Moral Voice," *Informal Logic* 17, no. 3 (1995): 347–63.

10. The nature of an internal relationship in Wittgenstein's work is interpreted and debated by G. P. Baker and P. M. S. Hacker in *Wittgenstein: Rules, Grammar, and Necessity: An Analytical Commentary on the Philosophical Investigations*, vol. 2 (Oxford: Basil Blackwell, 1985); and "Malcolm on Language and Rules," *Philosophy* 65 (1990): 167–79. See also P. M. S. Hacker, "Critical Notice," *Philosophical Investigations*, 10, no. 2 (1987): 142–50; Norman Malcolm, *Nothing Is Hidden: Wittgenstein's Criticism of His Early Thoughts* (Oxford: Basil Blackwell, 1986); and "Wittgenstein on Language and Rules," *Philosophy* 64 (1989): 5–28. Of relevance also is Malcolm, "Wittgenstein: The Relation of Language to Instinctive Behaviour," *Philosophical Investigations* 5, no. 1 (1982): 3–22. Malcolm expands on and defends the "community conception" that foregrounds the importance of social, or more broadly, public, regularities in providing a framework for linguistic usage, while Baker and Hacker develop a view that stresses regularities in personal behaviour such that, in an overworked trope, a solitary Crusoe might develop a language for his sole use. Although I cannot fully defend this here, I believe that Malcolm develops the stronger position.

11. Alison M. Jaggar, "Love and Knowledge: Emotion in Feminist Epistemology," in *Gender/Body/Knowledge: Feminist Reconstructions of Being and Knowing*, ed. Alison Jaggar and Susan Bordo (New Brunswick: Rutgers University Press, 1989), 145–71.

12. Karen Warren, "Critical Thinking and Feminism," *Informal Logic* 10, no. 1 (1988).

13. Linda Alcoff's important and influential "Cultural Feminism Versus Post-Structuralism: The Identity Crisis in Feminist Theory" (*Signs* 13, no. 3 [1988]: 405–36) develops a Wittgenstein-influenced argument for "the concept of woman as positionality" (434) by which she means to indicate that both women's subjective experience and social identity are constituted by their fluid sociohistorical positioning, but also that they actively construct meaning for themselves from out of this positionality. Wendy Lee-Lampshire endorses Alcoff's argument for positionality but goes further with her awareness that a Wittgensteinian account must also take stock of women as "thinking bodies" (324) and so contend with all of the "chaos" and indeterminacy that makes up our lives. This, she holds, entails an abandonment of the "objectivity" that characterizes masculinist historical work. While Lee-Lampshire has not got precisely the concept of woman as soul that is being developed in my essay, it seems to me that she has moved significantly closer to it than has Alcoff. See Lee-Lampshire, "History as Genealogy: Wittgenstein and the Feminist Deconstruction of Objectivity," *Philosophy and Theology*, 5, no. 4 (1991): 313–31.

14. Alison M. Jaggar's *Feminist Politics and Human Nature* (New Jersey: Rowman and Allenhead, 1983) remains the most comprehensive survey of mainstream modernist feminist theory (she surveys liberal, Marxist, radical, socialist theories) and is especially attentive to the economic and political positions of each and their attempts to address the public/private split, or failure to do so. More recently, Linda J. Nicholson has shown that the mapping of gender onto the public/private form of social organization was historically dependent on the development of abstract formalism in mathematical reasoning that itself developed out of specific patterns of economic exchange. Abstract formalism, which separates form and content, enables not only mathematical reasoning but also abstraction in moral thinking and other human endeavors. The historical development of this form

of reasoning and the appropriation of it for public-sphere male activities has had far-reaching consequences for the development of culture. See Nicholson, "Women, Morality, and History," in Mary
Jeanne Larrabee, *An Ethic of Care: Feminist and Interdisciplinary Perspectives* (New York: Routledge,
1993), 102–7.

15. Plato, *The Symposium*, trans. Walter Hamilton (Harmondworth: Penguin, 1981), 90–95 details Diotima's survey of the products of human generative action.

16. Plato, *Symposium*, 8–89.

17. Luce Irigaray, "Sorcer Love: A Reading of Plato, Symposium, Diotima's Speech," in *An
Ethics of Sexual Difference*, trans. Carolyn Burke and Gillian C. Gill (Ithaca: Cornell University
Press, 1993), 20–33. In response to Irigaray, see Andrea Nye, "The Hidden Host: Irigaray and
Diotima at Plato's Symposium," *Hypatia* 3, no. 3 (1989): 45–61. See also my "Diotima, Witt-
genstein, and a Language for Liberation," in *Beliefs, Bodies, and Being: Feminist Reflections on Embodi-
ment*, ed. Kathleen Earl, Lopez McAlister, and Eileen Kahl, and Carista P. Rainwater (Lanham, Md.:
Rowman and Littlefield, 2001).

18. In "Diotima, Wittgenstein, and a Language for Liberation," I address in fuller detail the
fundamental flaw of linguistic theories and techniques founded on a Saussurian model; his failure to
understand language games vitiates his linguistic theory and contaminates the work of his followers
and critics to the extent that they incorporate it into their own. I argue there that the Saussurain
model has prevented Irigaray's hearing Diotima's words on her own terms and so recovering her
meaning.

19. This is defended in my "Diotima, Wittgenstein, and a Language for Liberation."

20. Andrea Nye, "Rethinking Male and Female: The Pre-Hellenic Philosophy of Mortal Opinion," *History of European Ideas* 9, no. 3 (1988): 261–80.

21. Plato, *Symposium*, 87. See also Andrea Nye, "The Subject of Love: Diotima and her Critics,"
Journal of Value Inquiry 24 (1990): 139–41.

22. Plato, *Symposium*, 85.

23. Plato, *Symposium*, 93. In describing beauty here, Diotima's language seems at its most Platonic as she uses such descriptors as "absolute, existing alone with itself, unique, eternal" (94).

24. Audre Lorde, in *Sister Outsider: Essays and Speeches* (Freedom, Calif.: Crossing Press, 1984),
53–59.

25. Zora Neale Hurston develops a powerful depiction of the spiritual erotic in the life of women
in her novel *Their Eyes Were Watching God*. I develop a philosophical reading of this text in "The
Crone as Lover and Teacher: A Philosophical Reading of Hurston's Their Eyes Were Watching
God,"*Journal of Feminist Studies in Religion* 18, no. 1 (2002).

26. Mary Daly, *Gyn/Ecology: The Metaethics of Radical Feminism* (Boston: Beacon Press, 1978).
See especially Adrienne Rich, "Compulsory Heterosexuality and Lesbian Existence" in *Blood, Bread,
and Poetry: Selected Prose 1979–1985* (New York: Norton, 1986), 23–75.

27. Judith Butler's *Gender Trouble: Feminism and the Subversion of Identity* (New York: Routledge,
1990) is the most influential exponent of this trend.

28. Nancy Hartsock has pointedly asked, "Why is it that just at the moment when so many of
us who have been silenced begin to demand the right to name ourselves, to act as subjects rather than
as objects of history, that just then the concept of subjecthood becomes problematic?" ("Foucault on
Power: A Theory for Women," in *Feminism/Postmodernism* [New York: Routledge, 1990], 163). Her
point is that poststructuralist theories deny subjectivity and participatory rights just as effectively as
did Enlightenment Othering.

29. Gad Horowitz, "The Foucaultian Impasse: No Sex, No Self, No Revolution," *Political Theory*
15, no. 1 (1987): 61–80.

30. Diana Fuss, *Essentially Speaking: Feminism, Nature, and Difference* (New York: Routledge,
1990).

31. See Susan Bordo, *Unbearable Weight: Feminism, Western Culture, and the Body* (Berkeley and

Los Angeles: University of California Press, 1993) and Teresa de Lauretis, *Technologies of Gender: Essays on Theory, Film and Fiction* (Bloomington: Indiana University Press, 1987).

32. Anne Klein, "Finding a Self: Buddhist and Feminist Perspectives," in *Shaping New Visions: Gender and Values in American Culture*, Clarissa W. Atkinson and Constance H. Buchanan, and Margaret R. Miles (Ann Arbor, Mich.: UMI Research Press, 1987), 193. See also Klein, "Presence with a Difference: Buddhists and Feminists on Subjectivity," *Hypatia* 9, no. 4 (1994): 112–30.

33. A detailed account of this middle way for feminists is described in Klein, "Presence with a Difference."

34. While there are radical philosophical differences between the Buddhist philosophy that Klien discusses and the Hinduism that grounds Kaplan's yoga, as technologies of the self their practices and goals are by and large compatible, often identical.

35. Laura Duhan Kaplan, "Physical Education for Domination and Emancipation: A Foucauldian Analysis of Aerobics and Hatha Yoga," in *Philosophical Perspectives on Power and Domination: Theories and Practices*, ed. Laura Duhan Kaplan and Lawrence F. Bond (Amsterdam: Rodopi, 1997). A useful, less strictly philosophical approach to Buddhism and meditation is provided in Sandy Boucher, *Opening the Lotus: A Woman's Guide to Buddhism* (Boston: Beacon Press, 1997).

36. Klein, in "Finding a Self," 210–14, discusses the failure of Buddhist culture to liberate women.

16

"No Master, Outside or In":

Wittgenstein's Critique of the Proprietary Subject

Janet Farrell Smith

In the *Philosophical Investigations*, Wittgenstein criticizes the view that we need to explain the unity of our experiences by appealing to an internal proprietary subject. One who visually experiences a room might be said to be the "owner" of a visual room. So also, a subject, on the epistemological model he criticizes becomes an owner of "his own" experiences just as the owner of a house has title to it and its rooms. After exposing and deriding this view, Wittgenstein concludes section 398 by saying, "For, one might say, 'There is no master, outside or in.'"

In this essay, after briefly explaining Wittgenstein's point in sections 1

My thanks to the following people for suggestions: A. Diller, B. Houston, J. Martin, B. Nelson, J. Radden, N. Scheman, M. Yudkin, and J. Broackes.

and 2, I turn to my main question here: what happens when we extend Wittgenstein's insight into a sphere he neither featured nor intended to comment upon, namely, the political one? Viewed from a perspective of what has been called political epistemology, does an assumption of a universal owner-subject even make sense? In section 3, I explore Wittgenstein's point that a presupposition of embodied speakers in linguistic communities or forms of life features agency over subjectivity. In section 4 I ask whether there is a political sense in which we need or do not need the internal "master/owner". Finally, in section 5, I explore agency and what I call "masterless subjectivities" without requiring the notion of an internalized, hierarchical master.

1. Summary of Interpretation

Wittgenstein's purpose in examining these concepts and analogies is to sharpen awareness about the various ways in which we talk about our experiences. He urges us, especially in philosophical ventures, to see how we invent allegedly universal entities that both fail to be needed and fail to explain what they are supposed to. Accordingly, Wittgenstein ridicules the view that we can take the notion of a owner of real property and transfer it from the outside social world to the "inner world" of perceptual impressions, in other words, that we can posit some internal owner of experience to account for why experiences "belong" to certain people and not to others.

Such an internal owner fails to be a plausible model of experience, because, in Wittgenstein's rather special way of framing the point, this internal owner amounts to an absurd assumption: it is absurd to think that as perceivers we unify our experience in the same way the owner of property manages and controls "his own" rooms and houses. The relation of property ownership does not and cannot apply, because it presupposes the very relation of unified perceptual experience it is supposed to explain. The relation between my awareness and its objects does not rest on a dichotomy of "inside versus outside." Finally, the assumption of a proprietary subject is not needed. Instead of being a functional element in an explanation, the notion of a proprietary subject is an idle wheel, applied needlessly to organisms that already function perfectly well without it, in the human community of embodied speakers whose agency is inextricably intertwined with forms of life.

At the outset, however, let me sign a cautionary note. I am not saying that Wittgenstein propounds "theses" that "hold" in the political as well as an epistemological or metaphysical sense. First of all, Wittgenstein's method involves stringent critical observations, designed to stimulate insight or in part to dissolve pseudo-problems, not to erect "theses" that "hold" or "do not hold," as analytic philosophers might say.[1] Moreover Wittgenstein is criticizing the very idea of "having and holding." His insight is just that, an extended investigation into a way of speaking embedded in philosophy for centuries.

So, is there a political sense to Wittgenstein's statement "There is no master, outside or in"? The "answer" to whether the "no master" applies in a political sense turns out, in true Wittgensteinian spirit, to be multiple and contextualized. "The answer," if such a notion makes sense, depends: on context, use, function, forms of life, social relations, speaking and action, ongoing at a particular time. Clearly, on the level of social relations, there do exist and have existed social owners and masters, who dominate and control both real property and actual human beings. Wittgenstein never denies this. Nor do I interpret him in that way. Nor is Wittgenstein saying that such an internal master never exists on a psychic level. That, incidentally, would fail to recognize both authoritarian personalities who have internalized domination, and neurotics driven obsessively by internal "masters." As Freud notes, the ego serves three "masters," the id, the superego, and external reality, whose demands vary in intensity and frequency depending on circumstances.[2]

Wittgenstein criticizes a model of epistemology, a picture of what happens, in a certain manner of speaking, "inside the head of a knower." From the standpoint of a political epistemology, Wittgenstein's fundamental insight does apply in a political sense as well as to the standard model of certain theories of knowledge. The import of "There is no master, outside or in" might be paraphrased as the inner master does not exist, it is a figment, if *master* is meant to designate a universal epistemological subject.

But Wittgenstein is also setting down another observation: The term *owner* or *master* signifies an analogy that misfires when it is transferred by philosophers out of its home territory in everyday social relations and reified into the ontological centerpiece of a certain epistemic model of experience. Moreover, there is no need for such a universal proprietary subject of experiences because the very terms of our discourse presuppose that we already know to whom my, [or "your" or "our"] experiences belong. We already know this, even to be capable of sensibly articulating the philosophical question, What makes my experiences belong to me? Who is the "me" who questions to whom "my" experiences belong, for example, in the preceding question?

2. Wittgenstein's Epistemological Approach

Does experience need an owner? Does it need a master? Wittgenstein rejects the notion that it does. Of the experience of looking around a room, "a visual room," he says, "The description of the latter need not mention an owner, in fact it need not have any owner. But then the visual room cannot have any owner. 'For'—one might say—'it has no master, outside or in.'"[3]

What does Wittgenstein mean by this vivid claim? I suggest here that he means to reject a conception of self as owner or "master" of its visual impressions of a room (a visual room). He does so by debunking the notion that we "have" experiences. In other words, Wittgenstein casts doubt on the master/owner concept of a subject of experience by first scrutinizing the "having" and "holding" which gives rise to it.

The surface grammar of everyday language ("I have pain in my foot" or "I have a sense of vivid red") habituates us to a certain model of speaking. This surface structure then iterates into a philosophical theory in exhibiting a three-part matrix of subject—relation—object, ("The subject has an impression"). This matrix then takes on a life of its own, which is then projected into a picture or model of experience as possessions held by an owner who is the master of its experience. The matrix also becomes embedded in the implicit metaphors and metaphysical postulates of the model. The possessor relation is then invoked to "explain" why experience is unified into parcels "had" by certain subjects. The model and its structure then give rise to pseudoquestions such as, Why can only I have my experience and you not have it?

In other words, as I reconstruct Wittgenstein's point, the following statements illustrate the false parallelism he is trying to expose. The *have* in (*a*) I have a sense of red

bears a superficial resemblance to the *have* in

(*b*) I have a house with a room

The import of (*a*) becomes generalized to the basic form

(*d*) Subject *has* an impression

which in turn is misleadingly modeled on the "having" of property, in other words, by analogy from

(*c*) The owner *has* a house.

So, finally, the mistaken epistemic model of experience has conflated and then fused two senses of *have* into

(*e*) The owner or master of experience *has* experiences of "his own."

Although they appear as parallel structures and similar usages, the *having* in each differs, as Wittgenstein relentlessly points out. Because the use of *have* in "I have experience" implies nothing of possession, indeed it could be phrased as "I experience red," or, without the first person, as "red appears."[4]

Wittgenstein's notion of "owner" or "master" is designed to elicit a conception of self that is the center of attachment to perceptual impressions (objects) of which it is conscious.[5] But alongside his critique of a possessive self and a proprietary subject he is also gives a diagnosis its source in the relation of "having" that he detects repeatedly in his several discussions of what can loosely be called the problem of self-unity. For example, Wittgenstein asks, "Does the body *have* a soul?" He scrutinizes the claim "Only I have GOT this!" at the beginning of *Philosophical Investigations,* 398. He compares the grammar of "having a cigar" with the grammar of "having a pain in my foot."

While my task is to elaborate Wittgenstein's challenges to this proprietary model, some might question why a proprietary element enters in at all. Why should Wittgenstein propose that a proprietary relation yields such power over our ordinary and our philosophical conceptions? Doesn't this mean that he himself privileges possessive or proprietary relations? I do not believe that this is so, because the misleading parallel usage between perceptual having and possessive having already exists in our language. Wittgenstein is merely bringing forward to our scrutiny analogies that are already in the language but may be submerged from critical view.

Wittgenstein's repudiation of a proprietary subject amounts to a critique of thinking in which what we have or possess assumes greater significance than what we do. To accommodate the latter, however, we have to shift our perspective in favor of what philosophy has traditionally called Homo Faber, instead of the reified possessor, the proprietary sub-ject. We have to look more clearly at what we do than at what we have. Agency, in other words, becomes the primary foundation for what we know and how we constitute ourselves.

3. Self-Unity and Agency: Embodied Speakers Rather Than the Abstract Owner-Self

As Wittgenstein makes the concept of a person primary over the concept of self, so he also makes the notion of an embodied speaking person primary over the concept of subjectivity.[6] Instead of appealing to tran-scendental entities or notions of necessity, Wittgenstein appeals to the concreteness of embodied speakers. Since feminist and communitarian thinkers have criticized a "disembodied self," one might think that the contrast term, "embodied self," would be preferable. But this, on a Witt-gensteinian approach, would be a mistake. The notion of primacy of self or subject posits consciousness apart from an embodied speaker as the primary epistemological fact or foundation of all experience. And such an approach, Wittgenstein argues over and over, is profoundly misguided.

Wittgenstein's vantage point could be described as a set of observa-tions on the tendencies of classic epistemology and metaphysics, not an attempt to add another theory to the list. His basic point is that once subject and object of mental experience are split up into ontologically distinct entities, "named" by "terms," appealing to the classic name-rela-tion, then any attempt to put together what epistemology or metaphysics has artificially torn asunder will emerge as arbitrary, artificial, and beset by bad or inappropriate metaphors.

The attempt to make a proprietary "having" relation hook up subject and object especially fails as a purported account of the universality of normal mental experiences. Although Wittgenstein himself did not make the following observation, we may note that proprietary and posses-sive relations vary enormously between those groups of individuals who do and do not own property, who are allowed to own estates and who are barred from holding or receiving estates. Those not of the "master" class, for example, those of a given gender, economic status, or ethnic or racial composition, may not stand in the line of inheritance.

So, there are deep questions about how possession or ownership could be said to apply universally to each social subject. Indeed, some have observed that these notions are so diverse that it is questionable even whether the same concept of possession or ownership applies across certain cultural or social grouping. Given these doubts, how could such a notion function successfully as the foundation of self-unity universally across all subjects? Even to suppose that the core concept—owning one's experience—merely leans as a metaphor in the outer, public world, falls prey to the same criticisms on cultural and social differentials. Even if we attempt to formulate some alleged core notion of my experience belonging to me by means of successive attempts to strip away social meanings or metaphoric allusion until we finally approximate a "pure" concept unalloyed by social influence, we would still, in the end, lean on some significant level of cultural assumptions within a notion of proprietary belonging. There is no culturally and socially neutral or "pure" concept of proprietorship.[7]

Wittgenstein remains skeptical of the drive to postulate entities to answer to a supposed need for a necessary unity. He remains puzzled by the drive to answer fundamental mysteries of the unity or disunity of human life by postulating universal or essential notions or universal or essential entities. The ego or subject is one of these and metaphysically or transcendentally necessary self-unity is another.

Wittgenstein rejects a notion of thinking, sensing, or imagining, as "an incorporeal process which lends life and sense to speaking" (339). This is the very philosopher's myth that leads us into positing an abstract center of consciousness—a self, subject, or soul as owner—upon which to predicate these mental processes. Rather, it is the other way round. Speaking, in collective contexts, lends life and sense to thinking, to perceiving, to imagining. Speaking, which is comprehensible only from a public collective and within a form of life, allows us to see from whose mouth a statement issues. Such an embodied, speaking, communicating person is distinct conception (and produces different language games) from "this person who 'has' a body."

We perceive others by locating them in physical-linguistic space ("Someone else sees who is in pain from the groaning" [404]). Or, they see us from the pain-behaviors and actions, expressions of pain in spoken sentences, in yelps, or whatever. When I utter a groan or some expression of pain, as in "I have pain in my foot," I do not need to identify myself for my own purposes. Rather, the point is to call attention to myself, in a verbal fashion, somewhat like the British phrase "I say, . . ." Wittgenstein stresses that not only am I capable of recognizing others from their embodied expression as speakers, I am also capable of recognizing myself, and experiencing what I do, and expressing what I experience.[8]

The point is, expression in human communication has a physical dimension. It comes out of the mouth of a speaker, and that speaker is embodied within a community, a form of life, that identifies its participants within the collective matrix of human recognition. In sum, as Wittgenstein makes the concept of a person primary over the concept of self, so he also makes the notion of an embodied speaking person primary over the concept of subjectivity.

4. "No Master" in a Political Sense

In the following, I want to sketch some rather speculative ideas inspired by Wittgenstein's challenge to the proprietary subject. These differ from what he actually said or probably even thought about, but I believe that they arise in the spirit of a Wittgensteinian reflection.[9] My question is, What can we learn from Wittgenstein? What insight can we get here from Wittgenstein's philosophy if we shift into a more political interpretation of "master"? What form does such insight take? I would draw the following parallel insight: just as Wittgenstein argues that it is needless, useless, and senseless to take in (the picture of) an external master from the public arena into the "private" internal theater of subjective, personal experience, so from a political and feminist perspective, we may observe that in order to emerge from oppressive situations, it may be not needed, not useful, and contrary to our ideals to take the model of the external master into our personal, or so-called private, experience.[10] The recognition that what is personal incorporates power relations from the political level also resonates with Wittgenstein's insight.

"There is no master outside or in," should also be interpreted to include the assertion "There is no outside . . . or in," in other words, that we do not need a dichotomy of outside versus inside. At least there is no "outside" versus "in" dichotomy in a way that separates public communication from private, logically exclusive subjectivity.

In addition, we do not need an outside-inside dichotomy that requires us to replicate social relations of public structures into the subject's internal mental theater. This whole way of conceiving the matter is misguided. Neither of these two assumptions, as Wittgenstein has shown, makes sense. Dividing "outside" from "in" amounts to a dichotomy of public and so-called private that disallows connection between public communication and personal experience, as in Wittgenstein's refutation of the sense of private language in which the private object belongs exclusively and uniquely to a proprietary subject. Importing social relations from the "outside" to the mental "inside" correspondingly amounts to an illegitimate transfer from one realm, the sociopolitical, into another, an alleged interior mental realm.[11]

As late twentieth-century feminist thinkers, we could understand this point positively as our not needing to import certain political assumptions—dealing with controlling master over a subordinate—into our interpretations of our experience. The point is not that it is illegitimate *ever* to apply political structures to internal experience, but that it is illegitimate to assume them *tout court* without critical scrutiny.

One may grant that within internal experience many of us carry an undetected, unreflective, and uncritical "master." We might have internalized a master, yet be unaware of its implications or effects. So the force of the statement should not be taken to deny that we must scrutinize, explore, become critically aware, and cast it out. Rather the force of Wittgenstein's saying could be understood as this: once revealed, we do not need to allow the hierarchical, dominating "master" consciousness to remain within.

To be sure, there are many situations where master-subjugated relationships do describe, in an accurate and articulate manner, actual social relations. These relations may also be mirrored within persons' psychological lives. Moreover, it may be a step forward to discover and reflect upon this fact. Master-slave, or some generic sense of master-subordinate, relations do in many specific cases impute from the public to the individual domains, and from the social to psychic levels. As a master class dominates in political relations, so the internalized master dominates within. As a violent man intimidates his wife from venturing assertively into public space, so she begins to feel she has no capacity to do so, or that she has "no private life," in other words, that she cannot control access to her own thoughts, that even her inner thoughts are controlled by him.

But that is not a reason to assume that such proprietal relations are inevitable, inherent, or that they constitute a subcurrent of struggle in an inevitable way. My point is that the master or owner relations cannot be inferred or analogized *in a general way* to every description we give in language to our psychological or so-called inner states.

Inspired by Wittgenstein, I would point out that we hang on to the proprietary metaphors and relations when we don't have to do so. We don't need in every case to interpret what we call "self-mastery" in the language of proprietary relations. Nor need we appeal to a "picture" or model of master relations to make sense of what is termed in everyday language "self-mastery." This point is not as paradoxical as it sounds. We do not need to assume that one part of the psyche or the knowing faculty dominates another. Some feminist philosophers have criticized and would discard a classical hierarchical concept of the soul as part of an interpretation of self-mastery. Others, and here I would agree, recognize a benign notion of mastery in moral psychology that is more akin to integrity. One may exhibit integrated, balanced motives, desires, and cognitive capacities, in an undisturbed, harmonious unity. Everyday language may describe this as "self-possession" or "self-mastery," but there is not need to draw in some generalized proprietary relation to explain these attributes. We may "have" a certain heritage without needing to assume that it claims us in some proprietary way or, on the other hand, that we claim it in some proprietary way. In other words, we do not need to infer a need for proprietary "having" from a merely descriptive "having."

A related point has been made recently by feminist philosophers, interpreting an oft-quoted saying from Freud: "Where Id was there Ego shall be." This has been taken to imply the replacement of the uncivilized and passion-driven "Id" by the civilizing and mediating function of Ego. But *Id* in German translates to "it" and *Ego* to "I." So, in Scheman's reconstruction of this famous quote, we have "Where 'it' was there 'I' shall be." Rather than some universalized Ego-function, which serves the same purposes for all types or groups, including gender groups, there can be different "I" functions at different times for different purposes. Indeed, as Scheman puts it "[U]nity of the self is an illusion of privilege," not an assumed condition.[12] From the standpoint of this analysis one might say, "Proprietary unity of the subject is a product of a presumed propertied subjectivity, not some universal, transempirical notion."

5. "Masterless Subjectivities"

We may recognize the possibility of "masterless subjectivities." I have devised this term to indicate multiple subjectivities that do not incorporate a master-servant relationship. Nor do they incorporate dominance-subordinate relations, whether on the political or psychic level or both. Rather these masterless subjectivities, in individuals or collectivities, achieve moving states of balance, integration, and coordination. Such equilibria allow attainment of robust self-development, artistic, physical or mental creativity, and nonexploitative interpersonal relationships. What keeps such persons on an even keel is not some proprietary self or internal "master," like a captain of a ship. Rather what keeps them balanced and on target is their ability to be responsive, adaptive, and focused on the task at hand.

Masterless subjectivities are neither rudderless nor undirected. They have attained focused, and even assertive, action, but discarded the need to depend on dominance relations in order to maintain such action. They have discarded not only the subordinate position, but also the master position, that is, the master relations themselves. Although this may strike some as ideal or utopian, it is not that at all. Rather, most people, if they think about it, can find at least moments of freedom from internal dominance that allow action and insight to flourish at its highest level. Not driven by some external demand or some internal master, these can be moments of creativity, of insight, in concerted action. These might be the mastery of artistic creation or performance or simply unfettered realization.

The term *subjectivities* is used advisedly, in the plural. It indicates that, contrary to a tendency to postulate 'the subject' or make room for 'subjectivity', Wittgenstein, in his antiessentialist vein continually points out our misguided cravings: for generality, for "natures," for uniform, neatly wrapped generalizations that apply across the board.[13]

Of course "masterless subjectivities" does not mean subjectivities separate in consciousness from forms of life, from activities, from action, from agency, or, especially, from social life. On the contrary, to sustain these sorts of relations, the persons and collectivities who carry the diverse forms of subjectivity must participate in forms of social life that support such subjectivities. Since agency resides not in some substance that amounts to a ghostly metaphysical center, but in socially embedded persons, with publicly recognizable actions by socially recognizable criteria, we must see subjectivities of whatever sort in connection with their social, practical lives.

Let us now make these observations more concrete. How, for example, would an individual person overcome political subordination? Wouldn't she need an internalized master that she saw as making a rightful (proprietary) claim of her "own" heritage, her rightful heritage? However, to respond by positing or assuming such an internal proprietary subject might create another set of problems. Such an internal master might deny or negate another, equally important part of one's subjectivity. Moreover, the internal master, one's internal proprietary subject modeled on the external one, does not overcome, but simply replicates, the subordination one attempts to overcome. So, the question arises: How can such overcoming be accomplished by an internal master that represents, or simply is, the legacy of the external political master itself?

For, as many have observed, and as Mary Prince pointed out in her 1763 narrative about slavery, the master is as degraded as the slave in the sense that the one who is subordinated does not create the evil of the subordination.[14] This is done by the master himself, who is thereby more degraded because he conceives, initiates, and executes the disempowerment of another. The slave—or other subordinated individual or group—simply receives it. The master may claim "Mine" but the slave is, in effect, not allowed to use the language of "mine" or "ours." The slave is forced to receive subjugation, yet has the power to reject it, even if only in resistance, and, simultaneously, by observing the degradation, envision another ideal.[15] "The master's tools will never dismantle the master's house," as Audre Lorde has observed.[16]

Furthermore, the master relation over other human beings can be seen as strongly differing from the master relation over oneself. When, under the institution of slavery, one is or becomes the master of another, then one enslaves another. However, when one masters oneself, one does not enslave oneself in the same sense. Therefore, a dissimilarity emerges between the master-slave relation applied to self-other relations and to oneself-self. What can plausibly be said to emerge from the one way of speaking (the master enslaves the slave) cannot plausibly be said to emerge from the other way of speaking (I master myself). What does this dissimilarity imply?

One answer is that the concept of 'master' in *self-mastery* or the root concept of possessor in *self-possession* is a metaphor or analogy for certain forms of control. These forms of control have one set of implications when applied by one person over another persons or group of persons and another set of implications, depending on context and circumstances, when applied within one person. The forms of control, however, differ when we consider what it is for one person to have mastery over herself. The notion of "master" has a loose association with *mastery*. When we speak of a slave owner or estate owner, then he is a master in the sense of a superior over other persons, and hence in a position to control them, as in the process of enslaving them. However, when we speak of mastery over oneself, we don't mean that the person is a superior over himself, and hence in a position to control himself. We may mean that a person is in a position to control and direct herself in contrast to some master (internal or external) controlling and directing oneself. Then we have a separate evaluative question to decide: Which sort of control takes place at a given time frame? Hierarchical, dominating, oppressive control over a being? Or, in contrast, self-directed, healthy control issuing from a free being with integrity?

Master, mastery, master of others, mastery of self, mastery of a skill, mastery of objects, mastery of nature: this series relates, as Wittgenstein might say, by family resemblance, not synonymy. No one core notion, essential and synonymous through the whole chain, ties it together. The 'master' in the "Master" of a servant or slave and the 'master' in *self-mastery*, as used by groups resisting subordination, have different functions and draw on not only different senses but different kinds of meanings. They may also have different linguistic functions: Designation (naming) as opposed to analogical significance. The terms *owner, possessor,* or *master* may have a designating function as in "one who owns or dominates." But in *self-mastery* the 'mastery' root draws analogically on the notion of control. So to reject the "owner-master" as a model of a metaphysical subject or any subject or agency for that matter, is not to reject a notion of "self-mastery" but to open the possibility of new meanings, new developments, new tools to dismantle the master's house.

Furthermore, the notion of control is not monolithic but highly variable. The term *self-mastery* or *self-possession* may have evolved so far beyond the sense of owner-master that no overlapping strands of meaning remain, as in the strands of a rope that ravel over one another, but with none extending from beginning to end. Furthermore, if the kernel of 'master' in *self-mastery* has not so evolved, but retains some original sense of a dominating ruler, then perhaps this is dangerous: such an internalized 'master' needs to be challenged, assessed, crucially evaluated, because it is more likely to demand the kind of harsh, unbending, uncritical submission to authority that produces abuses.

These points can be extended into a criticism of taking the 'master', in the sense of dominating ruler, into one's psyche as a liberatory form. To take in the form of the external ruler-master psychologically as the powerful aspect of one's subjectivity is to risk furthering one's subordination on an internal level. However, it is possible to rise above that subordination with an entirely different and new relation that discards the master-subordinate inequality altogether. This riddle—the paradox of overcoming subordination—underlies each liberatory effort.[17] What Wittgenstein teaches us is that we must be careful about invoking the same dynamic that gives rise to the problem in attempting to overcome the problem.

Dispossession invites repossession and reclaiming. Dispossession of a group of its full status of personhood invites the language of possession and ownership, with its attendant metaphors reversing the traditional master-subjugated hierarchy. As *mine* or *ours* is unrightfully denied to a person who is enslaved or subjugated, and the words are used by an external master, so after manumission or liberation, the emancipated person uses the words *mine* or *ours* in a new sense.[18] As the ordinary, everyday assertion of mine and ours by disinherited groups is muffled by legal prohibitions sanctioning their disinheritance, so these groups' active rejection of the sanctions and active assertion of equal freedom reflects their sense of integrity in the person and in the political sphere. It need not designate some newly found sense of inner proprietorship modeled on the master "outside."

Most significant, these active assertions by subjugated groups need not be seen as self-proprietorship claimed by some internal master modeled on the one that formerly dominated them. Nor need it be presupposed that some internal master within the formerly enslaved possesses its experiences on the same model as the former master possessed its real property, its chattels, including its slaves.

Since masters are also degraded in the master-slave relation, why should it be regarded as an advantage to take the notion of external master into the position of internal master of one's experience? Consider the saying attributed to Abraham Lincoln "As I would not be a slave so I would not be a master. This is the true meaning of democracy." It is the very notion of master, and the relations which accompany it, which we must reject.

In "On Being the Object of Property," Patricia Williams, about to enter law school, recounts how her mother "said, in a voice of secretive reassurance, 'The Millers were lawyers, so you have it in your blood.'" She was referring to the great-great-grandfather, Austin Miller, who impregnated her great-great-grandmother, twelve-year-old Sophie, whom he had just purchased. Her mother, Williams says, "meant it defiantly, . . . that no one should make me feel inferior because someone else's father was a judge." But this identity and its reclamation turn out to be contradictory, in Williams's words: "She wanted me to reclaim that part of my heritage from which I had been disinherited, and she wanted me to use it as a source of strength and self-confidence. At the same time she was asking me to *claim a part of myself; she was asking me to deny that disenfranchised little black girl of myself that felt powerless, vulnerable and, moreover, rightly felt so*" (emphasis added).[19]

Williams's point is that the adoption of the master identification results in a contradictory valuing and devaluing identification. It does not represent "the subject's" smooth, continuous line of proprietorship. As the master devalues and oppresses his slave, so the internal master identification devalues and oppresses the identification with the little black girl.

By taking the master inside herself, a woman creates a questionable line of power, one that empowers one aspect of herself at the expense of another, and the more woman-based, aspect of herself. Why should this represent a step forward, as a basis for knowledge, as a basis for political freedom?

Williams comprehends her mother's message. Her identity and her heritage include not only the slave (female, nonprivileged and subjugated, follower) but also the master (male, privileged, dominant, leader, professional). Not only do you recognize the slave heritage, her mother says, you must also remember you have the master lineage. In seeking to develop further our understanding of Williams, how might her reaction be framed? As one of ambivalence? Part of her wants to deny the master heritage because she disidentifies with the master line's history of inflicting subjugation. The master line has subjugated and inflicted suffering on many persons generally but specifically for Williams on the lineage that constitutes another part of her heritage. Yet on the other hand, in one way her mother is right: this master part of her lineage is also a constituent of her personage. Is there no way out of this dilemma raised by addressing one's divided heritage—a condition that many share to a greater or lesser degree?

To overcome a subjugation one must acknowledge it. We might overcome the preceding dilemma by distinguishing between acknowledging and identifying. Identification means that one models part of one's self or identity on someone or something outside oneself. From a philosophical viewpoint, it means that one absorbs or takes in as part of one's self-conception (one's view of who or what one is) an empathetic or mimetic relation with a prior figure, role model, tradition. But here is precisely where the problem lies: to say "This is my legacy," in the sense that *"This is part of me,"* as a taking into my internal psychic structure the same relations that were part of the outer historical political structure. To replicate the historical political relations of subjugation within one's internal psychic identificatory structure becomes exactly what Williams and many others refuse to do.[20]

One way out of this dilemma is to acknowledge without identifying, to leave off the empathetic or mimetic affect regarding the oppressive elements in one's legacy. One may recognize one's history without putting oneself into emotional alignment with certain parts of it. One may acknowledge one's lineage or genealogy without having to take it in, replicate or imitate some element of it. One need not identify to recreate the external hierarchy in internal fashion, as in a point-by-point correlation between external points of power and internal elements in one's self-conception. There is no need to incorporate the master function standing "over" some subjugated material or constituent.[21] We may recognize history and leave its structures in the past, not incorporate it in the present. A person may face her heritage, positive and negative, subjugator and subjugated, without replicating its hierarchy inside herself.

But, then, one might ask in a Wittgensteinian fashion, what is inside? Do we need the "inside"-"outside" distinction? The answer, in parallel manner, is, there is no fruitful division of inside or out here, and no master "inside" is necessary. We can understand Williams's conflict without creating an inside-outside dichotomy or attributing one to her. What might this mean? If one's internal mental or psychic theater had parts corresponding one to one with figures in her history, then a woman might have a master part in her psyche corresponding to the master part in her lineage. There might be a slave part in her psyche corresponding to a subjugated part in her psyche.

But such assumptions are not necessary, nor do we need to look at the situation in this manner. One need not structure oneself in precisely the order one sees in political reality or history. Nor need one see oneself as, in the end, mirroring it. We need to recognize history in order to leave its structure in the past, not incorporate it in the present. A woman may, upon reflection and self-examination, recognize her past and historical legacy without incorporating its hierarchy within herself.

Now we may see from another angle why Wittgenstein's challenge to a general metaphysical subject or a generalized account of the subject or subjectivity may indeed have liberatory implications. Wittgenstein helps us see that the proprietary element—allegedly generic, uniform, pure, and stripped of political implications—may not in fact not present a uniform "nature" at all. Rather, its alleged metaphysical uniformity dissolves to striking variations in practice between master status or subordinated status.

The master status, representing a seamless, harmonious identity of one who has never been subordinated, emerges in sharp contrast with the conflicted, divided, identification of one who has.[22] Striking contrasts in experiences of proprietorship appear tied to strong differentials in social status. In my view, a more liberatory conception would not appeal to the master function in order to steer, to unify, to encompass, or even to claim as one's "own." Individuality (so-called self-unity) or the cohesiveness of a collectivity rests not on an internal master-subject or hierarchical structure, but on subjectivities, as embodied speakers, as they reside in forms of life.

This is not an ontology of bodies who "have" attributes of speech, or mental predicates, a conception that after all is dualistic, as Jennifer Teichmann observes. Nor does it posit some uniform epistemological structure throughout all subjectivity. There is no basis and no necessity for that. Rather, it is collective practical life that provides the basis for the unifying subjectivities. Instead of 'the subject' we find diverse subjectivities, not amenable to one general structural description, and ranging widely over hugely variant cultural and historical circumstances. Even 'the body' emerges as a philosophical abstraction from the multifarious cultural constructions put upon it and the discourses that give it meaning and shape, as anthropologist Mary Douglas observes in her *Symbol and Ritual*.

Uniform subjectivities in individual persons, or within or across groups, are not assumed starting points, they are achieved and constructed points of reference moving in equilibrium across a variety of untidy and contradictory experience. The "I" does not stand alone, but grounds its use and evolves its force in a community. For Wittgenstein, this insight takes 'the subject', a reified and generalized metaphysical entity, out of its abstract metaphysical realm and grounds it in a relational setting. For feminist thinkers such as Baier and Code, the "I" stands as a second person conditional upon its relationship to a first person, the primary giver of warmth, recognition, and identity.[23] So, severing the "I" from the "we" involves carving away the very ties which make "I" meaningful. Individuality depends on an alternating identification of subjectivities between the individual and the collective level: the "I that becomes a we and we that becomes an I," as Hegel says.[24]

The view that I suggest stands in contrast to the picture of a sole proprietor with exclusive access to its own subjective experience, who cannot easily participate in collective social life. It is very difficult to connect the proprietary subject, exclusive in the sense that it has unique subjective access to its own experience, to a political collectivity. In brief, it is difficult to reconcile subjective individualist epistemologies with democratic structures, which is why certain thinkers speak of a "political epistemology" that addresses such problems.[25] Traditional contract liberalism solves the problem by aggregating these lone proprietors into an uneasy, rationalized, alliance of sole proprietors, connected only by their adversarial calculations.

We may note that, instead of inventing a sole individual proprietor to "have" its experiences, some thinkers have invented collective entities, such as Rousseau's general will or Hegel's *Geist*.[26] In a Wittgensteinian spirit, concerning a collective subjective entity, we could say of it: we do not need that either. We do not need the postulate of a collective proprietary subject any more than we need the postulate of a sole individual proprietary subject.

Yet what about a collectivity rising up and claiming what has been unjustly denied to it? How can we, in light of this critique of proprietary language, view what some might call the language of rightful possession? Persons sometimes use the language of "mine" and "ours" as in a cry to "give us what is ours." Or, consider Thurgood Marshall's famous response to the winning the U.S. Supreme Court *Brown v. Board of Education* decision: "What we got is ours by right, simple justice."

The claim of "ours" refutes the historical line of disinheritance of a whole group. It expresses the claim to political equality from the vantage point of the first-person plural. It draws on a metaphor of possession. But it need not, any more than the first-person singular in Wittgenstein's example of "my house," depend on a generalized metaphysical collective entity-subject that has an inherent proprietary relation to its "own" experience. The "ours" in Marshall's statement refers back[27] and forward in time to an actual, embodied cultural-social-racial collectivity defined historically as a group by the very state-sanctioned processes over which it was then victorious, in a legal sense, in *Brown v. Board of Education*. The use of *ours* here reinforces the claim of "our freedom."

6. Conclusion: Final Significance of Wittgenstein's Imagery

Wittgenstein's property and ownership analogies help to implode the concept of self-ownership from the inside. Something that I "have *got* . . . which my neighbor has not" and about which I say, "only I have got THIS," is something private to me, to which I have exclusive access. Then the "I" possesses the private datum must by inference, be an owner of its property, a possessor of its 'things', a holder to ensure the "holding."

Weaving presents one compelling counterimage to property, evoking the historically female practice of weaving in preference to the historically male juridical structure of exclusive holdings. After citing William James's notion of 'self' as "peculiar motions in the head and between the head and the throat" (413), Wittgenstein describes the philosophical theory of self as sitting at an empty loom "going through the motions of weaving" (414). This passage invokes the image of the gear that does not turn, namely, the uselessness of alleged explanatory concepts on which nothing turns and that gives no information. If we try to "weave" this supposedly explanatory notion into our lives and our thinking, it is as if we were doing nothing, pursuing a fruitless endeavor. This applies to collective notions as much as to individual ones.

In sum, Wittgenstein makes the metaphysical proprietary subject the target of an extended critical investigation. But instead of concluding with a denial of its existence, Wittgenstein suggests rather that the hypothesis merely turns out to be an "idle wheel." Once we recognize the misguided tendencies of positing an inner-outer framework, the temptations from grammar to postulate such a subject, and the analogies hidden within our language that lead us to infer proprietary relations and a proprietary master-subject to sustain them, these very tendencies can be left aside. The issue of the existence or nonexistence of such a metaphysical postulate fades or evaporates, since the problem itself has dissipated.

Notes

1. The distinction has been made between *destructive*, in other words, mainly critical; and *constructive*, or theory building, analytic philosophers, with Wittgenstein cast in the former role.

2. Sigmund Freud, *New Introductory Lectures on Psychoanalysis*, trans. James Strachey (first published 1933; New York: Norton, 1965), 77.

3. . Ludwig Wittgenstein, *Philosophical Investigations*, 398. References to section numbers in the *Philosophical Investigations*, part I, are noted in parentheses.

4. The latter has sometimes been referred to as a no-ownership theory of experience, or the Strawson-Wittgenstein theory. However, my belief is that the critique of an owner-self has been hopelessly conflated with Wittgenstein's critique of any self at all, and that Wittgenstein's view is much more subtle than has been recognized heretofore. I pursue this complex subject elsewhere.

5. Wittgenstein uses standard German terminology: *Besitzer*, which is translated as "owner"; and *Herr*, which is translated "master."

6. In placing the idea of person as primary over the notion of self, I agree with interpreters such as J. Teichmann and B. Williams.

7. Even if we do manage to formulate a "pure" asocial concept of self unity—perhaps Kant's "I think," which accompanies all experience—we face cultural associations again in multiple forms. We face it in the divorce of reason from the passions, of cognition from affection, in the notion that necessity must itself be asocial, that metaphysical insight must transcend sociality in order to achieve objectivity.

8. In this essay, I do not go into the complex topic of self-reference versus reference to others.

9. My discourse shifts, quite deliberately, from a metaphysical or epistemic level to a political level, without making any claim that the implications of the first have direct or indirect implications for the second, namely, that a critique of a metaphysical self implies defects in a model of self for political analysis.

In this essay I want to avoid the thorny issue of whether a metaphysical self is implied in a given political theory, an issue that constitutes the crux of a disagreement between Sandel and Rawls. See Michael Sandel, *Liberalism and the Limits of Justice* (Cambridge University Press, 1982), and J. Rawls, *Political Liberalism* (New York: Columbia University Press, 1993). Also see the insightful analysis by Marilyn Friedman in *Friendship and Community* (Ithaca: Cornell University Press, 1994).

We must be careful to avoid conflating a metaphysical theory of an inner proprietary subject with a political theory of self-proprietor. On my interpretation here, Wittgenstein criticizes a metaphysical or epistemological proprietary subject, not a theory of self-ownership in the political sense. But that still leaves open the possibility that some of his insights on absurdities in the epistemic notions may apply to liberal theory, a topic I pursue elsewhere.

10. We may take Wittgenstein's critique of this internal proprietor in a metaphysical or epistemolgoical sense, as another line of criticism of subjectivist, individualist "foundations" for knowledge, allied with other critiques in postpositivist philosophy of science (Hansen, Kuhn) and feminist epistemology (Code, Longino, Haraway).

11. See Linda Nicholson's astute writings on the private and public, and the domestic-public dichotomy (*Gender and History: The Limits of Social Theory in the Age of the Family* [New York: Columbia University Press, 1986]).

12. Naomi Scheman, *Engenderings: Constructions of Knowledge, Authority, and Privilege* chap. 6, "Paranoia and Liberal Epistemology," 98. See also Nancy Julia Chodorow, "Toward a RelationalIndividualism: The Mediation of Self Through Psychoanalysis," in *Reconstructing Individualism: Autonomy, Individuality, and the Self in Western Thought*, ed. Thomas Heller, Morton Sosna, and David Wellbery (Stanford: Stanford University Press), 197–207.

13. In my analysis I agree with Wendy Lee-Lampshire in her Wittgensteinian critique of a predetermined subjectivity. Nevertheless, from Wittgenstein's viewpoint, I believe that one should emphasize *subjectivities* in the plural more than in the singular *subjectivity*. See Wendy Lee-Lampshire, "Moral 'I': The Feminist Subject and the Grammar of Self-Reference," *Hypatia* 2, no. 1 (1992).

14. Masters are as degraded as slaves, perhaps more. This is meant not in the sense that their suffering or the physical and psychic violence is equal, but in the sense that the evil of slave oppression is caused by the master, not the slave; the agency of slavery is due to the master, not the slave. (Note that it was not necessary to use the term *victim* here.) As the masters are themselves degraded by carrying out such dehumanized actions in the system of slavery, so is the master position a degraded and flawed one. See Mary Prince, "The History of Mary Prince, A West Indian Slave, Related by Herself," in *The Classic Slave Narratives*, ed. Henry L. Gates, Jr. (New York: New American Library, 1987), 187–215; also, Charles Davis and Henry L. Gates, Jr., ed., *The Slave's Narrative* (New York: Oxford University Press, 1985).

15. Angela Y. Davis, "Unfinished Lecture on Liberation, II," in *Philosophy Born of Struggle*, ed. Leonard Harris (Boulder, Colo.: Westview, 1972).

16. Audre Lorde, *Sister Outsider* (Trumansberg, N.Y.: Crossing Press, 1984). 110–13. See discussion in Scheman, *Engenderings*, 223–24.

17. A related point has been made by Patricia Williams both in political psychological terms as a "paradox" (see 217) and in legal theory. She argues that simply to adopt the bourgeois law (the master law) is not an adequate alternative to the abolition of slave law. See Williams, *The Alchemy of Race and Rights* (Cambridge: Harvard University Press, 1991), chap. 12, 216–36. Psychoanalyst and critical theorist Jessica Benjamin makes an analogous point: "The structure of individuation which permeates our culture, and which privileges separation over dependence, cannot simply be countered by its mirror opposite. Rather it must be criticized in light of a balance in which neither pole dominates the other, in which paradox is sustained" (*The Bonds of Love: Psychoanalysis, Feminism, and the Problem of Domination* [New York: Pantheon, 1988], 80–81).

18. The sense changes if and because the social practices change, not solely because the term has a new meaning in someone's mind.

19. *The Alchemy of Race and Rights*, 216–17.

20. My point, made in a political-philosophical analysis, may be similar to that of Jessica Benjamin: "Women's search for identificatory love . . . often leads to submission." ®MDUL Bonds of Love: Psychoanalysis, Feminism and the Problem of Domination (New York: Pantheon, 1988), 107 n. 1.

21. This may imply an alternate (nonhierarchical) analysis of what some moral philosophers call "will" but I do not undertake that project here.

22. Indeed, perhaps whether there even exists such a proprietorship, or an a priori substantial ego, may depend on one's status in social life. But I shall not argue that here.

23. Lorraine Code, *What Can She Know? Feminist Theory and the Construction of Knowledge* (Ithaca: Cornell University Press, 1991); Annette Baier, *Moral Prejudices: Essays on Ethics* (Cambridge: Harvard University Press, 1994).

24. G. W. F. Hegel, *Phenomenology of Spirit*, 110, quoted in Charles Taylor, *Multiculturalism and "The Politics of Recognition"* (Princeton: Princeton University Press, 1992) 58.

25. See Scheman, *Engenderings*, chap. 6, "Paranoia and Liberal Epistemology," esp. 75–77.

26. Such collective entities would also be subject to the same kind of Wittgensteinian antiessentialist critique made here. However, the critique allied to the private language argument (as I interpret it here) would not apply. Wittgenstein's generalized critique, which sees the subject not "in" the world, but its limit or condition, would be relevant to the philosophical instinct to create a *Res*, a thing, that can "explain" how consciousness comes to be.

27. Since *I* is not a name, according to Wittgenstein. See *PI*, 410; neither, it seems, would *we* be considered a name in his terms. But, in the sense of cross-reference, *ours* refers back to or coordinates with the grammatical subject, "We, African-Americans, who have claimed our rights. . . ." The first-person plural need not refer, as a name, anymore than the first-person singular does.

Section V

Feminism's Allies:
New Players, New Games

17

Wittgensteinian Vision(s) and "Passionate Detachments":

A Queer Context for a Situated Episteme

Wendy Lynne Lee

Passionate Constructions: Situating an Episteme

A number of feminist philosophers have recently begun to develop situated epistemes, or what philosopher Donna Haraway calls "situated knowledges."[1] Neither objectivist nor relativist, a situated episteme seeks to locate knowing in the complex, nuanced relationship between a knower, her/his specific and concrete situation within a context, that about which a knowledge claim is being made, and whom such claims empower—or disempower. In her essay "Situated Knowledges: The Science Question in Feminism and the Privilege of Partial Perspective,"[2] Haraway suggests that we imagine knowing as a kind of vision or sight—a *perspective*—through which knowing subjects "see" the world: "In these [visual] metaphors we find means for appreciating simultaneously both the concrete, 'real' aspect and the aspect of semiosis and production in what we call scientific knowledge."[3]

For Haraway, the real and the semiotic, the objective and the constructed, the imaginary and the rational, are not opposites, but rather always contestable aspects of knowing. Haraway tells us that she

> wants to argue for a doctrine and a practice of objectivity that privileges contestation, deconstruction, passionate construction, webbed connections, and hope for transformation of systems of knowledge and ways of seeing. But not just any partial perspective will do; we must be hostile to easy relativisms and holisms built out of summing and subsuming parts. "Passionate detachment" requires more than acknowledged and self-critical partiality. We are also bound to seek perspective from those points of view, which can never be known in advance, that promise something quite extraordinary, that is, knowledge potent for constructing worlds less organized by axes of domination. . . . The imaginary and the rational—the visionary and objective vision—hover close together.[4]

Not correctly understood as something that knowers merely have, to know is to practice the "passionate construction" of claims whose epistemic value privileges contest and revision as well as defense or substantiation. Because such vision is always and recognizably partial, it prompts us to seek perspectives that, in virtue of their difference, prod us to examine even the most rigidly established of our assumptions, especially those that contribute to heteropatriarchal or racist social orders. To practice "passionate detachment," it is not enough simply to acknowledge partiality—regardless how self-critically such an undertaking might be conducted. For this to have meaning *as knowing*, the critical self-reflection that grounds it must be accompanied by endeavors to envision how epistemic position informs and is informed by the contexts in which knowing is made possible, how context informs whatever possible knowledge claims may be made relevant to it, and last, how recognizing partiality can substantiate a claim to objectivity, yet—and in virtue of the same recognition—remain open to contest and revision.

For Haraway, the objective vision promised by partial perspective cannot be captured by the notion of a disembodied Cartesian eye hovering above the seen or scene, but rather belongs to the embodied "eyes" of potential knowers epistemically situated within concrete and intersubjective configurations of experience embedded in specific biological, psychological, historical, social, political, economic, ethnic, religious, sexual, and cultural contexts. Such an objectivity is not properly conceived as a "given" of rationality, but rather as a criteria-governed activity of knowing subjects. No crude relativist or holist, Haraway claims that "[t]he moral is simple: only partial perspective promises objective vision."[5] That is, for Haraway a situated episteme offers the most viable justificatory grounds for knowledge claims precisely because it takes seriously those relationships among knowers situating the multiplicity of possible perspectives, and in so doing offers the best opportunity to take responsibility not merely for recognizing the perspectives of others, but for responding to them as potential sites of situated knowledge. The aim of such an objectivity is thus not conquer or appropriation, but rather knowledge—passionately constructed, open to revision, and ethically defensible in light of its being able to account for its epistemic situation.

My project here is to amplify Haraway's notion of a situated episteme by attempting to address the following questions: How can we articulate the notion of a *partial* perspective? What does it mean to say that the "passionate constructions" of such a perspective promise *objective* vision? What does it mean to be a *knower*, given the possibility of situated knowledges? Undoubtedly, there are many roads we might consider in the pursuit of such a project; I have, however, chosen a road perhaps less traveled, though as I hope to demonstrate, most promising, namely, one that travels a text both rich in example and highly suggestive of the kind of situated episteme Haraway has in mind, namely, the later Wittgenstein's *Remarks on Colour*.

Through a contextualized exploration of the myriad possible uses of color terms such as *blue, black,* or *primary color,* Wittgenstein exemplifies a rich and variegated epistemic topography within which the usefulness of color words is intimately bound to the many and complex "webbed connections" that animate that use. What Wittgenstein demonstrates here as elsewhere is just how pervasively perspective is informed by those linguistic practices through which knowing is made possible as an *intersubjective or communicative* activity, and hence how deeply perspective is informed by the epistemic contexts within which such practices, or *language games,* evolve, become stagnate, are disrupted, empower, and disempower.

Such perspectives *are* partial or located, but this does not imply the failure to attain the universality promised by Cartesianism, nor does it imply what lies on the other side of this "God's-eye view," namely, crude subjectivism or relativism. What Wittgenstein shows is that passionate detachment originates in the potential for that critical self-reflection that prods us to examine the myriad ways in which language mediates the relationship between knowledge claims and the contexts in which they are made. Such relationships are reflected not only in the semantic content of a language, but also in its *grammar*, that is, in the more or less invisible rules for playing the language games relevant to those contexts. To understand a grammar is to begin to understand how epistemic situation informs and is informed by the sometimes consistent, sometimes conflicted perspectives played within and through it.

From a Wittgenstienian point of view, partiality is intimately bound to language games whose exploration offers a window onto epistemic situation conceived not merely as limited, but, in the best of possible epistemic worlds, as self-critically located, passionately detached, and always revisable in light of new experience; and in the worst, as unreflectively compartmentalized, rigidly myopic, fragmented, or parochial. Given this range of possibilities, then, how can we articulate an episteme that demonstrably avoids the "easy relativism" of which Haraway warns us? That is, is it possible to grant Wittgenstein's descriptive point about the relationship between epistemic situation and language and yet eschew epistemic relativism? Can we cultivate partiality as *passionate* detachment *and* sustain a robust objectivity?

I think so. Indeed, my argument is that an objectivity reconceived and revalued in terms of partiality can provide far *better* criteria upon which to assess knowledge claims than either objectivist or relativist epistemes. On this view, to be objective is to take responsibility not only for the content of one's perspective, but for *how* that perspective reflects and is reflected by the language games relevant to the context(s) one occupies as a uniquely situated, linguistically mediated knower. To know is to understand not merely how to play a language game but how the play reflects, mediates, sustains, and potentially conflicts with the relationships fundamental to that game. Acknowledging partiality constitutes, then, a first genuinely objective act of knowing—a passionate detachment—insofar as it begins to take into account how knowing situates itself or *happens* from that perspective. An act both epistemic and ethical in character, partiality prods us to take responsibility for understanding how knowledge claims are situated, dynamic, contestable, and passionate *constructions*. As Haraway might put it, to know is to know *how* the imaginary and the rational, the real and the semiotic, "hover close together"; my aim, then is to show how both of these pairs "hover close together" in *language*.

Clearly, many potential problems haunt such an account. For whom, for example, might a situated episteme prove to be useful?[26] Can this view of knowing provide genuinely critical tools for the assessment of knowledge claims in light of factors that inform the positions from which they are made? What does a situated episteme imply for moral action or decision? Following Haraway, should we regard such a view as feminist? Can such a view be of use to those for whom intersubjective agreement is not a given? Can such an approach be useful to knowers whose political, sexual, ethnic, cultural, or economic situations are not consistently recognized as sites of epistemic authority by those empowered to grant such recognition? And perhaps most important, can the idea of a situated knowledge be instantiated self-critically enough that the temptation to merely appropriate whatever is regarded as "other," and then deem that sufficient to epistemic responsibility, be resisted?

In my view, it is the answer to this latter question that most clearly identifies a situated episteme as feminist in the sense that the models that best exemplify, at least nascently, features most crucial to such an approach orient themselves around explicitly feminist issues. In the attempt, for example, to describe their situations as *multiply situated and signified* or, as Haraway might put it, *coded as different*, feminist philosophers Elisabeth Daumer and María Lugones exemplify how the conflict or *dissonance* that characterizes the sociopolitical positions of nonmale and/or nonstraight and/or nonwhite knowers encourage the development of alternative ways of knowing and being. By taking into account the situations from which each sees her "world" as well as those of others, Daumer and Lugones effectively practice partial perspective.[7] My aim, then, is to make this practice explicit by viewing epistemic situation through a Wittgensteinian "optics," that is, by attempting to read such worlds through Wittgenstein's insights on language games. In so doing, I will show not only how Daumer and Lugones embody the knowers of a situated episteme, but also how the dissonance that imbues the sociopolitical, sexual, and epistemic situations of those least privileged can motivate the "passionate construction" of a more objective vision.

Epistemic Vision: Wittgenstein and the Queer Grammar of Colors

Consider the following passage from Wittgenstein's *Remarks on Colour* in light of the question, How can we articulate partial perspective? "What is there in favour of saying that green is a primary colour and not a mixture of blue and yellow? Is it correct to answer: 'You can only know it directly, by looking at the colours'? But how do I know that I mean the same by the words 'primary colours' as someone else who is inclined to call green a primary colour? No, here there are language games that decide these questions."[8] In this passage as in many others, Wittgenstein portrays a specific linguistic practice, or language game. His purpose, however, is not merely to exhibit such games but to prod his readers to question what they take to be given in them.[9] "What is in favour of saying that green is a primary colour?" Wittgenstein suggests that we could not know this "directly," that is, the answer is not given by merely "looking at the colours," but rather is "decided by a language game."

At first glance this suggestion seems strange in that we are inclined to take our experience of color to be among the most "direct," given or unmediated of all experience. It "strikes us as obvious" that the words *primary color* refer to the same colors for anyone who knows what the words mean,[10] and that producing evidence of this requires little more than being able to correctly point to samples.[11] To someone who asks, "What is in favour of saying that green is a primary colour?" we would likely respond by pointing to samples of yellow or blue paper or cloth saying, "Here is a sample of the primary colour yellow, here blue. If you mix them you get the secondary colour green." If they still insisted that green was primary, we would say that they didn't understand how we were using the words *primary color* and thus didn't recognize what we were pointing at.[12] Why then does Wittgenstein ask "How do I know I mean the same by the words 'primary colour' as someone else who is inclined to call green a primary colour?" I know because there really are such things as primary colors, green is a secondary color, and to think otherwise is just mistaken.[13] What remains to be "decided by a language game"?

The answer to these questions may be found in the notion of "use." As these examples tacitly suggest, we understand what someone else means, and whether they mean the same as we do, not by looking directly, but by how they use the terms *yellow, blue,* or *primary color.* We doubt the understanding of someone who refers to green as a primary color not because they are not looking in the right location, but because they do not use these words in the same way. Pointing turns out to be of little help, for when I point to a yellow-colored piece of paper saying, "Here is a sample of the primary colour yellow," someone can as easily respond, "Yes, I understand" or "No, I don't." But in neither case could I tell whether what they are looking at is even the *color* of the paper (and not its shape or size) other than by the way they use the word *yellow* in succeeding sentences such as "So yellow is primary like blue, mix them and you get green."[14]

Hence, the question "What is in favour of saying that green is a primary colour?" is "decided" by a language game in which we must be able to answer a prior question: "How do I know I mean the same as someone else?" The answer to this question is not simply given because "[t]here is no such thing as *the* pure colour concept," samples of which can be found by looking directly.[15] We know that we mean the same as someone else only insofar as "[i]t is a fact that we can communicate with one another about the colours of things."[16] Similar use exemplifies the *agreement* fundamental to playing this language game; in other words, it exemplifies a game's grammar—its *communicative* "form of life,"[17] through which "things are put in a certain order."[18] Were it not for this agreement, "our concept [of color] *would* not exist" for then there would be nothing in which this communication could *consist*.[19]

What Wittgenstein's remarks suggest is that agreement concerning how words are used is fundamental not only to color language but to all language games. For what we discover is that at its most basic—perceiving objects—experience is mediated through language. Language games do not directly mirror the world at all; rather, they reflect in their own complexity and indeterminacy the complex contexts in which the meanings of words evolve through use.[20] The important question is not, What piece of reality does the use of a word represent? but rather, What does the use of a word accomplish, preserve, or alter? What does it communicate? As Wittgenstein remarks: "Would it be correct to say that our concepts reflect our life? They stand in the middle of it."[21] That is, concepts stand "in the middle of" the perspectives from which we look, they reflect at once the uniqueness of our situations *and* the agreement in relation to which *situatedness* becomes possible. For Wittgenstein, "[p]ractices give words their meaning," they situate us within a context.[22] Hence to say that I mean "the same as someone else" is to say not only that we both know the rules for playing a particular language game, but that we share a linguistically mediated *perspective*, the grammar of which "permeate[s] our life."[23]

If Wittgenstein is correct, then someone who calls green a primary color may not be mistaken, but is simply playing a different language game; in this case, her/his perspective is *partial* to a different game, a different context.[24] Does acknowledging this lead to Haraway's "easy relativism"? Are we bound to value all perspectives equally, thus producing an "easy holism"? Not necessarily. But what does come out here is that "knowledge is related to a decision."[25] For we could choose to ignore Wittgenstein's insights and maintain that we have prelinguistic access to a real world in which the concept of a pure color corresponds to colors such as yellow and blue. Or we could decide that the "world" consists in a "mere" multiplicity of language games within which knowing is merely knowing how to play particular games.[26]

However, there is a third possible choice: we could acknowledge the extent to which our perspectives are informed by the language games we play, and at the same time *decide to take responsibility* for understanding not merely how to play them, but for how a context may influence the evolution of a language game, how specific word usage can perpetuate, affect, and alter perspective, and how the way a language game is played can both reflect and determine how subjects are situated within specific contexts. In other words, we could adopt an *epistemic vision* in which knowing is conceived not in terms of *what* can be known (such as whether green is *really* a primary color), but rather in terms of taking responsibility for understanding *how knowing happens*: how knowing is partial to perspective, how perspective is situated within context, and how the perspectives of some situate those of others.

Primate Vision: Haraway and the Colors of Power

What do the following remarks suggest about the language game(s) in which they are played? What perspective(s) might they reflect? Whom might these games empower?

> If black merely made things dark, it could be clear; but because it smirches things, it can't be.[27]

Runge says that black "dirties"; what does that mean? Is that an emotional effect which black has on us? Is it an *effect* of the addition of black colour that is meant here?[28]

Runge: "Black dirties." That means it takes the brightness out of a colour, but what does it mean? Black takes away the luminosity of a colour.[29]

In one sense, to say that "black dirties" is no different from saying that yellow and blue are primary colors. For we could say that *dirty* describes black's location within a language game just as *primary* describes blue and yellow, or that "black dirties" is simply one of multiple ways to use the word *black*, depending upon which game is being played. There is something about the tone of these passages, however, that suggests something more about this use, namely, a sense of disapproval, corruption, or baseness.

In Western culture to say that something "dirties" implies a judgment that it is corrupting, or that what it dirties is made inferior or substandard. To call something dirty is a common way of expressing prejudice, hence one finds *dirty* prefacing *nigger*, *Jew*, *spic*, *geek*, *dyke*, or *queer*, and those so labeled viewed as dishonest or disreputable. Just as calling someone a "dirty Redskin," a "pink fag," or a "yellow Jap" is no neutral use of *red*, *pink, or yellow*, so too *black dirties* connotes the devaluation of persons perceived as "black."

References to color have long been a part of language games played to justify disappropriating, enslaving, raping, or exterminating the "dark other" of the paradigmatic "white man." In westerns, white hats are associated with good cowboys [*sic*], and black with bad ones, just as virginal (good) women wear white to their weddings and sexually active (bad) women are expected to wear the darker colors of lesser repute. The association of women's presumed intellectual inferiority with bodily "dirt" is as much a commonplace in Western culture as references to "women's nature" symbolized in such images as the black widow, the shadowy unkempt wicked witch, or the slovenly welfare queen (stereotypically portrayed as a dark-skinned woman).

My point, however, is not just that such phrases as "black dirties" express prejudice, but that they indicate the extent to which a use of language as apparently given as that of *blue*, *green*, and *black* is itself social, political, cultural, economic, racial, and sexual. In *Primate Visions*

Haraway argues that within primatology and paleoanthropology, knowledge is constructed according to a series of sociopolitically charged binarisms. Notice the role that color plays here: "Empathy is part of the Western scientific tool kit, kept in constant productive tension with its twin objectivity. Empathy is coded dark, covert or implicit, and objectivity light, acknowledged or explicit. But each constructs the other in the history of modernity. 'Western' science, just as nature-culture and man-woman are mutually constructed on a logic of appropriation and progress."[30] Empathy, however, is more than merely "coded dark," for were darkness not already coded "bad" or "inferior" within the epistemic context of this comparison the comparison, itself would make no sense. "Coded" or ordered as binarisms, empathy and objectivity take their place in a language game that mediates culture/nature, man/woman, good/evil by reference to the given, in this case the binarism light/dark. In this context light codes for the cultured, objective, seeing, male mind, while dark codes for the primitive, subjective, passive, female body.[31]

The binary grammar of the objectivity/empathy game defines "how things are put in order," that is, how things are *seen* within particular contexts. Haraway remarks that "[v]ision is *always* a question of the power to see—and perhaps of the violence implicit in our visualizing practices."[32] This violence, however, may not occur only among those "visualizing practices" (such as primatology) within which knowledge claims remain contestable, but among practices long taken for granted and that hence, like color, tend to remain invisible to critical inquiry. Haraway argues that binary pairs such as light/dark, empathy/objectivity, and mind/body structure the narrative of "stories"[33] such as man-hunter/woman-gatherer, humanity-cultured/animals-primitive, white-human/black-simian:

> Women and animals are set up as body with depressing regularity in the working of the mind/body binarisms in story fields, including scientific ones. The man/animal binarism is crosscut by two others which structure the narrative possibilities: mind/body and lighter/dark. White women mediate between "man" and "animals" in power-charged historical fields. Colored women are often so closely held by the category animal that they can barely function as mediators in texts produced within white culture. In these cultural fields, colored women densely code sex, animal, dark, dangerous, fecund, pathology. . . . The body is nature to the mind

of culture; in primate narratives white women negotiate the chasm.[34]

Notice how thoroughly color permeates this passage. It operates both visibly and invisibly, explicitly and implicitly. White women "negotiate" the man/animal "chasm" *because* they embody the objectivity/empathy binarism, itself color-coded lighter/darker. "Colored women" "can barely function as mediators" *because* they are associated by white men with the "category animal," itself color-coded as the inferior dark side of the man/animal binarism, and white men bring enlightenment legitimated by their possession of undirtied, disembodied, and invisible mind.

In Haraway's narratives, color both codes for difference and forms a crucial aspect of its play. *The* difference between mind and body, man and woman, man and animal, colored woman and white woman is not only *played out* in color language, but *constructed through* the play of light/dark, black/white, primary/secondary whose binary relationships are taken to be given, thus natural. Haraway argues that "primatology is about an order, a taxonomic and therefore political order that works by the negotiation of boundaries achieved through ordering *differences. . . .* The two major axes structuring the potent scientific stories of primatology that are elaborated in these practices are defined by the interacting dualisms, sex/gender, nature/culture."[35] This "ordering of differences," however, can only be "negotiated" through language games whose binarisms appear to be given and thus part of the natural epistemic framework within which order is made possible. *For the appearance of givenness confers the authority to order what is to be counted as real.* The construction of "man" as the enlightened, white knower of the real in opposition to "his" "other(s)" is legitimated not only by the "ordering of differences" but by the language games *through which* differences *can* be ordered. As "he" who just knows that green is not a primary color, that black dirties, and that "his" vision mirrors the real, "man" guarantees the invisibility of those language games that authorize his own construction as the empowered side of the sex/gender, nature/culture binarism.[36]

Within the language game of "man" Haraway herself occupies an epistemic situation that situates her as neither knower nor known.[37] She is a *woman*, and hence within *this* game can neither adopt the "view from nowhere"[38] nor escape her place among the to-be-known. For by the same token that the language game of "man" privileges (some) men *as men* by legitimating the invisibility of their epistemic situations *to them-*

selves (and others) as objective knowers, women in this binary logic become the visible object of questions such as, What does a woman want? To become an object of knowledge in this game is, in effect, to become the feminized, visible other to those men whose givenness as knowers is confirmed by the very authority with which they assume that their knowing is not situated, but universally valid.[39]

Haraway, however, rejects the binary logic within which male privilege is conferred and maintained, choosing instead to make her situation as scientist, woman, feminist, writer, and spectator critical to her epistemic vision. For Haraway, like Wittgenstein, "knowledge is related to a decision" not of one pole over another, but of the epistemic situations knowers occupy. To decide for one's situation is to confirm it neither as "the" objective perspective on the real, nor an empathetic opposite; rather, it is to take responsibility for the partiality of one's perspective as it reflects and is reflected by the language games of particular sociopolitical contexts. Haraway argues that "unlocateable knowledge is irresponsible."[40] I would like to add to this that knowing consists in becoming accountable to the epistemic situation from which one sees; but more than this, to know is to become able to locate oneself as a knower among the language games through which vision is constructed and through which passionate detachment is made possible.[41]

Queerly Situated Knowledges: Responsibility and Dissonance

If my account so far is plausible, those most likely to assume their vision to be paradigmatic are in fact the least likely candidates for objective knowers. Haraway remarks: "Gender, race, sexuality and class are not less structuring for men, or white people, or heterosexuals, or middle-class people. Rather the structure is less *visible*, and it takes a different kind of work to learn to see than for those at a less privileged node in a complex, hierarchically organized field."[42] Less likely to be visible to some men, whites, straights, or middle-class people are (to return to an earlier example) answers to such questions as why "black dirties" describes an "emotional effect." For some knowers this "effect" may be as given as associations such as that of white with purity or blue with primary, its sociopolitical roots buried in the binary grammars of language games taken to represent the real. Such games not only do remain invisible but must remain so, for visibility risks exposing the extent to which they are rooted not in nature but in power.[43] Ironically then, those who are most likely to take their vision to be paradigmatic are of necessity those who do not and cannot "see" without a radically "different kind of work."

Could those less privileged be better situated with respect to the production of knowledge? Perhaps. The sociopolitical situations of some nonmale, nonstraight, nonwhite, or non-middle-class people may make their epistemic situations less conducive to sustaining language games that support the privileges of others. By the same token, such situations may also encourage progress toward developing alternative knowledges that stem from and take into account sociopolitical difference. This is not to say that sheer lack of privilege in and of itself adequately facilitates the development of alternative knowledges, but that the epistemic situations of those for whom "givenness" authorizes oppression are more likely to generate the *dissonance* that sometimes motivates critique, resistance, and the desire for more responsible ways of "passionately constructing" the world.

In her essay "Queer Ethics; or, The Challenge of Bisexuality to Lesbian Ethics," Elisabeth Daumer articulates the dissonance experienced by the fictional Cloe, who, viewing herself as neither heterosexual, lesbian, or bisexual, tries to *say* who/what/where/how she *is*:[44] "Her own sense of the fissures and contradictions (between sexual and political identities, political and personal, emotional commitments, etc.) that attend her way of being in the world has produced in her a hunger for language differentiated enough to capture the wealth of contradictions that pervades the efforts of individual men and women to subvert or modify dominant constructions of gender and sexuality."[45] Cloe's "hunger" for a different language (or perhaps a language of difference) stems from the dissonance, the "fissures and contradictions" that attend her desire to say who she is within a language ordered around binary pairs. Like the binary pair man/woman, straight/gay ascribes greater value to straightness, associating it with the clear, decisive, and masculine. Like Haraway, Cloe finds that her epistemic situation does not easily fit such binarisms. In fact, the attempt to fit may even reinforce compulsory heterosexuality to the extent that one acts as if such language games are, as it were, the only games "in town." "I have so far resisted calling Cloe 'bisexual,'" writes Daumer, "because it seems to me that the term 'bisexuality,' rather than broadening the spectrum of available sexual identifications, holds in place

a *binary framework* of two basic and diametrically opposed sexual orientations."[46]

By the same token, however, that "bisexuality" helps to legitimate this
"binary framework," it is also legitimated within it. For like objectivity/
empathy or culture/nature, *bisexual* is encoded within a "framework"
grounded in binarisms far less likely to generate sociopolitical dissonance.
In Anglo-American culture, for instance, dressing babies in blue or pink
aids the maintenance of heterosexual norms through the association of
these colors with binarisms such as masculine/feminine. Encoded as
"pink," girls are taught sexual and political subordination; boys are taught
not to be "pink"; and gays are taught that crossing heterosexual lines
makes them perversely "pink." There is little doubt that reinforcing
straight/gay, male/female, is crucial to maintaining the power available to
those who fit the "right" half of each binary pair. What is easily missed
is the extent to which these binary pairs are themselves sustained by
others such as blue/pink whose apparent naturalness effectively conceals
their sociopolitical roots.

The dissonance that provokes Cloe's "hunger," then, is epistemic, ethical, and political; it is epistemic because it is not at least obvious that
she can know (in the sense articulated here) who she is within this binary
framework, ethical because Cloe is committed to being honest about the
complexities of her sexual identity, and political because the binary language games that sustain the framework are themselves grounded in the
power of those whose privilege derives from its invisibility. Daumer asks
whether "increased visibility would contribute to our struggle against homophobia, sexism, and heterosexism."[47] The answer to this question must
be no, for *visibility is not vision;* what this struggle requires is the cultivated
ability to *see* not only how heterosexuality is coded, but how it is encoded
in the "color" of a language. As Daumer points out, "as long as it is
politically essential to maintain oppositional cultures—based on sexuality as much as on gender—the effort to disambiguate bisexuality and
elevate it into a sign of integration might counteract the subversive potential of bisexuality as a moral and epistemological force."[48]

By attempting to accommodate it to the existing binary framework,
the move to normalize bisexuality may actually diminish its potential for
creating a different language, for envisioning a different perspective.[49]
Daumer proposes, then, that we "assume bisexuality, not as an identity
that integrates heterosexual and homosexual orientations, but as an epis-

temological as well as ethical vantage point from which we can examine and deconstruct the bipolar framework of gender and sexuality."[50] Initiated in Cloe's experience of difference, but self-critically appropriated in light of its potential for epistemic dissonance, Daumer's vantage point exemplifies a way to take responsibility for understanding how, as Haraway might put it, an axis of domination continues to be encoded within language games that privilege heterosexuality.[51]

In effect, what Daumer recommends is a passionate detachment born not only of experience but of the willingness to seek perspective from points of view less rigidly organized around what are, in fact, not merely binary pairs, but axes of domination. By conceiving herself as epistemically situated in this way, Cloe is empowered to reenvision her sexual identity as an intimate aspect of a unique location from which she may "examine and deconstruct" the language games that code her as "bisexual," as well as passionately (re)construct a more integrated, though always revisable, conception of herself. Coded as a dissonant or even subversive epistemic location, Cloe can both resist normalization and work to articulate a "different language," namely, a language that promises to be more objective because, as Daumer puts it, "it is able to shed light on the gaps and contradictions of all identity, on what we might call the difference *within* identity."[52] It is more "potent" because knowledge conceived as a "passionate construction" is always open to contest, and thus less likely to become encoded as the dominating vision.

Moreover, an objectivity understood in terms of epistemic responsibility offers a perspective from which to deconstruct the disembodied Cartesian knower without thereby embracing an "easy relativism." As Haraway suggests, while "the subjugated have a decent chance to be on to the god trick," this does not mean that partial perspectives are "exempt from critical examination" or that they claim to be "innocent."[53] Quite to the contrary. Such a perspective is "preferred because [it] seem[s] to promise [a] more adequate, sustained, objective, transforming account of the world."[54] That is, by taking responsibility for understanding the binary framework in which she is inscribed as bisexual, Cloe enacts a self-critical as well as self-affirming posture. By critically examining her perspective with respect to her own sexual identity, she locates herself among others and, as Haraway puts it, resists "the politics of closure."[55] For Cloe, as for Haraway, and by implication Wittgenstein, "[s]ituated knowledges are about communities, not about isolated individuals."[56]

Knowing as Playing: "World Traveling" and Passionate Detachment

In her essay "Playfulness, 'World'-Travelling, and Loving Perception," feminist philosopher María Lugones elaborates on what I will here characterize as an example of a situated episteme that, I suggest, accents several important aspects of this approach to knowledge.[57] From a Wittgensteinian perspective, Lugones's central theme, "world traveling" offers us a way to describe the knowing subject of a situated episteme not only as self-critical[58] and self-affirming,[59] but also as a *fundamentally communicative* inhabitant of one or more "worlds." Lugones describes a "world" as something "inhabited" by "flesh and blood" people, and possibly by the imaginary or the dead.[60] A "world" may be part of a society or the whole of it (168), complete or incomplete (168–69); it may be differentiable from other "worlds" according to sexuality, gender, race, and so forth (167–70) . What is crucial to understanding Lugones' conception of a "world" is that it is deeply *experiential*, an "ontologically problematic" notion:

> In describing my sense of a "world," I mean to be offering a description of experience, something that is true to experience even if it is ontologically problematic. Though I would think that any account of identity that could not be true to this experience of outsiders to the mainstream would be faulty even if ontologically unproblematic. Its ease would constrain, erase, or deem aberrant experience that has within it significant insights into non-imperialistic understanding between people. (170)

I am not entirely sure what Lugones means by "ontologically unproblematic," but if she is referring to some notion of a necessarily existent world "behind" our experiential "worlds," this is just the sort of problem a situated episteme is well suited to address. For if language does not mirror reality but instead reflects in its grammar the evolving and complex relationships that animate particular contexts, then questions about whether there exists any real world "underlying" these relationships, reference to which creates either ease (170–71) or dissonance in our experience, is at least unanswerable if not nonsensical.

Such worries are, moreover, largely mooted when we recognize that in the attempt to understand what is "ontologically problematic" about what seems "true to experience" we engage in what are in fact language games, namely, games in which words such as *real* become the subject of our attention. That is, if *reality* is itself defined in terms of its communicative usefulness, then to recognize this can only raise questions such as "useful to whom?" questions that promise to make visible the deeply sociopolitical character of binarisms such as reality/appearance. Instead, then, of making ontological commitments, the approach I have taken here advises passionate detachment; that is, the notion that a "world" need not consist in something-I-know-not-what outside the language games of its players or inhabitants; rather, a "world" consists in *some* implicit or explicit, recent or long past, accepted or contested *agreement* that situates its inhabitants, and insures the possibility of communication—however consistent or conflicted—among its players.

For example, Lugones describes a scenario in which two friends, in the course of a walk through a near-dry riverbed, playfully crash stones together in order to see the beautiful colors brought out by the wet inside the stones. They share an agreement marked by "the attitude that carries us through the activity" (176). The attitude Lugones describes is one of playfulness; it "turns the activity into play."[61] The game the two friends are playing is not bound by a particular set of rules, yet insofar as they agree, that is, insofar as they are able to communicate with each other in mutual playfulness, their play is bounded by the language games that make the construction of this "world" possible. What allows for their playfulness within a "world," in other words, is their ability to play a common language game; the playful *attitude* that "carries" them is made possible precisely *because* they inhabit a particular *linguistic* "world."

As Lugones readily acknowledges, there are worlds in which one can be playful, and worlds in which one cannot (173–74). In "worlds," for example, wherein one is constructed as the inferior side of binarisms such as light/dark, male/female, straight/gay, one cannot be playful without risking rejection, humiliation, and oppression (173, 178). There are also "worlds" in which one is not comfortable, in which one does not yet know how to play the language games.[62] Depending on one's perspective, however, this "world" may present itself as an opportunity rather than as a risk: "In attempting to take a hold of oneself and of one's relation to others in a particular 'world,' one may study, examine and come to understand oneself. One may then see what the possibilities for play are for the being one is in that 'world.' One may even decide to inhabit that self fully in order to understand it better and find its creative possibilities" (177). Lugones's conception of knowing oneself in the course of coming to know a "world" other than one's own is very similar to Haraway's notion of situatedness or Daumer's "vantage point." For to "take hold of oneself" is to try to see oneself as a player in that other "world" whatever dissonance the attempt may or may not generate. One could go even further and suggest that to view the attempt to fit into a "world" radically different from those in which one is "at ease" as a kind of play (170–74) is subversive in that to play is to assume that a "world" is not given, that the rules of its language games are not necessarily "sacred" (177 or "written in stone."[63]

Lugones' notion of "play" offers another way in which we may take responsibility for understanding how "worlds" may come to be passionately constructed. Cloe, for example, "takes hold of herself" by taking responsibility for coming to know the play of both her own "world" and those of others. Cloe's play with the words *bisexual*, *straight*, and *lesbian* may help to fulfill part of her "hunger" for a different language, for in the midst of playing these binary games she also questions the rules, a subversively ethical act that generates the dissonance that motivates Cloe to travel to different "worlds" (or "worlds" of difference).

Lugones remarks that "[k]nowing other women's "worlds" is part of knowing them and knowing them is part of loving them" (178). Not unlike Haraway's promise of "something quite extraordinary," knowing other women's worlds requires a kind of objective vision not readily available to those who benefit from the maintenance of binary-dominated language games grounded in Cartesian concepts of the real—at least not without "a different kind of work." Knowing conceived as a kind of loving well comprehends the notion that objectivity is best understood as a kind of embodied epistemic vision. For to be willing to be held accountable for understanding how one is situated in all of one's "worlds" is to take the tremendous risk of embracing difference, of loving the embodied sensual "world," and of knowing, that is, seeking where one fits or doesn't with respect to the "worlds" of others. Perhaps this kind of work is more possible for those of us whose travel to the "worlds" of others is a matter of "necessity and survival" (169). For not having the "privilege"[64] of ignoring either our own "worlds" or those of others, we are not only more likely to take seriously our epistemic locations, but perhaps more likely to envision knowing as a way of taking responsibility for the actions, beliefs, and dissonances that color our forms of life.

Epilogue: Seeing Beautiful "Worlds" from Where I Work, and Play, and Hope, and Am

Throughout this essay I have been employing the royal *we* as a stylistic device to entice/incite my audience. Couldn't "we," however, quite rightly ask to whom *we* refers? Perhaps my use of *we* renders this text self-deconstructing to the extent that I have employed just the sort of universal that I am seeking to undermine and dispel. This could be, but to see this is itself to begin to practice a situated episteme. For discomfort with the use of *we* stems from the recognition that one somehow does not fit it, that *we* does not describe one's epistemic situation, that one is not located *here*.

From my own contestable partial perspective, I could not possibly be "we." I am neither male, nor straight, and yet find that *lesbian* and *queer* and *gay* don't quite all mean the same thing either. I am a white middle-class mother. I am a woman, a lesbian, a philosopher, a teacher, and a passionate feminist—no comfortable bedfellows. Like Daumer's Cloe, I find a good deal of dissonance in all this, and like Lugones, I am always trying to learn how to better travel to the "worlds" of others. But mostly, like Wittgenstein, I worry about the language that forms the sometimes murky, sometimes barbed, sometimes too safe boundaries of my "world" and whether any of the words I use to describe "my" world get even close to capturing its beauty, its complexity, and its pain. Surely they do not, for language does not *capture* the world; it "stands in the middle of it" permeating my work and dreams, coloring my living all the while I try to become accountable for what I see from a "here" so deeply imbued by wonder that it cannot help but erupt into words. And I cannot help but hope that "we" have this much in common.

Notes

1. There are *many* feminist philosophers whose work would fit well with the following discussion. Some of these include Linda Alcoff, Naomi Scheman, Sarah Lucia Hoagland, Joyce Trebilcot, Marilyn Frye, and Edwina Franchild. For this essay, however, I have chosen to focus on Elisabeth Daumer and María Lugones. I would also like to acknowledge the community of women, girls, and lesbians whose lives so richly situate my own, especially Carley Aurora Lee-Lampshire, Gloria Cohen-Dion, Sarah Towne, and Nancy Lineman.

2. Donna Haraway, "Situated Knowledges: The Science Question in Feminism and the Privilege of Partial Perspective," *Feminist Studies* 14, no. 3 (1988): 575–99.

3. Haraway, "Situated Knowledges," 589; Haraway, *Primate Visions: Race, Gender and Nature in the World of Modern Science* (New York: Routledge, 1989) (hereafter *PV*), 116: "Semiosis is politics by other means."

4. Haraway, "Situated Knowledges," 584–85; see also 581.

5. Haraway, "Situated Knowledges," 583; see also 582, and *PV*, 4.

6. In her essay "On the Logic of Pluralist Feminism," in *Feminist Ethics*, ed. Claudia Card (University of Kansas Press, 1991), 43, María Lugones writes: "When I do not see plurality stressed in the very structure of a theory, I know that I will have to do lots of acrobatics . . . to have this theory speak to me without allowing the theory to distort me in my complexity." What I hope to accomplish here is some step toward a theory that not only stresses plurality but takes it to be at the heart of what it means to be a knower; see Wendy Lee-Lampshire, "Decisions of Identity: Feminist Subjects and Grammars of Sexuality," *Hypatia* 10, no. 4 (1995), or Lee-Lampshire, "Spilling All Over the "Wide Fields of Our Passions": Frye, Butler, Wittgenstein, and the Context(s) of Attention, Intention, and Identity," *Hypatia* 14, no. 3 (1999).

7. Specifically, I will be looking at Elisabeth Daumer, "Queer Ethics; or, The Challange of Bisexuality to Lesbian Ethics," *Hypatia* 7, no. 4 91–105; and María Lugones, "Playfulness, 'World'-Traveling, and Loving Perception," in *Lesbian Philosophy and Culture*, ed. Jeffner Allen (New York: State University of New York Press, 1990), 159–80 (originally published in *Hypatia* 2, no. 2).

8. Ludwig Wittgenstein, *Remarks on Colour*, ed. G. E. M. Anscombe, trans. Linda L. McAlister and Margarete Schattle (Berkeley and Los Angeles: University of California Press, 1977) (hereafter *RCI-III; RCI*), par. 158, 6.

9. Ludwig Wittgenstein, *Philosophical Investigations*, trans. G. E. M. Anscombe (New York: Macmillan, 1953) (hereafter *PI*), par. 238.

10. *RCIII*, par. 26–29; Ludwig Wittgenstein, *Zettel*, ed. G. E. M. Anscombe and G. H. von Wright (Berkeley and Los Angeles: University of California Press, 1967) (hereafter *Z*), par. 444; *Remarks on the Philosophy of Psychology*, vol. 1, ed. G. E. M. Anscombe and G. H. von Wright, trans. G. E. M. Anscombe (Chicago: University of Chicago Press, 1980) (hereafter *RPPI*), par. 622, 1107.

11. *PI*, par. 16 (note ostensive definition); also see *RCIII*, par. 102.

12. *RCIII*, par. 30; *PI*, note p. 14e; also see Haraway on what the taxidermist and the photographer see in their representations of the real in *PV*, 30–45.

13. Also see *RCIII*, par. 123 and 34.

14. *RCI*, par. 59–60, 68; *RCIII*, par. 53; *PI*, par. 239, 429; *RPPI*, par. 964.

15. *RCIII*, par. 73; 108; *RCI*, par. 17, 56; *PI.II*, p. 216.

16. *RCIII*, par. 52; *PI*, par. 340.

17. *PI*, par. 241; *RCIII*, par. 301; *Z*, par. 173, 175; Haraway, *PV*, 8, and "Situated Knowledges," 583.

18. *RCIII*, par. 110; *PI*, par. 61, 240–44, 491.

19. Ludwig Wittgenstein, *Remarks on the Philosophy of Psychology*, vol. 2, ed. G. H. von Wright and Heikki Nyman, trans. C. G. Luckhardt and M. A. U. Aue (Chicago: University of Chicago Press, 1980) (hereafter *RPPII*), par. 393; 684.

20. *PI*, par. 525, 652, and p. 188e; *Z*, par. 170; *RPPI*, par. 923; *RPPII*, par. 426–28; one could argue that the whole of Wittgenstein's work instantiates this claim, but this is another paper.

21. *RCIII*, par. 302.

22. *RCIII*, par. 317.

23. *RCIII*, par. 303; *PI*, par. 80–85, 224–26, p. 226e.

24. *RCIII*, par. 293, 296; 75; 32; 86; 154; *RCII*, par. 9–11; *RPPI*, par. 640–45; *RPPII*, par. 658.

25. Ludwig Wittgenstein, *On Certainty*, ed. G. E. M. Anscombe and G. H. von Wright, trans. Denis Paul and G. E. M. Anscombe (New York: Harper and Row, 1972) (hereafter *OC*), par. 362.

26. We might call this the sophist game although I think that at least the Protagoras of Plato's *Protagoras* and *Theatetus* may actually subscribe to a kind of relativism much closer to Haraway and Wittgenstein than he is generally credited for.

27. *RCIII*, par. 94.

28. *RCIII*, par. 105.

29. *RCIII*, par. 156.

30. Haraway, *PV*, 293.

31. *RPPII*, par. 684; Haraway, *PV*, 297; would it be stretching too far to associate man with the primary blue sky "up there" and woman with secondary green grassy Earth "down here"?

32. Haraway, "Situated Knowledges," 585.

33. Haraway, *PV*, 188.

34. Haraway, *PV*, 153–54; also see *PV*, 142–46.

35. Haraway, *PV*, 10, my emphasis.

36. For a particularly good example of man's/"man's" self-construction, see Haraway's account of "Man the hunter" in *PV*, 187–217.

37. Haraway, *PV*, 3.

38. Wendy Lee-Lampshire, "Moral 'I': The Feminist Subject and the Grammar of Self-Reference," *Hypatia*, 7, no. 1 (1992): 36–39; Haraway, *PV*, 13, 41.

39. Haraway, *PV*, 310.

40. Haraway, "Situated Knowledges" 583; *PV*, 13, 62, 309–35.

41. For a slightly different angle on this theme, see Wittgenstein's remarks on the nature of description, in *RPPI*, par. 1079–80; Wendy Lee-Lampshire, "Decisions of Identity," 11–15; "Women-Animals-Machines: A Grammar for a Wittgensteinian Ecofeminism," *Journal of Value Inquiry*, 29, no. 1 (1995); and Lee-Lampshire, "Moral 'I,'" 46–50.

42. Haraway, *PV*, 297, my emphasis.

43. For a brief discussion of the desire for power as it informs conceptions of certainty, see Lee-Lampshire, "Moral 'I,'" 40.

44. Elisabeth Daumer, "Queer Ethics; Or, The Challenge of Bisexuality to Lesbian Ethics." *Hypatia* 7, no. 4, 92.

45. Daumer, "Queer Ethics," 96.

46. Daumer, "Queer Ethics," 96, my emphasis.

47. Daumer, "Queer Ethics," 97.

48. Daumer, "Queer Ethics," 97–98.

49. Normalization is a very important theme in much current lesbian philosophy; see Bat-Ami Bar On's "The Feminist 'Sexuality Debates' and the Transformation of the Political" *Hypatia* 7, no. 4, 45–58.

50. Daumer, "Queer Ethics," 98.

51. Haraway, "Situated Knowledges," 585.

52. Daumer, "Queer Ethics," 98.

53. Haraway, "Situated Knowledges," 584.

54. Haraway, "Situated Knowledges," 584; also see 590.

55. Haraway, "Situated Knowledges," 590.

56. Haraway, "Situated Knowledges," 590.

57. María Lugones, "Playfulness," 159–80.

58. See Lugones's description of "arrogant perception," in "Playfulness," 160–67.

59. See Lugones's description of Hispanic "worlds" and the becoming of lesbian "worlds," in "Playfulness," 168.

60. Lugones, "Playfulness," 168. Page references to this work appear parenthetically in the text.

61. Lugones, "Playfulness," 176. An interesting comparison might be drawn here between Lugones's example of the crashing stones and Wittgenstein's builder's game (*PI*, par. 2–23) where instead of words such as *slab* or *pillar*, we might examine the use of *stone* or *wet* in light of the agreement that must already be in place among the games' participants in order for any "play" (in many senses of that term) to occur. For further analysis of this theme, see Wendy Lee-Lampshire's "The Sound

of Little Hummingbird Wings: A Wittgensteinian Investigation of Forms of Life as Forms of Power," *Feminist Studies*, 25, no. 2 (1999): 409–26.

62. Lugones, "Playfulness," 171, especially her discussion of poodle skirts.

63. At least not stones that cannot be broken in order to see the beautiful colors inside.

64. Within a situated episteme, privilege becomes "privilege," for, as we have seen, power as it has been traditionally justified in Cartesian terms requires precisely lack of vision. The disembodied eye is also blind. For more on this theme, see my discussion of Nagel in "Moral 'I.'"

18

Wittgenstein's *Remarks on Colour* as Remarks on Racism

Bruce Krajewski

Colours spur us to philosophize.

—Ludwig Wittgenstein[1]

Subjective and objective, physically fixed and culturally
constructed, absolutely proper and endlessly displaced,
color can appear as an unthinkable scandal.

—Stephen Melville[2]

Our studies must take us, in every case, beyond the
obvious or most immediate meaning of the text.

—Emmanuel Levinas[3]

With the words of Levinas in mind, I want to explore what might happen
if someone were to make Wittgenstein's *Remarks on Colour* speak to the
present, in a context about which Wittgenstein probably did give some
thought, given his own family's "race" negotiations with the National
Socialists in Germany during 1938–39,[4] and in which "people of color"[5]
have a stake. Can Wittgenstein be added to a list of those who make us
more aware of issues connected to color and racism? Is John Gage right
that "colour is almost everybody's business"?[6]

The use of the word *color* in the previous sentence has a wider and
more potent range of meaning than it might have had in Wittgenstein's

My thanks to Laurentian University for financial support to complete this essay.

world. That is but one of the myriad reasons that some, especially philosophers, could object to reading Wittgenstein out of his time (even mind).
Remarks on Colour is a minor book for students of Wittgenstein, far down
the shelf from the numerous studies of the *Tractatus Logico-Philosophicus*
(1921) and *Philosophical Investigations* (1953). Before dealing with some
of the objections that will naturally arise, I urge readers to imagine a
situation in which, for instance, a black South African living under
apartheid picks up *Remarks on Colour* and begins reading. Is it not plain
that the ways this person takes certain passages will be different from
those of a "white," North American philosopher employed at a university? My guess is that this hypothetical reader might see Wittgenstein's
remarks as an allegory, as something speaking otherwise about the present. Picture such a reader coming across the following remark: "I can
imagine how a human being would behave who regards that which is
important to me [color] as unimportant. But can I imagine his *state?*—
What does that mean? Can I imagine the state of someone who considers
important what I consider important?"[7] Isn't this reader living where
some people cannot imagine her having a state (adding a political meaning to that word) in which color is unimportant (in other words, nonex-
clusionary)? The point is to see the richness and pertinence of
Wittgenstein's remarks when placed in the new context, in which everyone has a stake in color, not just blacks, because that hypothetical reader's life is baldly linked to the fact of that person's "coloredness."
Suddenly, Wittgenstein's little book of remarks accrues (and reflects) values that might have been thought absent.

The current bilingual edition of *Remarks on Colour*, edited by G. E. M.
Anscombe, has been, say, purified, apparently with some direction provided by Wittgenstein himself, through the separation of color from its
links to the world. Anscombe writes, "Part III of this volume reproduces
most of a MS book written in Oxford in the Spring of 1950. I have
left out material on 'inner-outer', remarks about Shakespeare, and some
general observations . . . ; all this both [?] was marked as discontinuous
with the text . . . [*All dieses war von Wittgenstein als nicht zum Text gehörig
gekennzeichnet*]." How to understand this? One way seems to be to suppose
that as Wittgenstein wrote about color other things occurred to him,
thoughts about Shakespeare, for instance. On one reading, someone
might call these occurrences losses of concentration, on another, illuminating allusions, analogies, convergences. Anscombe tells us that Wittgenstein marked certain remarks as "not belonging [*gehörig*] to the text,"

yet they remained part of the text, part of a whole, yet—one would guess, after the fact of the initial writing—parenthetical, in a sense. Would it prove fruitful to work out possible connections between the *hören* (to hear, to listen) in *gehörig* and the *merken* (to mark, to listen to) in these *Bemerkungen* (remarks), to say something about philosophy as a kind of listening that is at first open, undifferentiated, in other words, a voice about color entering the mind's ear alongside, perhaps just after or just before, a voice from Shakespeare? Is this philosophy's task to separate out the world from texts, to make sure that thoughts about (voices from) Shakespeare, and all sorts of other seemingly impertinent thoughts (what Anscombe calls "*Reflexionen allgemeiner Art*," what Shakespeare scholars might call "asides") are marked as detours from a retrospectively conceived univocal, linear path? The philosophical studies of Wittgenstein's text seem to answer yes.

What follows will not be a "feminist reading" of *Remarks on Colour* in any easily recognizable sense, though Wittgenstein and feminism have been brought together in enlightening ways by others. Some recent work by Wendy Lee-Lampshire would be paradigmatic on that count.[8] At present, *Remarks on Colour*, in particular, has not attracted feminist scholars who have attended to Wittgenstein. Thus, my effort here justifies its appearance, in part, by falling into the category of a "rereading," in keeping with the series' title.

The two main recent studies that deal directly with Wittgenstein's text—by Alasdair MacIntyre and Jonathan Westphal—leave things at the literal level, and speak of color not in relationship to human beings, but as an abstract, psychological, and physiological phenomenon.[9] That humans have color never comes up in these studies, though my contention is that Wittgenstein's remarks implicitly address human color and its consequences at numerous points. A thoughtful text, which happens to incorporate several passages from *Remarks on Colour*, is Derek Jarman's *Chroma*, and he too notices the impoverishment in recent writings on color. He writes, "Pliny is as eloquent as any of the ancient writers. The reason for this is not just his insatiable curiosity, but because he puts himself and his prejudices so strongly into his writing. Most later books on color fail to do this, and therefore remain colourless."[10] Jarman's book is colorful, partly because his meditations on color result from watching his AIDS-infected body produce color changes. Jarman's reactions to Wittgenstein are colored by his own being, for one, the link between his body and his body of work; the AIDS virus and Jarman's film *Blue*; the homosexuality and Jarman's film *Wittgenstein,* in which Wittgenstein is brought out of the closet, opening the question of whether Wittgenstein's interest in color has anything to do with his homosexuality, as it seems to for Jarman, though in most of the secondary literature on Wittgenstein his homosexuality is kept separate from the philosophy. Stanley Cavell's work seems to be an exception. Cavell says, for instance, "I suppose that what I am expressing here is the fact that I am from time to time haunted—I rather take it for granted that this is quite generally true of male heterosexual philosophers—by the origin of philosophy (in ancient Greece) in an environment of homosexual intimacy."[11] Thus perhaps (who knows? who but Cavell would admit it?) the standard academic move among philosophers who write about Wittgenstein is to keep him closeted, not allow him to appear as a colorful (flamboyant) philosopher. Jarman's interest in Wittgenstein, like his interest in color, is not academic. As he says in "This is Not a Film of Ludwig Wittgenstein," "I have much of Ludwig in me."[12]

Perhaps something needs to be said about the apparent lateness of Jarman's attention to Wittgenstein, the lateness of the publicity of Wittgenstein's sexuality, and the lateness of the matter of color for Wittgenstein himself, who wrote his *Bemerkungen* on color just before his death in 1951. This temporality in relation to color strikes me as significant because it is the first thing that occurs to Wittgenstein to say about color, to fashion a double language game with a proposition about color from each, and to note some differences in the propositions, one of them being the difference between the temporal (or timely) and the timeless, between the *zeitlich* and the *zeitlos* (RC, I, #1), the contextual and the perennial.

Remarks on Colour is a rich text for thinking through the ways in which color determines communities, separates people into groups and classes, and heightens people's awareness of their own color-blindness, as well as their resistance to and fears of what is nonidentical.[13] Color is of special concern to "whites" who often imagine themselves to be colorless, in part because white is considered the norm, though technically, according to Edward Averill, "[W]hite and black are not spectral colours. . . . If a white surface is one that reflects all light and a black surface is one that absorbs all light, then a white surface is really a combination of all colors and a black surface is colorless."[14] As Richard Dyer says:

> In the realm of categories, black is always marked as a colour (as the term "coloured" egregiously acknowledges), and is always

particularising; whereas white is not anything really, not an identity, not a particularising quality, because it is everything—white
is no colour because it is all colours. This property of whiteness,
to be everything and nothing, is the source of its representational
power. . . . [W]hite domination is reproduced by the way that
white people "colonise the definition of normal."[15]

As we will see, Wittgenstein's text turns on the contrast between white
and black, which makes it relevant for the points Dyer raises. What
David Bloor calls Wittgenstein's "social theory of knowledge" needs to
be extended to Wittgenstein's reflections on color, if only to develop a
more complete picture of Wittgenstein as a philosopher of culture(s).[16]
Furthermore, while it might be tempting later on to say that having a
different skin color represents having a different "form of life," I take
Cavell's point that the phrase "form of life" has been given almost exclusively an ethnological reading: "The ethnological, or horizontal direction
. . . emphasizes differences between cultures, for example, in whether they
count or measure or sympathize as we do. The biological, or vertical,
direction emphasizes differences between, we might rather say, life forms,
for example, as between lower and higher, perhaps expressed in the presence or absence of a hand."[17] What Cavell says immediately after this
quotation makes me think that he means that lower and higher "life
forms" can be distinguished by their lower and higher powers of understanding, so that to be primitive in a Wittgensteinian sense might mean
that one continues to exhibit a low form of understanding. Later, I might
want to call that low form of understanding "bad prejudice" (about color).

Wittgenstein's text can help a reader to undo discussion about color
divorced from lived experience, such as MacIntyre and Westphal's, and
also help one to understand the consequences of color, what can happen
to people who interpret color as either irrelevant or definitive. Many of
Wittgenstein's remarks deal with issues about what happens to people
who interpret a color one way rather than another. An instance of this is
a person who calls white a colour in a community that has no specific
identification(s) with "whiteness." As Dyer says, this would be a community in which "white is no color." To make the case for Wittgenstein as
a relevant figure in current discussions of race (in other words, in cases
that equate race with color), color, discrimination, and prejudice, I must
attempt to recuperate some ancient ways of understanding, because my
reading of *Remarks on Colour* could rightly be called allegorical, though I

mean it to be more than that.[18] My hope is that some people will think it possible for a contemporary reader to reread Wittgenstein with a new set of concerns in mind regarding color, just as Wittgenstein reread Goethe's book on color, *Farbenlehre*, while writing on the topic.[19]

Much of the discussion about Wittgenstein's work, with the exception of the *Tractatus* and *Philosophical Investigations*, is problematic, because Wittgenstein's *Nachlass* has been edited in sometimes idiosyncratic ways. Jaakko Hintikka has explained the problem in a 1990 *Times Literary Supplement* article.[20] The upshot of Hintikka's view is that there will never be an "authorized" edition of Wittgenstein's notebooks. We will have only a partial view of what was important to Wittgenstein. Further, given that Wittgenstein apparently never planned to publish a book called *Remarks on Colour*, the collection of remarks that has appeared under that title looks dubious.

> He [Wittgenstein] noted that he read colour into a black and white photo. White had not been white since Newton discovered the Spectrum. White is colour full.
>
> The boy in the photo was blonde. Ludwig knew that. Was he wearing a red dress? Did he imagine the red dress in the achromatic greys? Colour glimmered in the mind's eye. Nothing was quite what it seemed. It was another language.[21]

Part of the inspiration for looking at *Remarks on Colour* as remarks on racism comes from Marjorie Perloff's reading of the *Tractatus* as a "war book."[22] Her case is rooted in Wittgenstein's own statements and in evidence provided by Wittgenstein's friends, acquaintances, and biographers. Perloff's article is a striking example of what can be accomplished by placing a Wittgenstein text in another context (in this case, partially putting it back into its original context of the World War I). However, what I propose here has almost no backing from Wittgenstein, nor from friends or biographers. Still, some biographical information leads one to think that Wittgenstein knew something about the effects of people treating others as representative of a particular ethnic or racial category that is not part of a majority. Wittgenstein was a Jew in some sense, though Cavell says in a different context that "what or who Wittgenstein is is, of course, not determined" (*Philosophical Passages*, 128); nonetheless, the following statement by Wittgenstein seems to serve as a gloss on the point Dyer makes, noted earlier, about black-white relations: "Within the history of the peoples of Europe the history of the Jews is not treated as circumstantially as their interventions in European affairs would actually merit, because within this history they are experienced as a sort of disease, and anomaly, and no one wants to put a disease on the same level as normal life."[23] Recall Dyer's declaration that "white domination is reproduced by the way that white people 'colonise the definition of normal,'" and then substitute *non-Jewish*, or equally plausibly *Christian*, for *white* in Dyer's phrasing. In fact, Sander Gilman makes the case that at least as far back as the nineteenth century, some Europeans attempted to equate blacks and Jews. As Gilman says, "The image of the Jews as black is, however, not merely the product of the racist biology of the late nineteenth century. . . . For the association of the Jews with blackness is as old as Christian tradition. Medieval iconography always juxtaposed the black image of the synagogue, of the Old Law, with the white of the church."[24] In light of Gilman's claims, it is perhaps more than possible that Wittgenstein was familiar with the link between blackness and Jewishness.

It is likely that no one would claim that all the items in *Remarks on Colour* can be read as remarks on racism, but a number of them leap out at a reader interested in such issues. As in many parts of North America, the emphasis in Wittgenstein's remarks is mainly on the relation of white to black, or some might say "white" to "people of color," and the mood of the text is exploratory rather than assertive. Questioning pervades the remarks, questioning that leads toward thinking through distinctions that could help in refining and understanding the matter at hand (making discriminations that do not lead to discrimination), as well as showing the matter in a more complete complexity, providing considerations for and against thinking a particular way.[25] Wittgenstein's way of presenting the remarks is illustrative precisely of someone who is not prejudiced (or racist), of someone who retains an open mind on an issue, which is not to say that Wittgenstein is without presuppositions about color (he has Goethe's book on color in mind at various points, for instance), but the point is that a reader of these remarks could become dislodged from predictable stances on color, even if one reads the text in an entirely academic way without regard to human color. "In every serious philosophical question uncertainty extends to the very roots of the problem. We must always be prepared to learn something totally new" (*RC*, I, #15). "Totally" (*ganz*) is italicized in the original, as if there are gradations of newness, from the merely new to the totally new—would it be going too far to call the *totally* new the *sui generis?*—something that had not occurred to one before, even in a hinting, shadowy way, something that calls for us to learn (*lernen*), and we must "always be prepared" for this calling.

My sense of *Remarks on Colour* includes the idea that readers cannot help but be aware continually of another totality at work in the remarks, namely a word that suggests totality: *blindness*. *Color-blindness* does not suggest the same. The partiality explicit in Wittgenstein's repeated appeals to color-blindness, and the varieties of color-blindness, needs to be set against an implicit presupposition about the totality of the state of most forms of color-blindness, that is, that some people are born with a certain (common) kind of color-blindness (not the extremely rare form of *total* color-blindness known as cerebral achromatopsia) and will retain that state permanently. The genetic nature of most color-blindness highlights again Wittgenstein's emphasis on the way we learn about colors, and the differences in life forms that such blindness produces. "The lives of the blind are different from those of the sighted" (*RC*, III, #319). This point might seem trivial, except that I believe that it corroborates Cavell's statement regarding "the remarkable fact of the presence of the figure of the child in Wittgenstein's thoughts" (*Philosophical Passages*, 167), with the child as a figure of adaptability and malleability. The human learning or training about color is an activity of childhood, and any undoing of that training disrupts, perhaps necessarily, the totality of what must look for all the world like a natural state, in other words, seeing things in a particular way, talking about them in a particular way that seems understandable to others. Thus, for instance, Oliver Sacks's attraction to Jonathan I, a painter who "had become colorblind—after sixty-five years of seeing colors normally—totally colorblind, as if 'viewing a black and white television screen. . . .' At this point the magnitude of his loss overwhelmed him. He had spent his life as a painter; now even his art was without meaning, and he could no longer imagine how to go on."[26] The totality of this change in adult life has profound effects, externally as well as internally: "He knew the colors of everything, with an extraordinary exactness (he could give not only the names but the numbers of colors as these were listed in a Pantone chart of hues he had used for many years). He could identify the green of van Gogh's billiard table in this way unhesitatingly. He knew all the colors in his favorite paintings, but could no longer see them, either when he looked or in his mind's eye"[27] (*Anthropologist*, 7). The change at this late date in Jonathan

I's life resulted in several weeks of "almost suicidal" depression, some-thing Sacks is quick to point out does not usually happen to people born color-blind (*Anthropologist*, 33). At first, Jonathan I did not know "how to go on," but later he was able "to construct the world anew, to construct his own sensibility and identity anew" (*Anthropologist*, 35). The construc-tion of the normality of the color world points back to Dyer's claim about the constructedness of race, and likewise dramatizes the degree of change Wittgenstein is likely calling for when he says: "We [he must mean adults] must be always be prepared to learn something totally new." A change in our childhood training about color (about anything?), and maybe in our philosophical conceptions about color, might mean some-thing as radical, as total, as having to construct the world anew, to learn how to go on (again).

I worry that the view of a "social construction" of color here might not be the issue on which the reader should focus (see reference to Slavoj Žižek, note 28), as much as "construction" might mesh well with Witt-genstein's use of "building" examples, calling for slabs, and the like. Given the surprising consensus among "cultural theorists" and racist "multiculturalists"[28] about "social constructivism"—even Sacks writes about "the parts of the brain that 'construct' the sensation of color"[29]—I may be in the same space as Wittgenstein describes at the beginning of his comments on Frazer's *Golden Bough*: "The very idea of wanting to explain a practice—for example, the killing of the priest-king—seems wrong to me. All that Frazer does is to make them plausible to people who think as he does."[30] My aim is more than seeking out the like-minded, and making the essay's title plausible.

Remarks on Colour begins with a reminder that color talk is one of a series of "language-games" (*Sprachspiele*). Color talk registers the en-twinement of color and its social construction, an instance being Adrian Piper's cousin's efforts to appear "black enough" to satisfy black peers who might question her skin color. Piper writes, "My maternal cousin, who resembles Michelle Pfeiffer, went through adolescence in the late 1960s and had a terrible time. She tried perming her hair into an Afro . . . , adopted a black working-class dialect . . . , and counted among her friends young people who criticized high scholastic achievers for 'act-ing white'" (PWPB, 7–8). This points up that classifying human beings according to color consists *of a variety of characteristics beyond skin pigmen-tation*, though this point must not be put into suspension at the cost of Slavoj Žižek's argument, putting cases of "passing" aside, about skin pigmentation being part of the real "inside" that is excessive, and thus "spilling" outside, and the tendency to draw back from that excess, say in repulsion or fear. Žižek says that racism's

> ultimate problem is precisely how to 'contain' the threatening inside from 'spilling out' and overwhelming us. . . . Is the presence of African-Americns not felt as threatening precisely insofar as it is experienced as too massive, too close . . . ? [T]he racist fantasmatic duality of blacks and whites coincides with the duality of formless stuff and shadowy-spectral-impotent form without stuff. . . . The ultimate problem in intersubjectivity is precisely the extent to which we are ready to accept the other . . . in the real of his or her existence. . . . The problem, of course, is that, in a sense, life itself is 'ugly'. . . . So, in order to survive, we do need a minimum of the real—in a contained, gentrified condition. ("Abyss," 24–25)

Even in *Remarks on Colour*, Wittgenstein does not deal with people's real skin color, in the way that Žižek speaks of it here, for, in part, Wittgenstein displaces this real into linguisticality. As students of Wittgenstein know, the notion of language-game prepares the reader for understanding that linguistic statements are integrated into patterns of activity, and that the understanding of statements is relative to one's community, or one's "form of life," even when that form of life goes on within other forms of life, and it is important not to follow a common slippage by allowing "forms of life" to become synonymous with pluralism. The *Remarks* highlight the relationship between black and white, and if a reader concentrates on relations between "blacks" and "whites," that focus would yield a coherence and suggestiveness that another (say on yellows and whites) would not.

This is not to say that other colors could not accomplish what Wittgenstein does by concentrating on black and white. I am thinking here of some interesting artwork by Byron Kim, a New York artist who works not with painterly colors but with skin tones. For instance, his piece called *Synecdoche* consists of two hundred small monochrome panels that are all different shades of brown, tan, or beige. Each panel matches the skin tone of one of the artist's friends.[31]

"State the relationship between the lightness of certain shades of colour" (*RC*, I, #1). Is it not an issue among people of color that the darkness or lightness of one's skin matters? One need only think of the controversy surrounding Michael Jackson's shift of skin color toward white, or of attempts to establish guidelines of racial purity, or of talk about someone being "lily white," or Piper's essay on "passing" for white. This latter point takes us to another early remark: "Lichtenberg says that very few people have ever seen pure white" (*RC*, I, #3). Of course, Lichtenberg did not have Nazis or the Ku Klux Klan in mind, but with those groups in the picture it seems fair to say not only that some people believe that they have seen pure white, but also that these groups claim to *know* what it means *to be* "pure white," so that the rest of the world appears tainted. Wittgenstein says that "[Lichtenberg] constructed an ideal use from the ordinary one. And that is not say a better one, but one that has been refined along certain lines and in the process something has been carried to extremes." A contemporary reader could take this statement as one critical of claims regarding racial purity (for example, purity of color). There is some more evidence in Wittgenstein's citation of Runge's remark that "White water which is pure is as inconceivable as clear milk" (*RC*, I, #21). To speak of the color concept "white" as pure (*rein*) does not make sense if one thinks of purity as uncoded, clear, since one calls milk white, though milk is opaque. (Here again, Žižek is pertinent: "Today, one likes to evoke our loss of contact with the authentic reality of external (as well as our internal) nature—we are so accustomed to aseptic, pasteurized milk that milk direct from a cow is unpleasant. This 'true milk' necessarily strikes us as too dense, disgusting, undrinkable" ["Abyss," 23]).

The matter is more cloudy than the purists imagine. "Whites" are not pure white; there are gradations of whiteness just as there are of blackness. On this reading, "whites" are "people of color" as well, and the notion of "pure white" is nonsensical. However, Wittgenstein says that when we think of white as a color of a substance, things turn out differently: "White as a colour of substances (in the sense in which we say snow is white) is lighter than any other substance-colour; black darker. *Here* colour is a darkening, and if all such is removed from the substance, white remains, and for this reason we can call it 'colourless'" (*RC*, I, #52). The deictic "here" indicates that the "purity" of whiteness is being seen in a different context, one perhaps closer to views normally associated with Nazis and Ku Klux Klan members, who seem to imagine themselves as "colorless," untainted by "colored" races. These people seem to believe, as Runge says in Wittgenstein's text, that black "dirties" (*RC*,

III, #105), and then Wittgenstein asks: "[W]hat does that mean? Is that an emotional effect which black has on us?" For Nazis and Ku Klux Klan members, "white" is a special color. As Wittgenstein says, "[P]eople reserve a special place for a given point on the colour wheel, and that they don't have to go to a lot of trouble to remember where the point is, but always find it easily" (RC, III, #7). This "finding" sounds very much like Dyer's point in his "White" article that color differences are sometimes *constructed* in what Žižek would call the realm of the Real.

It is also easy for people to notice what we would call color awareness in the cases of Nazis or Ku Klux Klan members, though color awareness is not restricted to "whites," nor does color awareness mean that which is "colored" is treated with more sensitivity. It happens that noticing someone's color can mean that person gets ignored, discounted, shunned. However, Wittgenstein thinks often about color-blindness, which seems to be another clue regarding the contemporary importance of this text. There are at least two ways of taking this color-blindness. One could read the term as reinforcing the perspective of Nazis, Ku Klux Klan members, and other "whites" who think of themselves as "colorless," and thus are blind to their own *real* pigmentation, and hence see everyone else as different. When one color dominates, that color (like gender) can become the standard against which other colors are judged, according to Catharine MacKinnon, who presents a powerful argument against embracing color-blindness in the law as an ameliorative move:

> In a society that is anything but sex-blind and color-blind, courts insist on color blindness and sex blindness as the rule for discerning inequality and enforcing equality. The moment you complain in court about discrimination is probably the first moment in your life when your color, your race, your ethnicity, or your sex becomes "irrelevant." This is supposed to be a principled and neutral stance. But the white man's standard for equality is: are you equal to *him*? That is hardly a neutral standard. It is a racist and sexist standard. . . . The white man's meaning of equality is being equal to him, which is the same as being the same as him [sic].[32]

Remarks on Colour can be read in a way that acknowledges MacKinnon's point.

A second, perhaps idealistic, way of approaching the issue of color-blindness is to place it in the ongoing conversation (of which MacKinnon's remark is indeed part) about equity among people of varying races that includes a recognition of the world's pied beauty—though this quickly begins to smack of multiculturalist claptrap—of the importance of racial heritage, while also insisting that certain situations (say, legal ones) might call for color-blindness, all the while keeping in mind that this particular form of color-blindness might be no more than what Žižek calls a "fantasmatic frame." Is it fair to say that the current North American context values color-blindness over color awareness? Is not color-blindness one of the elements of nondiscrimination? The image of justice is a blindfolded woman holding a scale, though blindfolds do not *necessarily* prevent color perception, as Goethe pointed out in his discussion of afterimages;[33] or as the Jarman epigraph says, color can glimmer in the mind's eye. Perhaps the blindfold's depiction is a preliminary recognition of the etymology of color (to cover, hide), so that covering the eyes in light of the law can be seen as an aid to ensure that people receive a hearing.

Wittgenstein suggests a thought-experiment: "Imagine a group [*Volk*] of colour-blind people, and there could easily be one. They would not have the same colour concepts as we do. For even assuming they speak, e.g. English [the original says *Deutsch*], and thus have all the English colour words, they would still use them differently than we do and would *learn* their use differently" (*RC*, I, #17). As a person who is red-green color-blind, I know this to be true, for I do not have the same color concepts as people who are not color-blind. Usually, people think of my color-blindness as a defect, but Wittgenstein says otherwise, and the image of justice as blind also seeks to demonstrate something positive, such as that a group of people working through legal matters can make themselves selectively blind, make themselves use words differently in a legal context in which one's color should not be a factor. "[T]he colour concepts of colour-blind people too deviate from those of normal people, and not every deviation from the norm must be a blindness, a defect" (*RC*, I, #9). This might be especially significant in places where a majority harbors color biases about those in a minority, and think that minority viewpoints must necessarily be "defective." In short, those in a majority often hold the belief that those in a minority need to adapt themselves to "our" (a majority's) way of life, the call to assimilation, as if a minority were not part of the "our," a point recently made by Cornel West in *Race Matters*.[34]

In other words, we need to rethink the famous image of the blindfolded woman of justice who holds the scales, a version of Astraea, the goddess of justice in Greek mythology. The blindfold indicates that the woman is most likely not blind, but shows that she is trying to *see* in a particular way. How could a sculpture represent a blind person? Can we tell who is blind from looking at a person in a photograph? The recognition of who is blind might depend on motion, say, putting the scales of justice in motion, watching the blind person in action, or listening to the blind person talk about the world. The sculpture of the blindfolded woman brings something important to light: the legal context is a special occasion, and the sculpture could be directing our attention to an ideal situation, though MacKinnon and others can justly complain that the ideal might be achieved only rarely, or inappropriately, say by erasing color from a picture in which a person brought into court has been painted into a corner. Normally, we take human forms represented in sculpture to be sighted. Wittgenstein writes: "Someone who describes the phenomena of colour-blindness in a book describes them in the concepts of the sighted" (*RC*, III, #55), and it is the color-blind who make the "normally" sighted aware of a different way of seeing, so that the non-color-blind people come to realize an aspect of their *unknownness to themselves*.

Color awareness reigns, because most people are not color-blind and are unaccustomed to color-blind descriptions and ways of acting. "But would it ever occur to colour-blind people to call themselves 'colour-blind'?—Why not? But how could 'normally sighted people' learn the 'normal' use of colour words, if they were the exceptions in a colour-blind population?—Isn't it possible that they just use colour words 'normally,' and perhaps, in the eyes of others they make certain mistakes, until the others finally learn to appreciate their unusual abilities[?]" (*RC*, III, #286). Once one flips this back to the "normal" situation in which color-blindness is exceptional, one sees that Wittgenstein suggests that color-blindness is an ability (*eine Fähigkeit*, see *RC*, I, #14), a form of competence—and one that non-color-blind people (including those who see only other people's color) can practice! The image of justice as a blindfolded woman conveys that sense that, though the world is normally sighted, and draws particular (sometimes hasty) conclusions from looking, to know something about color-blindness just might mean not taking looking for seeing (a lesson, to use *Oedipus* as an example, that Teiresias presents to both Oedipus, and later, to Creon. The Western tradition of the blind man—rarely the blind woman—as wise visionary is partially traced in Jacques Derrida's *Memoirs of the Blind*). "[L]ooking does not teach us anything about the concepts of colours" (*RC*, I, #72).

That last remark about looking directs our attention to the edifying nature of Wittgenstein's text, his effort to reeducate (when *lernen* in his text means training, raising up) us regarding color by suggesting that we think about color-blindness (a state of justice?), and seek out mutual understanding about color issues, which does not mean that one completely ignores color as a determining ingredient in someone's life, particularly if that person claims that color has been decisive. Wittgenstein says, "That I can be someone's friend rests on the fact that he [*sic*] has the same *possibilities* as I myself have, or similar ones" (*RC*, III, #301), and this can include the possibility of understanding that people can share color just as they can share bloodlines. Piper directs "white" attention to this possibility that those who imagine themselves "snow white" can be covered by the drift of color: "The ultimate test of a person's repudiation of racism is not what she can contemplate *doing* for or on behalf of black people, but whether she herself can contemplate calmly the likelihood of *being* black" (PWPB, 19). At least in the United States, this likelihood has been a live one, particularly with respect to what is called "the one-drop rule," which until recently, defined "as black a person with as little as a single drop of 'black blood,'" a notion derived from a misplaced belief that each race has its own blood type.[35]

Like Piper, Wittgenstein encourages us to rethink our "bad prejudices" (to borrow a phrase from John McDowell), and the prejudices at work in our words (*RC*, III, #101). "We could say people's concepts show what matters to them and what doesn't. But it's not as if this *explained* the particular concepts they have. It is only to rule out the view that we have the right concepts and other people the wrong ones" (*RC*, III, #293).

Wittgenstein suggests here that the color-aware and the color-blind occupy the same space, even that a single person can be color-aware at one moment and color-blind the next, and that these two kinds of people can benefit by communicating with each other, to keep each other aware of multiple ways of seeing (for example, the duck/rabbit from the *Philosophical Investigations*), thus increasing visual agility (the way a blindfold does), without sinking into an empty, racist pluralism. One can depend on the other for a degree of self-understanding and solidarity, which Wittgenstein puts this way: "And remember, too, that a human being might go through life without his colour-blindness being noticed, until some special occasion brings it to light" (*RC*, III, #31).

The current discussions about color and race have made many "whites" aware of their color. West says, "[W]e must focus our attention on the public square—the common good that undergirds our national and global destinies. The vitality of any public square ultimately depends on how much we *care* about the quality of our lives together" (West, *Race Matters*, 6). Alluding to James Ellison, West also underscores the importance of language in a warning: "Either we learn a new language of empathy and compassion, or the fire this time will consume us all" (8). This seems to be an echo of Wittgenstein's statement: "What I actually want to say is that here too it is not a matter of the *words* one uses or of what one is thinking when using them, but rather of the difference they make at various points in life" (RC, III, #317). And the difference that color words can make in the present lies almost entirely outside the boundaries of philosophy, where color perception from philosophy's perspective does not seem to have anything to do with human relationships, nor with politics. Taking Wittgenstein's *Remarks on Colour* as remarks on racism is a step toward bringing this text out of the university and into the street discussion about color and race going on among the mottled masses.

Notes

1. Ludwig Wittgenstein, *Culture and Value*, trans. Peter Winch (Chicago: University of Chicago Press, 1980), 66e. The German is *"Farben regen zum Philosophieren an,"* and the German verb *anregen* means "to stimulate," or "to animate." As Stanley Cavell suggests, Wittgenstein is a philosopher who seeks to awaken us, as if we are sometimes dead to the world. (This deadness might be especially true for "whites." See Richard Dyer, "White," *Screen* 29 [Autumn 1988]: 44–64, particularly his discussion of *Night of the Living Dead*.)

For more on Cavell and Wittgenstein, see note 2 below, as well as Stephen Mulhall, *Stanley Cavell: Philosophy's Recounting of the Ordinary* (Oxford: Clarendon Press, 1994), 164–65.

2. Stephen Melville, "Color Has Not Yet Been Named: Objectivity in Deconstruction," in *Deconstruction and the Visual Arts: Art, Media, Architecture*, ed. Peter Brunette and David Wills (New York: Cambridge University Press, 1994).

3. "Revelation in the Jewish Tradition," trans. Sarah Richmond, in *The Levinas Reader*, ed. Sean Hand (Cambridge: Basil Blackwell, 1989), 193.

4. See Ludwig Wittgenstein, *Cambridge Letters: Correspondence with Russell, Keynes, Moore, Ramsey, and Sraffa*, ed. Brian McGuinness and (Oxford: Blackwell, 1995), 300.

5. By the end of this essay, my hope is that it will be clear that the phrase "people of color" means all the people, including "whites." The phrase might be no less offensive than other terms, as Adrian Piper points out: "[C]ooking up new ways to classify those whom we degrade ultimately changes nothing but the vocabulary of degradation." See Piper's "Passing for White, Passing for Black," *Transition* 58 (1991): 30; hereafter cited as PWPB followed by page number. My thanks to Naomi Scheman for making this article available to me.

6. John Gage, *Color and Culture: Practice and Meaning from Antiquity to Abstraction* (Toronto: Little, Brown, 1993), 7. Gage's splendid text is a history of color, but again, human color is not

addressed. In a sense, Gage's book is an expanded, scholarly version of Derek Jarman's *Chroma* (London: Century, 1994). Another Gage essay worth noting is "Colour and Culture," in *Colour: Art and Science*, ed. Trevor Lamb and Janine Bourriau (New York: Cambridge University Press, 1995).

Another book like Gage's but of a more interdisciplinary nature is Charles A. Riley's *Color Codes: Modern Theories of Color in Philosophy, Painting, and Architecture, Literature, Music, and Psychology* (Hanover: University Press of New England, 1995).

For what might be called a materialist reading of color, see Manlio Brusatin *A History of Colors*, trans. Robert H. Hopcke and Paul Schwartz (Boston: Shambhala, 1991).

7. Ludwig Wittgenstein, *Remarks on Colour*, ed. G. E. M. Anscombe, trans. Linda L. McAlister and Margarete Schättle (Berkeley and Los Angeles: University of California Press, 1977); hereafter cited in the text as *RC* followed by the section and the number of the remark. For some of the remarks, I have slightly altered the translations to make them more literal.

8. Wendy Lee-Lampshire, "The Sound of Little Hummingbird Wings: A Wittgensteinian Investigation of Forms of Life as Forms of Power," *Feminist Studies* 25, no. 2 (1999): 409–26. Were it important for readers to know my own position regarding feminism, I would point such readers to Geoff Waite's *Nietzsche's Corps/e: Aesthetics, Politics, Prophecy, or the Spectacular Technoculture of Everyday Life* (Durham: Duke University Press, 1996). See my review of Waite's book in *Dialogue: Canadian Philosophical Review* 36 (1998): 125–28.

9. Alasdair MacIntyre, "Colors, Cultures, and Practices," in *Midwest Studies in Philosophy XVII: The Wittgenstein Legacy*, ed. Peter A. French et al. (Notre Dame: University of Notre Dame Press, 1992), 1–23; and Jonathan Westphal, *Colour* (Oxford: Oxford University Press, 1987). See also C. L. Hardin's *Color for Philosophers: Unweaving the Rainbow* (Indianapolis: Hackett, 1988). Wittgenstein plays almost no role in the two-volume collection titled *Readings on Color* (vol. 1: *The Philosophy of Color* and vol. 2: *The Science of Color*), ed. Alex Byrne and David R. Hilbert (Cambridge: MIT Press, 1997).

10. Jarman, *Chroma*, 27.

11. Stanley Cavell, "Postscript (1989): To Whom It May Concern," *Critical Inquiry* 16 (Winter 1990): 256. In another passage in this article, Cavell connects color, particularly the philosopher's color—purple—to Wittgenstein: "Now when I said, just now, that in Wittgenstein's closet there are bouts or fears of madness and cited his purple remarks about spider's webs and bewitchment and destruction of importance and unrelieved torment, I meant those citations as depictions of the closet, not as instances of what is expressed there. [Where is Wittgenstein's closet?] Those purple or 'excessive' expressions are possible only from one who knows the closet, that is, knows the philosophical door, hence wall, between the ordinary and something that sides against it" (259).

12. In Derek Jarman, *Wittgenstein: The Terry Eagleton Script, the Derek Jarman Film* (London: BFI, 1993), 67.

13. Some of these fears are wonderfully spelled out in Adrian Piper's "Two Kinds of Discrimination," *Yale Journal of Criticism* 6 (1993): 25–74. While Piper's discussion of discrimination is compelling, I cannot recommend her urgings about using art to combat certain forms of discrimination (see 68–69). Her Kantian picture of the static, "impersonal" work of art leaves art at the level of object for the viewer, and thus remains another of the spectator theories of art.

14. Edward Averill, "Color and the Anthropocentric Problem," *Journal of Philosophy*, 82 (June 1985): 293.

15. Dyer, "White," 45. The last phrase in the quotation comes from a video titled *Being White*. See also Thomas DiPiero, "White Men Aren't," *Camera Obscura* 30 (May 1992): 113–37. My thanks to Caryl Flinn for bringing Dyer's essay to my attention, and for her insightful commentary on an earlier draft of this essay.

16. Stanley Cavell has tried to make the case for Wittgenstein as a philosopher of culture in "Declining Decline: Wittgenstein as a Philosopher of Culture," in *This New Yet Unapproachable America: Lectures After Emerson After Wittgenstein* (Albuquerque: Living Batch Press, 1989), 29–75.

17. Stanley Cavell, *Philosophical Passages: Wittgenstein, Emerson, Austin, Derrida* (Cambridge: Blackwell, 1995), 158.

18. I have the following works in mind: E. K. Rand, *Founders of the Middle Ages* (New York: Dover, 1928); Robert Lamberton, *Homer the Theologian: Neoplatonist Allegorical Reading and the Growth of the Epic Tradition* (Berkeley and Los Angeles: University of California Press, 1986); David Dawson, *Allegorical Readers and Cultural Revision in Ancient Alexandria* (Berkeley and Los Angeles: University of California Press, 1992). All three of these works will serve as the proof texts, and will clarify the dialectic at work in allegory—both readers and texts appropriating each other. Rand deals with the ways in which the early Christian church had to cope with people immersed in a pagan culture. Given that the Christians could not ignore the pagan culture, the task was, as Rand puts it, to "reconcile" the old with the new, and one of the forms of reconciliation was for Christians to see that pagan texts could speak to the new Christian context. As the title of Lamberton's book suggests, it was not impossible for later people to look at Homer as a theologian. Lamberton demonstrates the ways in which Homer was "reread" with a new set of concerns in mind, so that the texts come alive again in a new context, and reveal themselves to have a capacity for being understood in a variety of ways. Dawson presents the case forcefully:

> [S]ome ancient pagan, Jewish, and Christian interpreters used allegory to endorse, revise, and subvert competing world views and forms of life. . . . [A]ncient allegory is best understood not only as a way of reading texts, but also as a way of using that reading to reinterpret culture and society . . . , [and] to promote alternative ways of being in the world. . . . The very tensions between literal and nonliteral readings that characterized ancient allegory stemmed from efforts by readers to secure for themselves and their communities social and cultural identity, authority, and power. (*Allegorical Readers*, 1–2)

The interpreters Dawson has in mind come to texts not to determine authorial intention, nor to lay bare the methodology of a text, but to reinscribe what matters to those reading allegorically. (Part II of Dawson's book is called "The Reinscription of Reality.") The presupposition at work here is that alien cultures make sense, and that alien texts have relevance in unforeseen circumstances. The interpreters see the alien texts as belonging to the present, hear the texts as speaking again, and then refigure things to help the alien texts participate in contemporary affairs. In current literary theory this process is more frequently called appropriation. The allegorizer of note for Dawson is Philo Judaeus, the Greek who translates the Hebrew Bible. (See Gerald Bruns, "Allegory as Radical Interpretation" in his *Hermeneutics Ancient and Modern* [New Haven: Yale University Press, 1992], 83–103. Bruns says, "I think of Philo as the greatest allegorist in antiquity, one of history's great masters of commentary and in many ways foundational for the history of interpretation, but I'm not sure anyone agrees with this" [86]). Philo does not spend time attempting to recover the original meaning of the text, but in commenting on the Hebrew Bible in light of his (Greek) community's concerns.

19. Johann Wolfgang von Goethe, *Theory of Colours*, trans. Charles Lock Eastlake (Cambridge: MIT Press, 1970). Here again, a book about color is more than it seems. In Nicholas Boyle's biography of Goethe, he says that the occasion of Goethe's decision to take up a study of color "has more than once been compared to a religious conversion. . . . A recent exegesis, of great brilliance, has shown that the underlying structure of Goethe's unwearying argument for a new chromatics is that of a defence of Arianism—the heretical belief that Christ was not divine—against the tyrannical sophistries of the established Trinitarian Christology. Light is tortured, indeed crucified, with the instruments of the scientists, who, like a churchful of theologians parroting inherited dogmas, endeavour to split up the pure simplicity of divinity into seven colours or three persons or some other magical number in which they would rather put their trust than in what their eyes and their reason tell them." See Boyle, *Goethe: The Poet and His Age*, vol. 1 (Oxford: Oxford University Press, 1992), 645.

See also Claudia J. Brodsky, "The Coloring of Relations: *Die Wahlverwandtschaften* as *Farbenlehre*" in her *The Imposition of Form: Studies in Narrative Represenation and Knowledge* (Princeton: Princeton University Press, 1987), 88–138. David Adams kindly told me about this connection.

20. Jaakko Hintikka, "Obstacles to Understanding," *Times Literary Supplement* 4565 (September 28–October 4, 1990): 1030. See also David G. Stern "The Availability of Wittgenstein's Philosophy," in *The Cambridge Companion to Wittgenstein*, ed. Hans Sluga and David G. Stern (Cambridge: Cambridge University Press, 1996), 442–76. The first part of the Bergen Electronic Edition of Wittgenstein's *Nachlass* (Oxford: Oxford University Press, 1998) is now available, but volume 1 does not help explicitly with sorting out *Remarks on Colour*. One seemingly significant erasure takes place in *Philosophische Bemerkungen* (band 17, item 121, p. 29v), where Wittgenstein has crossed out "*Rasse*" and used "*Volk*" instead.

21. Derek Jarman, *Wittgenstein*, 63.

22. Marjorie Perloff, "Toward an Avant-Garde *Tractatus*: Russell and Wittgenstein on War," *Common Knowledge* 2 (Spring 1993): 15–34.

23. Wittgenstein, *Culture and Value*, p. 20e.

24. Sander L. Gilman, *Jewish Self-Hatred: Anti-Semitism and the Hidden Language of the Jews* (Baltimore: Johns Hopkins University Press, 1986), 7. My thanks to Richard Heinemann for this reference.

25. For more on Wittgenstein's openness, see the chapter "Andgame: Wittgenstein, Bakhtin, and Literary Theory," in my *Traveling with Hermes: Hermeneutics and Rhetoric* (Amherst: University of Massachusetts Press, 1992), 72–83.

26. Oliver Sacks, *An Anthropologist on Mars: Seven Paradoxical Tales* (New York: Knopf, 1995), 6.

27. This phrase about seeing color "in the mind's eye" has particular importance for John McDowell's discussion of Wittgenstein in *Mind and World* (Cambridge: Harvard University Press, 1994).

28. See Slavoj Žižek's essay "The Abyss of Freedom," in Slavoj Žižek /F. W. J. von Schelling, *The Abyss of Freedom/Ages of the World* (Ann Arbor: University of Michigan Press, 1997). He writes that "multiculturalism suspends the traumatic kernel of the Other, reducing it to an aseptic folklorist entity. . . . [H]earing "The Star-Spangled Banner" gives no thrill, yet what does give a thrill is listening to some ritual of Native Americans, of African-Americans" (26–27).

29. Oliver Sacks, *The Island of the Colorblind* (New York: Knopf, 1997), 6. The relevant text for thinking about some intrinsic philosophical problems with "social construction" is Ian Hacking's *The Social Construction of What?* (Cambridge: Harvard University Press, 1999). Despite its sometimes patronizing and pedantic tone, Hacking's book does point to some fundamental difficulties with "social construction." Hacking writes, "The trouble is that social construction has become a part of the very discourse that it presents itself as trying to undo" (36).

30. Ludwig Wittgenstein, *Philosophical Occasions, 1912–1951*, ed. James Klagge and Alfred Nordmann (Indianapolis: Hackett, 1993), 28.

31. My thanks to Charles Riley for bringing Byron Kim's work to my attention.

32. Catharine A. MacKinnon, *Feminism Unmodified: Discourses on Life and Law* (Cambridge: Harvard University Press, 1987), 65. See also Amy Gutmann, "Must Public Policy Be Color Blind?" in K. Anthony Appiah and Amy Gutmann, *Color Conscious: The Political Morality of Race* (Princeton: Princeton University Press, 1996), 118–38.

33. For more on this, see Jonathan Crary, *Techniques of the Observer: On Vision and Modernity in the Nineteenth Century* (Cambridge: MIT Press, 1990), 67–99.

34. See the introduction to Cornel West, *Race Matters* (Boston: Beacon Press, 1993), 1–8.

35. Lawrence Wright, "Annals of Politics: One Drop of Blood," *New Yorker*, 25 July 1994, 48. This article outlines the problems the Census Bureau has had trying to categorize people by race. As Wright explains, "The categories became political entities, with their own constituencies, lobbies, and vested interests. What was even more significant, they caused people to think of themselves in new ways—as members of 'races' that were little more than statistical devices" (52–53). This corroborates Dyer's claims above.

19

Culture, Nature, *Ecosystem* (or Why Nature Can't Be Naturalized)

Rupert Read

"Man is born natural and is everywhere in culture."

My quasi-epigraph might very naturally lead us to consider the following question: If it is true that humans are or were at the outset natural, and that it is our cultures and civilizations that have led to the earth's increasing devastation, then how should such we react to this devastation, if not by affirming Nature and severely interrogating Culture? I want to suggest that there is something very problematic about the phrasing of

A previous version of this paper was given on 17 April 1993 at the Binghamton, New York, "Nature, Truth, and Culture" conference—thanks to those present for insightful questions. I also wish to thank Gordon Bleach, Shelly Fitzgerald, John Fritzman, Anne De Vivo, Tobyn De Marco, Jeff Buechner, Simon Stevens, Naomi Scheman, Richard Rorty, and an anonymous referee for comments and encouragement. 'Naturally', any and all infelicities in the text are entirely my own such questions as this. They continue a venerable intellectual tradition, which we may term for convenience the "Culture versus Nature" debate. This debate involves further questions such as, Which is responsible for the other? Does Nature provide the substance, and Culture just a few trimmings? Or is Nature fully constructed by Culture, materially and metaphysically a human artifact?

I wish to subvert the conversation that would have us continue to act as if the question, Does Nature make Culture, or vice versa? were a live one. I contend that the question is actually deeply moribund—though *not* because it can be decisively answered one way or another. Rather, we need to reorient the conversation.

It will be my contention that some of the major innovations in Western philosophical thought in the twentieth century have long since provided the materials with which to thoroughly *evade* the Nature-versus-Culture debate, to dissolve the profound philosophical problematic it purports to pursue.[1] I shall concentrate here on briefly setting out the sense and degree to which *Wittgenstein* (and also both twentieth-century U.S. Pragmatism and much twentieth-century feminist philosophy) have made vital (and substantially unrecognized) progress in the direction of not perpetuating obfuscation through the use of terms such as *Nature* and *Culture*.[2] Are there more positive reasons why we should wish to end the Nature-versus-Culture debate? I believe so, and that they have to do with being able to say and do things that are environmentally ethical and yet politically pragmatic (which is *not* to be equated with *compromised*). Concretely, the possibility for which I will argue is that it is possible to reforge our environment (including ourselves) in the best ways possible without trying forlornly to separate out which elements in that environment are "genuinely natural."

What follows then is an effort, in the spirit of Wittgenstein, thoroughly to interrogate the Nature-versus-Culture debate, much as Wittgenstein interrogated the supposed question of the "outer" versus the "inner," and associated pseudodebates in philosophy such as that between "behaviorists" and "dualists," or "rationalists" and "empiricists."

Somebody, a literary theorist eager to resolve interdisciplinary misunderstandings perhaps, might at this point wish to intervene to say: "I can help end the debate: Why not simply stress Culture, given the ubiquity of human construction of the world we live in? After all, the 'hardest' of hard scientists is still at work in a community of inquiry, in a cultural setting; all of us are in the final analysis *really* creators and analyzers of texts." All the world's a text, and men and women merely its authors, as it were.

A reply must center on the point that the conceptualization of Culture as all-pervasive, as if everything that humans touch turns to Culture, is highly problematic. The problem is: such a totalization of Culture, if intended to play an explanatory or foundational role with regard to Nature, is ultimately *empty*.

Now, to see this, one has to face a systematic ambiguity in the term *construct* that alone gives the hypothetical intervention *any* plausibility. Namely, is it being envisaged that Civilization now limitlessly (re-)constructs Nature physically/materially, through our rapacious biotechnological power; or is a more fundamental sense of *metaphysical* construction—through representational/epistemic categories—being envisaged?[3] In the former sense, it is fairly obvious that some elements at least of Nature will remain impervious to or antecedent to human construction. That is, humans cannot literally create or construct all or even most phenomena that we are inclined to call "natural," even if it is possible to alter or destroy—to reconstruct, perhaps—many. As for the latter sense of *construct*: if *everything* is culturally constructed then nothing is *explained* merely by the invoking of this "social/cultural construction."[4] To say that nature is totally culturally constructed in this sense is as yet actually to *say* nothing. This is so even if we think of the construction in question as being through the kind of idealized formalization that overtook nature with the scientific revolution[5]—that is, if the cultural construction in question is through *scientific* culture. For such construction can only be reconstruction, of *some* things; if it is supposed to extend to *everything* then we are only expressing our determination not to allow anything to be described in terms other than scientific terms—we are not yet saying anything in those (or any other) terms.

There is any plausibility to a strong Culturalist/constructionist thesis[6] only before its inherent ambiguity is unmasked—in other words, before we realize that such a thesis is either false (if taken in the material sense) or vacuous (if taken in the metaphysical sense).[7]

Let us now consider a related ambiguity in 'Nature'. As has already been hinted, some life-scientists and environmentalists tend to run together at least two senses of the word *Nature*—one, in which Nature is *everything*, is inescapable and all-encompassing, because (emptily) totalized; a second, in which Nature is something certainly not wholly dominated by "Man," and is (at least potentially) separable from Culture (we might designate what those who thus equivocate have in common "Naturalist").[8] Only in the second sense can Nature have a normative role—as something to destroy, to fight, to master, to explore, to protect, to cherish, to *become* one with. In the first sense, everything we do, no matter what it is, is natural, to be described and explained "naturalistically." So one can draw no conclusions about whether to protect or respect something because it is part of nature, in this sense. Someone who totalizes nature has nothing to say to an opponent who claims, for instance, that aggression is a natural drive, or even that causing mass devastation is just humankind's (or AIDS's) natural mission.

It is the second sense of *nature* that is of particular interest in the present essay, because it has more ethical attractions—it might well with some justice be thought to allow for the "defense of Nature" position mentioned at the start of this essay.[9] But again, this cuts both ways—for Nature as the not human can as easily be attacked as defended. This second sense of *Nature,* then, is arguably one in which Nature has assumed the figure of "Woman." To take an instance of this, consider "Gaia" imagery—doesn't it always run the real risk of buying into the very stereotypes that one is trying elsewhere in one's work and life to overcome?[10] The worry is this: that Nature will be alternately respected, romanticized, raped, and reclaimed repeatedly at least until this conceptualization of "Her" is emended or ended. I am claiming that a risk *intrinsic* to the rhetoric of many ecologists, to (for example) the rhetoric of "Mother Earth," is an immediate consequence of this being in the main only the flip side of the old rhetoric and strategies of "mastering," "conquering," and "husbanding" (the last in particular a term extremely ripe for feminist analysis and deconstruction in this context!). Those who support and cherish *Nature* (in the second sense given above) risk supporting only the long-running dialectic of adoration versus debasement, a "dialectic" unlikely to rescue us from the ongoing devastation of the earth. . . . If one sees plainly the disambiguated senses of *nature* which actually undergird this side of the debate, one will opt for neither; which, once again, is why those who invoke the figure of "Nature" figured female—whether to disrespect her, or to discover her, or to defy her, or to deify Her, or to delight in her—often take care, again, not to effect such disambiguation.[11]

Now, of course, some feminists employ the rhetoric of Mother Earth. Whether or not one does, one ought at least to show an awareness of the dangers of relying on *either* sense of *nature* as given earlier (or, worse still, on systematic ambiguity between them). Radical Feminist Mary Daly is a major example of a feminist philosopher who has shown just such an acute awareness. The twin risks of making whatever happens natural (and therefore "OK") on the one hand, and of viewing/figuring the earth as female on the other, come together in Daly's unexpectedly savage critique of the "Gaia hypothesis." The Gaia hypothesis apparently glorifies the beauty and wonder of the "organism" that is the Earth-Goddess, while potentially allowing that (say) nuclear holocaust *could* be part of the natural process of our planet's "development." In other words, it is compatible with the Gaia hypothesis that the earth might "protect herself" by fomenting mass destruction, mass extinction. One could read Daly's gyn-ecological quest as that of the finding of a path toward making sense of *our* being 'always already' not just interdependent with, but part of, the planet, and even of one another, and so forth. A sense of this profound nonalienation is what this essay is all about. By contrast, the "respect and love" adduced for Gaia by the proponents of the Gaia hypothesis reeks of a deep othering.[12] It is as though these latter who are studying (for example, like some life-scientists) or glorifying (for example, some deep ecologists and—in this respect—some non-Dalyian feminists) the biosphere cannot succeed in coherently and deeply envisioning themselves as *part* of it.

According to my analysis thus far, then, proenvironmental thinkers and activists, those who truly ("deeply") understand themselves to be *of* the world, have reason to be strongly suspicious of the invocation of terms such as *Cultural Construction* and *Nature*. And one might worry that, even were our discourse or at least our understandings of these terms to be recast to take account of such suspicion, there might still be certain undesirable aspects of the Nature-versus-Culture debate that we would be unable to avoid perpetuating. Particularly, the alienation between the two central terms of the debate or any replacements for them, their "object versus subject" orientation. And thus the discursive situation would remain substantively the same, even though we might have appeared to move on to a less intrinsically problematic position. Although I cannot hope to illustrate this in every actual or possible case, let me tackle once more an apparent counterexample to my suggestion that invoking (for example) "Nature" in a novel way is not enough to free one from the vicissitudes of the Nature-versus-Culture dualism. The apparent *counterexample* is of certain major strands in the Green movement, in contemporary ecological consciousness and practice.

I wish to build here on the arguments of Jim Cheney, in particular on his article "The Neo-Stoicism of Radical Environmentalism."[13] While disagreeing with his conclusion, which is (insofar as I can grasp it) that what we *really* need in order to save our planet is "a politics of difference," I would endorse the bulk of his arguments, which are directed against the strands in (particularly) Deep Ecology which *perpetuate* humans' alienation from our environment. Cheney puts it as follows: "[Fox, Devall, Sessions, and others] contribute, in certain of their theoretical formulations, to the continuation of the very alienation from nature that they consciously oppose,"[14] such that "[w]ith the exception of tribal peoples, the voices of oppressed people are disenfranchised by [them]. . . . Ecological consciousness is the consciousness of modernist alienation seeking reconnection with that from which it has lost touch. To that extent it is going in the right direction. But it speaks from alienation and does not escape it. The remedy is not . . . salvational politics."[15]

I follow Cheney in holding that one can only seriously foster or follow an ethic of becoming-one-with-nature, or of putting the earth first, if one conceives of the relation between humans and natural environment as in the first instance an *adversarial* one. Such an adversarial picture, which unfortunately we find in the "alienated" "salvational" politics of some Deep Ecologists, runs roughly as follows: Nature, unalloyed and untouched by human hands (let alone human minds/language/cultures), must be rigorously distinguished from and set against Humankind. . . . It is said that "Man," the destructive animal, will technologize and colonize Nature into oblivion—unless a lesson of peace with the planet, of reunion with the oceanic Maternal figure is achieved. The point is that the Green movement runs the *risk*, the danger, of presupposing exactly the alienation of culture, of humans, from their/our natural surroundings that it *exists* to oppose and overcome (except—for contemporary Westerners—possibly in some fantasized long-past era). The rhetoric of achieving peace with the planet, or of putting the earth first . . . all of this, its tactical value notwithstanding, is a problematic rhetoric still of *subject and object*, of alienation.

My present suggestion is that we—philosophers, literary critics, feminists, life scientists, environmentalists—set aside envisioning this general terrain as one of Nature and Culture(s), that we endeavor *to overcome the Nature versus Culture debate altogether*. And this means, among other things, foreswearing so far as is possible any affirmative invocation of Nature and the natural, per se.

"Inhabitants of the world unite: you have nothing to lose but (human) culture."

A key question for the remainder of the essay is in effect whether this quasi-epigraph has any more use than—or makes any more sense than—that with which I commenced the essay.

But if one's suspicions that it does not are well founded, still, *how* are we to evade the Nature-versus-Culture debate and the confusing academic culture that it has bred?

The core of the proposal lying in some of the greatest philosophizing of the first half of the twentieth century (and explored in more-concrete terms in some feminist and other political thought and activism, as briefly discussed later) is simple—almost, but not quite, too simple. We have to overcome the trick of language that seduces us into seeing human cultures as in any sense necessarily opposed to "what surrounds us." But this is best affected *not* by totalizing Nature, as we saw earlier, nor yet by totalizing Culture. We have instead to gain a clear view—an *übersicht*—of our practices (including, but not only, our linguistic practices), and of what these presuppose—*our "engulfment" in "the world,"* or more prosaically, our being a part of it; rather than either cultivating *or* directly countering a fantasized alienation from it.

Let me turn to the philosophers who were I think the first fully to recognize this: *Dewey* and, perhaps less directly but more crucially, because more diagnostically effectively, *Wittgenstein*. This recognition facilitates the abandonment of uses of the theoretical linguistic practices that tend to perpetuate the Nature-versus-Culture problematic.

Dewey argued in various works that, if one was to talk about nature and culture at all, then cultures were best understood as, very roughly, "special cases" of nature.[16] That is, he held human behavior to be the most complex and rapidly evolving of all phenomena, but not qualitatively distinguishable from other animal behavior. Insofar as it could make sense to distinguish between cultures and "the natural world" *at all*, then, the distinction would be one of degree—more "versus" less complex; and more "versus" less malleable.

Thus if one wishes to talk, as philosophers and some others are strongly inclined to do, of Culture, or Nature, or "the World," one should talk— one would be best advised so to talk, if one wishes to avoid potentially disabling philosophical and ultimately political confusions—roughly as follows: human cultures are communities of organisms that have reached a certain level of complexity and organization. They are not set against the natural (world) in the sense that there is some special feature unique to the human (Culture), which others (for example, "primitive" humans, animals) lack. And one should emphasize that it is (overlapping) communities actively coping with the conditions that they meet that are engulfed in or a part of this world. This is crucial because one can then evade the worry that in doing away with Nature versus Culture one is doing away with sociality altogether.[17]

When one combines attention to Wittgenstein with this Deweyan perspective, a view of humans as *copers* with their context (including crucially their sociolinguistic surroundings), becomes much more achievable still.[18] And "context" and "surroundings" are *not*, in Wittgenstein, found in the misleading and potentially dangerous guise of either Nature *or* Culture. Rather, what Wittgenstein termed our "forms of life"/"patterns of living"[19] are *internally* related to . . . "the world"? Perhaps, but— perhaps better still—a word more appropriate for what we are necessarily, undifferentiatedly engulfed in, and engaged in, is . . . our *environment(s)*. Wittgenstein held that each of the following three formulations amounts to much the same:[20] that we judge similarly; that we share a pattern of living (or "form of life"); and that we (in other words, any community of speakers/hearers/copers) simply *share a common environment* that we are always already a part of, an environment in which the "cultural" elements and the "natural" elements are *not qualitatively distinguishable*.

To see this, consider the following: in virtue of what might one consider that a group of animals has a culture? Possibly we would say that a bunch of dolphins or baboons held in cages "under laboratory conditions" do not; but what would be the ground for saying this of such a bunch acting in a context that did not prevent their *interaction*? Only, I think, the reasonable presumption that by and large they don't have *language:*

"It is sometimes said that animals do not talk because they lack the mental capacity. And this means: 'they do not think, and that is why they do not talk.' But—they simply do not talk. Or to put it better: they do not use language—if we accept the most primitive forms of language."[21]

"All" this comes to is the following: the "linguistic" behavior engaged in by nonhuman animals is not of sufficient complexity to earn the name of "language"; but beyond this brute facticity we have no reason for denying that nonhuman animals can have / can be part of culture, for some

do have reproducible "social systems" of a kind that involve mutual engagement in and with their environment, an environment that they partially constitute and continually modify. But if this description is sound,
then *on what principled basis* is the dividing line between culture and
nonculture to be drawn?

In Dewey's works the very term *environment* is used in precisely the
way indicated earlier, as marking and involving an *inextricability* of what
have been called cultural and natural elements.[22] And while Wittgenstein's practice involved no such explicit usage of the term, a conception of existence as active engagement as a part(icipant) in a whole or
wholes is among the most crucial of his later philosophical insights. It is
common ground between Wittgenstein and Dewey then that the envi-
ronment(s) of human animals are inextricably cultural/natural, and this
is the locus of "a connection of a man [*sic*], in the way of both dependence and support, with the enveloping world."[23]

But it might seem as though *the environment* were not a term different
enough from *nature* to terminate the Nature-versus-Culture debate, and
involve us in more productive conversation or action. Some might say
that the preexisting affirmative *environmentalist* appropriation of the term
is enough to remove it from any possibility of significantly re-orienting
our debate(s). Alternatively: isn't it true not only that the word *environment* is already saturated with meaning(s), but that our media culture is
saturated with the discourse of "environment," and it just isn't working?[24]
Perhaps most crucially of all, as we shall discuss later: Is "environment"
not a concept that tends to refer to or at least to connote something
standing outside of one in much the same way as "Nature"?

Allow me to begin a response to these concerns somewhat obliquely.
Dewey has on occasion been called a scientific naturalist;[25] Wittgenstein,
a deflationary naturalist.[26] These terms may be happy enough, so long
as (in Dewey's case) they don't distract one into thinking of scientific
naturalism after the fashion of a Quine or a Chomsky[27]—if Dewey is a
scientific naturalist, he is so only in that his *rhetoric* included the adoption by philosophy of "scientific methods," while Wittgenstein's did not;
and that Dewey's philosophy of science called for attention to the realities of experimental science,[28] while Wittgenstein was simply not in any
direct sense a philosopher of science. Much more significant is *their agreement* on the repudiation of any supernaturalism (now very widely shared),
and on there being no gap between "the sociocultural" and "the natural."

A comparison of the following quotations illustrates this crucial latter point:

> [A human] is naturally a being that lives in association with others in communities possessing language, and therefore enjoying a transmitted culture.[29]

> Commanding, questioning, recounting, chatting, are as much a part of our natural history as walking, eating, drinking, playing.[30]

On the Dewey-Wittgenstein conception, if humans' culture is to be "naturalized" thus, and if nonhuman animals cannot be said plainly not to have a culture, but at most only not to have a sophisticated language, *what is left* to be distinctively and definitively Cultural?

Now, Wittgenstein would have disliked being called a 'naturalist'—but just because he could not stand being dubbed an "——ist," *simpliciter*. And because he would have thought that this risked one's appearing to say that "'Culture' is really nature"—a philosophical thesis of dubious worth (like all such theses). His most prolific of interpreters, Gordon Baker and Peter Hacker, have written that his perspective might accurately and be summed up as "culturally naturalist," and this seems OK, providing we understand this term in a deflationary fashion, not as connoting adherence to any "thesis."[31] Now, the term Dewey chose for himself is more or less explicitly an effort to evade or supersede Nature versus Culture; this term was "cultural naturalist."[32]

But perhaps there are still happier terms available; perhaps what Dewey and Wittgenstein suggest to us is that we self-identify as small-*e* *environmentalists*.

The advantages of the term *environment* begin with the observation that this term may have the capacity to displace *both culture* and *nature*. And we have now seen why such displacement is necessary; for if there is no opposition between the terms *nature* and *culture*, then there is point neither in holding that "everything is natural," nor in finding nature to be normative. Ironically enough, Nature can neither be naturalized (that is, taken to refer by reduction or by some other theoretic means to some actually existing entity), nor usefully invoked in ethical discourse. The term *environment* can help us succeed where the dualistic terms have failed if we understand ourselves as already *part of* most environments that we describe. And if we understand *environment* not as a near-synonym for *nature*, talk of one's environment *need not* be an attempt to *discriminate* between first nature, second nature, and nonnature.

A further advantage of the term then is that its pluralization is much more straightforward than in the case of *nature*—it can make perfect sense to talk of environments of massively different scales, and forms.

But there remains one simple but crucial problem, one reason why the queries raised earlier concerning the usefulness of "environment" may finally be telling: it is *still* just a little too easy to see one's environment as something *external* to one (compare the frequent use among [say] politicians of the phrase "the natural environment" as a quasi-synonym for *nature*). There is a term available that circumvents this difficulty while retaining all the advantages of *environment* detailed earlier, and remaining true to the insights of Wittgenstein and company: *ecosystem*. It is built into the concept that one cannot sustain an external perspective toward one's ecosystem(s).

My proposal, my suggestion, then, comes down this: that we try refraining completely from the vocabulary of nature and culture, and instead work seriously and passionately with the vocabulary of different, and in most cases of *preferable/less preferable ecosystem(s)*. The latter notion is harmlessly parasitic upon actually preferred and not preferred ecosystems (by which is meant that normative judgments require no transcendental foundations, but are "grounded" simply in our concrete practices of judging and acting).[33]

Imagine at this point the following objection: "But then has anything been achieved? For everything will rest on who does the designating of 'preferable' and 'not preferable.' And will there not run throughout a deep anthropocentrism—which is to prejudge against the biocentrism that many Deep Ecologists, among others, endorse?"

The worry motivating the latter question simply *has no substance* unless one *first* sets up an antithesis of humans versus nature—for, beyond this antithesis, humans (and also those organisms that humans have changed, introduced, and so on) are *part* of the "bios" that one talks of centering. And the former question *similarly* fails to appreciate the point that we have *nowhere* to begin but with ways that we would have or experience our surroundings, if we could. The exact identity of this "we" will simply have to be contested, where it is contestable, through whatever sociopolitical channels are available. For instance, the inclusion of nonhuman animals in a "we" will have to be attested to and contested for, generally on a case-by-case basis. What I am suggesting here and will further argue below is that to focus on our ecosystem(s) (including us) as a whole(s), to which we can (and inevitably will) make a difference, can be *empowering*, and sanguine.

Roughly this line of response to roughly these questions is already available in the work of various thinkers on the environment / on ecology who have been influenced by Wittgenstein (and by feminism). Let me focus in on Elizabeth Harlow's "The Human Face of Nature: Environmental Values and the Limits of Nonanthropocentrism."[34] She draws on Wittgenstein and others to outline a deflationary holism that offers "to blur the lines between fact and value, and nature and culture, and with these, the line between human and environmental values."[35] While her use of Wittgenstein is sometimes exegetically problematic, the achievement of her article lies in the way she draws out the connection between the kind of issues around which my argument thus far has centered on the one hand, and the apparent clash between "human" and "ecosystemic" values on the other.[36] For her conclusion is that the idea of such a generalized clash is and must be *merely* apparent.

Specifically, once we are nonanthropocentric to the extent of saying that "the value of natural objects and processes is not reducible to human interests or preferences," nor to "the value of the human experiences or forms of consciousness excited by them,"[37] then "environmental ethics is inescapably human-centered [only] in a way that blurs the distinction between purely 'human" and purely "environmental" values."[38] Exactly. Any more "radical" effort at theorizing and practicing a value-system "independent" of humans founders on the incoherent notion of human animals judging and acting via criteria totally independent of themselves. What I am suggesting Wittgenstein and Dewey and their authentic successors in philosophy (and even in activism) suggest is the deflation of both Culture *and* Nature, *via* the suggestion that we think and talk instead simply in terms of (local, regional, global and so on) ecosystem(s), and (of course) that we conceive of ourselves as part of those ecosystems, but not as unable to make judgments about that which we co-constitute, nor as having to judge and value without reference to ourselves—which latter is logically impossible.

At this point, we should deal with a quasi-Pragmatist objection: "But might we not reinstate Nature as that which should be changed less, and is harder to change, and Culture as that which should be changed more, and is easier to change?" *No*, for two reasons. First, historically based feminist arguments can be made that intimate that this formulation may be empty, as apparently "socially/culturally constructed" phenomena are often *more* intransigent than "purely natural" phenomena—namely, changing technologies of sex tend to outstrip our societal capabilities to transform gender stereotypes. In other words: while biotechnologies and so on render the changing of *bodies* increasingly straightforward, it is the changing of *minds* that becomes, relatively, an increasingly difficult goal. . . . And second, one simply has to *judge what should be changed, and when, in the specificity of individual situations*—and there are probably many such in which a cultural phenomenon, such as making more widely available education about politics or feminism, is arguably worth its natural costs, such as the great amount of physical resources needed to supply paper, educational materials, and so forth to facilitate this. Pick your own favorite example if you don't like this one. The point—that judgments of the worth of cultural artifacts as compared to natural ones cannot be made with full generality and a priori—is important, and hard to resist.

What I want now provisionally to suggest is that, though the rough-and-ready distinction between the *natural* and the *cultural* may stay in our ordinary language, we would do well to ignore or abjure it entirely when in engaged in any form of "theorizing," and stick to talking of the environment(s), or (often better) of the ecosystem(s), as approximately "defined" earlier. For *natural* and *cultural* have turned out not to be terms that we can reliably *hang* anything one. (The terms *nature* and *culture*, as we have seen, are in fact just too prone to lead to philosophical trouble.)

This suggestion may be hard to implement—for even the likes of Harlow and Cheney retain the term *nature* and its cognates.[39] Thus Cheney valorizes the notions of identity and difference "even though culturally constructed," and writes of the debate between Deep Ecologists and their detractors "as occurring within nature."[40] And attentive readers will already have noticed that Harlow oscillates between retaining the term *nature* and using *environmental* as a near-synonym for *natural* on the one hand—rather than in the Pragmatist-Wittgensteinian sense outlined earlier, on the other. To recapitulate: if the line of argument of the present essay is sound, then these authors would do well to consider using the term *ecosystem* for the *indissolubly* cultural/natural, and simply dropping any residual affection or nostalgia for the ideas of unalloyed Nature, or Culture.

Again, I have not argued for the elimination from our ordinary language of the terms *natural, manmade, cultural,* and so forth. After Wittgenstein, far be it from a philosopher to attempt to *legislate* language use. Rather I have tried to emphasize that qua "theorists" we would do well to notice something we often fail to appreciate and need (in Wittgenstein's sense) to be reminded of—namely, that we are deeply embedded in our ecosystem(s) prior to setting up the binary oppositions through which we structure many of our less immediately practical language-games, oppositions such as nature versus culture. We are "thrown" into the world if you like—but from *within* it, as a part of it—it makes no *sense* to think of us as opposed to it. As long as language is used, terms such as *nature, technology,* and *human* will probably have a meaning, a use—but *that* doesn't imply that, qua "theorists," and (even) when putting our "theories" into action, we should use them. And that is all. What I am suggesting is that the differences between *nature* and *culture* in our language not be inflated into a kind of *quasi-Real* or theoretical or even *rhetorical* problematic.[41]

We should, then, move on beyond romantic or "deep" defenses of nature, with their structural attendant dangers of valorizing "the norm" in the same breath as "the natural environment" is normatively affirmed (compare: "heterosexual sex and reproduction is *natural, is normal*"); and, of course, we simultaneously move beyond the reverse image (to the defense of Nature)—the exploitation and domination of Nature. There can be no *pre*judgment either for or against technoscientific interventions in ecosystem(s)—each case is to be judged on its merits, pragmatically.

"Is this not covertly to judge against the ecological stability and survival of the planet, for are we not all-too-familiar with the masquerades of technological reason as value-free/neutral, as itself involving no prejudgments?"[42]

These "masquerades" should indeed be challenged, particularly in respect of the underlying complicity of "free market" ideology with the threats to and worsening of many of our ecosystems, but I think that the only *prejudgment* that can be made against technoscientific interventions is the very common-or-garden point that in general one shouldn't expend time and energy and precious resources on projects whose perhaps risk-laden effects one is deeply uncertain of, and so on. Such truisms are arguably all one can generate from an environmental ethic prior to getting one's hands "dirty" with empirical details, normative commitments, and hard decisions, unless one is prepared to endorse one of the extreme/incoherent perspectives criticized earlier. (Thus we can diagnose any alleged antianthropocentric biocentrism as among other things a perhaps-gendered attempt to escape from the "dirty," "messy" realities of living in a world, with others, committed to things, trying to make difficult decisions, sometimes making mistakes, and so on) The hope must be that *an up-front emphasis on all aspects of our ecosystem(s), not just the natural or the manmade, will enable us (at the margin) to make better ecological decisions*. For by the time we are faced with trying to make an ethical/ political choice between competing ecosystemic goods, it is already too late to turn to Nature as a final basis on which to decide. At the point of our making such choices the (alleged) naturalness of 'Nature' may even be quite beside the point. For again, Nature cannot be naturealized; any more than reason can. Both are contested, regulative (though arguably gendered and not, fortunately, indispensable) ideals.

The dysfunctional environmental practices of many, both locally and globally, should be still more obvious than they are at present, if my proposal is acted upon; while there need be no knee-jerk reactions against technological means of improving our ecosystems. Consider the following point: is one really going to object to applying any technology whatsoever (provided such technology is itself not very harmful) to the pressing task of *redressing what we judge to be harms done to our ecosystems* (by, for instance, past technoecological catastrophes)?[43] But then consider this: What principled grounds there are for distinguishing qualitatively between *changes to an ecosystem constituting the redressing of past harms done to it, and changes constituting alterations of an ecosystem for the better, but where there is no redressing of any particular past harm?* If one *agrees* with the arguments given in the present piece, one will agree that this is become—*ceteris paribus*—a distinction without a (relevant) difference, and that it is possible to judge that a human-altered ecosystem is preferable to one in its natural state. (A possibly controversial example might be the English Lake District's "improvement" by its partial deforestation and valley-floor draining a thousand years ago. The Lake District has arguably been beautified in a manner whose negative consequences for *some* flora and fauna are not overwhelming.)

If one *disagrees*, one is left in the uncomfortable position of having to explain on a philosophical/theoretical basis why only *some* deliberately engineered alterations in the environment constitute harms, and which do; why in particular we did not 'let things take their natural course' (a telling phrase) after, for instance, Chernobyl, rather than send in damage-control teams and environmental clean-up crews. There is no *road* back from technology *per se*; for any such road, even if we truly wished to take it (as surely no-one who has really thought about it actually does), could only be a technological one.

There are only different technologies, and serious reasons for believing that *certain* technologies must be abandoned or resisted. This is what I have been saying: any general philosophico-theoretical naturalization of these hard decisions is untenable. We have to face up to being in a world where being Green is not simple.

To recap: I contend that the cash value of looking at questions of how to organize our activities in the world after the fashion that I am suggesting is twofold:

(1) Extreme views of this may get ruled out as just obviously inadequate, because they incoherently fail even rudimentarily to observe our ecological interdependence (to give another for instance: most—cynical—"Wise Use" advocates, who seem actually just to be covering for the worsening of some beautiful and rich lands in the cause of short-term economic growth).

(2) We are forced to address more directly and less obscurantically reasons for one course of action or another. We have to explain how some action will improve the ecosystem in question (in terms of aesthetics, sustainability, and so on), and enhance the lives of those we take to be of relevance. As poll data has intimated, "quality of environment(s)" is a major factor in how citizens of the contemporary West are prepared to structure their life-choices—a democratic faith would enjoin us to frame ecological questions in a manner resembling that which I am proposing, and would not require that citizens be regaled with overarching reasons for exploiting *or for defending* Nature.[44] I would argue that it is education, mass activism, and a mass challenge to the so-called economic imperatives shaping our ecosystems right now that are required—not new theories of the nature or rights of Nature (or, indeed, even of Culture). *If* we are "required," for the sake of short-term ecopolitical goals, to speak with the naturealists, to speak of "despoiling/wounding Nature" and so forth, then so be it. But to paraphrase Rorty (on feminism); although this may be so, Greens would profit from at least *thinking* (*and,* insofar as one does so at all, *theorizing*) with the Pragmatist-Wittgensteinians.

Of course, point (2) above will not *settle* questions a priori; the core of my proposal is terminological, not *substantively* ethical. Terms such as *ecosystem* and *community* will remain essentially contested. But at least they promise not to be irremediably confused or confusing, and at least they bring with them few of the risks of the rhetoric of Nature (and Culture) identified earlier.

And so: there has been no effort here to seek to *regain* an original unity; only to find ways of understanding just how a certain unity of all part(icipant)s in the ecosystem(s) has never been threatened (because conceptually—grammatically—it cannot be threatened), has always been available to us. Literary theorists, feminists, life-scientists and ecoactivists need not be *threatened* by the argument of this piece—what has been proposed is simply that we "clarify" what we are doing when we "theorize" about ecology.[45] I don't believe that philosophy can dictate to one one's ethical commitments and political actions; but philosophy can help us gain a clear view of what we are already in one way or another committed to.[46]

I do not intend then to have hubristically outlined a general political strategy here, nor even to have protested against many of the ideas and rallying calls of "gynocentrism" or "biocentrism." On the former, I hope my invocation of and support of Daly and Collard is clear enough. On the latter, let me remark that I too love and value "wild nature." I love and value much old (as well as some new) wilderness. I would like to see a Buffalo Commons in the United States, and wolves back in Scotland. I just don't think that philosophy or any form of theorizing can tell us that we ought to have a Buffalo Commons, or wolves back in Scotland. Philosophy leaves these things as they are—but, at its best, gives us a better opportunity for changing ourselves, and them . . . in fact, for creating, anew, rather than merely returning to an (often fantasized) past. The center of my philosophical point has been this: a philosophical antianthropocentrism is nonsensical, and that a philosophical "foundation" for Green practice is not required.[47] We can advocate (for example) a Buffalo Commons without imagining, absurdly, that we are literally going Back to Nature.

Thus Wittgenstein (and Pragmatism) are I think natural allies to ecofeminism. Ecofeminists who avoid essentialism care concretely (locally and globally) about the inextricable mutual interleavedness of women, humans, creatures, and their encompassing ecosystems, in a manner that renders any general antihumanism absurd and any general philosophical foundationalism unnecessary.

A final possible "epigraph," possibly suggests itself, then: *Neither Nature, nor Culture, but forward to (international) ecologism.* For the sake of the avoidance of conceptual confusion and of needless endless discussion, and for the sake of what we are already often happy enough to call "the Environment," let us consider not the construction of Nature by Culture or vice versa, but rather what ecosystem(s) we wish to live in and to secure for future inhabitants of this ecosystem/of this planet, and how to achieve these goals.[48] That is, through both the requisite use of "linguistic practices" (such as this essay hopes in its small way to be) and of "nonlinguistic practices" (for example, changing our eating habits, producing genuinely ecological art, boycotting the stock of the nuclear industry and of other Greenpeace targets, monkey-wrenching if and when and where necessary . . .).

Notes

1. I employ the term *evade* in Cornel West's affirmative sense; vide *The American Evasion of Philosophy: Genealogy of Pragmatism* (Madison: University of Wisconsin Press, 1989), 36 and 87–96 and passim.

2. Wittgenstein enables us to seriously ask whether perhaps the philosophical questions one can find oneself asking are actually largely not profound, but empty. This is a hard lesson to learn, or to teach. I draw it from the later works; particularly paragraphs 81–133 of *Philosophical Investigations* trans. E. Anscombe (New York: Macmillan, 1958); and I argue it in "The Real Philosophical Discovery," *Philosophical Investigations* 18, no. 4 (1995):362–70. The later Putnam might put this point thus: "'Pragmatist-Wittgensteinism' is enough to free us from the confines of a bipolar opposition of metaphysical realism versus metaphysical constructionism/idealism.

3. Echoes of J. S. Mill contra "psychological hedonism" though one should note that "metaphysics" is being countenanced here in my text only ad hominem; in other words, it is hard to interpret others as engaged in anything other than metaphysical projects, though I would see no point or chance of success in any such project (see also note 2, above, and notes 20 and 42, below).

4. This point has been understood by some philosophers/sociologists of scientific knowledge—particularly by Bruno Latour (see particularly Latour and S. Woolgar, *Laboratory Life*, 2d ed. [Princeton: Princeton University Press, 1986], 281), who is now interested in "the construction of scientific facts" (conceived of as set of concrete processes involving the lives of certain people permuted by those objects that they are finding/creating, in certain institutional and material contexts), not in separating out the sociocultural elements in their construction from other elements, nor in grandiosely proclaiming metaphysical theses such as that "everything is socioculturally constructed," as though that could tell us anything. Critiques of Latour as an "unreconstructed" social constructionist (such as J. R. Brown, "Latour's Prosaic Science," *Canadian Journal of Philosophy* 21, no. 2

[1991]: 245–61) are thus well off target—Latour did not drop the "the word 'Social' from the title on the grounds that it is so obvious as not to need mentioning" (Brown, "Latour's Prosaic Science," 245), but, on the contrary, because it is so potentially misleading as not to deserve singling out. (A recent analysis in substantial sympathy with Latour, but that pushes harder on "constructionalists" to make clear what they are talking about, and to avoid empty totalizations, is Ian Hacking, *The Social Construction of What?* [Cambridge: Harvard University Press, 1999].)

5. This process has been described many times—a particularly useful account for present purposes is that of Neil Evernden, in his *The Social Creation of Nature* (Baltimore: Johns Hopkins University Press, 1992), 61. Cf. also parts of V. Plumwood's argument in "Women, Humanity and Nature," *Radical Philosophy* 48 (1988): 6–24.

6. Similarly, the "strong program" in sociology of science has often been ambiguous between quasi-material construction (social pressures as dictating the content of scientific theories and results, through structuring scientific institutions, communities and so on) and metaphysical construction (sociality as contaminating or saturating the category of "science"), as shown in the course of a nevertheless sympathetic discussion by Mary Hesse, "The Strong Thesis of Sociology of Science," in her *Revolutions and Reconstructions in the Philosophy of Science* (Bloomington: Indiana University Press, 1980), 29–62 (and cf. note 4, above).

7. Elizabeth Harlow writes, in her "The Human Face of Nature: Environmental Values and the Limits of Nonanthropocentrism," *Environmental Ethics* 14, no. 1 (1992):28–42, that what is not wanted is "idealist denials of the objective existence of nature or processes in nature: the natural world is not created by human mental activity" (39, her italics). Surely this is right on target in spirit (though I will later query her continued employment of the term *nature*). There is a more polemical way of making her point: what hubris to talk of (culture) literally making nature!

8. One such account is Evernden, *The Social Creation of Nature*, chap. 2 and passim.

9. The most theoretically compelling such defense is perhaps Paul Taylor, *Respect for Nature: A Theory of Environmental Ethics* (Princeton: Princeton University Press, 1986); vide 80–118 for his problematic use of the term *nature*. In particular, compare his naturalistic biocentrism including humans at 101 with his depiction of a clash between human Culture and its 'Other'—Nature—at 258.

10. This is effectually argued in Patrick Murphy, "Sex-Typing the Planet: Gaia Imagery and the Problem of Subverting Patriarchy," *Environmental Ethics* 10, no. 2 (1988): 155–68.

11. One should note that some indigenous cultures and some seriously practiced religions that have pursued a continuous path of "ecologism" rather than returned to it/to nature after an (imagined) rupturing from it are likely to escape my criticism here. Compare Ed McGaa, *Mother Earth Spirituality: Native American Paths to Healing Ourselves and Our World* (New York: HarperCollins, 1990). Booth and Jacobs, in "Ties That Bind: Native American Beliefs as a Foundation for Environmental Consciousness," *Environmental Ethics* 12, no. 1 (1990): 27–44 claim that Native American cultures are among the best places to look for live ecologism involving a reverence for nature that is not unavoidably reactive and compromised (but cf. also note 15, below). My point holds so far as one is dealing with questions of environmentalism in a context not restricted to that internal to indigenous "ecologistic" cultures—and the contemporary Western context is not so restricted. Again, take the instance of Gaia (as discussed by Mary Daly in *Pure Lust* (London: Women's Press, 1984, 56–57), and by Patrick Murphy, in "Sex-Typing the Planet."

12. See Daly, *Pure Lust*. A careful reading of Andrée Collard's (with J.Contrucci) severe radical ecofeminist masterpiece, *Rape of the Wild: Man's Violence Against Animals and the Earth* (Bloomington: Indiana University Press, 1989) (see esp. 142f.) indicates much the same: the rhetoric of loving or reuniting with the earth (flirted with less cautiously by "Cultural" Feminists) can so easily be an obstacle to achieving a sound ecologistic vision. Thus I find Collard to be quite compatible with the antiessentialist ecoeminism found, for example, in most of the essays in Karen Warren, ed., *Ecological Feminism* (London: Routledge, 1994), including notably V. Davion, "Is Ecofeminism Feminist?" and

D. Slicer, "Wrongs of Passage: Three Challenges to the Maturing of Ecofeminism." G. Gaard, "Misunderstanding Ecofeminism," *Z Papers* 3, no. 1 (1994): 20–24 provides a useful contemporary overview of the increasingly strong strand in feminist Green thought here with which I am strongly in sympathy; see particularly 21: "[The ecofeminism] I know . . . acknowledges the association patriarchy has traditionally made between women and nature, and shapes an analysis of oppression that is based on hierarchy and domination. . . . [This is] the only logical way to go. Subjected to critical scrutiny, the culture/nature dualism . . . is pretty silly." We need to understand ourselves as—completely—an element of what it is that we value; we need to absorb the "fact" of our deeper-than-deep nonalienation from the earth, not act as if there is some irrevocable gap between us and "the environment."

13. Jim Cheney, "The Neo-stoicism of Radical Environmentalism," *Environmental Ethics* 11, no. 4 (1989): 293–326. See also his "Nature/Theory/Difference: Ecofeminism and the Reconstruction of Environmental Ethics," in Warren, *Ecological Feminism*.

14. Cheney, "Neo-stoicism," 294.

15. Ibid., 318–19. Cheney may be too generous here to Devall and Sessions on the question of their respect for indigenous peoples' voices too—see M. Lewis, *Green Illusions: An Environmentalist Critique of Radical Environmentalism* (London: Duke University Press, 1992), 55. (Let me note that the possibility of continuing to use the rhetoric of biocentrism, without endorsing its more problematic historical formulations and theoretical commitments, is discussed below.)

16. Consult John Dewey, *Logic: The Theory of Inquiry* (New York: Holt, Rinehart, Winston, 1938); *A Common Faith* (New Haven: Yale Press, 1934); *Experience and Nature* (La Salle, Ill.: Open Court, 1925); and *Democracy and Education* (Toronto: Collier-MacMillan, 1916), particularly the first four chapters. Throughout the *Logic* in particular, Dewey emphasizes both the continuity of inquiry with (other) organic behavior, and the "profound interpenetration" of the physical and the cultural, which are ultimately dispensable idealizations.

17. This interpretation of Dewey stands opposed to Beth Singer's reading, in "Dewey's Concept of Community: A Critique," *Journal of the History of Philosophy* 23, no. 4 (1985): 555–70. Unlike Singer, I read Dewey as making a space for the seeing of instincts as on a continuum with habitual/social action. Thus one ought not in all contexts to qualitatively distinguish human cultures/communities from those found among nonhuman animals (see below); Singer fails to see this (e.g., 556) because she mistakes Dewey's ideal of a (deeply democratic) community for a necessary condition for being a community at all. (To say this is not to deny what Wittgensteinians stress in other contexts: the assimilation of the understanding of people to the explaining of nature [for example, in positivistic social science] inevitably risks serious philosophical confusion. This point is, for example, the valid product, in my opinion, of the lifework of P. Winch.)

18. Other texts with which one could supplement the Dewey-Wittgenstein axis here include Maurice Merleau-Ponty's *Phenomenology of Perception*, trans. C. Smith (London: Routledge and Kegan Paul, 1962); see also Soori and Gill, *A Post-Modern Epistemology: Language, Truth, and Body* (Lewiston: Edwin Mellen, 1989); some portions of Heidegger's oeuvre; large portions of the work of feminist philosophers such as Daly, Susan Bordo, and Vandana Shiva; and perhaps William Poteat, *Polanyian Meditations: In Search of a Post-Critical Logic* (Durham: Duke University Press, 1985). Our embodiedness in a world not alien to us is foregrounded in these texts to a greater extent than one usually finds in Dewey and Wittgenstein (though it is also to be found there). But the clear emphasis of pragmatist-Wittgensteinians on practice, combined with the fact that they largely wrote first, suggested the near restriction of attention (henceforth) to them, in the present context.

19. There is a (too?) vast "literature" on *Lebensformen*; see, e.g., Newton Garver, "Form of Life in Wittgenstein's Later Work" *Dialectica* 44 (1990): 175–201; and Kathleen Emmett, "Forms of Life" *Philosophical Investigations* 13, no. 3 (1990): 213–31, for the fairly recent recent state of play. My point in the text is both that mine is a most useful way to understand the interrelation of "form-of-life" with environs, and that Wittgenstein's posttranscendental argument for the conditions of actu-

ality of communication being a shared form-of-life is an essential supplement to Dewey's conception of the co-constitution of organism and environment. For more detail on how to understand the term 'form of life' unmisleadingly and postmetaphysically, see my (with J. Guetti), "Meaningful Consequences," *Philosophical Forum* 30 (Winter 1999): 289–315.

20. *Philosophical Investigations*, pars. 240 to 242—I intend these three formulations to capture the spirit of those pivotal three paragraphs in Wittgenstein's "argument."

21. Ibid., par. 25. Implicit in Wittgenstein here is a perhaps proto-Harawayian resistance to the attractions both of the thought that nonhuman animals are to be understood as deficient humans (would-be humans who "can't think well enough") and of the thought that human animals are simply animals, that there is no "value-added" whatsoever via the sophistications of language (see notes 31 and 45, below). For a fascinating document of the reason for finding some nonhuman animals to share important characteristics with humans, see the aptly named *Chimpanzee Cultures* (Cambridge: Harvard University Press, 1994), edited by Richard Wrangham et al.

22. Compare, for instance, the following quotation from Dewey, *Democracy and Education*, 11: Dewey tells us that the word *environment* denotes "something more than surroundings which encompass an individual. [It denotes] the specific continuity of the surroundings with [the individual's] own active tendencies." In this book, and in greater depth in the *Logic*, Dewey makes also the fairly obvious and useful move of pluralizing *environment*. That is to say, of discussing the various environments, local and global, which organisms are constituted by and co-constitute. (For an acute discussion, vide Richard Levins and Richard Lewontin, *The Dialectical Biologist* [Cambridge: Harvard University Press, 1985], 99–104).

23. Dewey, *A Common Faith*, 53.

24. Cf. Marc Cooper, "A Crack in the World," *Village Voice*, 23 June 1992, on the failure of the Rio conference: "[A]s one Brazilian newspaper put it on the day after Bush's speech, 'Everyone's an Environmentalist.' And if that's true, then no one is a polluter."

25. For example, by Singer, "Dewey's Concept of Community," 555.

26. For example, by Jerry Katz, in *The Metaphysics of Meaning* (Cambridge: MIT Press, 1991).

27. Katz's (ibid.) explanation of "scientific naturalism" in Quine and Chomsky is enough for present purposes.

28. As explained by Ian Hacking, in *Representing and Intervening* (Cambridge: Cambridge University Press, 1983), 61–63.

29. Dewey, *Logic*, 19.

30. Wittgenstein, par. 25—this is the continuation of the earlier quotation on animals.

31. See Gordon Baker and Peter Hacker, *Rules, Grammar, and Necessity* (Oxford: Blackwell, 1985), 240. It is salient that Baker and Hacker try generally to distance Wittgenstein, as he occasionally did himself, from pragmatism. I think the meeting of minds and words implied here would surprise all three. They might be still more surprised, were one to go on, as there is not space to do here (but see below), to lay out how close Dewey-Wittgenstein cultural naturalism (or environmentalism) puts one to the thinking of many feminist thinkers, such as perhaps even those who have rethought disciplines such as primatology as necessarily involving politics in the understanding of the "natural" environment/world.

32. Dewey, *Logic*, 20. Further, compare West, *The American Evasion of Philosophy*, 95–96, in which West discusses Dewey's intentions to rewrite (and retitle) *Experience and Nature*, making more obvious the bankruptcy of the nature-versus-culture dichotomy.

33. As in *Philosophical Investigations*, par. 654, "[T]his language-game is played."

34. Harlow, "The Human Face of Nature"; C. Manes, "Philosophy and the Environmental Task," *Environmental Ethics* 10, no. 1 (1988): 75–82 argues similarly that any identification of nonanthropocentric intrinsic value is impossible at a theoretical or philosophical level, and is actualized only in the course of concrete environmental tasks. For thoughts similar to Harlow's (and Manes's) from an explicitly ecofeminist point of view, rejecting the claim that Deep Ecology thinks deeply and

tenably-nonanthropocentrically, see Christine Cuomo, "Ecofeminism, Deep Ecology, and Human Population," in Warren, *Ecological Feminism;* Warren, "The Power and Promise of Ecological Feminism," *Environmental Ethics* 14, no. 3 (1990): 125–46; and C. Merchant, "Ecofeminism and Feminist Theory," in *Reweaving the World: The Emergence of Ecofeminism,* ed. Irene Diamond and Gloria Orenstein (San Francisco: Sierra Club Books, 1990).

35. Harlow, "The Human Face of Nature," 27 and 39. Incidentally, this "blurring" foregrounds an area of extreme mutual conduciveness between feminist theory on the one hand and (for example) Wittgenstein on the other. The fear of contamination across vague boundaries, of abyssal inexactitude, which is arguably a fear of the female, is simply not present in Wittgenstein's later work; while it is endemic in most Western philosophy. Wittgenstein's "defense" of vagueness in *Philosophical Investigations* is instructive in this regard. The mode of employment by Wittgenstein of the term *family resemblance* is also highly revealing: here the personal is philosophical, as it were, only it is hardly a hierarchical (let alone patriarchal) personal: for the connections between the components of a family-resemblance concept are loose and nonessentialist, barely even genealogical. Contrast what are in effect "inheritance from (the name of) the father" models of concepts that prevail elsewhere in analytic philosophy, in which a primary Essential sense is central.

36. For instance, while plainly I think, after Rorty, that the likes of N. Goodman and D. Davidson offer invaluable neopragmatist supplements to Wittgensteinian (and Deweyian) insights, still, I think that naming as the main "contemporary interpreters" of Wittgenstein "Thomas Kuhn, Donald Davidson, Daniel Dennett and Richard Rorty" (as Harlow does, in "The Human Face of Nature," 38) is eccentric—none of the four has ever written a book on Wittgenstein, and it is clear enough that their interpretations of him in each case involve strong misreading. (For example, on Kuhn's Wittgensteinianism—and his failure to see it through—see my [with W. Sharrock] *Thomas Kuhn: The Philosopher of Scientific Revolution* [Oxford: Polity, 2002]; and for a self-evidently failed attempt to bring together Dennett and Wittgenstein, see W. Lee-Lampshire, "Women-Animals-Machines: A Grammar for a Wittgensteinian Ecofeminism," in *Ecofeminism, Women, Culture, Nature,* ed. Karen Warren [Indianapolis: Indiana University Press, 1997].) In the context of this volume, on feminist (re-)readings of Wittgenstein, it looks particularly odd to ignore (the very many tremendously important women) interpreters of Wittgenstein such as Diamond, Anscombe, Murdoch, Lovibond, Foot, and others.

37. Ibid., 28.

38. Ibid., 29. I believe that Harlow (in concert with the present essay) also effectively rebuts the suspicion that, insofar as Social Ecology may perhaps have failed to overcome an arrogant anthropocentrism, such failure is endemic to ethical outlooks, which do not explicitly "respect Nature." Robyn Eckersley, in "Divining Evolution: The Ecological Ethics of Murray Bookchin," *Environmental Ethics* 11, no. 2 (1989): 101, objects to social ecology, claiming that "Bookchin's organismic philosophy may have transcended the nature / culture schism, but it has only partly undermined the idea that we should dominate nature. In particular . . . he develops his distinction between first and second nature (corresponding to the nonhuman and human realms respectively) [in an objectionable way]." There may or may not be something to the criticism as applied to Bookchin's oeuvre—but what would Eckersley be willing to count as "not dominating nature"? One fears that, beyond the kind of moves I make in the present essay, there is only the impossible invitation to abrogate technology altogether. And, disregarding its many flaws for a moment, we have to concede to M. Lewis, in *Green Delusions,* that he makes well the case (which I elaborate on briefly here) for sometimes using technology to combat ecological dangers.

39. For Harlow, see note 7, above.

40. Cheney, "Neo-stoicism," 318. (And cf. his "Eco-Feminism and Deep Ecology," *Environmental Ethics* 9 (1987): 115–46; and note 13, above.) As noted by Peter Losin, in Callicott such a usage is sometimes more clearly unhelpful, as when the latter claims that "nature is not amoral," that "intelligent moral behavior is natural behavior." Losin rightly urges, rather, "If human beings are

part of nature . . . then it is true that intelligent moral behavior is natural behavior. But so is foolish immoral behavior" (Review of *Companion to a Sand County Almanac*, by J. Baird Callicott. *Environmental Ethics* 10, no. 2 [1988]: 173). Two further points to note here: first, Callicott has actually fallen onto the first horn of the dilemma over the disambiguation of 'nature' discussed early in this essay—through totalizing Nature, he has (whether willingly or unwillingly, as Losin shows) evacuated it of normative content. Second, Losin himself does not escape fully from making the mistake he identifies: for in the ellipsis of the preceding quotation (ibid., 173), one finds the words "as of course they are." I would ask Losin what is gained by this assertion that humans are "part of nature"? For how does 'nature' have a sense here, except in contradistinction to (humans') culture, as in the writings of virtually the entire tradition from early Christianity through Rousseau to Deep Ecology? Better to settle on a new term, to leave behind the stale dialectic of nature versus culture (cf. note 43, below).

41. This paragraph is an effort at a Pragmatist-Wittgensteinian summation of the central point of the essay. If one were to prefer perhaps more strictly Wittgensteinian terms (after Diamond and Cavell), one might say rather: there is no word that does not have a perfectly fine everyday use(s), but we can't metaphysically "lean on" words (for example, on *culture* and *nature*). We go astray when we take (such) words to mark something deep. (For detail, see Martin Stone's essay "Wittgenstein and Deconstruction," in *The New Wittgenstein*, ed. Alice Crary and Rupert Read [London: Routledge, 2000]). In most particular contexts, we know what we mean, we mean most of what we say, what we say and mean is quite ordinary (as opposed to would-be metaphysical). But when we attempt to abstract from context and get at what *nature* and *culture* "really" refer to, we go astray. In my essay I have investigated, from both within and without, that going astray.

42. There have been various and repeated claims made along the lines of this (made-up) quotation; namely, for an influential example, Jerry Mander, *The Failure of Technology and the Survival of Indian Nations*, *Mother Jones* 16, no. 6 (1991): 69–70 (excerpt). Mander's view resembles Lovelock's, in the sense that 'nature' is contradictorily figured as all encompassing but yet simultaneously normative. This is simply self-contradiction—unless you are quite prepared to say of 'nature' what we can say of 'the environment' (or indeed of 'the ecosystem') even if we are supposedly not speaking of any local environment in particular: namely, that we can literally (re-)construct different and better and worse nature(s). The idea of our making nature itself better while it remains nature is liable to smell of self-contradiction or ungrammaticality; not so for the environment, providing that the latter term is not narrowly understood as "the natural environment" (in other words, here we see again the cash value of switching to *ecosystem*, a term less open to being understood so as to exclude humans).

43. The aim here, again, is not to assimilate pro-ecological reasoning to instrumental/techno-logic, if that is conceived as enabling us to take a wholly external orientation toward what we are interacting with and manipulating. Once more I am Pragmatist-Wittgensteinian in taking this latter to be a dispensable conception of instrumental reason, albeit one sometimes invoked by philosophers. Joseph Rouse has written that "[s]ocial ecologists, deep ecologists, ecological feminists, Marcusean critical theorists and perhaps some defenders of animals . . . [take] . . . non-instrumental relations to the natural world as irreducible goods" ("Interpretation in Natural and Human Science," in *The Interpretive Turn*, ed. David Hiley et al. [Ithaca: Cornell University Press, 1991], 53). Whether one concurs with Rouse in taking these groups at perhaps their own usual self-description or (preferably) prefers my rendering in terms of co-constitution with (and choices as to how to reorient) our ecosystem(s), the point remains that it would indeed be wrong to place all such "within the dominant parameters of our understanding of scientific rationality" (ibid.), unless one were to (re-)understand that rationality along roughly Wittgensteinian lines.

44. Compare the *Gallup Poll Monthly*, April 1991, 6–12, in which (during a recession, recall) 71 percent of respondents said that the environment was worth curbing economic growth for; 78 percent of respondents considered themselves environmentalists; 86 percent claimed to voluntarily recycle; 73 percent judged that "the government" was "not worried enough about the environment";

79 percent would pay higher prices for goods if CFCs were banned; while 78 percent would support new environmental taxes to the same end; and so on.

45. Sociobiologists, however, should be worried—this is yet another challenge to the coherency of the enterprise of those who would deduce the organization of human societies from "our natural endowment." Sociobiologists (and "evolutionary psychologists"), for all their apparent attention to language as a pivotal biological category, usually fail to understand humans as truly sophisticated, as truly what they (we) are, in their interdependence with other language-users and with their environment; because at the end of the day the fundamental "unit" of biological nature is taken to be the individual (or even the gene).

46. Wittgenstein considered his philosophizing a contribution to human understanding (in a de-divinized world, roughly) of one's (ethical) relations to other humans, fauna, and flora; like many feminist critics, he saw scientistic rhetoric as absurdly perpetuating an "external" and "confrontational" attitude toward the latter. In fact, I hope my essay has brought out just how self-evidently (naturally?) Wittgenstein and ecofeminism, in for example their use of wholistic and nondualistic thinking, work together. The nature-versus-culture debate has been thoroughly problematized by nonessentialist feminists, by philosophers such as Daly, Collard, Warren, Cuomo, Cheney, and others cited in this essay, the heirs of radical feminism, who have anti-anti-anthropocentrically resisted "naturealism," and the concomitant (perhaps sometimes politically/rhetorically useful but deeply risky and philosophically troubled) strands of ecofeminism that are full-bloodedly essentialist about Woman and Nature.

47. In particular, environmental ethics neither requires nor can be given a foundation—contra for instance Susan Armstrong-Buck, "Whitehead's Metaphysical System as a Foundation for Environmental Ethics," *Environmental Ethics* 8, no. 3 (1986): 241–59. I take her claims that "Environmental Ethics would greatly benefit from an adequate metaphysical foundation," and that "a metaphysical theory can give penetration to and a wider and consistent application of our intuitive and feeling-based apprehensions" (241), to reflect how far some of us still are from comprehending the contemporary state of 'metaphysics', and from realizing the kinds of things that actually need to be done to have some affirmative effect in our ecosystems. Ecosystemic goods that we recognize (but which there is no point in trying to theorize, to found; commensurating them is hard enough) include: biodiversity, preservation of uniqueness (not only of species), existence of (some) ecosystems with little human involvement, beauty, comfortableness to humans of ecosystems that they (we) are substantially involved in, and so on. For more, see R. Paden, "Against Grand Theory in Environmental Ethics," *Environmental Values* 3, no. 1 (1994): 61–70.

48. For further discussion/exemplification, see my "A Sketch of a Case-Study in Wittgensteinian 'Eco-Philosophy': PETA vs. TNC" (unpublished); and my "The Priority of Environmental Ethics to Epistemology and Metaphysics" (forthcoming), a quasi-Rortian coda to the present essay.

20

Moving to New Boroughs:

Transforming the World by Inventing Language Games

Peg O'Connor

Overview

In this essay, I explore one sense of Wittgenstein's claim that the limits of language are the limits of the world. I explore two cases where the language available to individuals limits the meanings they can make of their experiences, and thus limits their worlds. I then focus on two processes that involve the creation of new meanings through language and examine how these new meanings open up new worlds. These two processes are breaking silence about sexual abuse and coming out as gay, lesbian, or bisexual. "Breaking silence" means a person's finding her voice after having been silent or silenced during and after abuse. "Coming out" is understood as a process in which a person names to herself or to others her sexual orientation. My approach to these two processes is greatly influenced by Wittgenstein, and so I argue that these processes and activities are only possible *with* or *through* language. True to Wittgensteinian form, I have an interlocutor who makes himself known at various times in various ways. My aim in this essay is to show how the creation of new language games engenders new meanings and how these new meanings enable people to make sense of their lives in ways that can be validating and liberating.

The Limits of the World

Wittgenstein writes in the *Tractatus* that "[t]he limits of my language mean the limits of my world"[1] (5.6). Don't just think about those cases where you make a simple mistake in describing some aspects of a past experience, but rather think about those cases where the sense you had made of something is radically different from the sense you are now able to make of it. It is not the case that you could not make any sense, but that sense is now seen as dubious and perhaps hopelessly inadequate. In hindsight, it might seem that no matter how rich and robust your language, it somehow failed in your making sense of your experiences. I can think of two cases where language limits the world.

First is the case of a child who has been sexually abused. With a very young child, she may have neither the language nor the mental and emotional capacities to make sense of her experiences. In this instance, it is not the case that she has all the words in her head but simply cannot express them. Rather, she has no language beyond the most primitive (crying, for example) with which to express herself. While this case is extremely important, I want to focus on the case of an older child, aged nine or so, who does have a good deal of language to use. She does have a language with which to make sense of herself, and the sense she is able to make is that she is a bad, dirty person. Her grasp of language use is new and somewhat tenuous and her repertoire of concepts is limited. But where she can apply these concepts, she applies them without exception.

She is silent for many reasons—fear of discovery by other people, fear of the judgments of others, and fear of the perpetrator. Her world is largely defined by these experiences and she thinks that she is the only one who could ever do the things she has done. No one else would ever do such things. She lives in a world of one, and a world that is limited by her inability to give other meanings to her experiences.

The second case is that of a young teenager who feels quite different from all her friends, but she cannot locate the source of this difference nor can she express it. The one thing she often does know is that she doesn't want for this difference to be known. Her world becomes claustrophobic and the fear of discovery (of what, even she isn't sure) is all too real. She spends a great deal of energy hiding and misdirecting. In many ways, her world is reduced to a world of one, because she is sure, after all, that she is the only person around her who feels this way. The sense she may be able to make of herself is as some sort of freak or pervert.

Unpacking the Essentialisms

Sensing that you are somehow different without knowing the nature of that difference lends itself to essentialist interpretations. I should admit at this point that I have an essentialist interlocutor lurking within. An essentialist coming out story would go something like this:

> The reason why the young woman is aware of something different is that *something is*. This difference is a consequence of her genetic makeup or the level of the androgen spritz she received in utero.
>
> The desire is already present in her like a plant is already present in the seed. The latency and potentiality become manifest in actuality. It is a foregone conclusion that she come to identify as lesbian or bisexual. No big mystery here—destiny is simply unfolding its lovely lavender self.

(My interlocutor on this issue is always a gay man who read Aristotle as an undergrad.)[2] I call this my Essentialust Account.[3]

While some might find biological accounts of homosexuality comforting, such accounts are not without their price. When the trait or behavior in question is considered undesirable by that part of society whose norms are dominant, then those people who manifest this trait or behavior can take the tack that they did not choose to be this way and therefore they should not be blamed. This position does little to challenge the presumption that one sexuality should be normative and leaves those with the "deviant" sexuality apologizing for it. Furthermore, genetics is accorded huge explanatory power and the chain of explanation is quite direct. Genetic makeup explains one's sexuality, which in turn explains everything else about a person.[4]

This essentialist account presupposes much of what Wittgenstein rejects, in particular, the claim that we individuals have privileged access to our sensations (or differences, in this case) and that this privileged access guarantees that we are naming such sensations correctly. How does he know what his sensation is only from his own experience? He is like the person who has a box with something in it, which we call a "beetle." No one can look into another's box and he knows what a beetle is only by looking at *his* beetle. "The thing in the box has no place in the language-game, not even as a *something* because the box might be empty (*PI*, §293).

The strength of the essentialist hold is a consequence of a variety of factors. One is a desire to be an unimpeachable authority on something, in this case, the working of one's internal mechanisms. Another factor is the desire to have control over something, again in this case, your thoughts, feelings, desires, and so on. No matter what sort of external constraints are placed on a person, one is still free to think and feel however one chooses, according to this account.

The first case, of the abused child, involves an essentialism of a different kind and reveals a perverse relationship between blame and responsibility. The person who has been abused often thinks that she is a horrible, awful, bad person. Her nature is essentially bad and this explains all that has happened to her. She is somehow responsible for everything that has happened to her; she has brought it all on herself. Her character is accorded huge explanatory power and anything that she does or that happens to her is further confirmation of her true nature.

In both these cases, essentialism and secretiveness are linked through the need to control access to oneself. The essentialisms in both these cases are about privileged access to what are taken as the facts of the matter. In the case of the young woman sensing her difference from all her friends, she takes it as fact that she *just is* a freak or pervert. This fact or "true self" must somehow remain hidden from view, so she needs to have complete control over access to her thoughts. Being secretive is a way to control access. With the child who has been abused, the secrecy may have to do with hiding so that no one can see her shameful true nature and all the bad things she has done. Again, being secretive is a way to control access, and the need for such control may be heightened when so much access to her has been beyond her control.

In the remainder of this essay, I offer Wittgensteinian discussions of self-identity, linguistic training, and the acquisition of worldviews, both to describe how the individuals in my examples reach the conclusions they do about their natures and identities, and to provide the grounds for creating new languages having new meanings with which to make different senses of their experiences.

Acquiring Worldviews and Following Rules

Acquisition of Worldviews

A Wittgensteinian account of self-identity has no essential "I" to which all my beliefs, values, judgments, and concepts attach. (Such an essentialist account would make those beliefs and judgments accidental to my self-identity rather than constitutive of it.) In a significant portion of *On Certainty*, Wittgenstein examines the acquisition of worldviews by individuals. Self-identity involves a dynamic interactive process whereby identity is created, reinforced, and modified by participation in a wide variety of language games. Self-identity is a function of our social interaction and participation with other persons, broader communities, social institutions, and the world. These interactions are done *with* or *through* language. Playing multiple language games is what constitutes the scaffolding of individuals' thoughts. A person's genealogy or self-identity is assembled through such activities. Self-identities are assembled piecemeal from worldviews, and should not be thought of as monolithic entities.[5] It is language that allows a person, to a very large degree, to interact in meaningful ways. We learn particular languages and we come to learn about ourselves as members of particular families and later as members of larger social groups. We learn to become members of this family, this group, and speakers of this language. We learn to play a variety of language games, and this diversity of language games means that we do not learn to be abstract, atomistic, and generic people. Rather, we learn that we are particular people who stand in a multitude of relationships and have memberships in a variety of communities.

The goal of linguistic training is the initiation of a person into a community that is bound by an allegiance to the rules of the symbolic system. This goal of initiation is realized through individuals' acquisition and inheritance of judgments, concepts, and beliefs that are held by the community at large. These beliefs, concepts, and judgments constitute a worldview.

A shared worldview is a shared background that is necessary for the formulating and the following of rules. By our saying and doing similar things under similar circumstances, the basis for agreement and disagreement is maintained. The shared worldview and judgments are something that we as socially constituted individuals inherit or acquire. We acquire totalities of judgments, systems of verification, and hosts of beliefs. According to Wittgenstein, when we first come to believe anything, what we believe is a whole system of propositions and not single propositions (OC, §141). And these systems or totalities of judgments are acquired by means of observation and instruction. Wittgenstein intentionally does not say that one "learns" these systems (OC, §279). But while one does not learn whole systems, one does learn to do particular things. For example, we learn to make judgments and recognize that *this is* judging while *that is* describing (OC, §129). Even our practice of making empirical judgments, for example, relies on our having been taught judgments and their connection with other judgments. A totality of judgments is made plausible to us (OC, §140). One skill children learn early is how to judge others. And some children become quite skilled in judging themselves against standards that they cannot possibly understand. The child sees these standards and judgments holding for all people at all times. The standards and judgments are often transmitted and then taken as absolutes, allowing for no exceptions, mitigating factors, or alternative interpretations. A child is not yet in a position to see gray areas or the importance of mitigating factors; she does not yet possess the ability to make discriminations.

The standards and judgments she acquires are transmitted by certain authorities. Wittgenstein asks, "So is this it: I must recognize certain authorities in order to make judgments at all?" (OC, §493). Certain persons, in virtue of their position as parents and teachers, are accorded intellectual authority. Structured institutions such as universities are also taken as possessing intellectual authority. In general, children are taught to obey their elders. Children do not regard all adults as authorities, and some children are brought up to believe they are superior to and have authority over adults of different sexes, races, ethnicities, religions. But even in light of that, even those children so raised will treat some adults as authorities. In many cases of sexual abuse, the child knows the abuser and knows him or her in a context where that person already is seen as some sort of authority figure. The abuser comes to have a greater authority over the child throughout and after the abuse. He or she is the one who would be believed, were accusations ever to be made; he or she is the one who determines whether the child is good or bad, what kind of "love" or "punishment" is deserved, what count as "natural" and "special" ways to love. The abuser is the one who tells the child what kind of person she really is. The child learns by believing the adult and further, Wittgenstein says "I learned an enormous amount and accepted it on human authority, and then I found some things confirmed or disconfirmed by my own experience" (OC, §161). Understanding what counts as confirmation and knowing how to go about it in particular instances depends on my already having accepted a whole range of beliefs. The abused child's sense of herself as dirty and bad is confirmed with every abusive act. Further, nothing or very little will count as evidence against what she believes to be true.

These worldviews or systems acquired by us and others allow our correct following of a rule to be acknowledged. And further, according to Wittgenstein, "I did not get my picture of the world by satisfying myself of its correctness; nor do I have it because I am satisfied of its correctness. No: it is the inherited background against which I distinguish between true and false" (OC, §94). Questions of correctness, truth or falsity, and justification can only meaningfully be asked by someone within a system. The system provides the ground and makes possible the very conditions for asking and answering such questions. Our vast network of beliefs and judgments that we "take on" in virtue of being members of particular communities constitute the background against which other propositions are believed, knowledge claims are made, and claims to knowledge are grounded and justified. The vast networks of beliefs individuals have acquired are constitutive of self-identity.

I do not think it is inaccurate to say that a significant percentage of adults in the late twentieth-century United States have world views that are homophobic. There are degrees of homophobia, and it can be characterized in a variety of ways depending on the specific issues in question. The fiercely contested battles over the ordination of gays, lesbians, and bisexuals; gay marriage; adoption; the inclusion (or exclusion) of gays, lesbians, and bisexuals from civil rights protection; and the inclusion of gay, lesbian, and bisexual themes in school curricula are all evidence for homophobic worldviews. Adults are the ones fighting over these issues, but children are neither immune to nor unaware of these battles. In the course of the battles, children come to acquire many beliefs and judgments. I do not mean to imply that all children receive identical judgments. That would be patently false. But while there may be differences in particulars, certain general themes emerge. A partial list includes

1. Homosexuality is unnatural and its unnaturalness makes it sinful;
2. Gays and lesbians seduce and recruit individuals—pedophilia is the extreme form;
3. Gays, lesbians, and bisexuals think about sex all the time—they are promiscuous;
4. Lesbians are man-haters who because either they want to be men or can't get a man, hate all men; and
5. AIDS is God's revenge (or nature's revenge).

All kinds of sexual activity, and not just homosexual activity, are surrounded by judgments, prohibitions, and prescriptions. There are judgments made about sex outside of marriage, reasons for sex, selling sex, having sex with people of a different race, class, and so on. Some of the judgments transmitted to children include:

1. Sex is dirty and only dirty people have it;
2. Women who have many partners or enjoy it too much are sluts while men are real studs;
3. Boys can't control their sexual drives—they are at the mercy of their biology in a way that girls are not;
4. Girls are the ones responsible for sexual activity—they can stop it; and
5. Having sex means being loved.

This list, and the preceding one, hardly begin to expose the tip of the iceberg. That I and others are capable of generating such lists is a consequence of our being adults who have inherited such views and who now are in a position and possess the ability to deconstruct and pull out particular pieces. Such a list most likely could not be made by a child unless she has heard these things over and over and has spent a significant amount of time evaluating herself against them. A child who can make such list has had to pay too much attention to it.

The child learns to believe a host of things and learns to act according to those beliefs. Gradually, a system is formed of what is believed. Some propositions such as "the earth has existed for more than one hundred years" or "every human has parents" are beliefs that stand fast and are unlikely to shift. And "[w]hat stands fast does so, not because it is intrinsically obvious or convincing; it is rather held fast by what lies around it" (OC, §144). Also included as standing-fast judgments could be any or all the judgments about sexuality and sexual practice listed above.

It is only after a person has learned a whole set of propositions where some are held fast that she can realize that these propositions are like an axis around which a body rotates. The axis is held immobile by the movement around it and not because anything stationary holds it fast (OC, §152). Wittgenstein argues that those propositions that are held fast and more fixed are removed from the traffic of questioning and doubt (OC, §210). And that we have a system of beliefs where some are more firmly held and far less likely to be given up is what gives us the scaffolding of our thoughts (OC, §211). This scaffolding is not privately constructed and is only possible through publicly shared beliefs. It is this scaffolding that allows us to be competent participants in a language game.

Competency is generally taken to be a good thing; incompetence is a condition to be overcome. But in the case of an abused child and a homophobic teenager, the competency each possesses is a bad thing. In these cases, the competency is in judging and hating oneself. These are things in which no one should be made competent.

Following the Rules in Language Games

The question whether someone is following a rule can only be answered within a language game. A language game includes a range of activities and practices, and these practices have a certain uniformity. Rule-following is only possible within a language game. Wittgenstein asserts that "the term language-*game* is meant to bring into prominence the fact that the *speaking* of a language is part of an activity, or of a form of life" (PI, §23). Utterances play a role in language games but they do not constitute the whole range of possibilities within language games. Talking is but one move in a language game and its meaning comes from the rest of our proceedings (OC, §229). This uniformity of practices is necessary for answering the question whether or not a rule has been followed. This uniformity of practices is reinforced and preserved when rules are followed in the same way. Rule-following is ultimately practical.

The necessary uniformity of practice is maintained by people doing the same sorts of things, such as continuing the series in the same way or saying "red" when presented with a particular color patch. In other words, the uniformity of practice is maintained by people following rules in the same way.

Wittgenstein's discussion of rule-following is primarily limited to simple mathematical examples, such as "add two" but his treatment can be extrapolated for nonmathematical examples. There are many rules around desire—who can desire whom, when this desire can be acted upon, how can this desire be expressed, and so forth. Desiring is as rule governed an activity as is mathematics, and these rules are human creations enforced and perpetuated by individuals' actions. Rule-following also depends on the existence of authority relations. It is those who are in authority who judge whether a particular rule is being followed correctly. The rules are not the same for all people; they vary depending on race, gender, and class, and double standards are common. It is difficult to follow a rule correctly when the criteria for doing so are not applied uniformly or when the criteria appear to be uniform and consistent but really are not.

We are not as obviously and overtly trained to desire as we are to count and to write cursive letters, but we are trained nevertheless. Similar power mechanisms are in place, and children have already inherited a host of judgments. Wittgenstein is remarkably silent about the uses and abuses of power by those institutions and individuals possessing authority. In learning to follow a particular rule such as "add two" Wittgenstein mentions "holding a person back" or "allowing him to go on" when he continues the sequence correctly (RFM, p. 405).[6] But there needs to be a much more sophisticated and sustained discussion of the operations of power. This issue of power is central to how oppressive backgrounds are maintained.[7]

Girls get all sorts of messages about "boys being boys" and that little girls should find all attention from boys pleasing. They'd better not find them too pleasing though.

The message that girls and women should not only desire men but also make themselves desirable to men is so familiar that it is invisible.

Women should not desire women. A woman who has an object of her desire another woman is not only perverted; she is overstepping her boundaries as a woman. She is, in effect, desiring what she has no right to desire. Sanctions follow when rules are disobeyed, and these sanctions can take a variety of forms. And further, individuals impose sanctions on themselves when they realize that they are acting in ways that, on their accounting, are wrong. These self-imposed sanctions can be the most devastating and destructive of any imposed. There is no reprieve from yourself.

Acquiring these worldviews and learning how to follow rules that are most often not made explicit and are given in veiled language make it inevitable that a child who has been sexually abused believes that she is a bad, dirty person responsible for what has happened. All evidence she has comes from various authority relations, and nothing could count against her beliefs. Similarly, the woman who has internalized all sorts of messages and rules about whom and how she is supposed to desire, is going to feel different from her friends. In both cases, their differences cannot (and should not, according to the dominant language games) be validated. The means or avenues for validation are not available to them.

One important consideration to keep in mind about rules is that they are human constructions. Unlike the laws of nature that have to be accepted and to which we adjust, rules "not only can be changed without contravening laws of nature, but occur already in many variations. Rather than our having to adjust to rules, we can adjust the rules instead."[8] Rules do not compel us nor leave no choice about how to act. The laws of gravity do compel us and really don't give us a choice—I cannot really be said to be disobeying the laws of gravity. Rules, however, leave something open; it is not as if the use or the application is already determined. It is not the case that the steps are *really* already taken (*PI*, §189). The steps are no more determined by the rules or formula than the movements or actions of a machine are determined. With regard to the machine, "[w]e talk as if the parts could only move in this way, as if they could not do anything else." What we forget, according to Wittgenstein, is that it is quite possible that the various parts might melt, bend, or break off (*PI*, §193). The movements of the machine are not inevitable. That the machine has moved in these ways does not entail that it will always do so. Similarly, it is not inevitable that once a person sees herself as bad or perverse she will always see herself so. Parts of the scaffolding of her thoughts can melt or break off, no less so than the parts of the machine.

What was previously taken as a difference marking one as bad or perverted can be reinterpreted.

Breaking Off a Piece of the Machine

The Weaves of Life and Changes in Seeing the World

So how does one begin to name and find validation for these differences?
Is it possible that the naming and validation can be done privately, that
is, independently of a social context? My gay male interlocutor, who has
been stifling himself for quite some time, pipes up: "Each person has his
own ViewMaster. I can put my thoughts or feelings or differences on
display for myself. I can click to the feeling or difference any time I
want—pretty much giving myself a private display. I need only to know
where to look." This position makes my gay male interlocutor a private
exhibitionist, but such a *private* exhibition is an illusion (*PI*, §311). Private access to one's feelings does not ensure validation or even that you
are getting it right about what you are experiencing. Rather, one must
make use of concepts and meanings that are socially constituted and
acquired. Wittgenstein says that "[s]eeing life as a weave, this pattern
(pretence, say) is not always complete and is varied in a multiplicity of
ways. But we, in our conceptual world, keep seeing the same, recurring
with variations. That is how our concepts take it. For concepts are not
for use of a single occasion" (*Zettel*, §568; see also §657). The weaves and
patterns of our lives are not always recognizable to us. There are times
when we are unable to recognize a pattern because it is staring us in the
face. Its very familiarity is what obscures it (*PI*, §129). As we begin to
change our perspectives, literally and metaphorically, we begin to see
patterns in different ways and we may undergo a shift in what we take to
be significant within a pattern.

The patterns we perceive may be quite familiar to us, so familiar, in
fact that we fail to perceive that they are patterns. We are not encouraged
to see the world in different ways when we already see it the *right* way.
What would be the point? It is difficult, if not impossible, for a child on
her own to see aspects of her life as abusive. For her, because certain
things are familiar and have always been done in certain ways, these are

"normal." She may be quite convinced that *this* just is how children are (and should be) treated. She may not be able to see the abusiveness of a situation until she somehow becomes aware of different ways children can be loved. And even when she does see these ways, she may spend a significant amount of energy reinterpreting her experiences so that they, too, are like those loving ways.

Language games are not fixed, and new ones come into existence while other become obsolete and forgotten (*PI*, §23). Language-games, like any other games, can undergo changes. Wittgenstein asserts that "the rules of grammar are arbitrary in the sense that the rules of a game are arbitrary. We can make them differently. But then it is a different game" (*Lectures*, 1930–32, p. 57). He specifically links the grammar of "language" with the grammar of "invent." Further, new language games can be invented for specific purposes and the purposes of language use are countless. There is a prodigious diversity of our language games and it is possible to invent new ones because there are already a multitude of games being played (*PI*, §204). Language-games are human activities and so they do undergo change, perhaps gradually, as time passes (*OC*, §256). Furthermore, when we imagine the facts otherwise than how they are, then certain language games lose importance while others become more important.

New language games can develop spontaneously, as we see things anew. Wittgenstein says that "[s]omething new (spontaneous, 'specific') is always a language-game" (*PI*, p. 224). The appearance of new perspectives and new ways of seeing are responsible for changes in our language games. We can decide to invent new language-games, and their "newness" belongs with the new ways of looking at things (*PI*, §401).

When language games are altered, then there is a "change in concepts, and with concepts the meanings of words change" (*OC*, §§63–65). These new language games make new meanings possible and these new meanings allow people to make a different kind of sense to themselves and to others. The activities associated with breaking silence and coming out are two new language games that have been invented for specific reasons and in response to seeing the world differently. In many ways, they both represent shifts in how people are oriented in the world. "Shifts in orientations" is a useful way to think about these processes. New language games enable people to think about their identities and relations with others in new ways because they have new concepts and meanings to use.

Oppositional Discourses

In many ways, these new language games are opposed to the other language games that people had previously played and used to understand themselves. They are what Nancy Fraser has identified as opppostional discourses.[9] Oppositional discourses are concerned to politicize needs or issues that previously had not been regarded as political. A need is politicized when it is contested across a wide range of discursive arenas and among a wide range of discourse publics. Distinct discourse publics can be distinguished along a number of axes, including race, gender, class, sexual orientation, ability, or any particularly mobilizing issue (Fraser, *Unruly Practices*, 167). Some publics have more power and exert a more direct influence on the formation and reinforcement of hegemonic world views. Such publics also have a greater say in what counts as political. Counterhegemonic publics do not have the power to politicize needs in the same way. An oppositional discourse is one where the needs talk is politicized from below. Such discourses tend to challenge the traditional boundaries of "the economic" and "the domestic" and "the political." They offer alternative interpretations, descriptions, and understandings of experience. By doing this, they challenge and undermine hegemonic worldviews. Oppositional discourses contribute to the crystallization of new social identities on the part of subordinated social groups. They can also lead to the adoption of new social identities (171). Oppositional discourses also provide a ground from which to challenge and undermine dominant language games and worldviews. Wittgenstein says in *On Certainty* that a group can use their language game as a base from which to combat others (§609). The language games of coming out and breaking silence, with all their attendant activities and newly created recognizable meanings are, in many ways, loci from which to fight against the dominant language games we have all played. By being visible, by fighting for inclusion in all sorts of ways, by exposing the logics of dominant language games, gays, lesbians, bisexuals, and people who have been abused and survived are creating, maintaining, and reinforcing meanings and concepts that are more broadly available. These new language games provide alternatives to the dominant world. Achieving a shift in orientation—of how one sees oneself and one's relations to others—allows a person to examine, criticize, and discard some of the propositions that had stood fast and replace them with others.

Co-optation and Reclamation

Wittgenstein uses the metaphor of a city to describe language. He says, "Our language can be seen as an ancient city: a maze of little streets and squares, of old and new houses, and of houses with additions from various periods; and this surrounded by a multitude of new boroughs with straight regular streets and uniform houses" (*PI*, §18). Oppositional discourses are, in many ways, the boroughs or suburbs of the older city. Suburbs are not completely detached from the city, but they are clearly recognizable as different from the city. Because they are newer and in many ways more planned, for example, the streets are more uniform. In a similar manner, the meanings of words in an oppositional discourse will be more uniform and planned. What happens, though, is that as other people make use of these same words and phrases and begin to apply them to situations other than the ones for which they were created, their meanings change. The meanings of words, as Wittgenstein constantly notes, are in their use. Who is using these words, in what circumstances they are being used, and for what purposes, all affect the meaning of these words. The "straight original" meanings become twisty.

A potential danger that follows from the creation of new language games and meanings and vocabularies is co-optation. Co-optation in language games happens when those new meanings and vocabularies created in new language games are adopted and used by those very people or institutions against whom they were initially created.[10] Co-optation happens through the machinations of "reprivatization" discourses. Reprivatization discourses contest the politicization of needs by oppositional discourses. Reprivatization is concerned to depoliticize issues and return them to the appropriate economic or domestic arena. What reprivatization discourses do is

> blend the old and the new. On the one hand, they seem merely to render explicit those need interpretations that could earlier go without saying. But, on the other hand, by the very act of articulating such interpretations, they simultaneously modify them. Because reprivatization discourses respond to competing, oppositional interpretations, they are internally dialogized, incorporating reference to the alternatives they resist, even while rejecting them. (Fraser, *Unruly Practices*, 172)

In this reprivatization, there is an appropriation of the oppositional discourse that caused a matter to be politicized in the first place. Reprivatization functions not only to force a need back into a "private" arena, but also to negate any influence the oppositional discourse may have had by co-opting its vocabulary. And quite often it happens that the very vocabulary is then used to reinscribe and reinforce the dominance of the worldviews originally challenged.

The flip side of co-optation is reclamation. Certain words such as *queer* and *dyke*, for example, have a history of oppressive uses. These words have been used to insult, torment, and stigmatize gays, lesbians, and any one else who does not, in whatever way, meet certain expectations. However, gays, lesbians, and bisexuals have reclaimed these words. Their being reclaimed makes them suitable for cultivation and habitation. In our using them to name ourselves on our own terms, their meanings are transformed. These reclaimed words play radically different roles in our new language games and allow many to inhabit a new orientation.

Conclusion

New language games and oppositional discourses have been vital for people who have been sexually abused in seeing themselves as survivors, and for people who have felt outlaw or unnatural desires in seeing themselves positively as gay, lesbian, or bisexual. Such shifts in self-perception and orientation have been, for many, life affirming if not life saving.[11] The threat of co-optation leaves oppositional publics with a multitude of tasks: continuing to provide alternative interpretations and descriptions of experiences, creating new concepts and vocabularies for articulating experiences, reclaiming words, and most fundamentally, being visible, so that no child or young person thinks she is the only one who has ever done or had done to her these things and has felt these ways.

Notes

1. *Tractatus Logico-Philosophicus*, trans. D. F. Pears and B. F. McGuinness (London: Routledge, 1974).

2. That my interlocutor on this particular issue is a gay man does not surprise me, though I do find it rather interesting. The gay men with whom I have spoken about this issue most often embrace these biological accounts of hormonal levels and genes, saying that such accounts best describe and explain their experiences. Some even go so far as to say, "I always knew." My tendency is to adopt a Wittgensteinian attitude: "*What* did you know? What do you think is this object of knowledge?" Their sense of certainty is supposed to indicate the truthfulness of the claim. When the issue of choice arises, they often do say that they make a choice, but that the choice is whether or not to act on this desire. The choice to act on an already existing desire is quite different from the choice to desire in certain ways.

I wonder if the willingness to embrace these essentialist biological accounts also has something to do with the fact that the research being done on the "causes of homosexuality" (never the causes of heterosexuality) is being done on their sexuality. Lesbian sexuality is erased by science. I must admit, though, that keeping lesbian sexuality off the microscope slide of the inquiring neuroendocrinologist is not all bad. But one consequence is that any accounts of homosexuality that are advanced will be modeled on male sexuality. The use of Simon LeVay's work on the hypothalami of gay males provides a good example of this phenomenon.

3. This term wasn't so much coined as it was the result of a serendipitous typo. Its genesis aside, it is useful because it highlights the emphasis placed on desire when coming out is taken to mean the public naming of what you already privately knew. Later in this essay, I suggest that coming out is better understood as coming to inhabit an orientation.

4. Sex becomes epistemic—it is something about ourselves that we can know and discover. As Michel Foucault asserts, "For that is the essential fact: since Christianity, the Western world has never ceased saying: 'To know who you are, know what your sexuality is.' Sex has always been the forum where both the future of our species and our 'truth' as human subjects are decided" (111). Sex becomes an object of examination—it is a key locus of inquiry. See Foucault, "Power and Sex," in *Politics Philosophy Culture: Interviews and Other Writings, 1977–1984* (New York: Routledge, 1991).

5. For a genealogical account of self-identity, see Wendy Lee-Lampshire, "Moral 'I': The Feminist Subject and the Grammar of Self-Reference," *Hypatia* 7, no. 1 (1992): 34–51 as well as my "The Moral Beast: Understanding Moral Practices as Characteristic of Human Life" (work in progress).

6. *Remarks on the Foundations of Mathematics*, ed. G. H. von Wright, R. Rhees, and G. E. M. Anscombe (Cambridge: MIT Press, 1978).

7. The works of Paulo Freire, Michel Foucault, Nancy Fraser, and Marilyn Frye are all good places to start. Such an endeavor, however, is beyond the scope of this essay.

8. Newton Garver, *This Complicated Form of Life: Essays on Wittgenstein* (Chicago: Open Court Press, 1993), 232.

9. Nancy Fraser, *Unruly Practices: Power, Discourse, and Gender in Contemporary Social Theory* (Minneapolis: University of Minnesota Press, 1989). See esp. her chapter "Struggle over Needs."

10. See my essay "Clarence Thomas and the Survival of Sexual Harassment," in *Proceedings of the Berkeley Women and Language Conference* (April 1992). In that essay, I examine how the language created by survivors of sexual abuse was used in a *People* magazine article to make sense of Clarence Thomas's experience of having been accused of sexual harassment. The headline in large bold print above the cover photo of Clarence Thomas announces, "How We Survived." The "we" in this case is Clarence Thomas and his wife, Virginia Thomas. The phrases that appear throughout the article include "telling our story" and "empowerment," and also mentioned is the "sense of betrayal" that goes along with someone close to you (Anita Hill) doing such a terrible thing (charging sexual harassment).

11. My discussion in this chapter has been greatly and deeply influenced by the powerful first-person accounts of survivors of sexual abuse and other forms of sexual violence and the coming out stories of gay, lesbian, bisexual, and transgender people. There are a number of excellent books published in the past ten years, which is itself evidence of the ways these practices have been brought

out of the "private" and become more a part of our social and political discourse. They are objects of public discussion in ways that they never have been before. Once they become so public, it is more difficult to force them back out of view. This is part of their transformative power.

On the subject of childhood sexual abuse, I highly recommend Ellen Bass and Louise Thorton, eds., *I Never Told Anyone: Writings by Women Survivors of Childhood Sexual Abuse* (New York: Harper-Perennial, 1991); Ellen Bass and Laura Davis, *The Courage to Heal: A Guide for Women Survivors of Childhood Sexual Abuse* (New York: HarperPerennial, 1994); Jennifer Freyd, *Betrayal Trauma: The Logic of Forgetting Childhood Sexual Abuse* (Cambridge: Harvard University Press, 1996); and Judith Herman, *Trauma and Recovery: The Aftermath of Violence from Domestic Abuse to Political Terror*, rev. ed. (New York: Basic Books, 1997).

One of the most moving books about coming out, in part because of the accompanying photographs, is about young adults. See Adam Mastoon, *The Shared Heart: Portraits and Stories Celebrating Lesbian, Gay, and Bisexual Young People*, photographs by Adam Mastoon (New York: William Morrow, 1997). See also Julia Penelope, ed., *The Original Coming Out Stories* (Freedom, Calif.: Crossing Press, 1989); Patrick Merla, ed., *Boys Like Us: Gay Writers Tell Their Coming Out Stories* (New York: Avon Books, 1997); Lisa C. Moore, ed., *Does Your Mama Know? An Anthology of Black Lesbian Coming Out Stories* (Washington, D.C.: Redbone Press, 1998); and Joan Larkin, ed., *A Woman Like That: Lesbian and Bisexual Writers Tell Their Coming Out Stories* (New York: HarperPerennial, 2000).

Bibliography

Barker, Victoria. 1997. "Definition and the Question of Woman." *Hypatia* 12, no. 2:185–215.

Bowden, Peta. 1998. *Caring: Gender-Sensitive Ethics*. New York: Routledge.

Brill, Susan. *Wittgenstein and Critical Theory: Beyond Postmodern Criticism and Toward Descriptive Investigations*. Athens: Ohio University Press.

Colebrook, Claire. 1997. "Feminist Philosophy and the Philosophy of Feminism: Irigaray and the History of Western Metaphysics." *Hypatia* 12, no. 1:79–98.

Crary, Alice. "Wittgenstein's Philosophy in Relation to Political Thought." In *The New Wittgenstein*, ed. Alice Crary and Rupert Read. New York: Routledge.

————. 2001. "A Question of Silence: Feminist Theory and Women's Voices." *Philosophy* 76: 371–95.

Davidson, Joyce, and Mick Smith. 1999. "Wittgenstein and Irigaray: Gender and Philosophy in a Language (Game) of Difference." *Hypatia* 14, no. 2:72–96

Eagleton, Terry. 1982. "Wittgenstein's Friends." *New Left Review* 135:64–90.

Ferguson, Kennan. 1999. *The Politics of Judgment*. Lexington, Mass.: Lexington Books.

Green, Judith Mary, and Blanche Radford Cury. 1991. "Recognizing Each Other Amidst Diversity: Beyond Essentialism in Collaborative Multi-Cultural Feminist Theory." *Sage* 8, no. 1:39–49.

Hekman, Susan. 1983. "Some Notes on the Universal and Conventional in Social Theory: Wittgenstein and Habermas." *Social Science Journal* 20, no. 2:1–15.

————. 1995. *Moral Voices Moral Selves: Carol Gilligan and Feminist Moral Theory*. University Park: Penn State Press.

————. 1999. "Backgrounds and Riverbeds: Feminist Reflections." In *The Future of Differences: Truth and Method in Feminist Theory*. New York: Polity Press.

Heyes, Cressida. 2000. *Line Drawings: Defining Women Through Feminist Practice*. Ithaca: Cornell University Press.

————, ed. Forthcoming, 2002. *The Grammar of Politics: Wittgenstein and Political Philosophy*. Ithaca: Cornell University Press.

Janik, Allan. 1985. "Wittgenstein, Marx, and Sociology." In *Essays on Wittgenstein and Weininger*. Amsterdam: Rodopi.

Jones, K. 1986. "Is Wittgenstein a Conservative Philosopher?" *Philosophical Investigations* 9, no. 4:274–87.

Koggel, Christine M. 1998. *Perspectives on Equality: Constructing a Relational Theory*. Lanham, Md.: Rowman and Littlefield.

Lamb, David. 1980. "The Philosophy of *Praxis* in Marx and Wittgenstein." *Philosophical Forum* 11, no. 3:273–98.

Lee-Lampshire, Wendy. 1991. "History as Genealogy: Wittgenstein and the Feminist Deconstruction of Objectivity." *Philosophy and Theology* (Summer): 313–31.

———. 1992. "Moral I: The Feminist Subject and the Grammar of Self-Reference." *Hypatia* 7, no. 1:34–51.

———. 1995. "Decisions of Identity: Feminist Subjects and Grammars of Sexuality." *Hypatia* 10, no. 4:32–45.

———. 1995. Women-Animals-Machines: "A Grammar for a Wittgensteinian Ecofeminism." *Journal of Value Inquiry* 29, no. 1:89–101.

———. 1999. "The Sound of Little Hummingbird Wings: A Wittgensteinian Investigation of Forms of Life as Forms of Power." *Feminist Studies* 25, no. 2:409–26.

———. 1999. "Spilling All Over the 'Wide Fields of Our Passions': Frye, Butler, Wittgenstein, and the Context(s) of Attention, Intention, and Identity (or: From an Arm Wrestling Duck to Abject Being to Lesbian Feminist")." *Hypatia* 14, no. 3:1–16.

Lehtinen, Ullaliina. 1998. "How Does One Know What Shame Is? Epistemology, Emotions, and Forms of Life in Juxtaposition." *Hypatia* 13, no. 1:56–77.

Lovibond, Sabina. 1983. *Realism and Imagination in Ethics*. Minneapolis: University of Minnesota Press.

———. 1989. "Feminism and Postmodernism." *New Left Review* 178: 5–28.

Lugg, Andrew. 1985. "Was Wittgenstein a Conservative Thinker?" *Southern Journal of Philosophy* 23, no. 4:465–75.

Martin, Bill. 1995. "'To the Lighthouse' and the Feminist Path to Postmodernity." *Philosophy and Literature* 13:307–15.

Moi, Toril. 1999. "What Is a Woman? And Other Essays." Oxford: Oxford University Press.

Mouffe, Chantal. 1994. "Politics, Democratic Action, and Solidarity." *Inquiry* 38:99–108.

———. 2000. *The Democratic Paradox*. New York: Verso.

Nicholson, Linda. 1999. "Interpreting Gender." *The Play of Reason: From the Modern to the Postmodern*. Ithaca: Cornell University Press.

Nye, Andrea. 1987. "Woman Clothed with the Sun: Julia Kristeva and the Escape from/ to Language." *Signs* 12, no. 4:664–86.

O'Connor, Peg. 2002. *Oppression and Responsibility: A Wittgensteinian Approach to Social Practices and Moral Theory*. University Park: Penn State Press.

Orr, Deborah. 1995. "On Logic and Moral Voice." *Informal Logic* 17, no. 3:347–63.

———. 2001. "Diotima, Wittgenstein, and a Language for Liberation." In *Beliefs, Bodies, and Beings: Feminist Reflections on Embodiment*, ed. Kathleen Earl, Linda Lopez McAlister, Eileen Kahl, and Christa P. Rainwater. Lanham, Md: Rowman and Littlefield.

Peters, Michael, and James Marshall. 1999. *Wittgenstein: Philosophy, Postmodernism, Pedagogy*. Westport, Conn.: Bergin.

Pitkin, Hanna Fenichel. 1972. *Wittgenstein and Justice: On the Significance of Ludwig Wittgenstein for Social and Political Thought*. Berkeley and Los Angeles: University of California Press.

Rooney, Phyllis. 1991. "Gendered Reason: Sex Metaphor and Conceptions of Reason." *Hypatia* 6, no. 2:77–103.

———. 1993. "Feminist-Pragmatist Revisionings of Reason, Knowledge, and Philosophy." *Hypatia* 8, no. 2:15–37.
———. 1995. "Rationality and the Politics of Gender Difference." *Metaphilosophy* 28 no. 1/2:22–45.
Schatzki, Theodore R. 1996. *Social Practices: A Wittgensteinian Approach to Human Activity and the Social*. Cambridge: Cambridge University Press.
Scheman, Naomi. 1978. "Individualism and Philosophy of Mind." In *Wittgenstein and His Impact on Contemporary Thought*, ed. E. Leinfellner et al. Vienna: Holder-Pichler-Tempsky.
———. 1993. *Engenderings: Constructions of Knowledge, Authority and Privilege*. New York: Routledge.
———. 1995. "Feeling Our Way Toward Moral Objectivity." In *Mind and Morals*, ed. Andy Clark, Marilyn Friedman, and Larry May. Cambridge: MIT Press.
———. 1996. "Forms of Life: Mapping the Rough Ground." In *The Cambridge Companion to Wittgenstein*, ed. Hans Sluga and David G. Stern. Cambridge: Cambridge University Press.
———. 2000. "Against Physicalism." In *Cambridge Companion to Feminism in Philosophy*, ed. Miranda Fricker and Jennifer Hornsby. Cambridge: Cambridge University Press.
———. 2001. "Non-negotiable Demands: Metaphysics, Politics, and the Discourse of Needs." In *Future Pasts: Reflections on the History and Nature of Analytic Philosophy*, ed. Juliet Floyd and Sanford Shieh. Oxford: Oxford University Press.
Tibbetts, Frederick. 1988. "Irigaray and the Language of Wittgenstein." *Critical Matrix* 4 (Fall/Winter): 83–110.
Tully, James. 1995. *Strange Multiplicity: Constitutionalism in an Age of Diversity*. Cambridge: Cambridge University Press.
Zerilli, Linda M. G. 1998. "Doing Without Knowing: Feminism's Politics of the Ordinary." *Political Theory* 26, no. 4:435–58.

Index

abstract formalism, feminist theory and, 341 n.
14
additive analyses, Wittgenstein's concept of,
201–5
Adorno, T., 85–86
Adventures of Priscilla, Queen of the Desert, The,
230–31
aesthetics, ethics and, 165–73
agency: moral and political discourse and,
290–94; politics of obviousness and,
297–98; proprietary subject and, 348–49;
self-unity and, 349–51
*Alchemy of Race and Rights: The Diary of a Law
Professor,* 306–19
Alcoff, Linda, 341 n. 13
*Allegorical Readers and Cultural Revision in An-
cient Alexandria,* 406 n. 18
American Evasion of Philosophy, The, 428 n. 32
"Annals of Politics: One Drop of Blood," 407 n.
35
Anscombe, Elizabeth, 1–20, 125–26, 146, 429
n. 36
Anscombe, G. E. M., 390–91
Anthropologist, 397
antiessentialism: ecological ethics, 426 n. 12;
feminist spiritual erotics and, 331–39; femi-
nist theory and, 201–11; proprietary subject
and, 364 n. 26
anti-Semitism: color theory and, 394–95; in
Wittgenstein's work, 61–62, 69–74, 77–80,
82, 90 nn. 3–4, 9, 139, 146–47
APA Newsletter on Feminism and Philosophy, 155
n. 7
Appiah, Anthony, 156 n. 28, 157 n. 36
Arendt, Hannah, 290, 293
Arianism, 406 n. 19

Aristotle: on equality and justice, 245–50, 257
n. 9; essentialism and, 153, 434, 448 n. 2;
misogyny of, 226; moral and political discourse and, 293
Armstrong-Buck, Susan, 431 n. 47
"arrogant perceivers" concept, 115 n. 24
Augustine (Saint), 326–29
authorship, mimesis in context of, 68
Averill, Edward, 392
Ayer, A. J., 233 n. 8

Babbit, Susan, 247, 253
Baber, Harriet, 155 n. 5
Baier, Annette, 319 n. 1, 360
Baker, Gordon P., 341 n. 10, 417, 428 n. 31
Baker, Nancy, 6, 48–63
Bass, Ellen, 449 n. 11
beliefs: ethics and, 166–73; worldview acquisition and, 436–40
Benhabib, Seyla, 68, 85–90, 242–43, 255, 303
n. 3
Berkeley, 145
Berlin, Bernard, 272–74, 282 n. 16
"bewitchment," Wittgenstein's image of, 37–38,
41–45
Bhushan, Nalini, 12, 15, 259–81
Big Typescript, 41–42
binary logic: color theory and, 374–78; queer
ethics on bisexuality and, 379–81
biocentrism, 427 n. 15
biological model: categorization research and,
278–79; essentialist feminism and, 334–39
biomedical research, women's health issues ignored in, 98, 113 n. 3
bisexuality, queer ethics concerning, 379–81
Bishop, Elizabeth, 94 n. 36

Black, Max, 34, 36–37, 146
black separatism, contextualization of, 128, 135 n. 4
blindfold metaphor, color theory and, 402
blindness metaphor, color theory and, 396–404
Bloor, David, 393
Blue, 391–92
Blue and Brown Books, The, methodology of language games in, 161–62
Blue Book, The, language discussed in, 42–43
Boghossian, Paul, 186–87
Bookchin, Murray, 429 n. 38
Borch-Jacobsen, Mikkel, 93 n. 36
Bordo, Susan, 215–17, 221, 320 n. 2, 427 n. 18
Borges, Jorge Luis, 82
Boyle, Nicholas, 406 n. 19
Braaten, Jane, 10, 176–92
Bradford, Judith, 14, 287–303
Brecht, Bertolt, 52
Brodsky, Claudia J., 406 n. 19
Brown v. Board of Education, 361–62
Bucciarelli, Louis, 190
Buddhism. *See* Mahayana Buddhism
builders' analogy: gender difference and, 250–54; Lugones' "crashing stones" compared with, 387 n. 61; theory of meaning and, 237–40, 243–45, 256 nn. 3–4
Butler, Judith, 117 n. 38, 342 n. 27; essentialism and, 11–12, 209; gender theory and, 214–17, 219–20, 233 n. 6; mimesis and, 68, 76–77, 85, 87–88, 93 n. 36; parodic women, language-game of, 229–31

Callicott, J. Baire, 429 n. 40
care theory, gender difference and, 251–52
"care voice," moral language game and, 164–65
Cartesian dualism: categorization research and, 276–79; moral language theory, 171–73; pictures, grammar, and language-games and, 326; Wittgenstein's critique of, 60, 145–47
Casteñeda, Hector-Neri, 233 n. 8
categorical imperative, moral theory and, 171–72
categorization: Buddhism linked to, 275–79; family resemblances and, 262–64; functional diversity and uniform appearances and, 264–68; psychology and, 261, 281 n. 3; samples versus prototypes, theories of, 268–71; universal versus culture-specific

color categories, 272–75; Wittgenstein's discussion of, 259–81
Cavell, Stanley, 4, 92, 225, 289, 291, 430 n. 41; on color, 393–94, 404 n. 1, 405 n. 11
Celestial Emporium of Benevolent Knowledge, 271
Cheney, Jim, 413, 420, 427 nn. 13–15, 429 n. 40, 431 n. 46
Cher, 230
children: categorizations by, 266–68, 281 n. 10; language learning by, 329–31; moral and political discourse and, 301–2; worldview acquisition by, 437–40
choice, linguistic theory of, 326–31
Chow, Ray, 132–33
Chroma, 391–92
Churchill, Sandra W., 15, 305–19
city metaphor, Wittgenstein's use of, 10, 188–92
clarity, in language, 44, 47 n. 20
Clark, Andy, 281 n. 4
class structure, proletarian "standpoint" and, 101
Code, Lorraine, 115 n. 18, 116 n. 33, 360
cognitive science: grammar and, 326–31; metaphor and, 34–38; Wittgensteinian paradigms for, 259–81
Cohen, Daniel, 9–10, 138–55
Collard, Andrée, 424, 426 n. 12, 431 n. 46
color: categorization theory and, 268–71, 281 n. 12; feminist theory and, 374–78; queer grammar of, 372–74; racism and, 389–404, 404 n. 5; universal versus color-specific categories, 272–75; Wittgenstein's discussion of, 369–71, 389–404
Color and Culture: Practice and Meaning from Antiquity to Abstraction, 404 n. 6
Common Faith, A, 427 n. 16
Commonplace Book, The, 125–26
community conception: feminist skepticism and, 108–12; language theory and, 240, 256 n. 6, 341 n. 10
Companion to a Sand County Almanac, 430 n. 40
conceptual rearing, 15; differences and, 317–18; picture theory and, 312–13; Wittgenstein's discussion of, 305–19
conceptual separatism, uncertainty and, 123–24, 135 n. 5
Confessions, 326–27
consciousness: material conditions and, 101; self-unity and agency in, 350–51

construct terminology, nature versus culture and, 410–11, 426 n. 4
co-optation, language games and, 446–47
Cornell, Drucilla, 69, 85–86, 89
Craker, Tim, 7, 69–90
Crary, Alice, 8–9, 19
Crawford, Cindy, 229
creativity, language-game theory and, 332–39
cross-dressing, parodic women, language-game of, 229–31
"Cultural Feminism versus Post-Structuralism: The Identity Crisis in Feminist Theory," 341 n. 13
culture: categorization theory and, 261–62, 265–68, 281 n. 10; color categories and, 272–75; color theory and, 375–78, 397–404; conceptual rearing and, 312–13; gender differences and, 69–74, 90 n. 3; logic and influence of, 315–17; moral theory and practice and, 171–73; nature and ecosystem and, 408–24; Wittgenstein's view of, 7–10, 393; women's identity in context of, 195–99, 205–8; work in context of, 73–74
Culture and Value, 57–58, 61–62; categories of identity in, 157 n. 39; discourse examined in, 69–74; ethics and, 166–73; "Jewishness" discussed in, 78–80, 155 n. 3; Shakespeare discussed in, 80–85

Daly, Mary, 179, 336, 412, 424, 426 n. 12, 427 n. 18, 431 n. 46
Dani language, Rosch's research on, 282 n. 17
Daumer, Elizabeth, 18, 371, 379–81, 384–85
Davidson, Donald, 180–81, 429 n. 36
Dawson, David, 406 n. 18
Deep Ecology movement, 413, 420, 428 n. 34, 429 n. 40
"Defense of Common Sense," 119–35
Democracy and Education, 427 n. 16
Dennett, Daniel, 182, 429 n. 36
depth grammar, Wittgenstein's concept of, 327–31
Derrida, Jacques, 46 n. 13, 65–66, 402–3
Descartes, René: essentialism and, 153; language theory and, 326–31; modernist philosophy and, 168; on semantics, 186–87
Devall, M., 413, 427 n. 15
Dewey, John, 19, 414–24, 427 nn. 17–19, 428 n. 22

"Dewey's Concept of Community: A Critique," 427 n. 17
Diamond, Cora, 4, 429 n. 36, 430 n. 41
diarist metaphor, private language theory and, 218–20, 233 n. 8
diegesis, mimesis and, 74–76
difference: color theory and, 377–78; conceptual rearing and, 317–18; logic of sameness and, 314–15; moral and political implications, 249–54
Diotima of Mantinea, 15, 323–24, 331–39, 342 n. 18
discourse: community interpretations and, 110–12; contestations of political thought, 294–96; feminist skepticism and, 108–12; mimesis and Wittgenstein's discussion of, 65–90; moral and political concepts of, 288–94; politics of the obvious and, 296–98; worldview acquisition and, 445
discrimination, color theory and, 405 n. 13
dispossession, masterless subjectivity and, 357–61
dissonance: partiality and, 371; queer ethics on bisexuality and, 379–81, 385
"Divining Evolution: The Ecological Ethics of Murray Bookchin," 429 n. 38
domestic labor, feminist epistemology concerning, 98–100, 113 n. 1
"door" metaphor, individual identity and, 202–5
Douglas, Mary, 360
drag performance, parodic women, language-game of, 229–31
Dworsky, Nancy, 190
Dyer, Richard, 392–95, 397

Eckersley, Robyn, 429 n. 38
ecofeminism, nature versus culture and, 412–25, 426 n. 12, 431 n. 46
economic theory: environmentalist philosophy and, 422–25, 430 n. 44; feminist epistemology and, 98–100
ecosystem theory, culture and nature and, 408–25
education, exclusion of women from, 98, 113 n. 4
Einstein, Albert, 125–26
Ellison, James, 404
Emmett, Kathleen, 427 n. 19
empathy, color theory and, 376–78

Enlightenment, rationalism and, 151–55
environment, language and culture and, 415–25
epistemology: feminist standpoint theory and, 101–6; feminist theory and, 97–112, 367–85; Wittgenstein's critique of, 346–49
equality: conceptual framework for, 128–29; features of, 240–45; feminist theory and, 251–56; language theory and, 254–56; theory of meaning and, 236–40; Wittgenstein's discussion of, 235–56
Equal Rights Amendment, 227–29
eroticism, feminist theory and, 331–39
Essay Concerning Human Understanding, 32–33
essentialism: Appiah's discussion of, 157 n. 36; boundaries of, 205–8; versus constructionalism, 245; equality and justice and, 246–50, 253–56; feminist spiritual eroticism and, 335–39; feminist standpoint theory and, 102–6, 114 n. 16; feminist theory and, 199–201; language games concerning, 434–36, 448 n. 2; objectivity in context of, 99–100, 114 n. 10; Philosophical Investigations and, 139; Russell's discussion of, 152–53; Wittgenstein's discussion of, 11, 195–211
ethics: environmental ethics, 411–24, 426 n. 9; equality and, 241–45; moral language game and, 165–73; semantics and, 149–55; Wittgenstein's denial of, 142–47
Evernden, Neil, 426 n. 5
exactness, Wittgenstein's critique of, 57–63
exclusion, theme of: coalition building and, 226–29; feminist theory and, 6–7; Wittgenstein's discussion of, 48–63
experience, Wittgenstein on ownership of, 347–49
Experience and Nature, 427 n. 16
experiential foundationalism, 320 n. 3

Failure of Technology and the Survival of Indian Nations, 430 n. 42
false beliefs, mistakes and, 123–24
family resemblance: categorization theory and, 260–64; feminist theory and, 201–5; functional diversity and uniform appearances and, 264–68; masterless subjectivity and, 356–61; Wittgenstein's concept of, 10–13, 139, 155 n. 5, 165–73; women as group and theory of, 222–24
Farbenlehre, 394, 406 n. 19

femininity: boundaries of, 205–8; conceptual traps regarding, 121–23; family resemblance and, 222–24; mimesis as, 75–76; Weininger's discussion of, 146–47
feminist empiricists, 105–6, 116 n. 36
feminist objectivism: legitimacy of, 112; principles of, 103–6, 115 n. 26; Wittgenstein's philosophy and, 106–12, 117 nn. 37–38
Feminist Politics and Human Nature, 341 n. 14
feminist postmodernism, assessment of, 103–6, 115 n. 28
feminist spiritual erotics, 15, 322, 331–40
feminist standpoint theory: essentialism and, 102–6, 114 n. 16, 115 n. 18; objectivists and skeptics and, 100–106
feminist theory: additive analyses and family resemblances, 201–5; antiessentialism and, 209–11; contestations of political thought and, 294–96; criticism of, 105–6, 116 n. 35; Diotima's contribution to, 333–39; double standard for, 116 n. 34; ecological ethics and, 412–24, 426 n. 12, 429 n. 35; epistemology and, 97–100; equality and, 235–56; essentialism and, 11, 195–211; intellectual activism and, 306, 320 n. 2; language-game and, 213–32; language in context of, 44–45; as legitimate philosophy, discussion of, 25–30; mimesis in context of, 65–70; moral language game and, 159–73; nonliteralist theory of meaning and, 176–92; objectivity and, 98–100, 113 n. 8, 114 n. 9; proprietary subject and, 352–53; survey of current trends in, 331–32, 341 n. 14; Tractatus Logico-Philosophicus and principles of, 138–55; Western canon and, xi–xiii; Wittgenstein's legacy and, 16–20, 48–63; woman as politics and, 220–22
Ficker, S., 165
Finch, M., 146
Findlay, J., 146
Flax, Jane, 248
Fliess, W., 135 n. 7
"form-of-life" concept, Wittgenstein's use of, 415, 427 n. 19, 428 n. 20
Foucault, Michel, 91 n. 12, 220, 288, 295–98, 338, 448 nn. 4, 7
foundations as axes, Wittgenstein's concept of, 206–8
Founders of the Middle Ages, 406 n. 18
Fraser, Nancy, 116 n. 29, 295, 445–47, 448 n. 7

Frege, G., 39, 145
Freire, Paulo, 448 n. 7
Freud, Sigmund, 87, 130, 135 n. 7, 346, 353
Froman, Creel, 306
Frye, Marilyn, 4, 115 n. 24, 133, 448 n. 7
functional diversity, category boundaries and, 264–68
Fuss, Diana, 155 n. 5

Gaard, G., 427 n. 12
Gadamer, H. G., 177–78
Gage, John, 389, 404 n. 6
Gaia hypothesis, 412
Gallup Poll Monthly, 430 n. 44
game imagery: categorization and, 263–64; co-alition building, language-game and, 226–29; color as language-game, 272–75, 372–74, 397–98; feminist theory and, 201–5; international transformation through language-games, 432–47; language-game and feminist theory, 213–32; language-game of 'woman' and, 224–31; learning concept of, 225–26; moral language and, 159–74; nonliteralism and, 182–87; parodic women, language-game of, 229–31; rules of language and, 440–43; theory of meaning and, 239–40; Wittgenstein's discussion of language and, 54–63, 83–85; worldview acquisition and language games, 436–40
Garver, Newton, 427 n. 19
Gauss, Karl, 189–90
Geist, Hegel's concept of, 361
gender: abstract formalism concerning, 341 n. 14; environmental ethics and, 411, 426 n. 10; essentialism and, 200–201; exclusions of philosophy and, 48–63; feminist categorizations of, 10–13, 214–15; language games and, 183–87, 190–92; masculiniza-tion of philosophy and, 27–30; metaphor and, 31–38, 46 n. 13; neutrality of, for Wittgenstein, 152–55; parodic women, language-game of, 229–31; sexual roles and, 154, 157 n. 38; signifying practice and, 215–17; as social construct, 206–8; Witt-genstein's philosophy and, 10
Gender Trouble, 89, 214, 216–17, 233 n. 6, 342 n. 27
generativity, Diotima's concept of, 333–39
Genette, Gerard, 74

genius: "heroic" characterization of, 72–74, 91 n. 9; "Jewishness" and, 77–80, 147, 156 nn. 17, 19; suicide and, 146–47
Germain, Sophie, 189–90
Gilligan, Carol: essentialism and, 209–10, 251–52, 254; justice voice and, 159–60; moral language game and, 164, 167–70
Gilman, Sander, 395
Girard, René, 75
Godel's theorem, 130
Goethe, J. F. W., 93 n. 21, 394–95, 401, 406 n. 19
Golden Bough, The, 57–58, 397
Goodman, N., 429 n. 36
grammar: body and lived experience in context of, 323–24; categorization research and, 277–79; epistemological theory and, 347–49; language games and, 162–73, 444; pictures and language-games, 326–31; situ-ated knowledge and, 369–71
Grayling, 146
Green Delusions, 429 n. 38
Green movement, ecofeminism and, 412–13
Griffin, A., 146

Habermas, Jürgen, 10, 177–82, 185–87, 192, 303 n. 3
Hacker, P. M. S., 146, 341 n. 10, 417, 428 n. 31
Hacking, Ian, 12, 248–50, 407 n. 29
Haraway, Donna, 18, 115 n. 18, 297–98, 302, 367–71, 374, 384; color theory and, 374–81
Harding, Sandra, 102–3, 308, 320 nn. 3–4
Harlow, Elizabeth, 419–20, 426 n. 7, 428 n. 34, 429 nn. 35–38
Hartsock, Nancy, 101–2, 114 n. 16, 342 n. 28
Haslanger, Sally, 115 n. 24
"Have We Got a Theory for You!," 213
Hegel, G. W. F., 50, 53–65, 361
hegemonic discourse, feminist theory and, 10
Heidegger, Martin, 427 n. 18
Hekman, Susan, 9, 159–74, 242, 255
hermeneutics, nonliteralist theory of meaning, 177–78
Hesse, Mary, 426 n. 6
Heyes, Cressida, 11, 195–211
Hill, Anita, 127
Hintikka, Jaakko, 394, 407 n. 20
Hipparchia's Choice, 45
history: discourse in context of, 74, 91 n. 12;

feminist contributions to, 98–100, 113 n. 2; feminist interpretation of Wittgenstein and, 4; nominalist view of, 248–50; Wittgenstein on philosophy and, 57–63

Hoagland, Sarah, 9, 19, 119–35

Hobbes, Thomas, 326–28, 341 n. 6

Homer the Theologian: Neoplatonist Allegorical Reading and the Growth of the Epic Tradition, 406 n. 18

homoiosis, mimesis and, 84

homosexuality: color theory and, 391–92; "door" metaphor concerning, 202–5; essentialism and, 434–36, 448 nn. 2–3; parodic women, language-game of, 229–31, 234 n. 27; responsibility and dissonance and theories of, 378–81; rules of language and, 441–43; Wittgenstein's discussion of, 132–35, 138–39, 146–47, 151, 155, 157 n. 33; worldview acquisition and, 438–40. *See also* bisexuality

Horowitz, Gad, 336

"Human Face of Nature: Environmental Values and the Limits of Nonanthropocentrism," 419, 426 n. 7, 428 n. 34, 429 n. 35

human relations, feminist interpretations of Wittgenstein and, 13–16, 21 n. 9

Hume, David, 142, 145

Humpty-Dumpty theory of language, 217–20, 224

Hurston, Zora Neale, 342 n. 25

hysteria: mimesis and, 75–76; sexual abuse and, 135 n. 7

Iglesias, Teresa, 257 n. 8

illness metaphor of philosophy, Wittgenstein's use of, 53–54, 62–63

indigenous peoples, eco-philosophy and, 413, 427 n. 15

Inessential Woman, 200–202

intellectual activism, transformative undoing as, 306, 319 n. 1

Interpretive Turn, The, 430 n. 43

Investigations, 17

Irigaray, Luce: language theory and, 332, 342 n. 18; mimesis discussed by, 7, 75–77, 84–90; rules of language and, 187; Wittgenstein and, 69–74

Jaggar, Alison, 329–30, 341 n. 14

James, William, 145

Janik, Allan, 72–73, 90 n. 9

Jarman, Derek, 391–92, 401

"Jewishness": genius and, 77–80; participation and alienation and, 132–35; Weininger's discussion of, 146–47; Wittgenstein's discomfort with, 61–62, 69–74, 90 nn. 3–4, 9, 139, 155 n. 3

judgment: color categorization and, 273–75; theory of meaning and, 239–40; worldview acquisition and, 436–40

justice: equality and, 245–50; proprietary subject and, 361–62

justice voice, 159–60

justification, Wittgenstein's discussion of, 18–20

Kant, Immanuel, 69, 145, 167–69, 171–73, 363 n. 6, 405 n. 13

Kaplan, Laura, 337–39

Kay, Paul, 272–74, 282 n. 16

Kenny, Anthony, 41–42, 146, 233 n. 10

Kim, Byron, 398–99

Kittay, Eva Feder, 34

Klein, Anne, 337–39

knowledge: categorization theory and, 271; color and Wittgenstein's social theory of, 393; Haraway's discussion of, 367–71; moral language game and, 162–73; passionate detachment and, 382–85; scientific models of, 320 n. 4; uncertainty and, 119–35; Wittgenstein's concept of, 9, 55–63; women's exclusion from pursuit of, 98–100

Koggel, Christine, 12, 235–56

Krajewski, Bruce, 18, 389–404

Kraus, A., 72

Kripke, Saul, 117 n. 42, 183, 186

Kuhn, Thomas, 172–73, 429 n. 36

Ku Klux Klan, 399–400

Lacan, Jacques, 179

Lacoue-Labarthe, Philippe, 75–78

Lakoff, George, 262–63, 281 n. 13

Lamberton, Robert, 406 n. 18

Lang, k. d., 229

language and linguistics: categorization theory and, 261–62; coalition building, language-game and, 226–29; color as game of, 272–75, 372–74, 397–98; co-optation and reclamation and, 446–47; embodied self in context of, 323–24; environmental philosophy and, 420–25; epistemological theory and, 347–49; equality and, 254–56; essentialism and, 200–211; international transformation through games of, 432–47; "Jewishness" in context of, 78–80; language-game of 'woman' and, 224–31; language-game theory, Wittgenstein's development of, 203–32, 324–31; logic and, 307–9; mimesis of Irigaray and, 67–90; moral theory and, 159–74; nature-versus-culture theory and, 415–25; nonliteralist theory of meaning, 176–92; parodic women, language-game of, 229–31; pedagogy and politics and, 299–300; phallocentric theory of, 179; picture theory of, 309–12, 326–31; politics of naming and, 180–82; private language, Wittgenstein's concept of, 217–20; Rosch's research on prototypes and, 269–71, 281 n. 13; of Shakespeare, Wittgenstein's discussion of, 81–85; skepticism and, 129–30; textual placement of women in, 32–38; theory of meaning and, 237–40, 242–45; Wittgenstein's philosophy of, 8–10, 13–16, 25–45; worldview acquisition and games of, 436–40

"languaged reality" concept, 306

Latour, Bruno, 425 n. 4

learning: moral and political discourse and, 301–2; theory of meaning and, 238–40

Lebensformen, Wittgenstein on, 415, 427 n. 19

"Lecture on Ethics," 165

Lectures, 1930–32, 444

LeDoeuff, Michèle, 6, 31–32, 34–35, 37, 45, 46 n. 13, 48–49; Wittgenstein discussed by, 49–63

Lee, Wendy Lynne, 18, 367–85, 387 n. 61

Lee-Lampshire, Wendy, 127, 129–30, 135 n. 6, 341 n. 13, 364 n. 14, 391, 429 n. 36

LeRider, Jacques, 90 n. 3

lesbianism: essentialism and, 434–36, 448 n. 2; "other" concept in, 132–35; queer ethics and, 379–81

Levinas, Emmanuel, 389

Lewis, M., 429 n. 38

Lichtenberg, 72, 399

Lincoln, Abraham, 357

Lloyd, Elizabeth, 116 n. 34

Locke, John, 32–35, 38, 46 n. 13

logic: "big dogs, little dogs, universal dogs" exer-
cise and, 306–9; conceptual rearing and, Wittgenstein's discussion of, 305–19; contradictions in, 129–30; cultural effects and, 315–17; moral and political discourse and, 291–94; patriarchal power and, 332–33; picture theory of meaning and, 309–12; power and, 313–15; of sameness, 312–13; Wittgenstein's view of, 109–12

Logic: The Theory of Inquiry, 427 n. 16, 428 n. 22

logical atomism, 142–47

logical positivism, moral theory and, 162–73

logico-linguistic analysis, ethics and, 149–55

logocentrism, in Wittgenstein's *Tractatus*, 141–42

Lorde, Audre, 15, 314–17, 320 n. 2, 323–24, 335–39, 355

Losin, Peter, 429 n. 40

loss, mimesis and, 93 n. 36

Lovelock, 430 n. 42

Lovibond, Sabina, 4, 117 n. 37, 220

Ludwig Wittgenstein: The Duty of Genius, 242–45, 256 n. 7

Lugones, María, 14, 18, 133–34, 204–5, 213, 215, 300, 371, 382–85, 386 n. 6

Lukács, Georg, 101

Lurie, Yuval, 72–73, 90 n. 3

MacIntyre, Alasdair, 391, 393

MacKinnon, Catharine, 115 n. 24, 178–79, 209–10, 234 n. 27, 400–402

Madhyamika, categorization research and, 276–79

Mahayana Buddhism, 15, 260; categorization theory and, 275–79; feminist spiritual eroticism and, 337–39

Malcolm, Norman, 233 n. 8, 341 n. 10

"Male Lesbians and the Postmodernist Body," 207

Mander, Jerry, 430 n. 42

Manes, C., 428 n. 34

Marshall, Thurgood, 361–62

Martin, Biddie, 132–33

Marxist theory: capitalism critiqued in, 101; gender and, 220; Wittgenstein and, 4

masculine imagery: conceptual traps regarding, 122–23; philosophy in context of, 53–63

masquerade metaphor, environmentalist philosophy and, 421–22 masterless subjectivity, proprietary subject and, 353–62

materialist theory, color in context of, 405 n. 6

Maternal Thinking: Towards a Politics of Peace, 319, 320 n. 6

mathematics: contradictuion in, 129–30; language games and, 189–92, 329–31

McDowell, John, 407 n. 27

meaning: equality and Wittgenstein's theory of, 236–40, 248–50; nonliteralist theory of, 176–92; relativity theory and, 125–26; Wittgenstein's discussion of, 107–12

Melville, Stephen, 389

Mendelssohn, Felix, 73–74, 84

mental illness, meaning in context of, 125–29

mentalist, Wittgenstein's discussion of, 60

Merleau-Ponty, Maurice, 282 n. 18. 427 n. 18

metaphor: cognitive role of, 32–38, 46 n. 12; Wittgenstein's discussion of, 38–45

metaphysics: exclusion of women from, 50–63; nature versus culture and, 410, 425 n. 3; proprietary subject and, 363 n. 9

Meyerhoff, Barbara, 3

Mill, John Stuart, 425 n. 3

Miller, Austin, 357–58

mimesis: feminist theory and, 7; inheritance of, 85–90; "Jewishness" in context of, 78–80; logic and, 305–9; Wittgenstein's philosophy in context of, 69, 74–77, 92 n. 15

mind/body bifurcation, Wittgenstein's discussion of grammar and, 323–24

Minnich, Elizabeth, 309, 320 n. 2

Minow, Martha, 247, 249

mistakes, false beliefs and, 123–24

"Misunderstanding Ecofeminism," 427 n. 12

modernism, moral language game and, 166–73

Mohanty, Chandra, 131–33

Monk, Ray, 62, 69, 72–73, 139, 146 n. 17, 155 n. 2, 157 n. 33, 242, 256 n. 7

Moore, G. E., 119–35, 143, 221

moral theory: difference in context of, 250–54; equality and, 246–50; language game and, 159–74, 242–45, 257 n. 8; Wittgenstein's philosophy of, 287–303

Mother Earth metaphor, environmental ethics and, 411–12

Myth of the Twentieth Century, The, 77–78

Nachlass, 394

Nagarjuna, 15, 260, 275–79, 337

naming: feminist theory and, 187–92; politics of, 180–82

National Socialism, 389, 399

natural history: culture and ecosystem theory and, 408–25; depth grammar and, 327–28; moral language game and, 164–73; Wittgenstein's discussion of, 12–13, 15

nature, ambiguity in, 410–11, 426 n. 7

Nelson, Hilde Lindemann, 11–12, 213–32

"Neo-Stoicism of Radical Environmentalism, The," 413, 427 nn. 13–15

Nicholson, Linda J., 116 n. 29, 341 n. 14

Nietzsche, Friedrich, 46 n. 13, 288, 303 n. 1

Nineteenth Amendment, 247

nominalism: equality and, 248–50; realism versus, 12, 244–45

nonanthropocentrism, environmentalism and, 419–24, 426 n. 7, 428 n. 34, 429 n. 35

nonliteralist theory of meaning, feminist theory, 176–92

normativity, rules of language and, 183–87

Notebooks 1914–1916, 157 n. 39

Nussbaum, Martha, 116 n. 35, 246, 257 n. 9

Nye, Andrea, 332–34

Oakeshott, Michael, 171–73

objectivity: color categorization and, 272–75, 282 nn. 14–15; color theory and, 376–78; feminist standpoint theory and, 102–3; feminist theory and, 8–9, 98–100, 105–6, 113 n. 8, 114 n. 9. 116 n. 33; "high" and "low" objectivity, Wittgenstein's discussion of, 308–9, 316–17, 319, 320 n. 4; moral and political discourse and, 290–94; "passionate detachments" and, 365–71; postmodernism and, 103–4, 116 nn. 29–30; queer ethics on bisexuality and, 379–81; skepticism and, 100–106; Wittgenstein's discussion of, 18–20

obviousness, politics of, 296–98

O'Connor, Peg, 10, 19, 432–47

Odyssey, 149

Oedipus, 402

Office of Research on Women's Health, 113 n. 3

"On Being the Object of Property," 357–58

On Certainty, 9, 60–63, 119–35, 234 n. 16; logic discussed in, 306; moral language game and, 167–73; objectivity discussed in, 309; oppositional discourse in, 445; pictures, grammar, and language-games in, 325–31; rule-following discussed in, 256 n. 6; worldview acquisition in, 436–40, 444

On the Logic of the Social Sciences, 179–80

oppositional discourse, worldview acquisition and, 445

oppression, self-complicity of women in, 115 n. 24

Orr, Deborah, 15, 322–40

"other": inheritance of mimesis and, 86–90; uncertainty concerning, 131–35; woman as, in philosophy, 27–30

ownership/mastery, Wittgenstein's concept of, 346–49

pain-behavior, language-games and, 329–31

"paradigm of thought," Williams' concept of, 308–9

Parmenides, 332–33

parody, mimesis and, 76

partiality: color-blindness and, 396; situated knowledge and, 369–71

Parton, Dolly, 229

Pascal, Blaise, 52

Pateman, Carole, 127–28

patriarchal bias: conceptual traps and, 122–23; environmental ethics and, 411; language and, 179; logic and, 332–36; philosophy's exclusion of feminism and, 49–63; soul in context of, 324

pedagogy, politics in context of, 298–300

Peirce, C. S., 35–38

Pensées, 52

Perloff, Marjorie, 394

Pfeiffer, Michelle, 397

phallocentric theory of language, 179

phenomenological tradition, categorization research and, 282 n. 18

Phenomenology of Percept, 427 n. 18

Philosophical Grammar, language discussed in, 40, 83–84

Philosophical Imaginary, The, 31–32

Philosophical Investigations: additive analyses and family resemblances, 201–5; antiessentialism in, 139; categorization theory and, 260–62; coalition building and, 228–29; color theory and, 390, 394; co-optation and reclamation in, 446–47; essentialism in, 199–201; family resemblance and, 222–24; feminist interpretations of, 195–99; lan-

guage discussed in, 41–45, 53–63, 83–84, 161–73; logic discussed in, 306; moral and political theory in, 288–303; morality in, 243–45; nature and culture in, 425 n. 2; nonliteralist theory of meaning and, 178–92; pedagogy and politics in, 299–301; picture theory and, 310–12, 326–31; private language concept and, 218–20; proprietary subject in, 344–45, 348–49; regress argument in, 111–12, 118 n. 50; rule-following in, 215–32, 442–43; *Tractatus Logico-Philosophicus* and, 141, 152–53; vagueness defended in, 429 n. 35; worldview acquisition in, 443–44

Philosophical Passages, 394, 396

philosophical therapy, multilingualism and, 300

philosophy: language and, Wittgenstein's discussion of, 25–45; as male prerogative, 25–30, 98–100, 113 n. 6; moral and political discourse concerning, 287–303; Wittgenstein's philosophical subject and, 5–7

philosophy, Wittgenstein's hostility toward, 310–12, 320 n. 5

picture theory of meaning, 148–49, 156 n. 25; grammar and language-games and, 325–31, 340 n. 3; language and, 309–12; logic and power and, 313–15; in Wittgenstein's work, 52–63

Piper, Adrian, 397–99, 403–4, 405 n. 13

Pitkin, Hannah, 14, 287–303

Plato, 67, 74, 78, 86–87, 163, 331–32, 386 n. 26

play, Lugones' concept of, 382–85

"Playfulness, 'World'-Travelling, and Loving Perception," 382–85

Pleck, Elizabeth, 113 n. 2

poetry: mimesis and, 74–75; Wittgenstein on Shakespeare and, 80–85

"point-of-viewlessness," Wittgenstein's philosophy and, 110–12

Polanyi, Michael, 320 n. 4

politics: coalition building, language-game of, 226–29; contestations of, 294–96; difference in context of, 250–54; feminist theory and, 6, 21 n. 4; gender theory and, 214–15; limits of identity in, 201–5; of naming, 180–82; nonliteralist theory of meaning and, 178–92; of the obvious, 296–98; pedagogy and, 298–300; proprietary subject and, 351–53, 363 n. 9; reprivatization in, 446–47; Wittgenstein's interpretations of,

14–16, 287–303; woman defined as, 220–22; women's role in, 98–100, 113 n. 2

Politics, 246

Politics of Reality: Essays in Feminist Theory, The, 115 n. 24

positionality, of women, 341 n. 13

Post-Modern Epistemology: Language, Truth, and Body, 427 n. 18

postmodernism: feminist theory and, 103–6, 115 n. 28, 116 n. 29; pragmatist feminism and, 231–32

poststructuralism, feminist theory and, 342 n. 28

Postures of the Mind, 319 n. 1

Poteat, William, 427 n. 18

power: color theory concerning, 374–78; contestations of political thought and, 294–96; erotic as, 335–39; feminist theory and, 128–29, 135 n. 6; logic and, 313–15; versus privilege, 388 n. 64; rules of language and, 441–43; situated knowledge and, 379–81

pragmatism: concepts of difference and, 231–32; environmentalism and, 417–24, 430 nn. 41,43; language-game of 'woman' and, 224–31; woman as politics and, 220–22, 224

Pratt, Minnie Bruce, 132–33

primatology, color theory and, 374–78

Prince, Mary, 355

private language: feminist theory and, 217–20, 233 n. 8; Wittgenstein's discussion of, 60–63

private property, as foundational concept, 135 n. 3

privilege, versus power, 388 n. 64

"Proof of an External World," 119–35

property, Wittgenstein's concept of, 15–16, 345–47, 362–63

proprietary subject, Wittgenstein's critique of, 344–62; masterless subjectivity and, 353–62; politics and, 351–53, 363 n. 9; self-unity and agency and, 349–51

Protagoras, 386 n. 26

prototypes: categorization theory and, 264–68, 281 n. 5; Rosch's research on, 268–71

"psychological hedonism," nature versus culture and, 425 n. 3

psychology: categorization research and, 259–81, 281 n. 3; color theory and, 391

purity, Wittgenstein's discussion of, 57–58

"Queer Ethics; or, the Challenge of Bisexuality to Lesbian Ethics," 379–81

queer theory, situated knowledges and, 378–81

Quine, Willard V. O., 237, 256 n. 3

Race Matters, 401–3

racism: color theory and, 375–78, 376–78, 395–404; logic and, 307–9, 315–17; Wittgenstein's *Remarks on Colour* and, 389–404; in Wittgenstein's work, 90 n. 9, 98, 113 n. 6

Rand, E. K., 406 n. 18

rationality, exclusion of women from, 51–52

Read, Rupert, 12, 18–19, 408–24

realism: equality and, 244–45, 247–50; feminist interpertation of Wittgenstein and, 2–20; "languaged reality," 306; versus nominalism, 12

Realism and Imagination in Ethics, 4

Realistic Spirit: Wittgenstein, Philosophy, and the Mind, The, 4

reason, Wittgenstein on idealization of, 58–63

reclamation, language games and, 446–47

reductio ad absurdum, Wittgenstein's philosophy and, 110–12

relativism, feminist theory and, 8–9

relativity theory, knowledge in context of, 124–26

religion, in Wittgenstein's work, 52–63

Remarks on Colour, 18, 272–75, 369–70, 372–74; bilingual edition of, 390–91, 405 n. 7; racism and, 389–404

"Remarks on Frazer's *Golden Bough,*" 57–58

Remarks on Psychology, 188

Remarks on the Foundations of Mathematics, 123–24, 129–30, 303, 441

representation, categorization and, 275–79

reprivatization, co-optation and reclamation and, 446–47

Republic, 67, 74, 84

resistance, mistake and mental illness as, 127–29

Respect for Nature: A Theory of Environmental Ethics, 426 n. 9

responsibility, ethic of, 166

"Rethinking Male and Female," 333–34

Rich, Adrienne, 336

Riddick, Sara, 319, 320 n. 6

rightness, Wittgenstein on "standard" of, 218–20

Ring, Merril, 340 n. 4

ritual, feminist theory and, 3–4

riverbed metaphor, Wittgenstein's use of, 135 n. 1, 168–73, 328–31, 341 n. 7
Romantic tradition, Wittgenstein influenced by, 73–74
Rooney, Phyllis, 6, 25–45
Rorty, Richard, 429 n. 36
Rosch, Eleanor, 12–13, 15, 259–81
Rosenberg, Alfred, 77
Rouse, Joseph, 430 n. 43
Rousseau, Jean-Jacques, 50, 53, 361
Rowbotham, Sheila, 113 n. 5
Ruddick, Sara, 4
Rules, Grammar, and Necessity, 428 n. 31
rules of language: categorization and, 263–64; community interpretations and, 240, 256 n. 6; games and, 440–43; language-game of 'woman' and, 224–31; private language concept and, 217–20; worldview acquisition and, 436–40
Runge, 399–400
Rush, Florence, 135 n. 7
Russell, Bertrand, 39, 130, 142–48, 150, 152–53, 155 n. 8, 156 nn. 11–12,17

sabotage thesis, conceptual traps and, 121–23
Sacks, Oliver, 396–97, 407 n. 29
St. John, James Augustus, 33–38
samples, Wittgenstein on categorization and, 268–71
Scheman, Naomi, 1–20, 117 n. 37, 135 n. 1, 316–17, 319, 320 n. 2, 353
Schiller, Friedrich, Wittgenstein's discussion of, 72–73, 80–85, 92 n. 21
Schopenhauer, Arthur, 69, 90 n. 4, 145
science: cultural effects on, 316–17; Dewey's discussion of, 416–17; logic in, 308–9, 320 n. 4; moral and political discourse and, 290–94; nature versus culture and, 410, 425 nn. 4–5; philosophy and, 143–47, 154–55; sociology of, 410–11, 426 n. 6
Scott, Nancy, 113 n. 2
secrecy, essentialism and, 435–36
"self-evident" logic, concept of, 315–17
self identity: agency and, 349–51; categories of, 154–55, 157 n. 39; feminist interpretations of Wittgenstein and, 13–16; masterless subjectivity and, 358–62; women's disconnect concerning, 113 n. 5; worldview acquisition and, 436–40

self-mastery: masterless subjectivity and, 355–61; proprietary subject and, 353
self-unity, agency and, 349–51, 363 n. 7
semantic irrealism, 186–87
semantics, ethics and, 149–55
separatism, feminist theory and, 9, 128–29, 135 n. 5
Sessions, P., 413, 427 n. 15
Sex and Character, 7, 70–74, 90 n. 9
sexism: color theory and, 376–78; logic and, 307–9, 315–17
sexual abuse: hysteria and, 135 n. 7; language games concerning, 433–36, 443–44, 448 n. 11
sexuality: Diotima's discussion of, 334–39; epistemology of, 435–36, 448 n. 4; queer ethics on bisexuality and, 379–81
Shakespeare, William, 70, 72–73, 78, 80–85, 91 n. 9, 92 n. 21, 390–91
"Shameful Face of Philosophy, The," 49
Shiva, Vandana, 427 n. 18
Shrage, Laurie, 291
signifying practice, gender theory and, 215–17
signs, Wittgenstein's discussion of meaning and, 107–12
Signs, 213
Singer, Beth, 417 n. 17
Sister Outsider, 335
situated knowledge, Haraway's discussion of, 367–71; queer theory and, 378–81
"Situated Knowledges: The Science Question in Feminism and the Privilege of Partial Perspective," 367–68
skepticism: conceptual traps of, 121–23; essentialism and, 204–5; feminist objectivism and, 100–106, 116 n. 31; uncertainty and, 129–30; Wittgenstein's discussion of, 60–63, 107–12, 117 n. 42
slavery: legal theory and, 364 n. 17; proprietary subject concept and, 354–62, 364 n. 14
Slicer, D., 427 n. 12
Smith, Janet Farrell, 15, 344–62
social construction of color, 397–404, 407 n. 29
Social Construction of What?, The, 407 n. 29
Social Creation of Nature, The, 426 n. 5
Social Ecology movement, 419–20, 429 n. 38
social relations: language-games and, 329–31; moral and political discourse and, 290–94; moral language game and, 166–73; objectivity in context of, 102–6; property con-

cepts and, 346–47; situated knowledge and, 379–81

sociobiology, environmentalist theory and, 424, 430 n. 45

Socrates: on definitions, 55; on mimesis, 74–75

"Song of Myself," 89–90

soul, Wittgenstein's discussion of, 142–47, 149–55, 322–40

speech acts, Wittgenstein on complexity of, 237, 239, 256 n. 5

Spelman, Elizabeth V., 200–205, 213, 224, 300

Stamp, Terence, 230–31

Stone, Martin, 430 n. 41

Streng, F. J., 276–79

structuralist tradition, categorization research and, 282 n. 18

subjectivity: embodied speaker and, 349–51; moral language theory and, 160–73; proprietary subject and, 363 n. 10; Wittgenstein's discussion of discourse and, 71–74

suicide, Wittgenstein's discussion of, 146–47, 156 n. 16

surface grammar, Wittgenstein's concept of, 327–31

Symbol and Ritual, 360

symbolic logic, Wittgenstein influenced by, 35–36, 39

Symposium, 331

Synecdoche, 398–99

taste preferences, moral language-game and, 172–73

taxonomies, Rosch's research on, 265–66, 281 n. 9

Taylor, Paul, 426 n. 9

technology, environmentalist philosophy and, 419–25

Teichmann, Jennifer, 360

textual placement of women, in Western canon, 30–38

Theateus, 386 n. 26

Their Eyes Were Watching God, 342 n. 25

theory: constructive versus destructive building of, 346–47, 363 n. 1; versus practice, Wittgenstein's distinction concerning, 264–65, 281 nn. 4, 7

third world cultures, feminist theory and, 131–35

Thomas, Clarence, 448 n. 10

Thomas, Virginia, 448 n. 10

Thomas Kuhn: The Philosopher of Scientific Revolution, 429 n. 36

Thompson, Evan, 272, 275–76, 280, 282 n. 18

Thorton, Louise, 449 n. 11

Tohidi, Nayereh, 132

Tolstoy, Leo, 145

Tong, Rosemarie, 320 n. 2

toolbox metaphor: categorization theory and, 261–62; theory of meaning and, 237–40; Wittgenstein's discussion of language and, 83–84, 163–73

Tractatus Logico-Philosophicus, 10, 138–55; color theory and, 390, 394; equality discussed in, 241–45; language discussed in, 29–30, 39–45, 326–31, 340 n. 3; limits of language in, 433; logic discussed in, 305–9; moral language game and, 165–73, 257 n. 8; propositions discussed in, 309–12; role of philosophy in, 29–30

transfeminism: gender boundaries and, 207–8; parodic women, language-game of, 230–31

transformative undoing, 306, 319 n. 1; conceptual rearing and, 317–18

Trinitarian Christology, 406 n. 19

Tronto, Joan, 257 n. 11

truth: Einstein's relativity and, 125–26; Tractatus Logico-Philosophicus and discussion of, 140–55; Wittgenstein's discussion of, 17–20; worldview acquisition and, 438–40

Tuana, Nancy, 30–31, 130, 136 n. 7, xi–xiii

"Two Kinds of Discrimination," 405 n. 13

übersicht, Wittgenstein's discussion of language and, 40

uncertainty: feminist theory and, 130–35; Wittgenstein's discussion of, 119–35, 168–73

uniform appearances, category boundaries and, 264–68

universality: of color categorization, 272–75; logic and, 308–9; situated knowledge and, 369–71

Unruly Practices, 445–47

usage: color as language-game and, 372–74; family resemblance theory and, 223–24; logic of linguistics and, 328–31, 341 n. 10; rules of language and, 184–87

"Uses of the Erotic: The Erotic as Power," 335

utterances, rules of language and, 440–43

vagueness, Wittgenstein's defense of, 429 n. 35

Vanity Fair, 229

Varela, Francisco, 272, 275–76, 280, 282 n. 18
Vienna Circle, 144
Von Wright, G. H., 69

Walker, Margaret U., 290, 297
Warren, Karen, 331, 429 n. 36, 435 n. 46
Weber, Max, 166
Weininger, Otto: anti-Semitism of, 7, 69–74,
    78–80, 82, 90 nn. 3–4, 9; Wittgenstein in-
    fluenced by, 145–47, 156 n. 17
West, Cornel, 401–4, 425 n. 1, 428 n. 32
Westen, Peter, 235–36, 241
Western canon, omission of women from, xi–xiii
Westphal, Jonathan, 391, 393
"Whitehead's Metaphysical System as a Founda-
    tion for Environmental Ethics," 431 n. 47
Whitman, Walt, 89–90
Whorfian hypothesis, color categorization and,
    272–75
Whose Science? Whose Knowledge, 320 n. 4
"Why 'Physics' is a Bad Model for Physics," 320
Williams, Patricia, 15–16, 305–19, 320 n. 2,
    357–58, 364 n. 17
"Wise Use" policy, environmentalist philoso-
    phy and, 423
Wittgenstein, 392
Wittgenstein, Ludwig: Dewey and, 416–24; on
    European culture, 7–10; feminist objectiv-
    ism and, 106–12, 117 nn. 37–38; feminist
    theory and, 1–20, 16–20; homosexuality
    of, 132–35, 138–39, 146–47, 151, 155, 157
    n. 33; Irigaray and, 69–90; Moore and,
    119–35; moral language game and, 159–73;
    on objectivity, 100; Schiller and, 80–85, 92
    n. 21; *Tractatus* of, 138–55

*Wittgenstein: Rules, Grammar, and Necessity: An
    Analytical Commentary on the Philosophical
    Investigations,* 341 n. 10
"Wittgenstein and Deconstruction," 430 n. 41
Wittgenstein and Justice, 287
Wittig, Monique, 234 n. 27
"Woman and Philosophy," 48–63
women: coalition building, language-game and,
    226–29; exclusion from philosophy of,
    49–63; grammatical limits of language con-
    cerning, 218–20; "ideal" of, 195–99;
    language-games concerning, 224–31; as
    "other" in philosophy, 27–30; parodic
    women, language-game of, 229–31; *Philo-
    sophical Investigations* and definitions of,
    195–99; positionality of, 341 n. 13; textual
    placement of, 30–38
Women's Health Initiative, 113 n. 3
work, cultural value of, Wittgenstein's discus-
    sion of, 71–74
world picture, Wittgenstein's concept of,
    328–31
worldviews: acquisition of, 436–40; differences
    in, 443–44
Wright, Lawrence, 407 n. 35
"Wrongs of Passage: Three Challenges to the
    Maturing of Ecofeminism," 427 n. 12

yoga, feminist theory and, 337–39
Young, Iris, 213–15, 222

Zettel, 325, 443
Zita, Jacquelyn, 207
Zizek, Slavoj, 397–401, 407 n. 28

Contributors

NANCY E. BAKER has been teaching Wittgenstein's *Philosophical Investigations* (and occasionally *On Certainty*) in small, yearlong seminars at Sarah Lawrence College for twenty-five years. She has recently finished essays on *On Certainty* and is currently working on Wittgenstein's views on the connection between human and animal behavior. She also teaches a course on gender.

NALINI BHUSHAN received a B.A. in economics and an M.A. and M.Phi. in philosophy from Madras University, Chennai, India; and her Ph.D. in philosophy from the University of Michigan in Ann Arbor. She is currently associate professor of philosophy at Smith College. Her research interests lie at the intersection of mind and language, with a special focus on categorization. She has published in the journals *Cognitive Science* and *Philosophical Investigations*, among others, and has co-edited an anthology in the philosophy of chemistry titled *Of Minds and Molecules* for Oxford University Press (2000). She is currently working on the chemical senses, on chemical kinds, and on the philosopher Jiddu Krishnamurti.

JANE BRAATEN was tenured in philosophy at the College of Charleston in 1996, and then left the profession to pursue philosophical work in a more public vein, as well as landscape painting. She is studying computational geography for the sake of income, and is working with several local antiracist groups. Her new book, a *Critique of Pure America: A Philosophical Tortoise*, is nearing completion.

JUDITH BRADFORD is an independent philosopher who studied at Fordham University, where she received her M.A. Bradford has taught at Fordham University and at St. Mary's University in San Antonio. She has published on the politics of knowledge and on American philosophy.

SANDRA W. CHURCHILL is a master certified coach trained by Coach University and the Newfield Network. She also holds a Ph.D. in philosophy, with an emphasis on feminism, language, and culture. She has experience coaching and working with academics (both faculty and administrators), creatives (writers, musicians, and journalists), managers, senior executives, and women and men in all phases of life and career transitions (early career, midlife, and retirement). In her telephone-based coaching practice, Life Directions, she is dedicated to serving individuals and groups in the business of life and work fulfillment.

DANIEL COHEN is professor of philosophy at Colby College. His areas of professional interests are Wittgenstein, philosophy of language, metaphors, and most recently, argumentation theory. His articles have appeared in *Philosophia, Metaphilosophy, Journal of Philosophical Logic, Teaching Philosophy,* and *International Journal of Philosophical Studies,* among others.

TIM CRAKER is an associate professor in the Department of Humanities in the School of Education at Mercer University. He has published two essays on Wittgenstein. ("Der Sprache ins Auge sehen: Wittgenstein und Bedeutung als Physiognomie," in *Geschichten der Physiognomik,* edited by R. Campe and M. Schneider [Rombach Verlag, 1995]; and "Fragments," *International Studies in Philosophy,* 27:4 [1995]).

ALICE CRARY is assistant professor of philosophy at the New School. She is co-editor of *The New Wittgenstein* (Routledge, 2000). She has published articles on moral philosophy, feminist theory, and the philosophy of Wittgenstein. She recently published an article on J. L. Austin in *Inquiry.* Her work has appeared in *Philosophical Investigations, Philosophy,* and other places.

SUSAN HEKMAN teaches political theory and graduate humanities at the University of Texas at Arlington. She has published in the areas of the methodology of the social sciences and feminist theory. Her books include *Gender and Knowledge* (1990); *Moral Voices, Moral Selves* (1995); and *The Future of Differences* (1999).

CRESSIDA J. HEYES is assistant professor of philosophy at the University of Alberta. She is the author of *Line Drawings: Defining Women Through Feminist Practice* (Cornell University Press, 2000) and the editor of *The Grammar of Politics: Wittgenstein and Political Philosophy* (Cornell University Press, 2002). With a grant from the Social Sciences and Humanities Research Council of Canada, she is currently writing a series of essays on the feminist politics of sexual subjectivity.

SARAH LUCIA HOAGLAND is a Chicago dyke and philosopher. She is a member of the Institute of Lesbian Studies, a community-based collective in Chicago, and the Escuela Popular Norteña, a popular education school in Valdez, New Mexico. She is professor of philosophy and women's studies at Northeastern Illinois University in Chicago. She wrote *Lesbian Ethics,* and co-edited *For Lesbians Only* with Julia Penelope. More recently she has co-edited the Mary Daly volume in this Re-Reading the Canon series with Marilyn Frye and has a chapter in the Sartre volume. An essay titled "Resisting Rationality," moving on from the Wittgenstein chapter in this volume, appears in *Engendering Rationalities,* edited by Nancy Tuana and Sandra Morgen (State University of New York Press, 2001).

CHRISTINE M. KOGGEL teaches in the Department of Philosophy at Bryn Mawr College. Her main research interests are in the areas of moral theory, practical ethics, social and political philosophy, and feminism. In addition to publishing several chapters and journal articles, she is the author of *Perspectives on Equality: Constructing a Relational Theory* (Rowman and Littlefield, 1998); co-editor of the fourth edition of *Contemporary Moral Issues* (McGraw-Hill, 1997); and editor of *Moral Issues in Global Perspective* (Broadview, 1999).

BRUCE KRAJEWSKI is professor in and chair of the Department of Literature and Philosophy at Georgia Southern University. His most recent book is a cooperative effort with Douglas Parker titled *William Roye's "A Brefe Dialoge Bitwene a Christen Father and his Stobborne Son": The First Protestant Catechism Published in English* (University of Toronto Press, 1999). He is also editor of *Gadamer's Repercussions: Philosophical Hermeneutics Reconsidered* (forthcoming from University of California Press).

WENDY LYNNE LEE is professor of philosophy at Bloomsburg University of Pennsylvania. Her areas of specialization include philosophy of language, philosophy of mind, feminist philosophy, and philosophy of ecology. Her work can be found in journals such as *Hypatia, Journal of Mind and Behavior, Journal of Philosophy and Theology, Ethics and the Environment*, and *Feminist Studies*. She has also published on Aristotle in *Apeiron* and the *Canadian Philosophical Review*. She is the author of *On Marx: A Critical Introduction* (Wadsworth, 2001) She is currently working on a Wittgensteinian feminist critique of John Searle's application of his philosophy of mind to the construction of social institutions.

HILDE LINDEMANN NELSON is associate professor in the Department of Philosophy at Michigan State University. For five years an editor at the *Hastings Center Report*, she is the co-author, with James Lindemann Nelson, of *The Patient in the Family* (Routledge, 1995) and *Alzheimer's: Answers to Hard Questions for Families* (Doubleday, 1996). She has edited two collections—*Feminism and Families* and *Stories and Their Limits: Narrative Approaches to Bioethics* (both Routledge, 1997)—and co-edited *Meaning and Medicine: A Reader in the Philosophy of Health Care* (Routledge, 1999). She also co-edits the Reflective Bioethics Series for Routledge and the Feminist Constructions Series for Rowman and Littlefield. Her most recent book is *Damaged Identities, Narrative Repair* (Cornell University Press, 2001). Her articles in feminist ethics have appeared in *Hypatia* and a number of edited collections. Her articles in bioethics have appeared in *Hastings Center Report; Journal of Clinical Ethics; Kennedy Institute of Ethics Journal; Journal of Law, Medicine, and Ethics;* and *Bioethics*.

PEG O'CONNOR is director of the women's studies program at Gustavus Adolphus College. She is the author of *Oppression and Responsibility: A Wittgensteinian Approach to Social Practices and Moral Theory* (Pennsylvania State University Press, 2002). Her most recent work continues the examination of the "grammar of violence," in particular sexual abuse against women and children. She is co-editor (with Lisa Heldke) of *Philosophers on Holiday*, a quarterly 'zine in the philosophical travel/leisure travel genre.

DEBORAH ORR is a philosopher with the Division of Humanities, York University, Ontario. Her teaching and research interests include issues of gender, ethics, and the body as a site of wisdom and knowledge production. Her primary research interest currently is the rich pedagogic potential of yoga and meditation for addressing oppressive discourses. She has published in the areas of Wittgenstein, gender, ethics, and pedagogy. She is a longtime practitioner of meditation and yoga and teaches in Toronto.

RUPERT READ is a lecturer in philosophy at the University of East Anglia. He is the author of *Thomas Kuhn: The Philosopher of Scientific Revolution?* (forthcoming) and co-editor of *The New Wittgenstein* (Routledge, 2000). With an award from the Arts and

Humanities Research Board of Great Britain, he is currently working on a book titled *The Hidden Greatness of the Canon: Re-reading Modern Western Philosophy Through Wittgenstein*.

PHYLLIS ROONEY is associate professor of philosophy at Oakland University in Michigan. Much of her work is in feminist epistemology, and she has special interests in the reason question in feminism. She has published articles in *Hypatia, American Philosophical Quarterly, Philosophical Forum, Metaphilosophy*, and *Proceedings of the Philosophy of Science Association* and essays in *Epistemology: The Big Questions*, edited by L. M. Alcoff (Blackwell, 1998); and *Feminists Doing Ethics*, edited by P. DesAutels and J. Waugh (Rowman and Littlefield, 2001). She is currently working on two book projects: an introduction to feminist epistemology, and a book on reason and gender.

NAOMI SCHEMAN is professor of philosophy and women's studies and associate dean of the Graduate School at the University of Minnesota. Wittgenstein has been central to her philosophical identity since she encountered him as a prefeminist undergraduate at Barnard College in 1965, and he has remained an odd but always stimulating fellow traveler throughout her wanderings in feminist, antiracist, and queer theory.

JANET FARRELL SMITH is associate professor of philosophy at the University of Massachusetts at Boston. Her research interests are in the areas of philosophy of language, philosophy of medicine, theories of justice, and family ethics. Within family ethics, she is concerned with children's rights and racial and ethnic policies in child placement. Professor Smith has argued against preadoptive genetics testing of children.